Where To Stay
in the

*A*MERICAN
SOUTHWEST

Phil Philcox

HUNTER
PUBLISHING, INC

Hunter Publishing, Inc.
300 Raritan Center Parkway
Edison, NJ 08818
(908) 225 1900
Fax (908) 417 0482

ISBN 1-55650-650-3

© Phil Philcox 1995

Cover photograph:
Carson Valley NV (Superstock)

Contents

Introduction

If you're headed to the southwest for business or pleasure, this is the last word on finding a place to bed down for the night. Need a convenient downtown hotel within walking distance of the Convention Center or a motel along the tourist strip with lighted tennis courts and a heated swimming pool? Prefer a high-rise apartment or private home rental for an extended stay? How about a private rental home far away from the maddening crowds or a guest ranch with rates that include three meals a day and a host of activities? Whether your choice is an out-of-the-way bed and breakfast or a hotel suite in the center of the business district, you'll find something to your liking – and budget – in this guide.

Included are the names and telephone numbers of regional rental sources that handle an assortment of accommodation options –from private homes to condos and apartments. These agencies are excellent sources of information on what's available in each area at different price levels and most have toll-free numbers you can call for information.

Call the toll-free and fax numbers to request literature, rate cards and reservations. Many properties will fax their literature directly to your machine.

As of press time, the rates were current, based on interviews with the property owners. Rates are constantly changing and vary considerably with location and season, so use the rates listed to determine the price range of the property and always call prior to arrival. Use the toll-free number when available. Most toll-free numbers listed are valid from all states but some properties have outside-their-state numbers or in-state numbers. If you reach an invalid number, check with the toll-free operator at 800-555-1212.

Also included is a list of chain hotels and motels (you can contact them for free accommodations directories), their locations and descriptions of their special clubs and offerings.

To keep future editions up to date, we request you submit any new listing, changes in information and current rates to: The Where-To-Stay Book, 131B North Bay Drive, Lynn Haven FL 32444. Please include all telephone numbers (including fax and toll-free) along with number of rooms, facilities, rates and other information of interest to travelers.

Abbreviations Used In This Guide:

SGL – single room – rate for one person
DBL – double room – rate for two people sharing one room
EFF – efficiency, usually one room with kitchen or kitchenette
STS – suites

1BR, 2BR, 3BR – one- , two- , or three-bedroom condo, apartment, villa or townhouse, usually with full kitchen facilities, washer/dryer, etc.

A/C – air conditioning

NS ROOMS – rooms available for non-smokers

NS – smoking not permitted on the property

FREE BREAKFAST – a free continental or full American breakfast is included in the room rate

AIRPORT COURTESY CAR – free transportation to and from local airports

AIRPORT TRANSPORTATION – transportation is available to and from local airports for a fee

LOCAL TRANSPORTATION – free transportation is available to local attractions

MEETING FACILITIES – the property can provide facilities for meetings and conference

RESTAURANT – indicates there is a restaurant on the property, across the street or adjacent to the property

AMERICAN PLAN – all meals included in rates

MODIFIED AMERICAN PLAN – some meals included in room rates, usually breakfast and dinner

CC – accepts major credit cards

X – rate for a third person

$00-$000 – daily rate span

$W-$W – weekly rate span

$00-$W – daily rate followed by weekly rate

AP – charge for an additional person in the room

Chain Hotels

Locations and Special Deals

($) indicates there is a cost for membership

American International
18202 Minnetonka Blvd.
Deephaven MN 55391
Reservations: 800-634-3444

The Inn-Pressive Club for frequent travelers pays guest $35 for every 10 nights they stay at an American, a free upgrade to the next room type when available, a complimentary newspaper, check cashing privileges, no charge for local telephone calls and car rental discounts.

Best Western
Box 10203
Phoenix AZ 85064
Reservations: 800-528-1234

The Gold Crown Club International Card earns points redeemable for room nights and other awards. Many locations offer a 10% discount to senior travelers on a space-available basis with advanced reservations. The Government-Military Travel Program provides discounts to federal employees and military personnel.

Budget Host Inns
2601 Jackboro Highway
Fort Worth TX 76114
Reservations: 800-BUD-HOST

Budgetel Inns
212 West Wisconsin Avenue
Milwaukee WI 53203
Reservations: 800-428-3438

Budgetel Inns offers a free room-delivered continental breakfast, extra long beds, free satellite movies 24-hours, in-room VCRs, free local calls, executive conference center with speaker phones, in-room computer and fax hookups and children stay free with parents. The Road Runners Club offers a free night's stay after 12 paid nights.

Clarion-Choice Hotels
10750 Columbia Pike
Silver Spring MD 20901
Reservations: 800-221-2222

Clarion and Choice Hotels consist of Sleep Inns, Comfort Inns, Friendship Inn, Econo Lodges, Rodeway Inns, Quality Inns and Clarion Hotels and Resorts.

Special discounts of 10%-20% are available at participating locations for members of AAA. The Small Organizations Savings (SOS) Program is available to companies with over 10 employees and offers a 10% discount off the first 15 rooms used by company employees. The Weekender Rate Program offers special room rates of $20, $30 or $35 per night with an advanced reservation. All local, state and federal government employees and military personnel receive special per diem rates and upgrades when available at participating hotels. The Family Plan allows children to stay free when sharing a parent's room. Prime Time and Prime Time Senior Saver for people over age 60 offers a 10% discount at all hotels year-round and a 30% discount at limited locations when you call 800-221-2222 and ask for the Prime Time Senior Saver rate.

Days Inn
2751 Buford Highway
Atlanta GA 30324
Reservations: 800-325-2525

The September Days Club ($) offers travelers over the age of 50 up to 40% discount on rooms, 10% discount on food and gifts, a quarterly club magazine, seasonal room discounts and special tours and trips. The Inn Credible Card is designed for business travelers and provides up to 30% savings on room rates, free stays for spouses and other benefits. The Days Gem Club is a travel club for military personnel and government employees that offers up to 30% savings on room rates. School Days Club for academic staff and educators offers a minimum of 10% savings on room rates, special group rates and additional benefits. The Sport Plus Club is designed for coaches and team managers who organize team travel and offers 10% discounts on room rates, special team rates and late check-outs.

Doubletree-Compri Hotels
410 North 44th St.
Phoenix AZ 85008
Reservations: 800-528-0444

Doubletree operates 38 hotels in the United States, including Doubletree Club Hotels that provide oversized rooms, complimentary, cooked-to-order breakfasts, club rooms and hosted evening receptions. Family Plans allow up to two children under the age of 18 to stay free when they share the rooms with their parents. For the business traveler, most hotels offer secretarial services, photocopying, fax machines and computer hook-up capabilities. A special discounted rate is available to seniors. A Corporate Plus Program is available at all business center locations.

Business Class offers quick check-in and check-out, complimentary breakfast in a private lounge, complimentary newspaper and additional benefits. The Entree Gold floor provides concierge services, an exclusive lounge for use by guests, complimentary breakfast and cocktail hour and use of a private boardroom.

Drury Inns
10801 Pear Tree Lane
St. Louis MO 63074
Reservations: 800-325-8300

The Perfect Ten program provides one free night with every 10 paid nights. Guests over the age of 50 receive a 10% discount. Special rates are available to motorcoach travelers, school groups, athletic teams and members of associations. Information on group discounts is available by calling 800-444-4421.

Embassy Suites
222 Las Colinas Boulevard
Irving TX 75039
Reservations: 800-528-1100

Embassy Suites offer two-room suites with living room, bedroom and kitchenettes. Complimentary breakfasts are served daily and a two hour complimentary beverage program is offered nightly.

Guest Quarters Suite Hotels
30 Rowes Wharf
Boston MA 02110
Reservations: 800-424-2900

Hampton Inns
6800 Poplar
Memphis TN 38138
Reservations: 800-426-7866

Hampton Inns offer free continental breakfasts, free local calls. Children under 18 stay free in same room with parents. Most Hampton Inns offer a Hospitality Suite that can be used as a small meeting facility. The LifeStyle 50 Club provides discounts for guests over age 50, with no charge for a third person staying in the room.

Hawthorne Suites Hotels
400 Fifth Avenue
Waltham MA 02154
Reservations: 800-527-1133

Hawthorne Suites Hotels offer a free breakfast buffet, evening reception with complimentary refreshments and no charge for children under 18 occupying the same suite with their parents. Each suite is equipped with a refrigerator, microwave, coffee and coffee makers and tableware. Small meeting facilities are available at all locations for groups of up to 60.

Hilton Hotels and Resorts
9336 Civic Center Drive
Beverly Hills CA 90209
Reservations: 800-HILTON

Zip-Out-Quick Check-Out is available to travelers using major credit cards. An itemized statement of charges is provided the night before departure. Many Hilton locations have hotels-within-hotels, Tower and Executive accommodations offering room upgrades, use of a private lounge, access to business services, complimentary cocktails and continental breakfast and use of telex, fax machines and photocopying equipment.

The HHonors Guest Reward Program is a free program that earns points toward free or discounted stays at participating properties and members-only privileges that include rapid check-inns, free daily newspaper, free stay with spouse and free use of health club facilities when available.

The Corporate Rate Program offers business travelers guaranteed rates annually, speed reservations, Tower and Executive accommodations and Quick Check-Out facilities.

Hilton's Senior HHonors offers special amenities to travelers over the age of 60. Included are room discounts up to 50%, a 20% dinner discount and money-back guarantee, a private toll-free reservation number and automatic enrollment in Hilton's Guest Reward Programs. Bounce Back Weekend offers a free, daily continental breakfast, children free in parents' rooms and special rates for Thursday to Sunday with a Saturday stay. During the summer, these discounted rates apply Monday to Wednesday.

Hilton Leisure Breaks includes packages for honeymoons and special occasions with special rates. Hilton Meeting 2000 is a network of business meeting facilities available at some locations and includes special meeting room, audiovisual system, refreshments and assistance in setting up meeting rooms and programs.

Holiday Inn
1100 Ashwood Pkwy.
Atlanta GA 30338
Reservations: 800-HOLIDAY

Holiday Inn Preferred Senior Traveler offers a 20% savings on the single-person rate and a 10% discount at participating restaurants. Members of the American Association of Retired Persons receive a 10% discount at participating hotels.

Best Break Bed and Breakfast packages are offered at participating hotels and include a guest room and a breakfast coupon worth $12.

Great Rates are offered with advance reservations and include discounts of at least 10%. Most Holiday Inns offer Government/Military rates based on the per diem rate for government employees and contractors. Many hotels participate in the Government/Military Amenities program which offers coupons redeemable for free local phone calls with a $5 limit, 10% dinner discounts and a free continental breakfast.

The Priority Club is designed for frequent travelers and provides points that can be exchanged for travel and merchandise awards.

Homewood Suites
3742 Lamar Avenue
Memphis TN 38195
Reservations: 800-225-5466

Hospitality International Inns
1726 Montreal Circle
Tucker GA 30084
Reservations: 800-251-1962

Hospitality International consists of Red Carpet Inns, Scottish Inns, Master Host Inns, Passport Inns and Downtowner Motor Inns.

The Identicard Program provides room discounts at participating inns and resorts.

Howard Johnson
3838 East Van Buren
Phoenix AZ 85038
Reservations 800-654-2000

The Howard Johnson Road Rally Program offers discounts to senior travelers over the age of 60 and members of AARP and other national senior's organizations. With advanced reservations, a 30% discount is available at some locations. The Family Plan lets children under the age of 12 stay free at all locations, with some properties extending the age limit to 18.

Government Rate Programs offer special rates to federal employees, military personnel and government contractors. The Corporate Rate Program offers special rates to companies and business travelers. Howard Johnson Executive Section offers guests special rooms, complimentary wake-up coffee and newspapers and snacks. Kids Go Hojo provides children with free FunPacks filled with toys, puzzles, coloring books and games.

Hyatt Hotels International
Madison Plaza, 200 West Madison
Chicago IL 60606
Reservations: 800-228-9000

Hyatt Gold Passport provides earned credits for free stays, a private toll-free reservation number, express check-in, special members-only rooms, free newspaper daily, complimentary morning coffee and use of fitness centers when available. Hyatt Reserved Upgrade coupon booklets are available for confirmed room upgrades. Hyatt Gold Passport At Leisure is available at over 155 locations worldwide and includes invitations to private receptions, room amenities, priority room and dining reservations and a quarterly newsletter with member-only offers.

The Regency Club is a hotel within a hotel offering VIP accommodations. Located on the topmost floors of participating hotels, the rooms are reached by special elevators requiring a passkey. Also included is a free morning paper, complimentary breakfast, afternoon hors d'oeuvres, wine and cocktails.

Camp Hyatt is for children and their parents. Upon arrival at any Hyatt hotel or resort, children receive a free cap, frequent travel passport and a registration card. The program offers special childrens' menus in the dining room, room discounts, kitchen tours and other pastimes.

Independent Motels of America
Box 202
Winner SD 57580
Reservations: 800-341-8000

InnSuites Hotels
1651 West Baseline Rd.
Tempe AZ 85283
Reservations: 800-842-4242

Kempenski Hotels
750 Lexington Ave.
New York NY 10022
Reservations: 800-426-3135

Knights Court
26650 Emery Pkwy.
Cleveland OH 44128
Reservations: 800-843-5644

LaQuinta Inns
10010 San Pedro
San Antonio TX 78279
Reservations: 800-531-5900

Special rates are available to business travelers, government and military employees, seniors over the age of 55 and families.

La Quinta Returns Club offers discounted room rates, credit for a free night stay, guaranteed reservations and check cashing privileges.

La Quinta Senior Class ($) is available to travelers over the age of 60 and offers a 20% discount on room rates, credit for free night stays and guaranteed reservations.

La Quinta Per Diem Preferred offers credits and discounts to military personnel, U.S. government workers and cost-reimbursable contractors. La Quinta Returns earns credits for free nights, special room rates, guaranteed reservation for late arrivals, account summaries and $50 check cashing privileges.

Lexington Hotels and Suite Connections
2120 Walnut Hill Lane
Irving TX 75038
Reservations: 800-537-8483

Loews Hotels
One Park Avenue
New York NY 10016
Reservations: 800-235-6397

Marriott
Marriott Drive
Washington DC 20058
Reservations: *Marriott Hotels* 800-228-9290; *Courtyard by Marriott* 800-321-2211; *Fairfield Inns* 800-228-2800; *Residence Inns* 800-331-3131

Marriott consists of Marriott Hotels and Resorts, Marriott Suites, Courtyard by Marriott, Fairfield Inns, and Residence Inns. SuperSaver rates offer discounts on weekday and weekend stays at participating hotels. Discounts range from 10% and up. The TFB program (Two For Breakfast) offers discounts for weekend stays for two adults that includes complimentary breakfasts.

Advance Purchase Rates are discounts of up to 50% for advance, prepaid, non-refundable reservations 7, 14, 21 and 30 days in advance. Senior Citizen discounts for members of AARP and other senior groups are available at all participating hotels.

The Marriott Honored Guest Award offers special upgrades to members at participating hotels. After a 15-night stay during a 12-month period, members receive express checkout services, complimentary newspaper, check cashing privileges, free luggage tags and discounts.

Motel 6
14651 Dallas Pkwy.
Dallas TX 75240
Reservations: 800-437-7486

National 9 Inns
2285 South Main
Salt Lake City UT 84115
Reservations: 800-524-9999

Omni Hotels
515 Madison Avenue
New York NY 10022
Reservations: 800-THE-OMNI

The Omni Club Program is available at selected hotels and offers concierge service, private lounge facilities, complimentary breakfast, evening cocktails and hors d'oeuvres and specially-appointed rooms.

The Omni Hotel Select Guest Program provides special services, priority room availability, accommodations upgrade, complimentary coffee and morning newspaper and a newsletter announcing additional programs. The Omni Hotel Executive Service Plan is available to corporate members and includes a variety of special benefits. For planning and scheduling meetings, the Omni Hotels Gavel Service and Omni-Express Programs provide assistance by experienced meeting planners. City'scapes is a special weekend package that offers discounts and special amenities.

Park Inn International Hotels
4425 West Airport Freeway
Irving TX 75062
Reservations: 800-437-PARK

The Silver Citizens Club offers a 20% room discount and 10% food discount at participating hotels, free morning paper and coffee, special directory, all-night emergency pharmacy telephone number and personal check cashing.

Preferred Hotels
1901 South Meyers Road
Oakbrook Terrace IL 60181
Reservations: 800-323-7500

Radisson Hotels International
Carlson Pkwy.
Minneapolis MN 55459
Reservations: 800-333-3333

Radisson operates 270 hotels and affiliates worldwide. Plaza Hotels are usually located in the city center or suburban locations. Suite Hotels have oversized rooms with living room, mini-bar and kitchenettes. Resort Hotels usually include locations near beaches, golf course and recreational facilities.

Ramada Inn
1850 Parkway Place
Marietta GA 30067
Reservations: 800-2-RAMADA

Ramada Inn has 700 locations world-wide consisting of Ramada Inns, Ramada Hotels and Ramada Renaissance Hotels. The Hotels are designed to five-star international standards and include convention and banquet facilities, restaurants, 24-hour room service, entertainment and lounges. Most Renaissance Hotels offer a club floor with concierge services, upgraded room amenities and lounge.

Membership in the Ramada Business Card Program earns points for trips and merchandise based on dollars spent at Ramada properties. The card is available free. Membership includes favorable rates, automatic room upgrade when available, express check-in and check-out, free newspaper on business days, free same-room accommodations for your spouse when you travel together, extended check-out times, newsletter and points redeemable for hotel stays, air travel, car rentals and over 10,000 Service Merchandise catalog items.

Participating Ramada Inn properties offer SuperSaver Weekend discounts. These rates apply on Friday, Saturday and Sunday for one- , two- and three-night stays. Extra-person rates may apply for a third or fourth person in the room. Because some hotels limit availability on some dates, reservations are recommended.

When traveling with family or friends, the Ramada 4-for-1 Program permits up to four people to share the same room and pay the single rate. At participating properties, the Best Years Seniors Program provides travelers over the age of 60 who are members of AARP, the Global Horizons Club, Catholic Golden Age, The Golden Buckeye Club, Humana Seniors Association, The Retired Enlisted Association, The Retired Officers Association and United Airlines Silver Wings Plus with a 25% discount off regular room rates.

The Ramada Per Diem Value Program is available at more than 350 locations. Properties honor the maximum lodging per diem rates set by the U.S. General Services Administration. Federal employees, military personnel and employees of cost-reimbursable contractors traveling on official government business are eligible. In addition to the per diem limits for lodging, the single person room rate at participating locations includes full American breakfast and all applicable taxes. All Ramada properties provide corporate customers favorable rates. Companies need a minimum of 10 travelers with a combined total of 100 room nights per year.

Red Lion Hotels and Inns
4001 Main St.
Vancouver WA 98666
Reservations: 800-547-8010

Red Roof Inns
4355 Davidson Road
Hilliard OH 43026
Reservations: 800-843-7663

Redi Card membership offers 8 p.m. holds on reservations, complimentary *USA Today* newspaper, member-only newsletter, first priority advance room requests, check cashing privileges up to $50 per stay, express check-in and check-out and complimentary late stays upon request.

Ritz Carlton Hotels
3414 Peachtree Road NE
Atlanta GA 30326
Reservations: 800-241-3333

Sheraton Hotels, Inns and Resorts
60 State St.
Boston MA 02109
Reservations: 800-325-3535

ITT Sheraton Hotels, Resorts and All-Suite hotels are located in major gateway cities and business centers. All-Suites feature two-room suites with living and dining areas, bedroom, bath and additional features like sofa beds, wet bars and microwave ovens.

ITT Sheraton Inns are Sheraton's budget hotels, generally smaller in size and more informal in design than ITT Sheraton Hotels. Inns average from 125 to 250 guest rooms and are usually located in medium to large cities and in suburban area. All inns offer a full restaurant and professional meeting planner services.

ITT Sheraton Club International ($) additional guest services at over 400 participating hotels worldwide. Benefits include: automatic room upgrade whenever available; guaranteed 4 p.m. late check-out; Double Club points and free nights in select hotels throughout the year; Express pass check-in and check-out service with key ready upon arrival.

Shilo Inns
11600 Southwest Barnes Rd.
Portland OR 97225
Reservations: 800-222-2244

Stouffer Hotels
29800 Bainbridge Road
Cleveland OH 44139
Reservations: 800-HOTELS-1

Super 8 Motels
1910 8th Avenue NE
Aberdeen SD 57402
Reservations: 800-800-8000

Travelers Inns
1800 East Imperial Highway
Brea CA 92621
Reservations: 800-633-8300

TraveLodge
1973 Friendship Drive
El Cajon CA 92020
Reservations: 800-255-3050

The Business Break Club Program offers a 10% discount off the lowest published room rate, express check-in and check-out, free local telephone call and morning coffee and a special 800-number for fast reservations. The Corporate Business Break Club provides a 10% room discount off the lowest published rate, free morning coffee, newsletters and car rental discounts.

The Classic Travel Club is available to travelers over the age of 50. It offers room discounts of 15%, a quarterly newsletter, check cashing privileges, free morning coffee, car rental discounts and express check-in, check-out services.

Coaches, Athletic Directors and Educators are eligible for Team TraveLodge, which offers a free stay with groups of 10 or more, a minimum 10% discount, upgrades for group leaders, late check-out, free morning coffee, newsletter and car rental discounts.

All federal, state and local government employees and members of the armed forces and their families traveling on official government business or pleasure receive special rates equal to or less than the prevailing per diem rates. Information on these rates is available from 800-GOVT-RES.

Under the Family Plan, there is no charge for children under the age of 17 when sharing a room with their parents. The Government Traveler-Value America Plan offers rates equal to or less than the prevailing per diem rates paid and is available to federal employees, military personnel and contractors on government business.

Westin Hotels and Resorts
The Westin Building
Seattle WA 98121
Reservations: 800-228-3000

At Westin hotels or resorts there is no charge for children under the age of 18 when they share the same room with parents or guardians. If more than one room is required to accommodate a family, the single guest room rate will apply to each room, regardless of the number of people occupying the room.

Wyndham Hotels and Resort
2001 Bryan St., Suite 2300
Dallas TX 75210
Reservations: 800-822-4200

Accommodations Directory

Arizona

Rental and Reservation Services:

A Apartment Locators (3202 East Greenway, 85032; 992-300, 800-955-7545) rental apartments, condos, townhouses and private homes.

Bed and Breakfast in Arizona (Scottsdale 85252; 800-266-7829) inns, bed and breakfasts and rental homes.

Ajo
Area Code 602

Guest House Inn (3 Guest House Rd., 85321; 387-6133) 4 rooms, restaurant, free breakfast, NS, A/C, TV, wheelchair access, 1920s inn, no pets, CC. SGL/DBL$60-$70.

Marine Motel (1966 2nd Ave., 85321; 387-7626) 20 rooms, A/C, TV, NS rooms, wheelchair access, in-room refrigerators, children free with parents, CC. SGL/DBL$30-$70.

Mine Managers House (1 Greenway Dr., 85321; 387-6505, Fax 387-6508) 5 rooms, free breakfast, whirlpools, lighted tennis court, gift shop, laundry facilities, antique furnishings, wheelchair access, NS rooms, no pets, senior rates, CC. SGL/DBL$65-$100.

Apache Junction
Area Code 602

Apache Junction Motel (1680 West Apache Trail, 85220; 982-7702) 15 rooms, in-room refrigerators and microwaves, pets OK, A/C, TV, NS rooms, wheelchair access, CC. SGL/DBL$25-$58.

Gold Canyon Ranch (6100 South Kings Ranch Rd., 85219; 982-9090, Fax 830-5211, 800-624-6445) 57 rooms and efficiencies, restaurant, lounge, pool, whirlpools, exercise center, lighted tennis courts, no pets, VCRs, kitchenettes, A/C, TV, NS rooms, in-room refrigerators, wheelchair access, room service, meeting facilities, CC. SGL/DBL$95-$220.

Benson
Area Code 602

Best Western Quail Hollow Inn (699 North Ocotillo St., 85602; 586-3646, 800-528-1234) 69 rooms, restaurant, pool, exercise center, children free with parents, A/C, NS rooms, TV, laundry facilities, wheelchair access, in-room refrigerators, free local calls, pets OK, senior rates, meeting facilities, CC. SGL/DBL$40-$52.

Bisbee
Area Code 602

Bisbee Grand Hotel (61 Main St., 85603; 432-5900, 800-421-1909) 8 rooms and suites, free breakfast, lounge, NS, antique furnishings, 1908 inn, A/C, TV, NS rooms, wheelchair access, CC. SGL/DBL$50-$75, STS$90.

Busboy Inn (45 OK St., 85603; 432-5131) 18 rooms, free breakfast, pets OK, TV, laundry facilities, 1917 inn, NS, CC. SGL/DBL$29-$39.

Copper Queen Hotel (11 Hail Ave., 85603; 432-2216, 800-247-5829) 45 rooms, restaurant, lounge, entertainment, outdoor heated pool, A/C, TV, NS rooms, wheelchair access, meeting facilities, CC. SGL/DBL$65-$100.

The Greenway House (401 Cole Ave., 85603; 432-7170, 800-253-3325) 8 efficiencies, free breakfast, 1906 home, antique furnishings, NS, kitchenettes, no pets, TV, NS rooms, CC. SGL/DBL$75-$125.

Bullhead City
Area Code 602

Best Western Grand Vista Inn (1817 Arcadia Plaza, 86442; 763-3300, Fax 763-4447, 800-528-1234) 80 rooms, pool, whirlpools, children free with parents, local transportation, A/C, NS rooms, TV, laundry facilities, wheelchair access, no pets, senior rates, meeting facilities, CC. SGL/DBL$53-$78.

Days Inn (2200 Karis Dr., 86442; 758-1711, Fax 758-7937, 800-325-2525) 70 rooms and suites, restaurant, free breakfast, outdoor pool, whirlpools, children free with parents, room service, laundry service, A/C, TV, free local calls, pets OK, fax, wheelchair access, NS rooms, senior rates, CC. SGL/DBL$35-$75, STS$60-$110.

Econo Lodge Riverside (1717 Hwy. 95, 84662; 758-8080, Fax 758-8283, 800-4-CHOICE) 77 rooms and suites, free breakfast, pool, children under 12 free with parents, no pets, senior rates, NS rooms, wheelchair access, A/C, TV, senior rates, CC. SGL/DBL$32-$78, STS$55-$95.

Holiday Inn (839 Landon Dr., 86462; 754-4700, Fax 754-1225, 800-HOLI-DAY) 155 rooms, restaurant, lounge, pool, exercise center, children under 19 free with parents, wheelchair access, A/C, TV, NS rooms, fax, room service, pets OK, airport transportation, laundry service, meeting facilities for 400, senior rates, CC. SGL/DBL$35-$50.

Lake Mohave Resort and Marina (Bullhead City 86430; 754-3245, 800-752-9669) 51 rooms and suites, restaurant, lounge, pool, kitchenettes, airport transportation, pets OK, A/C, TV, NS rooms, children free with parents, wheelchair access, senior rates, CC. SGL/DBL$60-$85.

Super 8 Motel (Bullhead City 86430; 754-4651, Fax 754-2259, 800-888-6228, 800-800-8000) 120 rooms and suites, outdoor pool, no pets, children under 12 free with parents, free local calls, A/C, TV, in-room refrigerators and microwaves, fax, laundry facilities, local transportation, NS rooms, senior rates, wheelchair access, meeting facilities, CC. SGL/DBL$38-$55.

TraveLodge (2340 4th St., 86430; 754-3000, Fax 754-5234, 800-578-7878) 88 rooms, restaurant, lounge, free breakfast, pool, whirlpools, wheelchair access, complimentary newspaper, laundry service, TV, A/C, free local calls, fax, NS rooms, in-room refrigerators and microwaves, local transportation, children under 18 free with parents, pets OK, meeting facilities, senior rates, CC. SGL/DBL$45-$65.

Camp Verde
Area Code 602

Best Western Cliff Castle Lodge (Camp Verde 86322; 567-6611, Fax 567-9455, 800-528-1234) 80 rooms, restaurant, lounge, whirlpools, exercise center, children free with parents, A/C, NS rooms, in-room refrigerators and microwaves, TV, laundry facilities, wheelchair access, pets OK, senior rates, meeting facilities, CC. SGL/DBL$50-$65.

Super 8 Motel (1550 Hwy. 260, 86322; 567-2622, 800-800-8000) 42 rooms and suites, no pets, children under 12 free with parents, free local calls, A/C, TV, in-room refrigerators and microwaves, fax, NS rooms, senior rates, wheelchair access, meeting facilities, CC. SGL/DBL$40-$50.

Carefree
Area Code 602

Boulders Resort and Club (34631 North Tom Darlington Dr., 85377; 488-9009, Fax 488-4118, 800-553-1717) 136 villas and townhouses, restaurant, lounge, pool, exercise center, sauna, whirlpools, A/C, TV, NS rooms, wheelchair access, airport transportation, in-room refrigerators and coffee makers, laundry facilities, children free with parents, no pets, modified American plan available, senior rates, meeting facilities, CC. SGL/DBL$450-$525.

Casa Grande
Area Code 602

Best Western Casa Grande Suites (665 Via del Cielo, 85222; 836-1600, Fax 836-7242, 800-528-1234) 80 rooms, restaurant, free breakfast, lounge, pool, exercise center, children free with parents, A/C, NS rooms, TV, laundry facilities, wheelchair access, pets OK, meeting facilities, senior rates, CC. SGL/DBL$45-$100.

Francisco Grande Resort and Golf Club (26000 Gila Bend Hwy., 85222; 836-6444, 800-237-4238) 112 rooms and suites, restaurant, lounge, entertainment, pool, exercise center, tennis courts, A/C, TV, NS rooms, wheelchair access, airport transportation, pets OK, CC. SGL/DBL$56-$106.

Holiday Inn (777 North Pinal Ave., 85222; 426-3500, Fax 836-4728, 800-HOLIDAY) 14 rooms and suites, restaurant, lounge, entertainment, outdoor heated pool, exercise center, whirlpools, children under 19 free with parents, wheelchair access, A/C, TV, local transportation, NS rooms, fax, room service, gift shop, in-room refrigerators, pets OK, laundry service, meeting facilities, senior rates, CC. SGL/DBL$65-$71.

Chambers
Area Code 602

Best Western Chieftain Inn (Chambers 86502; 688-2754, 800-528-1234) 52 rooms, restaurant, pool, exercise center, children free with parents, A/C, NS rooms, TV, laundry facilities, wheelchair access, pets OK, senior rates, meeting facilities, CC. SGL/DBL$53-$70.

Chandler
Area Code 602

Aloha Motel (445 North Arizona Ave., 85224; 963-3403) 26 rooms and efficiencies, outdoor heated pool, restaurant, kitchenettes, A/C, TV, NS rooms, wheelchair access, CC. SGL/DBL$40-$60.

Sheraton San Marcos (1 San Marcos Pl., 85224; 963-6655, Fax 899-5441, 800-325-3535) 296 rooms and suites, restaurant, lounge, entertainment, heated pool, exercise center, whirlpools, gift shop, local transportation, car rental desk, room service, NS rooms, A/C, TV, children free with parents, wheelchair access, 25,000 square feet of meeting and exhibition space, 17 meeting rooms, meeting facilities for 700, CC. SGL/DBL$180-$210, STS$250-$575.

Super 8 Motel (7171 West Chandler Blvd., 85226; 961-3888, Fax 961-3888 ext 400, 800-800-8000) 75 rooms, heated outdoor pool, pets OK, free local calls, NS rooms, A/C, TV, in-room refrigerators and microwaves, children free with parents, wheelchair access, meeting facilities, CC. SGL$43-$58, DBL$48-$63.

Wyndham Garden Hotel (7475 West Chandler Blvd., 85226; 961-4444, Fax 940-0269, 800-822-4200) 159 rooms and suites, restaurant, lounge, heated pool, whirlpool, exercise center, airport transportation, A/C, TV, NS rooms, wheelchair access, room service, meeting facilities, senior rates, CC. SGL/DBL$110-$130, STS$120-$140.

Chinle
Area Code 602

Canyon de Chelly Motel (Chinle 86503; 674-5875) 102 rooms, restaurant, indoor heated pool, A/C, TV, NS rooms, wheelchair access, CC. SGL/DBL$56-$98.

Holiday Inn (Chinle, 86503; 674-5000, Fax 674-5683, 800-HOLIDAY) 110 rooms, restaurant, lounge, outdoor pool, exercise center, children under 19 free with parents, wheelchair access, A/C, TV, NS rooms, fax, room service, pets OK, laundry service, meeting facilities, senior rates, CC. SGL/DBL$60-$110.

Cottonwood
Area Code 602

Best Western Cottonwood Inn (993 South Main St., 86326; 634-5575, Fax 255-0259, 800-528-1234) 64 rooms and suites, restaurant, free breakfast, lounge, heated pool, exercise center, whirlpools, children free with parents, A/C, NS rooms, TV, in-room refrigerators, laundry facilities, wheelchair access, pets OK, senior rates, meeting facilities, CC. SGL/DBL$50-$83.

Country Elegance Bed and Breakfast (Cottonwood 86326; 634-4470) 3 rooms, free breakfast, TV, no pets, NS, CC. SGL/DBL$70-$95.

Quality Inn (302 West Hwy. 89A, 86326; 634-4207, Fax 634-5764, 800-221-2222) 51 rooms and suites, restaurant, lounge, heated pool, exercise center, whirlpools, children free with parents, A/C, TV, room service, laundry service, wheelchair access, NS rooms, meeting facilities, senior rates, CC. SGL/DBL$60-$70.

View Motel (818 South Main St., 86326; 634-7581) 34 rooms, heated pool, kitchenettes, A/C, TV, NS rooms, wheelchair access, CC. SGL/DBL$34-$42.

Willow Tree Inn (1089 Hwy. 260, 86326; 634-3678) 30 rooms and efficiencies, no pets, A/C, TV, NS rooms, wheelchair access, CC. SGL/DBL$36-$58.

Douglas
Area Code 602

Motel 6 (111 16th St., 85607; 364-2457, 505-891-6161) 137 rooms, pool, free local calls, children under 17 free with parents, NS rooms, wheelchair access, pets OK, A/C, TV, CC. SGL/DBL$35-$44.

TraveLodge (1030 19th St., 85607; 364-8434, Fax 364-5687, 800-578-7878) 29 rooms, restaurant, lounge, free breakfast, pool, wheelchair access, complimentary newspaper, laundry service, TV, A/C, free local calls, fax, NS rooms, in-room refrigerators and microwaves, airport transportation, children under 18 free with parents, no pets, meeting facilities, CC. SGL/DBL$32-$39.

Eagar
Area Code 602

Best Western Sunrise Inn (128 North Main St., 85925; 333-2540, 800-528-1234) 40 rooms, restaurant, free breakfast, lounge, pool, spa, exercise center, children free with parents, A/C, NS rooms, TV, laundry facilities, wheelchair access, pets OK, senior rates, meeting facilities for 30, CC. SGL/DBL$40-$75.

Ehrenberg
Area Code 602

Best Western Flying J Motel (Ehrenberg 85334; 923-9711, Fax 923-8335, 800-528-1234) 83 rooms and suites, restaurant, lounge, heated pool, whirlpool tub, children free with parents, A/C, NS rooms, TV, laundry facilities, in-room refrigerators and microwaves, wheelchair access, pets OK, senior rates, meeting facilities, CC. SGL/DBL$35-$57.

Eloy
Area Code 602

Super 8 Motel (3945 West Houser Rd., 85231; 466-7804, 800-392-5026, 800-800-8000) 42 rooms and suites, pool, kitchenettes, no pets, children under 12 free with parents, free local calls, A/C, TV, in-room refrigerators and microwaves, fax, NS rooms, senior rates, wheelchair access, meeting facilities, CC. SGL/DBL$43-$50.

Flagstaff
Area Code 602

Americana Motor Hotel (2650 Route 66 East, 86001; 526-2200) 89 rooms, pool, A/C, TV, NS rooms, wheelchair access, CC. SGL/DBL$21-$55.

Arizona Motel (910 South Milton Rd., 86001; 774-7171) 26 rooms, restaurant, A/C, TV, kitchenettes, NS rooms, wheelchair access, CC. SGL/DBL$36-$44.

Autolodge Motel (1313 South Milton Rd., 86001; 774-6621) 20 rooms, A/C, TV, NS rooms, wheelchair access, CC. SGL/DBL$32-$62.

Best Western Pony Soldier Inn (3030 Hwy. 66, 86004; 526-2388, Fax 527-8329, 800-528-1234) 90 rooms, restaurant, lounge, free breakfast, lounge, indoor pool, exercise center, children free with parents, A/C, NS rooms, TV, laundry facilities, wheelchair access, gift shop, pets OK, senior rates, meeting facilities, senior rates, CC. SGL/DBL$42-$72.

Budget Host Saga Hotel (820 West Route 66, 86001; 779-3631, 800-283-4678) 29 rooms, restaurant, lounge, heated pool, laundry facilities, NS rooms, wheelchair access, A/C, TV, senior rates, children free with parents, CC. SGL/DBL$26-$46.

Comfi-Cottages of Flagstaff (1612 North Aztec St., 86001; 774-0731) cottages, free breakfast, kitchenettes, pets OK, CC. SGL/DBL$65-$85.

Country Club Condos and Resort (2380 North Oakmont Dr., 86004; 526-4287) 1- to 3-bedroom condominiums, outdoor heated pool, kitchenettes, A/C, TV, NS rooms, wheelchair access, CC. SGL/DBL$100-$180.

Days Inn (1000 West Hwy. 40, 86001; 774-5221, 800-325-2525) 157 rooms and suites, restaurant, outdoor pool, children free with parents, room service, laundry service, A/C, TV, free local calls, pets OK, fax, wheelchair access, NS rooms, senior rates, CC. SGL/DBL$55-$79, STS$88.

Dierker House (423 West Cherry Ave., 86004; 774-3249) 3 rooms, free breakfast, A/C, NS rooms, no pets, no children, antique furnishings, TV, CC. SGL/DBL$30-$40.

Econo Lodge East (Lockette and Santa Fe, 86004; 527-1477, Fax 527-0228, 800-4-CHOICE) 52 rooms, restaurant, pool, whirlpools, children under 12 free with parents, no pets, NS rooms, wheelchair access, A/C, TV, senior rates, CC. SGL/DBL$60-$100.

Evergreen Inn (1008 Route 66, 86004; 774-7356) 139 rooms and efficiencies, outdoor pool, hot tubs, A/C, TV, NS rooms, wheelchair access, pets OK, CC. SGL/DBL$24-$65.

Fairfield Inn by Marriott (2005 South Milton Rd., 86001; 773-1300, 800-228-2800) 135 rooms, restaurant, free breakfast, children under 18 free with parents, NS rooms, remote control cable TV, free local calls, laundry service, A/C, wheelchair access, fax, meeting facilities, fax, senior rates, CC. SGL/DBL$66-$88.

Family Inn (121 South Milton Rd., 86001; 774-8820) restaurant, lounge, pets OK, A/C, TV, NS rooms, wheelchair access, CC. SGL/DBL$45-$65.

Flagstaff Inn (2285 East Butler Ave., 86004; 774-1821, 800-533-8992) 100 rooms and efficiencies, restaurant, whirlpools, sauna, pets OK, A/C, TV, NS rooms, wheelchair access, CC. SGL/DBL$35-$80.

Hampton Inn (3603 East Lockett Rd., 86004; 526-1885, 800-HAMPTON) 56 rooms, free breakfast, indoor heated pool, whirlpools, exercise center, children under 18 free with parents, NS rooms, wheelchair access, in-room computer hookups, fax, TV, A/C, free local calls, no pets, meeting facilities, CC. SGL/DBL$45-$100.

Holiday Inn (2320 Lucky Lane, 86004; 526-1150, Fax 779-2610, 800-HOLIDAY) 157 rooms, restaurant, lounge, entertainment, outdoor heated pool, exercise center, wheelchair access, children under 19 free with parents, wheelchair access, A/C, TV, NS rooms, fax, room service, no pets, in-room refrigerators, fireplaces, laundry service, airport transportation, meeting facilities for 100, senior rates, CC. SGL/DBL$90-$100, STS$110-$165.

Hidden Village Motel (822 West Route 66, 86004; 774-1443) pool, A/C, TV, NS rooms, wheelchair access, pets OK, CC. SGL/DBL$33-$45.

Highland Country Inn (223 South Milton Rd., 86004; 774-5041) 42 rooms and efficiencies, pool, kitchenettes, pets OK, A/C, TV, NS rooms, wheelchair access, CC. SGL/DBL$55-$65.

Howard Johnson Hotel (2200 East Butler Ave., 86004; 779-6944, Fax 779-6944 ext 341, 800-I-GO-HOJO) 100 rooms and suites, restaurant, lounge, entertainment, indoor pool, sauna, children free with parents, wheelchair access, NS rooms, TV, A/C, pets OK, laundry facilities, fireplaces, senior rates, meeting facilities, CC. SGL/DBL$62-$82.

The Inn at Four Ten (410 North Lerous St., 86003; 774-0088) free breakfast, NS rooms, A/C, TV, CC. SGL/DBL$55-$85.

Little America North (2515 East Butler Ave., 86004; 779-2741, Fax 779-7983, 800-352-4386) 248 rooms and suites, restaurant, lounge, pool, exercise center, sauna, whirlpools, A/C, TV, NS rooms, wheelchair access, airport transportation, in-room refrigerators and coffee makers, fireplaces, gift shop, laundry facilities, children free with parents, no pets, senior rates, meeting facilities, CC. SGL/DBL$90-$100, STS$110-$186.

Master Hosts Five Flags Inn (2610 East Route 66, 86004; 526-1388, 800-251-1962) 87 rooms, restaurant, lounge, heated pool, in-room refrigerators, NS rooms, A/C, TV, children under 18 free with parents, pets OK, senior rates, meeting facilities, senior rates, CC. SGL/DBL$35-$63.

Monte Vista Hotel (100 North San Francisco St., 86004; 779-6971, Fax 779-2904) 35 rooms, restaurant, A/C, TV, NS rooms, wheelchair access, CC. SGL/DBL$25-$110.

Motel 6 West (2500 East Lucky Lane, 86004; 779-6184, 505-891-6161) 121 rooms, pool, free local calls, children under 17 free with parents, NS rooms, A/C, wheelchair access, pets OK, TV, CC. SGL/DBL$27-$44.

Motel 6 (2745 South Woodlands Village, 86001; 779-3757, 505-891-6161) 150 rooms, pool, free local calls, children under 17 free with parents, wheelchair access, pets OK, NS rooms, A/C, TV, CC. SGL/DBL$38-$41.

Quality Inn (2000 South Milton Rd., 86001; 774-8771, Fax 774-0216, 800-221-2222) 96 rooms, restaurant, free breakfast, heated pool, exercise center, children free with parents, A/C, TV, room service, laundry service, NS rooms, pets OK, meeting facilities, senior rates, CC. SGL/DBL$75-$100.

Quality Suites (706 South Milton Rd., 86001; 774-4333, Fax 774-0216, 800-221-2222) 102 suites, restaurant, free breakfast, heated pool, exercise center, whirlpools, children free with parents, A/C, TV, room service, laundry service, gift shop, no pets, NS rooms, meeting facilities, senior rates, CC. SGL/DBL$95-$175.

Relax Inn Motel (1416 East Route 66, 86004; 774-5123) 30 rooms, outdoor heated pool, pets OK, A/C, TV, NS rooms, wheelchair access, CC. SGL/DBL$18-$70.

Rodeway Inn East (2350 East Lucky Lane, 86004; 779-3614, 800-424-4777) 101 rooms, pool, wheelchair access, NS rooms, children free with parents, free local calls, A/C, TV, senior rates, CC. SGL/DBL$38-$95.

Super 8 Motel (3725 Kasper Ave., 86004; 526-0818, Fax 526-8786, 800-800-8000) 86 rooms and suites, restaurant, whirlpools, sauna, pets OK, children under 12 free with parents, free local calls, A/C, TV, in-room refrigerators and microwaves, wheelchair access, fax, NS rooms, senior rates, wheelchair access, meeting facilities, senior rates, CC. SGL/DBL$35-$55.

TraveLodge Grand Canyon (2520 East Lucky Lane, 86004; 779-5121, Fax 774-3809, 800-578-7878) 140 rooms and suites, pool, wheelchair access, complimentary newspaper, laundry service, TV, A/C, free local calls, fax, NS rooms, in-room refrigerators and microwaves, children under 18 free with parents, no pets, meeting facilities, senior rates, CC. SGL/DBL$42-$78.

Florence
Area Code 602

Blue Mist Motel (40 South Pinal Pkwy., 85232; 868-5875) 22 rooms and efficiencies, A/C, TV, NS rooms, wheelchair access, CC. SGL/DBL$25-$45.

Forest Lakes
Area Code 602

Forest Lakes Lodge (Forest Lake 85931; 535-4727) 20 rooms, no pets, children free with parents, in-room refrigerators and microwaves, TV, NS rooms, wheelchair access, CC. SGL/DBL$39-$59.

Gila Bend
Area Code 602

Best Western Space Age Lodge (401 East Pima, 85337; 683-2273, 800-528-1234) 41 rooms, restaurant, free breakfast, lounge, pool, exercise center, whirlpools, children free with parents, A/C, NS rooms, TV, laundry facilities, wheelchair access, pets OK, senior rates, meeting facilities, CC. SGL/DBL$45-$68.

Super 8 Motel (I-8 and Hwy. 85, 85337; 683-6311, Fax 683-2120, 800-800-8000) 63 rooms and suites, restaurant, outdoor heated pool, no pets, children under 12 free with parents, free local calls, A/C, TV, in-room refrigerators and microwaves, fax, NS rooms, senior rates, wheelchair access, meeting facilities, CC. SGL/DBL$33-$55.

Glendale
Area Code 602

Best Western Sage Inn (5940 Northwest Grand Ave., 85301; 939-9431, Fax 939-9431 ext 146, 800-528-1234) 83 rooms, restaurant, free breakfast, lounge, pool, exercise center, children free with parents, A/C, NS rooms, TV, laundry facilities, wheelchair access, pets OK, senior rates, meeting facilities, CC. SGL/DBL$55-$65.

Globe
Area Code 602

Cloud Nine Motel (1649 East Ash St., 85501; 425-5741) 71 rooms, heated pool, whirlpools, in-room refrigerators, no pets, TV, NS rooms, wheelchair access, CC. SGL/DBL$47-$55.

Copper Manor Motel (637 East Ash St., 85501; 425-7124) 39 rooms, outdoor heated pool, children free with parents, TV, NS rooms, wheelchair access, pets OK, in-room refrigerators, CC. SGL/DBL$42-$52.

Goodyear
Area Code 602

Best Western Inn (1100 North Litchfield Rd., 85338; 932-3210, 800-528-1234) 78 rooms, pool, exercise center, children free with parents, A/C, NS rooms, TV, laundry facilities, wheelchair access, pets OK, senior rates, meeting facilities, CC. SGL/DBL$50-$82.

Comfort Inn (1770 North Dysart Rd., 85338; 932-9191, 800-221-2222) 160 rooms, restaurant, lounge, free breakfast, pool, sauna, fax, wheelchair access, NS rooms, no pets, children under 18 free with parents, A/C, TV, meeting facilities, senior rates, CC. SGL/DBL$45-$100.

Grand Canyon Lodge (85338; 638-2611) 201 rooms and cabins, restaurant, lounge, no pets, NS rooms, CC. SGL/DBL$55-$75.

Grand Canyon National Park (South Rim)
Area Code 602

Best Western Grand Canyon Squire Inn (Grand Canyon National Park, 86023; 638-2681, 638-2782, 800-528-1234) 250 rooms, restaurant, lounge, outdoor heated pool, exercise center, whirlpools, sauna, game room, children free with parents, A/C, NS rooms, TV, laundry facilities, wheelchair access, airport transportation, gift shop, pets OK, senior rates, meeting facilities, CC. SGL/DBL$100-$120.

Bright Angel Lodge (West Rim Dr., 86023; 638-2631, Fax 638-9247) 89 rooms and cabins, restaurant, lounge, entertainment, gift shop, fireplaces, kitchenettes, barber and beauty shop, A/C, TV, NS rooms, pets OK, wheelchair access, CC. SGL/DBL$$50-$205.

El Tovar (Grand Canyon National Park, 86023; 638-2631, Fax 638-9247) 78 rooms and suites, restaurant, lounge, entertainment, gift shop, 1905 inn, A/C, children free with parents, pets OK, TV, NS rooms, wheelchair access, CC. SGL/DBL$105-$165, STS$165-$255.

Kachina Lodge (Grand Canyon National Park 86023; 638-2401, Fax 638-9247) 48 rooms, restaurant, TV, NS rooms, wheelchair access, children free with parents, pets OK, meeting facilities, CC. SGL/DBL$90-$100.

Moqui Lodge (Grand Canyon National Park 86023; 638-2424) 136 rooms, TV, no pets, CC. SGL/DBL$70-$80.

Quality Inn at Grand Canyon (Hwys. 64 and 180, 86023; 638-2673, Fax 638-9537, 800-221-2222) 176 rooms and suites, pool, exercise center, whirlpools, children free with parents, A/C, TV, room service, laundry service, gift shop, no pets, NS rooms, meeting facilities, senior rates, CC. SGL/DBL$105-$110.

Red Feathers Lodge (Grand Canyon National Park 86023; 638-2412, Fax 638-9216, 800-538-2345) 106 rooms, restaurant, A/C, TV, NS rooms, wheelchair access, airport transportation, gift shop, CC. SGL/DBL$110.

Yavapai Lodge (Mather Center, 86023; 638-2631, Fax 638-9247) 358 rooms, restaurant, lounge, children free with parents, TV, pets OK, wheelchair access, CC. SGL/DBL$70-$88.

Green Valley
Area Code 602

Quality Inn (111 South La Canada, 85614; 625-2250, 800-221-2222) 109 rooms and suites, restaurant, pool, exercise center, children free with parents, A/C, TV, room service, laundry service, NS rooms, meeting facilities, senior rates, CC. SGL/DBL$69-$105.

Greer
Area Code 601

Greer Lodge (Greer 85927; 735-7515) 16 rooms and cabins, restaurant, free breakfast, fireplaces, water view, TV, NS rooms, kitchenettes, wheelchair access, CC. SGL/DBL$90-$150.

Hereford
Area Code 692

Ramsey Canyon Inn (31 Ramsey Canyon; 85615; 378-3010) 9 rooms and cottages, free breakfast, NS, A/C, TV, NS rooms, wheelchair access, CC. SGL/DBL$75-$85.

Holbrook
Area Code 602

Best Western Adobe Inn (615 West Hopi Dr., 86025; 524-3498, Fax 524-3612, 800-528-1234) 54 rooms, restaurant, free breakfast, lounge, pool, exercise center, children free with parents, A/C, NS rooms, TV, laundry facilities, wheelchair access, pets OK, senior rates, meeting facilities, CC. SGL/DBL$42-$61.

Comfort Inn (2602 East Navajo Blvd., 86025; 524-6131, 800-221-2222) 83 rooms, restaurant, free breakfast, pool, wheelchair access, NS rooms, no pets, children under 18 free with parents, A/C, TV, meeting facilities, senior rates, CC. SGL/DBL$42-$68.

Days Inn (2601 Navajo Blvd., 86025; 524-6949, Fax 524-6665, 800-325-2525) 54 rooms and suites, free breakfast, outdoor pool, children free with parents, room service, laundry service, A/C, TV, free local calls, in-room refrigerators and microwaves, pets OK, fax, wheelchair access, NS rooms, senior rates, CC. SGL/DBL$44-$70, STS$70-$90.

Econo Lodge (2596 Navajo Blvd., 86025; 524-1448, 800-4-CHOICE) 40 rooms, restaurant, pool, children under 12 free with parents, no pets, NS rooms, wheelchair access, A/C, TV, senior rates, CC. SGL/DBL$30-$55.

Holiday Inn (1308 Navajo Blvd., 86025; 524-1466, 800-HOLIDAY) 59 rooms, restaurant, lounge, entertainment, indoor pool, exercise center, whirlpools, children under 19 free with parents, wheelchair access, A/C, TV, NS rooms, fax, room service, pets OK, laundry service, meeting facilities, senior rates, CC. SGL/DBL$45-$58.

Motel 6 (2514 Navajo Blvd., 86025; 524-6101, 505-891-6161) 126 rooms, pool, free local calls, children under 17 free with parents, wheelchair access, pets OK, NS rooms, A/C, TV, CC. SGL/DBL$36-$48.

Rainbow Inn (2211 East Navajo Blvd., 86025; 524-2654) 40 rooms, A/C, in-room refrigerators, TV, NS rooms, pets OK, senior rates, CC. SGL/DBL$30-$48.

Ramada Inn (2604 East Navajo Blvd., 86025; 524-2566, 800-2-RAMADA) 37 rooms and suites, pool, sauna, wheelchair access, NS rooms, no pets, A/C, TV, children under 18 free with parents, room service, laundry facilities, meeting facilities, senior rates, CC. SGL/DBL$35-$66.

Kayenta
Area Code 602

Holiday Inn (Hwys. 160 and 163, 86033; 697-3221, 800-HOLIDAY) 160 rooms and suites, restaurant, lounge, pool, exercise center, children under 19 free with parents, wheelchair access, A/C, TV, NS rooms, fax, room service, no pets, laundry service, gift shop, meeting facilities, senior rates, CC. SGL/DBL$90-$105, STS$100-$115.

Wetherhill Inn (Kayenta 86033; 697-3231) 54 rooms, A/C, TV, no pets, NS, CC. SGL/DBL$45-$80.

Kingman
Area Code 602

Best Western A Wayfarer's Inn (2815 East Andy Devine Ave., 86401; 753-6271, Fax 753-9608, 800-548-5695, 800-528-1234) 100 rooms and suites, restaurant, lounge, heated pool, exercise center, whirlpools, in-room refrigerators and microwaves, children free with parents, A/C, NS rooms,

TV, laundry facilities, wheelchair access, pets OK, senior rates, meeting facilities, CC. SGL/DBL$38-$85.

Days Inn West (3023 Andy Devine Ave, 86401; 753-7500, Fax 753-4686, 800-325-2525) 60 rooms and suites, outdoor pool, jacuzzis, children free with parents, room service, laundry service, A/C, TV, kitchenettes, free local calls, pets OK, airport transportation, fax, wheelchair access, NS rooms, senior rates, CC. SGL/DBL$35-$75.

High Desert Inn (2803 East Andy Devine Ave., 86401; 753-2935) 15 rooms and 2-bedroom suites, A/C, TV, no pets, CC. SGL/DBL$20-$30.

Hill Top (1901 East Andy Devine Ave., 86401; 753-2198) 29 rooms, restaurant, heated pool, in-room refrigerators, A/C, pets OK, laundry facilities, TV, NS rooms, wheelchair access, CC. SGL/DBL$25-$45.

Holiday Inn (3100 East Andy Devine Ave., 86401; 753-6262, 800-HOLI-DAY) 120 rooms, restaurant, lounge, pool, exercise center, children under 19 free with parents, wheelchair access, A/C, TV, NS rooms, fax, room service, airport transportation, pets OK, laundry service, meeting facilities, senior rates, CC. SGL/DBL$50-$70.

National 9 Imperial Inn (1911 Andy Devine Ave., 86401; 753-2176, 800-524-9999) 25 rooms, heated pool, NS rooms, wheelchair access, A/C, TV, children free with parents, senior rates, CC. SGL/DBL$30-$36.

Quality Inn (1400 East Andy Devine Ave., 86401; 753-4747, 800-221-2222) 98 rooms and suites, restaurant, lounge, pool, exercise center, whirlpools, children free with parents, A/C, TV, room service, local transportation, laundry service, NS rooms, meeting facilities, senior rates, CC. SGL/DBL$45-$55.

Rodeway Inn (411 West Beale St., 86401; 753-5521, 800-424-4777) 37 rooms, restaurant, pool, wheelchair access, NS rooms, children free with parents, A/C, TV, senior rates, CC. SGL/DBL$26-$42.

Sunny Inn (3275 East Andy Devine Ave., 86401; 757-1188) 65 rooms, pool, whirlpools, laundry facilities, A/C, TV, NS rooms, wheelchair access, no pets, CC. SGL/DBL$25-$40.

Super 8 Motel (3401 East Andy Devine Ave., 86401; 757-4808, Fax 757-4808 ext 324, 800-800-8000) 61 rooms and suites, no pets, children under 12 free with parents, free local calls, A/C, TV, in-room refrigerators and microwaves, fax, NS rooms, senior rates, wheelchair access, meeting facilities, CC. SGL/DBL$30-$45.

Lake Havasu City
Area Code 602

Acoma Inn (89 Acoma Blvd., 86403; 855-2084) 25 rooms, pool, spa, A/C, TV, NS rooms, wheelchair access, laundry facilities, CC. SGL/DBL$39-$85.

Blue Danube Inn (2176 Birch Sq., 86403; 855-5566) 48 rooms and apartments, pool, spa, laundry facilities, A/C, kitchenettes, TV, NS rooms, wheelchair access, CC. SGL/DBL$45-$140.

Bridgeview Motel (101 London Bridge Rd., 86403; 855-5559) 37 rooms, pool, pets OK, A/C, TV, NS rooms, wheelchair access, CC. SGL/DBL$35-$70.

El Aztec Motel and Apartments (2078 Swanson Ave., 86403; 453-7172) 16 rooms and 1-bedroom apartments, pool, laundry facilities, kitchenettes, A/C, TV, NS rooms, wheelchair access, senior rates, CC. SGL/DBL$34-$59.

Havasu Motel All-Suite Inn (2035 Acoma Blvd., 86403; 855-2311) 24 suites, kitchenettes, laundry facilities, A/C, TV, NS rooms, wheelchair access, senior rates, CC. SGL/DBL$20-$45.

Hidden Palms All-Suite Inn (2100 Swanson Ave., 86403; 855-7144) 22 1-bedroom suites, pool, kitchenettes, A/C, TV, NS rooms, laundry facilities, senior rates, wheelchair access, CC. SGL/DBL$45-$75.

Holiday Inn (245 London Bridge Rd., 86403; 855-4071, Fax 855-2379, 800-HOLIDAY) 162 rooms and suites, restaurant, lounge, heated pool, exercise center, children under 19 free with parents, wheelchair access, A/C, TV, NS rooms, fax, airport courtesy car, in-room refrigerators, room service, pets OK, laundry service, meeting facilities, senior rates, CC. SGL/DBL$45-$88, STS$100-$135.

Island Inn Hotel (1300 McCulloch Blvd., 86403; 680-0606) 115 rooms, restaurant, lounge, heated pool, whirlpools, children free with parents, pets OK, laundry facilities, airport transportation, limousine service, A/C, TV, NS rooms, wheelchair access, CC. SGL/DBL$52-$85.

Lakeview Motel (440 London Bridge Rd., 86403; 855-3605) 14 efficiencies, pets OK, A/C, TV, NS rooms, wheelchair access, senior rates, CC. SGL/DBL$24-$45.

Nautical Inn and Townhouses (1000 McCulloch Blvd., 86403; 855-2141, 800-892-2141) 120 rooms and 2-bedroom townhouses, restaurant, lounge, pool, spa, laundry facilities, A/C, TV, NS rooms, wheelchair access, 4 meeting rooms, meeting facilities for 400, senior rates, CC. SGL/DBL$50-$150.

Pecos II Condominiums (465 Lake Havasu Ave. North, 86403; 855-7444) 15 2-bedroom condominiums, pool, spa, pets OK, kitchenettes, A/C, TV, NS rooms, wheelchair access, CC. 2BR$350W.

Pioneer Hotel (271 Lake Havasu Ave., 86403; 855-1111, 800-528-5169) 200 rooms and suites, restaurant, lounge, entertainment, pool, spa, pets OK, laundry facilities, airport transportation, fax, A/C, TV, NS rooms, wheelchair access, 2 meeting rooms, meeting facilities for 250, senior rates, CC. SGL/DBL$35-$69.

Sandman Inn (1700 McCulloch Blvd., 86403; 855-7841, 800-835-2410) 89 rooms and suites, pool, pets OK, laundry facilities, A/C, fax, TV, NS rooms, wheelchair access, meeting facilities for 50, senior rates, CC. SGL/DBL$25-$95.

Sands Resort Hotel (2040 Mesquite Ave., 86403; 855-1388, 800-521-0360) 42 1- and 2-bedroom suites, pool, tennis courts, laundry facilities, VCRs, A/C, TV, NS rooms, wheelchair access, CC. SGL/DBL$50-$200.

Shakespeare Inn (2190 McCulloch Blvd., 86403; 855-4157) 32 rooms and suites, restaurant, lounge, pool, A/C, TV, NS rooms, wheelchair access, meeting facilities for 150, senior rates, CC. SGL/DBL$23-$85.

Tamarisk Inn (3101 London Bridge Rd., 86403; 764-3033) 18 suites, pool, laundry facilities, A/C, kitchenettes, fax, TV, NS rooms, wheelchair access, CC. SGL/DBL$39-$120.

TraveLodge (480 London Bridge Rd., 86403; 680-9202, Fax 680-1511, 800-578-7878) 37 rooms, restaurant, lounge, free breakfast, pool, wheelchair access, complimentary newspaper, laundry service, TV, A/C, free local calls, fax, NS rooms, in-room refrigerators and microwaves, children under 18 free with parents, no pets, meeting facilities for 25, senior rates, CC. SGL/DBL$40-$150.

Windsor Inn (451 London Bridge Rd., 86403; 855-4135, 800-245-4135) 64 rooms and suites, pool, spa, pets OK, kitchenettes, A/C, TV, NS rooms, wheelchair access, in-room refrigerators, CC. SGL/DBL$26-$49.

Xanadu Condo Resort (276 South Lake Havasu Ave., 86403; 855-8300) 75 suites, heated pool, spa, whirlpools, beauty shop, laundry facilities, A/C, TV, NS rooms, wheelchair access, meeting facilities for 60, CC. SGL/DBL$70-$150.

Lakeside

Area Code 602

Bartram's White Mountain Bed and Breakfast (Lakeside 85929; 367-1408) 3 rooms, free breakfast, no pets, NS rooms, A/C, TV, senior rates, CC. SGL/DBL$40-$80.

84
4rgm

8**Lazy Oaks Resort** (Lakeside 85929; 368-6203) 15 rooms and 1- and 2-bedroom cottages, laundry facilities, fireplace, children free with parents, TV, kitchenettes, CC. SGL/DBL$50-$100.

Litchfield Park
Area Code 602

The Wigwam Resort and Country Club (300 East Indian School Rd., Litchfield Park 85340; 935-3811, Fax 935-3737, 800-323-7500) 331 rooms and suites, restaurant, lounge, entertainment, heated pool, lighted tennis courts, exercise center, whirlpools, sauna, gift shop, barber and beauty shop, fireplaces, 24-hour room service, airport transportation, fireplaces, A/C, TV, meeting facilities for 1,100, CC. SGL/DBL$200-$280, STS$335-$420.

Lukeville
Area Code 602

Gringo Pass Motel (Lukeville 85341; 254-9284) 12 rooms and efficiencies, laundry facilities, pool, kitchenettes, A/C, TV, NS rooms, wheelchair access, CC. SGL/DBL$50-$65.

Marble Canyon
Area Code 602

Cliff Dweller's Lodge (Marble Canyon 86036; 355-2228, 800-433-2543) 20 rooms, restaurant, lounge, A/C, no pets, TV, NS rooms, wheelchair access, CC. SGL/DBL$50-$65.

Marble Canyon Lodge (Marble Canyon 86036; 355-2225, 800-726-1789) 58 rooms and efficiencies, restaurant, lounge, pets OK, in-room coffee makers, kitchenettes, local transportation, A/C, TV, NS rooms, wheelchair access, CC. SGL/DBL$40-$90.

Mesa
Area Code 602

Arizona Golf Resort and Conference Center (425 South Power Rd., 85206; 832-3202, Fax 981-0151, 800-528-8282) 162 rooms and suites, restaurant, lounge, entertainment, heated pool, jacuzzi, golf, lighted tennis courts, in-room refrigerators, A/C, TV, NS rooms, wheelchair access, airport transportation, pets OK, airport transportation, meeting facilities, CC. SGL/DBL$100-$155, STS$150-$285.

Best Western Mesa Inn (1625 East Main St., 85204; 964-8000, 800-528-1234) 99 rooms, restaurant, lounge, pool, exercise center, children free with parents, A/C, NS rooms, TV, laundry facilities, wheelchair access, pets OK, senior rates, free local calls, meeting facilities, CC. SGL/DBL$48-$64.

Days Inn (5531 East Main St., 85205; 981-8111, Fax 396-8027, 800-325-2525) 61 rooms and suites, free breakfast, outdoor pool, whirlpools, children free with parents, room service, laundry service, A/C, TV, free local calls, pets OK, fax, wheelchair access, NS rooms, senior rates, CC. SGL/DBL$35-$79.

Days Inn (333 West Juanita Ave., 85202; 844-8900, 800-325-2525) 124 rooms and suites, free breakfast, outdoor pool, jacuzzis, children free with parents, room service, laundry service, A/C, TV, free local calls, pets OK, fax, wheelchair access, NS rooms, senior rates, CC. SGL/DBL$40-$55.

Dobson Ranch Inn and Resort (1666 South Dobson Rd., 85201; 831-7000) 212 rooms and 1-bedroom suites, restaurant, lounge, heated pool, whirlpools, children free with parents, A/C, TV, NS rooms, wheelchair access, in-room refrigerators and microwaves, CC. SGL/DBL$65-$115.

Hilton Pavilion Hotel (1011 West Holmes Ave., 85210; 833-5555, Fax 649-1886, 800-HILTONS) 263 rooms and suites, restaurant, two lounges, pool, whirlpools, golf, concierge, NS rooms, A/C, TV, wheelchair access, in-room computer hookups, no pets, car rental desk, airport transportation, airline ticket desk, gift shop, beauty shop, business services, 11 meeting rooms, meeting facilities for 1,500, CC. SGL/DBL$99-$109, STS$115-$300.

Holiday Inn (1600 South Country Club Dr., 85210; 964-7000, 800-HOLI-DAY) 245 rooms and 2-room suites, restaurant, lounge, entertainment, indoor and outdoor pools, sauna, jacuzzi, A/C, TV, pets OK, in-room refrigerators, children free with parents, NS rooms, CC. SGL$49-$59, DBL$59-$69.

Lexington Hotels Suites and Inns (1410 South Country Club Dr., 85210; 964-2897, Fax 833-0536, 800-927-8483) 120 1- and 2-bedroom suites, free breakfast, heated pool, whirlpools, A/C, no pets, TV, fax, laundry facilities, NS rooms, children free with parents, wheelchair access, meeting facilities, senior rates, CC. SGL/DBL$50-$150.

Maricopa Inn Motor Hotel (3 East Main St., 85210; 834-6060) 62 rooms, outdoor pool, pets OK, children free with parents, A/C, TV, NS rooms, wheelchair access, CC. SGL/DBL$30-$50.

Motel 6 South (1511 South Country Club Dr., 85202; 834-0066, 505-891-6161) 91 rooms, pool, free local calls, children under 17 free with parents, NS rooms, wheelchair access, pets OK, A/C, TV, CC. SGL/DBL$36-$46.

Rodeway Inn (5700 East Main St., 85205; 985-3600, 800-424-4777) 88 rooms, restaurant, lounge, pool, exercise center, wheelchair access, NS rooms, children free with parents, A/C, TV, senior rates, CC. SGL/DBL$39-$99.

Saguaro Lake Ranch Resort (13020 Bush Hwy., 85205; 984-2194) 25 rooms and cottages, pool, A/C, TV, CC. SGL/DBL$66-$96.

Sheraton Mesa Hotel (200 North Centennial Way, 85201; 898-8300, Fax 964-9279, 800-325-3535) 275 rooms and suites, restaurant, lounge, entertainment, heated pool, exercise center, spa, lighted tennis courts, whirlpools, in-room refrigerators, NS rooms, A/C, TV, children free with parents, wheelchair access, 45,000 square feet of meeting and exhibition space, meeting facilities for 1,800, CC. SGL/DBL$90-$150.

Miami
Area Code 602

Best Western Copper Hills Inn and Resort (Hwy. 60, 85539; 425-7151, Fax 425-2504, 800-528-1234) 68 rooms, restaurant, lounge, pool, exercise center, children free with parents, A/C, NS rooms, TV, laundry facilities, in-room refrigerators, gift shop, wheelchair access, pets OK, senior rates, meeting facilities, CC. SGL/DBL$57-$70.

Nogales
Area Code 602

Americana Motel (639 North Grand Ave., 85621; 287-7211, Fax 287-5188, 800-874-8079) 97 rooms, restaurant, lounge, heated pool, pets OK, room service, barber and beauty shop, A/C, TV, children free with parents, NS rooms, wheelchair access, meeting facilities, senior rates, CC. SGL/DBL$55-$70.

Best Western Siesta Motel (673 North Grand Ave., 85621; 287-4671, Fax 287-9616, 800-528-1234) 47 rooms, restaurant, free breakfast, lounge, heated pool, spa, exercise center, children free with parents, A/C, NS rooms, TV, laundry facilities, wheelchair access, pets OK, senior rates, meeting facilities, CC. SGL/DBL$58-$65.

Rico Resort (1064 Camino Caralamp, 85621; 281-1901, Fax 281-7132, 800-288-4746) 175 rooms and suites, restaurant, lounge, heated pool, sauna, whirlpools, exercise center, lighted tennis courts, room service, A/C, TV, NS rooms, wheelchair access, senior rates, CC. SGL/DBL$70-$300.

Super 8 Motel (547 West Mariposa Rd., 85621; 281-2242, 800-800-8000) 116 rooms and suites, restaurant, lounge, pool, whirlpools, no pets, children under 12 free with parents, free local calls, A/C, TV, in-room refrigerators and microwaves, fax, NS rooms, wheelchair access, meeting facilities, senior rates, CC. SGL/DBL$42-$55.

Oracle
Area Code 602

Inn at the Biosphere (Oracle 85623; 825-6222) 27 rooms, restaurant, lounge, pool, whirlpools, lighted tennis courts, children free with parents, no pets, in-room refrigerators, laundry facilities, A/C, TV, NS rooms, wheelchair access, CC. SGL/DBL$50-$80.

Villa Cardinale (1315 West Oracle Ranch Rd., 85623; 896-2516, Fax 896-2304) 4 rooms, free breakfast, fireplaces, children free with parents, pets OK, A/C, TV, CC. SGL/DBL$45-$55.

Page
Area Code 602

Best Western Weston Inn (201 North Lake Powell Blvd., 86040; 645-2451, Fax 645-9552, 800-528-1234) 91 rooms, restaurant, free breakfast, lounge, pool, exercise center, airport courtesy car, children free with parents, A/C, airport courtesy car, NS rooms, TV, laundry facilities, wheelchair access, pets OK, senior rates, meeting facilities, CC. SGL/DBL$32-$90.

Econo Lodge (121 South Lake Powell Blvd., 86040; 645-2488, 800-4-CHOICE) 62 rooms and suites, pool, children under 12 free with parents, no pets, senior rates, NS rooms, wheelchair access, A/C, TV, in-room refrigerators, senior rates, CC. SGL/DBL$48-$52.

Empire House (107 South Lake Powell Blvd., 86040; 645-2451, Fax 645-9552) 69 rooms, restaurant, lounge, pool, A/C, TV, NS rooms, pets OK, gift shop, airport transportation, wheelchair access, CC. SGL/DBL$50-$63.

The Inn at Lake Powell (716 Rimview Dr., 86040; 645-2466, Fax 645-2466 ext 501, 800-826-2718) 103 rooms and suites, restaurant, lounge, pool, whirlpools, pets OK, children free with parents, airport transportation, A/C, TV, NS rooms, wheelchair access, CC. SGL/DBL$40-$95.

Lake Powell Motel (Page 86040; 645-2477, 800-528-6154) 24 rooms, pool, pets OK, airport transportation, children free with parents, A/C, TV, NS rooms, pets OK, wheelchair access, CC. SGL/DBL$55-$65.

Wahweap Lodge and Marina (Page 86040; 645-2433) 350 rooms and suites, restaurant, lounge, entertainment, heated pool, whirlpools, local transportation, in-room refrigerators, pets OK, A/C, TV, NS rooms, wheelchair access, room service, CC. SGL/DBL$58-$110.

Parker

Area Code 602

Holiday Inn (604 California Ave., 85344; 669-2133, Fax 669-6676, 800-HOLIDAY) 41 rooms, restaurant, lounge, pool, exercise center, children under 19 free with parents, wheelchair access, A/C, TV, NS rooms, fax, in-room refrigerators, children free with parents, room service, no pets, laundry service, meeting facilities, senior rates, CC. SGL/DBL$55-$65.

Kofa Inn (1700 California Ave., 85344; 669-2101) 41 rooms, pool, A/C, TV, NS rooms, wheelchair access, CC. SGL/DBL$31-436.

Patagonia

Area Code 602

The Stage Stop Inn (Patagonia 85624; 394-2211) 43 rooms and efficiencies, restaurant, pool, A/C, TV, NS rooms, wheelchair access, children free with parents, meeting rooms, CC. SGL/DBL$40-$50.

Payson

Area Code 602

Majestic Mountain Inn (602 East Hwy. 260, 85541; 474-0185) 25 rooms, whirlpools, children free with parents, pets OK, in-room refrigerators and coffee makers, A/C, TV, NS rooms, wheelchair access, CC. SGL/DBL$35-$75.

Payson Pueblo Inn (809 East Hwy. 260, 85541; 474-5241) 31 rooms, whirlpools, A/C, TV, in-room refrigerators, NS rooms, wheelchair access, senior rates, CC. SGL/DBL$37-$63.

TraveLodge (101 West Phoenix St., 85541; 474-4526, Fax 474-4526, 800-578-7878) 39 rooms, restaurant, lounge, free breakfast, pool, wheelchair access, complimentary newspaper, laundry service, TV, A/C, free local calls, fax, NS rooms, in-room refrigerators and microwaves, children under 18 free with parents, pets OK, meeting facilities, CC. SGL/DBL$32-$75.

Phoenix

Area Code 602

Rental and Reservation Services

Evans Withycombe (4455 East Camelback Rd., 85018; 840-1040)

Phoenix-Scottsdale Hotel Reservations (800-528-0483)

Arizona Association of Bed and Breakfast Inns (3661 North Campbell Ave., Tucson, 85719; 231-6777)

Bed and Breakfast In Arizona (Box 8628, Scottsdale 85252; 995-2831, 800266-STAY)

Downtown Phoenix

Budget Lodge (402 West Van Buren St., 85003; 254-7247) 65 rooms, A/C, TV, laundry facilities, CC. Near the Convention Center. SGL$20, DBL$22.

Days Inn (502 West Camelback Rd., 85013; 264-9290, Fax 264-3068, 800-688-2021) 166 rooms and suites, restaurant, lounge, entertainment, heated pool, hot tub, whirlpools, in-room refrigerators, pets OK, airport transportation, A/C, TV, meeting facilities, senior rates, CC. Eight miles from the airport. SGL/DBL$60-$80, STS$130-$160.

Econo Lodge (5050 North Black Canyon Hwy., 85011; 242-8011, 800-446-6900) 40 rooms, free breakfast, jacuzzi, pets OK, A/C, TV, meeting facilities, CC. SGL/DBL$45-$68.

Hyatt Regency Phoenix (122 North Second St., 85004; 252-1234, Fax 254-9472, 800-228-9000, 800-233-1234) 711 rooms, restaurant, heated pool, exercise center, spa, whirlpools, NS rooms, A/C, TV, room service, wheelchair access, boutiques, children free with parents, car rental desk, business service, meeting facilities, CC. Near the Phoenix Civic Center. SGL/DBL$165-$190, STS$250-$700.

Lexington Hotels Suites and Inns (100 West Clarendon, 85013; 279-9811, Fax 631-9358, 800-927-8483) 167 rooms and suites, free breakfast, heated pool, exercise center, whirlpools, sauna, airport transportation, boutiques, pets OK, children free with parents, A/C, TV, fax, laundry facilities, NS rooms, wheelchair access, CC. SGL/DBL$75-$110.

Maricopa Manor (Box 7186, 85011; 274-6302) 5 suites, bed and breakfast, spa, A/C, TV, NS, 1920s inn, children free with parents, kitchenettes, meeting facilities, CC. Near the Convention Center. SGL/DBL$4129-$144.

Motel 6 East (5313 East Van Buren St., 85008; 267-8555) 85 rooms, pool, A/C, laundry facilities, TV, CC. SGL/DBL$43-$45.

Park Central Motor Hotel (3033 North Seventh Ave., 85013; 227-2621) 99 rooms and apartments, restaurant, heated pool, pets OK, A/C, TV, laundry service, in-room refrigerators, CC. SGL/DBL$56-$73.

Radisson Midtown Madison Hotel (3738 North Fourth Ave., 85013; 234-2464, 800-333-3333) 106 rooms and suites, restaurant, lounge, free breakfast, heated pool, exercise center, jacuzzi, children free with parents, airport courtesy car, wheelchair access, NS rooms, A/C, TV, meeting facilities, CC. SGL/DBL$115-$138, STS$110-$135.

Ramada Hotel Downtown (401 North First St., 85004; 258-3411, Fax 258-3171, 800-2-RAMADA) 160 rooms, heated outdoor pool, lounge, free breakfast, entertainment, NS rooms, A/C, TV, wheelchair access, room service, children free with parents, airport transportation, meeting facilities for 300, CC. Near the Convention Center, Symphony Hall and Sports Arena. SGL/DBL$60-$260.

Ritz Carlton (2401 East Camelback Rd., 85016; 468-0700, Fax 468-0793, 800-241-3333) 281 rooms and suites, Ritz Carlton Club, restaurant, lounge, entertainment, pool, spa, exercise center, tennis courts, whirlpools, room service, NS rooms, gift shop, A/C, TV, local transportation, 7,728 square feet of meeting and exhibition space, 9 meeting rooms, CC. SGL/DBL$150-$375.

North Phoenix

The Arizona Biltmore (24th St. and Missouri, 85016; 955-6600, Fax 381-7600, 800-950-0086, 800-228-3000, 800-528-3696) 502 rooms and suites, four restaurants, two lounges, three heated pools, whirlpools, sauna, exercise center, lighted tennis courts, golf, car rental desk, complimentary newspaper, no pets, 24-hour room service, wheelchair access/rooms, NS rooms, A/C, TV, 19 meeting rooms, meeting facilities for 2,000, CC. Located near Biltmore Fashion Park Shopping Center, 8 miles from the downtown area, seven miles from the airport. SGL$210-$290, STS$600-$1,050, X$25.

Comfort Inn North (1711 West Bell Rd., 85023; 866-2089, 800-221-2222) 147 rooms and suites, restaurant, free breakfast, heated outdoor pool, sauna, no pets, local transportation, in-room refrigerators, meeting facilities, senior rates, CC. 10 minutes from the downtown area, 6 miles from Sun City. SGL/DBL$54-$89.

Corner Inn and Suites (4301 North 24th St., 85016; 954-9220) 122 2-room suites, free breakfast, pool, pets OK, in-room refrigerators and microwaves, airport courtesy car, A/C, TV, meeting facilities, CC. SGL/DBL$45-$125.

Crown Sterling Suites Biltmore (2630 East Camelback Rd., 85016; 955-3992, 800-433-4600) 233 suites, restaurant, lounge, free breakfast, heated pool, golf, whirlpools, A/C, TV, wheelchair access, NS rooms, children free with parents, local transportation, meeting facilities, senior rates, CC. 5 miles from the airport. SGL/DBL$160-$195.

La Quinta Inn (2510 West Greenway Rd., 85023; 993-0800, Fax 789-9172, 800-531-5900) 149 rooms and suites, restaurant, free breakfast, lounge, pool, lighted tennis courts, sauna, complimentary newspaper, free local calls, fax, laundry service, NS rooms, in-room refrigerators, wheelchair access, remote control TV, A/C, meeting facilities, senior rates, CC. SGL/DBL$75-$130.

Northeast Phoenix

Ambassador Inn (4727 East Thomas Rd., 85018; 840-7500, 800-624-6759) 170 efficiencies, restaurant, lounge, heated pool, kitchenettes, airport courtesy car, A/C, TV, meeting facilities, CC. Five miles from the airport. SGL/DBL$30-$60.

InnSuites Phoenix Central (3101 North 32nd St., 85018; 956-4900, 800-842-4242) 76 suites, free breakfast, lounge, heated pool, jacuzzi, exercise center, spa, kitchenettes, airport courtesy car, fax, business services, A/C, TV, meeting facilities for 70, CC. SGL/DBL$42-$72.

Wooley Suites Hotel (3211 East Pinchot, 85018; 957-1350) 104 suites, free breakfast, heated outdoor pool, airport transportation, A/C, TV, meeting facilities. SGL/DBL$49-$69; SGL/DBL$54-$74.

Northwest Phoenix

The Crescent Hotel at Koll Center (2520 West Dunlop, 85021; 943-8200, 800-423-4126, 800-221-6222) 342 rooms and suites, restaurant, lounge, entertainment, heated pool, exercise center, whirlpools, lighted tennis courts, airport courtesy car, boutiques, gift shop, children free with parents, wheelchair access, NS rooms, in-room refrigerators, A/C, TV, meeting facilities. SGL$120-$500.

Hampton Inn (8101 North Black Canyon Hwy., 85021; 864-6233, Fax 995-7503, 800-426-7866, 800-HAMPTON) 149 rooms, free breakfast, heated pool, whirlpools, children free with parents, NS rooms, A/C, TV, wheelchair access, computer hookups, fax, pets OK, free local calls, meeting facilities, CC. Near the Metrocenter Mall, 13 miles from the airport. SGL/DBL$75-$80.

The Pointe at Squaw Park (7677 North 16th St., 85020; 997-2626, 800-528--0428) 600 2-room suites, restaurant, lounge, free breakfast, pool, exercise center, spa, tennis courts, A/C, TV, meeting facilities, CC. SGL/DBL$179.

The Pointe at Tapatio Cliffs (11111 North Seventh St., 85020; 866-7500, 800-876-4683) 600 2-room suites, restaurant, lounge, entertainment, free breakfast, pool, exercise center, spa, tennis courts, golf, A/C, TV, meeting facilities, CC. SGL/DBL$159.

Travelers Inn (I-17 and Northern Ave., 85051; 995-8451, 800-633-8300) 126 rooms and suites, pool, free local calls, NS rooms, A/C, TV, wheelchair access, meeting facilities, CC. 5 miles from the downtown area, 10 miles from the Phoenix airport and State Capital building. SGL$40, DBL$45.

TraveLodge Metro Central (8617 North Black Canyon Hwy., 85021; 995-9500, Fax 995-0150, 800-255-3050) 171 rooms, restaurant, free breakfast, lounge, pool, spa, whirlpools, car rental desk, laundry service, local transportation, fax, A/C, TV, meeting facilities, CC. Near the MetroCenter Mall and Recreational Center, 10 miles from the airport, 9 miles from the downtown area, 15 miles from Sun City. SGL/DBL$50-$65.

Westcourt Hotel (10220 North Metro Pkwy., 85051; 997-5900, 800-858-1033) 284 rooms and 2-room suites, Executive Floor, restaurant, lounge, heated pool, exercise center, sauna, lighted tennis courts, children free with parents, boutiques, wheelchair access, NS rooms, A/C, TV, meeting facilities, senior rates, CC. SGL/DBL$$95-$250.

West Phoenix

Embassy Suites Westside (3210 Northwest Grand Ave., 85017; 2793211, 800-326-2779, 800-EMBASSY) 167 2-room suites, restaurant, free breakfast, pool, exercise center, spa, NS rooms, A/C, TV, room service, pets OK, business services, 7 meeting rooms, CC. SGL$57-$92, DBL$67-$92.

Hilton Suites Phoenix Plaza (10 East Thomas Rd., 85034; 222-1111, Fax 2654841, 800-HILTONS) 226 2-room suites, restaurant, lounge, free breakfast, pool, exercise center, spa, in-room refrigerators, VCRs, NS rooms, A/C, TV, wheelchair access, fax, gift shop, business services, 6 meeting rooms, meeting facilities for 250, CC. 5 miles from the airport, 2 miles from the Phoenix Civic Center. SGL/DBL$80-$170.

Holiday Inn (1500 North 51st St., 85043; 484-9009, Fax 484-9009 ext 505, 800-HOLIDAY) 144 rooms, restaurant, lounge, entertainment, indoor and outdoor pools, exercise center, spa, sauna, wheelchair access, pets OK, A/C, TV, meeting facilities for 300, CC. SGL/DBL$65-$75.

Motel 6 Airport (214 South 24th St., 85034; 244-1155, 891-6161) 61 rooms, pool, free local calls, children under 17 free with parents, NS rooms, wheelchair access, pets OK, A/C, TV, CC. SGL/DBL$38-$44.

Rodeway Inn Grand (3400 Grand Ave., 85017; 264-9164, Fax 264-7633, 800-228-2000) 132 rooms, restaurant, lounge, pool, whirlpools, children free with parents, A/C, TV, meeting facilities, CC. SGL/DBL$36-$52.

Travelers Inn (150 and 51st Ave., 85043; 233-1988, 800-633-8300) 125 rooms and suites, pool, free local calls, NS rooms, wheelchair access, A/C, TV, meeting facilities, CC. 4 miles from the downtown area, 10 miles from the airport and State Capital building. SGL/DBL$35-$55.

Airport Area

Best Western Airport Hotel (2425 South 24th St., 85034; 273-7251, Fax 273-7180, 800-528-1234) 114 rooms, restaurant, lounge, pool, NS rooms, A/C, TV, children free with parents, CC. SGL$49-$67, DBL$54-$67.

Comfort Inn Airport (4120 East Van Buren Pkwy., 85008; 275-5746, 800-- 221-2222) 47 rooms, restaurant, pool, no pets, children free with parents, A/C, kitchenettes, TV, meeting facilities, senior rates, CC. SGL$46-$52, DBL$52-$58.

Days Inn Airport (3333 East Van Burne, 85008; 244-8244, Fax 244-8240, 800-325-2525) 206 rooms and suites, restaurant, lounge, two pools, spa, exercise center, room service, pets OK, wheelchair access, limousine service, NS rooms, A/C, TV, fax, pets OK, airport transportation, meeting facilities, senior rates, CC. 2 miles from the airport, 3 miles from the Civic Plaza, 2 miles from the Phoenix Zoo. SGL/DBL$54-$79.

Double Tree Suites at Phoenix Gateway Center (320 North 44th St., 85008; 225-0500, Fax 225-0957, 800-528-0444) 242 suites, restaurant, free breakfast, 2 lounges, outdoor pool, sauna, spa, tennis courts, exercise center, airport courtesy car, children free with parents, NS rooms, A/C, TV, 8 meeting rooms, meeting facilities for 360, CC. 2 miles from the airport. SGL/DBL$90-$150.

Embassy Suites Camelhead (1515 North 44th St., 85008; 244-8800, Fax 244-8800 ext 7534, 800-447-8483, 800-EMBASSY) 229 2-room suites, restaurant, lounge, free breakfast, pool, whirlpools, sauna, laundry service, in-room refrigerators and microwaves, A/C, TV, wheelchair access, NS rooms, gift shop, airport transportation, room service, business service, CC. 1.5 miles from the airport, 4 miles from the Phoenix Zoo. SGL/DBL$135-$150.

Hampton Inn Airport (4234 South 48th St., 85040; 438-8688, Fax 431-8339, 800-HAMPTON) 132 rooms, restaurant, free breakfast, pool, airport transportation, children free with parents, NS rooms, A/C, TV, wheelchair access, computer hookups, fax, pets OK, free local calls, meeting facilities, CC. Near the Diablo Stadium, 5 minutes from Phoenix University, 15 minutes from the downtown area, 10 minutes from the airport. SGL$59, DBL$65.

Hilton Hotel (2435 South 47th St., 85043; 894-1600, 800-HILTONS) 255 rooms and suites, Executive Level, restaurant, lounge, entertainment, free breakfast, heated pool, spa, whirlpools, exercise center, concierge, airport courtesy car, NS rooms, A/C, TV, wheelchair access, gift shop, 24-hour room service, business services, 17 meeting rooms, meeting facilities for 500, CC. 1.5 miles from the airport, 3 miles from Arizona State University, 6 miles from the downtown area. SGL/DBL$125-$275.

Howard Johnson Lodge (124 South 24th St., 85034; 244-8221, 800-I-GO-HOJO) 101 rooms and suites, restaurant, lounge, heated pool, airport courtesy car, children free with parents, NS rooms, pets OK, airport courtesy car, A/C, TV, car rental desk, meeting facilities, CC. 1 mile from airport, 2 miles from the downtown area and Convention Center. SGL$44-$89.

Palma Viva Bed and Breakfast (4540 North 44th St., 85016; 955-0943, Fax 957-6979) 2 rooms, free breakfast, CC. SGL/DBL$85-$95.

Pyramid Inn (3307 East Van Buren St., 85008; 275-3691) 134 rooms, heated pool, airport courtesy car, CC. Five minutes from the airport and American West Arena. SGL/DBL$35-$40.

Quality Inn Desert Sky Airport (3541 East Van Buren Pkwy., 85008; 273-7121, 800-221-2222) 90 rooms, restaurant, lounge, entertainment, heated pool, car rental desk, NS rooms, A/C, TV, meeting facilities, CC. 3 miles from the airport. SGL$29-$45, DBL$39-$73.

Rodeway Inn Airport West (1202 South 24th St., 85043; 273-1211, 800-228-2000) 139 rooms, restaurant, lounge, pool, exercise center, in-room computer hookups, pets OK, airport transportation, CC. At the airport, 4 miles from the downtown area, 10 miles from the Phoenix Zoo and Desert Botanical Gardens. SGL/DBL$50-$75.

Select Suites Apartment Hotel (4221 East McDowell Rd., 85008; 267-7917, 800-845-3020) 275 1-bedroom suites, kitchenettes, pool, tennis courts, A/C, TV, laundry facilities, wheelchair access, CC. SGL/DBL$249W.

Wyndham Garden Hotel Airport (427 Northwest 44th St., 85008; 220-4400, Fax 231-8703, 800-822-4200) 214 rooms, restaurant, lounge, outdoor heated pool, whirlpools, exercise room, in-room coffee makers, room service, airport courtesy car, wheelchair access, NS rooms, 2,100 square feet of meeting space, A/C, TV, meeting facilities for 130, senior rates, CC. 1 mile from the airport, 5 minutes from the Convention Center and Sun Devil Stadium. SGL/DBL$59-$129.

Other Locations

Best Western Grace Inn (10831 South 51st St., 85044; 893-3000, 800-528-1234) 160 rooms and suites, restaurant, lounge, entertainment, pool, exercise center, spa, pets OK, barber and beauty shop, airport transportation, wheelchair access, A/C, TV, meeting facilities, senior rates, CC. SGL/DBL$100-$175.

Holiday Inn Corporate Center North (2532 West Peoria Ave., 85029; 943-2341, 800-HOLIDAY) 248 rooms, restaurant, lounge, entertainment, outdoor pool, exercise center, whirlpools, local transportation, wheelchair access, NS rooms, A/C, TV, pets OK, meeting facilities for 750, CC. 18 miles from the airport, 6 miles from the downtown area, 15 miles from the Scottsdale Shopping Center. SGL/DBL$55$95.

La Quinta Inn (2725 North Black Canyon Hwy., 85009; 258-6271, Fax 3409225, 800-531-5900) 139 rooms, restaurant, free breakfast, heated pool, meeting facilities, free local calls, NSrooms, A/C, TV, wheelchair access, fax, complimentary magazines, laundry service, pets OK, meeting facilities, CC. 5 miles from the downtown area and Civic Center, 9 miles from the airport. SGL/DBL$60-$73.

Holiday Inn (111 North Central Ave., 85004; 257-1525, Fax 253-9755, 800-HOLIDAY) 534 rooms, restaurant, lounge, entertainment, outdoor pool, exercise center, whirlpools, gift shop, children under 19 free with parents, wheelchair access, A/C, TV, NS rooms, fax, room service, pets OK, laundry service, meeting facilities for 1,500, senior rates, CC. SGL/DBL$58-$65.

The Pointe on South Mountain (7777 South Pointe Pkwy., 85040; 438-9000, Fax 438-0577, 800-528-0428, 800-876-4683) 640 2-room suites, restaurant, free breakfast, pool, exercise center, jacuzzi, tennis courts, airport courtesy car, audiovisual equipment, A/C, TV, meeting facilities, 85,000 square feet of meeting and exhibition space, CC. 10 minutes from the airport. SGL/DBL$215-$450.

Ramada Inn Metrocenter (12027 North 28th Dr., 85029; 866-7000, Fax 942-7512, 800-272-6232, 800-2RAMADA) 167 rooms and suites, restaurant, lounge, pool, spa, jacuzzi, children free with parents, kitchenettes, wheelchair access, in-room refrigerators and microwaves, NSrooms, A/C, TV, pets OK, airport transportation, meeting facilities for 200, senior rates, CC. 1 mile from the Metrocenter Mall. SGL/DBL$65-$90, STS$85-$110.

Westways Private Boutique Resort Inn (Box 41624, 85080; 582-3868, Fax 581-9844) 6 rooms and suites, free breakfast, no pets, senior rates, CC. SGL/DBL$61-$150.

Wyndham Garden Hotel North Phoenix (2641 West Union Hills Dr., 85027; 978-2222, Fax 978-9139, 800-822-4200) 166 rooms and suites, restaurant, lounge, outdoor heated pool, whirlpools, exercise center, room service, wheelchair access, pets OK, NS rooms, A/C, TV, in-room coffee makers, 5 meeting rooms, 2,500 square feet of meeting space, meeting facilities for 140, CC. 10 miles from the downtown area, 20 miles from the airport. SGL/DBL$100-$120.

Pinetop
Area Code 602

Best Western Inn (404 South White Mountain Blvd., 85935; 367-6667, Fax 367-6672, 800-528-1234) 41 rooms, restaurant, lounge, pool, exercise center, children free with parents, A/C, NS rooms, TV, laundry facilities, airport transportation, wheelchair access, pets OK, senior rates, meeting facilities, CC. SGL/DBL$50-$115.

Buck Springs Resort (Pinetop 85935; 369-3554) 24 rooms and 1- to 3-bedroom cottages, TV, in-room refrigerators, kitchenettes, no pets, children free with parents, NS rooms, wheelchair access, CC. SGL/DBL$48-$123.

Lakeside Inn (Pinetop 85935; 368-6600, 800-843-4792) 56 rooms, free breakfast, whirlpools, in-room refrigerators, A/C, TV, NS rooms, children free with parents, wheelchair access, fireplaces, no pets, senior rates, CC. SGL/DBL$60-$85.

Mountain Hacienda Lodge (1024 East White Mountain Blvd., 85935; 367-4146) 24 rooms, children free with parents, no pets, A/C, TV, NS rooms, wheelchair access, CC. SGL/DBL$33-$49.

Northwood Resort (165 East White Mountain Blvd., 85935; 367-2966) 10 rooms and 1- to 3-bedroom cottages, laundry facilities, fireplaces, TV, kitchenettes, pets OK, CC. SGL/DBL$45-$98.

Prescott
Area Code 602

Best Western Prescottonian (1317 East Gurley St., 86301; 445-3096, Fax 778-2976, 800-528-1234) 121 rooms and suites, restaurant, lounge, pool, exercise center, whirlpools, children free with parents, A/C, NS rooms, TV, laundry facilities, wheelchair access, in-room refrigerators, pets OK, senior rates, meeting facilities, CC. SGL/DBL$50-$85.

Comfort Inn (1290 White Spar Rd., 86303; 778-5770, 800-221-2222) 61 rooms and efficiencies, restaurant, lounge, entertainment, pool, whirlpools, wheelchair access, NS rooms, no pets, children under 18 free with parents, kitchenettes, A/C, TV, meeting facilities, senior rates, CC. SGL/DBL$45-$80.

Cottages at Prescott Country Inn (503 South Montezuma St., 86303; 445-7991) 12 rooms and 2-bedroom suites, A/C, TV, NS rooms, wheelchair access, fireplaces, kitchenettes, CC. SGL/DBL$80-$125.

Hassayampa Inn (122 East Gurley St., 86301; 778-9434, Fax 778-9434 ext 109, 800-322-1927) 67 rooms and suites, restaurant, free breakfast, lounge, 1920s inn, A/C, TV, NS rooms, wheelchair access, meeting facilities, no pets, antique furnishings, CC. SGL/DBL$90-$160.

Hotel Vendome (230 South Cortez St., 86303; 776-0900) 21 rooms and suites, restaurant, free breakfast, lounge, children free with parents, 1917 inn, A/C, TV, NS rooms, wheelchair access, CC. SGL/DBL$60-$100.

Lynx Creek Farm (Prescott 86303; 778-9573) 4 rooms, free breakfast, NS rooms, pets OK, CC. SGL/DBL$95-$110.

Mark's House (203 Eat Union St., 86303; 778-4682) 4 suites, free breakfast, NS, 1890s home, antique furnishings, TV, CC. SGL/DBL$80-$135.

Prescott Pines Inn (901 White Spar Rd., 86303; 445-7270) 13 rooms, free breakfast, A/C, TV, kitchenettes, no pets, fireplaces, CC. SGL/DBL$50-$180.

Sheraton Resort and Conference Center (1500 Hwy. 69, 86301; 776-1666, Fax 776-8544, 800-325-3535) 161 rooms and suites, restaurant, lounge, entertainment, pool, exercise center, tennis courts, spa, sauna, gift shop, NS rooms, A/C, barber and beauty shop, TV, children free with parents, airport transportation, wheelchair access, 8,000 square feet of meeting and exhibition space, meeting facilities for 850, senior rates, CC. SGL/DBL$96-$160.

Prescott Valley
Area Code 602

Days Inn (7875 East Hwy. 69, 86314; 772-8600, Fax 772-0942, 800-325-2525) 59 rooms and suites, restaurant, free breakfast, outdoor pool, whirlpools, children free with parents, room service, laundry service, A/C, TV, free local calls, pets OK, fax, wheelchair access, NS rooms, meeting facilities, senior rates, CC. SGL/DBL$40-$145.

Rio Rico
Area Code 602

Rio Rico Resort and Country Club (1069 Camino Caralampi, 85648; 281-1901, Fax 281-7132) 175 rooms and suites, restaurant, lounge, heated pool, whirlpools, sauna, lighted tennis courts, A/C, TV, children free with parents, no pets, laundry facilities, VCRs, in-room refrigerators, NS rooms, wheelchair access, CC. SGL/DBL$55-$80.

Safford
Area Code 602

Best Western Inn (1391 Thatcher Blvd., 85546; 428-0521, Fax 428-7653, 800-528-1234) 70 rooms, restaurant, lounge, heated pool, exercise center, children free with parents, A/C, NS rooms, TV, laundry facilities, wheelchair access, in-room coffee makers, local transportation, pets OK, senior rates, meeting facilities, CC. SGL/DBL$58-$75.

Comfort Inn (1578 West Thatcher Rd., 85546; 428-5851, 800-221-2222) 44 rooms, free breakfast, pool, wheelchair access, NS rooms, no pets, children under 18 free with parents, A/C, TV, meeting facilities, senior rates, CC. SGL/DBL$45-$70.

Scottsdale

Area Code 602

Rental and Reservation Services:

Action Apartment Locators (4613 East Thomas Rd., 85008; 952-1496, 800-541-4254) rental apartments.

ABC Resort Suites (6824 East 4th St., 85251; 994-0375) 25 1- and 2-bedroom apartments, heated pool, laundry facilities, no pets, tennis courts, A/C, TV, wheelchair access, CC. SGL/DBL$65-$145.

□□□

Abode Apartment Hotel (3635 North 68th St., 85251; 945-3544, Fax 954-3544 ext 114) 12 1- to 3-bedroom apartments, heated pool, spa, A/C, TV, wheelchair access, CC. SGL/DBL$55-$80.

Best Western Papago Inn and Resort (7017 East McDowell Rd., 85257; 947-7335, Fax 994-0692, 800-528-1234) 58 rooms, restaurant, lounge, pool, exercise center, sauna, spa, in-room refrigerators, children free with parents, A/C, NS rooms, TV, laundry facilities, wheelchair access, pets OK, senior rates, meeting facilities, CC. SGL/DBL$88-$110.

Camelback Resort (6302 East Camelback Rd., 85251; 947-3300, Fax 994-0594) 111 suites, restaurant, lounge, entertainment, heated pool, exercise center, whirlpools, no pets, A/C, TV, NS rooms, wheelchair access, CC. SGL/DBL$65-$95.

Camelview (7601 East Indian Bend Rd., 85250; 991-2400, Fax 998-2261, 800-852-5205) 200 rooms and suites, restaurant, lounge, heated pool, in-room refrigerators and coffee makers, A/C, TV, NS rooms, no pets, airport transportation, gift shop, wheelchair access, 7,700 square feet of meeting and exhibition spaces, CC. SGL/DBL$200-$265.

Courtyard by Marriott (13444 East Shea Blvd., 85259; 860-4000, Fax 860-4308, 800-321-2211) 124 rooms and suites, restaurant, lounge, heated pool, exercise center, whirlpools, local transportation, children free with parents, laundry service, A/C, in-room refrigerators, NS rooms, TV, meeting facilities, senior rates, CC. SGL/DBL$100-$125.

Embassy Suites (5001 North Scottsdale Rd., 85250; 949-1414, Fax 947-2675, 800-EMBASSY) 311 2-room suites, restaurant, lounge, free breakfast, lounge, heated pool, whirlpool, exercise center, sauna, lighted tennis courts, room service, laundry service, wheelchair access, complimentary newspaper, free local calls, NS rooms, gift shop, local transportation, business services, 10,000 square feet of meeting and exhibition space, senior rates, CC. SGL/DBL$145-$163.

Fairfield Inn by Marriott (13440 North Scottsdale Rd., 85254; 483-0042, 800-228-2800) 133 rooms, free breakfast, outdoor pool, whirlpools, children under 18 free with parents, NS rooms, remote control TV, free cable TV, free local calls, laundry service, A/C, wheelchair access, fax, meeting facilities, fax, senior rates, CC. SGL/DBL$85-$95.

Holiday Inn (7353 East Indian School Rd., 85251; 994-9203, Fax 941-2567, 800-HOLIDAY) 206 rooms, restaurant, lounge, entertainment, outdoor pool, jacuzzi, wheelchair access, tennis court, gift shop, no pets, A/C, TV, meeting facilities for 400, CC. .2 miles from Old Town Scottsdale and the Stadium. SGL/DBL$65-$80.

Hospitality Suite Resort (409 North Scottsdale Rd., 85257; 949-5115, Fax 941-8014, 800-445-5115) 209 rooms and efficiencies, restaurant, lounge, entertainment, heated pool, whirlpools, lighted tennis courts, pets OK, children free with parents, laundry facilities, in-room refrigerators, A/C, TV, NS rooms, wheelchair access, 1,000 square feet of meeting and exhibition space, senior rates, CC. SGL/DBL$100-$134.

Howard Johnson (5101 North Scottsdale, 85251; 945-4392, Fax 947-3044, 800-I-GO-HOJO) 216 rooms, restaurant, free breakfast, lounge, heated pool, spa, gift shop, children free with parents, wheelchair access, NS rooms, TV, A/C, no pets, laundry facilities, senior rates, meeting facilities, CC. SGL/DBL$59-$119.

Hyatt Regency Scottsdale Resort (7500 East Doubletree Ranch Rd., 85258; 991-3388, Fax 483-5550, 800-233-1234) 493 rooms and suites, restaurant, lounge, entertainment, pool, whirlpools, exercise center, tennis courts, room service, no pets, airport transportation, in-room refrigerators, TV, A/C, NS rooms, wheelchair access, 23 meeting rooms, meeting facilities for 1,500, senior rates, CC. SGL/DBL$285-$325, STS$400-$2,500.

The Inn at the Citadel (8700 East Pinnacle Peak Rd., 85255; 585-6133, Fax 585-3436, 800-585-6133) 11 suites, restaurant, free breakfast, room service, children free with parents, antique furnishings, A/C, TV, NS rooms, wheelchair access, fireplaces, 4,000 square feet of meeting and exhibition space, CC. SGL/DBL$200-$265.

Loloma Vista Resort (6929 East 2nd St., 85251; 994-8217) 18 1- to 3-bedroom apartments, heated pool, laundry facilities, A/C, TV, wheelchair access, CC. SGL/DBL$50, 1BR$65, 2BR$75, 3BR$100.

Marriott Mountain Shadows Resort and Country Club (5641 East Lincoln Dr., 85253; 948-7111, Fax 951-5430, 800-228-9290) 338 rooms and suites, restaurant, lounge, entertainment, heated pool, exercise center, whirlpools, sauna, tennis courts, wheelchair access, TV, A/C, NS rooms, laundry service, gift shop, barber and beauty shop, pets OK, children free with parents, airport transportation, meeting facilities, senior rates, CC. SGL/DBL$200-$750.

Marriott Scottsdale Suites (7325 East 3rd Ave., 85251; 945-1550, Fax 945-2005, 800-228-9290) 251 suites, restaurant, lounge, entertainment, pool, exercise center, whirlpools, wheelchair access, TV, A/C, NS rooms, in-room refrigerators, laundry service, gift shop, children free with parents, meeting facilities, senior rates, CC. SGL/DBL$170-$225.

Orange Tree Golf and Conference Resort (10601 North 56th St., 85254; 948-6100, 800-228-0386) 160 suites, restaurant, lounge, pool, A/C, TV, NS rooms, wheelchair access, CC. SGL$200-$220, DBL$220-$240.

The Phoenician (6000 East Camelback Rd., 85251; 941-8200, Fax 947-4311, 800-888-8234) 580 rooms and suites, restaurant, lounge, entertainment, indoor and outdoor heated pool, exercise center, sauna, whirlpools, lighted tennis courts, A/C, TV, NS rooms, wheelchair access, airport transportation, in-room refrigerators and coffee makers, laundry facilities, children free with parents, no pets, 60,000 square feet of meeting and exhibition space, senior rates, CC. SGL/DBL$290-$435, STS$840-$4,400.

Ramada Inn (6850 Main St., 85251; 945-6321, Fax 947-5270, 800-2-RAMADA) 289 rooms and suites, restaurant, lounge, entertainment, pool, whirlpools, exercise center, wheelchair access, NS rooms, pets OK, A/C, TV, children under 18 free with parents, room service, laundry facilities, meeting facilities for 400, senior rates, CC. SGL/DBL$70-$325.

Red Lion Inn (4949 East Lincoln Dr., 85253; 952-0420, Fax 840-8576, 800-547-8010) 264 rooms, restaurant, lounge, entertainment, heated pool, sauna, exercise center, tennis courts, whirlpools, in-room refrigerators, beauty shop, laundry facilities, airport courtesy car, A/C, TV, wheelchair access, NS rooms, pets OK, 17,000 square feet of meeting and exhibition space, 17 meeting rooms, meeting facilities for 800, senior rates, CC. SGL/DBL$175-$250, STS$750-$1,000.

Regal McCormick Ranch (7401 North Scottsdale Rd., 85235; 948-5050, Fax 948-9113, 800-243-1332) 175 rooms and 2- and 3-bedroom villas, restaurant, lounge, entertainment, heated pool, whirlpools, lighted tennis courts, airport transportation, gift shop, fireplaces, A/C, TV, NS rooms, wheelchair access, 5,000 square feet of meeting and exhibition space, senior rates, CC. SGL/DBL$150-$500.

The Registry (7171 North Scottsdale Rd., 85253; 991-3800, Fax 948-1381, 800-247-9810) 326 rooms, cottages and suites, restaurant, lounge, entertainment, heated pools, whirlpools, sauna, game room, no pets, in-room refrigerators, A/C, TV, NS rooms, wheelchair access, 30,000 square feet of meeting and exhibition space, CC. SGL/DBL$250-$350, STS$500-$650.

Resort Suites (7677 East Princess Blvd., 85255; 585-1234, Fax 585-1457, 800-541-5203) 297 suites, restaurant, lounge, heated pool, exercise center, whirlpools, in-room coffee makers, A/C, TV, NS rooms, wheelchair access, meeting facilities, senior rates, CC. SGL/DBL$170-$600.

Rodeway Inn (7110 East Indian School Rd., 85251; 946-3456, 800-424-4777) 62 rooms and suites, free breakfast, heated pool, whirlpools, wheelchair access, NS rooms, children free with parents, A/C, TV, senior rates, CC. SGL/DBL$84-$125.

Safari Resort (4611 North Scottsdale Rd., 85251; 945-3456, Fax 946-4248) 188 rooms and suites, restaurant, free breakfast, lounge, heated pool, whirlpools, pets OK, laundry service, gift shop, A/C, TV, NS rooms, wheelchair access, senior rates, CC. SGL/DBL$95-$145.

Scottsdale Fifth Avenue Inn (6935 Fifth Ave., 85251; 994-9461, Fax 947-1695) 92 rooms, heated pool, A/C, no pets, in-room refrigerators, TV, NS rooms, wheelchair access, CC. SGL/DBL$35-$77.

Scottsdale Inn (7707 McDowell Rd., 85257; 941-1202, Fax 990-7873, 800-238-8851) 120 rooms, restaurant, free breakfast, heated pool, whirlpools, pets OK, laundry facilities, children free with parents, A/C, TV, NS rooms, wheelchair access, CC. SGL/DBL$75-$83.

Scottsdale Plaza Resort (7200 North Scottsdale Rd., 85253; 948-5000, Fax 998-5971, 800-832-2025) 404 rooms and suites, restaurant, lounge, entertainment, indoor and outdoor heated pool, exercise center, sauna, whirlpools, in-room refrigerators, gift shop, airport transportation, pets OK, beauty shop, A/C, TV, NS rooms, wheelchair access, airport transportation, in-room refrigerators and coffee makers, laundry facilities, children free with parents, no pets, senior rates, meeting facilities, CC. SGL/DBL$210-$2,500.

Stouffer Cottonwoods Resort (Scottsdale 85253; 991-1414, Fax 951-3350, 800-HOTELS-1) 170 rooms and suites, restaurant, free breakfast, lounge, heated pool, exercise center, whirlpools, pets OK, airport courtesy car, wheelchair access, NS rooms, complimentary newspaper, TV, A/C, room service, children under age 18 free with parents, fax, in-room refrigerators, meeting facilities, CC. SGL/DBL$200-$300.

Sunburst Hotel and Conference Center (4925 North Scottsdale Rd., 85251; 945-7666, Fax 946-4056, 800-528-7867) 208 rooms and suites, restaurant, free breakfast, lounge, entertainment, heated pool, exercise center, sauna, whirlpools, A/C, TV, NS rooms, wheelchair access, airport transportation, in-room refrigerators and coffee makers, laundry facilities, children free with parents, no pets, senior rates, meeting facilities, CC. SGL/DBL$135-$180, STS$190-$300.

Wyndham Paradise Valley Resort Hotel (5401 North Scottsdale Rd., 85250; 947-5400, Fax 946-1524, 800-822-4200) 387 rooms and suites, restaurant, lounge, pool, whirlpool, exercise center, A/C, TV, NS rooms, wheelchair access, room service, meeting facilities, CC. SGL/DBL$180-$390.

Sedona
Area Code 602

A Touch of Sedona (595 Jordan Rd., 86339; 282-6462) 4 rooms, free breakfast, no pets, NS, antique furnishings, shared baths, CC. SGL/DBL$80-$95.

A Touch of the Southwest Suites (296 Schnebly Rd., 86335; 282-4747) 6 rooms and suites, kitchenettes, A/C, TV, in-room coffee makers, no pets, NS rooms, wheelchair access, CC. SGL/DBL$95-$105.

Bed and Breakfast at Saddle Rock Ranch (255 Rock Ridge Dr., 86339; 282-7640) 3 rooms, free breakfast, pool, whirlpools, no pets, NS, A/C, TV, NS rooms, fireplace, antique furnishings. SGL/DBL$90-$125.

Bell Rock Inn (6246 Hwy. 179, 86336; 282-4161) 47 rooms, restaurant, lounge, entertainment, heated pool, A/C, TV, NS rooms, wheelchair access, meeting facilities, CC. SGL/DBL$55-$95.

Black Forest House (50 Willow Way, 86336; 282-2835) 12 rooms, A/C, no pets, in-room refrigerators and microwaves, VCRs, TV, NS rooms, wheelchair access, CC. SGL/DBL$30-$80.

Briar Patch Inn (Sedona 86336; 282-2342) 15 rooms and 2-bedroom suites, free breakfast, fireplaces, A/C, TV, CC. SGL/DBL$125-$165.

Canyon Portal Motel (280 Hwy. 89A, 86336; 542-8484, Fax 282-1825, 800-542-8484) 20 rooms and 2-bedroom apartment, restaurant, heated pool, pets OK, game room, in-room refrigerators, A/C, TV, NS rooms, wheelchair access, CC. SGL/DBL$60-$90.

Canyon Villa Bed and Breakfast (400 North Hwy. 89; 86336; 284-1226, Fax 284-2114, 800-453-1166) 11 rooms, free breakfast, heated pool, whirlpools, fireplaces, NS, no pets, A/C, TV, heated pool, children free with parents, wheelchair access, CC. SGL/DBL$85-$155.

Cedars Resort (Sedona 86336; 282-7010) 39 rooms, heated pool, in-room refrigerators, NS, A/C, TV, NS rooms, wheelchair access, CC. SGL/DBL$40-$70.

Cimarron Inn (2991 West Hwy. 89, 86336; 282-9166) 66 rooms and 1-bedroom suites, heated pool, whirlpools, no pets, A/C, TV, NS rooms, wheelchair access, in-room refrigerators, CC. SGL/DBL$38-$58.

Desert Quail Inn (6626 Hwy. 179, 86336; 284-1433) 20 rooms, A/C, children free with parents, in-room refrigerators and coffee makers, pets OK, TV, NS rooms, wheelchair access, CC. SGL/DBL$55-$80.

Enchantment Resort (525 Boynton Canyon, 86336; 282-2900, Fax 282-9249, 800-826-4180) 175 rooms and 2-bedroom villas, restaurant, lounge, heated pool, exercise center, sauna, whirlpools, A/C, TV, NS rooms, wheelchair access, airport transportation, laundry facilities, children free with parents, no pets, senior rates, meeting facilities, CC. SGL/DBL$185-$500.

Graham Bed and Breakfast Inn (150 Canyon Circle Dr., 86336; 284-1425, 800-228-1425) 6 rooms, free breakfast, pool, whirlpools, fireplaces, antique furnishings, wheelchair access, A/C, TV, CC. SGL/DBL$85-$190.

Junipine Resort (8351 North Hwy. 89, 86336; 282-3375) 29 rooms and 1- and 2-bedroom condominiums, restaurant, lounge, kitchenettes, children free with parents, A/C, no pets, fireplaces, TV, NS rooms, wheelchair access, CC. SGL/DBL$110-$250.

Matterhorn Motor Lodge (230 Apple Ave., 86336; 282-7176) 21 rooms, heated pool, whirlpools, in-room coffee makers, pets OK, A/C, TV, NS rooms, wheelchair access, CC. SGL/DBL$50-$85.

Orchards at L'Auberge (Sedona 86336; 282-7131, Fax 282-2885) 41 rooms, restaurant, lounge, heated pool, whirlpools, children free with parents, A/C, no pets, in-room refrigerators, modified American plan available, TV, NS rooms, wheelchair access, CC. SGL/DBL$100-$160.

Poco Diablo Resort (Sedona 86336; 282-7333, Fax 282-2090, 800-528-4275) 109 rooms and suites, restaurant, lounge, heated pool, lighted tennis courts, whirlpools, airport courtesy car, A/C, TV, NS rooms, in-room refrigerators and coffee makers, fireplaces, wheelchair access, senior rates, CC. SGL/DBL$115-$170, STS$250-$350.

Rose Tree Inn (376 Cedar St., 86336; 282-2065) 4 rooms, whirlpools, no pets, CC. SGL/DBL$60-$116.

Sedona Motel (Sedona 86336; 282-7187) 13 rooms, A/C, TV, NS rooms, wheelchair access, no pets, CC. SGL/DBL$50-$75.

Sky Ranch Lodge (Sedona 86336; 282-6400) 94 rooms and cottages, heated pool, whirlpool tub, in-room refrigerators, pets OK, children free with parents, fireplaces, A/C, TV, NS rooms, wheelchair access, CC. SGL/DBL$45-$95.

Show Low
Area Code 602

Best Western Painted Pony Lodge and Convention Center (581 West Deuce of Clubs, 85901; 537-5773, 800-528-1234) 32 rooms, restaurant, free breakfast, lounge, pool, exercise center, children free with parents, A/C, NS rooms, TV, laundry facilities, wheelchair access, pets OK, senior rates, meeting facilities for 500, CC. SGL/DBL$69-$95.

Kiva Motel (261 East Deuce of Clubs, 85901; 537-4542) 20 rooms, whirlpools, pets OK, in-room refrigerators and coffee makers, A/C, TV, NS rooms, wheelchair access, CC. SGL/DBL$35-$45.

Sierra Vista
Area Code 602

Motel 6 (1551 East Fry Blvd., 85635; 459-5035, 505-891-6161) 103 rooms, pool, free local calls, children under 17 free with parents, NS rooms, wheelchair access, pets OK, A/C, TV, CC. SGL/DBL$36-$48.

Ramada Inn (2047 South Hwy. 92, 85635; 459-5900, Fax 458-1347, 800-2-RAMADA) 149 rooms and suites, restaurant, free breakfast, lounge, entertainment, pool, wheelchair access, NS rooms, pets OK, A/C, TV, children under 18 free with parents, in-room coffee makers, airport transportation, limousine service, room service, laundry facilities, meeting facilities, senior rates, CC. SGL/DBL$50-$100.

Sierra Suites (391 East Fry Blvd., 85635; 459-4221, Fax 459-8449) 100 rooms and suites, free breakfast, lounge, heated pool, whirlpools, A/C, TV, in-room refrigerators, NS rooms, wheelchair access, meeting facilities, senior rates, CC. SGL/DBL$45-$70.

Thunder Mountain Inn (1631 South Hwy. 92, 85635; 458-7900) 105 rooms, restaurant, lounge, pool, whirlpools, in-room refrigerators, no pets, children free with parents, A/C, TV, NS rooms, wheelchair access, CC. SGL/DBL$45-$48.

Springerville
Area Code 602

El-Jo Motor Inn (Springerville 85938; 333-4314, 800-638-6114) 36 rooms, restaurant, lounge, pets OK, A/C, TV, NS rooms, wheelchair access, pets OK, CC. SGL/DBL$24-$32.

Super 8 Motel (Hwy. 60 West, 85938; 333-2655, Fax 333-5149, 800-800-8000) 42 rooms and suites, no pets, children under 12 free with parents, free local calls, A/C, TV, in-room refrigerators and microwaves, fax, NS rooms, senior rates, wheelchair access, meeting facilities, CC. SGL/DBL$40-$51.

Sun City
Area Code 602

Best Western Inn (11201 Grand Ave., 84636; 933-8211, 800-528-1234) 75 rooms, restaurant, heated pool, exercise center, children free with parents, A/C, NS rooms, TV, laundry facilities, wheelchair access, pets OK, senior rates, meeting facilities, CC. SGL/DBL$38-$68.

Surprise
Area Code 602

Windmill Inn (12545 West Bell Rd., 85347; 583-0133) 127 suites, heated pool, whirlpools, laundry facilities, pets OK, children free with parents, in-room microwaves, A/C, TV, NS rooms, wheelchair access, meeting facilities, senior rates, CC. SGL/DBL$55-$89.

Taylor
Area Code 602

Best Western Whiting Motor Inn (Taylor 85939; 536-2600, 800-528-1234) 34 rooms, free breakfast, exercise center, whirlpools, sauna, in-room refrigerators and microwaves, children free with parents, A/C, NS rooms, TV, laundry facilities, wheelchair access, pets OK, senior rates, meeting facilities, CC. SGL/DBL$46-$63.

Tempe
Area Code 602

The Buttes Hotel (2000 Westcourt Way, 85282; 225-9000, Fax 438-8622, 800-843-1968) 350 rooms and suites, restaurant, lounge, heated pool, lighted tennis courts, exercise center, sauna, children free with parents, pets OK, gift shop, A/C, TV, in-room refrigerators and coffee makers, NS rooms, wheelchair access, meeting facilities, senior rates, CC. SGL/DBL$200-$225, STS$375-$1,500.

Country Suites (1660 West Elliot Rd., 85283; 345-8585, Fax 345-7461) 139 efficiencies, free breakfast, pool, whirlpools, lighted tennis courts, pets OK, airport courtesy car, laundry facilities, A/C, TV, NS rooms, wheelchair access, meeting facilities, senior rates, CC. SGL/DBL$75-$95.

Days Inn (1221 East Apache Blvd., 85281; 968-7793, Fax 966-4450, 800-325-2525) 100 rooms and suites, free breakfast, outdoor pool, whirlpools, children free with parents, room service, laundry service, A/C, free local calls, TV, free local calls, pets OK, fax, wheelchair access, NS rooms, senior rates, CC. SGL/DBL$45-$70.

Econo Lodge Arizona State University (2101 East Apache Blvd., 85281; 966-5832, Fax 921-2648, 800-4-CHOICE) 39 rooms, free breakfast, pool, children under 12 free with parents, no pets, senior rates, NS rooms, wheelchair access, A/C, TV, senior rates, CC. SGL/DBL$29-$65.

Fiesta Inn (2100 South Priest Dr., 85282; 967-1441, 800-528-6481) 269 rooms, restaurant, lounge, heated pool, jacuzzi, exercise center, airport courtesy car, A/C, in-room refrigerators, wheelchair access, in-room refrigerators and coffee makers, local transportation, TV, meeting facilities, senior rates, CC. SGL/DBL$75-$120.

Holiday Inn (915 East Apache Blvd., 85281; 968-3451, Fax 968-6262, 800-HOLIDAY) 190 rooms and suites, restaurant, lounge, pool, exercise center, whirlpools, children under 19 free with parents, wheelchair access, A/C, TV, NS rooms, fax, room service, gift shop, airport transportation, car rental desk, pets OK, laundry service, meeting facilities, senior rates, CC. SGL/DBL$80-$110.

Howard Johnson Hotel (225 East Apache Blvd., 85281; 967-9431, Fax 967-9431 ext 299, 800-I-GOHOJO) 138 rooms, restaurant, pool, exercise center, children free with parents, room service, car rental desk, wheelchair access, fax, A/C, TV, meeting facilities for 130, CC. 5 miles from the airport, 10 miles from the downtown area; near Arizona State University and the Sun Devil Stadium. SGL/DBL$52-$89.

Innsuites Airport (1651 West Baseline Rd., 85283; 897-7900, Fax 491-1008, 800-841-4242) 170 rooms and suites, restaurant, heated pool, jacuzzi, whirlpools, exercise center, lighted tennis courts, laundry service, free local calls, in-room coffee makers and microwaves, business services, fax, A/C, TV, meeting facilities for 120, CC. SGL/DBL$72.

Marriott Residence Inn Airport (5075 South Priest Dr., 85282; 7562122, 800331-3131) suites, free breakfast, meeting facilities, in-room refrigerators, laundry service, fireplaces, wheelchair access, NS rooms, A/C, TV, pets OK, VCRs, CC. 5 miles from the airport. SGL/DBL$85-$119.

Motel 6 Broadway (513 West Broadway Rd., 85282; 967-8696, 505-891-6161) 61 rooms, pool, free local calls, children under 17 free with parents, NS rooms, wheelchair access, pets OK, A/C, TV, CC. SGL/DBL$44-$48.

Radisson Mission Palms (60 East 5th St., 85281; 894-1400, Fax 968-7677, 800-333-3333) 303 rooms and suites, restaurant, lounge, entertainment, pool, exercise center, lighted tennis courts, airport transportation, no pets, in-room refrigerators, microwaves and coffee makers, children free with parents, VCRs, wheelchair access, NS rooms, TV, A/C, children free with parents, meeting facilities, senior rates. CC. SGL/DBL$100-$250.

Ramada Hotel Sky Harbor (1600 South 52nd St., 85281; 967-6600, Fax 829-9427, 800-2RAMADA) 215 rooms, restaurant, lounge, entertainment, indoor and outdoor pools, spa, airport courtesy car, children free with parents, wheelchair access, NS rooms, A/C, TV, airport transportation, meeting facilities for 400, CC. 3 miles from Arizona State University and Old Town. SGL/DBL$65-$125.

Rodeway Inn Airport East (1550 South 52nd St., 85281; 967-3000, 800-424-4777) 100 rooms, free breakfast, pool, whirlpools, airport transportation, wheelchair access, NS rooms, children free with parents, A/C, TV, meeting facilities for 50, senior rates, CC. SGL/DBL$51-$79.

Tempe University TraveLodge (1005 East Apache Blvd., 85281; 968-7871, 800-255-3050) 56 rooms, restaurant, free breakfast, lounge, heated pool, laundry service, car rental desk, complimentary newspaper, in-room refrigerators and microwaves, free local calls, fax, pets OK, meeting facilities, CC. Near Arizona State University. SGL/DBL$34-$59.

Tolleson
Area Code 602

Coachman Inn (1520 North 84th Dr., 85353; 936-4667) 120 rooms, heated pool, laundry facilities, A/C, TV, NS rooms, wheelchair access, senior rates, CC. SGL/DBL$40-$60.

Tombstone
Area Code 602

Best Western Lookout Lodge (Tombstone 85638; 457-2223, Fax 457-3870, 800-528-1234) 40 rooms, free breakfast, children free with parents, A/C, NS rooms, TV, laundry facilities, wheelchair access, pets OK, senior rates, meeting facilities, CC. SGL/DBL$55-$70.

Tucson
Area Code 602

Northeast Tucson

Arizona Inn (2200 East Elm St., 85719; 325-1541, 800-933-1093) 80 rooms and cottages, restaurant, lounge, entertainment, pool, tennis courts, 5 meeting rooms, meeting facilities for 200, A/C, TV, CC. SGL$124-$152, DBL$134-$162.

Canyon Ranch Spa (8600 East Rockcliff Rd., 85715; 749-9000, Fax 749-7755, 800-742-9000) 80 rooms and cottages, restaurant, lounge, pool, exercise center, spa, tennis courts, beauty salon, airport transportation, 6 meeting rooms, meeting facilities for 30, American plan available, A/C, TV, CC. SGL/DBL$400-$500.

El Conquistador Golf and Tennis Resort (10000 North Oracle Rd., 85737; 742-7000, Fax 797-1522, 800-325-7832, 800-325-3535) 440 rooms and suites, 6 restaurants, 2 lounges, entertainment, 4 heated outdoor pools, exercise center, hot tubs, golf course, lighted tennis courts, NS rooms, wheelchair access, A/C, TV, free airport transportation, 30,000 square feet of meeting and exhibition space, 18 meeting rooms, meeting facilities for 1,200, CC. 15 miles from Old Tucson and the Sonora Desert Museum, 24 miles from the airport. SGL/DBL$215, STS$250.

Hacienda Del Sol (5601 North Hacienda del Sol, 85718; 229-1501) 47 rooms and cottages, restaurant, heated pool, jacuzzi, exercise center, tennis courts, in-room refrigerators, meeting facilities for 200, A/C, TV, CC. SGL/DBL$85-$115.

Loews Ventana Canyon Resort (7000 North Resort Dr., 85715; 299-2020, Fax 299-6832) 366 rooms and suites, restaurant, lounge, pool, exercise center, A/C, TV, NS rooms, wheelchair access, 37,000 square feet of meeting and exhibition space, meeting facilities for 1,300, senior rates, CC. SGL/DBL$65-$125.

North Campbell Suites Hotel (2925 North Campbell Ave., 85719; 323-7378) 22 rooms and 4-room suites, pool, A/C, TV, free local calls, CC. 1 mile from the University of Arizona. SGL/DBL$105.

Quality Inn Tanque Verde (7007 East Tanque Verde Rd., 85715; 298-2300, 800-228-5151) 89 rooms, free breakfast, pool, jacuzzi, spa, in-room refrigerators, airport courtesy car, meeting facilities for 150, A/C, TV, CC. SGL/DBL$38-$68.

Ramada Inn Foothills (6944 East Tanque Verde, 85715; 886-9595, Fax 7218466, 800-2-RAMADA) 102 rooms and suites, restaurant, lounge, free breakfast, heated pool, spa, sauna, children under 18 free with parents, wheelchair access, NS rooms, airport transportation, free local calls, A/C, TV, 5 meeting rooms, CC. In the shopping and entertainment district. SGL/DBL$60-$88.

Ranch Del Rio Resort and Tennis Club (2800 North Sabino Canyon Rd., 85715; 722-2800) 12 rooms, restaurant, lounge, free breakfast, heated pool, tennis courts, A/C, TV, CC. SGL/DBL$65.

Tanque Verde Guest Ranch (Route 8, 85748; 296-6275, Fax 721-9426, 800-234-DUDE) 88 rooms and cottages, restaurant, free breakfast, heated outdoor pool, exercise center, jacuzzi, tennis courts, NS rooms, wheelchair access, laundry service, children free with parents, in-room refrigerators, 2 meeting rooms, meeting facilities for 125, A/C, TV, CC. SGL$225-$275, DBL$250$300, STS$280-$355.

Ventana Canyon Golf and Racquet Club (6200 North Clubhouse Lane, 85715; 577-1400, Fax 299-0256, 800-828-5701) 48 1- and 2-bedroom suites, restaurant, lounge, entertainment, heated pool, exercise center, whirlpools, sauna, lighted tennis courts, in-room refrigerators, beauty shop, wheelchair access, NS rooms, children free with parents, airport transportation, boutiques, meeting facilities for 70, A/C, TV, CC. 1BR$255-$360, 2BR$350-$412.

Windmill Inn at St. Philip's Plaza (4250 North Campbell Ave., 85718; 5770007, 800-547-4747) 127 1-bedroom suites, free breakfast, free local calls, NS rooms, wheelchair access, meeting facilities for 300, A/C, TV, CC. SGL/DBL$85-$95.

Airport Area

Best Western Airport (7060 South Tucson Blvd., 85706; 746-0271, Fax 889-7391, 800-5281234) 150 rooms, restaurant, free breakfast, in-lounge, pool, jacuzzi, exercise center, tennis court, airport courtesy car, A/C, TV, in-room refrigerators and microwaves, 4 meeting rooms, meeting facilities for 40, A/C, TV, CC. SGL/DBL$58-$123.

Clarion Hotel Airport (6801 South Tucson Blvd., 85706; 746-3932, Fax 8899934, 800-526-0550) 194 rooms and suites, restaurant, free breakfast, lounge, heated pool, whirlpools, in-room refrigerators, wheelchair access, NS rooms, pets OK, children free with parents, airport courtesy car, 6 meeting rooms, 2,800 square feet of meeting and exhibition space, A/C, TV, CC. SGL/DBL$69-$115.

Embassy Suites Airport (7051 South Tucson Blvd., 85706; 573-0700, Fax 7419645, 800-362-2779) 204 suites, restaurant, lounge, free breakfast, heated pool, exercise center, jacuzzi, children free with parents, wheelchair access, NS rooms, pets OK, in-room refrigerators, laundry facilities, airport courtesy car, 10 meeting rooms, 10,000 square feet of meeting and exhibition space, meeting facilities for 600, A/C, TV, CC. SGL/DBL$75-$125.

Park Inn International Tucson (2803 East Valencia Rd., 85706; 294-2500, 800-437-PARK) 90 rooms, restaurant, lounge, heated outdoor pool, complimentary newspaper, in-room refrigerators, wheelchair access, NS rooms, airport courtesy car, A/C, TV, 2 meeting rooms, meeting facilities for 100, CC. 12 miles from the Old Tucson area and Arizona Sonora Desert Museum, 1 mile from the airport. SGL/DBL$75-$95.

Ramada Inn Palo Verde (5251 South Julian Dr., 85706; 294-5250, Fax 294-5250 ext 7322, 800-2-RAMADA) 169 rooms, restaurant, lounge, free breakfast, heated outdoor pool, exercise center, jacuzzi, children under 18 free with parents, wheelchair access, NS rooms, airport transportation, in-room coffee makers, 4 meeting rooms, meeting facilities for 400, CC. Near the airport and the Air Museum. SGL/DBL$55-$105.

Northwest Tucson

Best Western Ghost Ranch (801 West Miracle Mile, 85705; 791-7565, Fax 791-3898, 800-5281234) 81 rooms and cottages, restaurant, lounge, free breakfast, pool, jacuzzi, spa, laundry service, kitchenettes, pets OK, 3 meeting rooms for 40, A/C, TV, CC. SGL/DBL$50-$85.

Country Suites (7411 North Oracle Rd., 85704; 575-9255, Fax 575-8671, 800-456-4000) 155 suites, restaurant, heated outdoor pool, airport courtesy car, laundry service, children free with parents, wheelchair access, NS rooms, meeting facilities, A/C, TV, senior rates, CC. SGL/DBL$75-$155.

La Siesta Motel (1602 North Oracle Rd., 85705; 624-6491) 13 rooms, free breakfast, pool, A/C, TV, CC. SGL/DBL$45.

Lazy K Bar Ranch (8401 North Scenic Dr., 85743; 297-0702) 23 rooms, restaurant, lounge, entertainment, heated pool, tennis courts, jacuzzi, local transportation, children free with parents, meeting facilities for 40, A/C, TV, CC. SGL/DBL$130-$250.

Paul's Hideaway Lodge (255 West Flores Ave., 85705; 624-2221) 17 rooms, heated pool, laundry service, in-room refrigerators, A/C, TV, CC. SGL/DBL$65.

Tucson National Golf and Conference Resort (2727 West Club Dr., 85741; 297-2271, Fax 742-2452, 800-528-4856) 170 rooms and cottages, three restaurants, two lounges, pool, exercise center, tennis courts, jacuzzi, children free with parents, wheelchair access, NS rooms, in-room refrigerators, barber and beauty shop, no pets, airport courtesy car, gift shop, 13 meeting rooms, meeting facilities, A/C, TV, CC. SGL/DBL$195-$205, STS$205.

Vista del Sol (1458 West Miracle Mile, 85705; 293-9270) 29 rooms and suites, pool, laundry service, in-room refrigerators, A/C, TV, CC. SGL/DBL$125.

Wayward Winds Lodge (707 West Miracle Mile, 85705; 791-7526) 41 rooms and efficiencies, free breakfast, heated outdoor pool, in-room refrigerators, laundry service, children free with parents, A/C, TV, CC. SGL/DBL$85-$135.

Westwood Look Resort (245 East Ina Rd., 85704; 297-1151, Fax 297-9023, 800-722-2500) 244 rooms and suites, restaurant, lounge, entertainment, heated pool, jacuzzi, tennis courts, wheelchair access, NS rooms, in-room refrigerators, children free with parents, gift shop, airport transportation, 11 meeting rooms, 10,000 square feet of meeting and exhibition space, meeting facilities for 400, A/C, TV, CC. SGL/DBL$200, STS$225.

White Stallion Ranch (9251 West Twin Peaks Rd., 85743; 297-0252, Fax 7442786, 800-782-5546) 30 rooms and suites, restaurant, lounge, entertainment, heated pool, jacuzzi, tennis courts, laundry service, in-room refrigerators, children free with parents, airport courtesy car, A/C, TV, CC. SGL/DBL$210-$280.

Southeast Tucson

Best Western Aztec Inn (102 North Alvernon Way, 85711; 695-0330, Fax 326-2111, 800-528-1234) 156 rooms, restaurant, lounge, heated pool, tennis courts, beauty shop, free local calls, NS rooms, no pets, in-room refrigerators, 10 meeting rooms, meeting facilities for 250, A/C, TV, CC. SGL/DBL$55-$90.

Candlelight Suites Motor Lodge (1440 South Craycroft Rd., 85711; 747-1440, Fax 750-0144, 800-233-1440) 70 2-room suites, free breakfast, wheelchair access, NS rooms, pets OK, in-room refrigerators, meeting facilities for 25, A/C, TV, CC. SGL/DBL$125.

Courtyard by Marriott (2505 East Executive Dr., 85706; 573-0000, Fax 5730470) 149 rooms and suites, restaurant, lounge, heated outdoor pool, airport courtesy car, in-room refrigerators, children free with parents, laundry service, wheelchair access, NS rooms, 2 meeting rooms, meeting facilities for 50, A/C, TV, CC. SGL/DBL$89-$109.

Days Inn (3700 East Irvington Rd., 85714; 571-1400, 800-325-2525) 116 rooms, restaurant, heated pool, spa, whirlpools, children under 12 free with parents, wheelchair access, NS rooms, fax, pets OK, A/C, TV, airport transportation, free local calls, 2 meeting rooms, meeting facilities for 125, CC. 14 miles from Old Tucson, 4 miles from the airport. SGL/DBL$50-$95.

Doubletree Hotel At Randolph Park (445 South Alvernon Way, 85711; 881-4200, Fax 323-5225, 800-528-0444) 295 rooms and suites, 2 restaurants, lounge, entertainment, outdoor heated pool, golf, exercise center, lighted tennis courts, jogging trail, children under 12 free with parents, NS rooms, A/C, TV, 16 meeting rooms, 25,000 square feet of meeting and exhibition space, meeting facilities for 1,200, CC. 10 minutes from the downtown area and 15 minutes from the airport. SGL/DBL$135-$165.

Econo Lodge (1165 North Stone Ave., 85705; 62-7763, 800-4-CHOICE) 44 rooms, free breakfast, pool, children under 12 free with parents, no pets, senior rates, NS rooms, wheelchair access, A/C, TV, senior rates, CC. SGL/DBL$26-$89.

El Presidio Bed and Breakfast Inn (297 North Main Ave., 85701; 623-6151) 6 rooms and suites, restaurant, free breakfast, A/C, 1870s inn, antique furnishings, NS, TV, CC. SGL/DBL$70-$100.

Embassy Suites (5335 East Broadway, 85711; 745-2700, Fax 790-9232) 142 efficiencies, restaurant, free breakfast, outdoor heated pool, whirlpools, wheelchair access, NS rooms, children free with parents, airport courtesy car, 3 meeting rooms, meeting facilities for 180, A/C, TV, CC. SGL/DBL$70-$100.

Hilton East (7600 East Broadway, 85710; 721-5600, Fax 721-5696, 800-445-8667) 239 rooms and suites, Executive Floor, restaurant, lounge, pool, exercise center, sauna, no pets, tennis courts, wheelchair access, NS rooms, gift shop, room service, 9 meeting rooms, 12,000 square feet of meeting and exhibition space, meeting facilities for 700, A/C, TV, CC. SGL/DBL$99-$125, STS$165-$240.

Holiday Inn Broadway (181 West Broadway, 85701; 624-8711, Fax 623-8121, 800-HOLIDAY) 308 rooms and suites, restaurant, lounge, entertainment, heated pool, jacuzzi, sauna, exercise center, children free with parents, pets OK, wheelchair access, NS rooms, game room, airport courtesy car, 17 meeting rooms, 30,000 square feet of meeting and exhibition space, meeting facilities for 1,000, A/C, TV, CC. SGL/DBL$65-$95.

Howard Johnson Lodge (1025 East Benson Hwy., 85714; 623-7792, Fax 620-1556, 800-654-2000, 800-446-4656) 136 rooms, Executive Floor, restaurant, lounge, entertainment, outdoor heated pool, sauna, whirlpools, NS rooms, A/C, TV, wheelchair access, fax, room service, airport courtesy car, no pets, meeting facilities, CC. 4 miles from the downtown area, 5 miles from the airport. SGL/DBL$39-$125.

La Quinta Inn (6404 East Broadway, 85710; 747-1414, Fax 745-6903, 800-531-5900) 140 rooms, restaurant, free breakfast, heated outdoor pool, jacuzzi, exercise center, children free with parents, wheelchair access, NS rooms, meeting facilities, A/C, TV, CC. SGL/DBL$55-$90.

Lodge On The Desert (306 North Alvernon Way, 85773; 325-3366, Fax 327-5834, 800-223-0888) 38 rooms and 1-bedroom suites, restaurant, lounge, free breakfast, heated pool, in-room refrigerators, 6 meeting rooms, meeting facilities for 100, A/C, TV, senior rates, CC. SGL$74-$84, STS$125.

Motel 6 (755 East Benson Hwy., 85713; 622-4614, 505-891-6161) 120 rooms, pool, free local calls, children under 17 free with parents, NS rooms, wheelchair access, pets OK, A/C, TV, CC. SGL/DBL$33-$42.

Marriott Residence Inn (6477 East Speedway Blvd., 85710; 721-0991, Fax 290-8323, 800-331-3131) 128 1- and 2bedroom suites, kitchens, in-room refrigerators, laundry service, airport transportation, room service, wheelchair access, NS rooms, pets OK, in-room VCRs, 2 meeting rooms, meeting facilities for 60, CC. 9 miles from the downtown area, 21 miles from Old Tucson. SGL/DBL$65-$135.

Palm Court Inn (4425 East 22nd St., 85711; 745-1777, 800-331-1650) 198 rooms, free breakfast, pool, in-room refrigerators, no pets, 2 meeting rooms, meeting facilities for 80, A/C, TV, CC. SGL/DBL$75-$105.

Plaza International Hotel (1900 East Speedway Blvd., 85719; 327-7341, 800-843-8052) 150 rooms, pool, jacuzzi, children free with parents, airport transportation, in-room refrigerators, wheelchair access, NS rooms, 7 meeting rooms, A/C, TV, CC. 12 minutes from the airport. SGL/DBL$71-$81, STS$150.

Quality Inn East (6161 Benson Hwy., 85706; 294-3191, 800-228-5151) 47 rooms, pool, meeting facilities, A/C, TV, CC. SGL/DBL$74-$90.

Rodeway Inn (810 Benson Hwy., 85713; 884-5800, 800-228-2000) 99 rooms, restaurant, free breakfast, pool, airport courtesy car, laundry service, pets OK, free local calls, children free with parents, NS rooms, A/C, TV, CC. SGL/DBL$29-$83.

Smuggler's Inn (6350 East Speedway Blvd., 85710; 296-3292, 800-525-8852, 800-362-5170 in Arizona) 150 rooms and suites, restaurant, lounge, entertainment, heated outdoor pool, lighted tennis courts, jacuzzi, children free with parents, airport courtesy car, NS rooms, golf course, 3 meeting rooms, meeting facilities for 200, A/C, TV, CC. SGL/DBL$89-$99, STS$150.

Super 8 Motel (1990 South Craycroft Rd., 85711; 790-6021, 800-800-8000) 40 rooms and suites, restaurant, outdoor pool, no pets, children under 12 free with parents, free local calls, A/C, TV, in-room refrigerators and microwaves, fax, NS rooms, senior rates, wheelchair access, meeting facilities, CC. SGL/DBL$43-$94.

Viscount Suite Hotel (4855 East Broadway, 85711; 745-6500, Fax 7905114) 216 rooms, two restaurants, lounge, free breakfast, pool, sauna, local transportation, wheelchair access, NS rooms, in-room refrigerators, 8 meeting rooms, meeting facilities for 350, A/C, TV, CC. SGL/DBL$185.

Southwest Tucson

Best Western Royal Sun Inn and Suites (1015 North Stone Ave., 85705; 622-8871, Fax 623-2267, 800-5281234) 79 rooms, restaurant, heated pool, sauna, exercise center, hot tubs, children free with parents, airport transportation, in-room refrigerators, NS rooms, no pets, wheelchair access, meeting facilities for 40, A/C, TV, CC. SGL/DBL$63-$185.

Comfort Inn (715 West 22nd St., 85713; 791-9282, Fax 798-1458) 68 rooms, pool, whirlpools, children free with parents, wheelchair access, NS rooms, room service, A/C, TV, senior rates, no pets, CC. SGL/DBL$45-$75.

Congress Hotel (311 East Congress St., 85701; 622-8848, 800-722-8848) 40 rooms, restaurant, lounge, A/C, TV, CC. SGL$35.

Days Inn (222 South Freeway, 85745; 791-7511, Fax 622-3481, 800-325-2525) 122 rooms and suites, outdoor pool, children free with parents, room service, laundry service, A/C, TV, free local calls, pets OK, VCRs, fax, wheelchair access, NS rooms, meeting facilities for 50, senior rates, CC. SGL/DBL$39-$95.

Discovery Inn (1010 South Freeway, 85745; 622-5871, Fax 620-0097, 800-521-5243) 143 rooms, restaurant, lounge, heated pool, laundry service, airport courtesy car, 4 meeting rooms, meeting facilities for 160, CC. Near the University of Arizona. SGL/DBL$85.

La Quinta Motor Inn (664 North Freeway, 85745; 622-6491, 800-531-5900) 126 rooms, heated outdoor pool, NS rooms, free local calls, A/C, TV, CC. SGL/DBL$65.

Motel 6 South (960 South Freeway, 85745; 628-1339, 505-891-6161) 111 rooms, pool, free local calls, children under 17 free with parents, NS rooms, wheelchair access, pets OK, A/C, TV, CC. SGL/DBL$40-$44.

Quality Inn University (1601 North Oracle Rd., 85705; 623-6666, Fax 884-7422, 800-228-5151) 184 rooms and efficiencies, restaurant, lounge, entertainment, heated outdoor pool, gift shop, pets OK, NS rooms, in-room refrigerators, children free with parents, 8 meeting rooms, meeting facilities for 1,000, A/C, TV, CC. SGL/DBL$59-$95.

Ramada Inn Downtown 2 (475 North Granada, 85701; 622-3000, Fax 623-8922, 800-2-RAMADA) 297 rooms and suites, restaurant, free breakfast, lounge, pool, children under 18 free with parents, wheelchair access, NS rooms, A/C, TV, airport transportation, beauty shop, 13 meeting rooms, meeting facilities for 1,200, CC. Near the historic downtown area and Government Center, 2 miles from the University of Arizona. SGL/DBL$60-$128.

Regal 8 Inn (1222 South Freeway, 85713; 624-2516, 800-851-8888) 99 rooms, pool, NS rooms, children free with parents, free local calls, wheelchair access, A/C, TV, CC. SGL/DBL$50-$58.

Rodeway Inn North (1365 West Grant Rd., 85745; 622-7791) 148 rooms, restaurant, lounge, pool, jacuzzi, sauna, exercise center, children free with parents, pets OK, wheelchair access, NS rooms, airport courtesy car, 4 meeting rooms, meeting facilities for 150, A/C, TV, CC. SGL/DBL$60-$100.

TraveLodge (1136 North Stone Ave., 85705; 622-6714, 800-255-3050) 48 rooms, restaurant, lounge, free breakfast, pool, wheelchair access, complimentary newspaper, laundry service, free local calls, room service, in-room refrigerators and microwaves, no pets, A/C, TV, CC. SGL$52-$74, DBL$56-$78, X$4$6.

University Inn (950 North Stone Ave., 85705; 791-7503, 800-233-8466) 38 rooms, restaurant, free breakfast, pool, laundry service, in-room refrigerators, pets OK, children free with parents, A/C, TV, CC. SGL/DBL$85.

Tubac

Area Code 602

Tubac Golf Resort (Tubac 84646; 398-2211, 800-848-7893) 32 rooms and efficiencies, restaurant, lounge, heated pool, in-room refrigerators and coffee makers, fireplaces, pets OK, A/C, TV, NS rooms, wheelchair access, CC. SGL/DBL$105-$130.

Best Western Ranch Grande Motel (293 East Wickenburg Way, 85358; 684-5445, Fax 684-7380, 800-528-1234) 80 rooms, restaurant, free breakfast, lounge, pool, exercise center, children free with parents, A/C, NS rooms, airport transportation, TV, laundry facilities, wheelchair access, pets OK, senior rates, meeting facilities, CC. SGL/DBL$52-$88.

Flying E Ranch (2801 West Wickenburg Way, 85358; 684-2690, Fax 684-5305) 16 rooms, restaurant, entertainment, exercise center, in-room refrigerators and coffee makers, airport courtesy car, A/C, TV, NS rooms, wheelchair access, meeting facilities, senior rates, CC. SGL/DBL$120-$220.

Rancho de los Caballeros (1551 South Vulture Mine Rd., 85390; 684-5484, Fax 684-2267) 73 rooms, restaurant, no pets, children free with parents, A/C, TV, NS rooms, wheelchair access, in-room refrigerators and coffee makers, no pets, CC. SGL/DBL$130-$335.

Wickenburg Inn (Wickenburg 85358; 684-7811, Fax 684-2981, 800-528-4227) 47 rooms and villas, restaurant, lounge, entertainment, heated pool, whirlpools, tennis courts, fireplaces, airport transportation, A/C, TV, NS rooms, wheelchair access, CC. SGL/DBL$155-$350.

Willcox

Area Code 602

Best Western Plaza Inn (1100 West Rex Allen Dr., 85643; 384-3556, Fax 384-2679, 800-528-1234) 92 rooms, restaurant, free breakfast, lounge, pool, exercise center, children free with parents, A/C, NS rooms, beauty shop, TV, laundry facilities, wheelchair access, pets OK, senior rates, meeting facilities, CC. SGL/DBL$48-$95.

Econo Lodge (724 North Busboy Ave., 85643; 384-4222, 800-826-4152, 800-4-CHOICE) 73 rooms, pool, exercise center, children under 12 free with parents, no pets, senior rates, NS rooms, wheelchair access, A/C, TV, senior rates, CC. SGL/DBL$35-$98.

Motel 6 (921 North Busboy Ave., 85643; 384-2201, 505-891-6161) 123 rooms, pool, free local calls, children under 17 free with parents, NS rooms, wheelchair access, pets OK, A/C, TV, CC. SGL/DBL$36-$46.

Williams
Area Code 602

Best Western Inn (1901 West Bill Williams Ave., 86046; 635-4400, Fax 635-4488, 800-528-1234) 78 rooms, heated pool, laundry facilities, A/C, TV, no pets, A/C, TV, meeting facilities, senior rates. SGL/DBL$70-$113.

Budget Host Inn (620 West Bill Williams Ave., 86046; 635-4415) 26 rooms, A/C, TV, children free with parents, pets OK, senior rates, CC. SGL/DBL$20-$28.

Canyon Country Inn (442 West Bill Williams Ave., 86046; 635-2349) 13 rooms, free breakfast, A/C, NS rooms, no pets, TV, CC. SGL/DBL$35-$95.

Comfort Inn (911 West Bill Williams Ave., 86046; 635-4045, 800-221-2222) 54 rooms, free breakfast, indoor heated pool, whirlpools, wheelchair access, NS rooms, no pets, children under 18 free with parents, A/C, TV, meeting facilities, senior rates, CC. SGL/DBL$40-$65.

Days Inn (2488 West Bill Williams Ave., 86046; 635-4051, Fax 635-4411, 800-325-2525) 73 rooms and suites, restaurant, indoor pool, children free with parents, room service, laundry service, A/C, TV, free local calls, pets OK, fax, wheelchair access, NS rooms, meeting facilities for 35, senior rates, CC. SGL/DBL$39-$150.

Econo Lodge (302 East Bill Williams Ave., 86046; 635-4085, 800-4-CHOICE) 42 rooms, pool, children under 12 free with parents, no pets, senior rates, NS rooms, wheelchair access, A/C, TV, senior rates, CC. SGL/DBL$28-$89.

El Ranch Motel (617 East Bill Williams Ave., 86046; 635-2552, Fax 635-4173, 800-228-2370) 25 rooms and suites, restaurant, heated pool, in-room refrigerators, pets OK, airport courtesy car, A/C, TV, NS rooms, wheelchair access, senior rates, CC. SGL/DBL$50-$100.

Highlander Motel (533 West Bill Williams Ave., 86046; 635-2541) 12 rooms, A/C, pets OK, TV, NS rooms, wheelchair access, CC. SGL/DBL$25-$49.

Holiday Inn (831 West Bill Williams Ave., 86046; 635-9000, Fax 645-9472, 800-HOLIDAY) 51 rooms, restaurant, lounge, indoor heated pool, exercise center, whirlpools, children under 19 free with parents, wheelchair access,

A/C, TV, NS rooms, fax, room service, no pets, laundry service, meeting facilities, senior rates, CC. SGL/DBL$45-$95.

Mountain Side Inn (642 East Bill Williams Ave., 86046; 635-4431, 800-462-9381) 96 rooms, restaurant, lounge, entertainment, heated pool, whirlpools, A/C, TV, children free with parents, pets OK, senior rates, NS rooms, wheelchair access, CC. SGL/DBL$65-$125.

Norris Motel (1001 Bill Williams Ave., 86046; 635-2202, Fax 635-9202, 800-341-8000, 34 rooms, whirlpools, in-room refrigerators, airport transportation, children free with parents, A/C, TV, NS rooms, wheelchair access, CC. SGL/DBL$55-$65.

Quality Inn Mountain (I-40 and Route 1, 86046; 635-2693, 800-221-2222) 73 rooms and suites, restaurant, pool, exercise center, tennis courts, children free with parents, A/C, TV, room service, laundry service, no pets, NS rooms, meeting facilities, senior rates, CC. SGL/DBL$50-$100.

Ramada Inn (710 West Bill Williams Ave., 86046; 635-4464, Fax 635-4814, 800-2-RAMADA) 47 rooms and suites, restaurant, wheelchair access, NS rooms, pets OK, A/C, TV, children under 18 free with parents, room service, laundry facilities, meeting facilities, senior rates, CC. SGL/DBL$30-$80.

Rodeway Inn (750 North Grand Canyon Blvd., 86046; 635-9127, 800-424-4777) 19 rooms and 2-bedroom apartments, pool, wheelchair access, NS rooms, children free with parents, A/C, in-room refrigerators and microwaves, TV, senior rates, CC. SGL/DBL$30-$100.

Super 8 Motel (2001 East Bill Williams Ave., 86046; 635-4700, 800-800-8000) 40 rooms and suites, pets OK, children under 12 free with parents, free local calls, A/C, TV, in-room refrigerators and microwaves, fax, NS rooms, senior rates, wheelchair access, meeting facilities, CC. SGL/DBL$50-$80.

TraveLodge (430 East Bill Williams Ave., 86046; 635-2651, Fax 635-4296, 800-578-7878) 41 rooms, restaurant, lounge, outdoor heated pool, jacuzzi, wheelchair access, complimentary newspaper, laundry service, TV, A/C, free local calls, fax, NS rooms, in-room refrigerators and microwaves, children under 18 free with parents, pets OK, meeting facilities, senior rates, CC. SGL/DBL$29-$129.

Winslow

Area Code 602

Best Western Adobe Inn (1701 North Park Dr., 86047; 289-4638, 800-528-1234) 72 rooms, restaurant, lounge, indoor pool, exercise center, children free with parents, A/C, NS rooms, TV, laundry facilities, wheelchair access, room service, pets OK, senior rates, meeting facilities, CC. SGL/DBL$46-$60.

Best Western Town House Inn (1914 West 3rd St., 86047; 289-4611, 800-528-1234) 68 rooms, restaurant, free breakfast, lounge, pool, exercise center, children free with parents, A/C, NS rooms, local transportation, TV, laundry facilities, wheelchair access, pets OK, senior rates, meeting facilities, CC. SGL/DBL$44-$64.

Comfort Inn (520 Desmond St., 86047; 289-9581, 800-221-2222) 55 rooms, free breakfast, indoor heated pool, whirlpools, wheelchair access, NS rooms, no pets, children under 18 free with parents, A/C, TV, meeting facilities, senior rates, CC. SGL/DBL$40-$70.

Econo Lodge (1706 North Park Dr., 86047; 289-4687, 800-4-CHOICE) 73 rooms and suites, heated pool, children under 12 free with parents, no pets, senior rates, NS rooms, wheelchair access, A/C, TV, senior rates, CC. SGL/DBL$38-$53.

Super 8 Motel (1916 West 3rd St., 86047; 289-4606, 800-800-8000) 46 rooms and suites, restaurant, pets OK, children under 12 free with parents, free local calls, A/C, TV, in-room refrigerators and microwaves, fax, NS rooms, senior rates, wheelchair access, meeting facilities, CC. SGL/DBL$35-$50.

Youngtown
Area Code 602

Motel 6 Sun City (11133 Grand Ave., 85363; 977-1318, 505-891-6161) 62 rooms, pool, free local calls, children under 17 free with parents, NS rooms, wheelchair access, pets OK, A/C, TV, CC. SGL/DBL$38-$42.

Yuma
Area Code 602

Airporter Inn (711 East 32nd St., 85365; 726-4721, Fax 344-0452) 80 rooms, restaurant, lounge, pool, lighted tennis courts, children free with parents, laundry facilities, A/C, TV, NS rooms, wheelchair access, meeting facilities, senior rates, CC. SGL/DBL$55-$70.

Best Western Chilton Inn and Conference Center (300 East 32nd St., 85365; 344-1050, Fax 344-4877, 800-528-1234) 49 rooms and suites, restaurant, free breakfast, lounge, pool, exercise center, children free with parents, room service, free local calls, complimentary newspaper, A/C, NS rooms, TV, VCRs, in-room refrigerators and microwaves, laundry facilities, wheelchair access, pets OK, senior rates, meeting facilities, CC. SGL/DBL$40-$60, STS$60-$110.

Best Western Coronado Motor Hotel (233 4th Ave., 85364; 783-4453, Fax 782-7487, 800-528-1234) 49 rooms, restaurant, free breakfast, lounge, pool, exercise center, children free with parents, A/C, NS rooms, gift shop, in-room refrigerators and microwaves, TV, laundry facilities, wheelchair access, pets OK, senior rates, meeting facilities, CC. SGL/DBL$40-$110.

Best Western Inn Suites Hotel Yuma (Yuma 85365; 783-8341, Fax 783-1349, 800-528-1234) 166 rooms, restaurant, free breakfast, lounge, pool, exercise center, jacuzzi, tennis courts, in-room refrigerators and microwaves, children free with parents, A/C, NS rooms, TV, laundry facilities, wheelchair access, pets OK, senior rates, meeting facilities, CC. SGL/DBL$61-$95.

Cabana Motel (2151 South 4th Ave., 85364; 783-8311) 63 rooms and efficiencies, heated pool, children free with parents, A/C, TV, NS rooms, wheelchair access, free local calls, kitchenettes, in-room refrigerators, children free with parents, senior rates, CC. SGL/DBL$25-$65.

Holiday Inn (3181 South 4th Ave., 85364; 344-1420, Fax 341-0158, 800-HOLIDAY) 120 rooms, restaurant, lounge, outdoor pool, exercise center, children under 19 free with parents, wheelchair access, A/C, TV, NS rooms, fax, in-room refrigerators, microwaves and coffee makers, airport transportation, room service, pets OK, laundry service, meeting facilities, senior rates, CC. SGL/DBL$65-$80.

La Fuente Inn (1513 East 16th St., 85365; 329-1814, 800-841-1814) 95 rooms and suites, free breakfast, restaurant, heated pool, exercise center, whirlpools, children free with parents, laundry facilities, in-room refrigerators, microwaves and coffee makers A/C, TV, NS rooms, wheelchair access, senior rates, CC. SGL/DBL$70-$90.

Motel 6 Downtown (1640 Arizona Ave., 85364; 782-6561, 505-891-6161) 201 rooms, pool, free local calls, children under 17 free with parents, NS rooms, wheelchair access, pets OK, A/C, TV, CC. SGL/DBL$34-$39.

Motel 6 East (1445 East 16th St., 85365; 782-9521, 505-891-6161) 123 rooms, pool, free local calls, children under 17 free with parents, NS rooms, wheelchair access, pets OK, A/C, laundry facilities, TV, CC. SGL/DBL$38-$42.

Park Inn International (2600 South 4th Ave., 85364; 726-4830, Fax 726-4830 ext 388, 800-437-PARK) 164 suites, restaurant, free breakfast, lounge, heated pool, exercise center, A/C, TV, in-room refrigerators and microwaves, airport transportation, wheelchair access, NS rooms, CC. SGL/DBL$85-$95.

Shilo Inn (1550 South Castle Dome Rd., 85365; 782-9511, Fax 783-1538) rooms and suites, restaurant, lounge, outdoor heated pool, spa, exercise center, airport courtesy car, in-room refrigerators, A/C, TV, NS rooms, laundry facilities, wheelchair access, children under 12 free with parents, meeting facilities for 450, senior rates, CC. SGL/DBL$66-$106.

Torch Lite Lodge (2501 South 4th Ave., 85364; 344-1600) 40 rooms and efficiencies, restaurant, heated pool, A/C, TV, NS rooms, wheelchair access, CC. SGL/DBL$27-$39.

TraveLodge (2050 South 4th Ave., 85364; 782-3831, Fax 783-4616, 800-578-7878) 48 rooms, restaurant, lounge, free breakfast, pool, wheelchair access, complimentary newspaper, laundry service, TV, A/C, free local calls, fax, NS rooms, in-room refrigerators and microwaves, children under 18 free with parents, no pets, meeting facilities, senior rates, CC. SGL/DBL$32-$82.

Colorado

Rental and Reservations Services

Bed and Breakfast Rocky Mountain (11170 Black Forest Rd., Denver 80209; 303-744-8415, 800-733-8415) represents 175 bed and breakfast in Colorado.

Akron
Area Code 303

Crestwood Manor Motel (625 East 1st St., 80720; 345-2231) 14 rooms, A/C, TV, NS rooms, wheelchair access, pets OK, CC. SGL/DBL$25-$32.

Alamosa
Area Code 719

Best Western Alamosa Inn (1919 Main St., 81101; 589-2567, Fax 589-0767, 800-528-1234) 121 rooms, restaurant, lounge, indoor heated pool, exercise center, children free with parents, A/C, NS rooms, TV, laundry facilities, wheelchair access, in-room refrigerators, pets OK, senior rates, meeting facilities, CC. SGL/DBL$48-$160.

The Cottonwood Inn (123 Santa Fe Ave., 81101; 589-5833, Fax 589-4412) 6 rooms and suites, free breakfast, airport transportation, antique furnishings, NS, TV, CC. SGL/DBL$50-$70.

Days Inn (224 O'Keefe Pkwy., 81101; 589-9037, Fax 589-3585, 800-325-2525) 33 rooms and suites, outdoor pool, children free with parents, room service, laundry service, A/C, TV, free local calls, pets OK, fax, wheelchair access, NS rooms, senior rates, CC. SGL/DBL$32-$50.

Holiday Inn (333 Santa Fe Ave., 81101; 589-5833, Fax 589-4412, 800-HOLI-DAY) 127 rooms and suites, restaurant, lounge, entertainment, indoor pool, exercise center, whirlpools, airport transportation, gift shop, children under 19 free with parents, wheelchair access, A/C, TV, NS rooms, fax, room service, pets OK, laundry service, meeting facilities for 500, senior rates, CC. SGL/DBL$60-$115.

Super 8 Motel (2505 Main St., 81101; 589-6447, 800-800-8000) 37 rooms and suites, restaurant, pets OK, children under 12 free with parents, free local calls, A/C, TV, in-room refrigerators and microwaves, fax, NS rooms, senior rates, wheelchair access, meeting facilities, CC. SGL/DBL$35-$58.

Almont
Area Code 303

Char-B Resort (Almont 81210; 641-0751, 800-641-2873) 16 1- to 5-bedroom cottages, hot tub, in-room refrigerators, TV, NS rooms, wheelchair access, fireplaces, CC. SGL/DBL$60-$100.

Aspen
Area Code 303

Aspen Bed and Breakfast (311 West Main St., 81611; 925-7650, Fax 925-5744, 800-36-ASPEN) 38 rooms, free breakfast, heated pool, whirlpools, fireplaces, in-room refrigerators, children free with parents, fireplaces, pets OK, A/C, TV, senior rates, CC. SGL/DBL$80-$200.

Aspen Club Lodge (709 East Durant, 81611; 925-6760, Fax 925-6778) 90 rooms, restaurant, lounge, heated pool, whirlpools, sauna, exercise center, in-room refrigerators, airport transportation, A/C, TV, NS rooms, wheelchair access, CC. SGL/DBL$95-$650.

Aspen Hotel (110 West Main St., 81611; 925-3441, 800-527-7369) 45 rooms, free breakfast, heated pool, whirlpools, local transportation, pets OK, kitchenettes, in-room refrigerators, A/C, TV, NS rooms, wheelchair access, CC. SGL/DBL$165-$245.

Aspen Manor (411 South Monarch St., 81611; 925-3001) 22 rooms, free breakfast, heated pool, sauna, whirlpools, pets OK, TV, NS rooms, wheelchair access, CC. SGL/DBL$50-$175.

Aspen Square (617 East Cooper, 81611; 925-1000, Fax 925-1017, 800-862-7736) 105 rooms and 3-bedroom condominiums, restaurant, heated pool, whirlpools, sauna, pets OK, laundry facilities, A/C, TV, NS rooms, wheelchair access, CC. SGL/DBL$220-$350.

Boomerang Lodge (500 West Hopkins, 81611; 925-3416, 800-992-8852) 35 rooms and 2- and 3-bedroom suites, free breakfast, heated pool, whirlpools, sauna, fireplaces, A/C, TV, NS rooms, in-room refrigerators, pets

OK, wheelchair access, local transportation, senior rates, CC. SGL/DBL$105-$210.

Cresthaus Inn (1301 East Cooper, 81611; 925-7081, 800-344-3853) 31 rooms, free breakfast, pool, sauna, whirlpools, laundry facilities, local transportation, pets OK, fireplaces, A/C, TV, NS rooms, wheelchair access, CC. SGL/DBL$125-$175.

The Inn at Aspen (38750 Hwy. 82, 81611; 925-1500, Fax 925-9037, 800-952-1515) 188 efficiencies, restaurant, lounge, pool, sauna, whirlpools, A/C, TV, in-room refrigerators and microwaves, gift shop, airport transportation, game room, NS rooms, wheelchair access, meeting facilities, senior rates, CC. SGL/DBL$120-$450.

Innsbruck Inn (233 West Main St., 81611; 925-2980, 800-772-7903) 31 rooms and 2-bedroom suites, free breakfast, heated pool, sauna, whirlpools, children free with parents, A/C, TV, NS rooms, in-room refrigerators, pets OK, wheelchair access, senior rates, CC. SGL/DBL$115-$210.

Jerome Hotel (330 East Main St., 81611; 920-1000, Fax 925-2784, 800-331-7213) 94 rooms and suites, restaurant, lounge, heated pool, whirlpools, antique furnishings, pets OK, airport transportation, in-room refrigerators, A/C, TV, NS rooms, wheelchair access, CC. SGL/DBL$200-$700.

Lenado Hotel (200 South Aspen St., 81611; 925-6246, Fax 925-3840) 10 rooms, free breakfast, lounge, hot tubs, in-room refrigerators, A/C, TV, NS rooms, wheelchair access, meeting facilities, CC. SGL/DBL$215-$285.

Lift One Condominiums (131 East Furant Ave., 81611; 925-1670, Fax 925-1152) 27 2- and 3-bedroom condominiums, outdoor pool, whirlpools, sauna, pets OK, laundry facilities, A/C, TV, NS rooms, wheelchair access, CC. SGL/DBL$75-$260.

Limelite Lodge (228 East Cooper, 81611; 925-3025, Fax 925-5120, 800-433-0832) 34 rooms and 2-bedroom efficiencies, free breakfast, heated pool, whirlpools, sauna, VCRs, pets OK, laundry facilities, children free with parents, A/C, TV, NS rooms, wheelchair access, CC. SGL/DBL$70-$170.

Little Nell Hotel (675 East Durant Ave., 81611; 920-4600, Fax 920-4670, 800-525-6200) 92 rooms and suites, restaurant, lounge, entertainment, heated pool, exercise center, airport courtesy car, boutiques, A/C, TV, NS rooms, wheelchair access, fireplaces, pets OK, CC. SGL/DBL$160-$425.

Molly Gibson Lodge (101 West Main St., 81611; 925-3434, 800-356-6559) 53 rooms and efficiencies, lounge, heated pool, whirlpools, pets OK, in-room refrigerators, A/C, TV, kitchenettes, fireplaces, NS rooms, wheelchair access, meeting facilities, airport transportation, senior rates, CC. SGL/DBL$90-$400.

Ritz Carlton (315 Dean St., 81611; 555-5555, 800-241-3333) 256 rooms and suites, restaurant, lounge, entertainment, heated pool, exercise center, sauna, 24-hour room service, wheelchair access, A/C, TV, NS rooms, wheelchair access, children free with parents, airport transportation, pets OK, meeting facilities, CC. SGL/DBL$165-$700.

Sardy House (128 East Main St., 81611; 920-2525, Fax 920-4478, 800-321-3457) 20 rooms and suites, restaurant, free breakfast, lounge, heated pool, whirlpools, sauna, in-room refrigerators, antique furnishings, A/C, TV, NS rooms, wheelchair access, CC. SGL/DBL$250-$550.

Snowflake Inn (221 East Hyman Ave., 81611; 925-3221, 800-247-2069) 38 rooms and suites, free breakfast, heated pool, sauna, whirlpools, airport transportation, children free with parents, in-room coffee makers, A/C, TV, NS rooms, wheelchair access, CC. SGL/DBL$130-$150, STS$160-$650.

Ullr Lodge (520 West Main St., 81611; 925-7696, Fax 920-4339) 24 rooms and 1- and 2-bedroom apartments, free breakfast, pool, whirlpools, laundry facilities, A/C, TV, NS rooms, wheelchair access, in-room refrigerators, pets OK, meeting facilities, CC. SGL/DBL$95-$190.

Aurora

Area Code 303

Hampton Inn (1500 South Abilene, 80012; 369-8400, Fax 369-0324, 800-HAMPTON) 132 rooms, restaurant, free breakfast, pool, exercise center, children under 18 free with parents, NS rooms, wheelchair access, in-room computer hookups, fax, TV, A/C, free local calls, pets OK, meeting facilities, CC. SGL/DBL$52-$75.

Holiday Inn Denver SouthTech (3200 South Parker Rd., 80014; 695-1700, 800-962-7672) 479 rooms and suites, restaurant, lounge, entertainment, outdoor heated pool, exercise center, children free with parents, wheelchair access, TV, A/C, NS rooms, fax, room service, pets OK, airport courtesy car, gift shop, beauty shop, 19 meeting rooms, 21,000 square feet of meeting and exhibition space, meeting facilities for 2,000, CC. SGL/DBL$83-$93.

La Quinta Aurora (1011 South Abilene St., 80012; 337-0206, Fax 750-9738, 800-531-5900) 122 rooms, restaurant, lounge, heated pool, complimentary newspaper, free local calls, fax, NS rooms, airport transportation, wheelchair access, TV, A/C, laundry service, meeting facilities, CC. SGL/DBL$57-$62.

Avon

Area Code 303

Charter at Beaver Creek (Avon 81620; 949-6660, Fax 949-6709, 800-525-6660) 170 rooms and suites, restaurant, indoor and outdoor pools, exercise center, sauna, whirlpools, A/C, TV, NS rooms, wheelchair access, beauty shop, fireplaces, kitchenettes, children free with parents, pets OK, CC. SGL/DBL$135-$995.

Comfort Inn Beaver Creek (161 West Beaver Creek Blvd., 81620; 949-5511, 800-221-2222) 146 rooms, restaurant, free breakfast, pool, whirlpools, wheelchair access, NS rooms, pets OK, children under 18 free with parents, local transportation, A/C, in-room refrigerators and microwaves, TV, meeting facilities, senior rates, CC. SGL/DBL$70-$225.

Hyatt Regency Beaver Creek Resort (Avon 81620; 949-1234, Fax 949-4164, 800-233-1234) 300 rooms and suites, restaurant, lounge, entertainment, heated pool, whirlpools, exercise center, tennis courts, room service, TV, A/C, NS rooms, wheelchair access, airport transportation, pets OK, barber and beauty shop, children free with parents, in-room coffee makers, 23,000 square feet of meeting and exhibition space, senior rates, CC. SGL/DBL$285-$550, STS$850-$2,300.

The Inn at Beaver Creek (Avon 81620; 845-7800, Fax 949-2308) 45 rooms and suites, free breakfast, lounge, entertainment, heated pool, sauna, whirlpools, TV, NS rooms, wheelchair access, in-room refrigerators and coffee makers, laundry service, CC. SGL/DBL$200-$250.

Pines Lodge (141 Scott Hill Rd., 81620; 845-7900, Fax 845-7809) 60 rooms, restaurant, lounge, entertainment, heated pool, whirlpools, sauna, in-room refrigerators, laundry facilities, pets OK, airport transportation, A/C, TV, NS rooms, wheelchair access, CC. SGL/DBL$120-$425.

Basalt

Area Code 303

Best Western Aspenalt Lodge (Basalt 81621; 927-3191, 800-528-1234) 35 rooms, restaurant, free breakfast, lounge, pool, hot tub, exercise center, whirlpools, children free with parents, A/C, NS rooms, TV, laundry facilities, wheelchair access, pets OK, in-room refrigerators, senior rates, meeting facilities, CC. SGL/DBL$45-$100.

Bayfield

Area Code 303

Bear Paw Lodge (18011 Hwy. 501, 81122; 884-2508) cabins, kitchenettes, pets OK, TV, NS rooms, wheelchair access, CC. SGL/DBL$58-$75.

Circle S Lodge (18022 Hwy. 501, 81122; 884-2473) cabins, kitchenettes, laundry facilities, pets OK, A/C, TV, NS rooms, wheelchair access, CC. SGL/DBL$60-$75.

D'Mara Resort (1213 Hwy. 500, 81122; 884-9806) cabins, kitchenettes, A/C, TV, NS rooms, wheelchair access, CC. SGL/DBL$80-$115.

Elk Point Lodge (21730 Hwy. 501, 81122; 884-2482) cabins, kitchenettes, A/C, TV, NS rooms, wheelchair access, CC. SGL/DBL$50-$100.

Forest Lake Resort (82 Alpine Forest Dr., 81122; 884-2411) cabins, kitchenettes, hot tubs, pets OK, A/C, TV, NS rooms, wheelchair access, CC. SGL/DBL$53.

Lake Haven Resort (14452 Hwy. 501, 81122; 884-2517) cabins, restaurant, pets OK, A/C, TV, NS rooms, wheelchair access, CC. SGL/DBL$44-$80.

Pine River Lodge (14443 Hwy. 501, 81122; 884-2563) cabins, kitchenettes, hot tubs, laundry facilities, A/C, TV, pets OK, NS rooms, wheelchair access, CC. SGL/DBL$140.

Saw Mill Lodge (14737 Hwy. 501, 81122; 884-2669) kitchenettes, pets OK, A/C, TV, NS rooms, wheelchair access, CC. SGL/DBL$55-$65.

Scotties Resort (17454 Hwy. 501, 81122; 884-2506) cabins, kitchenettes, pets OK, A/C, TV, NS rooms, wheelchair access, CC. SGL/DBL$45-$79.

Silver Streams (18645 Hwy. 501, 81122; 884-2770) cabins, restaurant, kitchenettes, pets OK, A/C, TV, NS rooms, wheelchair access, CC. SGL/DBL$55-$65.

Wilderness Trail Ranch (Bayfield 81122; 247-0722) 20 rooms and cabins, restaurant, lounge, entertainment, pool, hot tubs, jacuzzi, American plan available, game room, children free with parents, TV, NS rooms, wheelchair access, local transportation, laundry facilities, gift shop, CC. SGL/DBL$1,400W-$2,400W.

Wit's End Guest Ranch (Bayfield 81122; 884-4112) pool, hot tub, American plan, A/C, TV, NS rooms, wheelchair access, CC. SGL/DBL$105-$135.

Beaver Creek
Area Code 303

Borders Lodge (Beaver Creek 81620; 845-7911, Fax 845-5895) 20 rooms and 2- and 3-bedroom efficiencies, heated pool, whirlpools, A/C, TV, NS rooms, wheelchair access, laundry facilities, pets OK, senior rates, CC. SGL/DBL$145-$665.

Poste Montane (Beaver Creek 81620; 845-7500, Fax 845-5891) 24 rooms and efficiencies, sauna, whirlpools, pets OK, fireplaces, in-room refrigerators, A/C, TV, NS rooms, wheelchair access, CC. SGL/DBL$66-$485.

St. James Place (Beaver Creek 81620; 845-9300, Fax 845-0099) 42 rooms and efficiencies, restaurant, indoor heated pool, whirlpools, laundry facilities, pets OK, A/C, TV, NS rooms, wheelchair access, senior rates, CC. SGL/DBL$120-$500.

Trappers Cabin (Beaver Creek 81620; 845-5877, Fax 949-2308) 1 4-bedroom cabin, whirlpools, laundry facilities, pets OK, A/C, TV, NS rooms, wheelchair access, CC. SGL/DBL$450-$900.

Bellevue
Area Code 303

Big Horn Cabins (31635 Poudre Canyon, 80512; 881-2142) 5 2- and 3-bedroom cabins, kitchenettes, pets OK, TV, VCRs, CC. SGL/DBL$40-$72.

Boulder
Area Code 303

The Alps Boulder Canyon Inn (38619 Boulder Canyon, 80302; 444-5445) 12 rooms, whirlpools, pets OK, fireplaces, A/C, TV, NS rooms, wheelchair access, CC. SGL/DBL$80-$160.

Best Western Boulder Inn (770 28th St., 80303; 449-3800, 800-233-8469) 95 rooms, restaurant, free breakfast, lounge, outdoor heated pool, exercise center, whirlpools, children free with parents, A/C, NS rooms, TV, laundry facilities, wheelchair access, pets OK, airport transportation, VCRs, senior rates, meeting facilities, CC. SGL/DBL$48-$80.

Best Western Golden Bluff Lodge (1725 28th St., 80301; 442-7450, Fax 442-8788, 800-999-BUFF, 800-528-1234) 112 rooms, restaurant, free breakfast, lounge, pool, exercise center, kitchenettes, in-room refrigerators, children free with parents, A/C, NS rooms, TV, laundry facilities, wheelchair access, pets OK, senior rates, meeting facilities, CC. SGL/DBL$55-$100.

Bluebird Lodge (Main St., 80302; 443-6475) 9 rooms, free breakfast, A/C, TV, NS, pets OK. SGL/DBL$40-$50.

Boulder Mountain Lodge (91 Four Mile Canyon, 80302; 444-0882, 800-458-0882) 22 rooms and 2-bedroom efficiencies, heated pool, whirlpools, pets OK, A/C, TV, kitchenettes, NS rooms, wheelchair access, CC. SGL/DBL$35-$70.

Boulderado Hotel (2115 13th St., 80302; 442-4344, Fax 442-4378, 800-433-4344) 160 rooms and suites, restaurant, lounge, entertainment, pets OK, antique furnishings, in-room refrigerators, airport transportation, A/C, TV, NS rooms, wheelchair access, meeting facilities, senior rates, CC. SGL/DBL$110-$148.

Briar Rose Inn (2151 Arapahoe Ave., 80302; 442-3007) 9 rooms, free breakfast, antique furnishings, pets OK, NS, fireplaces, airport transportation, A/C, TV, CC. SGL/DBL$70-$110.

Broker Inn (555 30th St., 80303; 444-3330, 800-338-5407) 116 rooms and suites, restaurant, lounge, entertainment, heated pool, whirlpools, airport transportation, pets OK, local transportation, A/C, TV, NS rooms, wheelchair access, meeting facilities, senior rates, CC. SGL/DBL$100-$175.

Clarion Harvest House Hotel (1345 28th St., 80302; 443-3850, 800-221-2222) 270 rooms, restaurant, lounge, entertainment, free breakfast, indoor and outdoor pool, whirlpools, exercise center, airport transportation, in-room refrigerators, laundry facilities, pets OK, NS rooms, children under 18 free with parents, senior rates, meeting facilities, A/C, TV, CC. SGL/DBL$70-$100.

Courtyard by Marriott (4710 Pearl East Circle, 80301; 440-4700, Fax 440-8975, 800-321-2211) 147 rooms and suites, restaurant, lounge, indoor pool, exercise center, whirlpools, children free with parents, laundry service, A/C, NS rooms, TV, in-room refrigerators and coffee makers, airport transportation, pets OK, meeting facilities, senior rates, CC. SGL/DBL$70-$85.

Days Inn (5397 South Boulder Rd., 80303; 499-4422, Fax 494-0269, 800-325-2525) 74 rooms and suites, free breakfast, lounge, outdoor pool, children free with parents, room service, laundry service, A/C, TV, free local calls, pets OK, airport transportation, fax, wheelchair access, NS rooms, senior rates, CC. SGL/DBL$49-$84.

Foot of the Mountain Motel (200 Arapahoe Ave., 80302; 442-5688) 18 rooms, A/C, TV, NS rooms, pets OK, in-room refrigerators, wheelchair access, CC. SGL/DBL$40-$60.

Highlander Inn (970 28th St., 80303; 443-7800, Fax 443-7801, 800-525-2149) 72 rooms and efficiencies, heated pool, pets OK, in-room refrigerators, laundry facilities, A/C, TV, NS rooms, wheelchair access, CC. SGL/DBL$45-$80.

Holiday Inn (800 28th St., 80303; 443-3322, Fax 443-0397, 800-HOLIDAY) 165 rooms, restaurant, lounge, indoor pool, exercise center, children under 19 free with parents, wheelchair access, A/C, TV, NS rooms, fax, room service, pets OK, laundry service, airport transportation, meeting facilities for 250, senior rates, CC. SGL/DBL$75-$88.

Homewood Suites (4950 Baseline Rd., 80303; 499-9922, Fax 440-3796, 800-CALL-HOME) 1- and 2-bedroom suites, free breakfast, pool, whirlpools, exercise center, in-room refrigerators, coffee makers and microwaves, fireplace, fax, pets OK, TV, A/C, complimentary newspaper, NS rooms, wheelchair access, senior rates, meeting facilities, CC. SGL/DBL$95-$140.

Pearl Street Inn (1820 Pearl St., 80302; 444-5584, 800-232-5949) 7 rooms, restaurant, A/C, TV, NS rooms, wheelchair access, CC. SGL/DBL$60-$70.

Residence Inn (3030 Center Green Dr., 80301; 449-5545, Fax 449-2452, 800-331-3131) 128 suites, free breakfast, heated pool, whirlpools, in-room refrigerators, coffee makers and microwaves, laundry facilities, TV, A/C, VCRs, pets OK, complimentary newspaper, fireplaces, children free with parents, NS rooms, wheelchair access, meeting facilities, CC. SGL/DBL$110-$140.

Sandy Point Inn (6485 Twin Lakes Rd., 80301; 530-2939, 800-322-2939) 30 rooms, A/C, TV, NS rooms, wheelchair access, kitchenettes, laundry facilities, pets OK, CC. SGL/DBL$50-$75.

Silver Saddle Motel (90 West Araphaoe Ave., 80302; 442-8022, 800-525-9509) 32 rooms and 2-bedroom efficiencies, A/C, TV, NS rooms, wheelchair access, pets OK, CC. SGL/DBL$45-$75.

Skyland Motel (1100 28th St., 80303; 443-2650, 800-654-5220) 50 rooms, A/C, TV, NS rooms, wheelchair access, CC. SGL/DBL$32-$36.

University Inn Downtown (1632 Broadway, 80302; 442-3830, Fax 449-3777, 800-258-7917) 39 rooms, restaurant, free breakfast, pets OK, heated pool, A/C, TV, in-room refrigerators, laundry facilities, NS rooms, wheelchair access, CC. SGL/DBL$55-$65.

Breckenridge

Area Code 303

Allaire Timbers Inn (Breckenridge 80424; 453-7530, Fax 453-8864, 800-325-2342) 10 rooms, hot tubs, whirlpools, pets OK, A/C, TV, NS rooms, wheelchair access, CC. SGL/DBL$90-$210.

Beaver Run Hotel (620 Village Rd., 80420; 453-6000, Fax 453-4284, 800-288-1282) 438 rooms and suites, restaurant, lounge, entertainment, indoor and outdoor heated pool, whirlpools, sauna, exercise center, tennis courts, kitchenettes, pets OK, laundry facilities, A/C, TV, NS rooms, wheelchair access, fireplaces, meeting rooms, senior rates, CC. SGL/DBL$100-$325.

Cotton House Bed and Breakfast (Main St., 80424; 453-5509) 3 rooms, free breakfast, A/C, TV, NS, pets OK, CC. SGL/DBL$50-$90.

Hilton Hotel (550 Village Rd., 80424; 453-4500, Fax 453-0212, 800-HIL-TONS) 208 rooms and suites, restaurant, lounge, entertainment, indoor heated pool, exercise center, hot tubs, sauna, game room, children free with parents, NS rooms, wheelchair access, pets OK, room service, laundry facilities, A/C, TV, meeting facilities for 1,000, CC. SGL/DBL$85-$260.

River Mountain Lodge (100 South Park St., 80424; 453-4711, 800-325-2342) 55 condominiums, free breakfast, lounge, entertainment, whirlpools, sauna, airport transportation, pets OK, fireplaces, laundry facilities, A/C, TV, NS rooms, wheelchair access, senior rates, CC. SGL/DBL$60-$450.

Brighton
Area Code 303

Super 8 Motel (1020 Old Brighton Rd., 80601; 659-6063, Fax 659-9367, 800-800-8000) 39 rooms and suites, pets OK, children under 12 free with parents, free local calls, A/C, TV, in-room refrigerators and microwaves, fax, NS rooms, senior rates, wheelchair access, meeting facilities, CC. SGL/DBL$31-$40.

Brush
Area Code 303

Best Western Inn (1208 North Colorado Ave., 80723; 842-5146, 800-528-1234) 44 rooms, restaurant, lounge, heated pool, exercise center, children free with parents, A/C, NS rooms, TV, laundry facilities, wheelchair access, pets OK, senior rates, meeting facilities, CC. SGL/DBL$48-$70.

Budget Host Empire Motel (1408 Edison, 80723; 842-2876, 800-283-4678) 19 rooms, laundry facilities, NS rooms, wheelchair access, A/C, pets OK, TV, children free with parents, senior rates, CC. SGL/DBL$25-$38.

Buena Vista
Area Code 719

The Adobe Inn (303 North Hwy. 24, 81211; 395-6340) 7 rooms and suites, bed and breakfast, restaurant, free breakfast, whirlpools, pets OK, A/C, TV, fireplaces, in-room refrigerators, NS, 1880s inn, CC. SGL/DBL$55-$80.

Alpine Lodge (Buena Vista 81211; 395-2415) 13 rooms, restaurant, pets OK, A/C, TV, NS rooms, wheelchair access, CC. SGL/DBL$25-$40.

Great Western Sumac Lodge (Buena Vista 81211; 395-8111) 30 rooms, A/C, TV, NS rooms, wheelchair access, pets OK, kitchenettes, CC. SGL/DBL$32-$65.

Topaz Lodge (115 North Hwy. 24, 81211; 395-2427) 18 rooms, pets OK, in-room coffee makers, TV, NS rooms, wheelchair access, CC. SGL/DBL$40-$70.

Burlington
Area Code 719

Budget Host Chaparral (405 South Lincoln, 80807; 346-5361, 800-283-4678) 39 rooms, restaurant, heated pool, laundry facilities, NS rooms, wheelchair access, A/C, TV, pets OK, children free with parents, senior rates, CC. SGL/DBL$26-$38.

Econo Lodge (450 South Lincoln, 80807; 346-5555, 800-4-CHOICE) 112 rooms, restaurant, lounge, pool, children under 12 free with parents, pets OK, airport transportation, meeting facilities, senior rates, NS rooms, wheelchair access, A/C, TV, senior rates, CC. SGL/DBL$32-$52.

National 9 Sloan's Motel (1901 Rose Ave., 80807; 346-5333, 800-524-9999) 30 rooms, restaurant, lounge, indoor heated pool, NS rooms, wheelchair access, A/C, TV, children free with parents, senior rates, CC. SGL/DBL$26-$40.

Super 8 Motel (2100 Fay, 80807; 346-5627, 800-800-8000) 39 rooms and suites, restaurant, pets OK, children under 12 free with parents, free local calls, A/C, TV, in-room refrigerators and microwaves, fax, NS rooms, senior rates, wheelchair access, meeting facilities, CC. SGL/DBL$30-$42.

Byers

Area Code 303

Longhorn Motel (457 North Main st., 80103; 822-5205) 25 rooms, restaurant, heated pool, children free with parents, TV, A/C, free local calls, NS rooms, pets OK, meeting facilities, senior rates, CC. SGL/DBL$25-$40.

Canon City

Area Code 719

Best Western Royal Gorge Motel (1925 Fremont Dr., 81212; 275-3377, Fax 275-3931, 800-231-7317, 800-528-1234) 67 rooms and suites, restaurant, free breakfast, lounge, pool, exercise center, children free with parents, A/C, NS rooms, TV, laundry facilities, wheelchair access, pets OK, senior rates, meeting facilities, CC. SGL/DBL$48-$93.

Canon Inn (Hwy. 50, 81212; 275-8676, 800-525-7727 in Colorado) 152 rooms, restaurant, lounge, heated pool, spa, room service, laundry facilities, local transportation, in-room refrigerators, pets OK, A/C, TV, NS rooms, wheelchair access, meeting facilities, senior rates, CC. SGL/DBL$60-$90.

Days Inn (217 North Reynolds, 81212; 269-1100, Fax 275-8030, 800-325-2525) 29 rooms and 2-bedroom suites, free breakfast, children free with parents, room service, laundry service, A/C, TV, free local calls, pets OK, fax, wheelchair access, NS rooms, senior rates, CC. SGL/DBL$25-$43.

Holiday Motel (1502 Main St., 81212; 275-3317) 15 rooms and 2-bedroom efficiencies, heated pool, A/C, TV, NS rooms, wheelchair access, pets OK, in-room refrigerators, CC. SGL/DBL$22-$40.

Super 8 Motel (209 North 19th St., 81212; 275-8687, Fax 275-8687 ext 121, 800-800-8000) 41 rooms and suites, pets OK, children under 12 free with parents, free local calls, A/C, TV, in-room refrigerators and microwaves, fax, pets OK, NS rooms, senior rates, wheelchair access, meeting facilities, CC. SGL/DBL$30-$43.

Thunderbird of Royal Gorge (Hwy. 50, 81212; 275-3168) cabins, kitchenettes, pool, gift shop, A/C, CC. SGL/DBL$60.

Carbondale
Area Code 303

Crystal River Resort (7202 Hwy. 133, 81623; 963-2341) cabins, hot tub, sauna, fireplaces, kitchenettes, TV. SGL/DBL$65.

Days Inn (950 Cowen Dr., 81623; 963-9111, Fax 963-0759, 800-325-2525) 69 rooms and suites, free breakfast, indoor heated pool, jacuzzi, sauna, children free with parents, room service, laundry service, A/C, TV, free local calls, pets OK, fax, wheelchair access, NS rooms, in-room refrigerators, meeting facilities, senior rates, CC. SGL/DBL$50-$70.

Castle Rock
Area Code 303

Super 8 Motel (1020 Park St., 80104; 688-0880, 800-800-8000) 60 rooms and suites, restaurant, pets OK, children under 12 free with parents, free local calls, A/C, TV, in-room refrigerators and microwaves, fax, NS rooms, senior rates, wheelchair access, meeting facilities, CC. SGL/DBL$37-$48.

Cimmarron
Area Code 303

The Inn at Arrowhead (21401 Alpine Plateau Rd., 81220; 249-5634, Fax 249-2802) 12 rooms, restaurant, lounge, whirlpools, A/C, TV, NS rooms, wheelchair access, CC. SGL/DBL$60-$65.

Clark
Area Code 303

Glen Eden Resort Lodge (Clark 80428; 879-3907, 800-882-0854) 29 efficiencies, restaurant, lounge, heated pool, whirlpools, tennis courts, A/C, TV, NS rooms, wheelchair access, laundry facilities, local transportation, meeting facilities, senior rates, CC. SGL/DBL$90-$125.

Home Ranch (Clark 80428; 879-1780, Fax 879-1795, 800-223-7094) 14 rooms and cottages, restaurant, lounge, A/C, TV, NS rooms, wheelchair access, American plan available, laundry facilities, boutiques, local transportation, pets OK, in-room refrigerators, CC. SGL/DBL$80-$500.

Clifton
Area Code 303

Clifton Inn (Clifton 81520; 434-3400) 20 rooms, A/C, TV, NS rooms, wheelchair access, in-room refrigerators, CC. SGL/DBL$36-$46.

Colorado Springs
Area Code 719

Marland Court Townhouses (Colorado Springs Realty, 401 South Nevada Ave., 80903; 473-3325, 800-748-2085) rental 2- and 3-bedroom townhouses.

Alikar Garden Resort (1123 Verde Dr., 80910; 475-2564, 800-456-1123, 800-666-9997) 1- and 2-bedroom suites, outdoor heated pool, spa, exercise center, whirlpools, kitchenettes, A/C, TV, NS rooms, wheelchair access, airport transportation, laundry facilities, VCRs, senior rates, CC. SGL/DBL$70-$150.

Amarillo Motel (2801 West Colorado Ave., 80904; 635-86539, Fax 473-2609) 31 rooms and efficiencies, kitchenettes, pets OK, A/C, TV, NS rooms, wheelchair access, CC. SGL/DBL$36-$48.

American Inn (1703 South Nevada Rd., 80906; 632-7077) 78 rooms, restaurant, heated pool, A/C, TV, NS rooms, wheelchair access, senior rates, CC. SGL/DBL$40-$60.

American Youth Hostel (3704 West Colorado Ave., 80904; 475-9450, 800-248-9451) 48 beds and cabins, pool, hot tub, TV, CC. SGL/DBL$15-$18.

Apache Motel (3401 West Pikes Peak Ave., 80904; 471-9440) 13 rooms, kitchenettes, hot tub, A/C, TV, pets OK, NS rooms, wheelchair access, CC. SGL/DBL$27-$60.

Apollo Park Executive Suites (805 South Circle Dr., 80910; 634-0286, 800-666-1955) 1- and 2-bedroom suites, kitchenettes, heated pool, pets OK, A/C, TV, NS rooms, wheelchair access, CC. SGL/DBL$55-$65.

B n' B Motel (4918 Nevada Ave., 80918; 598-3816) 15 rooms, A/C, TV, pets OK, NS rooms, wheelchair access, CC. SGL/DBL$25-$40.

Bel Air Motel (4000 North Nevada Ave., 80907; 598-7057, 800-647-2002) 15 rooms, heated pool, kitchenettes, A/C, TV, NS rooms, wheelchair access, laundry facilities, CC. SGL/DBL$22-$40.

Best Western Palmer House (3010 North Chestnut St., 80907; 636-5201, 800-528-1234) 150 rooms, restaurant, free breakfast, lounge, heated pool, exercise center, children free with parents, A/C, NS rooms, TV, laundry facilities, wheelchair access, pets OK, room service, airport transportation, senior rates, meeting facilities, CC. SGL/DBL$49-$93.

Beverly Hills Lodge (6 El Paso Blvd., 80904; 632-0386) 12 rooms and cabins, kitchenettes, pets OK, A/C, TV, NS rooms, wheelchair access, kitchenettes, CC. SGL/DBL$23-$50.

The Broadmoor (1 Lake Circle, 80906; 634-7711, 800-634-7711) 551 rooms and suites, restaurant, lounge, entertainment, indoor and outdoor heated pool, exercise center, sauna, whirlpools, tennis courts, A/C, TV, NS rooms, wheelchair access, airport transportation, room service, laundry facilities, children free with parents, pets OK, senior rates, meeting facilities, CC. SGL/DBL$200-$250, STS$280-$1,600.

Bighorn Lodge (1018 South Nevada Ave., 80903; 632-7658) room and efficiencies, A/C, TV, NS rooms, wheelchair access, CC. SGL/DBL$36-$48.

Budget Inn (1440 Harrison Rd., 80906; 576-2371) 43 rooms, restaurant, pool, NS rooms, children free with parents, pets OK, A/C, TV, meeting facilities, CC. SGL/DBL$28-$38.

Buffalo Lodge (2 El Paso Blvd., 80904; 634-2851, 800-235-7416) 39 rooms, free breakfast, heated pool, hot tubs, 1890s inn, kitchenettes, A/C, TV, laundry facilities, NS rooms, wheelchair access, CC. SGL/DBL$40-$120.

Cheyenne Mountain Conference Resort (3225 Broadmoor Valley Rd., 80906; 576-4600) 266 rooms, restaurant, lounge, entertainment, indoor and outdoor pool, exercise center, sauna, whirlpools, tennis courts, A/C, TV, NS rooms, wheelchair access, airport transportation, in-room refrigerators and coffee makers, laundry facilities, children free with parents, pets OK, senior rates, meeting facilities, CC. SGL/DBL$65-$135.

Chief Motel (1624 South Nevada Ave., 80903; 634-1545) 43 rooms and 2-bedroom efficiencies, heated pool, kitchenettes, A/C, in-room refrigerators, TV, NS rooms, wheelchair access, senior rates, CC. SGL/DBL$24-$44.

Colorado Motel (2021 West Colorado Ave., 80904; 634-8452) 11 rooms and suites, kitchenettes, A/C, TV, NS rooms, wheelchair access, senior rates, CC. SGL/DBL$32-$80.

Comfort Inn Air Force Academy (8280 Hwy. 83, 80920; 598-6700, 800-221-2222) 110 rooms and suites, restaurant, free breakfast, outdoor heated pool, whirlpools, spa, free local calls, wheelchair access, NS rooms, pets OK, children under 18 free with parents, A/C, TV, meeting facilities, senior rates, CC. SGL/DBL$40-$78.

Dale Downtown Motel (620 West Colorado Ave., 80905; 636-3721, 800-456-3204) 28 rooms, heated pool, kitchenettes, A/C, TV, NS rooms, wheelchair access, CC. SGL/DBL$28-$74.

Days Inn (4610 Rusina Rd., 80907; 598-1700, Fax 592-9029, 800-325-2525) 62 rooms and suites, restaurant, lounge, free breakfast, outdoor pool, children free with parents, room service, laundry service, A/C, TV, free local calls, pets OK, fax, wheelchair access, NS rooms, meeting facilities, senior rates, CC. SGL/DBL$33-$78.

Doubletree Antlers Hotel (4 South Cascade Ave., 80903; 473-5600, Fax 389-0259, 800-828-7447) 290 rooms and suites, restaurant, lounge, entertainment, pool, exercise center, NS rooms, children under 18 free with parents, senior rates, A/C, TV, fax, in-room computer hookups, 21 meeting rooms, meeting facilities for 1,200, CC. SGL/DBL$65-$85.

Drury Inn Pikes Peak (8155 North Academy Blvd., 80920; 598-2500, 800-325-8300) 114 rooms and suites, restaurant, free breakfast, outdoor heated pool, whirlpools, exercise center, TV, children under 18 free with parents, NS rooms, A/C, wheelchair access, fax, laundry service, in-room computer hookups, free local calls, senior rates, CC. SGL/DBL$47-$74.

Econo Lodge Downtown (714 North Nevada Ave., 80903; 636-3385, 800-4-CHOICE) 37 rooms, pool, children under 12 free with parents, pets OK, NS rooms, wheelchair access, A/C, TV, kitchenettes, senior rates, CC. SGL/DBL$27-$59.

El Dorado Motel (3950 North Nevada Ave., 80907; 598-4434) 20 rooms, kitchenettes, pets OK, A/C, TV, NS rooms, wheelchair access, CC. SGL/DBL$28-$52.

Embassy Suites (7290 Commerce Center Dr., 80919; 599-9100, Fax 599-4644, 800-EMBASSY) 207 2-room suites, restaurant, lounge, free breakfast, lounge, indoor heated pool, whirlpool, exercise center, sauna, room service, laundry service, wheelchair access, complimentary newspaper, free local calls, NS rooms, gift shop, local transportation, meeting facilities, senior rates, CC. SGL/DBL$100-$120.

Fireside Manor Resort (620 North Murray Blvd., 80915; 597-6207, Fax 597-7483) 1- and 2-bedroom suites, kitchenettes, A/C, TV, NS rooms, wheelchair access, free local calls, senior rates, CC. SGL/DBL$60-$85.

Hampton Inn North (7245 Commerce Center Dr., 80919; 593-9700, Fax 598-0563, 800-HAMPTON) 128 rooms, restaurant, free breakfast, indoor heated pool, exercise center, children under 18 free with parents, NS rooms, wheelchair access, in-room computer hookups, pets OK, fax, TV, A/C, free local calls, senior rates, meeting facilities, CC. SGL/DBL$45-$60.

Hampton Inn (1410 Harrison Rd., 80906; 579-6900, Fax 579-0897, 800-HAMPTON) 112 rooms, restaurant, free breakfast, indoor pool, exercise center, children under 18 free with parents, NS rooms, wheelchair access, in-room computer hookups, fax, TV, A/C, free local calls, pets OK, meeting facilities, CC. SGL/DBL$58-$66.

Hearthstone Inn (506 North Cascade Ave., 80903; 473-4413, 800-521-1885) 23 rooms and suites, free breakfast, A/C, 1880s inn, fireplaces, NS, TV, private baths, antique furnishings, CC. SGL/DBL$80-$125.

Heidelberg Motel (2105 East Platte Ave., 80909; 636-5261) 18 rooms, heated pool, kitchenettes, A/C, TV, NS rooms, wheelchair access, senior rates, CC. SGL/DBL$36-$50.

Hilton Hotel (505 Pope's Bluff Trail, 80907; 598-07656, Fax 590-9623, 800-HIL-TONS) 197 rooms and suites, restaurant, lounge, entertainment, outdoor heated pool, exercise center, jacuzzi, lighted tennis courts, children free with parents, NS rooms, wheelchair access, pets OK, room service, laundry facilities, fax, A/C, TV, meeting facilities, CC. SGL/DBL$45-$85.

HoJo Inn (5056 North Nevada Ave., 80918; 598-7793, 800-I-GO-HOJO) 50 rooms, restaurant, free breakfast, lounge, heated pool, children free with parents, wheelchair access, NS rooms, TV, A/C, pets OK, laundry facilities, free local calls, airport transportation, senior rates, meeting facilities, CC. SGL/DBL$24-$49.

Holden House Bed and Breakfast (1102 West Pikes Peak Rd., 80904; 471-3980) 5 rooms and suites, free breakfast, 1902 home, A/C, TV, NS rooms, private baths, pets OK, CC. SGL/DBL$60-$90.

Holiday Inn Central (725 West Cimmaron St., 80905; 473-5530, 800-HOLI-DAY) 207 rooms and suites, restaurant, free breakfast, lounge, heated pool, exercise center, children under 19 free with parents, wheelchair access, A/C, TV, NS rooms, fax, room service, pets OK, laundry service, meeting facilities for 50, senior rates, CC. SGL/DBL$31-$83.

Holiday Inn North (3125 Sinton Rd., 80907; 633-5541, 800-HOLIDAY) 220 rooms and suites, restaurant, lounge, indoor heated pool, exercise center, whirlpools, children under 19 free with parents, wheelchair access, A/C, TV, NS rooms, fax, room service, pets OK, laundry service, meeting facilities, senior rates, CC. SGL/DBL$35-$90.

Iowa Motel (2508 East Platte Ave., 80909; 635-3509) 30 rooms and 2-bedroom efficiencies, heated pool, kitchenettes, A/C, TV, NS rooms, wheelchair access, pets OK, CC. SGL/DBL$30-$50.

J's Motor Hotel (820 North Nevada Ave., 80903; 633-5513) 50 rooms, restaurant, indoor heated pool, A/C, TV, NS rooms, wheelchair access, CC. SGL/DBL$38-$42.

La Quinta Inn (4385 Sinton Rd., 80907; 528-5060, Fax 598-0360, 800-531-5900) 105 rooms, restaurant, free breakfast, lounge, pool, complimentary newspaper, free local calls, fax, laundry service, NS rooms, wheelchair access, TV, A/C, meeting facilities, CC. SGL/DBL$40-$78.

LeBaron Hotel (314 West Bijou St., 80905; 471-8680, 800-477-8610) 206 rooms and suites, restaurant, lounge, entertainment, outdoor heated pool, exercise center, airport transportation, pets OK, A/C, TV, NS rooms, wheelchair access, meeting facilities for 350, senior rates, CC. SGL/DBL$55-$85.

Maple Lodge Value Inn (9 El Paso Blvd., 80904; 685-9230) cabins, heated pool, kitchenettes, A/C, TV, NS rooms, wheelchair access, CC. SGL/DBL$29-$89.

Marriott Hotel (5580 Tech Center Dr., 80919; 260-1800, Fax 260-1492, 800-228-9290) 310 rooms and suites, restaurant, lounge, entertainment, indoor and outdoor pool, exercise center, whirlpools, saunas, wheelchair access, TV, A/C, NS rooms, pets OK, laundry service, gift shop, children free with parents, meeting facilities, senior rates, CC. SGL/DBL$50-$90, STS$230-$300.

Mecca Motel (3518 West Colorado Ave., 80904; 475-9415, 800-634-2442) heated pool, A/C, TV, NS rooms, wheelchair access, CC. SGL/DBL$35-$85.

Mel Haven Lodge (3715 West Colorado Ave., 80904; 633-9435, 800-762-5832) 21 rooms and 2-bedroom suites, heated pool, pets OK, kitchenettes, pets OK, laundry facilities, A/C, TV, NS rooms, wheelchair access, CC. SGL/DBL$30-$65.

Motel 6 (3228 North Chestnut St., 80907; 520-5400, 505-891-6161) 84 rooms, pool, free local calls, children under 17 free with parents, NS rooms, wheelchair access, A/C, TV, CC. SGL/DBL$36-$44.

National 9 Inn (1623 South Nevada Ave., 80906; 632-6651, 800-524-9999) 40 rooms and suites, heated pool, NS rooms, wheelchair access, A/C, TV, children free with parents, senior rates, CC. SGL/DBL$35-$45, STS$53-$63.

Nevada Motel (1006 South Nevada Ave., 80903; 520-0016) 21 rooms, restaurant, A/C, TV, NS rooms, wheelchair access, CC. SGL/DBL$29-$65.

Quality Inn (555 West Garden of the Gods Rd., 80907; 593-9119, 800-221-2222) 157 rooms and suites, restaurant, heated pool, exercise center, children free with parents, A/C, TV, room service, laundry service, NS rooms, meeting facilities, senior rates, CC. SGL/DBL$50-$100.

Radisson Inn Airport (1645 Newport Dr., 80916; 597-7000, 800-333-3333) 139 rooms and suites, restaurant, free breakfast, lounge, entertainment, pool, exercise center, jacuzzi, hot tub, in-room refrigerators, microwaves and coffee makers, children free with parents, VCRs, wheelchair access, NS rooms, airport transportation, TV, A/C, pets OK, CC. SGL/DBL$100-$165.

Radisson Inn Colorado Springs North (8110 North Academy Blvd., 80920; 598-5770, 800-333-3333) 200 rooms and suites, restaurant, lounge, entertainment, indoor pool, exercise center, in-room refrigerators, microwaves and coffee makers, VCRs, wheelchair access, NS rooms, TV, A/C, children free with parents, pets OK, meeting facilities for 350, CC. SGL/DBL$70-$225.

Rainbow Motel (3709 West Colorado Ave., 80904; 632-4551) heated pool, laundry facilities, A/C, TV, NS rooms, wheelchair access, CC. SGL/DBL$28-$39.

Raintree Inn West (2625 Ore Mill Rd., 80904; 632-4600) 117 rooms, indoor heated pool, laundry service, pets OK, VCRs, A/C, TV, NS rooms, wheelchair access, CC. SGL/DBL$30-$60.

Ramada Inn (4440 North I-25, 80907; 594-0700, Fax 594-6458, 800-2-RAMADA) 154 rooms and suites, restaurant, lounge, entertainment, pool, wheelchair access, NS rooms, pets OK, A/C, TV, children under 18 free with parents, room service, laundry facilities, meeting facilities, senior rates, CC. SGL/DBL$36-$64.

Ramada Inn (520 North Murray Blvd., 80915; 596-7660, 800-2-RAMADA) 102 rooms and suites, restaurant, lounge, entertainment, heated pool, wheelchair access, NS rooms, pets OK, A/C, TV, children under 18 free with parents, room service, laundry facilities, meeting facilities, senior rates, CC. SGL/DBL$45-$80.

Red Lion Hotel (1775 East Cheyenne Mountain Blvd., 80906; 576-8900, Fax 576-4450, 299 rooms, restaurant, lounge, entertainment, indoor pool, exercise center, sauna, gift shop, airport transportation, room service, children free with parents, A/C, TV, NS rooms, wheelchair access, airport transportation, 14 meeting rooms, meeting facilities for 1,500, senior rates, CC. SGL/DBL$42-$54.

Regency Tower Apartments (912 Green Star Dr., 80906; 633-2121) 1- and 2-bedroom apartments, pool, CC. SGL/DBL$55-$85.

Residence Inn (3880 North Academy Blvd., 80917; 574-0370, 800-331-3131) 96 rooms and 1-bedroom suites, free breakfast, pool, spa, in-room refrigerators, coffee makers and microwaves, fireplaces, laundry facilities, TV, A/C, VCRs, pets OK, local transportation, fireplaces, children free with parents, pets OK, complimentary newspaper, NS rooms, wheelchair access, meeting facilities, CC. SGL/DBL$85-$135.

Rodeway Inn (2409 East Pikes Peak, 80909; 471-0990, 800-424-4777) 113 rooms, restaurant, lounge, heated pool, wheelchair access, NS rooms, children free with parents, pets OK, A/C, TV, senior rates, CC. SGL/DBL$40-$52.

Satellite Hotel (411 Lakewood Circle, 80910; 596-6800, 800-423-8409) 76 rooms, restaurant, lounge, heated pool, sauna, tennis courts, airport transportation, A/C, TV, NS rooms, wheelchair access, CC. SGL/DBL$54-$70.

Sheraton Colorado Springs Hotel (2886 South Circle Dr., 80906; 576-5900, 800-325-3535) 502 rooms and suites, restaurant, lounge, entertainment, indoor and outdoor pool, exercise center, lighted tennis courts, NS rooms, A/C, room service, TV, children free with parents, gift shop, pets OK, wheelchair access, airport transportation, meeting facilities, senior rates, CC. SGL/DBL$80-$195.

Springs Motor Inn (2850 South Circle Dr., 80906; 576-8020, 800-548-1059) 176 rooms, restaurant, lounge, indoor and outdoor pools, A/C, TV, NS rooms, wheelchair access, CC. SGL/DBL$35-$40.

Stagecoach Motel (1647 Nevada Ave., 80906; 633-3894) 18 rooms and 2-bedroom efficiencies, restaurant, in-room refrigerators, A/C, TV, NS rooms, wheelchair access, senior rates, CC. SGL/DBL$28-$42.

Star Motel (3920 North Nevada Ave., 80907; 598-4044) 29 rooms, kitchenettes, A/C, TV, NS rooms, wheelchair access, senior rates, CC. SGL/DBL$24-$36.

Super 8 Motel (3270 North Chestnut, 80907; 632-2681, 800-800-8000) 32 rooms and suites, pets OK, children under 12 free with parents, free local calls, A/C, TV, in-room refrigerators and microwaves, fax, NS rooms, senior rates, wheelchair access, meeting facilities, CC. SGL/DBL$30-$48.

Super 8 Motel (4604 Rusina Rd., 80907; 594-0964, Fax 599-8616, 800-800-8000) 52 rooms and suites, pets OK, children under 12 free with parents, free local calls, A/C, TV, in-room refrigerators and microwaves, fax, NS rooms, senior rates, wheelchair access, meeting facilities, CC. SGL/DBL$30-$45.

Super 8 Motel (605 Peterson Rd., 80915; 597-4100, 800-800-8000) 41 rooms and suites, pets OK, children under 12 free with parents, free local calls, A/C, TV, in-room refrigerators and microwaves, fax, NS rooms, senior rates, wheelchair access, meeting facilities, CC. SGL/DBL$32-$45.

Super 8 Motel (8135 North Academy Blvd., 80918; 528-7100, 800-800-8000) 33 rooms and suites, pets OK, children under 12 free with parents, free local calls, A/C, TV, in-room refrigerators and microwaves, fax, NS rooms, senior rates, wheelchair access, meeting facilities, CC. SGL/DBL$30-$55.

Super 8 Motel (8135 North Academy Blvd., 80918; 528-7100, 800-800-8000) 33 rooms and suites, pets OK, children under 12 free with parents, free local calls, A/C, TV, in-room refrigerators and microwaves, fax, NS rooms, senior rates, wheelchair access, meeting facilities, CC. SGL/DBL$30-$55.

Swiss Chalet (3410 West Colorado Ave., 80904; 471-2260) 17 cabins and suites, kitchenettes, A/C, TV, NS rooms, wheelchair access, laundry facilities, pets OK, in-room refrigerators, senior rates, CC. SGL/DBL$25-$65.

Timber Lodge Bed and Breakfast Rocky Mountain (3627 West Colorado Ave., 80904; 636-3941, 800-448-6762) 25 1-, 2- and 3-room cabins, heated pool, kitchenettes, A/C, TV, NS rooms, wheelchair access, CC. SGL/DBL$43-$91.

Travel Inn Motel (512 South Nevada Ave., 80903; 636-3986) 36 rooms, restaurant, lounge, free breakfast, pool, wheelchair access, complimentary newspaper, laundry service, TV, A/C, free local calls, fax, NS rooms, in-room refrigerators and microwaves, children under 18 free with parents, pets OK, meeting facilities, senior rates, CC. SGL/DBL$30-$45.

Travelers Uptown Motel (220 East Cimarron St., 80903; 473-2774) 48 rooms and 2-bedroom efficiencies, outdoor heated pool, A/C, TV, NS rooms, wheelchair access, pets OK, senior rates, CC. SGL/DBL$25-$45.

Treehaven Motel (3620 West Colorado Ave., 80904; 578-1968) 1- and 2-bedroom cottages, heated pool, kitchenettes, A/C, TV, NS rooms, wheelchair access, CC. SGL/DBL$35-$100.

Tree House and Spruce Berry Cabins (3011 Chamber Cir., 80904; 389-1461) 2 cabins, kitchenettes, CC. SGL/DBL$50-$60.

Twilight Canyon Ranch (3450 Old State Rd., 80906; 471-2048) fireplaces, A/C, TV, NS rooms, wheelchair access, CC. SGL/DBL$36-$56.

Wedgewood Cottage Inn (1111 West Pikes Peak Ave., 80904; 636-1829) 1 suite, free breakfast, A/C, TV, 1899 inn, antique furnishings, fireplace, TV, jacuzzi, CC. SGL/DBL$55-$75.

Copper Mountain
Area Code 303

Copper Mountain Resort (Copper Mountain 80443) 125 2- and 3-bedroom condominiums, restaurant, lounge, lounge, entertainment, pool, exercise center, sauna, whirlpools, A/C, TV, NS rooms, wheelchair access, airport transportation, in-room refrigerators, microwaves and coffee makers, laundry facilities, children free with parents, pets OK, senior rates, meeting facilities, CC. SGL/DBL$145-$270.

Cortez

Area Code 303

Anasazi Motor Inn (640 South Broadway, 81321; 565-3773, Fax 565-1027, 800-972-6232) 85 rooms, outdoor pool, hot tub, A/C, TV, NS rooms, wheelchair access, pets OK, laundry facilities, senior rates, CC. SGL/DBL$40-$69.

Aneth Lodge (645 East Main St., 81321; 565-3453) 30 rooms, pets OK, A/C, TV, NS rooms, wheelchair access, CC. SGL/DBL$29-$41.

Arrow Motor Inn (440 South Broadway, 81321; 565-7778, 800-727-7692) 30 rooms, outdoor pool, hot tubs, A/C, TV, NS rooms, wheelchair access, CC. SGL/DBL$36-$58.

Bel-Rau Lodge (2040 East Main St., 81321; 565-3738) 26 rooms, outdoor pool, hot tubs, laundry facilities, A/C, TV, NS rooms, kitchenettes, pets OK, wheelchair access, CC. SGL/DBL$$36-$58.

Best Western Sands Motel (1120 East Main St., 81321; 565-3761, Fax 564-9320, 800-438-9909, 800-528-1234) 81 rooms, restaurant, free breakfast, lounge, indoor pool, exercise center, children free with parents, A/C, NS rooms, TV, laundry facilities, wheelchair access, pets OK, senior rates, meeting facilities, senior rates, CC. SGL/DBL$48-$68.

Best Western Turquoise Motor Inn (535 East Main St., 81321; 565-3778, 800-547-3376, 800-528-1234) 46 rooms, restaurant, free breakfast, lounge, pool, exercise center, children free with parents, A/C, NS rooms, TV, laundry facilities, wheelchair access, pets OK, senior rates, meeting facilities, CC. SGL/DBL$50-$90.

Comfort Inn (2308 East Main St., 81321; 565-4528, 800-221-2222) 140 rooms, free breakfast, indoor pool, wheelchair access, NS rooms, pets OK, children under 18 free with parents, A/C, TV, laundry service, meeting facilities, senior rates, CC. SGL/DBL$58-$88.

Days Inn (Cortez 81321; 565-8577, Fax 565-0123, 800-628-2183, 800-325-2525) 77 rooms and suites, outdoor pool, children free with parents, room service, laundry service, A/C, TV, free local calls, pets OK, fax, wheelchair access, NS rooms, meeting facilities, senior rates, CC. SGL/DBL$38-$78.

El Capri Motel (2110 South Broadway, 81321; 565-3764) 16 rooms, outdoor heated pool, A/C, TV, NS rooms, wheelchair access, pets OK, CC. SGL/DBL$37-$60.

Holiday Inn Express (2121 East Main St., 81321; 565-6000, Fax 565-3438, 800-HOLIDAY) 100 rooms, restaurant, lounge, indoor pool, exercise center, whirlpools, local transportation, children under 19 free with parents, wheelchair access, A/C, TV, NS rooms, fax, room service, pets OK, laundry service, meeting facilities, senior rates, CC. SGL/DBL$45-$88.

Kelly Place (14663 Country Rd., 81321; 565-3125) 6 rooms, free breakfast, A/C, TV, CC. SGL/DBL$47-$60.

North Broadway Motel (510 North Broadway, 81321; 565-2481) 15 rooms, pets OK, A/C, TV, NS rooms, wheelchair access, CC. SGL/DBL$23.

Ramada Inn (2020 East Main St., 81321; 565-3474, Fax 565-0923, 800-2-RAMADA) 70 rooms and suites, restaurant, lounge, pool, wheelchair access, NS rooms, pets OK, A/C, TV, children under 18 free with parents, room service, laundry facilities, meeting facilities, senior rates, CC. SGL/DBL$36-$88.

Sand Canyon Inn (301 West Main St., 81321; 565-8562, 800-257-3699) 28 rooms, restaurant, outdoor pool, laundry facilities, A/C, TV, NS rooms, wheelchair access, senior rates, CC. SGL/DBL$38.

Super 8 Motel (505 East Main St., 81321; 565-8888, Fax 565-6595, 800-800-8000) 60 rooms and suites, restaurant, pets OK, children under 12 free with parents, free local calls, A/C, TV, in-room refrigerators and microwaves, fax, NS rooms, senior rates, wheelchair access, meeting facilities, CC. SGL/DBL$36-$58.

Tomahawk Lodge (728 South Broadway, 81321; 565-8521) 38 rooms, outdoor pool, A/C, TV, NS rooms, wheelchair access, pets OK, senior rates, CC. SGL/DBL$27-$47.

Ute Mountain Motel (531 South Broadway, 81321; 565-8507) 36 rooms, A/C, TV, NS rooms, wheelchair access, pets OK, CC. SGL/DBL$26-$46.

Craig
Area Code 303

A Bar Z Motel (2690 West Hwy. 40, 81625; 824-7088, 800-458-7228) 40 rooms, A/C, TV, NS rooms, pets OK, in-room coffee makers, children free with parents, wheelchair access, CC. SGL/DBL$35-$40.

Best Western Inn (755 East Victory Way, 81625; 824-8101, 800-528-1234) 33 rooms, free breakfast, children free with parents, A/C, NS rooms, TV, laundry facilities, wheelchair access, pets OK, senior rates, meeting facilities, CC. SGL/DBL$26-$44.

Black Nugget Inn (2855 West Victory Way, 81625; 824-8161, 800-727-2088) 20 rooms, A/C, TV, NS rooms, wheelchair access, laundry facilities, pets OK, CC. SGL/DBL$28-$32.

Craig Motel (894 Yampa Ave., 81625; 824-4491) 25 rooms and efficiencies, laundry facilities, pets OK, A/C, TV, NS rooms, wheelchair access, CC. SGL/DBL$22-$36.

Holiday Inn (300 South Colorado Hwy. 13, 81625; 824-4000, Fax 824-3950, 800-HOLIDAY) 167 rooms and suites, restaurant, lounge, indoor pool, exercise center, whirlpools, game rooms, children under 19 free with parents, wheelchair access, A/C, TV, NS rooms, fax, room service, pets OK, laundry service, meeting facilities for 200, senior rates, CC. SGL/DBL$40-$60.

Super 8 Motel (200 Hwy. 13 South, 81625; 824-3471, 800-800-8000) 59 rooms and suites, pets OK, children under 12 free with parents, free local calls, A/C, TV, in-room refrigerators and microwaves, fax, NS rooms, senior rates, wheelchair access, meeting facilities, CC. SGL/DBL$29-$75.

Crested Butte
Area Code 303

Elk Mountain Lodge (129 Gothic Ave., 81224; 349-7533, 800-374-6521) 16 rooms, free breakfast, whirlpools, TV, NS rooms, wheelchair access, NS, pets OK, children free with parents, CC. SGL/DBL$95-$105.

Grande Butte Hotel (500 Gothic Rd., 81224; 349-4000, Fax 349-6332, 800-642-4422) 261 rooms and suites, restaurant, lounge, entertainment, pool, whirlpools, exercise center, sauna, in-room refrigerators, A/C, airport transportation, pets OK, TV, NS rooms, wheelchair access, meeting facilities, senior rates, CC. SGL/DBL$80-$175.

Nordic Inn (Crested Butte 81224; 349-5542, Fax 349-6487) 28 rooms and efficiencies, free breakfast, hot tub, fireplace, TV, NS rooms, kitchenettes, wheelchair access, pets OK, kitchenettes, senior rates, CC. SGL/DBL$65-$140.

Old Town Inn (201 North 6th St., 81224; 349-6184) 33 rooms, free breakfast, hot tubs, pets OK, A/C, TV, NS rooms, wheelchair access, local transportation, meeting facilities, senior rates, CC. SGL/DBL$42-$90.

Cripple Creek
Area Code 719

Best Western Gold Rush Hotel and Casino (209 East Bennett Ave., 80813; 689-2646, Fax 689-3943, 800-235-8239, 800-528-1234) 14 rooms, restaurant, lounge, pool, exercise center, children free with parents, A/C, NS rooms, TV, laundry facilities, wheelchair access, pets OK, senior rates, meeting facilities, CC. SGL/DBL$60-$103.

Cripple Creek Hospitality House (600 North B St., 80813; 689-2513) beauty shop, TV, CC. SGL/DBL$36-$44.

Independence Hotel and Casino (151 East Bennett Ave., 80813; 689-2744) 7 rooms, restaurant, free breakfast, A/C, TV, NS rooms, wheelchair access, CC. SGL/DBL$55-$80.

Imperial Hotel and Casino (123 North 3rd St., 80813; 689-7777, 800-235-2922) 26 rooms, restaurant, lounge, entertainment, TV, NS rooms, wheelchair access, 1890s inn, senior rates, meeting facilities, CC. SGL/DBL$65-$80.

Palace Hotel and Casino (2nd and Bennett Ave., 80813; 689-2992) 15 rooms, restaurant, A/C, TV, CC. SGL/DBL$35-$55.

Wild Bill's Pub and Gaming Parlor (220 East Bennett Ave., 80813; 689-2707) 7 rooms, free breakfast, private baths, CC. SGL/DBL$55-$65.

Delta
Area Code 303

Best Western Sundance Inn (903 Main St., 81416; 874-9781, Fax 874-5440, 800-626-1994, 800-528-1234) 41 rooms, restaurant, lounge, outdoor heated pool, exercise center, hot tubs, children free with parents, A/C, NS rooms, TV, laundry facilities, wheelchair access, pets OK, senior rates, meeting facilities, CC. SGL/DBL$36-$54.

Riverwood Inn (677 Hwy. 50 North, 81416; 874-5787) 11 rooms, A/C, TV, NS rooms, wheelchair access, pets OK, laundry facilities, CC. SGL/DBL$35-$50.

Denver
Area Code 303

Rental and Reservation Services:

Bed and Breakfast Colorado (Box 12206, Boulder 80303; 494-4994, 800373-4995)

Bed and Breakfast Rocky Mountains (900 South Pearl St., 80209; 744-8415, 800-733-8415)

Metropolitan Suites (2000 South Colorado Blvd., 80222; 759-8577)

Downtown Denver

Best Budget Bar X Motel (5001 West Colfax, 80204; 534-7191) 14 rooms, A/C, TV. SGL$30, DBL$32.

Broadway Plaza Motel (1111 Broadway, 80203; 893-3501) 40 rooms, A/C, TV, CC. SGL$25, DBL$27.

The Brown Palace (321 17th St., 80202; 297-3111, Fax 293-9204, 800-321-2599, 800-323-7500) 230 rooms, 1- and 2-bedroom suites, restaurant, lounge, gift shop, 24-hour room service, meeting facilities for 600, CC. 15 minutes from the airport. SGL$149-$199, DBL$159-$215, 1BR$225-$575, 2BR$325-$675.

The Burnsley Hotel (1000 Grant St., 80203; 830-1000, Fax 830-7676, 800-231-3915) 82 suites, restaurant, lounge, entertainment, pool, wheelchair access, TV, A/C, NS rooms, local transportation, pets OK, meeting facilities, CC. Near the State Capital. SGL/DBL$95-$225, X$20.

Cambridge Club (1560 Sherman St., 80203; 831-1252, Fax 831-1252, 800-752-1252) 27 rooms and suites, restaurant, free breakfast, children free with parents, airport courtesy car, meeting facilities, CC. SGL/DBL$115$175.

Canon Inn (3075 East Hwy. 50, 80212; 275-8676, Fax 275-8675) 152 rooms, restaurant, lounge, indoor pool, A/C, TV, NS rooms, wheelchair access, senior rates, CC. SGL/DBL$45-$55.

Central YMCA (25 East 16th Ave., 80202; 861-8300) 112 rooms and dormitory accommodations, pool, exercise center, CC. SGL/DBL$25-$33.

Comfort Inn Downtown (401 17th St., 80202; 296-0400, Fax 293-9204, 800-228-5150) 229 rooms, restaurant, lounge, free breakfast, wheelchair access, TV, A/C, NS rooms, barber and beauty shop, pets OK, meeting facilities, CC. Near the Convention Center, 6 miles from the airport. SGL/DBL$60-$93.

Denver International Youth Hostel (630 East 16th Ave., 80203; 494-5255) Dormitory accommodations, laundry service, A/C, TV, CC. SGL$16.

Hotel Denver Downtown (1450 Glenarm Place, 80202; 573-1450, Fax 572-1113, 800-423-5128) 412 rooms and suites, restaurant, lounge, outdoor pool, wheelchair access, TV, A/C, NS rooms, pets OK, laundry service, barber and beauty shop, airport transportation, meeting facilities, CC. Near the Convention Center. SGL$69-$88, DBL$79-$88, X$10.

Embassy Suites (1881 Curtis St., 80202; 297-8888, Fax 298-1103, 800-EM-BASSY) 337 2-room suites, restaurant, free breakfast, pool, whirlpool, sauna, exercise center, wheelchair access, TV, A/C, NS rooms, room service, airport courtesy car, laundry service, meeting facilities for 1,000, CC. Near the State Capital, 8 miles from the airport. SGL/DBL$144-$156.

Executive Tower Inn (1405 Curtis St., 80202; 571-0300, Fax 825-4301, 800-525-6651) 336 rooms, indoor heated pool, exercise center, hot tubs, airport transportation, pets OK, tennis courts, 12 meeting rooms, A/C, TV, CC. SGL$107-$122, DBL$117-$132, AP $10.

Franklin House Bed and Breakfast (1620 Franklin St., 80218; 331-9106) 6 rooms, free breakfast, airport transportation, SGL/DBL$20-$40.

Gotham Hotel (1196 Grant St., 80203; 861-1177) 45 rooms and suites, A/C, TV, CC. SGL/DBL$20-$45.

The Holiday Chalet (1820 East Colfax Ave., 80218; 321-9975, 800-626-4497) 10 rooms, children free with parents, in-room refrigerators, free local calls, NS, pets OK, fax, A/C, TV, CC. SGL$49, DBL$54.

Holiday Inn Denver Sports Center (1975 Bryant, 80204; 433-8331, Fax 455-7061, 800-HOLIDAY) 167 rooms, restaurant, lounge, exercise center, children free with parents, wheelchair access, TV, A/C, NS rooms, fax, room service, laundry room, airport transportation, pets OK, 4 meeting rooms, CC. Near Mile High Stadium. SGL/DBL$58-$68.

Howard Johnson Lodge (4765 Federal Blvd., 80211; 433-8441, Fax 458-0863, 800-800-I-GO-HOJO) 92 rooms, restaurant, lounge, indoor heated pool, children free with parents, NS rooms, wheelchair access, TV, A/C, CC. 9 miles from the airport. SGL$30-$70.

Hyatt Regency Denver (1750 Welton St., 80202; 295-1234, Fax 292-2472, 800-233-1234) 540 rooms and suites, restaurant, lounge, outdoor pool, jogging track, tennis court, airport transportation, A/C, TV, wheelchair access, NS rooms, audiovisual equipment, 11 meeting rooms, 33,000 square feet of meeting space and exhibition space, CC. In the financial district near the Convention Center. SGL/DBL$65.

Marriott City Center Hotel (1701 California St., 80202; 297-1300, Fax 293-3736, 800-228-9290) 614 rooms and suites, Concierge Level, two restaurants, lounge, indoor pool, exercise center, sauna, jogging track, children free with parents, NS rooms, wheelchair access, TV, A/C, airline ticket desk, gift shop, 25 meeting rooms, 25,000 square feet of meeting and exhibition space, CC. Near the Convention Complex. SGL/DBL$135.

Marriott Residence Inn (I-25 and Seer Blvd. North 80211; 458-5318, 800-331-3131) 156 suites, in-room refrigerators, pool, jacuzzis, exercise center, laundry room, wheelchair access, TV, A/C, NS rooms, airport transportation, children free with parents, local transportation, pets OK, VCRs, meeting facilities for 450, CC. 9 miles from the airport. SGL$95-$150.

The Oxford Alexis Hotel (1600 17th St., 80202; 628-5400, Fax 628-5413, 800-228-5838) 80 rooms and suites, restaurant, lounge, pets OK, children free with parents, 24-hour room service, local transportation, barber and beauty shop, 5 meeting rooms, CC. Near Union Station. SGL$120, DBL$130, X$20.

Queen Anne Inn (2147 Tremont Place, 80205; 296-6666, Fax 296-2151, 800-432-INNS) 14 rooms and suites, free breakfast, free local calls, NS, wheelchair access, TV, A/C, pets OK, fax, meeting facilities for 12, CC. SGL/DBL$75$125, STS$150.

Radisson Hotel Denver (1550 Court Place, 80202; 893-3333, 800-333-3333) 750 rooms, two restaurants, two lounges, pool, exercise center, boutiques, barber and beauty shop, airport transportation, wheelchair access, TV, A/C, pets OK, NS rooms, 90,000 square feet of meeting and exhibition space, CC. SGL/DBL$119.

Ramada Inn Downtown (1150 East Colfax Ave., 80218; 831-7700, Fax 894-9192, 800-2-RAMADA) 142 rooms and suites, restaurant, lounge, pool, laundry service, local transportation, meeting facilities, CC. 1 mile from the State Capital and Convention Center, 5 miles from the airport. SGL$55-$65, DBL$60$70, STS$65, X$6.

Residence Inn by Marriott Downtown (2777 Zuni, 80211; 458-5318, 800-331-3131) 144 suites, free breakfast, pool, airport transportation, fireplaces, pets OK, meeting facilities for 45, CC. 9 miles from the airport, 4 miles from the Coliseum. SGL/DBL$60-$126.

Super 8 Motel Downtown (2601 Zuni St., 80211; 433-6677, Fax 455-1530, 800-800-8000) 160 rooms and suites, restaurant, lounge, outdoor pool, game room, pets OK, wheelchair access, TV, A/C, NS rooms, fax, free local calls, laundry room, children free with parents, gift shop, meeting facilities, CC. Near the Mile High Stadium, 1 mile from the Convention Center, 10 minutes from the airport. SGL/DBL$30-$42.

Warwick Hotel Denver (1776 Grant St., 80203; 861-2000, Fax 832-0329, 800-525-2888) 200 rooms, restaurant, lounge, free breakfast, pool, exercise center, room service, airport transportation, wheelchair access, TV, A/C, NS rooms, pets OK, local transportation, meeting facilities, CC. SGL/DBL$95-$150.

Westin Hotel Tabor Center (1672 Lawrence St., 80202; 572-9100, Fax 572-7288, 800-228-3000) 420 rooms, Executive Club Level, restaurant, lounge, indoor and outdoor pools, hot tub, sauna, exercise center, 24-hour room service, valet laundry, airline ticket counter, gift shop, pets OK, wheelchair access, TV, A/C, NS rooms, 14 meeting rooms and facilities for 80, CC. In the business, shopping and entertainment district, 7.5 miles from the airport. SGL$145$180, DBL$170-$199, STS$320-$1050, X$15.

Airport Area

Airport Budget Hotel (15100 East 40th St., 80239; 371-9102, 800-950-5507) 112 rooms, restaurant, lounge, outdoor pool, whirlpool, sauna, local transportation, pets OK, laundry service, in-room refrigerators, meeting facilities, A/C, TV, CC. SGL/DBL$38.

Best Western Airport Inn (4411 Peoria St., 80239; 373-5730, Fax 375-1157, 800-528-1234) 193 rooms, restaurant, lounge, heated pool, exercise center, children free with parents, A/C, NS rooms, TV, laundry facilities, gift shop, airport transportation, wheelchair access, pets OK, senior rates, meeting facilities, CC. SGL/DBL$54-$80.

Comfort Inn Airport (7201 East 36th Ave., 80207; 393-7666, Fax 393-7666, 800-221-2222) 119 rooms, restaurant, free breakfast, pool, exercise center, pets OK, NS rooms, airport courtesy car, wheelchair access, TV, A/C, CC. 6 miles from the Convention Center, 3 miles from the Museum of Natural History. SGL/DBL$53-$76.

Courtyard by Marriott Airport (7415 East 41st Ave., 80216; 800-321-2211) 146 rooms, restaurant, lounge, indoor pool, exercise center, wheelchair access, TV, A/C, NS rooms, local transportation, laundry service, meeting facilities, CC. SGL/DBL$85.

Days Hotel Airport (4590 Quebec St., 80216; 320-0260, 800-325-2525) 195 rooms and suites, restaurant, outdoor pool, whirlpool, exercise center, children free with parents, laundry facilities, gift shop, car rental desk, complimentary newspaper, airport transportation, fax, pets OK, NS-rooms, meeting facilities, CC. 2.5 miles from airport, 7 miles from the downtown area, 4 miles from the Coliseum. SGL/DBL$51-$110.

Embassy Suites Denver Airport (4444 North Havana St., 80239; 375-0400, Fax 371-4634, 800-345-0087) 212 suites, restaurant, free breakfast, pool, whirlpool, exercise center, room service, laundry service, airport transportation, wheelchair access, color TV, A/C, pets OK, meeting facilities, CC. At the airport, 10 miles from the downtown area, 12 miles from the State Capital. SGL/DBL$120.

Hampton Inn Denver Airport (4685 Quebec St., 80216; 388-8100, Fax 333-7710, 800-HAMPTON) 138 rooms, restaurant, lounge, free breakfast, children free with parents, airport transportation, NS rooms, wheelchair access, TV, A/C, in-room computer hookups, fax, free local calls, meeting facilities, CC. 5 minutes from the airport, 10 miles from the downtown area. SGL/DBL$55-$70.

Holiday Inn Denver (15500 East 40th Ave., 80239; 371-9494, Fax 371-9528, 800-HOLIDAY) 256 rooms, restaurant, 2 lounges, pool, exercise center, children free with parents, NS rooms, barber and beauty shop, airport transportation, wheelchair access, TV, A/C, pets OK, CC. SGL/DBL$66-$76.

Holiday Inn Denver Airport (4040 Quebec St., 80216; 321-6666, 800-HOLIDAY) 303 rooms, restaurant, lounge, pool, exercise center, children free with parents, wheelchair access, TV, A/C, NS rooms, fax, room service, airport transportation, 66,000 square feet of meeting and exhibition space, meeting facilities for 300, CC. 5 miles from the airport. SGL/DBL$65-$75.

La Quinta Inn Airport (3975 Peoria Way, 80239; 371-5640, 800-531-5900) 112 rooms, restaurant, lounge, pool, free local calls, NS rooms, wheelchair access, TV, A/C, fax, complimentary magazines, airport courtesy car, valet laundry, CC. 5 miles from airport. SGL/DBL$57-$62.

Motel 6 (12020 East 39th Ave., 80239; 371-1980) 137 rooms, outdoor pool, A/C, TV, CC. SGL/DBL$33-$38.

Motel 6 Denver (12033 East 38th Ave., 80239; 371-0740, 800-851-8888) 65 rooms indoor pool, NS rooms, pets allowed, wheelchair access, TV, A/C, CC. 2 miles from the airport, 5 miles from downtown area. SGL/DBL$26-$34.

Ramada Inn (3737 Quebec St., 80207; 388-6161, Fax 388-0426, 800-2-RAMADA) 148 rooms, restaurant, lounge, pool, pets OK, audiovisual equipment, airport courtesy car, 2 meeting rooms, CC. Near the airport, 2 miles from the Imax Theater, 10 miles from Cherry Creek Shopping Center, 8 miles from the downtown area. SGL$60-$70, DBL$68-$78, X$8.

The Red Lion Airport (3203 Quebec St., 80207; 321-3333, Fax 321-3333 ext 7175, 800-547-8010) 574 rooms and suites, restaurant, lounge, indoor heated pool, sauna, exercise center, hot tub, gift shop, wheelchair access, TV, A/C, NS rooms, 24-hour room service, in-room refrigerators, airport courtesy car, meeting facilities, CC. SGL/DBL$70-$125.

Sheraton Inn Denver Airport (3535 Quebec St., 80207; 333-7711, 800-325-3535) 200 rooms and suites, restaurant, lounge, indoor heated pool, jacuzzi, exercise center, airport transportation, wheelchair access, TV, A/C, NS rooms, children free with parents, 5,000 square feet of meeting and exhibition space, 8 meeting rooms, meeting facilities for 200, CC. Near the airport. SGL/DBL$69.

Stapleton Plaza Hotel and Fitness Center (3333 Quebec St., 80207; 321-3500, 800-950-6070) 300 rooms, restaurant, lounge, pool, exercise center, airport courtesy car, shopping arcade, room service, children free with parents, car rental desk, NS rooms, wheelchair access, TV, A/C, CC. 2 minutes from the airport. SGL/DBL$108, STS$205.

Stouffer Concourse (3810 Quebec St., 80207; 399-7500, 800-468-3571) 400 rooms, restaurant, lounge, indoor pool, sauna, exercise center, wheelchair access, TV, A/C, NS rooms, complimentary newspaper, gift shop, 24-hour room service, airport courtesy car, meeting facilities, CC. SGL/DBL$145-$165.

Super 8 Motel (5888 North Broadway, 80216; 296-3100, 800-800-8000) 100 rooms and suites, outdoor heated pool, pets OK, children under 12 free with parents, free local calls, A/C, TV, in-room refrigerators and microwaves, fax, NS rooms, senior rates, wheelchair access, meeting facilities, CC. SGL/DBL$30-$44.

Traveler's Inn (14200 East Sixth Ave., 80011; 366-7333, 800-633-8300) 149 rooms, pool, free local calls, NS rooms, wheelchair access, TV, A/C, meeting facilities, CC. Near airport, 25 minutes from the downtown area. SGL/DBL$31.

Travelers Inn (I-70 and Peoria St., 80239; 371-0551, 800-633-8300) 133 rooms and suites, pool, free local calls, NS rooms, wheelchair access, TV, A/C, meeting facilities, CC. 12 miles from the downtown area, 5 miles from airport. SGL/DBL$36.

North Denver

Best Western Capri Hotel Plaza (11 East 84th St., 80221; 428-5041, Fax 426-7134, 800-800-I-GO-HOJO) 100 rooms and suites, restaurant, lounge, entertainment, heated pool, children free with parents, NS rooms, pets OK, airport transportation, wheelchair access, TV, A/C, meeting facilities, CC. 10 miles from the airport and the downtown area, 30 minutes from Mile High Stadium. SGL/DBL$42-$67, X$5.

La Quinta Inn Central (3500 Fox St., 80216; 458-1222, Fax 433-2246, 800-531-5900) 106 rooms, restaurant, lounge, pool, complimentary newspaper, free local calls, fax, laundry service, airport transportation, NS rooms, wheelchair access, TV, A/C, meeting facilities, CC. 8 miles from the airport, within 10 miles of the Convention Center, Merchandise Mart and State Capital. SGL/DBL$53-$58.

The Regency Hotel (3900 Elati St., 80216; 458-0808, Fax 477-4255, 800-525-8748) 400 rooms, restaurant, lounge, indoor and outdoor pools, exercise center, sauna, lighted tennis courts, barber and beauty shop, wheelchair access, TV, A/C, NS rooms, airport transportation, CC. SGL/DBL$45, STS$100.

Rosedale Motel (3901 Elati St., 80216; 433-8345) 24 rooms, A/C, TV. Located 2 minutes from the downtown area. SGL/DBL$22-$38.

Travelers Inn (Hwy. 36 and Pecos St., 80221; 427-9400, 800-633-8300) 51 rooms, pool, free local calls, NS rooms, wheelchair access, TV, A/C, meeting facilities, CC. SGL/DBL$36-$38.

TraveLodge Hotel Denver North (200 West 48th St., 80216; 296-4000, Fax 296-4000 ext 850, 800-255-3050) 211 rooms, restaurant, lounge, pool, complimentary newspaper, wheelchair access, TV, A/C, meeting facilities for 245, senior rates, CC. Near the Merchandise Mart, 10 minutes from the airport. SGL/DBL$48-$65.

Vali Hi Motor Hotel (7320 Pecos, 80221; 429-3551) 55 rooms, restaurant, lounge, pool, free local calls, A/C, TV, CC. SGL$20, DBL$29, X$5.

Southeast Denver

Best Western Landmark Inn Hotel (455 South Colorado Blvd., 80222; 388-5561, Fax 388-7936, 800-528-1234) 279 rooms, restaurant, lounge, pool, exercise center, children free with parents, NS rooms, wheelchair access, TV, A/C, pets OK, laundry service, CC. 5 miles from the airport. SGL/DBL$42-$70.

Cherry Creek Inn (600 South Colorado Blvd., 80222; 757-3341) 323 rooms and suites, restaurant, lounge, pool, exercise center, laundry service, beauty shop, gift shop, meeting facilities, CC. Near the Cherry Creek Shopping Center. SGL/DBL$55.

Days Inn Midtown (1680 South Colorado Blvd., 80222; 691-2223, 800-554-1429) 165 rooms, free breakfast, indoor pool, wheelchair access, TV, A/C, children free with parents, fax, pets OK, CC. 1 mile from the University of Denver, 5 miles from the downtown area and Mile High Stadium, 7 miles from the airport. SGL$33-$60, DBL$45-$80, X$4.

Doubletree Hotel Denver (13696 East Liff Place, 80014; 337-2800, Fax 752-0296, 800-528-0444) 248 rooms and suites, restaurant, lounge, entertainment, indoor heated pool, whirlpool, exercise center, room service, children free with parents, NS rooms, 15 meeting rooms, meeting facilities for 500, CC. 11 miles from the airport. SGL/DBL$89, STS$140.

Econo Lodge (4760 East Evans Ave., 80222; 757-7601, 800-446-6900) 78 rooms, restaurant, lounge, pool, wheelchair access, TV, A/C, NS, pets OK, CC. SGL/DBL$30-$45.

Embassy Suites Southeast (7525 East Hampden Ave., 80231; 696-6644, Fax 337-6202, 800-525-3585, 800-EMBASSY) 207 2-room suites, restaurant, free breakfast, pool, sauna, whirlpool, exercise center, airport transportation, laundry service, NS rooms, wheelchair access, TV, A/C, CC. 10 miles from the airport, 7 miles from the downtown area. SGL/DBL$125.

Hyatt Regency Tech Center (7800 East Tufts Ave., 80237; 779-1234, Fax 850-7164, 800-233-1234) 450 rooms and suites, Regency Club Level, restaurant, two lounges, entertainment, heated indoor pool, whirlpool, sauna, exercise center, lighted tennis courts, wheelchair access, TV, A/C, NS rooms, complimentary newspaper, 12 meeting rooms, 20,000 square feet of meeting and exhibition space, CC. 10 miles from the airport. SGL/DBL$59.

La Quinta Inn Denver South (1975 South Colorado Blvd., 80222; 758-8886, 800-531-5900) 135 rooms and suites, restaurant, lounge, heated pool, complimentary newspaper, free local calls, NS rooms, wheelchair access,

TV, A/C, fax, laundry service, meeting facilities, CC. 12 miles from airport, 10 miles from the Denver Technical Center, the downtown area and Cherry Creek Mall. SGL/DBL$57-$62.

Loew's Giorgio Hotel (4150 East Mississippi, 80222; 782-9300, Fax 758-6542, 800-345-9172, 800-522-5455) 347 rooms and suites, restaurant, lounge, free breakfast, pool, exercise center, complimentary newspaper, wheelchair access, TV, gift shop, boutiques, A/C, airport courtesy car, NS rooms, meeting facilities for 1,200, CC. SGL/DBL$155, STS$175-$300.

Marriott SouthWest (6363 East Hampden Ave., 80222; 758-7000, Fax 758-6305, 800-228-9290) 595 rooms and suites, Concierge Level, restaurant, lounge, entertainment, indoor and outdoor heated pools, exercise center, whirlpool, NS rooms, pets OK, wheelchair access, TV, A/C, gift shop, airline ticket desk, meeting facilities, CC. 15 minutes from the downtown area. SGL/DBL$82.

Quality Inn South (6300 East Hampden Ave., 80222; 758-2211, Fax 753-0156, 800-647-1986) 184 rooms, restaurant, lounge, outdoor pool, sauna, jacuzzi, laundry room, valet service, room service, pets OK, wheelchair access, TV, A/C, meeting facilities. 7 miles from the Convention Center and the downtown area. SGL/DBL$60-$78.

Ramada Inn Denver Midtown (1475 South Colorado Blvd., 80222; 757-8798, Fax 758-0704, 800-228-2828) 250 rooms and suites, restaurant, lounge, entertainment, pool, pets OK, wheelchair access, TV, A/C, airport courtesy car, 5,000 square feet of meeting and exhibition space, meeting facilities, CC. 15 minutes from the airport, 2 miles from the Cherry Creek Shopping Center, 10 minutes from the downtown area. SGL$65-$78, DBL$69-$82, STS$85.

Sheraton Denver Tech Center (4900 DTC Pkwy., 80237; 779-1100, Fax 7706112, 800-552-7030) 627 rooms and suites, 3 restaurants, 2 lounges, entertainment, heated indoor and outdoor pools, whirlpool, exercise center, airport transportation, pets OK, wheelchair access, TV, A/C, NS rooms, 24 meeting rooms, 43,000 square feet of meeting and exhibition space, meeting facilities for 1,000, CC. 14 miles from the downtown area, 6 miles from the Cherry Creek Recreation Area and 14 miles from the airport. SGL/DBL$117.

Other Locations

Castle Marne Bed and Breakfast (1572 Race St., 80206, 331-0621, Fax 355-2255, 800-92-MARNE) 9 rooms, free breakfast, private baths, gift shop, pets OK, no children, NS, A/C, TV, CC. SGL$65-$145.

Chalet Motel (6051 West Alameda Ave., 80226; 237-7775, 800-288-7997) 19 rooms, heated outdoor pool, laundry service, pets OK, NS rooms, A/C, TV, CC. SGL$33, DBL$37.

Doubletree Hotel Denver (137 Union Blvd., 80228; 969-9900, 800-528-0444) 172 rooms and suites, free breakfast, lounge, heated outdoor pool, exercise center, spa, sauna, children free with parents, NS rooms, 3 meeting rooms, meeting facilities for 50, CC. 10 minutes from the downtown area, 14 miles from the airport. SGL/DBL$119.

Hampton Inn SouthWest (3605 South Wadsworth Blvd., 80235; 989-6900, 800-HAMPTON) 193 rooms and suites, restaurant, free breakfast, pool, exercise center, children under 18 free with parents, NS rooms, wheelchair access, in-room computer hookups, fax, TV, A/C, room service, gift shop, in-room refrigerators, free local calls, pets OK, meeting facilities, CC. SGL/DBL$50-$65.

Quality Inn North (110 West 104th Ave., 80234; 451-1234, 800-221-2222) 110 rooms, restaurant, lounge, entertainment, pool, whirlpool, wheelchair access, TV, A/C, meeting facilities, CC. 12 miles from the airport, 10 miles from the Museum of Natural History and Denver Zoo. SGL/DBL$55-$58.

Super 8 North (12055 Melody Dr., 80234; 451-7200, Fax 451-7200 ext 350, 800-800-8000) 116 rooms and suites, wheelchair access, TV, A/C, exercise center, spa, sauna, pets OK, NS rooms, fax, free local calls, children free with parents, car rental desk, meeting facilities, airport courtesy car, in-room refrigerators and microwaves, CC. 15 minutes from the airport, 11 miles from Colorado National Speedway, 10 miles from the Mile High Stadium. SGL/DBL$37.

Victoria Oaks (1575 Race St., 80206; 355-1818) 9 rooms, free breakfast, pets OK, NS rooms, A/C, TV, CC. SGL/DBL$40-$90.

White Swan Motel (6060 West Colfax, 80214; 238-1351, 800-257-9972) 20 rooms and efficiencies, free breakfast, heated outdoor pool, free local calls, wheelchair access, TV, A/C, airport transportation. SGL$29-$39, EFF$35.

Writer's Manor (1730 South Colorado Blvd., 80214; 756-8877, Fax 691-5972, 800-525-8072) 325 rooms, pool, jacuzzi, sauna, exercise center, tennis courts, wheelchair access, TV, A/C, NS rooms, airport transportation, gift shop, meeting facilities, CC. SGL/DBL$60-$90.

Dillon
Area Code 303

Aspen Canyon Ranch (Dillon 80435; 725-3518, Fax 473-8748, 800-321-1357) 12 rooms, whirlpools, pets OK, fireplaces, TV, NS rooms, American plan available, wheelchair access, CC. SGL/DBL$1140W-$1800W.

Best Western Ptarmigan Lodge (652 Lake Dillon Dr., 80435; 468-2341. Fax 468-6465, 800-842-5939, 800-528-1234) 69 rooms and efficiencies, restaurant, free breakfast, lounge, pool, exercise center, children free with parents, A/C, NS rooms, TV, laundry facilities, wheelchair access, pets OK, senior rates, meeting facilities, CC. SGL/DBL$45-$145.

Days Inn (580 Silverthorne Lane, 80435; 468-8651, Fax 468-5583, 800-325-2525) 72 rooms and suites, free breakfast, outdoor pool, children free with parents, room service, laundry service, A/C, TV, free local calls, pets OK, fax, wheelchair access, NS rooms, meeting facilities, senior rates, CC. SGL/DBL$70-$120.

Super 8 Motel (Dillon 80435; 468-8888, Fax 468-2086, 800-800-8000) 60 rooms and suites, pets OK, children under 12 free with parents, free local calls, A/C, TV, in-room refrigerators and microwaves, fax, NS rooms, senior rates, wheelchair access, meeting facilities, CC. SGL/DBL$40-$82.

Dolores
Area Code 303

Circle K Ranch (26916 Hwy. 145, 81323; 562-3808) 17 rooms, restaurant, laundry facilities, A/C, TV, NS rooms, wheelchair access, CC. SGL/DBL$32.

Dolores Mountain Inn (701 Hwy. 145, 81323; 882-7203, Fax 882-7011, 800-842-8113) 30 rooms and efficiencies, laundry facilities, A/C, TV, NS rooms, wheelchair access, CC. SGL/DBL$37-$60.

Historic Rio Grande Southern Hotel (101 South 5th St., 81323; 882-7527, 800-258-0434) 10 rooms, bed and breakfast, restaurant, free breakfast, A/C, NS rooms, TV, CC. SGL/DBL$45-$90.

Mountain View Bed and Breakfast (28050 County Rd., 81323; 882-7861, 800-228-4592) 8 rooms, free breakfast, hot tubs, A/C, TV, laundry facilities, CC. SGL/DBL$39-$75.

Outpost Motel (1800 Hwy. 145, 81323; 882-7271, 800-382-4892) 10 rooms and efficiencies, laundry facilities, pets OK, A/C, TV, NS rooms, wheelchair access, CC. SGL/DBL$33-$45.

Rag O'Muffin Ranch (26030 Hwy. 145, 81323; 562-3803) 2 rooms, free breakfast, A/C, TV, pets OK, CC. SGL/DBL$80.

Remuda Inn (1121 Central Ave., 81323; 882-4633) 9 rooms, A/C, TV, NS rooms, wheelchair access, pets OK, senior rates, CC. SGL/DBL$33-$46.

Rivers Edge (24507 Hwy. 145, 81323; 882-4188) 4 rooms, hot tubs, A/C, TV, NS rooms, wheelchair access, CC. SGL/DBL$50-$70.

Stoner Alpine Lodge (25134 Hwy. 145, 81323; 882-7825) 11 rooms, restaurant, A/C, TV, NS rooms, wheelchair access, CC. SGL/DBL$35-$45.

West Fork Lodge (Hwy. 535, 81323; 882-7959) 5 rooms, free breakfast, CC. SGL/DBL$36-$48.

Durango

Area Code 303

Adobe Inn (2178 Main Ave., 81301; 247-2743, 800-251-8773) 25 rooms and efficiencies, restaurant, heated pool, whirlpools, pets OK, A/C, kitchenettes, TV, NS rooms, wheelchair access, CC. SGL/DBL$65-$85.

Affordable Suites Motel (3131 Main Ave., 81301; 247-5460) TV, A/C, kitchenettes, CC. SGL/DBL$30.

Alpine Motel (3515 North Main Ave., 81301; 247-4042) 21 rooms and efficiencies, A/C, TV, NS rooms, wheelchair access, pets OK, CC. SGL/DBL$24-$64.

Best Western Durango Inn (Hwy. 160, 81301; 247-3251, 800-547-9090, Fax 385-4835, 800-547-9090, 800-528-1234) 56 rooms and 2-bedroom efficiencies, restaurant, free breakfast, lounge, indoor pool, exercise center, sauna, children free with parents, A/C, NS rooms, TV, laundry, local transportation, wheelchair access, pets OK, senior rates, meeting facilities, CC. SGL/DBL$49-$84.

Bed and Breakfast Rocky Mountain (3255 Main Ave., 81301; 247-5200, Fax 247-5200, 800-528-1234) 65 rooms, exercise center, indoor pool, jacuzzi, in-room refrigerators and microwaves, children free with parents, A/C, NS rooms, TV, laundry facilities, wheelchair access, pets OK, senior rates, meeting facilities, CC. SGL/DBL$52-$94.

Best Western Lodge at Purgatory (49617 North Hwy. 550, 81303; 247-9669, Fax 247-9681, 800-637-7727, 800-528-1234) 26 rooms and condominiums, restaurant, indoor pool, exercise center, children free with parents, A/C, NS rooms, TV, laundry facilities, wheelchair access, local transportation, pets OK, senior rates, meeting facilities, CC. SGL/DBL$60-$85.

Best Western Rio Grande Inn (400 East 2nd Ave., 81301; 385-4980, Fax 385-4980, 800-245-4466, 800-528-1234) 101 rooms, restaurant, lounge, free breakfast, jacuzzi, sauna, children free with parents, A/C, free local calls, NS rooms, TV, laundry facilities, wheelchair access, pets OK, senior rates, meeting facilities, CC. SGL/DBL$63-$105.

Brimstone at Purgatory (400 Sheol St., 81303; 259-1066, 800-323-SKI-2) 24 2-bedroom condominiums, hot tubs, fireplaces, A/C, TV, NS rooms, wheelchair access, CC. SGL/DBL$55-$135.

Budget Inn (3077 Main Ave., 81303; 247-5222, 800-257-5222) 37 rooms, outdoor pool, pets OK, A/C, TV, NS rooms, wheelchair access, CC. SGL/DBL$32-$57.

Caboose Motel (3363 Main Ave., 81303; 247-1191) 18 rooms and efficiencies, restaurant, pets OK, A/C, TV, in-room refrigerators and microwaves, NS rooms, wheelchair access, CC. SGL/DBL$28-$56.

Cascade Village (50827 Hwy. 550 North, 81303; 259-5960, 800-525-0896) 125 1- to 3-bedroom condominiums, hot tubs, sauna, laundry facilities, A/C, TV, NS rooms, wheelchair access, pets OK, local transportation, CC. SGL/DBL$55-$185.

Colorado Outback (2694 Hwy. 222, 81303; 259-2147) 3 rooms, free breakfast, A/C, private baths, fireplace, TV, CC. SGL/DBL$50.

Colorado Trails Ranch (12161 Hwy. 240, 81303; 247-5055, 800-323-DUDE) 33 rooms and cabins, restaurant, pool, hot tubs, jacuzzi, tennis courts, A/C, TV, airport transportation, children free with parents, game room, pets OK, NS rooms, wheelchair access, American plan available, CC. SGL/DBL$825W-$1150W.

Comfort Inn (2930 North Main Ave., 81301; 259-5373, 800-221-2222) 48 rooms, restaurant, free breakfast, heated pool, sauna, wheelchair access, NS rooms, pets OK, children under 18 free with parents, A/C, TV, meeting facilities, senior rates, CC. SGL/DBL$40-$88.

Country Sunshine Bed and Breakfast (35130 Hwy. 550 North, 81303; 247-2853, 800-383-2853) 6 rooms, free breakfast, whirlpools, NS, antique furnishings, private baths, fireplace, TV, CC. SGL/DBL$85-$125.

Days End (2202 Main Ave., 81303; 259-3311, 800-242-3297) 28 rooms and efficiencies, outdoor pool, jacuzzi, hot tub, laundry facilities, pets OK, A/C, TV, NS rooms, wheelchair access, CC. SGL/DBL$32-$57.

Days Inn (1700 Animas View Dr., 81301; 259-1430, Fax 259-5741, 800-325-2525) 94 rooms and suites, restaurant, lounge, indoor pool, jacuzzis, sauna, children free with parents, room service, laundry service, A/C, TV, free local calls, pets OK, fax, wheelchair access, NS rooms, senior rates, CC. SGL/DBL$39-$68.

Dollar Inn (2391 Main Ave., 81303; 247-0593, 800-727-DRGO) 23 rooms, A/C, TV, NS rooms, wheelchair access, CC. SGL/DBL$32-$66.

Durango Lodge (150 5th St., 81303; 247-0955, Fax 259-5741) 30 rooms, restaurant, outdoor pool, hot tubs, whirlpools, pets OK, in-room refrigerators, A/C, TV, NS rooms, wheelchair access, CC. SGL/DBL$35-$90.

East Rim Condominiums at Purgatory (44 Sheol St., 81303; 247-5528, 800-682-1293) 16 condominiums, hot tubs, laundry facilities, kitchenettes, A/C, TV, NS rooms, wheelchair access, CC. SGL/DBL$75.

Econo Lodge (2002 Main Ave., 81301; 247-4242, 800-4-CHOICE) 41 rooms, pool, whirlpools, kitchenettes, VCRs, children under 12 free with parents, pets OK, NS rooms, wheelchair access, A/C, TV, senior rates, CC. SGL/DBL$29-$82.

Farmhouse Village (281 South Silver Queen, 81303; 259-2812, 800-748-2502) 20 rooms and apartments, free breakfast, A/C, private baths, hot tubs, fireplaces, TV, CC. SGL/DBL$68-$120.

Four Winds (20797 Hwy. 160 West, 81301; 247-4512, 800-322-8029) 33 rooms, indoor pool, A/C, TV, NS rooms, wheelchair access, CC. SGL/DBL$32-$48.

The Gable House (805 East 5th Ave., 81303; 247-4982) 2 rooms, free breakfast, fireplaces, A/C, TV, CC. SGL/DBL$60-$65.

General Palmer Hotel (567 Main Ave., 81303; 247-4747, 800-523-3358) 39 rooms, and suites, free breakfast, 1890s inn, antique furnishings, in-room refrigerators, airport transportation, pets OK, children free with parents, A/C, TV, NS rooms, wheelchair access, CC. SGL/DBL$75-$250.

Holiday Inn (800 Camino del Rio, 81303; 247-5393, 800-HOLIDAY) 139 rooms, restaurant, lounge, heated pool, exercise center, whirlpools, sauna, children under 19 free with parents, wheelchair access, A/C, TV, NS rooms, fax, room service, pets OK, laundry service, meeting facilities, senior rates, CC. SGL/DBL$52-$99.

Iron House Inn (5800 North Main Ave., 81303; 259-1010, 800-748-2990) 141 rooms, restaurant, indoor heated pool, hot tubs, jacuzzis, laundry facilities, pets OK, A/C, TV, NS rooms, fireplaces, wheelchair access, airport transportation, game room, meeting facilities, senior rates, CC. SGL/DBL$65-$105.

Jarvis Suite Hotel (125 West 10th St., 81303; 259-6190, 800-824-1024) 22 rooms and 1- and 2-bedroom suites, restaurant, laundry facilities, A/C, TV, pets OK, airport transportation, NS rooms, wheelchair access, meeting facilities, senior rates, CC. SGL/DBL$65-$130.

Lake Mancos Ranch (Durango 81303; 533-7900, 800-325-9462) 17 rooms and cabins, restaurant, lounge, entertainment, heated pool, whirlpools, A/C, TV, NS rooms, pets OK, laundry facilities, airport transportation, wheelchair access, in-room refrigerators, game room, American plan available, CC. SGL/DBL$850W-$1,600W.

Landmark Motel (3030 Main Ave., 81303; 259-1333, 800-252-8853) 48 rooms and 2-bedroom efficiencies, indoor and outdoor heated pools, hot tubs, whirlpools, A/C, TV, NS rooms, pets OK, wheelchair access, CC. SGL/DBL$45-$84.

Logwood Bed and Breakfast (35060 Hwy. 550 North, 81303; 259-4395, 800-369-4082) 5 rooms, free breakfast, A/C, pets OK, NS, no children, fireplace, TV, pets OK, CC. SGL/DBL$75-$80.

National 9 Sunset Inn (2855 Main Ave., 81303; 247-2653, 800-524-9999) outdoor pool, jacuzzi, whirlpools, NS rooms, wheelchair access, A/C, TV, children free with parents, laundry facilities, senior rates, CC. SGL/DBL$24-$56.

Purgatory Village Hotel (1 Skier Pl., 81303; 247-9000, 800-TRY-PURG) 170 1- to 4-bedroom condominiums, restaurant, outdoor pool, jacuzzi, whirlpools, fireplaces, A/C, local transportation, TV, NS rooms, wheelchair access, CC. SGL/DBL$49-$110.

Red Lion Inn (501 Carmino del Rio, 81301; 259-6580, Fax 259-4398, 800-547-8010) 159 rooms and suites, restaurant, lounge, entertainment, indoor heated pool, spa, sauna, exercise center, airport courtesy car, A/C, TV, wheelchair access, NS rooms, laundry facilities, 5 meeting rooms, meeting facilities for 420, senior rates, CC. SGL/DBL$88-$150.

Redwood Lodge (763 Animas View Dr., 81303; 247-3895) 16 rooms and 2-bedroom efficiencies, sauna, hot tubs, A/C, TV, NS rooms, wheelchair access, pets OK, CC. SGL/DBL$28-$50.

Rodeway Inn (2701 Main Ave, 81301; 259-2540, 800-424-4777) 31 rooms, indoor heated pool, whirlpools, sauna, exercise center, pets OK, wheelchair access, NS rooms, children free with parents, A/C, TV, gift shop, airport transportation, senior rates, CC. SGL/DBL$120-$150.

Siesta Motel (3475 Main Ave., 81303; 247-0741) 22 rooms and efficiencies, pets OK, A/C, TV, NS rooms, wheelchair access, in-room refrigerators, CC. SGL/DBL$22-$52.

Silver Spruce Motel (2929 Main Ave., 81303; 247-2202) TV, A/C, pets OK, CC. SGL/DBL$19-$48.

Silver Spur Motel (3416 Main Ave., 81303; 247-5552, 800-748-1715) 35 rooms, restaurant, outdoor pool, A/C, TV, NS rooms, wheelchair access, laundry facilities, CC. SGL/DBL$30-$85.

Spanish Trails Motel ((3141 Main Ave., 81303; 247-4173) outdoor pool, laundry facilities, A/C, TV, NS rooms, wheelchair access, CC. SGL/DBL$49.

Steward Ranch Cabins (Durango 81303; 247-8962) cabins, kitchenettes, TV, wheelchair access, CC. SGL/DBL$45-$50.

Strater Hotel (699 Main Ave., 81303; 247-4431, 800-247-4431) 93 rooms, restaurant, lounge, entertainment, hot tub, laundry facilities, A/C, TV,

1880s inn, antique furnishings, boutiques, NS rooms, wheelchair access, CC. SGL/DBL$55-$140.

Super 8 Motel (20 Stewart Dr., 81301; 259-0590, Fax 247-5765, 800-800-8000) 85 rooms and suites, restaurant, pets OK, children under 12 free with parents, free local calls, A/C, TV, in-room refrigerators and microwaves, fax, NS rooms, senior rates, wheelchair access, meeting facilities, CC. SGL/DBL$37-$77.

Tall Timber Resort (Silverton Star Rt., 81303; 259-4813) 10 suites, restaurant, lounge, pool, whirlpools, exercise center, sauna, tennis courts, in-room refrigerators and coffee makers, A/C, TV, NS, wheelchair access, gift shop, fireplaces, pets OK, American plan available. SGL/DBL$1,200W-$2,400W.

Tamaroon Resort (40292 Hwy. 550 North, 81303; 259-2000, 800-678-1000) 325 condominiums, restaurant, lounge, entertainment, indoor and outdoor pool, tennis courts, sauna, whirlpools, American plan available, laundry facilities, A/C, TV, local transportation, no pets, NS rooms, wheelchair access, CC. SGL/DBL$85-$370.

Twilight View Condominiums (166 Sheol St., 81303; 247-8234, 800-433-3890) 17 condominiums, hot tubs, laundry facilities, fireplaces, A/C, TV, NS rooms, wheelchair access, CC. SGL/DBL$65-$130.

Western Star Motel (3310 Main Ave., 81303; 247-4895) 21 rooms and efficiencies, restaurant, indoor pool, jacuzzi, whirlpools, A/C, TV, NS rooms, laundry facilities, wheelchair access, CC. SGL/DBL$46-$70.

Wildcat Canyon Lodge (20280 Hwy. 160 West, 81303; 247-3350, 800-748-1711) 35 rooms and efficiencies, A/C, TV, NS rooms, wheelchair access, CC. SGL/DBL$30-$49.

Wilderness Trails Ranch (Durango 81303; 247-0722, Fax 247-1006) 13 cottages, heated pool, whirlpools, laundry facilities, pets OK, TV, NS rooms, wheelchair access, CC. SGL/DBL$895W-$1,850W.

Eagle

Area Code 303

Best Western Eagle Lodge (200 Loren Lane, 81631; 328-6316, Fax 328-2394, 800-528-1234) 48 rooms, restaurant, free breakfast, lounge, pool, exercise center, spa, children free with parents, A/C, NS rooms, TV, laundry facilities, wheelchair access, pets OK, senior rates, meeting facilities, CC. SGL/DBL$50-$125.

Edwards
Area Code 303

The Lodge at Cordillera (Edwards 81632; 926-2200, Fax 926-2486, 800-548-2721) 28 rooms and suites, restaurant, free breakfast, lounge, entertainment, pool, exercise center, sauna, whirlpools, NS rooms, wheelchair access, local transportation, pets OK, fireplace, meeting facilities, senior rates, CC. SGL/DBL$195-$250, STS$250-$350.

Englewood
Area Code 303

Clarion Hotel Southeast (7770 South Peoria St., 80112; 790-7770, 800-221-2222) 119 rooms, restaurant, lounge, free breakfast, pool, whirlpools, local transportation, pets OK, NS rooms, children under 18 free with parents, senior rates, meeting facilities, A/C, TV, CC. SGL/DBL$78-$105.

Courtyard by Marriott (6565 South Boston St., 80111; 721-0300, Fax 721-0037, 800-321-2211) 154 rooms and suites, restaurant, lounge, indoor pool, exercise center, whirlpools, children free with parents, laundry service, in-room refrigerators and coffee makers, local transportation, A/C, NS rooms, TV, meeting facilities, senior rates, CC. SGL/DBL$70-$105.

Embassy Suites Tech Center (10250 East Costilla Ave., 80112; 792-0433, 800-EMBASSY) 236 2-room suites, restaurant, lounge, free breakfast, lounge, heated pool, whirlpool, exercise center, sauna, room service, laundry service, wheelchair access, complimentary newspaper, free local calls, game room, NS rooms, gift shop, local transportation, meeting facilities, CC. SGL/DBL$80-$165.

Hampton Inn Southeast (9231 East Arapahoe Rd., 80112; 792-9999, 800-426-7866) 152 rooms, free breakfast, outdoor pool, exercise center, children free with parents, NS rooms, wheelchair access, TV, A/C, in-room computer hookups, fax, pets OK, free local calls, meeting facilities, CC. SGL/DBL$55-$77.

Denver Hilton South (7801 East Orchard Rd., 80111; 779-6161, Fax 850-0103, 800-HILTONS) 265 rooms and suites, indoor and outdoor pools, exercise center, sauna, in-room refrigerators, 24-hour room service, NS rooms, car rental desk, wheelchair access, TV, A/C, free local calls, meeting facilities for 700, CC. SGL/DBL$99-$109, STS$195-$275.

Radisson South (7007 South Clinton St., 80112; 799-6200, 800-333-3333) 263 rooms and suites, restaurant, lounge, entertainment, heated pool, exercise center, whirlpools, gift shop, room service, in-room refrigerators, microwaves and coffee makers, children free with parents, VCRs, wheelchair access, NS rooms, TV, A/C, children free with parents, pets OK, meeting facilities, senior rates, CC. SGL/DBL$70-$90.

Ramada Inn Denver Tech Center (5150 South Quebec, 80111; 721-1144, Fax 721-1245, 800-2-RAMADA) 235 rooms and suites, restaurant, lounge, entertainment, heated pool, jacuzzis, gift shop, laundry service, in-room refrigerators, 12 meeting rooms, meeting facilities for 1,200, CC. SGL$46-$56, DBL$50-$70, STS$95, X$6.

Residence Inn South (6565 South Yosemite, 80111; 740-7177, Fax 740-7177 ext 129, 800-331-3131) 128 efficiencies, free breakfast, in-room refrigerators, coffee makers and microwaves, laundry facilities, TV, A/C, VCRs, pets OK, complimentary newspaper, fireplaces, children free with parents, NS rooms, wheelchair access, meeting facilities, senior rates, CC. SGL/DBL$105-$130.

The Scanticon (200 Inverness Dr. West, 80112; 799-5800, 800-346-4891) 302 rooms and suites, three restaurants, four lounges, heated indoor and outdoor pools, hot tubs, exercise center, lighted tennis courts, gift shop, local transportation, room service, NS rooms, wheelchair access, TV, A/C, 33 meeting rooms, CC. SGL/DBL$$69-139, STS$169-$350.

Estes Park
Area Code 303

Rental and Reservation Services:

Alpine Meadows Vacation Homes (Estes Park 80517; 586-4507, 800-748-2181) rental 2- to 6-bedroom homes.

Valhalla Resort (Estes Park 80517; 586-3284) rental 1- , 2- and 3-bedroom homes.

Windcliff (Estes Park 80517; 800-748-2181) rental 1- , 2- and 3-bedroom homes.

□□□

Affairs of the Heart at Streamside (Estes Park 80517; 800-321-3303) 19 cabins, fireplace, kitchenettes, VCRs, CC. SGL/DBL$80.

Alpine Trail Ridge Inn (927 Moraine Ave., 80517; 586-4584, Fax 586-6249, 800-233-5023) 48 rooms and suites, restaurant, heated pool, A/C, TV, NS rooms, pets OK, kitchenettes, wheelchair access, CC. SGL/DBL$35-$90, STS$78-$98.

Amberwood (Estes Park 80517; 586-4385) 1- to 4-bedroom cabins, kitchenettes, pets OK, fireplace, meeting facilities. SGL/DBL$40-$158.

American Wilderness Lodge (481 West Elkhorn, 80517; 800-762-5968) 36 rooms and suites, indoor pool, sauna, jacuzzi, fireplaces, kitchenettes, A/C, TV, NS rooms, wheelchair access, CC. SGL/DBL$39-$44.

The Aspen Lodge (6120 Hwy. 7, 80517; 800-332-MTNS) 56 rooms and 2- and 3-bedroom, cabins, restaurant, lounge, entertainment, heated pool, whirlpools, lighted tennis courts, pets OK, modified American plan available, in-room refrigerators, CC. SGL/DBL$$32-$75.

The Ayerie on Eagle Cliff (Estes Park 80517; 586-9623, 800-828-9676) 10 rooms, cabins and 1- and 2-bedroom homes, A/C, TV, NS rooms, wheelchair access, 3,000 square feet of meeting and exhibition space, CC. SGL/DBL$90-$220.

The Baldplate Inn (Estes Park 80517; 586-6151) restaurant, free breakfast, fireplace, A/C, TV, NS rooms, wheelchair access, CC. SGL/DBL$65.

Best Western Estes Village Motor Inn (1040 Big Thompson Ave., 80517; 586-5338, 800-528-1234) 42 rooms, restaurant, heated pool, spa, exercise center, children free with parents, A/C, NS rooms, TV, laundry facilities, wheelchair access, pets OK, senior rates, meeting facilities, CC. SGL/DBL$35-$85.

Best Western Lake Estes Resort (1650 Big Thompson Ave., 80517; 586-3386, 800-292-VIEW, 800-528-1234) 57 rooms and suites, restaurant, whirlpools, kitchenettes, children free with parents, A/C, NS rooms, TV, laundry facilities, wheelchair access, pets OK, senior rates, meeting facilities, CC. SGL/DBL$45-$155.

Big Thompson Timberlane Lodge (Hwy. 36 West, 80517; 586-3137) 34 rooms and 1-, 2- and 3-bedroom cottages, indoor and outdoor pools, whirlpools, laundry facilities, pets OK, TV, water view, kitchenettes, wheelchair access, CC. SGL/DBL$39-$79, 1BR$39-$72, 2BR$59-$79, 3BR$125-$247.

Blackhawk Lodges (1750 Fall River Rd., 80517; 586-6100) 1- and 2-bedroom cabins, kitchenettes, TV, pets OK, wheelchair access, fireplaces, CC. SGL/DBL$85-$155.

Boulder Brook (1900 Fall River Rd., 80517; 586-0910) 16 rooms and efficiencies, whirlpools, pets OK, TV, NS rooms, wheelchair access, CC. SGL/DBL$100-$160.

Brookside Resort (Estes Park 80517; 586-4669) cottages, kitchenettes, A/C, TV, NS rooms, wheelchair access, pets OK, CC. SGL/DBL$35-$90.

Brynwood on the River (Estes Park 80517; 586-3475) 10 rooms and cottages, pool, whirlpools, TV, NS rooms, wheelchair access, kitchenettes,

Budget Host Four Winds Motor Lodge (1120 Big Thompson Ave., 80517; 586-3313, 800-283-4678) 50 rooms and suites, heated pool, hot tubs, in-room coffee makers, pets OK, laundry facilities, NS rooms, wheelchair access, A/C, TV, senior rates, children free with parents, CC. SGL/DBL$30-$70.

Castle Mountain Lodge (1520 Fall River Rd., 80517; 586-3664) 26 rooms and cottages, kitchenettes, in-room refrigerators, pets OK, fireplaces, TV, NS rooms, wheelchair access, CC. SGL/DBL$59-$360W.

Comfort Inn (1450 Big Thompson Ave., 80517; 586-2358, 800-221-2222) 60 rooms and efficiencies, free breakfast, pool, sauna, wheelchair access, NS rooms, pets OK, children under 18 free with parents, A/C, TV, meeting facilities, senior rates, CC. SGL/DBL$40-$140.

Cottonwood House (Estes Park 80517; 586-5104) free breakfast, A/C, TV, 1920s home, pets OK, NS, private baths, CC. SGL/DBL$55-$64.

Days Inn (1701 Big Thompson Ave., 80517; 586-5363, Fax 586-5365, 800-325-2525) 135 rooms and suites, indoor pool, children free with parents, room service, laundry service, A/C, TV, free local calls, pets OK, fax, wheelchair access, NS rooms, meeting facilities, senior rates, CC. SGL/DBL$42-$95.

Deer Crest Resort (1200 Fall River Rd., 80517; 586-2324) 26 rooms and cabins, heated pool, pets OK, TV, NS rooms, wheelchair access, CC. SGL/DBL$40-$95.

Four Seasons Inn (1130 West Elkhorn Ave., 80517; 586-5693, 800-779-4616) 8 rooms, hot tub, fireplace, in-room refrigerators and microwaves, CC. SGL/DBL$89.

Four Winds Motor Lodge (Estes Park 80517; 586-3313) 52 rooms and 2-bedroom efficiencies, heated pool, whirlpools, sauna, pets OK, TV, laundry facilities, NS rooms, wheelchair access, CC. SGL/DBL$25-$65.

Glacier Lodge (Estes Park 80517; 586-4401) 1- and 2-bedroom, cottages, restaurant, A/C, fireplaces, TV, NS rooms, wheelchair access, CC. SGL/DBL$40-$125.

Holiday Inn (101 South St., 80517; 586-2332, 800-HOLIDAY) 155 rooms, restaurant, lounge, indoor pool, exercise center, whirlpools, children under 19 free with parents, wheelchair access, A/C, TV, NS rooms, fax, room service, game room, pets OK, laundry service, meeting facilities for 450, senior rates, CC. SGL/DBL$70-$95.

The Inn at Rock n' River (Estes Park 80517; 443-4611) 17 rooms and 2-bedroom efficiencies, hot tubs, pets OK, TV, NS rooms, in-room refrigerators and microwaves, wheelchair access, CC. SGL/DBL$40-$135.

Lazy R Cottages (891 Moraine, 80517; 586-3708) 2- and 3-bedroom cottages, TV, VCR, kitchenettes, wheelchair access, CC. SGL/DBL$50-$150.

Lazy T Motor Lodge (1340 Big Thompson Ave., 80517; 586-4376) 2-bedroom apartments, restaurant, heated pool, fireplaces, kitchenettes, A/C, TV, NS rooms, wheelchair access, meeting facilities, CC. SGL/DBL$25-$40.

McGregor Mountain Lodge (2815 Fall River Rd., 80517; 586-3457) 27 rooms and cottages, hot tubs, fireplaces, in-room microwaves, pets OK, TV, NS rooms, wheelchair access, CC. SGL/DBL$55-$225.

Miles Motel (Estes Park 80517; 586-3185) 22 rooms, heated pool, pets OK, TV, kitchenettes, NS rooms, wheelchair access, CC. SGL/DBL$40-$125.

Olympus Lodge (Estes Park 80517; 586-8141) 18 rooms, lounge, kitchenettes, pets OK, TV, in-room refrigerators, CC. SGL/DBL$30-$125.

Park Lodge (2512 Hwy. 66, 80517; 586-3720) kitchenettes, A/C, TV, NS rooms, wheelchair access, CC. SGL/DBL$27-$55.

Ponderosa Lodge (Estes Park 80517; 586-4233) 19 rooms and 2-bedroom cottages, pets OK, TV, NS rooms, wheelchair access, CC. SGL/DBL$45-$105.

River Song (Estes Park 80517; 586-4666) 9 rooms, free breakfast, whirlpools, TV, NS, pets OK, private baths, hot tub, fireplaces, wheelchair access, airport transportation, in-room refrigerators, CC. SGL/DBL$60-$130.

Silver Saddle Motor Lodge (1260 Big Thompson Ave., 80517; 586-4476) 50 rooms and 2-bedroom efficiencies, restaurant, heated pool, whirlpools, pets OK, kitchenettes, A/C, TV, NS rooms, wheelchair access, CC. SGL/DBL$36-$100.

Streamside Cabins (1260 Fall River Rd., 80517; 586-6464) 1- and 2-bedroom cabins, jacuzzi, whirlpools, VCRs, pets OK, kitchenettes, fireplaces, TV, CC. SGL/DBL$65-$250.

Sundance Cottages (960 Riverside Dr., 80517; 586-3922) 1- , 2- and 3-bedroom cabins, TV, fireplaces, CC. SGL/DBL$66-$105.

Sunnyside Knoll Resort (1675 Fall River Rd., 80517; 586-5759) 14 rooms and cottages, heated pool, sauna, TV, NS rooms, wheelchair access, kitchenettes, pets OK, CC. SGL/DBL$80-$170.

Tellmark Resort (650 West Moraine, 80517; 586-4343, 800-669-0650) 22 cabins, kitchenettes, fireplace, TV, credit cards. SGL/DBL$65-$75.

Trappers Motor Inn (553 West Elkhorn, 80517; 586-2833) 20 rooms and 2-bedroom efficiencies, pets OK, TV, A/C, CC. SGL/DBL$25-$65.

Wanek's Lodge at Estes (560 Ponderosa Dr., 80517; 586-5851) free breakfast, A/C, TV, NS, pets OK, fireplaces, CC. SGL/DBL$45-$60.

The Woodlands on Fall River (1888 Fall River Rd., 80517; 586-0404) 16 1- and 2-bedroom suites, jacuzzis, hot tubs, kitchenettes, in-room refrigerators and coffee makers, fireplaces, TV, CC. 1BR$60-$90, 2BR$70-$105.

Evans
Area Code 303

Heritage Fata Suites Inn (3301 West Service Rd., 80620; 339-5900, Fax 339-5139) 73 rooms, restaurant, lounge, heated pool, whirlpools, pets OK, A/C, TV, NS rooms, airport transportation, wheelchair access, CC. SGL/DBL$45-$55.

Park Inn International (3301 Hwy. 85 South, 80620; 339-5656, Fax 339-5739, 800-437-PARK) 59 rooms and suites, restaurant, lounge, outdoor pool, A/C, TV, wheelchair access, NS rooms, meeting facilities for 175, CC. SGL/DBL$45-$55.

Winterset Inn (800 31st St., 80620; 339-2492) 49 rooms and 2-bedroom suites, lounge, A/C, TV, NS rooms, wheelchair access, laundry facilities, pets OK, CC. SGL/DBL$30-$48.

Evergreen
Area Code 303

Highland Haven Resort (4395 Independence Trail, 80439; 674-3577) 16 rooms and 2-bedroom efficiencies, in-room refrigerators, pets OK, TV, CC. SGL/DBL$45-$110.

Fairplay
Area Code 719

Western Inn (Fairplay 80440; 836-2026) 19 rooms, restaurant, TV, pets OK, CC. SGL/DBL$35-$45.

Florence
Area Code 719

National 9 Inn (136 East Front St., 81226; 800-524-9999) 48 rooms, pool, hot tubs, in-room refrigerators and microwaves, pets OK, free local calls, NS rooms, wheelchair access, A/C, TV, children free with parents, senior rates, CC. SGL/DBL$35-$50.

River Valley Inn (4540 Hwy. 67 South, 81226) rooms and suites, free local calls, A/C, TV, NS rooms, wheelchair access, CC. SGL/DBL$45-$55.

Fort Collins
Area Code 303

Best Western University Motor Inn (914 South College Ave, 80524; 484-1984, 800-528-1234) 74 rooms, restaurant, free breakfast, lounge, pool, exercise center, children free with parents, A/C, complimentary newspaper, NS rooms, TV, laundry facilities, wheelchair access, pets OK, senior rates, meeting facilities, CC. SGL/DBL$40-$55.

Budget Host Inn (1513 North College Ave., 80524; 484-0870, Fax 224-2998, 800-283-4678) 30 rooms and 2-room efficiencies, restaurant, hot tubs, pets OK, in-room coffee makers, laundry facilities, NS rooms, wheelchair access, A/C, TV, senior rates, children free with parents, CC. SGL/DBL$29-$50.

Comfort Inn (1638 East Mulberry St., 80524; 484-2444, 800-221-2222) 43 rooms and suites, free breakfast, pool, whirlpools, wheelchair access, NS rooms, pets OK, children under 18 free with parents, A/C, TV, meeting facilities, senior rates, CC. SGL/DBL$50-$83.

Days Inn (3625 East Mulberry, 80524; 221-5490, 800-325-2525) 77 rooms and suites, free breakfast, children free with parents, room service, laundry service, A/C, TV, free local calls, pets OK, VCRs, fax, wheelchair access, NS rooms, senior rates, CC. SGL/DBL$30-$45.

Econo Lodge (4333 East Mulberry, 80524; 493-9000, Fax 224-9636, 800-4-CHOICE) 120 rooms, restaurant, lounge, heated pool, whirlpools, children under 12 free with parents, airport transportation, pets OK, NS rooms, wheelchair access, A/C, TV, senior rates, CC. SGL/DBL$40-$55.

Elizabeth Street Guest House (202 East Elizabeth, 80524; 493-2337) free breakfast, 1905 home, antique furnishings, NS, pets OK, private baths, A/C, TV, CC. SGL/DBL$50-$65.

Helmshire Inn (1204 South College Ave., 80524; 493-4683) 26 rooms, free breakfast, A/C, TV, NS rooms, wheelchair access, meeting facilities, senior rates, CC. SGL/DBL$59-$64.

Holiday Inn I-25 Holidome (3836 East Mulberry, 80524; 484-4660, 800-HOLIDAY) 180 rooms, restaurant, lounge, indoor pool, exercise center, whirlpools, children under 19 free with parents, wheelchair access, A/C, TV, NS rooms, fax, room service, game room, pets OK, laundry service, meeting facilities for 450, senior rates, CC. SGL/DBL$45-$65.

Holiday Inn University Park (425 West Prospect Rd., 80524; 482-2626, 800-HOLIDAY) 259 rooms, restaurant, lounge, entertainment, indoor pool, exercise center, children under 19 stay free with parents, wheelchair access, airport transportation, A/C, TV, NS rooms, fax, room service, pets OK, laundry service, meeting facilities, senior rates, CC. SGL/DBL$75-$88.

Marriott Hotel (350 East Horsetooth Rd., 80524; 226-5200, 800-548-2536, 800-228-9290) 228 rooms and suites, restaurant, lounge, entertainment, indoor and outdoor pools, exercise center, whirlpools, airport transportation, wheelchair access, TV, A/C, NS rooms, laundry service, gift shop, children free with parents, meeting facilities, senior rates, CC. SGL/DBL$25-$45.

Motel 6 (3900 East Mulberry, 80524; 482-6466, 505-891-6161) pool, free local calls, children under 17 free with parents, NS rooms, A/C, TV, CC. SGL/DBL$36-$44.

National 9 Inn (3634 East Mulberry, 80524; 482-1114, 800-524-9999) 55 rooms, pool, NS rooms, wheelchair access, A/C, TV, children free with parents, senior rates, CC. SGL/DBL$35-$56.

Ramada Inn (3709 East Mulberry, 80524; 493-7800, 800-2-RAMADA) 133 rooms and suites, restaurant, lounge, indoor and outdoor pools, wheelchair access, NS rooms, pets OK, A/C, TV, children under 18 free with parents, room service, laundry facilities, 5 meeting rooms, meeting facilities for 300, senior rates, CC. SGL/DBL$45-$63.

Super 8 Motel (409 Centro Way, 80524; 493-7701, 800-800-8000) 71 rooms and suites, whirlpools, sauna, pets OK, children under 12 free with parents, free local calls, A/C, TV, in-room refrigerators and microwaves, fax, NS rooms, senior rates, wheelchair access, meeting facilities, CC. SGL/DBL$32-$49.

Fort Morgan
Area Code 303

Best Western Park Terrace Motor Hotel (725 Main St., 80701; 867-8256, Fax 867-8257, 800-528-1234) 23 rooms, restaurant, pool, exercise center, children free with parents, A/C, free local calls, NS rooms, TV, laundry facilities, wheelchair access, pets OK, senior rates, meeting facilities, CC. SGL/DBL$40-$68.

Central Motel (201 West Platte Ave., 80701; 867-2401) 17 rooms and suites, pets OK, children free with parents, A/C, TV, VCRs, pets OK, NS rooms, wheelchair access, in-room refrigerators, senior rates, CC. SGL/DBL$40-$58.

Econo Lodge (1409 Barlow Rd., 80701; 867-9481, 800-4-CHOICE) 40 rooms, restaurant, lounge, pool, children under 12 free with parents, pets OK, NS rooms, wheelchair access, A/C, TV, senior rates, CC. SGL/DBL$38-$83.

Madison Hotel (14378 Hwy. 34, 80701; 867-8208) 99 rooms, restaurant, lounge, indoor heated pool, sauna, A/C, TV, NS rooms, wheelchair access, pets OK, CC. SGL/DBL$36-$43.

Super 8 Motel (1220 North Main St., 80701; 867-9443, Fax 867-8658, 800-800-8000) 36 rooms and suites, pets OK, children under 12 free with parents, free local calls, A/C, TV, in-room refrigerators and microwaves, fax, NS rooms, senior rates, wheelchair access, meeting facilities, CC. SGL/DBL$34-$46.

Frisco
Area Code 303

Best Western Lake Dillon Lodge (1201 Summit Blvd., 80443; 668-5094, Fax 668-0571, 800-727-0607, 800-528-1234) 127 rooms and suites, restaurant, lounge, indoor heated pool, exercise center, children free with parents, A/C, NS rooms, TV, laundry facilities, wheelchair access, pets OK, senior rates, meeting facilities, CC. SGL/DBL$60-$125, STS$120-$210.

Galena Street Mountain Inn (106 Galena St., 80443; 668-3224) 15 rooms, whirlpools, TV, NS rooms, wheelchair access, pets OK, CC. SGL/DBL$70-$135.

Holiday Inn (1129 North Summit Blvd., 80443; 668-5000, 800-782-7669, 800-HOLIDAY) 218 rooms, restaurant, lounge, indoor heated pool, exercise center, whirlpools, hot tubs, tennis courts, gift shop, children under 19 free with parents, wheelchair access, A/C, TV, NS rooms, fax, room service, pets OK, laundry service, meeting facilities for 300, senior rates, CC. SGL/DBL$50-$135.

Luxury Inn (1205 North Summit Blvd., 80443; 668-3220, 800-745-1211) 28 rooms, restaurant, pets OK, A/C, TV, NS rooms, wheelchair access, CC. SGL/DBL$35-$65.

Sky View Motel (Frisco 80443; 668-3311) 26 rooms, indoor heated pool, whirlpools, pets OK, TV, NS rooms, CC. SGL/DBL$40-$85.

Snowshoe Motel (Frisco 80443; 668-3444) 37 rooms and efficiencies, restaurant, pets OK, kitchenettes, A/C, TV, NS rooms, wheelchair access, in-room refrigerators, CC. SGL/DBL$30-$65.

Georgetown
Area Code 303

The Lodge at Georgetown (Georgetown 89444; 569-3211) 54 rooms, restaurant, whirlpools, A/C, TV, NS rooms, wheelchair access, VCR, fireplaces, CC. SGL/DBL$45-$65.

Super 8 Motel (1600 Argentine St., 89444; 569-3211, 800-800-8000) 54 rooms and suites, restaurant, whirlpools, game room, pets OK, children under 12 free with parents, free local calls, A/C, TV, in-room refrigerators and microwaves, fax, NS rooms, senior rates, wheelchair access, meeting facilities, CC. SGL/DBL$39-$55.

Glenwood Springs
Area Code 303

Adducci's Inn (1023 Grand Ave., 81601; 945-9341) free breakfast, hot tub, sauna, local transportation, A/C, TV, CC. SGL/DBL$45.

Affordable Inns (Glenwood Springs 81601; 945-8888, Fax 945-6059) 60 rooms and efficiencies, whirlpools, in-room refrigerators and microwaves, A/C, TV, NS rooms, wheelchair access, pets OK, senior rates, CC. SGL/DBL$30-$80.

Best Western Antlers Inn (171 West 6th St., 81601; 945-8535, Fax 945-9388, 800-626-0609, 800-528-1234) 105 rooms and 2-bedroom efficiencies, restaurant, heated pool, exercise center, hot tub, children free with parents, A/C, NS rooms, TV, laundry facilities, wheelchair access, pets OK, senior rates, meeting facilities, CC. SGL/DBL$50-$155.

Best Western Caravan Inn (1826 Grand Ave., 81601; 945-7451, 800-945-5495, 800-528-1234) 68 rooms and 2-bedroom suites, restaurant, pool, exercise center, hot tub, kitchenettes, children free with parents, A/C, NS rooms, TV, laundry facilities, wheelchair access, pets OK, senior rates, meeting facilities, CC. SGL/DBL$50-$90.

Budget Host Motel (51429 Hwy. 6, 81601; 945-5682, 800-283-4678) 22 rooms and suites, restaurant, heated pool, airport transportation, pets OK, laundry facilities, NS rooms, wheelchair access, A/C, TV, senior rates, children free with parents, CC. SGL/DBL$25-$49.

Cedar Lodge Motel (2102 Grand Ave., 81601; 945-6579, 800-341-8000) 49 rooms and 2-bedroom efficiencies, heated pool, whirlpools, sauna, pets OK, A/C, in-room refrigerators, TV, NS rooms, wheelchair access, CC. SGL/DBL$43-$60.

Colonial Inn Motel (Glenwood Springs 81601; 945-6279) 14 rooms, A/C, TV, NS rooms, wheelchair access, pets OK, CC. SGL/DBL$50-$68.

Frontier Lodge (2834 Glen Ave., 81601; 945-5496) 25 rooms and efficiencies, restaurant, A/C, TV, NS rooms, wheelchair access, in-room refrigerators, pets OK, CC. SGL/DBL$40-$65.

Glenwood Motor Inn (141 West 6th St., 81601; 945-5438) 30 rooms, restaurant, whirlpools, pets OK, A/C, TV, NS rooms, wheelchair access, CC. SGL/DBL$35-$65.

Glenwood Springs Hostel (1021 Grand Ave., 81601; 945-8545) kitchenettes, laundry facilities, local transportation. SGL/DBL$10-$20.

The Hideout (1293 Rd. 117, 81601; 945-5621) cabins, kitchenettes, fireplaces, laundry facilities, TV. SGL/DBL$48.

Holiday Inn (51359 Hwy. 6, 81601; 945-8551, Fax 945-1279, 800-332-2233, 800-HOLIDAY) 123 rooms, restaurant, lounge, outdoor pool, exercise center, children under 19 free with parents, wheelchair access, A/C, TV, NS rooms, fax, room service, pets OK, laundry service, meeting facilities for 400, senior rates, CC. SGL/DBL$45-$65.

Hot Springs Lodge (415 6th St., 81601; 945-6571, Fax 945-6683, 800-537-7946) 107 rooms and suites, restaurant, lounge, pool, exercise center, sauna, whirlpools, A/C, TV, NS rooms, pets OK, wheelchair access, in-room refrigerators, laundry facilities, meeting facilities, CC. SGL/DBL$45-$75.

Kaiser House (932 Cooper Ave., 81601; 945-8827) 7 rooms, free breakfast, hot tubs, sauna, NS, local transportation, 1902 home, A/C, TV, CC. SGL/DBL$45-$125.

Knotty Pine Lodge (2706 South Grand Ave., 81601; 945-6446) cabins, TV, NS rooms, fireplace, laundry facilities, wheelchair access, CC. SGL/DBL$50.

National 9 Homestead Inn (52039 Hwy. 6, 81601; 945-8817, 800-456-6685, 800-524-9999) 35 rooms, pool, NS rooms, wheelchair access, A/C, TV, children free with parents, pets OK, senior rates, CC. SGL/DBL$47-$67.

Ponderosa Cottages (51793 Hwy. 6, 81601; 945-5058) cabins, kitchenettes, fireplaces, wheelchair access, TV, local transportation, pets OK, CC. SGL/DBL$43.

Ramada Inn (124 West 6th St., 81601; 945-2500, Fax 945-2530, 800-2-RAMADA) 123 rooms and suites, restaurant, lounge, entertainment, indoor pool, whirlpools, wheelchair access, NS rooms, pets OK, A/C, TV, children under 18 free with parents, VCRs, room service, laundry facilities, meeting facilities, senior rates, CC. SGL/DBL$50-$165.

Red Mountain Inn (51637 Hwy. 6, 81601; 945-6353) cabins, pool, fireplaces, kitchenettes, pets OK, TV, laundry facilities, CC. SGL/DBL$49.

Riverside Cottages (1287 County Rd. 154, 81601; 945-5509) cabins, kitchenettes, TV, fireplaces, laundry facilities. SGL/DBL$36-$46.

Silver Spruce Motel (162 West 6th St., 81601; 945-5458, 800-523-4742) 90 rooms and 2-bedroom suites, whirlpools, fireplaces, A/C, TV, NS rooms, in-room refrigerators and microwaves, VCRs, wheelchair access, pets OK, local transportation, CC. SGL/DBL$30-$70.

Sunlight Bavarian Inn (10252 Hwy. 117, 81601; 945-5225) bed and breakfast, restaurant, free breakfast, A/C, hot tubs, sauna, fireplaces, laundry facilities, local transportation, TV, CC. SGL/DBL$59.

Golden

Area Code 303

Days Inn (15059 West Colfax Ave., 80401; 277-0200, Fax 277-0209, 800-325-2525) 145 rooms and 1- and 2-bedroom suites, restaurant, outdoor pool, exercise center, whirlpools, children free with parents, room service, laundry service, A/C, TV, free local calls, pets OK, local transportation, fax, wheelchair access, NS rooms, 1,800 square feet of meeting and exhibition space, senior rates, CC. SGL/DBL$37-$125.

Dove Bed and Breakfast (711 14th St., 80401; 278-2209) 6 rooms, free breakfast, A/C, 1870s home, antique furnishings, pets OK, airport transportation, TV, CC. SGL/DBL$45-$60.

Holiday Inn (14707 West Colfax, 80401; 279-7611, Fax 78-1651, 800-HOLIDAY) 225 rooms, restaurant, lounge, entertainment, indoor pool, exercise center, children under 19 free with parents, wheelchair access, A/C, TV, NS rooms, local transportation, gift shop, in-room coffee makers, fax, room service, pets OK, laundry service, meeting facilities for 700, senior rates, CC. SGL/DBL$55-$73.

La Quinta Inn (3301 Youngfield Service Rd., 80401; 279-5565, Fax 279-5841, 800-531-5900) 129 rooms, restaurant, free breakfast, lounge, pool, complimentary newspaper, free local calls, fax, laundry service, NS rooms, wheelchair access, pets OK, TV, A/C, meeting facilities, CC. SGL/DBL$45-$60.

Marriott Denver West (1717 Denver West Marriott Blvd., 80401; 279-9100, Fax 271-0205, 800-331-3131) 307 rooms and suites, restaurant, lounge, entertainment, free breakfast, in-room refrigerators, coffee makers, microwaves, laundry facilities, TV, A/C, airport transportation, gift shop, game room, VCRs, pets OK, complimentary newspaper, fireplaces, children free with parents, NS rooms, wheelchair access, meeting facilities, senior rates, CC. SGL/DBL$60-$335.

Granby

Area Code 303

Beacon Landing Motel (Granby 80446; 627-3671, 800-864-4372) 1- and 2-bedrooms and trailer, kitchenettes, TV, fireplace, CC. 1BR$43, 2BR$53-$69.

Broken Arrow Motel (Granby 80446; 887-3532) 12 rooms, A/C, TV, NS rooms, wheelchair access, pets OK, local transportation, CC. SGL/DBL$25-$40.

C Lazy U Ranch (Granby 80446; 887-3344, Fax 887-3917) 45 rooms and cottages, restaurant, lounge, entertainment, pool, exercise center, local transportation, children free with parents, in-room coffee makers, pets OK. SGL/DBL$1,300W-$2,700W.

Circle H Lodge (6732 Hwy. 34, 80446; 887-3955) free breakfast, A/C, TV, CC. SGL/DBL$45-$50.

Drowsy Water Ranch (Granby 80446; 725-3456, 800-845-2292) 17 rooms and cottages, restaurant, heated pool, local transportation, pets OK, children free with parents, A/C, TV, NS rooms, wheelchair access, CC. SGL/DBL$875W-$1,600W.

Gala Marina and Motel (928 Grand County Rd. 64, 80446; 627-3220) 8 rooms, TV, pets OK, boat rentals, water view, CC. SGL/DBL$42-$47.

Little Tree Inn (Granby 80446; 887-2551) 47 rooms and efficiencies, whirlpools, pets OK, A/C, TV, NS rooms, wheelchair access, laundry facilities, senior rates, CC. SGL/DBL$66-$72.

Stillwater Valley Guest Ranch (1001 Country Rd. 452, 80446; 627-3556, 800-GUEST-RA) 2 cabins, TV, CC. SGL/DBL$80.

Grand Junction

Area Code 303

Best Value Inn (718 Horizon Dr., 81506; 243-5080) 138 rooms, outdoor pool, A/C, TV, NS rooms, wheelchair access, meeting facilities, CC. SGL/DBL$33-$50.

Best Western Horizon Inn (754 Horizon Dr., 81506; 245-1410, Fax 245-4039, 800-544-3782, 800-528-1234) 100 rooms, restaurant, free breakfast, lounge, indoor pool, exercise center, spa, sauna, in-room coffee makers, children free with parents, A/C, NS rooms, TV, laundry facilities, wheelchair access, pets OK, senior rates, meeting facilities, CC. SGL/DBL$44-$67.

Best Western Sandman Motel (708 Horizon Dr., 81506; 243-4150, Fax 243-1828, 800-528-1234) 79 rooms, restaurant, indoor pool, exercise center, children free with parents, A/C, NS rooms, TV, laundry facilities, wheelchair access, pets OK, local transportation, senior rates, meeting facilities, CC. SGL/DBL$38-$55.

Budget Host Inn (721 Horizon Dr., 81506; 243-6050, 800-283-4678) 54 rooms, restaurant, heated pool, laundry facilities, NS rooms, wheelchair access, A/C, TV, senior rates, children free with parents, CC. SGL/DBL$28-$45.

Cider House Bed and Breakfast (1126 Grand Ave., 81506; 242-9087) 3 rooms, free breakfast, A/C, TV, CC. SGL/DBL$28-$42.

Columbine Motel (2824 North Ave., 81506; 241-2908) 15 rooms, outdoor pool, pets are OK, A/C, TV, NS rooms, wheelchair access, CC. SGL/DBL$26-$50.

El Palomino Motel (2400 North Ave., 81506; 242-1826) 20 rooms, outdoor pool, A/C, TV, NS rooms, wheelchair access, CC. SGL/DBL$20-$48.

El Rio Rancho Motel (730 Hwy. 50 South, 81506; 242-0256) 18 rooms and efficiencies, A/C, TV, NS rooms, wheelchair access, pets OK, CC. SGL/DBL$30-$50.

Friendship Inn (733 Horizon Dr., 81506; 245-7200, 800-424-4777) 105 rooms, restaurant, pool, exercise center, A/C, TV, pets OK, NS rooms, children free with parents, wheelchair access, room service, airport transportation, meeting facilities, senior rates, CC. SGL/DBL$33-$64.

Gate House Bed and Breakfast (2502 North 1st, 81506; 242-6106) 4 rooms, free breakfast, no pets, A/C, TV, CC. SGL/DBL$46-$68.

Guest House Motel (2425 North 7th, 81506; 242-9571) 22 rooms and efficiencies, A/C, TV, NS rooms, wheelchair access, CC. SGL/DBL$26-$35.

Hilton Hotel (743 Horizon Dr., 81506; 241-8888, Fax 241-8888 ext 160, 800-HILTONS) 264 rooms and suites, restaurant, lounge, entertainment, outdoor pool, exercise center, tennis courts, children free with parents, NS rooms, wheelchair access, pets OK, room service, airport transportation, laundry facilities, A/C, TV, meeting facilities, CC. SGL/DBL$50-$140.

Holiday Inn (755 Horizon Dr., 81506; 243-6790, 800-HOLIDAY) 291 rooms and suites, restaurant, lounge, entertainment, indoor pool, exercise center, children under 19 free with parents, wheelchair access, A/C, airport courtesy car, TV, NS rooms, fax, room service, pets OK, laundry service, meeting facilities for 500, senior rates, CC. SGL/DBL$48-$60.

Howard Johnson Lodge (752 Horizon Dr., 81506; 243-5150, Fax 242-3692, 800-I-GO-HOJO) 100 rooms, restaurant, lounge, pool, exercise center, car rental desk, children free with parents, wheelchair access, NS rooms, TV, A/C, pets OK, room service, laundry facilities, senior rates, meeting facilities, CC. SGL/DBL$40-$60.

Junction Country Inn (861 Grand Ave., 81506; 241-2817) 4 rooms, free breakfast, A/C, TV, CC. SGL/DBL$35-$79.

LeMaster Motel (2858 North Ave., 81506; 243-3230) 75 rooms, restaurant, lounge, outdoor pool, A/C, TV, NS rooms, wheelchair access, pets OK, meeting facilities, CC. SGL/DBL$25-$38.

Melrose Hotel (337 Colorado Ave., 81506; 242-9636, 800-430-4555) 25 rooms, A/C, TV, NS rooms, wheelchair access, CC. SGL/DBL$16-$35.

Motel 6 (776 Horizon Dr., 81506; 243-2628, 505-891-6161) 100 rooms, pool, free local calls, children under 17 free with parents, NS rooms, wheelchair access, pets OK, A/C, TV, CC. SGL/DBL$38-$46.

Peachtree Inn (1600 North Ave., 81506; 245-5770, 800-525-0030) 75 rooms, outdoor pool, restaurant, lounge, pets OK, kitchenettes, A/C, TV, NS rooms, wheelchair access, CC. SGL/DBL$25-$38.

Prospector Motel (547 Hwy. 50 South, 81506; 241-3020, 800-453-9254) 100 rooms, restaurant, lounge, outdoor pool, pets OK, A/C, TV, NS rooms, wheelchair access, CC. SGL/DBL$32-$68.

Ramada Inn (2790 Crossroads Blvd., 81506; 241-8411, Fax 241-1077, 800-2-RAMADA) 157 rooms and suites, restaurant, lounge, entertainment, indoor pool, whirlpools, airport transportation, wheelchair access, NS rooms, pets OK, A/C, TV, children under 18 free with parents, room service, laundry facilities, meeting facilities, senior rates, CC. SGL/DBL$50-$78.

Riviera Motel (125 North Ave., 81506; 245-6754) 11 rooms and efficiencies, A/C, TV, NS rooms, wheelchair access, CC. SGL/DBL$22-$38.

Super 8 Motel (728 Horizon Dr., 81506; 248-8080, 800-800-8000) 132 rooms and suites, restaurant, outdoor pool, pets OK, children under 12 free with parents, free local calls, A/C, TV, in-room refrigerators and microwaves, fax, NS rooms, senior rates, wheelchair access, meeting facilities, CC. SGL/DBL$33-$52.

Trails End Motel (2925 North Ave., 81506; 242-3243) 11 rooms, restaurant, kitchenettes, A/C, TV, NS rooms, wheelchair access, CC. SGL/DBL$20-$35.

Travelers Inn (704 Horizon Dr., 81505; 245-3080, 800-633-8300) 125 rooms, A/C, TV, NS rooms, wheelchair access, CC. SGL/DBL$30-$44.

Value Lodge (104 White Ave., 81505; 242-0651) 45 rooms, restaurant, outdoor heated pool, pets OK, A/C, TV, NS rooms, wheelchair access, CC. SGL/DBL$32-$45.

West Gate Inn (2210 Hwy. 6, 81505; 241-3020, Fax 243-4516, 800-453-9253) 100 rooms, restaurant, lounge, heated pool, pets OK, laundry facilities, A/C, TV, NS rooms, wheelchair access, CC. SGL/DBL$30-$50.

. Grand Lake

Area Code 303

Rental and Reservation Services:

Grand Realty (Box 570, Grand Lake 80447; 627-3905) rental homes, town-houses and condos.

ReMax Resorts of Grand Lake (728 Grand Ave., 80447; 627-8001) rental cabins and homes.

Sun Valley Lake Retreat (6437 South Heritage Place West, Englewood CO 80111; 303-740-7441) rental homes.

□□□

Big Horn Lodge (613 Grand Ave., 80447; 627-8101, 800-621-5923) 20 rooms, restaurant, hot tubs, pets OK, A/C, TV, wheelchair access, CC. SGL/DBL$45-$75.

Driftwood Lodge (Grand Lake 80447; 627-3654) 17 rooms and 2-room suites, outdoor heated pool, hot tub, jacuzzi, kitchenettes, local transportation, pets OK, in-room refrigerators, A/C, TV, CC. SGL/DBL$49-$75.

Eagle Landing Condominiums (420 Ellsworth St., 80447; 627-3425) 1- and 2-bedroom condominiums, sauna, spa, fireplace, kitchenettes, A/C, TV, laundry facilities, pets OK, CC. 1BR$80-$100, 2BR$110-$150.

Grand Lake Lodge (Grand Lake 80447; 627-3967) 1- to 8-bedroom cabins, restaurant, lounge, entertainment, outdoor heated pool, gift shop, A/C, kitchenettes, pets OK, CC. SGL/DBL$125-$345.

Grandview Lodge (12429 Hwy. 34, 80447; 627-3914) 66 rooms and cabins, restaurant, lounge, entertainment, heated pool, local transportation, gift shop, game room, pets OK, TV, in-room refrigerators and microwaves, pets OK, children free with parents, meeting facilities, CC. SGL/DBL$40-$200.

Lake Forest Estates and Lodge (Grand Lake 80447; 800-800-6096) rental homes, pool, whirlpools, exercise center, hot tubs, kitchenettes, laundry facilities, TV, fireplaces, CC. SGL/DBL$150-$200.

Lemmon Lodge (Grand Lake 80447; 627-3314) 1- to 5-bedroom cabins, kitchenettes, NS rooms, pets OK, beach, TV, CC. SGL/DBL$50-$200.

Lonesome Dove Cottages (Grand Lake 80447; 627-8019) cottages, kitchenettes, TV, CC. SGL/DBL$40-$60.

Nature Valley Ranch (County Rd. 4480, 80447; 627-3425, 800-252-3425) 1- and 2-bedroom cabins, kitchenettes, pets OK, TV, CC. 1BR$70-$80, 2BR$100-$140.

Rocky Mountain Cabins (Grand Lake 80447; 627-3061) cabins, kitchenettes, CC. SGL/DBL$75-$155.

Soda Springs Ranch and Resort (9921 Hwy. 34, 80447; 627-8125) 1- to 3-bedroom condominiums, kitchenettes, pets OK, A/C, TV, children free with parents, CC. 1BR$57-$102, 2BR$88-$133, 3BR$110-$175.

Victoria Cottage (Grand Lake 80447; 627-8027) 2-room cabin, kitchenette, fireplace, CC. SGL/DBL$60.

Western Hills Cottages (12082 Hwy. 34, 80447; 627-3632) 8 1- and 2-bedroom cabins, fireplace, kitchenettes, water view, TV, CC. 1BR$50-$60, 2BR$70.

Western Riviera (419 Garfield Ave., 80447; 627-3580) 22 rooms and cabins, restaurant, fireplace, A/C, TV, NS rooms, kitchenettes, wheelchair access, pets OK, CC. SGL/DBL$55-$95.

Winding River Resort (Grand Lake 80447; 627-3215) 1-bedroom cabins, antique furnishings, TV, CC. SGL/DBL$65-$80.

Sun Valley Lake Estates (Grand Lake 80447; 627-3356) rental 3-bedroom home, kitchenette, TV, VCR, fireplace, CC. SGL/DBL$120-$750W.

Greely
Area Code 303

Best Western Ramkota Inn (701 8th St., 80631; 353-8444, Fax 353-4269, 800-528-1234) 148 rooms, restaurant, lounge, indoor pool, exercise center, in-room coffee makers, children free with parents, A/C, NS rooms, TV, laundry facilities, wheelchair access, pets OK, senior rates, meeting facilities, CC. SGL/DBL$52-$75.

Greeley Inn (721 13th St., 80631; 353-3216) 38 rooms, restaurant, pets OK, heated pool, A/C, TV, NS rooms, wheelchair access, CC. SGL/DBL$35-$45.

Holiday Inn (609 8th Ave., 80631; 356-3000, 800-HOLIDAY) 100 rooms, restaurant, lounge, heated pool, free local calls, children under 19 free with parents, wheelchair access, A/C, TV, NS rooms, fax, room service, pets OK, laundry service, meeting facilities for 300, senior rates, CC. SGL/DBL$55-$70.

Green Mountain Falls

Area Code 303

Columbine Inn (10755 Ute Pass Ave., 80819; 684-9063) 7 rooms, restaurant, A/C, TV, NS rooms, CC. SGL/DBL$28-$33.

Cottage-by-the-Stream (Green Mountain Falls 80819; 684-9759) 2- and 3-bedroom cottages, kitchenettes, fireplaces, CC. SGL/DBL$49-$55.

Hi-Vue Motel and Campground (19909 West Hwy. 24, 80819; 684-9044) 15 rooms, pool, A/C, TV, NS rooms, wheelchair access, pets OK, CC. SGL/DBL$35-$75.

Just-A-Mere Cottages (Green Mountain Falls 80819; 684-9797) 2- and 3-bedroom cottages, laundry facilities, kitchenettes, fireplaces, CC. SGL/DBL$45-$55.

Lakeside Cottages (10535 Foster Ave., 80819; 684-9576) 8 rooms, A/C, TV, NS rooms, wheelchair access, CC. SGL/DBL$45-$100.

Millwell Motel (1222 Manitou Ave., 80819; 685-9363) 19 rooms and 2-bedroom cottages, A/C, TV, NS rooms, wheelchair access, CC. SGL/DBL$40-$50.

Outlook Lodge Bed and Breakfast (6975 Howard St., 80819; 684-2303) 9 rooms, free breakfast, A/C, TV, NS, antique furnishings, pets OK, CC. SGL/DBL$45-$70.

Red Wing Motel (56 El Paso Blvd., 80819; 685-5656, 800-733-9547) 27 rooms, pool, A/C, TV, kitchenettes, NS rooms, wheelchair access, CC. SGL/DBL$46-$79.

Super 8 Motel (229 Manitou Ave., 80819; 685-5368, 800-800-8000) 38 rooms and suites, pool, pets OK, children under 12 free with parents, free local calls, A/C, TV, in-room refrigerators and microwaves, fax, NS rooms, senior rates, wheelchair access, meeting facilities, CC. SGL/DBL$60-$90.

Greenwood Village

Area Code 303

Motel 6 (9201 East Arapahoe Rd., 80111; 790-8220, 505-891-6161) 139 rooms, pool, free local calls, children under 17 free with parents, NS rooms, wheelchair access, pets OK, A/C, TV, CC. SGL/DBL$36-$56.

Gunnison
Area Code 303

Best Western Tomichi Village Inn (Gunnison 81230; 641-1131, Fax 641-1131, 800-528-1234) 49 rooms, restaurant, free breakfast, lounge, pool, exercise center, children free with parents, A/C, NS rooms, TV, laundry facilities, wheelchair access, local transportation, pets OK, senior rates, meeting facilities, CC. SGL/DBL$40-$75.

Days Inn (701 West Hwy. 50, 81230; 641-0608, Fax 641-2854, 800-325-2525) 45 rooms and suites, free breakfast, outdoor pool, children free with parents, room service, laundry service, A/C, TV, free local calls, pets OK, fax, wheelchair access, NS rooms, senior rates, CC. SGL/DBL$30-$45.

Friendship Inn West (400 East Tomichi, 81230; 641-1288, 800-424-4777) 50 rooms and suites, free breakfast, indoor heated pool, exercise center, whirlpools, A/C, TV, pets OK, NS rooms, children free with parents, wheelchair access, meeting facilities, senior rates, CC. SGL/DBL$40-$100.

Harmel's Guest Ranch (Gunnison 81230; 641-1740) 44 rooms, suites and cottages, restaurant, lounge, heated pool, pets OK, in-room refrigerators, laundry facilities, gift shop, game room, A/C, TV, NS rooms, wheelchair access, modified American plan available, CC. SGL/DBL$85-$170.

Hylander Inn (412 East Tomichi Ave., 81230; 641-0700) 23 rooms, restaurant, A/C, TV, NS rooms, wheelchair access, airport transportation, pets OK, CC. SGL/DBL$30-$58.

Mary Lawrence Inn (601 North Tylor St., 81230; 641-3343) 7 rooms and suites, free breakfast, 1880s inn, TV, NS rooms, wheelchair access, airport courtesy car, NS, CC. SGL/DBL$55-$120.

Powderhorn Ranch (Powderhorn Rd., 81230; 641-0220) 13 cabins, heated pool, whirlpools, kitchenettes, airport transportation, pets OK, in-room refrigerators, TV, wheelchair access, CC. SGL/DBL$720W-$1,550W.

Ramada Inn (1001 West Rio Grande, 81230; 641-2804, 800-2-RAMADA) indoor pool, sauna, wheelchair access, NS rooms, pets OK, A/C, TV, children under 18 free with parents, room service, laundry facilities, meeting facilities, senior rates, CC. SGL/DBL$38-$68, STS$60-$77.

Super 8 Motel (411 East Tomichi, 81230; 641-3068, Fax 641-1332, 800-800-8000) 49 rooms and suites, pets OK, children under 12 free with parents, free local calls, A/C, TV, in-room refrigerators and microwaves, fax, NS rooms, senior rates, wheelchair access, meeting facilities, CC. SGL/DBL$32-$63.

Water Wheel Inn (Gunnison 81230; 641-1650, 800-642-1650) 53 rooms, restaurant, free breakfast, whirlpools, exercise center, airport courtesy car, pets OK, kitchenettes, in-room refrigerators, NS, 1880s inn, CC. SGL/DBL$36-$73.

Waunita Hot Springs (8007 Hwy. 887, 81230; 641-1266) 22 rooms and 2-bedroom efficiencies, restaurant, heated pool, American plan available, pets OK, local transportation, game room, NS, A/C, laundry facilities, TV, NS, wheelchair access, CC. SGL/DBL$720W-$1,760W.

Gypsum
Area Code 303

7-W Guest Ranch (3412 City Rd. 151, 81637; 524-9328) cabins, restaurant, hot tub, sauna, local transportation, fireplaces, A/C, TV, NS rooms, wheelchair access, CC. SGL/DBL$139.

Henderson
Area Code 303

Super 8 Motel (9051 I-76, 80640; 287-8888, Fax 287-8881, 800-800-8000) 59 rooms and suites, pets OK, children under 12 free with parents, free local calls, A/C, TV, in-room refrigerators and microwaves, fax, NS rooms, senior rates, wheelchair access, meeting facilities, CC. SGL/DBL$34-$45.

Hesperus
Area Code 303

Blue Lake Ranch (16919 Hwy. 140, 81326; 385-4537) 7 rooms and 3-bedroom cabin, free breakfast, hot tub, whirlpools, pets OK, A/C, TV, private baths, fireplace, CC. SGL/DBL$85-$225.

Hot Sulphur Springs
Area Code 303

Canyon Motel (221 Byers Ave., 80451; 725-3395) 12 rooms, TV, NS rooms, wheelchair access, in-room refrigerators, pets OK, senior rates, CC. SGL/DBL$29-$45.

Hotchkiss
Area Code 303

Comfort Inn (406 Hwy. 133, 81419; 872-2200, 800-221-2222) 24 rooms, restaurant, wheelchair access, pets OK, laundry facilities, children free with parents, A/C, TV, NS rooms, wheelchair access, CC. SGL/DBL$30-$45.

Idaho Springs

Area Code 303

Argo Motor Inn (2622 Colorado Blvd., 80452; 567-4473) 22 rooms and efficiencies, hot tubs, fireplaces, A/C, TV, NS rooms, kitchenettes, pets OK, wheelchair access, laundry facilities, CC. SGL/DBL$45-$80.

H&H Motor Lodge (2445 Colorado Blvd., 80452; 567-2838, 800-445-2893) 19 rooms, hot tubs, sauna, kitchenettes, A/C, TV, in-room refrigerators, pets OK, NS rooms, wheelchair access, CC. SGL/DBL$30-$75.

Peoriana Motel (2901 Colorado Blvd., 80452; 567-2021) 31 rooms and efficiencies, restaurant, whirlpools, hot tubs, A/C, TV, NS rooms, pets OK, wheelchair access, CC. SGL/DBL$25-$35.

Rest Haven (2631 Colorado Blvd., 80452; 567-2242) spa, kitchenettes, A/C, TV, NS rooms, wheelchair access, CC. SGL/DBL$36-$48.

Riverside Bed and Breakfast (2130 Riverside Dr., 80452; 567-9032) 1- to 3-bedroom suites, free breakfast, A/C, TV, CC. SGL/DBL$40-$80.

Kremmling

Area Code 303

Latigo Ranch (201 Hwy. 1911, 80459; 724-9008, 800-227-9655) 10 cottages, restaurant, entertainment, heated pool, whirlpools, exercise center, children free with parents, gift shop, local transportation, laundry facilities, in-room coffee makers, A/C, TV, NS rooms, gift shop, American plan available, wheelchair access, game room, in-room refrigerators, pets OK, CC. SGL/DBL$90-$400.

La Junta

Area Code 719

Days Inn (27882 Frontage Rd., 81050; 384-4408, Fax 384-2236, 800-325-2525) 25 rooms and suites, free breakfast, children free with parents, room service, laundry service, A/C, TV, free local calls, pets OK, fax, wheelchair access, NS rooms, senior rates, CC. SGL/DBL$29-$45.

Friendship Inn (1325 East 3rd St., 81050; 384-2571, 800-424-4777) 30 rooms, pool, exercise center, A/C, TV, pets OK, NS rooms, children free with parents, wheelchair access, senior rates, CC. SGL/DBL$33-$45.

Stagecoach Inn (905 West 3rd St., 81050; 384-5476, Fax 384-9091) 30 rooms, free breakfast, pool, pets OK, children free with parents, A/C, TV, NS rooms, wheelchair access, CC. SGL/DBL$33-$40.

Lake City
Area Code 303

Cinnamon Inn (426 Gunnison Ave., 81235; 944-2641) 5 rooms and suites, free breakfast, 1870s inn, A/C, TV, NS, pets OK, wheelchair access, CC. SGL/DBL$60-$85.

Lakeview Resort (Lake City 81235; 944-2401, 800-645-0170) 1-, 2- and 3-bedroom cabins, kitchenettes, wheelchair access, CC. 1BR$65, 2BR$75, 3BR$90-$95.

Lakewood
Area Code 303

Denver Lakewood Inn (7150 West Colfax, 80215; 238-1251, Fax 238-7504, 800-321-7187) 122 rooms, restaurant, lounge, outdoor heated pool, children free with parents, pets OK, NS rooms, laundry service, fax, CC. 25 minutes to the airport, CC. SGL$32-$40, DBL$36-$46.

Econo Lodge West (715 Kipling St., 80215; 232-5000, 800-4-CHOICE) 145 rooms, free breakfast, pool, children under 12 free with parents, pets OK, in-room coffee makers, NS rooms, wheelchair access, A/C, TV, senior rates, CC. SGL/DBL$39-$47.

Just Arnolds (1165 Holland St., 80215) rental 3-bedroom home, kitchenette, laundry facilities, fireplace, TV, CC. SGL/DBL$110.

Lamar
Area Code 719

Best Western Cow Palace Inn (1301 North Main St., 81052; 336-7753, Fax 336-9598, 800-678-0344, 800-528-1234) 102 rooms, restaurant, indoor pool, exercise center, jacuzzi, children free with parents, A/C, NS rooms, TV, laundry facilities, wheelchair access, pets OK, senior rates, meeting facilities, CC. SGL/DBL$50-$68.

Blue Spruce Motel (1801 South Main St., 81052; 336-7454) 24 rooms, heated pool, A/C, TV, NS rooms, wheelchair access, pets OK, CC. SGL/DBL$28-$35.

El Mar Budget Host Motel (1210 South Main St., 81052; 336-4331, 800-283-4678) 40 rooms, restaurant, heated pool, laundry facilities, NS rooms, wheelchair access, A/C, airport transportation, pets OK, TV, senior rates, children free with parents, CC. SGL/DBL$26-$32.

Super 8 Motel (1201 North Main St., 81052; 336-3427, Fax 336-3427 ext 223, 800-800-8000) 43 rooms and suites, game room, pets OK, children under 12 free with parents, free local calls, A/C, TV, in-room refrigerators and microwaves, fax, NS rooms, senior rates, wheelchair access, meeting facilities, CC. SGL/DBL$29-$42.

Las Animas
Area Code 719

Best Western Bent's Fort Inn (81054; 456-0011, 800-528-1234) 38 rooms, restaurant, pool, exercise center, children free with parents, A/C, NS rooms, TV, laundry facilities, wheelchair access, pets OK, airport transportation, room service, meeting facilities, senior rates, CC. SGL/DBL$35-$65.

Leadville
Area Code 719

AAA Pan Ark Lodge (Leadville 80461; 486-1063, 800-443-1063) 48 rooms and efficiencies, pets OK, laundry facilities, fireplaces, A/C, TV, NS rooms, wheelchair access, CC. SGL/DBL$45-$55.

Delaware Hotel (700 Harrison, 80461; 486-1418, 800-748-2004) 36 rooms and suites, restaurant, free breakfast, private baths, hot tubs, A/C, TV, NS rooms, wheelchair access, CC. SGL/DBL$50-$65.

Leadville Country Inn (127 East 8th, 80461; 486-2354, 800-748-2354) free breakfast, private baths, hot tubs, NS, A/C, TV, CC. SGL/DBL$56-$76.

Peri and Ed's Mountain Hideaway (201 West 8th, 80461; 486-0716, 800-933-3715) 6 rooms and suites, free breakfast, hot tubs, A/C, TV, CC. SGL/DBL$40-$60.

Silver King Motor Inn (2020 North Poplar, 80461; 486-2610) 56 rooms, restaurant, lounge, laundry facilities, A/C, TV, NS rooms, wheelchair access, senior rates, CC. SGL/DBL$45-$60.

Timberline Motel (216 Harrison Ave., 80461; 486-1876, 800-352-1876) 15 rooms, pets OK, A/C, TV, in-room refrigerators, NS rooms, wheelchair access, CC. SGL/DBL$35-$45.

Woodhaven Manor (807 Spruce St., 80461; 486-0109, 800-748-2570) 4 rooms, free breakfast, A/C, TV, private baths, antique furnishings, CC. SGL/DBL$40-$80, DBL$50-$90.

Limon
Area Code 719

Econo Lodge (I-70 and Hwy. 24, 80828; 775-2867, 800-4-CHOICE) 47 rooms, children under 12 free with parents, pets OK, NS rooms, wheelchair access, A/C, TV, senior rates, CC. SGL/DBL$37-$67.

Limon Inn (250 East Main St., 80828; 775-2821) 40 rooms, A/C, TV, NS rooms, wheelchair access, pets OK, CC. SGL/DBL$34-$40.

MidWest Country Inn (Limon 80828; 775-2373) 30 rooms and suites, A/C, TV, NS rooms, wheelchair access, pets OK, CC. SGL/DBL$30-$44.

Preferred Motor Inn (Limon 80828; 775-2385, 800-341-8000) 42 rooms, indoor heated pool, sauna, whirlpools, pets OK, game room, A/C, TV, NS rooms, wheelchair access, CC. SGL/DBL$32-$56.

Red Carpet Inn (158 East Main St., 80828; 775-2385, 800-251-1962) indoor heated pool, whirlpools, children free with parents, TV, A/C, NS rooms, free local calls, pets OK, game room, meeting facilities, senior rates, CC. SGL/DBL$40-$58.

Safari Motel (637 Main St., 80828; 775-2363) 28 rooms and 2-bedroom efficiencies, restaurant, heated pool, laundry facilities, pets OK, A/C, TV, NS rooms, wheelchair access, CC. SGL/DBL$35-$44.

Super 8 Motel (Limon 80828; 775-2889, 800-800-8000) 31 rooms and suites, pets OK, children under 12 free with parents, free local calls, A/C, TV, in-room refrigerators and microwaves, fax, NS rooms, senior rates, wheelchair access, meeting facilities, CC. SGL/DBL$31-$50.

Longmont

Area Code 303

Briarwood Inn (1228 North Main St., 80501; 776-6622) 17 rooms, whirlpools, laundry facilities, pets OK, A/C, TV, NS rooms, wheelchair access, in-room refrigerators, CC. SGL/DBL$35-$55.

Budget Host Inn (3815 Hwy. 119, 80501; 776-8700, Fax 776-8700, 800-283-4678) 68 rooms, restaurant, indoor heated pool, game room, laundry facilities, NS rooms, wheelchair access, A/C, airport transportation, pets OK, TV, senior rates, children free with parents, CC. SGL/DBL$29-$49.

Raintree Plaza Hotel (1900 Diagonal Hwy., 80501; 776-2000, Fax 776-2000) 151 rooms, outdoor heated pool, exercise center, whirlpools, in-room refrigerators, pets OK, laundry facilities, airport transportation, A/C, TV, NS rooms, wheelchair access, CC. SGL/DBL$95-$100.

Super 8 Motel (2446 North Main St., 80501; 772-8106, 800-800-8000) 64 rooms and suites, pets OK, children under 12 free with parents, free local calls, A/C, TV, in-room refrigerators and microwaves, fax, NS rooms, senior rates, wheelchair access, meeting facilities, CC. SGL/DBL$37-$48.

Loveland
Area Code 303

Best Western Coach House (I-25 and Hwy. 34, 80537; 667-7810, Fax 667-1047, 800-528-1234) 88 rooms, restaurant, lounge, indoor and outdoor pools, exercise center, whirlpools, children free with parents, A/C, NS rooms, TV, laundry facilities, wheelchair access, pets OK, senior rates, meeting facilities, CC. SGL/DBL$33-$66.

Budget Host (2716 Southeast Frontage Rd., 80537; 667-5202, 800-283-4678) 31 rooms and efficiencies, restaurant, heated pool, laundry facilities, NS rooms, wheelchair access, A/C, TV, pets OK, in-room coffee makers, airport transportation, children free with parents, senior rates, CC. SGL/DBL$25-$31.

The Lovelander Bed and Breakfast (217 West 4th St., 80537; 669-0798) 9 rooms, free breakfast, restaurant, whirlpools, NS, pets OK, private baths, antique furnishings, A/C, TV, pets OK, CC. SGL/DBL$60-$110.

Super 8 Motel (1655 East Eisenhower Blvd., 80537; 663-7000, 800-800-8000) 48 rooms and suites, restaurant, pets OK, children under 12 free with parents, free local calls, A/C, TV, in-room refrigerators and microwaves, fax, NS rooms, senior rates, wheelchair access, meeting facilities, CC. SGL/DBL$30-$49.

Lyons
Area Code 303

Peaceful Valley Lodge (Lyons 80540; 747-2881, Fax 747-2167, 800-955-6343) 52 rooms and 2- and 3-bedroom suites, restaurant, lounge, indoor heated pool, sauna, whirlpools, tennis courts, laundry facilities, TV, NS rooms, wheelchair access, pets OK, CC. SGL/DBL$995W-$2,250W.

Mancos
Area Code 303

Blue Spruce Motel (40700 Hwy. 160, 81328; 533-7073) 12 rooms and efficiencies, A/C, TV, NS rooms, wheelchair access, CC. SGL/DBL$27-$50.

Echo Basin Dude Ranch (Mancos 81328; 533-7800, 800-426-1890) 18 rooms, pool, American plan, A/C, TV, NS rooms, wheelchair access, CC. SGL/DBL$280W-$420W.

Enchanted Mesa Motel (862 West Grand Ave., 81328; 533-7729) 10 rooms and efficiencies, A/C, TV, NS rooms, wheelchair access, CC. SGL/DBL$25-$43.

Lake Mancos Guest Ranch (Mancos 81328; 533-7900, 800-325-WHOA) 17 rooms, outdoor pool, American plan, A/C, TV, NS rooms, laundry facilities, wheelchair access, CC. SGL/DBL$70-$90.

Lost Canyon Lake Lodge (15472 Hwy. 35, 81328; 882-4913) free breakfast, A/C, TV, CC. SGL/DBL$65-$75.

Mesa Verde Motel (191 West Railroad Ave., 81328; 533-7741, 800-825-MESA) 15 rooms and efficiencies, restaurant, whirlpools, A/C, TV, NS rooms, wheelchair access, CC. SGL/DBL$26-$46.

Ponderosa Cabins (14050 County Rd., 81328; 882-7396) 3 rooms, free breakfast, A/C, TV, CC. SGL/DBL$40.

Tucker's Mountain Meadows (37951 Hwy. 184, 81328; 533-7664) 5 rooms, laundry facilities, A/C, TV, NS rooms, wheelchair access, CC. SGL/DBL$85-$125.

Manitou Springs
Area Code 719

Rental and Reservation Services:

Naturenest Cabin Rentals (636-3637) rental cabins

□□□

Alpine Motel (45 Manitou Ave., 80829; 685-5455, 800-289-5455) 25 rooms and efficiencies, pool, kitchenettes, A/C, TV, NS rooms, wheelchair access, CC. SGL/DBL$38-$70.

Beckers Lane Lodge (115 Beckers Lane, 80829; 685-1866) heated pool, A/C, TV, NS rooms, wheelchair access, CC. SGL/DBL$40-$50.

Black Forest Bed and Breakfast (11170 Black Forest, 80829; 495-4208) 4 rooms and suites, pool, exercise center, sauna, free breakfast, A/C, TV, private baths, fireplaces, wheelchair access, kitchenettes, CC. SGL/DBL$65-$85.

Budget Host Alpine Motel (45 Manitou Ave., 80829; 685-5455, 800-283-4678) 25 rooms, heated pool, laundry facilities, NS rooms, wheelchair access, A/C, TV, senior rates, children free with parents, CC. SGL/DBL$28-$58.

Cottonwood Court (120 Manitou Ave., 80829; 685-1312) 24 rooms, A/C, TV, NS rooms, pets OK, kitchenettes, wheelchair access, CC. SGL/DBL$35-$50.

Dillon Motel (134 Manitou Ave., 80839; 685-5225) 18 rooms, pool, A/C, TV, NS rooms, wheelchair access, CC. SGL/DBL$28-$65.

Eagle Motel (423 Manitou Ave., 80829; 685-5467, 800-872-2285) 25 rooms, spa, pets OK, A/C, TV, NS rooms, wheelchair access, CC. SGL/DBL$52-$72.

El Colorado Lodge (23 Manitou Ave., 80829; 685-5485, Fax 685-4645, 800-782-2246) 27 rooms and cabins, heated pool, kitchenettes, fireplaces, A/C, kitchenettes, fireplaces, TV, NS rooms, wheelchair access, CC. SGL/DBL$37-$78.

Foothills Lodge (626 Manitou Ave., 80829; 685-5616) 13 rooms, A/C, TV, NS rooms, wheelchair access, kitchenettes, pets OK, CC. SGL/DBL$32-$75.

Green Will Motel (328 Manitou Ave., 80829; 685-9997) 14 rooms, pets OK, kitchenettes, TV, NS rooms, wheelchair access, CC. SGL/DBL$28-$95.

Grey's Avenue Hotel (711 Manitou Ave., 80829; 685-1277) 10 rooms, free breakfast, private baths, fireplace, children over 10 welcome, NS rooms, meeting facilities, CC. SGL/DBL$45-$70.

LaFon Motel (123 Manitou Ave., 80829; 685-5488) 53 rooms, heated pool, kitchenettes, A/C, TV, NS rooms, wheelchair access, CC. SGL/DBL$38-$56.

McLaughlin Lodge (183 Crystal Park Rd., 80829; 685-5278) 20 rooms, A/C, TV, NS rooms, wheelchair access, pets OK, fireplaces, kitchenettes, CC. SGL/DBL$50W-$125W.

Onaledge Bed and Breakfast Inn (336 El Paso Blvd., 80829; 685-4265, 800-530-8253) 6 rooms, free breakfast, hot tubs, A/C, children over 10 welcome, fireplaces, TV, private baths, antique furnishings, CC. SGL/DBL$75-$125.

Prickly Pear Cottage (126 Via Vallecito, 80829; 685-5899) 1 suite, private bath, fireplace, kitchenettes, children over 7 welcome, A/C, TV, NS rooms, wheelchair access, CC. SGL/DBL$90-$95.

Red Crags Bed and Breakfast (302 El Paso Blvd., 80829; 685-1920) 6 rooms, free breakfast, hot tub, NS rooms, 1870 home, private baths, fireplaces, A/C, TV, CC. SGL/DBL$75-$150.

Red Eagle Mountain Bed and Breakfast Inn (616 Ruxton Ave., 80829; 685-4541; 800-686-8801) 3 rooms, free breakfast, hot tub, A/C, TV, fireplace, pets OK, in-room refrigerators and microwaves, private baths, CC. SGL/DBL$70-$80.

Red Stone Castle Bed and Breakfast Inn (Manitou Springs 80829; 685-5080) 1 rooms, free breakfast, A/C, TV, private baths, CC. SGL/DBL$90-$130.

Red Wing Motel (El Paso Blvd., 80829; 685-9547) 27 rooms, heated pool, kitchenettes, A/C, TV, NS rooms, wheelchair access, CC. SGL/DBL$42-$56.

Santa Fe Motel (3 Manitou Ave., 80829; 475-8185) 3 1- and 2-bedroom homes, heated pool, hot tub, kitchenettes, fireplace, A/C, TV, NS rooms, wheelchair access, CC. SGL/DBL$85-$150.

Silver Saddle Motel (215 Manitou Ave., 80829; 685-5611, 800-772-3353) 54 rooms, heated pool, hot tubs, A/C, TV, NS rooms, wheelchair access, CC. SGL/DBL$70-$105.

Skyway Motel (311 Manitou Ave., 80829; 685-5991) 14 rooms, A/C, TV, NS rooms, wheelchair access, pets OK, kitchenettes, CC. SGL/DBL$35-$60.

Super 8 Motel (229 Manitou Ave., 80829; 685-5898, Fax 685-5498, 800-800-8000) 38 rooms and suites, outdoor heated pool, pets OK, children under 12 free with parents, free local calls, A/C, TV, in-room refrigerators and microwaves, fax, NS rooms, senior rates, wheelchair access, meeting facilities, CC. SGL/DBL$50-$74.

Timber Lodge 3627 West Colorado Ave., 80829; 636-3941, 800-448-6762) 1- and 2-bedroom cabins, outdoor heated pool, kitchenettes, TV, NS rooms, wheelchair access, CC. SGL/DBL$2BR$45-$55, 2BR$68.

Town and Country Cottages (123 Crystal Park Rd., 80829; 685-5427, 800-685-5427) 10 cabins, pool, TV, NS rooms, wheelchair access, fireplaces, kitchenettes, CC. SGL/DBL$59-$80.

Two Sisters Inn (10 Otoe Pl., 80829; 685-9684) 5 rooms and cottages, free breakfast, private baths, fireplace, 1919 home, private baths, NS, pets OK, TV, CC. SGL/DBL$59-$90.

Ute Pass Motel (1128 West Manitou Ave., 80829; 850-5171, 800-845-9762, 800-845-9762) 17 rooms, kitchenettes, A/C, TV, NS rooms, wheelchair access, CC. SGL/DBL$41-$81.

Victoria's Keep (202 Ruxton Ave., 80829; 685-5354) 4 rooms, free breakfast, spa, A/C, private baths, fireplace, NS rooms, TV, CC. SGL/DBL$65-$125.

Villa Motel (481 Manitou Ave., 80829; 685-5492, 800-341-8000) 47 rooms, heated pool, kitchenettes, A/C, TV, NS rooms, wheelchair access, in-room coffee makers, pets OK, in-room coffee makers, CC. SGL/DBL$35-$84.

Western Cabins Resort (106 Beckers Lane, 80829; 685-5755, 800-873-4533) 11 cabins, heated pool, laundry facilities, A/C, TV, NS rooms, wheelchair access, CC. SGL/DBL$45-$89.

Wheeler House (36 Park Ave., 80829; 685-4100) 1- and 2-bedroom suites, heated pool, kitchenettes, A/C, TV, NS rooms, wheelchair access, meeting facilities, CC. SGL/DBL$31-$89.

Mesa
Area Code 303

Wagon Wheel Motel (1090 Hwy. 65, 81643; 268-5224) 8 rooms, restaurant, whirlpool tub, A/C, TV, NS rooms, wheelchair access, pets OK, laundry facilities, CC. SGL/DBL$40-$45.

Mesa Verde National Park
Area Code 303

Far View Lodge (Mesa Verde National Park 81330; 529-4421) 150 rooms, restaurant, pets OK, in-room refrigerators, TV, gift shop, NS rooms, wheelchair access, CC. SGL/DBL$75-$85.

Monarch
Area Code 719

Monarch Mountain Lodge (Monarch 81227; 539-2581, Fax 539-3909, 800-332-3668) 100 rooms and suites, restaurant, lounge, indoor heated pool, whirlpools, tennis courts, laundry facilities, pets OK, VCRs, TV, NS rooms, wheelchair access, CC. SGL/DBL$40-$100.

Monte Vista
Area Code 719

Best Western Movie Manor Motor Inn (2830 West Hwy. 160, 81144; 852-5921, Fax 852-0122, 800-528-1234) 60 rooms, restaurant, free breakfast, lounge, pool, exercise center, children free with parents, A/C, NS rooms, TV, laundry facilities, wheelchair access, pets OK, senior rates, meeting facilities, CC. SGL/DBL$42-$75.

Comfort Inn (1519 Grande Ave., 81144; 852-0612, 800-221-2222) 26 rooms, free breakfast, indoor pool, sauna, whirlpools, exercise center, wheelchair access, NS rooms, pets OK, children under 18 free with parents, A/C, TV, meeting facilities, senior rates, CC. SGL/DBL$55-$82.

Monte Villa Inn (925 1st Ave., 81144; 852-5166, 800-527-5168) 39 rooms, restaurant, lounge, rooms service, children free with parents, A/C, TV, pets OK, modified American plan available, NS rooms, wheelchair access, CC. SGL/DBL$35-$50.

Montrose

Area Code 303

Best Western Red Arrow Motor Inn (1702 East Main St., 81402; 249-9641, Fax 249-8380, 800-469-9323, 800-528-1234) 60 rooms and suites, restaurant, exercise center, spa, in-room refrigerators, children free with parents, A/C, NS rooms, TV, laundry facilities, wheelchair access, pets OK, senior rates, meeting facilities, CC. SGL/DBL$70-$165.

Black Canyon Motel (1605 East Main St., 81402; 249-3495) 60 rooms and 2-bedroom, suites, heated pool, jacuzzi, A/C, TV, wheelchair access, airport transportation, pets OK, meeting facilities for 350, CC. SGL/DBL$50-$56.

Country Lodge (1624 East Main St., 81401; 249-4567) 22 rooms and efficiencies, heated pool, hot tubs, airport transportation, children free with parents, A/C, TV, kitchenettes, in-room refrigerators and microwaves, NS rooms, wheelchair access, CC. SGL/DBL$45-$75.

Days Inn (1655 East Main, 81401; 249-3411, Fax 240-4882, 800-325-2525) 20 rooms and suites, free breakfast, children free with parents, room service, laundry service, A/C, TV, free local calls, pets OK, fax, wheelchair access, NS rooms, senior rates, CC. SGL/DBL$29-$47.

Log Cabin Motel (1034 East Main St., 81401; 249-7610) 14 rooms, kitchenettes, A/C, TV, CC. SGL/DBL$28-$33.

Mesa Motel (10 North Townsend Ave., 81401; 249-3773) 17 rooms, A/C, TV, CC. SGL/DBL$36-$45.

Red Barn Motel (1417 East Main St., 81401; 249-4507) 70 rooms, restaurant, lounge, heated pool, hot tub, sauna, exercise center, laundry facilities, pets OK, in-room coffee makers, NS, A/C, TV, CC. SGL/DBL$70.

San Juan Inn (1480 Hwy. 550 South, 81401; 249-6644) 50 rooms, restaurant, indoor heated pool, whirlpools, pets OK, A/C, TV, CC. SGL/DBL$35-$50.

Super 8 Motel (1705 East Main St., 81401; 249-9294, Fax 249-9294 ext 334, 800-800-8000) 42 rooms and suites, hot tubs, pets OK, children under 12 free with parents, free local calls, A/C, TV, in-room refrigerators and microwaves, fax, NS rooms, senior rates, wheelchair access, meeting facilities, CC. SGL/DBL$35-$53.

Trapper Motel (1225 East Main St., 81401; 249-3426, 800-858-5911) 27 rooms and 2-bedroom efficiencies, restaurant, NS rooms, airport transportation, A/C, TV, CC. SGL/DBL$28-$45.

Traveler's B&B Inn (502 South 1st, 81401; 249-3472) 15 rooms, free breakfast, TV, CC. SGL/DBL$40-$60.

Western Motel (1200 East Main St., 81401; 249-3481, 800-445-7301) 28 rooms and suites, heated pool, whirlpools, A/C, TV, NS rooms, wheelchair access, pets OK, local transportation, CC. SGL/DBL$35-$50, EFF$55-$75.

Will Rogers Motel (940 North Townsend Ave., 81401; 249-4891) 12 rooms, kitchenettes, A/C, TV, CC. SGL/DBL$37-$42.

Nathrop
Area Code 719

Deer Valley Ranch (16825 Hwy. 162, 81236; 395-2353) 29 rooms and cottage, restaurant, heated pool, whirlpools, sauna, children free with parents, in-room refrigerators, local transportation, modified American plan, meeting rooms, CC. SGL/DBL$100-$200.

Nederland
Area Code 303

The Goldminer Hotel (Nederland 80466; 800-422-4629) rooms and suites, free breakfast, local transportation, private baths. $60-$100.

Nederhaus (Nederland 80466; 800-422-4629) 800-422-4629 rooms and suites, kitchenettes, private bath, local transportation, antique furnishings, TV, NS rooms, wheelchair access, CC. SGL/DBL$51-$79.

Rocky Ledge Cabin (Nederland 80466; 800-422-4629) rental cabin, kitchenette, local transportation, fireplace, CC. SGL/DBL$80-$95.

Northglenn
Area Code 303

Days Inn (36 East 120th Ave., 80233; 457-0688, Fax 457-0152, 800-325-2525) 123 rooms, restaurant, outdoor pool, exercise center, children free with parents, fax, pets OK, CC. SGL/DBL$35-$62.

Ouray
Area Code 303

Alpine Motel (645 Main St., 81427; 325-4546) 12 rooms, restaurant, kitchenettes, TV, NS, pets OK, wheelchair access, in-room coffee makers, CC. SGL/DBL$45-$50.

Antlers Motel (Ouray 81427; 325-4589) 17 rooms and efficiencies, restaurant, pets OK, A/C, TV, NS rooms, wheelchair access, CC. SGL/DBL$50-$90.

Best Western Twin Peaks Motel (125 Third Ave., 81427; 325-4427, 800-528-1234) 49 rooms, children free with parents, A/C, NS rooms, TV, laundry facilities, wheelchair access, pets OK, senior rates, meeting facilities, CC. SGL/DBL$60-$100.

Box Canyon Lodge (45 3rd Ave., 81427; 325-4981, 800-327-5080) 38 rooms and efficiencies, whirlpools, fireplaces, children free with parents, pets OK, TV, NS rooms, wheelchair access, CC. SGL/DBL$45-$115.

Cascade Falls Lodge (191 5th Ave., 81427; 325-7203, 800-438-5713) 30 rooms, hot tub, whirlpools, pets OK, A/C, TV, NS rooms, children free with parents, wheelchair access, CC. SGL/DBL$54-$80.

Circle M Motel (Ouray 81427; 325-4394, 800-523-2589) 30 rooms, restaurant, whirlpools, TV, NS rooms, wheelchair access, pets OK, children free with parents, CC. SGL/DBL$45-$62.

Damn Yankee Bed and Breakfast (100 6th St., 81427; 325-4219, 800-845-7512) 8 rooms and suites, free breakfast, hot tubs, private baths, fireplace, NS, children free with parents, pets OK, A/C, TV, CC. SGL/DBL$82-$145.

Matterhorn Motel (201 6th Ave., 81427; 325-4938, 800-334-9425) 25 rooms and efficiencies, heated pool, whirlpools, pets OK, A/C, TV, NS rooms, wheelchair access, CC. SGL/DBL$45-$75.

Ouray Chalet Motel (510 Main St., 81427; 325-4331) 30 rooms, restaurant, whirlpools, local transportation, TV, pets OK, in-room coffee makers, NS rooms, wheelchair access, CC. SGL/DBL$65-$70.

Ouray Victorian Inn (50 3rd Ave., 81427; 325-7222, Fax 325-7225, 800-443-7361) 38 rooms and suites, free breakfast, whirlpools, children free with parents, pets OK, laundry facilities, A/C, TV, NS rooms, wheelchair access, meeting facilities, CC. SGL/DBL$70-$85.

Ouray's Wiesbaden Hot Springs Spa and Lodging (Ouray 81427; 325-4347) indoor and outdoor pool, sauna, jacuzzi, A/C, TV, NS rooms, local transportation, wheelchair access, CC. SGL/DBL$65-$130.

St. Elmo Inn (426 Main St., 81427; 325-4951) 9 rooms, restaurant, whirlpools, sauna, A/C, TV, NS rooms, wheelchair access, antique furnishings, 1890s inn, CC. SGL/DBL$46-$65.

Pagosa Springs
Area Code 303

Best Western Oak Ridge Motor Inn (158 Light Plant Rd., 81147; 264-4173, Fax 264-4472, 800-528-1234) 80 rooms, restaurant, lounge, children free with parents, A/C, NS rooms, TV, laundry facilities, wheelchair access, pets OK, senior rates, meeting facilities, CC. SGL/DBL$48-$75.

Echo Manor Inn (3366 Hwy. 84, 81147; 264-5646) 10 rooms and suites, free breakfast, A/C, TV, pets OK, private baths, American plan available, CC. SGL/DBL$50-$140.

High Country Lodge (3821 East Hwy. 160, 81147; 264-4181) 29 rooms and 2-bedroom suites, kitchenettes, whirlpools, A/C, TV, NS rooms, wheelchair access, pets OK, CC. SGL/DBL$35-$48.

First Inn (260 East Pagosa , 81147; 264-4161, Fax 264-4652) 33 rooms, restaurant, whirlpools, pets OK, A/C, TV, NS rooms, wheelchair access, laundry facilities, CC. SGL/DBL$35-$45.

Super 8 Motel (34 Piedra Rd., 81147; 731-4005, 800-800-8000) 25 rooms and suites, pets OK, children under 12 free with parents, free local calls, A/C, TV, in-room refrigerators and microwaves, fax, NS rooms, senior rates, wheelchair access, meeting facilities, CC. SGL/DBL$42-$58.

Parachute
Area Code 303

Super 8 Motel (252 Green St., 81635; 285-7936, Fax 285-9538, 800-800-8000) 98 rooms and suites, pets OK, children under 12 free with parents, free local calls, A/C, TV, in-room refrigerators and microwaves, fax, NS rooms, senior rates, wheelchair access, meeting facilities, CC. SGL/DBL$36-$53.

Powderhorn
Area Code 303

Powderhorn (Powderhorn 81243; 641-0220, 800-786-1220) 18 1- and 2-bedroom cabins, restaurant, lounge, entertainment, heated pool, whirlpool, game room, airport transportation, in-room refrigerators, pets OK, in-room refrigerators. SGL/DBL$800W.

Pueblo
Area Code 719

Best Western Town House Motor Hotel (730 North Santa Fe, 81003; 543-6530, Fax 543-6565, 800-528-1234) 88 rooms, restaurant, lounge, pool, exercise center, children free with parents, A/C, NS rooms, TV, laundry facilities, wheelchair access, pets OK, senior rates, meeting facilities, CC. SGL/DBL$44-$70.

Comfort Inn (Eagle Ridge Dr., 81008; 800-221-2222) 60 rooms, free breakfast, indoor heated pool, whirlpools, wheelchair access, NS rooms, pets OK, children under 18 free with parents, A/C, TV, meeting facilities, senior rates, CC. SGL/DBL$38-$73.

Days Inn (4201 North Elizabeth, 81008; 543-8031, Fax 546-1317, 800-325-2525) 37 rooms and suites, free breakfast, children free with parents, room service, laundry service, A/C, TV, free local calls, pets OK, fax, wheelchair access, NS rooms, senior rates, CC. SGL/DBL$40-$135.

Hampton Inn (4703 North Freeway, 81008; 544-4700, Fax 544-6526, 800-HAMPTON) 112 rooms, restaurant, free breakfast, pool, exercise center, children under 18 free with parents, NS rooms, wheelchair access, in-room computer hookups, fax, TV, A/C, free local calls, pets OK, meeting facilities, CC. SGL/DBL$48-$70.

Holiday Inn (4001 North Elizabeth, 81008; 543-8050, Fax 543-8050 ext 260, 800-HOLIDAY) 193 rooms and suites, restaurant, lounge, indoor pool, exercise center, children under 19 free with parents, wheelchair access, A/C, TV, NS rooms, fax, room service, game room, pets OK, laundry service, meeting facilities for 250, senior rates, CC. SGL/DBL$65-$150.

Motel 6 West (960 Hwy. 50 West, 81008; 719-543-8900) pool, free local calls, children under 17 free with parents, NS rooms, wheelchair access, pets OK, A/C, TV, CC. SGL/DBL$25-$31.

Motel 6 (4103 North Elizabeth St., 81008; 543-6221, 505-891-6161) 122 rooms, pool, free local calls, children under 17 free with parents, NS rooms, wheelchair access, pets OK, A/C, TV, CC. SGL/DBL$38-$44.

National 9 Rambler Motel (4400 North Elizabeth, 81008; 543-4183, 800-524-9999) 31 rooms and 2-bedroom efficiencies, heated pool, NS rooms, wheelchair access, A/C, TV, children free with parents, senior rates, CC. SGL/DBL$25-$36.

Super 8 Motel (1100 Hwy. 50 West, 81008; 545-4104, Fax 545-4104, 800-800-8000) 60 rooms and suites, pets OK, children under 12 free with parents, free local calls, A/C, TV, in-room refrigerators and microwaves, fax, NS rooms, senior rates, wheelchair access, meeting facilities, CC. SGL/DBL$29-$43.

Pueblo West

Area Code 719

Best Western Inn at Pueblo West (201 South McCulloch Blvd., 81007; 547-2111, Fax 547-0385, 800-448-1972, 800-528-1234) 80 rooms, restaurant, lounge, complimentary newspaper, children free with parents, A/C, NS rooms, TV, laundry facilities, wheelchair access, pets OK, senior rates, meeting facilities, CC. SGL/DBL$42-$73.

Rangely
Area Code 303

Escalante Trail Motel (117 South Grand St., 81648; 675-8461) 25 rooms, A/C, TV, NS rooms, wheelchair access, pets OK, CC. SGL/DBL$36-$42.

Red Cliff
Area Code 303

Pilgrim's Inn (101 Eagle St., 81649; 827-5333) free breakfast, A/C, NS, pets OK, private baths, hot tub, antique furnishings, TV, CC. SGL/DBL$75-$85.

Red Feather Lakes
Area Code 303

Rental and Reservation Services:

Poudre River Cabins (33059 Poudre Canyon Hwy., 80544; 881-2139) rental cabins

Beaver Meadows Resort (Red Feather Lakes 80545; 881-2459) rental cabins.

Redstone
Area Code 303

Cleveholm Manor (58 Redstone Blvd., 81623; 963-3463, 800-643-4873) 16 rooms and suites, restaurant, free breakfast, TV, wheelchair access, pets OK, NS, 1880s inn, antique furnishings, private baths, CC. SGL/DBL$80-$175.

Redstone Inn (82 Redstone Blvd., 81623; 963-2526, 800-748-2524) 35 rooms and suites, restaurant, heated pool, whirlpools, sauna, exercise center, game room, 1902 inn, antique furnishings, TV, NS rooms, wheelchair access, CC. SGL/DBL$32-4100, STS$100-$135.

Ridgeway
Area Code 303

Super 8 Motel (373 Palomino Tr., 81432; 626-5444, Fax 626-5898, 800-800-8000) 52 rooms and suites, indoor heated pool, jacuzzi, sauna, game room, pets OK, children under 12 free with parents, free local calls, A/C, TV, in-room refrigerators and microwaves, fax, laundry facilities, NS rooms, senior rates, wheelchair access, meeting facilities, CC. SGL/DBL$54-$88.

Rifle
Area Code 303

Rusty Cannon Motel (701 Taughenbaugh, 81650; 625-4004, Fax 625-3604, 800-341-8000) 88 rooms, restaurant, heated pool, sauna, pets OK, laundry facilities, A/C, TV, NS rooms, wheelchair access, children free with parents, senior rates, CC. SGL/DBL$38-$46.

Rocky Ford
Area Code 719

Melon Valley Inn (1319 Elm Ave., 81067; 254-3306) 40 rooms, restaurant, lounge, indoor heated pool, pets OK, A/C, TV, NS rooms, wheelchair access, senior rates, CC. SGL/DBL$36-$50.

Salida
Area Code 719

Aspen Leaf Lodge (7350 Hwy. 50 West, 81201; 530-6733) 17 rooms, whirlpools, A/C, TV, NS rooms, wheelchair access, pets OK, CC. SGL/DBL$28-$55.

Best Western Colorado Lodge (352 West Rainbow Blvd., 81201; 539-2514, Fax 539-4316, 800-528-1234) 35 rooms, restaurant, heated pool, exercise center, spa, tennis courts, children free with parents, A/C, NS rooms, TV, laundry facilities, wheelchair access, pets OK, senior rates, meeting facilities, CC. SGL/DBL$46-$80.

Circle R Motel (304 East Rainbow Blvd., 81201; 539-6296) 16 rooms, whirlpools, A/C, TV, NS rooms, wheelchair access, pets OK, laundry facilities, CC. SGL/DBL$25-$50.

Days Inn (407 East Hwy. 50, 81201; 539-6651, Fax 539-6240, 800-325-2525) 27 rooms and suites, free breakfast, children free with parents, room service, laundry service, A/C, TV, free local calls, pets OK, fax, wheelchair access, NS rooms, senior rates, CC. SGL/DBL$29-$47.

Friendship Inn Ranch House (7545 West Hwy. 50, 81201; 539-6655, 800-424-4777) 20 rooms, free breakfast, pool, exercise center, whirlpools, gift shop, local transportation, free local calls, A/C, TV, pets OK, NS rooms, children free with parents, wheelchair access, meeting facilities, senior rates, CC. SGL/DBL$32-$68.

National 9 Motel (1310 East Rainbow, 81201; 539-2895, 800-524-9999) 32 rooms and suites, spa, NS rooms, wheelchair access, A/C, TV, children free with parents, senior rates, CC. SGL/DBL$28-$81.

Rainbow Inn (105 Hwy. 50 East, 81201; 539-4444) 22 rooms and efficiencies, A/C, TV, NS rooms, wheelchair access, CC. SGL/DBL$40-$70.

Redwood Lodge (Salida 81201; 539-2528) 27 rooms and suites, heated pool, whirlpools, pets OK, in-room refrigerators, A/C, TV, NS rooms, wheelchair access, CC. SGL/DBL$40-$72.

Super 8 Motel (525 West Rainbow, 81201; 539-6689, Fax 539-7018, 800-800-8000) 26 rooms and suites, indoor heated pool, whirlpools, pets OK, children under 12 free with parents, free local calls, A/C, TV, in-room refrigerators and microwaves, fax, NS rooms, senior rates, wheelchair access, meeting facilities, CC. SGL/DBL$29-$70.

Western Holiday Motel (545 West Rainbow Blvd., 81201; 539-2553) 30 rooms and efficiencies, heated pool, whirlpools, pets OK, in-room refrigerators, A/C, TV, NS rooms, wheelchair access, CC. SGL/DBL$35-$60.

Woodland Motel (903 West 1st St., 81201; 539-4980) 18 rooms and efficiencies, whirlpools, pets OK, in-room refrigerators, A/C, TV, NS rooms, wheelchair access, CC. SGL/DBL$25-$66.

Sedalia
Area Code 303

Lost Valley Guest Ranch (Route 2, 80135; 647-2311) 24 1- to 3-bedroom cabins, restaurant, entertainment, heated pool, whirlpools, spa, tennis courts, fireplaces, children free with parents, kitchenettes, laundry facilities, A/C, TV, NS rooms, wheelchair access, local transportation, American plan available, meeting facilities, CC. SGL/DBL$100W-$150W.

Shawnee
Area Code 303

North Fork Ranch (Shawnee 80475; 838-9873, 800-843-7895) 13 rooms and cottages, restaurant, heated pool, whirlpools, kitchenettes, children free with parents, laundry facilities, TV, NS rooms, wheelchair access, American plan available, airport transportation, pets OK, CC. SGL/DBL$1,050W-$2,000W.

Silver Creek
Area Code 303

The Inn at Silver Creek (Silver Creek 80446; 887-2131, Fax 887-2350, 800-926-4386) 342 rooms and efficiencies, restaurant, lounge, pool, whirlpools, sauna, exercise center, A/C, TV, NS rooms, wheelchair access, pets OK, boutiques, laundry facilities, in-room refrigerators, fireplaces, local transportation, meeting facilities, senior rates, CC. SGL/DBL$100-$240.

Silverthorne
Area Code 303

Days Inn (580 Silverthorne Lane, 80498; 468-8661, Fax 468-5583, 800-325-2525) 72 rooms and suites, free breakfast, sauna, children free with parents, room service, laundry service, A/C, TV, free local calls, pets OK, local transportation, fax, wheelchair access, NS rooms, senior rates, CC. SGL/DBL$39-$185.

Summit Inn and Conference Center (Silverthorne 80498; 468-6200, Fax 468-7836) 18 efficiencies, restaurant, lounge, indoor heated pool, whirlpools, A/C, TV, NS rooms, wheelchair access, laundry facilities, pets OK, CC. SGL/DBL$35-$158.

Silverton
Area Code 303

Alma House Inn (220 East 10th St., 81443; 387-5336) 10 rooms and suites, restaurant, TV, NS rooms, local transportation, 1890s inn, pets OK, room service, antique furnishings, wheelchair access, CC. SGL/DBL$50-$80.

Christopher House Bed and Breakfast (821 Empire St., 81433; 387-5857) 3 rooms, free breakfast, A/C, TV, CC. SGL/DBL$40-$50.

Grand Imperial Motel (1219 Green St., 81433; 387-5527) 40 rooms and suites, restaurant, lounge, TV, NS rooms, wheelchair access, antique furnishings, 1880s inn, CC. SGL/DBL$50-$90.

Kendell Mountain Getaway Condominium (545 Resse St., 81433; 249-5711) condominiums, A/C, TV, NS rooms, wheelchair access, CC. SGL/DBL$85-$105.

Triangle Motel (864 Green, 81443; 387-5780) 216 rooms and efficiencies, TV, NS rooms, wheelchair access, CC. SGL/DBL$35-$65.

Wyman Inn (1371 Greene St., 81433; 387-5372) 11 rooms, restaurant, NS, A/C, TV, pets OK, NS, 1902 inn, antique furnishings, wheelchair access, CC. SGL/DBL$58-$78.

Snowmass Village
Area Code 303

Crestwood Hotel (400 Wood Rd., 81615; 923-2450, Fax 923-5018, 800-356-5946) 125 rooms and apartments, heated pool, exercise center, whirlpools, airport transportation, in-room refrigerators, fireplaces, children free with parents, A/C, TV, NS rooms, wheelchair access, CC. SGL/DBL$250-$490.

Mountain Chalet (Snowmass Village 81615; 923-3900) 64 rooms, heated pool, whirlpools, sauna, pets OK, TV, CC. SGL/DBL$50-$225.

Silvertree Hotel (100 Elbert Lane, 81615; 525-3520, Fax 923-5192, 800-525-9402) 261 rooms and suites, restaurant, lounge, entertainment, heated pool, exercise center, sauna, whirlpools, A/C, TV, NS rooms, wheelchair access, airport transportation, boutiques, in-room refrigerators, laundry facilities, children free with parents, pets OK, senior rates, meeting facilities, CC. SGL/DBL$140-$1,200.

Snowmass Lodge and Club (Snowmass Village 81615; 923-5600, Fax 923-6944, 800-525-6200) 135 rooms and villas, restaurant, lounge, entertainment, heated pool, exercise center, sauna, whirlpools, lighted tennis courts, gift shop, local transportation, A/C, TV, NS rooms, wheelchair access, in-room refrigerators, CC. SGL/DBL$130-$680.

Timberline Lodge (264 Snowmass Rd., 81615; 923-4000, Fax 923-3036) 96 condominiums, restaurant, lounge, whirlpools, sauna, fireplaces, TV, pets OK, laundry facilities, CC. SGL/DBL$65-$650.

Wildwood Hotel (40 Elbert Lane, 81615; 923-3550, 800-445-1642) 148 rooms and suites, restaurant, lounge, heated pool, children stay free with parents, airport transportation, A/C, in-room refrigerators, pets OK, modified American plan available, TV, NS rooms, wheelchair access, in-room refrigerators, meeting facilities, senior rates, CC. SGL/DBL$110-$324.

South Fork
Area Code 719

Wolf Creek Ski Lodge (31042 Hwy. 160 West, 81154; 873-5547, 800-874-0416) 49 rooms and efficiencies, restaurant, lounge, whirlpools, pets OK, airport courtesy car, TV, pets OK, modified American plan available, NS rooms, wheelchair access, meeting facilities, senior rates, CC. SGL/DBL$55-$65.

Steamboat Springs
Area Code 303

Alpiner Lodge (424 Lincoln Ave., 80477; 879-1430, Fax 879-0054, 800-538-7519) 32 rooms, restaurant, children free with parents, in-room coffee makers, local transportation, A/C, TV, NS rooms, wheelchair access, pets OK, CC. SGL/DBL$80-$90.

Best Western Ptarmigan Inn (2304 Apres Ski Way, 80477; 879-1730, Fax 879-6044, 800-538-7519, 800-528-1234) 77 rooms, restaurant, pool, exercise center, whirlpools, children free with parents, A/C, NS rooms, TV, laundry facilities, wheelchair access, pets OK, senior rates, meeting facilities, CC. SGL/DBL$60-$205.

Harbor Hotel and Condominiums (703 Lincoln Ave., 80477; 879-1522, Fax 879-1737) 109 rooms and suites, whirlpools, sauna, pets OK, TV, NS rooms, wheelchair access, kitchenettes, laundry facilities, CC. SGL/DBL$50-$185.

Holiday Inn (3190 South Lincoln, 80477; 879-2250, 800-654-3944, 800-HOLIDAY) 82 rooms, restaurant, lounge, heated pool, exercise center, whirlpools, game room, children under 19 free with parents, wheelchair access, A/C, TV, NS rooms, fax, local transportation, game room, room service, pets OK, laundry service, meeting facilities, senior rates, CC. SGL/DBL$110-$160.

The Inn at Steamboat (3070 Columbine Dr., 80477; 879-2600, 800-872-2601) 32 rooms, lounge, free breakfast, outdoor heated pool, sauna, children free with parents, game room, pets OK, local transportation, game room, laundry facilities, A/C, TV, NS rooms, wheelchair access, CC. SGL/DBL$50-$150.

The Overlook Lodge (1000 Highpoint Dr., 80477; 879-2900, Fax 879-7641) 117 rooms and efficiencies, restaurant, lounge, indoor heated pool, whirlpools, tennis courts, A/C, TV, kitchenettes, NS rooms, wheelchair access, CC. SGL/DBL$65-$180.

Rabbit Ears Motel (201 Lincoln Ave., 80477; 879-1150, 800-828-7702) 65 rooms, pool, VCRs, in-room refrigerators, pets OK, children free with parents, A/C, TV, NS rooms, wheelchair access, CC. SGL/DBL$38-$122.

The Ranch at Steamboat Springs (1 Ranch Rd., 80477; 879-3000, 800-525-2002) 88 condominiums, heated pool, sauna, tennis courts, whirlpools, local transportation, TV, NS rooms, wheelchair access, laundry facilities, CC. SGL/DBL$250-$450.

Sheraton Resort and Conference Center (2200 Village Inn Court, 80477; 879-2220, Fax 879-7686, 800-848-8878, 800-325-3535) 300 rooms and suites, restaurant, lounge, entertainment, outdoor heated pool, exercise center, tennis courts, hot tubs, sauna, NS rooms, A/C, TV, children free with parents, local transportation, pets OK, in-room refrigerators, wheelchair access, airport courtesy car, 16 meeting rooms, meeting facilities for 675, CC. SGL/DBL$80-$500.

Sky Valley Lodge (31490 East Hwy. 40, 80477; 879-7749, Fax 879-7749, 800-538-7510) 24 rooms, restaurant, lounge, whirlpools, pets OK, A/C, TV, NS rooms, wheelchair access, CC. SGL/DBL$55-$200.

Super 8 Motel (Hwy. 40 East, 80477; 879-5230, 800-800-8000) 60 rooms and suites, restaurant, sauna, pets OK, children under 12 free with parents, free local calls, A/C, TV, in-room refrigerators and microwaves, fax, NS rooms, senior rates, wheelchair access, meeting facilities, CC. SGL/DBL$39-$80.

Vista Verde Ranch (Steamboat Springs 80477; 879-3858, Fax 879-1413, 800-526-7433) 10 rooms and cabins, entertainment, pool, whirlpools, exercise center, sauna, American plan available, NS, TV, wheelchair access, in-room refrigerators, children free with parents, CC. SGL/DBL$$1,375W-$2,600W.

Western Lodge (1122 Lincoln Ave., 80477; 879-1050, Fax 879-2657) 35 rooms and suites, indoor heated pool, sauna, pets OK, A/C, TV, NS rooms, wheelchair access, CC. SGL/DBL$50-$125.

Sterling
Area Code 303

Best Western Sundowner Inn (Overland Trail St., 80751; 522-6265, 800-528-1234) 29 rooms and suites, restaurant, pool, hot tub, exercise center, children free with parents, A/C, NS rooms, TV, laundry facilities, wheelchair access, pets OK, senior rates, meeting facilities, CC. SGL/DBL$58-$84.

Colonial Motel (915 South Division St., 80751; 522-3382) 14 rooms, A/C, TV, NS rooms, wheelchair access, pets OK, CC. SGL/DBL$20-$35.

Days Inn (12881 Hwy. 61, 80751; 522-6660, 800-325-2525) 96 rooms and suites, restaurant, lounge, outdoor pool, children free with parents, room service, laundry service, A/C, TV, free local calls, pets OK, fax, wheelchair access, NS rooms, meeting facilities, senior rates, CC. SGL/DBL$23-$52.

National 9 Inn (I-76 and East Hwy. 6, 80751; 522-2626, 522-1321, 800-524-9999) 101 rooms, exercise center, airport transportation, NS rooms, wheelchair access, A/C, TV, children free with parents, meeting facilities for 200, senior rates, CC. SGL/DBL$40-$68.

Park Inn International (Sterling 80751; 522-2626, Fax 522-1321, 800-437-PARK) 101 rooms and suites, restaurant, lounge, indoor heated pool, whirlpools, pets OK, A/C, TV, wheelchair access, NS rooms, laundry facilities, CC. SGL/DBL$33-$68.

Ramada Inn (Sterling 80751; 522-2626, Fax 522-1321, 800-2-RAMADA) 100 rooms and suites, restaurant, lounge, indoor heated pool, whirlpools, sauna, exercise center, wheelchair access, NS rooms, pets OK, A/C, game room, TV, children under 18 free with parents, room service, laundry facilities, meeting facilities, senior rates, CC. SGL/DBL$38-$70.

Super 8 Motel (12883 Hwy. 61, 80751; 522-0300, Fax 522-8417, 800-800-8000) 72 rooms and suites, restaurant, indoor heated pool, pets OK, chil-

dren under 12 free with parents, free local calls, A/C, TV, in-room refrigerators and microwaves, fax, NS rooms, senior rates, wheelchair access,
meeting facilities, CC. SGL/DBL$35-$46.

Stratton
Area Code 719

Best Western Golden Prairie Inn (700 Colorado Ave., 80836; 348-5311,
Fax 348-5944, 800-528-1234) 40 rooms, restaurant, heated pool, hot tub,
children free with parents, A/C, NS rooms, TV, laundry facilities, wheelchair access, pets OK, senior rates, meeting facilities for 50, CC.
SGL/DBL$58-$65.

Telluride
Area Code 303

Bear Creek Inn (221 East Colorado Ave., 81435; 728-6681, 800-338-7064) 8
rooms, restaurant, free breakfast, A/C, TV, NS, pets OK, wheelchair
access, senior rates, CC. SGL/DBL$65-$146.

Doral Telluride Resort and Spa (134 Country Club Dr., 81435; 728-6800,
Fax 728-6567, 800-44-DORAL) 177 rooms and suites, restaurant, lounge,
entertainment, pool, exercise center, sauna, whirlpools, tennis courts,
A/C, TV, NS rooms, wheelchair access, airport transportation, gift shop,
in-room refrigerators and coffee makers, laundry facilities, children free
with parents, pets OK, senior rates, meeting facilities, CC. SGL/DBL$350-
$360, STS$485-$800.

Ice House Motel (310 South Fir St., 81435; 728-6300, 800-544-3436) 35
rooms and suites, free breakfast, restaurant, whirlpools, children free
with parents, TV, NS rooms, pets OK, wheelchair access, CC.
SGL/DBL$80-$350.

Manitou Hotel (333 South Fir St., 81435; 728-4011) 12 rooms, free
breakfast, whirlpools, TV, NS rooms, wheelchair access, children free
with parents, in-room refrigerators, antique furnishings, CC.
SGL/DBL$115-$190.

Pennington Mountain Village Inn (100 Pennington Ct., 81435; 728-5337,
800-543-1437) 12 suites, free breakfast, whirlpools, sauna, TV, NS rooms,
pets OK, game room, laundry facilities, wheelchair access, CC.
SGL/DBL$140-$250.

San Sophia Inn (330 West Pacific Ave., 81435; 728-3001, Fax 728-6226,
800-537-4781) 16 rooms, free breakfast, whirlpools, children free with
parents, TV, VCRs, wheelchair access, antique furnishings, NS, game
room, CC. SGL/DBL$85-$120.

Skyline Ranch (7214 Hwy. 145, 81435; 728-3757) 16 rooms and cottages, free breakfast, laundry facilities, gift shop, NS, TV, wheelchair access, CC. SGL/DBL$960W-$1,850W.

Victorian Inn (401 West Pacific Ave., 81435; 728-6601) 26 rooms and efficiencies, free breakfast, whirlpools, sauna, A/C, TV, NS rooms, wheelchair access, in-room refrigerators, CC. SGL/DBL$55-$90.

Thornton
Area Code 303

Motel 6 (6 West 83rd Pl., 80221; 429-1550, 505-891-6161) 121 rooms, pool, free local calls, children under 17 free with parents, NS rooms, wheelchair access, pets OK, A/C, TV, CC. SGL/DBL$38-$55.

Sheraton Inn Greystone Castle Denver North (83 East 120th Ave., 80233; 451-1002, Fax 451-1002 ext 608, 800-325-3535) 137 rooms and suites, restaurant, lounge, entertainment, indoor heated pool, exercise center, jacuzzi, sauna, airport courtesy car, gift shop, NS rooms, A/C, TV, children free with parents, wheelchair access, 11,600 square feet of meeting and exhibition space, 9 meeting rooms, meeting facilities for 1,500, CC. SGL/DBL$80-$105.

Trinidad
Area Code 719

Best Western Country Club Inn (900 West Adams St., 81082; 846-2215, 800-955-2215, 800-528-1234) 55 rooms, restaurant, lounge, pool, exercise center, whirlpools, gift shop, local transportation, children free with parents, A/C, NS rooms, TV, laundry facilities, wheelchair access, pets OK, senior rates, meeting facilities, CC. SGL/DBL$41-$69.

Budget Host (10301 Santa Fe Trail Dr., 81082; 846-3307, 800-283-4678) 16 rooms and suites, laundry facilities, NS rooms, wheelchair access, A/C, in-room coffee makers, pets OK, TV, children free with parents, senior rates, CC. SGL/DBL$25-$70.

Holiday Inn (Trinidad 81082; 846-4491, 800-HOLIDAY) 111 rooms and suites, restaurant, lounge, indoor pool, exercise center, whirlpools, hot tubs, gift shop, children under 19 free with parents, wheelchair access, A/C, TV, NS rooms, fax, room service, pets OK, laundry service, meeting facilities, senior rates, CC. SGL/DBL$40-$90.

Super 8 Motel (Freedom Rd., 81082; 800-800-8000) 42 rooms and suites, restaurant, indoor heated pool, whirlpools, pets OK, children under 12 free with parents, free local calls, A/C, TV, in-room refrigerators and microwaves, fax, NS rooms, senior rates, wheelchair access, meeting facilities, CC. SGL/DBL$50-$60.

Trinidad Motor Inn (702 West Main St., 81082; 846-2271) 60 rooms, restaurant, lounge, heated pool, laundry facilities, A/C, TV, NS rooms, wheelchair access, pets OK, senior rates, CC. SGL/DBL$30-$52.

Vail

Area Code 303

Antlers at Vail (680 West Lionshead Place, 81657; 476-2471, Fax 476-4146) 68 rooms and suites, restaurant, heated pool, sauna, whirlpools, pets OK, kitchenettes, VCRs, TV, NS rooms, wheelchair access, CC. SGL/DBL$85-$350.

Best Western Vailglo Lodge (701 West Lionshead Circle, 81658; 476-5506, Fax 476-3926, 800-541-9423, 800-528-1234) 34 rooms, restaurant, free breakfast, lounge, pool, exercise center, whirlpools, children free with parents, A/C, NS rooms, TV, laundry facilities, wheelchair access, pets OK, senior rates, meeting facilities, CC. SGL/DBL$65-$200.

The Black Bear Inn (2405 Elliott Rd., 81657; 476-1304) 12 rooms, restaurant, free breakfast, antique furnishings, NS, wheelchair access, TV. SGL/DBL$95-$150.

Christiania at Vail (356 East Hanson Ranch Rd., 81657) 22 rooms and suites, restaurant, free breakfast, heated pool, sauna, kitchenettes, antique furnishings, pets OK, CC. SGL/DBL$195-$400.

Gasthof Gramshammer (231 East Gore Creek Dr., 81657; 476-5626, Fax 476-8816) 28 rooms, restaurant, free breakfast, lounge, TV, NS rooms, wheelchair access, pets OK, in-room refrigerators, fireplaces, CC. SGL/DBL$195-$555.

Eagle River Inn (145 North Main St., 81657; 827-5761, Fax 827-4020) 12 rooms, restaurant, pets OK, TV, wheelchair access, pets OK, private baths, senior rates, CC. SGL/DBL$80-$195.

Holiday Inn (13 Vail Rd., 81657; 476-5631, Fax 476-2508, 800-451-9840, 800-HOLIDAY) 120 rooms and 1-, 2- and 3-bedroom suites, restaurant, lounge, heated pool, exercise center, whirlpools, sauna, local transportation, in-room refrigerators, children under 19 free with parents, wheelchair access, A/C, TV, NS rooms, fax, room service, pets OK, laundry service, meeting facilities for 200, senior rates, CC. SGL/DBL$165-$250.

Lion Square Lodge (660 West Lionshead Pl., 81657; 476-2281, Fax 476-7423, 800-525-5788) 111 rooms and townhouses, lounge, heated pool, whirlpools, sauna, in-room refrigerators and coffee makers, children free with parents, kitchenettes, TV, laundry facilities, pets OK, NS rooms, wheelchair access, CC. SGL/DBL$110-$970.

The Lodge at Vail (174 East Gore Creek Dr., 81657; 476-5011, Fax 476-7425, 800-331-5634) 60 rooms and suites, restaurant, free breakfast, lounge, entertainment, heated pool, whirlpools, sauna, exercise center, children free with parents, boutiques, A/C, TV, NS rooms, wheelchair access, local transportation, CC. SGL/DBL$290-$450, STS$550-$1,400.

Lodge Tower in Vail Village (200 Vail Rd., 81657; 476-9530, Fax 476-4093, 800-654-2517) 70 rooms and suites, restaurant, whirlpools, pets OK, TV, NS rooms, wheelchair access, CC. SGL/DBL$70-$250.

L'Ostello (705 West Lionshead Circle, 81657; 476-2050, 800-283-VAIL) 52 rooms and suites, restaurant, heated pool, whirlpools, in-room refrigerators, VCRs, laundry facilities, pets OK, TV, NS rooms, wheelchair access, CC. SGL/DBL$50-$250.

Manor Vail (595 East Vail Valley Dr., 81657; 476-5651, 800-950-VAIL) 217 rooms and suites, restaurant, lounge, heated pool, whirlpools, sauna, exercise center, pets OK, A/C, TV, NS rooms, wheelchair access, laundry service, children free with parents, CC. SGL/DBL$250-$700.

Radisson Resort Vail (715 West Lionshead Circle, 81657; 476-4444, Fax 476-1647, 800-333-3333) 350 rooms and suites, restaurant, lounge, entertainment, heated pool, exercise center, whirlpools, tennis courts, sauna, game room, wheelchair access, TV, A/C, NS rooms, beauty shop, in-room refrigerators and coffee makers, laundry service, gift shop, children free with parents, meeting facilities, senior rates, CC. SGL/DBL$225-$700.

The Pines Lodge (Vail 81657; 345-7900) 60 rooms and suites, restaurant, free breakfast, pool, exercise center, whirlpools, sauna, in-room refrigerators, TV, NS rooms, wheelchair access, children free with parents, pets OK, fireplaces, CC. SGL/DBL$275-$1,300.

Sitzmark Lodge (183 Gore Creek Dr., 81657; 476-5001, Fax 476-8702) 35 rooms, restaurant, lounge, free breakfast, heated pool, sauna, whirlpools, boutiques, TV, pets OK, laundry facilities, pets OK, local transportation, fireplaces, NS rooms, wheelchair access, CC. SGL/DBL$55-$220.

Sonnenalp Resort (20 Vail Rd., 81657; 476-565, Fax 476-1638, 800-654-8312) 186 rooms and villas, restaurant, free breakfast, lounge, pool, whirlpools, sauna, exercise center, children free with parents, A/C, TV, NS rooms, local transportation, room service, wheelchair access, meeting facilities, CC. SGL/DBL$225-$950.

Vail Athletic Club (352 East Meadow Dr., 81657; 476-0700, Fax 476-6451, 800-882-4754) 38 rooms and suites, restaurant, lounge, indoor heated pool, whirlpools, sauna, in-room refrigerators, laundry facilities, pets OK, TV, NS rooms, wheelchair access, CC. SGL/DBL$115-$400.

Westin Hotel and Resort (1300 Westhaven Dr., 81657; 476-7111, Fax 479-7020) 290 rooms and suites, restaurant, lounge, entertainment, heated pool, whirlpools, exercise center, sauna, children free with parents, in-room refrigerators, pets OK, A/C, TV, NS rooms, wheelchair access, local transportation, boutiques, meeting facilities, senior rates, CC. SGL/DBL$285-$325, STS$350-$700.

Westwind (548 South Frontage Rd., 81657; 476-9378) 25 rooms and apartments, restaurant, heated pool, whirlpools, sauna, pets OK, kitchenettes, TV, NS rooms, wheelchair access, fireplaces, CC. SGL/DBL$50-$475.

Vallecita
Area Code 303

Wit's End Guest Ranch (254 County Rd. 500; 884-4113, Fax 884-4114) 21 cabins, restaurant, lounge, entertainment, heated pool, whirlpools, lighted tennis court, pets OK, TV, NS rooms, wheelchair access, local transportation, fireplaces, gift shop, CC. SGL/DBL$2,400W.

Victor
Area Code 303

The Mother Lode (415 Victor Ave., 80860; 689-2147) 3 rooms, private baths, TV, CC. SGL/DBL$44-$56.

Walsenburg
Area Code 719

Best Western Rambler Inn (Walsenburg 81089; 738-1121, 800-528-1234) 32 rooms, heated pool, exercise center, children free with parents, A/C, NS rooms, TV, laundry facilities, local transportation, wheelchair access, pets OK, senior rates, meeting facilities, CC. SGL/DBL$46-$85.

Budget Host Country Host Inn (553 Hwy. 85, 81089; 738-3800, 800-283-4678) 17 rooms, restaurant, laundry facilities, NS rooms, wheelchair access, A/C, pets OK, TV, senior rates, children free with parents, CC. SGL/DBL$24-$49.

Days Inn (22808 West Hwy. 160, 81089; 738-2167, 800-325-2525) 36 rooms and suites, restaurant, lounge, free breakfast, outdoor heated pool, children free with parents, room service, laundry service, A/C, TV, free local calls, pets OK, fax, wheelchair access, NS rooms, senior rates, CC. SGL/DBL$36-$55.

Westcliffe
Area Code 719

Pines Guest Ranch (Westcliffe 81252; 800-446-WHOA) 20 rooms, restaurant, A/C, TV, NS rooms, wheelchair access, American plan available, CC. SGL/DBL$180-$220.

Westminster
Area Code 303

La Quinta Inn (8701 Turnpike Dr., 80030; 425-9099, Fax 427-5860, 800-531-5900) 130 rooms, restaurant, free breakfast, lounge, pool, complimentary newspaper, free local calls, fax, laundry service, NS rooms, wheelchair access, TV, A/C, meeting facilities, CC. SGL/DBL$45-$75.

Ramada Inn (8773 Yates Dr., 80030; 427-4000, Fax 426-1680, 800-2-RAMADA) 180 rooms and suites, restaurant, lounge, indoor pool, wheelchair access, NS rooms, pets OK, A/C, TV, barber and beauty shop, children under 18 free with parents, room service, laundry facilities, 8,500 square feet of meeting and exhibition space, senior rates, CC. SGL/DBL$85-$125.

Wheat Ridge
Area Code 303

Best Western Country Villa Inn Foothills (4700 Kipling St., 80033; 423-4000, Fax 424-7680, 800-528-1234) 117 rooms, restaurant, lounge, pool, exercise center, whirlpools, children free with parents, A/C, NS rooms, TV, laundry facilities, wheelchair access, pets OK, senior rates, meeting facilities, CC. SGL/DBL$44-$60.

Motel 6 North (9920 West 49th Ave., 80033; 424-0658, 505-891-6161) 92 rooms, pool, free local calls, children under 17 free with parents, NS rooms, wheelchair access, pets OK, A/C, TV, CC. SGL/DBL$40-$48.

Motel 6 West (10300 South I-70 Frontage Rd., 80033; 467-3172, 505-891-6161) 113 rooms, pool, free local calls, children under 17 free with parents, NS rooms, wheelchair access, pets OK, A/C, TV, CC. SGL/DBL$38-$49.

Super 8 Motel (10101 West 48th Ave., 80033; 424-8300, 800-800-8000) 125 rooms and suites, outdoor heated pool, whirlpools, sauna, game room, pets OK, children under 12 free with parents, free local calls, A/C, TV, in-room refrigerators and microwaves, fax, NS rooms, senior rates, wheelchair access, meeting facilities, CC. SGL/DBL$46-$55.

Winter Park
Area Code 303

Rental and Reservation Services:

Vacations Incorporated (Winter Park 80482; Fax 726-8004, 800-228-1025) rentals lodges, rooms and condominiums.

◻◻◻

Hi Country Haus Resort (Winter Park 80482; 726-9421, Fax 726-8004, 800-228-1025) 308 1- to 3-bedroom condos, indoor pool, whirlpools, sauna, A/C, TV, NS rooms, laundry facilities, kitchenettes, fireplaces, wheelchair access, meeting facilities, CC. 1BR$60-$165, 2BR$75-$240, 3BR$120-$350.

Mulligan's Mountain Inn (148 Fern Way, 80482; 887-2877) free breakfast, jacuzzis, NS, pets OK, children over 10 welcome, game room, A/C, TV, CC. SGL/DBL$40-$80.

Iron Horse Retreat (257 Winter Park Dr., 80482; 726-8851, Fax 726-8852 ext 6023, 800-621-8190) 126 condominiums, restaurant, lounge.

Vintage Resort (100 Winter Park Dr., 80482; 726-8801, 800-472-7017) 121 rooms and efficiencies, restaurant, lounge, entertainment, heated pool, sauna, whirlpools, laundry facilities, local transportation, pets OK, TV, NS rooms, wheelchair access, meeting facilities, senior rates, CC. SGL/DBL$110-$460.

Woodland Park
Area Code 719

Elwell's Cottage (2220 Lee Circle Dr., 80866; 687-9838) 1 cottage, kitchenettes, pets OK, CC. SGL/DBL$60-$65.

Pikes Peak Paradise Bed and Breakfast (236 Pinecrest Rd., 80866; 687-6656, 800-728-8282) 5 rooms, free breakfast, A/C, TV, fireplaces, hot tubs, limousine service, NS, pets OK, private baths, CC. SGL/DBL$85-$125.

Nevada

Battle Mountain
Area Code 702

Best Western Big Chief Inn (434 West Front St., 89820; 635-2416, 800-528-1234) 58 rooms, restaurant, free breakfast, lounge, pool, exercise center, children free with parents, A/C, NS rooms, in-room refrigerators and microwaves, pets OK, TV, laundry facilities, wheelchair access, meeting facilities, senior rates, CC. SGL/DBL$45-$55.

Colt Service Center (650 West Front St., 89820; 635-5424, 800-343-0085) 72 rooms, restaurant, children free with parents, A/C, TV, NS rooms, wheelchair access, CC. SGL/DBL$40-$50.

Holiday Inn Express (521 Front St., 89820; 635-5880, Fax 635-4854, 800-HOLIDAY) 72 rooms and suites, restaurant, lounge, heated pool, exercise center, whirlpools, in-room refrigerators and microwaves, airport transportation, children under 19 free with parents, wheelchair access, A/C, TV, NS rooms, fax, room service, pets OK, laundry service, meeting facilities, senior rates, CC. SGL/DBL$48-$58.

The Owl Club (155 South Reese St., 89820; 635-5155) 18 rooms, restaurant, A/C, TV, NS rooms, wheelchair access, CC. SGL/DBL$35-$40.

Beatty
Area Code 702

Burro Inn (Hwy. 95 South, 89003; 553-2225, Fax 553-2892, 800-843-2078) 62 rooms, restaurant, lounge, A/C, TV, NS rooms, wheelchair access, laundry facilities, CC. SGL/DBL$32-$40.

El Portal Motel (301 Main St., 89003; 553-2912, 800-742-7762) 30 rooms, A/C, TV, NS rooms, wheelchair access, CC. SGL/DBL$28-$35.

Exchange Club Motel (Beatty 89003; 553-2333) 44 rooms, restaurant, lounge, A/C, TV, NS rooms, wheelchair access, in-room refrigerators, laundry facilities, CC. SGL/DBL$38-$45.

Phoenix Inn (1st St. and Hwy. 95, 89003; 553-2250, 800-845-7401) 54 rooms, A/C, TV, NS rooms, wheelchair access, CC. SGL/DBL$44.

Stagecoach Hotel and Casino (Hwy. 95, 89003; 553-2419, Fax 553-2419, 800-4BIG-WIN) 32 rooms, A/C, TV, NS rooms, wheelchair access, CC. SGL/DBL$40.

Boulder City
Area Code 702

Best Western Lighthouse Inn and Resort (110 Ville Dr., 89005; 293-6444, Fax 293-6547, 800-528-1234) 70 rooms, restaurant, free breakfast, lounge, pool, exercise center, children free with parents, A/C, NS rooms, TV, laundry facilities, wheelchair access, no pets, meeting facilities, senior rates, CC. SGL/DBL$58-$70.

El Rancho Boulder Motel (725 Nevada Hwy. 89005; 293-1085, Fax 293-6685) 39 rooms and 2-bedroom efficiencies, restaurant, A/C, TV, in-room refrigerators, NS rooms, wheelchair access, meeting facilities, CC. SGL/DBL$60-$90.

Gold Strike Inn and Casino (Boulder City 89005; 293-5000, 800-245-6380) 155 rooms, restaurant, lounge, entertainment, water view, A/C, TV, NS rooms, wheelchair access, gift shop, senior rates, CC. SGL/DBL$29-$34.

Lake Mead Marina and Seven Crowns Resort (322 Lakeshore Rd., 89005; 293-3484, Fax 293-3002, 800-752-9669) rooms, A/C, TV, NS rooms, wheelchair access, CC. SGL/DBL$55-$65.

Nevada Inn (1009 Nevada Hwy., 89005; 293-2044, 800-638-8890) 55 rooms, A/C, TV, NS rooms, wheelchair access, CC. SGL/DBL$45-$55.

Sands Motel (809 Nevada St., 89005; 293-2589, Fax 293-7015) 25 rooms and 2-bedroom efficiencies, in-room refrigerators, no pets, A/C, TV, NS rooms, wheelchair access, CC. SGL/DBL$32-$48.

Super 8 Motel (704 Nevada Hwy. 89005; 294-8888, Fax 293-4344, 800-800-8000) 114 rooms and suites, restaurant, lounge, indoor heated pool, kitchenettes, pets OK, children under 12 free with parents, free local calls, A/C, TV, in-room refrigerators and microwaves, fax, NS rooms, senior rates, wheelchair access, meeting facilities, CC. SGL/DBL$38-$52.

Carson City
Area Code 702

Best Western Carson Station Hotel (900 South Carson St., 89701; 883-0900, 800-528-1234) 92 rooms and suites, restaurant, children free with parents, A/C, NS rooms, TV, laundry facilities, in-room refrigerators, wheelchair access, pets OK, meeting facilities, senior rates, CC. SGL/DBL$40-$60.

Best Western Trailside Inn (1300 North Carson St., 89701; 883-7300, 800-528-1234) 67 rooms, restaurant, pool, exercise center, children free with parents, A/C, NS rooms, TV, laundry facilities, wheelchair access, pets OK, meeting facilities, senior rates, CC. SGL/DBL$28-$56.

Carson Motor Lodge (1421 North Carson St., 89701; 882-3572) 15 rooms and efficiencies, A/C, TV, pets OK, NS rooms, wheelchair access, CC. SGL/DBL$25-$40.

City Center Motel (800 North Carson St., 89701; 882-5535) 81 rooms, restaurant, A/C, TV, NS rooms, wheelchair access, CC. SGL/DBL$30-$60.

Days Inn (3103 North Carson St., 89701; 883-3343, Fax 887-0446, 800-325-2525) 62 rooms and suites, free breakfast, children free with parents, room service, laundry service, A/C, TV, free local calls, pets OK, fax, wheelchair access, in-room refrigerators and microwaves, NS rooms, senior rates, CC. SGL/DBL$35-$100.

Desert Hills Motel (1010 South Carson St., 89701; 882-1932) 33 rooms and suites, restaurant, pets OK, A/C, TV, NS rooms, wheelchair access, CC. SGL/DBL$40-$65.

Downtowner Motel (801 North Carson St., 89701; 882-1333) 34 rooms, restaurant, A/C, TV, NS rooms, wheelchair access, CC. SGL/DBL$28-$36.

Forty Niner Motel (2450 North Carson St., 89701; 882-1123) 25 rooms, pool, pets OK, A/C, TV, NS rooms, wheelchair access, CC. SGL/DBL$40-$60.

Frontier Motel (1718 North Carson St., 89701; 882-1377) 51 rooms and suites, restaurant, kitchenettes, A/C, TV, NS rooms, wheelchair access, CC. SGL/DBL$35-$75.

Hardman House Motor Inn (917 North Carson St., 89701; 882-7744, 887-0321, 800-626-0793) 62 rooms and suites, in-room refrigerators, A/C, no pets, VCRs, TV, NS rooms, wheelchair access, laundry facilities, senior rates, CC. SGL/DBL$40-$65, STS$80-$100.

Mill House Inn (3251 South Carson St., 89701; 882-2715) 24 rooms, pool, children free with parents, A/C, TV, NS rooms, wheelchair access, senior rates, CC. SGL/DBL$40-$55.

Motel Orleans (2731 South Carson St., 89701; 882-2007) 58 rooms, pool, whirlpools, laundry facilities, A/C, TV, NS rooms, wheelchair access, no pets, CC. SGL/DBL$32-$48.

Motel 6 (2749 South Carson St., 89701; 885-7710, 505-891-6161) 82 rooms, pool, free local calls, children under 17 free with parents, NS rooms, wheelchair access, pets OK, A/C, TV, CC. SGL/DBL$30-$40.

The Nugget Motel (651 North Stewart St., 89701; 882-7711) 60 rooms, children free with parents, A/C, TV, NS rooms, wheelchair access, senior rates, CC. SGL/DBL$35-$55.

Ormsby House Hotel (600 Carson St., 89701; 882-1890) 200 rooms and suites, restaurant, pool, A/C, TV, NS rooms, wheelchair access, CC. SGL/DBL$40-$80.

Pioneer Motel (907 South Carson St., 89701; 882-3046) 35 rooms and suites, restaurant, pool, pets OK, A/C, TV, NS rooms, wheelchair access, CC. SGL/DBL$35-$80.

Plaza Motel (805 Plaza, 89701; 882-1518) 21 rooms and suites, restaurant, kitchenettes, A/C, TV, NS rooms, wheelchair access, pets OK, CC. SGL/DBL$35-$60.

Round House Inn (1400 North Carson St., 89701; 882-3446) 39 rooms and suites, restaurant, pool, A/C, TV, NS rooms, wheelchair access, pets OK, CC. SGL/DBL$40-$60.

Royal Crest Motel (1930 North Carson St., 89701; 882-1785) 58 rooms and suites, restaurant, A/C, TV, NS rooms, wheelchair access, CC. SGL/DBL$35-$70.

Sierra Sage Motel (801 South Carson St., 89701; 882-1419) 24 rooms, restaurant, A/C, TV, NS rooms, wheelchair access, CC. SGL/DBL$$35-$48.

Sierra Vista Motel (711 Plaza, 89701; 883-9500) 24 rooms and suites, restaurant, kitchenettes, A/C, TV, NS rooms, wheelchair access, CC. SGL/DBL$35-$60.

Silver Queen Inn (201 West Caroline, 89701; 882-5534) 34 rooms and suites, A/C, TV, NS rooms, wheelchair access, CC. SGL/DBL$32-$58.

Super 8 Motel (2829 South Carson St., 89701; 883-7800, Fax 883-0376, 800-800-8000) 63 rooms and suites, restaurant, pets OK, children under 12 free with parents, free local calls, A/C, TV, in-room refrigerators and microwaves, fax, NS rooms, senior rates, wheelchair access, meeting facilities, CC. SGL/DBL$32-$54.

Westerner Motel (555 North Stewart, 89701; 883-6565) 102 rooms, restaurant, pets OK, A/C, TV, NS rooms, wheelchair access, CC. SGL/DBL$28-$55.

Crystal Bay
Area Code 702

Cal Neva Lodge Resort Hotel and Casino (2 Stateline Rd., 89402; 832-4000, 800-CAL-NEVADA) 200 rooms, restaurant, pool, A/C, TV, NS rooms, wheelchair access, CC. SGL/DBL$69.

Club Tahoe Resort (914 Northwood Blvd., 89402; 831-5705, Fax 831-5177, 800-527-5154) 92 rooms and 2-bedroom suites, restaurant, lounge, kitchenettes, pool, whirlpools, lighted tennis courts, A/C, TV, NS rooms, wheelchair access, CC. SGL/DBL$110-$155.

East Ely

Area Code 702

Steptoe Valley Inn (220 East 11th St., 89315; 289-8687) 5 rooms, free breakfast, A/C, TV, NS, no children, no pets, CC. SGL/DBL$65-$78.

Elko

Area Code 702

Best Western Marquis Motor Inn (837 East Idaho St., 89801; 738-7261, Fax 738-0118, 800-528-1234) 49 rooms and suites, free breakfast, lounge, heated pool, exercise center, children free with parents, A/C, NS rooms, TV, laundry facilities, wheelchair access, pets OK, in-room refrigerators and microwaves, senior rates, meeting facilities, CC. SGL/DBL$44-$80.

Best Western Inn Red Lion Motor Inn (2050 Idaho St., 89801; 738-8421, Fax 738-1798, 800-528-1234) 151 rooms, restaurant, free breakfast, lounge, pool, exercise center, children free with parents, A/C, NS rooms, TV, laundry facilities, wheelchair access, pets OK, in-room refrigerators, meeting facilities, senior rates, CC. SGL/DBL$58-$75.

Days Inn (1500 Idaho St., 89801; 738-7245, Fax 753-9881, 800-325-2525) 33 rooms and suites, free breakfast, outdoor pool, children free with parents, room service, laundry service, in-room refrigerators and microwaves, airport transportation, A/C, TV, free local calls, pets OK, fax, wheelchair access, NS rooms, senior rates, CC. SGL/DBL$30-$54.

Econo Lodge (1785 Idaho St., 89801; 753-7747, 800-4-CHOICE) 61 rooms, whirlpools, children under 12 free with parents, no pets, NS rooms, wheelchair access, A/C, TV, in-room refrigerators and microwaves, senior rates, CC. SGL/DBL$40-$45.

Holiday Inn (3015 Idaho St., 89801; 738-8425, 800-HOLIDAY) 170 rooms and suites, restaurant, lounge, entertainment, indoor pool, exercise center, whirlpools, children under 19 free with parents, wheelchair access, A/C, TV, NS rooms, fax, in-room refrigerators, microwaves and coffee makers, room service, airport transportation, pets OK, laundry service, meeting facilities, senior rates, CC. SGL/DBL$60-$90.

Motel 6 (3021 Idaho St., 89801; 738-4337, 505-891-6161) 123 rooms, pool, free local calls, children under 17 free with parents, NS rooms, wheelchair access, pets OK, A/C, TV, CC. SGL/DBL$38-$48.

National 9 El Neva Motel (736 Idaho St., 89801; 738-7152, 800-348-0850, 800-524-9999) 28 rooms, pool, NS rooms, wheelchair access, A/C, TV, children free with in-room refrigerators and microwaves, no pets, senior rates, CC. SGL/DBL$30-$55.

National 9 Inn Toppers Motel (1500 Idaho St., 89801; 738-7152, 800-348-0850, 800-524-9999) pool, NS rooms, wheelchair access, A/C, TV, children free with parents, senior rates, CC. SGL/DBL$45-$59.

Red Lion Inn and Casino (2065 East Idaho St., 89801; 738-2111, Fax 753-9859, 800-547-8010) 223 rooms and 2-bedroom suites, restaurant, lounge, entertainment, heated pool, A/C, TV, wheelchair access, NS rooms, laundry facilities, gift shop, barber and beauty shop, game room, airport transportation, pets OK, meeting facilities, senior rates, CC. SGL/DBL$75-$255.

Rodeway Inn (1349 Idaho St., 89801; 738-7000, 800-424-4777) 65 rooms, restaurant, wheelchair access, NS rooms, children free with parents, in-room refrigerators, microwaves and coffee makers, no pets, A/C, TV, senior rates, CC. SGL/DBL$36-$60.

Shilo Inn (2401 Mountain City Hwy., 89801; 738-5522, Fax 738-6247, 800-222-2244) 70 rooms and suites, restaurant, lounge, indoor heated pool, whirlpools, exercise center, in-room refrigerators, A/C, TV, NS rooms, wheelchair access, pets OK, airport courtesy car, children under 12 free with parents, in-room refrigerators and microwaves, airport transportation, meeting facilities, senior rates, CC. SGL/DBL$70-$93.

Super 8 Motel (1755 Idaho St., 89801; 738-8488, Fax 738-4637, 800-800-8000) 75 rooms and suites, restaurant, pets OK, children under 12 free with parents, free local calls, A/C, TV, in-room refrigerators and microwaves, fax, NS rooms, senior rates, wheelchair access, meeting facilities, CC. SGL/DBL$38-$53.

Thunderbird Motel (345 Idaho St., 89801; 738-7115) 70 rooms, heated pool, A/C, TV, NS rooms, wheelchair access, CC. SGL/DBL$40-$57.

Ely

Area Code 702

Best Western Main Motel (1101 Aultman St., 89301; 289-4529, 800-528-1234) 19 rooms, restaurant, free breakfast, lounge, pool, exercise center, children free with parents, A/C, NS rooms, TV, laundry facilities, wheelchair access, pets OK, meeting facilities, senior rates, CC. SGL/DBL$35-$69.

Best Western Park Vue Motel (930 Aultman St., 89301; 289-4497, 800-528-1234) 21 rooms, restaurant, free breakfast, lounge, pool, exercise center, children free with parents, A/C, NS rooms, TV, laundry facilities, wheelchair access, pets OK, meeting facilities, senior rates, CC. SGL/DBL$43-$56.

The Copper Queen (701 Ave. I, 89301; 289-4884) 63 rooms, restaurant, indoor pool, whirlpools, airport courtesy car, A/C, TV, NS rooms, wheelchair access, senior rates, CC. SGL/DBL$45-$58.

Fireside Inn (McGill Hwy., 89301; 289-3765, 800-732-8288) 15 rooms, A/C, TV, NS rooms, wheelchair access, CC. SGL/DBL$41.

Jailhouse Motel and Casino (Ely 89301; 289-3033, 800-841-5430) 47 rooms, restaurant, A/C, TV, NS rooms, wheelchair access, senior rates, CC. SGL/DBL$40-$51.

Motel 6 (7th St. and Ave. O, 89301; 289-6671, 505-891-6161) 122 rooms, pool, free local calls, children under 17 free with parents, NS rooms, wheelchair access, pets OK, A/C, TV, CC. SGL/DBL$38-$44.

Fallon

Area Code 702

Best Western Bonanza Inn (855 West Williams Ave., 89406; 423-6031, 800-528-1234) 75 rooms and suites, restaurant, free breakfast, lounge, pool, exercise center, children free with parents, A/C, NS rooms, TV, laundry facilities, wheelchair access, pets OK, senior rates, meeting facilities, CC. SGL/DBL$40-$78.

Comfort Inn (1830 West Williams Ave., 89406; 423-5554, 800-221-2222) 49 rooms, free breakfast, pool, whirlpools, wheelchair access, NS rooms, no pets, children under 18 free with parents, in-room refrigerators, A/C, TV, meeting facilities, senior rates, CC. SGL/DBL$55-$60.

Days Inn (60 South Allen Rd., 89406; 423-7021, Fax 423-5039, 800-325-2525) 51 rooms and suites, free breakfast, children free with parents, room service, laundry service, A/C, TV, free local calls, pets OK, fax, wheelchair access, NS rooms, senior rates, CC. SGL/DBL$35-$80.

Econo Oasis Lodge (70 East Williams Ave., 89406; 423-2194, 800-4-CHOICE) 30 rooms, free breakfast, pool, children under 12 free with parents, no pets, NS rooms, wheelchair access, A/C, TV, in-room refrigerators, microwaves and coffee makers, senior rates, CC. SGL/DBL$35-$85.

Lariat Motel (850 West Williams Ave., 89406; 423-5118) 18 rooms, A/C, TV, NS rooms, wheelchair access, no pets, CC. SGL/DBL$35-$40.

Western Motel (125 South Carson St., 89406; 423-5118) 22 rooms, outdoor heated pool, pets OK, A/C, TV, NS rooms, wheelchair access, in-room refrigerators, senior rates, CC. SGL/DBL$32-$40.

Fernley
Area Code 702

Super 8 Motel (1350 West Newlands Dr., 89408; 575-5555, Fax 575-6546, 800-800-8000) 36 rooms and suites, no pets, children under 12 free with parents, free local calls, A/C, TV, in-room refrigerators and microwaves, fax, NS rooms, senior rates, wheelchair access, no pets, meeting facilities, CC. SGL/DBL$39-$45.

Rest Rancho Motel (325 Main St., 89408; 575-4452) 38 rooms, A/C, TV, NS rooms, wheelchair access, CC. SGL/DBL$38-$44.

Gardnerville
Area Code 702

The Nenzel Mansion (1431 Ezell St., 89410; 782-7644) 4 rooms, free breakfast, pets OK, A/C, TV, NS rooms, wheelchair access, antique furnishings, CC. SGL/DBL$80-$95.

Topaz Lodge and Casino (1979 Hwy. 395 South, 89410; 266-3338, 800-962-0732) 59 rooms, restaurant, lounge, A/C, TV, NS rooms, wheelchair access, pets OK, meeting facilities, CC. SGL/DBL$40-$50.

Village Motel (1383 Hwy. 395 North, 89410; 782-2624) rooms, A/C, TV, NS rooms, wheelchair access, CC. SGL/DBL$28-$36.

Westerner Motel (1353 Hwy. 95, 89410; 782-3602) 25 rooms, A/C, TV, NS rooms, pets OK, wheelchair access, CC. SGL/DBL$30-$45.

Genoa
Area Code 710

Genoa House Inn Bed and Breakfast (180 Nixon St., 89411; 782-7057) 4 rooms, free breakfast, A/C, TV, CC. SGL/DBL$45-$65.

Glenbrook
Area Code 702

Rental and Reservation Services:

Glenbook Resorts (2070 Pray Meadow Rd., 89413; 749-5663)

Hawthorne
Area Code 702

Best Western Desert Lodge (1402 East 5th St., 89415; 945-2600, Fax 945-3872, 800-528-1234) 39 rooms, restaurant, free breakfast, lounge, pool, exercise center, children free with parents, A/C, NS rooms, TV, laundry facilities, wheelchair access, pets OK, meeting facilities, senior rates, CC. SGL/DBL$39-$65.

El Capitan Lodge and Casino (Hawthorne 89415; 945-3321, Fax 324-6229) 103 rooms and 2-bedroom apartments, restaurant, lounge, heated pool, game room, A/C, TV, NS rooms, pets OK, wheelchair access, in-room refrigerators, meeting facilities, senior rates, CC. SGL/DBL$28-$45.

Sand n'Sage Motel (Hawthorne 89415; 945-3352) 37 rooms, pool, pets OK, in-room refrigerators, A/C, TV, NS rooms, wheelchair access, senior rates, CC. SGL/DBL$30-$40.

Henderson
Area Code 702

Best Western Lake Mead Inn (85 West Lake Mead Dr., 89015; 564-1712, Fax 564-7642, 800-528-1234) 58 rooms, restaurant, free breakfast, lounge, pool, exercise center, children free with parents, A/C, NS rooms, TV, laundry facilities, wheelchair access, pets OK, in-room refrigerators, senior rates, meeting facilities, CC. SGL/DBL$41-$58.

Outpost Motel (1104 North Boulder Hwy., 89015; 564-2664, Fax 565-77858) 12 rooms, A/C, TV, NS rooms, wheelchair access, CC. SGL/DBL$44-$56.

Railroad Pass Hotel and Casino (2800 Boulder Hwy., 89015; 294-5000, Fax 294-0129, 800-654-0877) 120 rooms, A/C, TV, NS rooms, wheelchair access, CC. SGL/DBL$19-$44.

Incline Village
Area Code 702

Rental and Reservation Services:

A Bella Properties (805 Tahoe Blvd., 89450; 831-5331, 800-GO-TAHOE) rental rooms and homes.

Blue Diamond Realty (865 Tahoe Blvd., 89450; 831-7177, 800-992-1008)

B.R.A.T. Realty Management (120 Country Club Dr., 89450; 831-3318, Fax 831-8668, 800-869-8308)

Coldwell Banker Realty (795 Mays Blvd., 89450; 831-1515, Fax 831-4827, 800-748-5919)

Forest Pines Rental Agency (123 Juanita Dr., 89450; 831-1307, 800-45-TAHOE)

◻◻◻

Haus Bavaria (593 North Dyer Circle, 89451; 831-6122, 800-GO-TAHOE) 5 rooms, free breakfast, children free with parents, NS, TV, CC. SGL/DBL$80-$90.

Hilton Regency Lake Tahoe Resort and Casino (Country Club Dr., 89450; 831-1111, Fax 831-7508, 800-HILTONS) 458 rooms, cottages suites, restaurant, lounge, entertainment, heated pool, exercise center, tennis courts, spa, children free with parents, NS rooms, wheelchair access, no pets, beach, room service, laundry facilities, A/C, TV, meeting facilities, CC. SGL/DBL$65-$125.

Hyatt Regency Lake Tahoe (Incline Village 89451; 832-1234, Fax 831-7508, 800-233-1234) 458 rooms and suites, restaurant, lounge, entertainment, heated pool, whirlpools, exercise center, tennis courts, children free with parents, in-room coffee makers, boutiques, room service, no pets, TV, A/C, NS rooms, wheelchair access, CC. SGL/DBL$240-$260, STS$500-$900.

The Inn at Incline and Condos (1003 Tahoe Blvd, 89451; 831-1052, 800-824-6391) 38 rooms and condominiums, free breakfast, indoor heated pool, whirlpools, exercise center, sauna, in-room refrigerators, no pets, children free with parents, TV, NS rooms, senior rates. SGL/DBL$55-$100.

Indian Springs
Area Code 702

Indians Springs Hotel and Casino (Hwy. 95, 89018; 384-7449) 45 rooms, restaurant, lounge, laundry facilities, pets OK, children free with parents, A/C, TV, NS rooms, wheelchair access, CC. SGL/DBL$35-$40.

Jackpot
Area Code 702

Cactus Pete's Hotel and Casino (Hwy. 93, 89825; 755-2321, 800-821-1103) 293 rooms, restaurant, lounge, entertainment, heated pool, lighted tennis courts, whirlpools, children free with parents, no pets, A/C, TV, NS rooms, wheelchair access, CC. SGL/DBL$40-$175.

Horseshu Hotel and Casino (Dice Rd., 89825; 755-7777) 120 rooms, restaurant, lounge, pool, whirlpools, A/C, TV, NS rooms, wheelchair access, children free with parents, pets OK, CC. SGL/DBL$30-$75.

Primadonna Resort and Casino (Jackpot 89193; 382-1212) 661 rooms, restaurant, lounge, entertainment, pool, whirlpools, A/C, TV, NS rooms, wheelchair access, children free with parents, no pets, meeting facilities, CC. SGL/DBL$20-$40.

Jean
Area Code 702

Gold Strike Hotel and Casino (1 Main St., 89109; 477-5000, 800-634-1359) 18 rooms, A/C, TV, NS rooms, wheelchair access, CC. SGL/DBL$18-$39.

Nevada Landing Hotel and Casino (Jean 89019; 387-5000, Fax 874-1583, 800-628-6682) 303 rooms, A/C, TV, NS rooms, wheelchair access, CC. SGL/DBL$18-$39.

Whiskey Pete's Hotel and Casino (Jean 89019; 382-4388, Fax 874-1554, 800-367-PETE) 726 rooms, restaurant, lounge, entertainment, pool, whirlpools, no pets, children free with parents, A/C, TV, NS rooms, wheelchair access, CC. SGL/DBL$20-$35.

Lake Tahoe
Area Code 702

Horizon Casino Resort (Lake Tahoe 89449; 588-6211, 800-322-7723) 539 rooms, A/C, TV, NS rooms, wheelchair access, CC. SGL/DBL$60.

Las Vegas
Area Code 702

Airport Inn (5100 Paradise Rd., 89119; 798-2777, 800-634-6439) 340 rooms, A/C, TV, NS rooms, wheelchair access, CC. SGL/DBL$40-$95.

Aladdin Hotel and Casino (3667 Las Vegas Blvd., 89114; 736-0111, Fax 734-3583, 800-634-3424) 1,100 rooms and suites, restaurant, lounge, pool, exercise center, A/C, TV, NS rooms, wheelchair access, room service, in-room refrigerators, children free with parents, senior rates, meeting facilities, CC. SGL/DBL$25-$55.

Alexis Park Resort (375 East Harmon Ave., 89109; 796-3300, Fax 796-4334, 800-453-8000) 500 rooms and 2-bedroom suites, restaurant, lounge, entertainment, heated pool, whirlpools, tennis courts, in-room refrigerators and coffee makers, in-room computer hookups, children under 18 free with parents, pets OK, A/C, TV, NS rooms, wheelchair access, CC. SGL/DBL$85-$600.

Algiers (2845 Las Vegas Blvd., South, 89109; 735-3311, 800-732-3361) 105 rooms, A/C, TV, NS rooms, wheelchair access, CC. SGL/DBL$45-$65.

Ambassador East Motel (916 East Fremont St., 89101; 384-8420, 800-634-6703) 308 rooms, A/C, TV, NS rooms, wheelchair access, CC. SGL/DBL$23-$32.

Arizona Charlie's Motel (740 South Decatur Ave., 89107; 258-5200, 800-342-2695) 100 rooms, restaurant, lounge, pool, gift shop, A/C, TV, NS rooms, airport transportation, children free with parents, no pets, wheelchair access, CC. SGL/DBL$30-$45.

Bally's Hotel (3645 Las Vegas Blvd., 89109; 739-4111, Fax 794-2413, 800-634-3434) 2,813 rooms and suites, restaurant, lounge, entertainment, heated pool, exercise center, sauna, whirlpools, lighted tennis courts, A/C, TV, NS rooms, wheelchair access, airport transportation, in-room refrigerators and coffee makers, game room, boutiques, barber and beauty shop, laundry facilities, children free with parents, no pets, senior rates, meeting facilities, CC. SGL/DBL$90-$1,500.

Barcelona Coast Hotel and Casino (3595 Las Vegas Blvd. South, 89132; 737-7111, Fax 737-6304, 800-634-6755) 200 rooms and suites, restaurant, lounge, in-room refrigerators, in-room computer hookups, no pets, A/C, TV, NS rooms, wheelchair access, CC. SGL/DBL$50-$130.

Barcelona Hotel and Casino (5011 East Craig Rd., 89115; 644-6300, 800-223-6330) 179 rooms, restaurant, lounge, entertainment, pool, whirlpools, kitchenettes, in-room refrigerators, laundry facilities, no pets, A/C, TV, NS rooms, wheelchair access, senior rates, CC. SGL/DBL$35-$55.

Best Western Main Street Inn (1000 North Main St., 89101; 382-3455, Fax 382-1428, 800-851-1414, 800-528-1234) 91 rooms, restaurant, free breakfast, lounge, pool, exercise center, children free with parents, A/C, NS rooms, in-room refrigerators, TV, laundry facilities, wheelchair access, pets OK, meeting facilities, senior rates, CC. SGL/DBL$40-$60.

Best Western Mardi Gras Inn (3500 Paradise Rd., 89109; 731-2020, 800-634-6501, 800-528-1234) 314 rooms and 1- and 2-bedroom suites, restaurant, free breakfast, lounge, pool, exercise center, whirlpools, airport transportation, children free with parents, A/C, NS rooms, TV, in-room refrigerators and coffee makers, wheelchair access, pets OK, meeting facilities, senior rates, CC. SGL/DBL$35-$100.

Best Western McCarren Inn (4970 Paradise Rd., 89119; 798-5530, Fax 798-7627, 800-528-1234) 97 rooms, restaurant, free breakfast, lounge, pool, exercise center, children free with parents, A/C, NS rooms, TV, laundry facilities, wheelchair access, airport courtesy car, pets OK, senior rates, meeting facilities, CC. SGL/DBL$65-$65.

Best Western Nellis Motor Inn (5330 East Craig Rd., 89115; 643-6111, 800-528-1234) 52 rooms, restaurant, free breakfast, lounge, pool, exercise center, children free with parents, A/C, NS rooms, TV, laundry facilities, wheelchair access, pets OK, meeting facilities, senior rates, CC. SGL/DBL$40-$55.

Best Western Parkview Inn (905 Las Vegas Blvd. North, 89101; 385-1213, 800-548-6122, 800-528-1234) 56 rooms, restaurant, free breakfast, lounge, pool, exercise center, children free with parents, A/C, NS rooms, TV, laundry facilities, wheelchair access, pets OK, meeting facilities, senior rates, CC. SGL/DBL$38-$58.

Binion's Horseshoe Hotel and Casino (128 East Freemont St., 89125; 382-1600, Fax 382-5750, 800-622-6468) 350 rooms, A/C, TV, NS rooms, wheelchair access, CC. SGL/DBL$40-$60.

Blair House Hotel (344 East Desert Inn Rd., 89109; 792-2222, 800-553-9111) 224 rooms, pool, whirlpools, kitchenettes, laundry facilities, VCRs, children free with parents, no pets, A/C, TV, NS rooms, wheelchair access, CC. SGL/DBL$65-$85.

Boardwalk Hotel and Casino (3750 Las Vegas Blvd., 89109; 735-1167) 201 rooms, restaurant, lounge, pool, pets OK, laundry facilities, A/C, TV, NS rooms, wheelchair access, CC. SGL/DBL$45-$90.

Caesers Palace (3570 Las Vegas Blvd., 89109; 731-7110, Fax 731-6636, 800-634-6001) 1,518 rooms and suites, restaurant, lounge, indoor and outdoor heated pool, exercise center, sauna, whirlpools, lighted tennis courts, A/C, TV, NS rooms, barber and beauty shop, wheelchair access, airport transportation, boutiques, in-room refrigerators and coffee makers, laundry facilities, children free with parents, no pets, senior rates, meeting facilities, CC. SGL/DBL$95-$900.

California Hotel and Casino (Las Vegas 89109; 385-1222, 800-634-6255) 635 rooms, restaurant, pool, A/C, TV, NS rooms, wheelchair access, no pets, gift shop, in-room refrigerators, children free with parents, meeting facilities, CC. SGL/DBL$40-$60.

Carriage House (105 East Harmon Ave., 89109; 798-1020, Fax 798-1020 ext 112) 150 2-bedroom efficiencies, restaurant, heated pool, kitchenettes, A/C, TV, NS rooms, wheelchair access, local transportation, kitchenettes, in-room microwaves and coffee makers, VCRs, no pets, children free with parents, laundry facilities, senior rates, CC. SGL/DBL$85-$190.

Casino Royale and Hotel (3419 Las Vegas Blvd., 89109; 737-3500) 160 rooms, no pets, A/C, TV, NS rooms, wheelchair access, CC. SGL/DBL$35-$70.

Center Strip Inn (3688 Las Vegas Blvd., 89109; 739-6066, 800-777-7737) 105 rooms and 2-bedroom suites, pool, in-room refrigerators and microwaves, VCRs, children free with parents, A/C, TV, NS rooms, no pets, wheelchair access, CC. SGL/DBL$30-$125.

Circus Circus Hotel and Casino (Las Vegas 89109; 734-0410, 800-634-3450) 2,800 rooms and suites, restaurant, lounge, heated pool, exercise center, sauna, whirlpools, A/C, TV, NS rooms, wheelchair access, airport transportation, in-room refrigerators and coffee makers, barber and beauty shop, boutiques, laundry facilities, children free with parents, no pets, senior rates, meeting facilities, CC. SGL/DBL$20-$100.

Comfort Inn Central (211 East Flamingo Rd., 89109; 733-7777, 800-221-2222) 320 rooms, restaurant, free breakfast, pool, wheelchair access, NS rooms, no pets, children under 18 free with parents, A/C, TV, meeting facilities, senior rates, CC. SGL/DBL$48-$183.

Comfort Inn South (5075 Koval Lane, 89119; 736-3600, 800-221-2222) 106 rooms, restaurant, free breakfast, pool, wheelchair access, NS rooms, no pets, children under 18 free with parents, A/C, TV, meeting facilities, senior rates, CC. SGL/DBL$36-$108.

Convention Inn (735 East Desert Inn, 89109; 737-1555) 73 rooms, A/C, TV, NS rooms, wheelchair access, pets OK, CC. SGL/DBL$55-$65.

Courtyard by Marriott (3275 Paradise Rd., 89109; 791-3600, Fax 796-7981, 800-321-2211) 149 rooms and suites, restaurant, lounge, heated pool, exercise center, whirlpools, children free with parents, laundry service, A/C, NS rooms, TV, in-room refrigerators and coffee makers, airport courtesy car, meeting facilities, senior rates, CC. SGL/DBL$85-$120.

Days Inn Downtown (707 East Fremont St., 89101; 388-1400, Fax 388-9622, 800-325-2525) 147 rooms and 1-bedroom suites, restaurant, lounge, outdoor pool, children free with parents, room service, laundry service, A/C, TV, free local calls, local transportation, pets OK, fax, wheelchair access, NS rooms, meeting facilities, senior rates, CC. SGL/DBL$36-$150.

Days Inn (3265 Las Vegas Blvd., 89109; 735-5102, Fax 735-0168, 800-325-2525) 126 rooms and suites, outdoor pool, children free with parents, room service, laundry service, A/C, TV, free local calls, pets OK, fax, complimentary newspaper, airport transportation, wheelchair access, NS rooms, senior rates, CC. SGL/DBL$45-$120.

Days Inn (4155 Koval Lane, 89109; 731-2111, Fax 731-1113, 800-325-2525) 357 rooms and suites, restaurant, lounge, entertainment, outdoor pool, children free with parents, room service, laundry service, gift shop, A/C, TV, free local calls, pets OK, fax, wheelchair access, NS rooms, senior rates, CC. SGL/DBL$29-$75, STS$75-$150.

Desert Inn (3145 Las Vegas Blvd., 89109; 733-4444, 800-634-6906) 821 rooms and suites, restaurant, lounge, pool, exercise center, sauna, whirlpools, lighted tennis courts, barber and beauty shop, boutiques, A/C, TV, NS rooms, wheelchair access, airport transportation, in-room refrigerators and coffee makers, laundry facilities, children free with parents, no pets, senior rates, meeting facilities, CC. SGL/DBL$90-$1,500.

Econo Lodge (1150 Las Vegas Blvd., 89104; 382-6001, 800-4-CHOICE) 127 rooms, pool, children under 12 free with parents, no pets, NS rooms, wheelchair access, A/C, TV, free local calls, kitchenettes, senior rates, CC. SGL/DBL$50-$95.

Econo Lodge Downtown (520 South Casino Center Blvd., 89101; 384-8211, 800-4-CHOICE) 48 rooms, children under 12 free with parents, no pets, NS rooms, wheelchair access, A/C, TV, in-room refrigerators and coffee makers, laundry facilities, senior rates, CC. SGL/DBL$35-$85.

El Cortez (600 East Fremont St., 89125; 385-5200, 800-634-6703) 308 rooms, restaurant, lounge, room service, boutiques, barber and beauty shop, A/C, TV, NS rooms, wheelchair access, CC. SGL/DBL$25-$40.

Excalibur (3850 Las Vegas Blvd, 89119; 597-7777, 800-937-7777) 4,032 rooms and suites, restaurant, lounge, entertainment, pool, exercise center, sauna, whirlpools, A/C, TV, NS rooms, wheelchair access, airport transportation, boutiques, barber and beauty shop, in-room refrigerators and coffee makers, laundry facilities, children free with parents, no pets, senior rates, meeting facilities, CC. SGL/DBL$39-$85, STS$100.

Fairfield Inn by Marriott (3850 Paradise Rd., 89109; 791-0899, 800-228-2800) 129 rooms, outdoor pool, children under 18 free with parents, NS rooms, TV, free cable TV, free local calls, laundry service, A/C, wheelchair access, meeting facilities, fax, airport transportation, senior rates, CC. SGL/DBL$44-$60.

Four Queens (202 East Fremont 89125; 385-4011, Fax 383-0631, 800-634-6045) 700 rooms and suites, restaurant, lounge, entertainment, A/C, TV, NS rooms, 24-hour room service, no pets, children free with parents, wheelchair access, meeting facilities, senior rates, CC. SGL/DBL$49-$100.

Fremont Hotel (200 East Fremont St., 89125; 385-3232, 800-634-6182) 452 rooms, restaurant, lounge, gift shop, A/C, TV, NS rooms, wheelchair access, CC. SGL/DBL$35-$60.

Friendship Inn King Albert (185 Albert Ave., 89101; 735-1741, 800-424-4777) 52 rooms and efficiencies, A/C, TV, no pets, NS rooms, laundry facilities, children free with parents, wheelchair access, senior rates, CC. SGL/DBL$35-$77.

Gold Coast Hotel (4000 West Flamingo Rd., 89103; 367-7111, Fax 367-8575, 800-331-5334) 722 rooms and suites, restaurant, lounge, entertainment, pool, whirlpools, 24-hour room service, children free with parents, barber and beauty shop, game room, A/C, TV, NS rooms, in-room refrigerators, wheelchair access, CC. SGL/DBL$35-$400.

Golden Nugget (129 East Freemont St., 89125; 385-7111, Fax 386-8362, 800-634-3454) 1,907 rooms and suites, restaurant, lounge, entertainment, heated pool, exercise center, saunas, whirlpools, gift shop, barber and beauty shop, A/C, TV, wheelchair access, NS rooms, no pets, children free with parents, meeting rooms, senior rates, CC. SGL/DBL$58-$125, STS$210-$750.

The Hacienda Resort (3950 Las Vegas Blvd., 89109; 739-8911, Fax 798-8289, 800-634-6713) 1,140 rooms and suites, restaurant, lounge, entertainment, pool, lighted tennis courts, boutiques, beauty shop, in-room refrigerators, A/C, TV, NS rooms, wheelchair access, CC. SGL/DBL$30-$80, STS$125-$350.

Harrah's (3475 Las Vegas Blvd., 89109; 369-5000, Fax 369-6014) 1,725 rooms and suites, restaurant, lounge, pool, exercise center, sauna, whirlpools, A/C, TV, NS rooms, wheelchair access, airport transportation, in-room refrigerators and coffee makers, laundry facilities, barber and beauty shop, boutiques, game room, children free with parents, no pets, senior rates, meeting facilities, CC. SGL/DBL$70-$125, STS$190-$350.

Hilton Flamingo Hotel (3555 Las Vegas Blvd. South, 89109; 733-3499, Fax 684-4550, 800-HILTONS) 3,530 rooms and suites, restaurant, lounge, entertainment, pool, exercise center, lighted tennis courts, spa, children free with parents, NS rooms, wheelchair access, no pets, room service, laundry facilities, A/C, TV, meeting facilities, CC. SGL/DBL$65-$135, STS$200-$400.

Hilton Las Vegas Hotel (3000 Paradise Rd., 89109; 732-5111, Fax 732-5424, 800-HILTONS) 3,174 rooms and suites, restaurant, lounge, entertainment, pool, exercise center, lighted tennis courts, whirlpools, in-room refrigerators, children free with parents, NS rooms, wheelchair access, no pets, room service, boutiques, barber and beauty shop, game room, laundry facilities, A/C, TV, meeting facilities, CC. SGL/DBL$85-$100, STS$265-$300.

Holiday Inn (325 East Flamingo Rd., 89109; 732-9100, Fax 731-9784, 800-832-7889, 800-HOLIDAY) 150 rooms, restaurant, lounge, indoor heated pool, exercise center, spa, whirlpools, children under 19 free with parents, wheelchair access, A/C, airport transportation, TV, NS rooms, fax, room service, no pets, laundry service, 3,500 square feet of meeting and exhibition space, senior rates, CC. SGL/DBL$70-$165.

Howard Johnson Lodge (3111 West Tropicana Ave., 89103; 798-1111, Fax 798-7138, 800-I-GO-HOJO) 150 rooms, restaurant, lounge, outdoor pool, jacuzzi, gift shop, game room, children free with parents, wheelchair access, NS rooms, TV, A/C, no pets, laundry facilities, airport transportation, senior rates, meeting facilities, CC. SGL/DBL$50-$140.

Howard Johnson Lodge (1322 Fremont St., 89101; 385-1150, Fax 385-4940, 800-I-GO-HOJO) 88 rooms, restaurant, lounge, pool, jacuzzi, children free with parents, wheelchair access, NS rooms, TV, A/C, no pets, laundry facilities, senior rates, meeting facilities, CC. SGL/DBL$48-$85.

Howard Johnson Plaza Suites (4255 Paradise Rd., 89109; 369-4400, Fax 369-3770, 800-I-GO-HOJO) 202 suites, restaurant, lounge, outdoor heated pool, exercise center, whirlpools, sauna, children free with parents, wheelchair access, NS rooms, TV, A/C, in-room coffee makers, gift shop, airport courtesy car, pets OK, laundry facilities, senior rates, meeting facilities, CC. SGL/DBL$100-$250.

Imperial Palace (3535 Las Vegas Blvd., 89109; 731-3311, Fax 735-8528, 800-634-6441) 2,700 rooms and suites, restaurant, lounge, pool, exercise center, sauna, whirlpools, A/C, TV, NS rooms, wheelchair access, airport transportation, in-room refrigerators and coffee makers, laundry facilities, children free with parents, no pets, boutiques, barber and beauty shop, senior rates, meeting facilities, CC. SGL/DBL$45-$350.

La Quinta Motor Inn (3782 Las Vegas Blvd., 89109; 800-531-5900) 114 rooms, outdoor heated pool, complimentary newspaper, free local calls, fax, laundry service, NS rooms, wheelchair access, remote control TV, airport courtesy car, A/C, meeting facilities, senior rates, CC. SGL/DBL$45-$70.

Lady Luck Casino (206 North 3rd St., 89101; 477-3000, Fax 477-3002, 800-523-9582) 791 rooms and suites, restaurant, lounge, pool, A/C, TV, NS rooms, wheelchair access, in-room refrigerators, no pets, airport transportation, laundry facilities, CC. SGL/DBL$50-$200.

Luxor Las Vegas Resort (3900 Las Vegas Blvd., 89119; 795-8118) 2,565 rooms, restaurant, lounge, whirlpools, sauna, A/C, TV, NS rooms, wheelchair access, room service, children free with parents, no pets, CC. SGL/DBL$50-$100.

MGM Grand Hotel Casino (3799 Las Vegas Blvd., 89109; 891-7777) 5,014 rooms and suites, restaurant, lounge, entertainment, pool, exercise center, sauna, whirlpools, A/C, TV, NS rooms, wheelchair access, airport transportation, in-room refrigerators and coffee makers, laundry facilities, children free with parents, no pets, senior rates, meeting facilities, CC. SGL/DBL$60-$1,500.

Mirage (3400 Las Vegas Blvd., 89109; 791-7111, Fax 791-7446, 800-627-6667) 3,049 rooms and suites, restaurant, lounge, entertainment, indoor and outdoor pool, exercise center, sauna, whirlpools, A/C, TV, NS rooms, wheelchair access, airport transportation, in-room refrigerators and coffee makers, boutiques, game room, laundry facilities, children free with parents, no pets, senior rates, meeting facilities, CC. SGL/DBL$80-$280, STS$300-$3,000.

Motel 6 (Desert Inn Rd., 89121; 457-8051, 505-891-6161) 161 rooms, pool, free local calls, children under 17 free with parents, NS rooms, wheelchair access, pets OK, A/C, TV, CC. SGL/DBL$34-$44.

Motel 6 (5085 South Industrial Rd., 89118; 739-6747, 505-891-6161) 139 rooms, pool, free local calls, children under 17 free with parents, NS rooms, wheelchair access, pets OK, A/C, TV, CC. SGL/DBL$36-$42.

Motel 6 (195 East Tropicana Ave., 89109; 798-0728, 505-891-6161) 88 rooms, pool, free local calls, children under 17 free with parents, NS rooms, wheelchair access, pets OK, A/C, TV, CC. SGL/DBL$38-$44.

Palace Station Hotel and Casino (2411 West Sahara, 89102; 367-2411, 800-634-3101) 1,028 rooms and suites, restaurant, lounge, entertainment, indoor and outdoor heated pool, whirlpools, gift shop, game room, children free with parents, A/C, TV, NS rooms, wheelchair access, CC. SGL/DBL$40-$100, STS$150-$750.

Quality Inn Sunrise Suites (4575 Boulder Hwy., 89121; 434-0848, 800-221-2222) 143 rooms and suites, restaurant, pool, exercise center, whirlpools, children free with parents, A/C, TV, room service, laundry service, NS rooms, meeting facilities, senior rates, CC. SGL/DBL$38-$123.

Quality Inn (377 East Flamingo Rd., 89109; 733-7777, 800-221-2222) 320 rooms and suites, restaurant, lounge, pool, whirlpools, exercise center, children free with parents, A/C, game room, TV, room service, laundry service, NS rooms, meeting facilities, senior rates, CC. SGL/DBL$38-$156.

Ramada San Remo Inn (115 East Tropicana Ave., 89109; 739-9000, Fax 736-1120, 800-2-RAMADA) 711 rooms and suites, restaurant, lounge, entertainment, heated pool, whirlpools, game room, gift shop, wheelchair access, NS rooms, pets OK, A/C, TV, children under 18 free with parents, room service, laundry facilities, meeting facilities, senior rates, CC. SGL/DBL$40-$100, STS$100-$350.

Residence Inn (3225 Paradise Rd., 89109; 796-9300, 800-331-3131) 192 rooms and suites, free breakfast, in-room refrigerators, coffee makers and microwaves, laundry facilities, TV, A/C, VCRs, pets OK, complimentary newspaper, fireplaces, children free with parents, airport transportation, NS rooms, wheelchair access, meeting facilities for 50, CC. SGL/DBL$90-$165.

Rio Suite Hotel and Casino (Las Vegas 89114; 252-7777, Fax 252-7670, 800-PLAY-RIO) 424 suites, restaurant, lounge, entertainment, heated pool, exercise center, game room, whirlpools, no pets, children free with parents, barber and beauty shop, in-room refrigerators, A/C, TV, NS rooms, wheelchair access, meeting facilities, senior rates, CC. SGL/DBL$85-$150.

Riviera Hotel (2901 Las Vegas Blvd., 89109; 734-5110, Fax 794-9663, 800-634-6753) 2,100 rooms and suites, restaurant, lounge, entertainment, heated pool, exercise center, sauna, whirlpools, lighted tennis courts, barber and beauty shop, boutiques, A/C, TV, NS rooms, wheelchair access, airport transportation, in-room refrigerators and coffee makers, laundry facilities, children free with parents, no pets, senior rates, meeting facilities, CC. SGL/DBL$60-$500.

Rodeway Inn (3786 Las Vegas Blvd. South, 89109; 736-1434, Fax 736-6058, 800-424-4777) 97 rooms and 2-bedroom suites, restaurant, heated pool, wheelchair access, NS rooms, children free with parents, pets OK, in-room coffee makers, A/C, TV, senior rates, CC. SGL/DBL$45-$150.

Sahara Hotel (2535 Las Vegas Blvd. South, 89109; 737-2111, Fax 791-2027, 800-634-6666) 2,035 rooms and suites, restaurant, lounge, entertainment, pool, exercise center, sauna, whirlpools, A/C, TV, NS rooms, wheelchair access, airport transportation, in-room refrigerators and coffee makers, laundry facilities, children free with parents, no pets, senior rates, meeting facilities, CC. SGL/DBL$50-$100, STS$200-$300.

Sam's Town (5111 Boulder Hwy., 89109; 456-7777, 800-634-6371) 197 rooms and suites, restaurant, lounge, entertainment, pool, boutiques, game room, no pets, children free with parents, A/C, TV, NS rooms, wheelchair access, CC. SGL/DBL$30-$50, STS$90-$100.

Sands Hotel (3355 Las Vegas Blvd., 89109; 634-6901, Fax 733-5620) 71 rooms and suites, restaurant, lounge, heated pool, whirlpools, exercise center, in-room refrigerators, boutiques, laundry service, airport transportation, room service, A/C, TV, NS rooms, wheelchair access, CC. SGL/DBL$30-$110, STS$150-$1,500.

Santa Fe Hotel and Casino (494 North Rancho Dr., 89103; 658-4900, 800-872-6823) 200 rooms, restaurant, lounge, entertainment, game room, gift shop, children free with parents, A/C, TV, NS rooms, wheelchair access, CC. SGL/DBL$40-$50.

Sheffield Inn (3970 Paradise Rd., 89109; 796-9000) 228 rooms and efficiencies, free breakfast, pool, whirlpools, A/C, TV, NS rooms, children free with parents, no pets, wheelchair access, airport courtesy car, in-room refrigerators and coffee makers, kitchenettes, VCRs, laundry facilities, CC. SGL/DBL$100-$200.

Showboat Hotel (2800 East Fremont, 89104; 384-9123, Fax 383-9238, 800-826-2800) 484 rooms and suites, restaurant, lounge, entertainment, heated pool, airport transportation, barber and beauty shop, gift shop, game room, children free with parents, A/C, TV, NS rooms, wheelchair access, CC. SGL/DBL$30-$85. STS$85-$255.

Stardust Hotel and Casino (3000 Las Vegas Blvd. South, 89109; 732-6111, Fax 732-6296, 800-634-6757) 2,341 rooms and suites, restaurant, lounge, entertainment, pool, exercise center, sauna, whirlpools, A/C, TV, NS rooms, wheelchair access, barber and beauty shop, boutiques, game room, airport transportation, in-room refrigerators and coffee makers, laundry facilities, children free with parents, no pets, senior rates, meeting facilities, CC. SGL/DBL$25-$100, STS$150-$225.

Super 8 Motel (5288 Boulder Hwy., 89122; 435-8888, Fax 435-6953, 800-825-0880, 800-800-8000) 150 rooms and suites, restaurant, lounge, outdoor pool, jacuzzi, game room, no pets, children under 12 free with parents, free local calls, A/C, TV, in-room refrigerators and microwaves, fax, NS rooms, senior rates, wheelchair access, meeting facilities, CC. SGL/DBL$30-$46.

Super 8 Motel (4435 Las Vegas Blvd. North, 89115; 644-5666, Fax 644-1219, 800-800-8000) 109 rooms and suites, restaurant, lounge, outdoor pool, jacuzzi, no pets, children under 12 free with parents, free local calls, A/C, TV, in-room refrigerators and microwaves, local transportation, fax, NS rooms, senior rates, wheelchair access, meeting facilities, CC. SGL/DBL$30-$53.

Super 8 Motel (4250 Koval Lane, 89109; 794-0888, Fax 794-3504, 800-800-8000) 289 rooms and suites, outdoor heated pool, whirlpools, sauna, game room, gift shop, boutiques, no pets, children under 12 free with parents, free local calls, A/C, TV, in-room refrigerators and microwaves, fax, NS rooms, senior rates, wheelchair access, meeting facilities, CC. SGL/DBL$36-$57.

TraveLodge Downtown (2028 East Fremont St., 89101; 384-7540, Fax 384-0408, 800-578-7878) 58 rooms and suites, restaurant, pool, wheelchair access, complimentary newspaper, laundry service, TV, A/C, free local calls, fax, local transportation, NS rooms, in-room refrigerators and microwaves, children under 18 free with parents, no pets, meeting facilities, CC. SGL/DBL$40-$80.

TraveLodge South Strip (3735 Las Vegas Blvd. South, 89109; 736-3443, Fax 736-1356, 800-578-7878) 128 rooms, restaurant, lounge, pool, wheelchair access, complimentary newspaper, laundry service, TV, A/C, free local calls, fax, NS rooms, in-room refrigerators and microwaves, children under 18 free with parents, no pets, meeting facilities, CC. SGL/DBL$50-$125.

TraveLodge Las Vegas Strip (2830 Las Vegas Blvd. South, 89109; 735-4222, Fax 733-7695, 800-578-7878) 100 rooms and suites, restaurant, lounge, pool, wheelchair access, complimentary newspaper, laundry service, TV, A/C, free local calls, fax, NS rooms, in-room refrigerators and microwaves, children under 18 free with parents, no pets, meeting facilities, CC. SGL/DBL$65-$125.

Tropicana Hotel (3801 Las Vegas Blvd, 89109; 739-2222, 800-634-4000) 1,900 rooms and suites, restaurant, lounge, entertainment, pool, exercise center, sauna, whirlpools, A/C, TV, NS rooms, wheelchair access, airport transportation, in-room refrigerators and coffee makers, barber and beauty shop, boutiques, laundry facilities, children free with parents, no pets, senior rates, meeting facilities, CC. SGL/DBL$55-$155.

Westward Ho Hotel and Casino (2900 Las Vegas Blvd., 89109; 731-2900, 800-634-6803) 777 rooms, restaurant, lounge, entertainment, indoor and outdoor pools, whirlpools, A/C, TV, NS rooms, wheelchair access, in-room refrigerators, room service, CC. SGL/DBL$37-$110.

Laughlin
Area Code 702

Bayshore Inn (1955 West Casino Dr., 89029; 299-9010) 105 rooms pool, whirlpools, children free with parents, A/C, TV, NS rooms, wheelchair access, no pets, senior rates, CC. SGL/DBL$25-$68.

Best Western Riverside Resort (1650 Casino Dr., 89029; 298-2535, Fax 298-2614, 800-528-1234) 660 rooms, restaurant, lounge, entertainment, pool, exercise center, children free with parents, A/C, NS rooms, TV, laundry facilities, wheelchair access, pets OK, room service, airport courtesy car, senior rates, meeting facilities, senior rates, CC. SGL/DBL$35-$65, STS$75-$300.

Colorado Belle Hotel (2100 Casino Dr., 89029; 298-4000, 800-458-9500) 1,232 rooms and suites, restaurant, lounge, entertainment, heated pool, whirlpools, boutiques, no pets, in-room refrigerators, game room, room service, A/C, TV, NS rooms, wheelchair access, airport courtesy car, CC. SGL/DBL$25-$70.

Edgewater Hotel and Casino (2020 Casino Dr., 89029; 298-2453, 800-677-4837) 1,450 rooms and suites, restaurant, lounge, entertainment, heated whirlpools, exercise center, A/C, airport transportation, in-room refrigerators, no pets, gift shop, TV, NS rooms, wheelchair access, CC. SGL/DBL$25-$55, STS$75-$125.

Gold River Gambling Hall and Resort (2700 South Casino Dr., 89029; 298-2242, 800-835-7903) 1,003 rooms and suites, restaurant, lounge, entertainment, heated pool, whirlpools, boutiques, game room, A/C, TV, NS rooms, airport courtesy car, wheelchair access, CC. SGL/DBL$25-$300.

Golden Nugget (2300 Casino Dr., 89029; 298-7111, 800-950-7700) 300 rooms and suites, restaurant, lounge, entertainment, whirlpools, sauna, boutiques, airport courtesy car, A/C, TV, NS rooms, wheelchair access, CC. SGL/DBL$25-$50, STS$150.

Harrah's Casino Hotel (2900 South Casino Dr., 89029; 298-4600) 1,658 rooms, restaurant, lounge, entertainment, pool, whirlpools, no pets, A/C, TV, NS rooms, wheelchair access, CC. SGL/DBL$55-$150.

Hilton Flamingo Hotel (1900 South Casino Dr., 89029; 298-5111, Fax 298-5129, 800-HILTONS) 2,000 rooms and suites, restaurant, lounge, entertainment, pool, exercise center, lighted tennis courts, beauty salon, gift shop, children free with parents, NS rooms, wheelchair access, no pets, room service, laundry facilities, A/C, TV, meeting facilities, CC. SGL/DBL$30-$275.

Pioneer Hotel and Casino (Casino Dr., 89029; 298-2442, 800-634-3469) 415 rooms and suites, restaurant, lounge, pool, exercise center, lighted tennis courts, game room, in-room refrigerators, A/C, TV, NS rooms, airport courtesy car, wheelchair access, CC. SGL/DBL$30-$45.

Ramada Express Hotel and Casino (2121 South Casino Dr., 89029; 298-4200, Fax 298-4619, 800-2-RAMADA) 1,500 rooms and suites, restaurant, lounge, entertainment, outdoor pool, jacuzzi, wheelchair access, NS rooms, no pets, gift shop, airport courtesy car, A/C, TV, children under 18 free with parents, room service, laundry facilities, meeting facilities, senior rates, CC. SGL/DBL$28-$83, STS$200-$275.

Lovelock
Area Code 702

Best Western Sturgeon's Inn (1420 Cornell Ave., 89419; 273-2971, Fax 273-2278, 800-528-1234) 42 rooms, restaurant, free breakfast, lounge, pool, exercise center, children free with parents, A/C, NS rooms, TV, laundry facilities, wheelchair access, pets OK, meeting facilities, senior rates, CC. SGL/DBL$39-$63.

Minden
Area Code 702

Carson Valley Inn (1627 Hwy. 395 North, 89423; 782-9711, 800-321-6983) 154 rooms, restaurant, lounge, entertainment, whirlpools, no pets, in-room refrigerators, A/C, TV, NS rooms, wheelchair access, children free with parents, no pets, senior rates, CC. SGL/DBL$60-$80.

Carson Valley Motor Lodge (1645 Hwy. 395 North, 89423; 782-9711) 74 rooms and suites, no pets, children free with parents, A/C, TV, NS rooms, wheelchair access, CC. SGL/DBL$40-$60.

Holiday Lodge (1591 Hwy. 395, 89423; 782-2288, 800-266-2289) 20 rooms and efficiencies, A/C, TV, NS rooms, pets OK, wheelchair access, CC. SGL/DBL$32-$50.

Overton
Area Code 702

Echo Bay Resort (North Shore Rd., 89040; 394-4000, 800-752-9669) 52 rooms, restaurant, lounge, pool, laundry facilities, pets OK, A/C, TV, NS rooms, wheelchair access, CC. SGL/DBL$70-$85.

Pahrump
Area Code 702

Pahrump Station Days Inn (Hwy. 160 Loop Rd., 89041; 727-5100, 800-325-2525) 44 rooms and suites, free breakfast, outdoor pool, children free with parents, room service, laundry service, A/C, TV, free local calls, pets OK, fax, wheelchair access, NS rooms, meeting facilities, senior rates, CC. SGL/DBL$45-$55.

Reno
Area Code 702

Adventure Inn (3575 South Virginia St., 89502; 828-9000, Fax 825-8338, 800-937-1436) 45 rooms, A/C, TV, NS rooms, wheelchair access, CC. SGL/DBL$70-$225.

Bed and Breakfast South Reno (136 Andrew Lane, 89511; 849-0772) 10 rooms, free breakfast, pool, A/C, TV, NS, private baths, children over 8 welcome, CC. SGL/DBL$58-$75.

Best Western Airport Plaza Inn (1981 Terminal Way, 89502; 348-6370, Fax 348-9722, 800-528-1234) 270 rooms and efficiencies, restaurant, free breakfast, lounge, pool, exercise center, children free with parents, A/C, NS rooms, TV, laundry facilities, airport transportation, game room, fireplaces, wheelchair access, pets OK, senior rates, meeting facilities, senior rates, CC. SGL/DBL$65-$105.

Best Western Continental Lodge (1885 South Virginia St., 89502; 329-1001, Fax 324-5402, 800-528-1234) 104 rooms, restaurant, free breakfast, lounge, pool, exercise center, children free with parents, A/C, NS rooms, TV, laundry facilities, wheelchair access, pets OK, meeting facilities, senior rates, CC. SGL/DBL$42-$78.

Best Western Daniel's Motor Lodge (375 North Sierra St., 89501; 329-1351, 800-528-1234) 82 rooms, restaurant, free breakfast, lounge, pool, exercise center, children free with parents, A/C, NS rooms, TV, laundry facilities, wheelchair access, pets OK, meeting facilities, senior rates, CC. SGL/DBL$40-$70.

Bob Cashell's Horseshoe Club (222 North Sierra St., 89501; 322-2178, 800-843-7403) 48 rooms, A/C, TV, NS rooms, wheelchair access, CC. SGL/DBL$35-$40.

Circus-Circus Hotel Casino (500 North Sierra St., 89513; 329-0711, Fax 329-0599, 800-648-5010) 1,624 rooms and suites, restaurant, lounge, entertainment, children free with parents, no pets, gift shop, game room, A/C, TV, NS rooms, wheelchair access, CC. SGL/DBL$38-$66.

Clarion Hotel Casino (3800 South Virginia, 89502; 825-4700, Fax 826-7860, 800-221-2222) 303 rooms and suites, restaurant, lounge, heated pool, exercise center, whirlpools, sauna, no pets, NS rooms, children under 18 free with parents, airport transportation, senior rates, meeting facilities, A/C, TV, CC. SGL/DBL$50-$295.

Colonial Hotel Inn and Casino (250 North Arlington, 89501; 322-3838, 800-336-7366) 168 rooms, restaurant, lounge, heated pool, sauna, A/C, no pets, TV, NS rooms, wheelchair access, meeting facilities, senior rates, CC. SGL/DBL$50-$60.

Colonial Motor Inn (232 West St., 89501; 786-5038, Fax 323-4588, 800-255-7366) 100 rooms, heated pool, sauna, exercise center, in-room coffee makers, A/C, TV, NS rooms, wheelchair access, CC. SGL/DBL$45-$55.

The Comstock Hotel and Casino (200 West 2nd St., 89501; 329-1880, 800-468-4866) 310 rooms and suites, restaurant, lounge, pool, whirlpools, sauna, exercise center, A/C, TV, NS rooms, wheelchair access, CC. SGL/DBL$50-$300.

Days Inn (701 East 7th, 89512; 786-4070, Fax 329-4338, 800-325-2525) 137 rooms and suites, outdoor pool, children free with parents, room service, laundry service, A/C, TV, free local calls, pets OK, fax, wheelchair access, NS rooms, senior rates, CC. SGL/DBL$32-$75.

Eldorado Hotel and Casino (345 North Virginia St., 89501; 786-5700, 800-648-5966) 783 rooms and suites, restaurant, lounge, heated pool, whirlpools, gift shop, in-room refrigerators, A/C, TV, children free with parents, no pets, airport transportation, NS rooms, wheelchair access, CC. SGL/DBL$70-$750.

Fitzgerald's Hotel and Casino (255 North Virginia St., 89501; 786-3663, Fax 786-7170, 800-648-5022) 351 rooms and suites, restaurant, lounge, entertainment, no pets, A/C, TV, NS rooms, wheelchair access, CC. SGL/DBL$35-$120.

Gateway Inn Complex (1275 Stardust St., 89503; 747-4220, 800-345-2910) 28 rooms, A/C, TV, NS rooms, wheelchair access, no pets, CC. SGL/DBL$35-$65.

Harrah's (210 North Center St., 89503; 786-3232, Fax 329-4455, 800-648-3773) 565 rooms and suites, restaurant, lounge, entertainment, heated pool, whirlpools, sauna, exercise center, pets OK, barber and beauty shop, boutiques, A/C, TV, NS rooms, wheelchair access, CC. SGL/DBL$85-$130, STS$210-$375.

Holiday Hotel and Casino (111 Mill St., 89504; 329-0411, Fax 329-3627, 800-648-5431) 190 rooms, A/C, TV, NS rooms, wheelchair access, CC. SGL/DBL$49.

Holiday Inn Downtown (1000 East 6th St., 89512; 786-5151, 800-648-4877, 800-HOLIDAY) 286 rooms, restaurant, lounge, pool, exercise center, children under 19 free with parents, wheelchair access, A/C, TV, NS rooms, fax, room service, pets OK, laundry service, airport transportation, car rental desk, meeting facilities for 550, senior rates, CC. SGL/DBL$55-$75.

Holiday Inn Convention Center (5851 South Virginia St., 89502; 825-9240, Fax 826-2825, 800-HOLIDAY) 153 rooms, restaurant, lounge, pool, exercise center, children under 19 free with parents, wheelchair access, A/C, TV, NS rooms, fax, room service, no pets, laundry service, meeting facilities, senior rates, CC. SGL/DBL$30-$60.

Hilton Flamingo Hotel (255 North Sierra St., 89501; 332-1111, Fax 785-7086, 800-HILTONS) 604 rooms and suites, restaurant, lounge, entertainment, pool, exercise center, children free with parents, NS rooms, wheelchair access, no pets, room service, laundry facilities, A/C, TV, meeting facilities, CC. SGL/DBL$60-$400.

Hilton Reno Hotel (2500 East 2nd St., 89595; 789-2000, Fax 789-2418, 800-HILTONS) 2,001 rooms and suites, restaurant, lounge, entertainment, pool, exercise center, lighted tennis courts, children free with parents, NS rooms, wheelchair access, barber and beauty shop, boutiques, airport courtesy car, no pets, room service, laundry facilities, A/C, TV, meeting facilities, senior rates, CC. SGL/DBL$70-$120, STS$130-$550.

La Quinta Airport Inn (4001 Market St., 89502; 348-6100, Fax 348-8794, 800-531-5900) 130 rooms, restaurant, free breakfast, lounge, pool, complimentary newspaper, free local calls, fax, laundry service, NS rooms, pets OK, wheelchair access, remote control TV, A/C, meeting facilities, CC. SGL/DBL$50-$68.

Motel 6 Central South (666 North Wells Ave., 89512; 329-8681, 505-891-6161) 97 rooms, pool, free local calls, children under 17 free with parents, NS rooms, wheelchair access, pets OK, A/C, TV, CC. SGL/DBL$38-$50.

Motel 6 South (1901 South Virginia Ave., 89502; 827-0255, 505-891-6161) 115 rooms, pool, free local calls, children under 17 free with parents, NS rooms, wheelchair access, pets OK, A/C, TV, CC. SGL/DBL$40-$53.

Motel 6 West (1400 Stardust St., 89503; 747-7390, 505-891-6161) 123 rooms, pool, free local calls, children under 17 free with parents, NS rooms, wheelchair access, pets OK, A/C, TV, CC. SGL/DBL$38-$45.

Nevada Inn (330 East 2nd St., 89501; 323-1005, 800-999-9686) 43 rooms, pool, A/C, TV, NS rooms, wheelchair access, CC. SGL/DBL$30-$35.

Peppermill Casino Hotel (2707 South Virginia St., 89502; 826-2121, Fax 825-5737, 800-648-6992) 632 rooms and suites, restaurant, lounge, entertainment, heated pool, exercise center, gift shop, airport courtesy car, barber and beauty shop, no pets, A/C, TV, NS rooms, wheelchair access, CC. SGL/DBL$50-$450.

Pioneer Inn Hotel and Casino (221 South Virginia St., 89501; 324-7777, 800-879-8879) 252 rooms, A/C, TV, NS rooms, wheelchair access, CC. SGL/DBL$36-$65.

Plaza Resort Club (121 West St., 89501; 786-2200, Fax 786-2384, 800-648-5990) 103 rooms, A/C, TV, NS rooms, wheelchair access, CC. SGL/DBL$89.

R&R Lodge (500 North Lake St., 89504; 788-2000, 800-648-3600) 200 rooms, A/C, TV, NS rooms, wheelchair access, CC. SGL/DBL$36-$66.

Ramada Inn (Sixth and Lake St., 89501; 788-2000, Fax 348-1860, 800-2-RAMADA) 232 rooms and suites, restaurant, lounge, pool, wheelchair access, NS rooms, pets OK, A/C, TV, children under 18 free with parents, room service, local transportation, game room, laundry facilities, meeting facilities, senior rates, CC. SGL/DBL$45-$160.

Reno Spa Resort Club (140 Court St., 89501; 329-4251, 800-634-6981) 80 rooms and 1-bedroom suites, A/C, TV, NS rooms, wheelchair access, CC. SGL/DBL$50-$60, STS$70.

Riverboat Hotel and Casino (34 West 2nd St., 89501; 323-8877, Fax 348-0926, 800-888-5525) 300 rooms and suites, restaurant, lounge, pool, room service, in-room refrigerators, children free with parents, A/C, TV, NS rooms, wheelchair access, meeting facilities, CC. SGL/DBL$47-$62.

River House Motor Lodge (2 Lake St., 89505; 329-0036) 33 rooms, pets OK, A/C, TV, NS rooms, wheelchair access, CC. SGL/DBL$30-$60.

Rodeway Inn (2050 Market St., 89502; 786-2500, 800-424-4777) 210 rooms and efficiencies, free breakfast, heated pool, whirlpools, sauna, wheelchair access, NS rooms, children free with parents, A/C, TV, laundry facilities, airport transportation, meeting facilities, senior rates, CC. SGL/DBL$57-$90.

Sands Regency Hotel and Casino (345 North Arlington Ave., 89501; 348-2200, 800-648-3553) 938 rooms and suites, restaurant, lounge, entertainment, pool, exercise center, sauna, whirlpools, A/C, TV, NS rooms, wheelchair access, airport transportation, in-room refrigerators and coffee makers, laundry facilities, children free with parents, no pets, senior rates, meeting facilities, CC. SGL/DBL$65.

Thunderbird Motel (420 North Virginia St., 89501; 329-3578) 27 rooms and 2-bedroom efficiencies, A/C, TV, NS rooms, wheelchair access, no pets, CC. SGL/DBL$75-$100.

TraveLodge Downtown (655 West 4th St., 89503; 329-3451, Fax 329-3454, 800-578-7878) 98 rooms and suites, restaurant, lounge, pool, wheelchair access, complimentary newspaper, laundry service, TV, A/C, free local calls, fax, NS rooms, in-room refrigerators and microwaves, children under 18 free with parents, no pets, meeting facilities, CC. SGL/DBL$29-$89.

Truckee River Lodge (501 West 1st St., 89503; 786-8888, 800-635-8950) 214 rooms, restaurant, lounge, exercise center, in-room refrigerators, A/C, TV, NS rooms, wheelchair access, NS, airport transportation, pets OK, senior rates, CC. SGL/DBL$30-$55.

Vagabond Inn (3131 South Virginia St., 89502; 825-7134) 130 rooms and 2-room suites, restaurant, free breakfast, heated pool, pets OK, A/C, TV, NS rooms, wheelchair access, local transportation, children free with parents, meeting facilities, senior rates, CC. SGL/DBL$40-$70.

Virginia Hotel and Casino (140 North Virginia St., 89501; 329-4664, Fax 329-2673, 800-874-5558).

Washoe Inn (75 Pringle Way, 89501; 328-5080) rooms, A/C, TV, NS rooms, wheelchair access, CC. SGL/DBL$36-$46.

Wonder Lodge (430 Lake St., 89501; 786-6840) 63 rooms, pool, A/C, TV, NS rooms, wheelchair access, no pets, CC. SGL/DBL$32-$55.

Sparks
Area Code 702

John Ascuaga's Nugget (1100 Nugget Ave., 89432; 356-3300, 800-648-1177) 157 rooms, restaurant, lounge, entertainment, indoor heated pool, exercise center, whirlpools, A/C, TV, NS rooms, wheelchair access, no pets, airport transportation, children free with parents, senior rates, CC. SGL/DBL$90-$115.

McCarren House Inn (55 East Nugget Ave., 89431; 358-6900, 800-548-5798) 220 rooms and suites, restaurant, lounge, pool, A/C, TV, NS rooms, wheelchair access, airport transportation, no pets, CC. SGL/DBL$40-$55.

Motel 6 (2405 B St., 89431; 358-1080, 505-891-6161) 95 rooms, pool, free local calls, children under 17 free with parents, NS rooms, wheelchair access, pets OK, A/C, TV, CC. SGL/DBL$45-$65.

Nendels Inn of Reno/Sparks (60 East B. St., 89431; 356-7770, 800-547-0106) 90 rooms, A/C, TV, NS rooms, wheelchair access, laundry facilities, CC. SGL/DBL$40-$50.

The Nugget Courtyard (1225 B St., 89431; 356-3300, Fax 356-4198, 800-648-1177) 157 rooms, restaurant, heated pool, airport courtesy car, A/C, TV, NS rooms, wheelchair access, CC. SGL/DBL$60-$75.

Silver Club Hotel and Casino (Sparks 89432; 358-4771, 800-648-1137) 207 rooms, restaurant, lounge, entertainment, A/C, TV, airport transportation, no pets, children free with parents, NS rooms, wheelchair access, senior rates, CC. SGL/DBL$25-$50.

Thunderbird Resort Club (200 Nichols Blvd., 89431; 359-1141, 800-821-4912) 159 1- and 2-bedroom apartments, A/C, TV, NS rooms, wheelchair access, no pets, children free with parents, CC. 1BR$54, 2BR$81.

Victorian Inn (1555 B St., 89431; 331-3203) 21 rooms, A/C, TV, NS rooms, wheelchair access, in-room refrigerators, microwaves and coffee makers, no pets, CC. SGL/DBL$30-$70.

Stateline

Area Code 702

Rental and Reservation Services:

Lake Tahoe Accommodations (255 Kingsbury Grade, 89449; 588-5684, Fax 542-1860, 800-228-6921)

Mountain View Management (680 Kingsbury Grade, 89449; 588-3300, Fax 588-2400, 800-541-3315)

Selective Accommodations (290 Kingsbury Grade, 89449; 588-8258, 800-242-5387)

Caesar's Tahoe (Stateline 89449; 588-3515, 800-648-3353) 440 rooms and suites, restaurant, lounge, entertainment, pool, exercise center, sauna, whirlpools, A/C, TV, NS rooms, wheelchair access, airport transportation, in-room refrigerators and coffee makers, laundry facilities, children free with parents, boutiques, barber and beauty shop, game room, in-room coffee makers, no pets, senior rates, meeting facilities, CC. SGL/DBL$115-$200, STS$650-$1,000.

Harrah's Hotel Casino (Stateline 89449; 588-6611, 800-648-3773) 534 rooms and suites, restaurant, lounge, entertainment, indoor heated pool, exercise center, sauna, whirlpools, A/C, TV, NS rooms, wheelchair access, airport transportation, barber and beauty shop, pets OK, boutiques, game room, in-room refrigerators and coffee makers, laundry facilities, children free with parents, no pets, senior rates, meeting facilities, CC. SGL/DBL$140-$175, STS$180-$850.

Harvey's Resort (Stateline 89449; 588-2411, 800-648-3361) 740 rooms and suites, restaurant, lounge, entertainment, heated pool, whirlpools, sauna, exercise center, airport transportation, barber and beauty shop, boutiques, game room, A/C, TV, NS rooms, wheelchair access, CC. SGL/DBL$100-$560.

Horizon Casino Resort (Stateline 89449; 588-6211) 539 rooms, restaurant, lounge, entertainment, pool, whirlpools, no pets, A/C, TV, NS rooms, wheelchair access, CC. SGL/DBL$85-$149.

Lake Tahoe Horizon (Stateline 89449; 588-6211, Fax 588-3110, 800-648-3322) 539 rooms and suites, restaurant, lounge, entertainment, pool, whirlpools, boutiques, barber and beauty shop, game room, A/C, TV, NS rooms, wheelchair access, meeting facilities, senior rates, CC. SGL/DBL$90-$400.

Lake Village Vacation Condominiums (Hwy. 50 and Lake Village Dr., 89448; 588-2481, 800-635-0066) 55 condominiums, A/C, TV, NS rooms, wheelchair access, no pets, children free with parents, CC. SGL/DBL$110-$225.

Lakeside Inn and Casino (Stateline 89449; 588-7777, Fax 588-4092, 800-624-7980) 123 rooms and suites, restaurant, lounge, entertainment, heated pool, game room, in-room coffee makers, children free with parents, A/C, TV, NS rooms, wheelchair access, senior rates, CC. SGL/DBL$70-$244.

Ridge Tahoe Resort (400 Ridge Club Dr., 89449; 588-3553, Fax 588-5242) 443 1- and 2-bedroom condominiums, pool, tennis courts, whirlpools, sauna, exercise center, no pets, gift shop, children free with parents, kitchenettes, A/C, TV, NS rooms, wheelchair access, CC. SGL/DBL$$225-$365.

Tonopah
Area Code 702

Best Western Desert Inn (320 South Main St., 89049; 482-3511, 800-528-1234) 62 rooms, free breakfast, pool, exercise center, whirlpools, children free with parents, A/C, NS rooms, TV, laundry facilities, wheelchair access, pets OK, senior rates, meeting facilities, CC. SGL/DBL$40-$60.

Butler Motel (100 South Main St., 89049; 482-3577, 800-635-9455) 25 rooms, A/C, TV, pets OK, NS rooms, wheelchair access, senior rates, CC. SGL/DBL$30-$36.

Silver Queen Motel (255 South Main St., 89049; 482-6291) 85 rooms and efficiencies, restaurant, pets OK, A/C, TV, NS rooms, wheelchair access, CC. SGL/DBL$28-$39.

Station House Hotel (1100 East Main St., 89049; 482-9777, Fax 482-8762) 75 rooms and suites, restaurant, lounge, entertainment, boutiques, local transportation, children free with parents, A/C, TV, NS rooms, wheelchair access, senior rates, CC. SGL/DBL$35-$80.

Unionville

Area Code 702

Old Pioneer Garden Guest Ranch (Unionville 89418; 538-7585) free breakfast, NS, private baths, children over 10 welcome, A/C, TV, CC. SGL/DBL$50-$65.

Verdi

Area Code 702

Boomtown Hotel and Casino (Garson Rd., 89439; 345-6000, 800-648-3790) 120 rooms, restaurant, pool, in-room refrigerators, no pets, children free with parents, A/C, TV, NS rooms, wheelchair access, CC. SGL/DBL$43-$47.

Wells

Area Code 702

Best Western Sage Motel (576 6th St., 89835; 752-3353, 800-528-1234) 24 rooms and efficiencies, heated pool, exercise center, children free with parents, A/C, NS rooms, TV, laundry facilities, wheelchair access, pets OK, meeting facilities, senior rates, CC. SGL/DBL$32-$52.

Motel 6 (I-80 and Hwy. 40, 89835; 752-2116, 505-891-6161) 122 rooms, pool, free local calls, children under 17 free with parents, NS rooms, wheelchair access, pets OK, A/C, TV, CC. SGL/DBL$36-$46.

Super 8 Motel (930 6th St., 89835; 752-3384, Fax 752-3384, 800-800-8000) 57 rooms and suites, outdoor heated pool, pets OK, children under 12 free with parents, free local calls, A/C, TV, in-room refrigerators and microwaves, fax, NS rooms, senior rates, wheelchair access, meeting facilities, CC. SGL/DBL$32-$49.

Wendover

Area Code 702

Nevada Crossing Hotel and Casino (Wendover 89883; 664-2900, 800-537-0207) 137 rooms and efficiencies, indoor heated pool, no pets, children free with parents, A/C, TV, NS rooms, wheelchair access, CC. SGL/DBL$40-$50.

Stateline Silversmith Hotel and Casino (100 Wendover Blvd., 89883; 664-2221, Fax 664-2526, 800-848-7300) 700 rooms, restaurant, lounge, pool, whirlpools, exercise center, room service, in-room refrigerators, A/C, pets OK, children free with parents, TV, NS rooms, wheelchair access, CC. SGL/DBL$34-$57.

Super 8 Motel (1325 Wendover Blvd., 89883; 664-2888, Fax 664-3051 ext 410, 800-800-8000) 74 rooms and suites, restaurant, lounge, pets OK, children under 12 free with parents, free local calls, A/C, TV, in-room refrigerators and microwaves, fax, NS rooms, senior rates, wheelchair access, meeting facilities, CC. SGL/DBL$34-$51.

Winnemucca

Area Code 702

Best Western Gold Country Inn (921 West Winnemucca Blvd., 89445; 623-6999, Fax 623-9190, 800-528-1234) 71 rooms, restaurant, free breakfast, lounge, pool, exercise center, children free with parents, A/C, NS rooms, TV, laundry facilities, wheelchair access, pets OK, senior rates, meeting facilities, CC. SGL/DBL$65-$75.

La Villa Motel (390 Lay St., 89445; 623-2334, Fax 623-0158) 37 rooms, A/C, TV, NS rooms, wheelchair access, pets OK, senior rates, CC. SGL/DBL$40-$65.

Model T Motel (1122 Winnemucca Blvd., 89445; 623-0222, Fax 623-0771, 800-645-5658) 75 rooms, restaurant, free breakfast, A/C, TV, no pets, children free with parents, NS rooms, wheelchair access, CC. SGL/DBL$48.

Motel 6 (1600 Winnemucca Blvd., 89445; 623-1180, 505-891-6161) 103 rooms, pool, free local calls, children under 17 free with parents, NS rooms, wheelchair access, pets OK, A/C, TV, CC. SGL/DBL$38-$44.

Pyrenees Motel (740 Winnemucca Blvd. West, 89445; 623-1116, 800-238-9754) 46 rooms, A/C, TV, in-room refrigerators and microwaves, no pets, NS rooms, wheelchair access, CC. SGL/DBL$35-$50.

Red Lion Inn and Casino (741 West Winnemucca Blvd., 89445; 623-2565, Fax 623-5702, 800-547-8010) 107 rooms and suites, restaurant, lounge, heated pool, A/C, TV, wheelchair access, NS rooms, laundry facilities, pets OK, game room, meeting facilities, senior rates, CC. SGL/DBL$70-$150.

Val-U-Inn Motel (125 East Winnemucca Blvd., 89445; 623-5248, 800-443-3661) 80 rooms heated pool, sauna, pets OK, A/C, TV, pets OK, NS rooms, wheelchair access, CC. SGL/DBL$45-$55.

Winners Hotel and Casino (185 Winnemucca Blvd. West, 89445; 623-2511, Fax 623-1207, 800-648-4770) 83 rooms, restaurant, lounge, pool, exercise center, A/C, TV, NS rooms, pets OK, children free with parents, wheelchair access, CC. SGL/DBL$38.

Zephyr Cove
Area Code 702

Rental and Reservation Services:

Lake Village Vacation Condominiums (Hwy. 50 and Lake Village Dr., 89448; 588-2481, Fax 588-10310, 800-635-0066)

Skyland Realty (Zephyr Cove, 89448; 588-5455, 800-822-2790)

New Mexico
Rental and Reservation Services:

Accommodations of New Mexico (Ranchos de Taos, 87557; 751-3153, 800-331-3153)

New Mexico Central Reservations (121 Tijeras Ave., Northeast, Albuquerque 87102; 766-9770, 800-466-7829)

Rio Grande Reservations (Pilar 87531; 758-0090, 800-999-PLUM)

Alamogordo
Area Code 505

All American Inn (508 South White Sands Blvd., 88310; 437-1850) 28 rooms, pool, no pets, A/C, TV, NS rooms, wheelchair access, CC. SGL/DBL$35-$65.

Best Western Inn (1021 South White Sands Blvd., 88310; 437-2110, Fax 437-1898, 800-528-1234) 100 rooms, free breakfast, heated pool, whirlpools, sauna, NS rooms, TV, laundry facilities, wheelchair access, pets OK, in-room refrigerators and microwaves, meeting facilities, senior rates, CC. SGL/DBL$40-$61.

Days Inn (907 South White Sands Blvd., 88310; 437-5090, Fax 434-5667, 800-325-2525) 40 rooms and suites, free breakfast, outdoor pool, children free with parents, room service, laundry service, A/C, TV, free local calls, pets OK, fax, wheelchair access, NS rooms, in-room refrigerators and microwaves, meeting facilities, senior rates, CC. SGL/DBL$38-$50.

Holiday Inn (1401 South White Sands Blvd., 88310; 437-7100, 800-HOLIDAY) 107 rooms, restaurant, lounge, entertainment, heated pool, exercise center, children under 19 free with parents, wheelchair access, A/C, TV, gift shop, beauty shop, car rental desk, NS rooms, fax, room service, pets OK, laundry service, meeting facilities, senior rates, CC. SGL/DBL$47-$66.

Satellite Inn (2224 North White Sands Blvd., 88310; 437-8454) 40 rooms and efficiencies, heated pool, in-room refrigerators, children free with parents, pets OK, A/C, TV, NS rooms, wheelchair access, CC. SGL/DBL$30-$40.

Super 8 Motel (3204 North White Sands Blvd., 88310; 434-4205, Fax 434-4205, 800-800-8000) 57 rooms and suites, pets OK, children under 12 free with parents, free local calls, A/C, TV, in-room refrigerators and microwaves, fax, NS rooms, senior rates, wheelchair access, meeting facilities, CC. SGL/DBL$28-$41.

Albuquerque
Area Code 505

Adobe Roses Bed and Breakfast (1011 Ortega Northwest, 87114; 898-0654) free breakfast, A/C, TV, wheelchair access, CC. SGL/DBL$30-$60.

Amberly Suite Hotel (7620 Pan American Freeway Northeast, 87109; 823-1300, Fax 823-2896, 800-333-9806) 170 suites, restaurant, lounge, heated pool, whirlpools, sauna, exercise center, pets OK, A/C, TV, NS rooms, children free with parents, wheelchair access, laundry facilities, in-room refrigerators, airport transportation, senior rates, CC. SGL/DBL$75-$95.

Barcelona Court Hotel (900 Louisiana Ave., Northeast, 87110; 255-5566, Fax 255-5566 ext 6116) 164 efficiencies, restaurant, free breakfast, indoor and outdoor pools, sauna, whirlpools, laundry facilities, gift shop, no pets, in-room refrigerators, A/C, TV, NS rooms, wheelchair access, meeting facilities, senior rates, CC. SGL/DBL$75-$125.

Best Western Inn (2910 Yale Blvd. Southeast, 87106; 843-7000, Fax 843-6307, 800-528-1234) 266 rooms and suites, restaurant, lounge, heated pool, exercise center, children free with parents, A/C, NS rooms, TV, laundry facilities, wheelchair access, pets OK, laundry facilities, gift shop, local transportation, in-room refrigerators, senior rates, meeting facilities, CC. SGL/DBL$85-$300.

Best Western Inn (12999 Central Ave. Northeast, 87123; 298-7426, Fax 298-0212, 800-528-1234) 76 rooms, restaurant, lounge, heated pool, whirlpools, children free with parents, in-room refrigerators, NS rooms, TV, laundry facilities, wheelchair access, pets OK, meeting facilities, senior rates, CC. SGL/DBL$41-$69.

Bottger Mansion (110 San Felipe Northwest, 87104; 243-639, Fax 883-8213) 3 rooms and suites, free breakfast, whirlpools, NS, no pets, A/C, TV, senior rates, CC. SGL/DBL$60-$90.

Budgetel Inn (7439 Pan American Freeway Northeast, 87109; 345-7500, 800-428-3438) 102 rooms and suites, free breakfast, children under 18 free with parents, A/C, wheelchair access, NS rooms, free local calls, in-room computer hookups, fax, in-room refrigerators, microwaves and coffee makers, laundry facilities, VCRs, TV, meeting facilities, CC. SGL/DBL$40-$51.

Casa de Montoya (Albuquerque 87184; 344-4342) rental home, A/C, TV, CC. SGL/DBL$125.

Casa de Suenos (310 Rio Granada Southwest, 87104; 247-4560, Fax 842-8493, 800-242-8987) 18 rooms and suites, free breakfast, antique furnishings, NS, A/C, TV, NS rooms, wheelchair access, children free with parents, no pets, CC. SGL/DBL$110-$225.

Clubhouse Inn (1315 Menaul Blvd. Northeast, 87107; 345-0010, 800-258-2466) 137 rooms and suites, free breakfast, heated pool, whirlpools, free local calls, A/C, no pets, TV, airport transportation, NS rooms, wheelchair access, in-room refrigerators, meeting facilities, senior rates, CC. SGL/DBL$58-$89.

Comfort Inn Airport (2300 Yale Blvd. Southeast, 87106; 243-2244, 800-221-2222) 115 rooms, restaurant, free breakfast, pool, whirlpools, airport transportation, wheelchair access, NS rooms, no pets, children under 18 free with parents, A/C, TV, meeting facilities, senior rates, CC. SGL/DBL$55-$75.

Comfort Inn East (13031 Central Ave. Northeast, 87123; 294-1800, 800-221-2222) 122 rooms, restaurant, pool, whirlpools, wheelchair access, NS rooms, pets OK, children under 18 free with parents, laundry facilities, A/C, TV, meeting facilities, senior rates, CC. SGL/DBL$45-$78.

Comfort Inn Midtown (2015 Menaul Blvd. Northeast, 87107; 881-3210, 800-221-2222) 151 rooms, pool, whirlpools, wheelchair access, NS rooms, no pets, children under 18 free with parents, A/C, TV, meeting facilities, senior rates, CC. SGL/DBL$49-$69.

Courtyard by Marriott (1920 Yale Southeast, 87106; 843-6600, Fax 843-8740, 800-321-2211) 150 rooms and suites, restaurant, lounge, pool, exercise center, whirlpools, children free with parents, laundry service, A/C, NS rooms, TV, airport courtesy car, in-room refrigerators and coffee makers, no pets, meeting facilities, senior rates, CC. SGL/DBL$75-$105.

Days Inn (6031 Iliff Rd. Northwest, 87105; 836-3297, Fax 836-1898, 800-325-2525) 81 rooms and suites, free breakfast, indoor pool, sauna, whirlpools, children free with parents, room service, laundry service, A/C, TV, free local calls, pets OK, fax, wheelchair access, NS rooms, senior rates, CC. SGL/DBL$30-$70.

Days Inn (10321 Hotel Ave. Northeast, 87123; 275-0599, Fax 275-0245, 800-325-2525) 77 rooms and suites, indoor pool, sauna, children free with parents, room service, laundry service, A/C, TV, free local calls, pets OK, fax, wheelchair access, NS rooms, senior rates, CC. SGL/DBL$36-$75.

Days Inn (13317 Central Ave., Northeast, 87123; 294-3297, 800-325-2525) 72 rooms and suites, indoor pool, sauna, children free with parents, room service, laundry service, A/C, TV, free local calls, pets OK, fax, wheelchair access, NS rooms, senior rates, CC. SGL/DBL$34-$70.

Doubletree Hotel (201 Marquette Ave. Northwest, 87102; 247-3344, Fax 247-7025, 800-828-7447) 294 rooms and suites, restaurant, lounge, pool, NS rooms, children under 18 free with parents, senior rates, A/C, TV, business services, fax, in-room computer hookups, local transportation, in-room refrigerators and microwaves, no pets, gift shop, meeting facilities, CC. SGL/DBL$70-$480.

Econo Lodge (10331 Hotel Ave., 87123; 271-8500, 800-4-CHOICE) 50 rooms, free breakfast, children under 12 free with parents, no pets, NS rooms, wheelchair access, A/C, TV, senior rates, CC. SGL/DBL$42-$78.

Econo Lodge East (13211 Central Ave. Northeast, 87123; 292-7600, 800-4-CHOICE) 58 rooms, restaurant, indoor heated pool, sauna, whirlpools, free local calls, children under 12 free with parents, no pets, NS rooms, wheelchair access, A/C, TV, senior rates, CC. SGL/DBL$29-$75.

Fairfield Inn by Marriott (I-40 and I-25, 87102; 889-4000, 800-228-2800) indoor pool, tennis courts, children under 18 free with parents, NS rooms, remote control TV, free cable TV, free local calls, laundry service, A/C, wheelchair access, fax, no pets, meeting facilities, senior rates, CC. SGL/DBL$60-$80.

Friendship Inn Downtown (717 Central Ave. Northwest, 87102; 247-1501, Fax 842-5067, 800-253-5012, 800-424-4777) 144 rooms, restaurant, lounge, pool, exercise center, A/C, TV, no pets, NS rooms, local transportation, children free with parents, wheelchair access, meeting facilities, senior rates, CC. SGL/DBL$30-$45.

Hampton Inn (5101 Ellison Northeast, 87109; 344-1555, Fax 345-2216, 800-HAMPTON) 125 rooms, restaurant, free breakfast, heated pool, exercise center, children under 18 free with parents, NS rooms, wheelchair access, in-room computer hookups, fax, TV, A/C, free local calls, pets OK, meeting facilities, senior rates, CC. SGL/DBL$45-$60.

Hilton Inn (1901 University Blvd. Northeast, 87109; 884-2500, Fax 889-9118, 800-HILTONS) 262 rooms and suites, restaurant, lounge, entertainment, indoor and outdoor heated pools, exercise center, children free with parents, NS rooms, wheelchair access, no pets, room service, laundry facilities, A/C, TV, airport courtesy car, meeting facilities, senior rates, CC. SGL/DBL$80-$120, STS$350-$475.

Holiday Inn (5151 San Francisco Rd. Northeast, 87109; 821-3333, 800-HOLIDAY) 311 rooms, restaurant, lounge, entertainment, indoor pool, exercise center, children under 19 free with parents, wheelchair access, A/C, TV, NS rooms, fax, room service, airport transportation, gift shop, pets OK, laundry service, meeting facilities for 1,500, senior rates, CC. SGL/DBL$100-$275.

Holiday Inn Midtown (202 Menaul Blvd. Northeast, 87107; 884-2511, Fax 884-5720, 800-545-0599, 800-HOLIDAY) 360 rooms, restaurant, lounge, entertainment, indoor heated pool, exercise center, whirlpools, sauna, game room, children under 19 free with parents, wheelchair access, A/C, TV, NS rooms, fax, room service, gift shop, airport transportation, pets OK, room service, laundry service, meeting facilities, senior rates, CC. SGL/DBL$80-$100.

Howard Johnson (15 Hotel Circle Northeast, 87123; 296-4852, 800-877-4852, 800-I-GO-HOJO) 150 rooms, restaurant, lounge, pool, exercise center, whirlpools, spa, airport transportation, room service, children free with parents, wheelchair access, NS rooms, TV, A/C, no pets, laundry facilities, senior rates, meeting facilities, CC. SGL/DBL$45-$71.

Howard Johnson Plaza Hotel (6000 Pan American Freeway Northeast, 87109; 821-9451, 800-I-GO-HOJO) 150 rooms, restaurant, lounge, entertainment, indoor and outdoor pool, exercise center, sauna, children free with parents, wheelchair access, NS rooms, TV, A/C, gift shop, local transportation, in-room refrigerators, room service, pets OK, laundry facilities, senior rates, meeting facilities, CC. SGL/DBL$46-$115.

Hyatt Regency (330 Tijeras Northwest, 87102; 842-1234, Fax 766-6710, 800-233-1234) 395 rooms and suites, restaurant, lounge, entertainment, pool, whirlpools, exercise center, room service, TV, A/C, NS rooms, wheelchair access, boutiques, beauty shop, local transportation, no pets, 19,000 square feet of meeting and exhibition space, senior rates, CC. SGL/DBL$105-$725.

La Posada de Albuquerque (125 2nd St. Northwest, 87102; 242-9090, Fax 242-8664) 114 rooms and suites, restaurant, lounge, entertainment, gift shop, airport courtesy car, A/C, TV, NS rooms, wheelchair access, no pets, in-room refrigerators, senior rates, CC. SGL/DBL$72-$225.

La Quinta Inn (2424 San Mateo Blvd. Northeast, 87110; 884-3591, Fax 881-3065, 800-531-5900) 105 rooms, restaurant, lounge, free breakfast, lounge, pool, complimentary newspaper, free local calls, fax, laundry service, NS rooms, wheelchair access, remote control TV, local transportation, A/C, meeting facilities, CC. SGL/DBL$45-$65.

La Quinta Inn North (5241 San Antonio Dr. Northeast, 87109; 821-9000, Fax 821-2399, 800-531-5900) 130 rooms, restaurant, free breakfast, lounge, pool, complimentary newspaper, free local calls, fax, laundry service, NS rooms, wheelchair access, remote control TV, A/C, meeting facilities, CC. SGL/DBL$48-$66.

La Quinta Airport Inn (2116 Yale Blvd., Southeast 87106; 243-5500, 800-531-5900) 105 rooms, pool, airport transportation, pets OK, children free with parents, free local calls, fax, laundry service, NS rooms, wheelchair access, remote control TV, A/C, meeting facilities, CC. SGL/DBL$48-$56.

LeBaron Inn and Suites (2120 Menaul Blvd., Northeast, 87107; 884-0250, Fax 883-0594, 800-444-7378) 189 rooms and suites, restaurant, free breakfast, pool, laundry facilities, A/C, TV, NS rooms, wheelchair access, in-room refrigerators, children free with parents, no pets, airport courtesy car, meeting facilities, senior rates, CC. SGL/DBL$45-$100.

Lorlodge Motel (801 Central Ave., East, 87102; 243-2891) 33 rooms, pool, children free with parents, A/C, TV, NS rooms, wheelchair access, pets OK, CC. SGL/DBL$20-$44.

Mauger Estate Inn (701 Roma Ave. Northwest, 87102; 242-8755) 8 rooms, free breakfast, TV, NS rooms, wheelchair access, pets OK, 1890s inn, CC. SGL/DBL$45-$65.

Marriott Hotel (2101 Louisiana Blvd. Northeast, 87110; 881-6800, Fax 888-2982, 800-228-9290) 411 rooms and suites, restaurant, lounge, entertainment, indoor and outdoor pool, exercise center, whirlpools, sauna, wheelchair access, TV, A/C, NS rooms, laundry service, gift shop, children free with parents, gift shop, airport courtesy car, meeting facilities, senior rates, CC. SGL/DBL$120-$135, STS$250-$500.

Monterey Motel (2402 Central Ave., Southwest, 87104; 243-3554) 15 rooms, laundry facilities, no pets, NS, A/C, TV, NS rooms, wheelchair access, CC. SGL/DBL$35-$59.

Motel 6 (3400 Prospect Ave. Northeast, 87107; 883-8813, 505-891-6161) 108 rooms, pool, free local calls, children under 17 free with parents, NS rooms, wheelchair access, pets OK, A/C, TV, CC. SGL/DBL$38-$46.

Motel 6 East (13141 Central Ave. Northeast, 87123; 294-4600, 505-891-6161) 123 rooms, pool, free local calls, children under 17 free with parents, NS rooms, wheelchair access, pets OK, A/C, TV, CC. SGL/DBL$38-$46.

Motel 6 Midtown (1701 University Blvd. Northeast, 87102; 843-9228, 505-891-6161) 118 rooms, pool, free local calls, children under 17 free with parents, NS rooms, wheelchair access, pets OK, A/C, TV, CC. SGL/DBL$38-$53.

Motel 6 (6015 Iliff Rd. Northwest, 87105; 831-3400, 505-891-6161) 130 rooms, pool, free local calls, children under 17 free with parents, NS rooms, wheelchair access, pets OK, A/C, TV, CC. SGL/DBL$34-$44.

Motel 6 (5701 Iliff Rd. Northwest, 87105; 831-8888, 505-891-6161) 111 rooms, pool, free local calls, children under 17 free with parents, NS rooms, wheelchair access, pets OK, A/C, TV, CC. SGL/DBL$40-$50.

Motel 6 Stadium (1000 Stadium Blvd. Southeast, 87102; 243-8017, 505-891-6161) 97 rooms, pool, free local calls, children under 17 free with parents, NS rooms, wheelchair access, pets OK, A/C, TV, CC. SGL/DBL$39-$56.

Old Town Bed and Breakfast (707 17th St. Northwest, 87104; 764-9144) free breakfast, A/C, TV, wheelchair access, CC. SGL/DBL$45-$55.

Plaza Inn (900 Medical Arts Ave. Northeast, 87102; 243-5693, Fax 843-6229, 800-237-1307) 120 rooms, restaurant, lounge, heated pool, exercise center, local transportation, laundry facilities, in-room refrigerators, A/C, TV, NS rooms, wheelchair access, pets OK, CC. SGL/DBL$65-$75.

Quality Hotel Four Seasons (2500 Carlisle Northeast, 87110; 888-3311, 800-221-2222) 356 rooms and suites, restaurant, lounge, entertainment, indoor and outdoor pools, exercise center, whirlpools, sauna, pets OK, children free with parents, A/C, TV, room service, laundry service, NS rooms, gift shop, barber and beauty shops, local transportation, game room, meeting facilities, senior rates, CC. SGL/DBL$70-$90, STS$105-$125.

Radisson Inn Airport (1901 University Southeast, 87106; 247-0512, Fax 843-7148, 800-333-3333) 150 rooms and suites, restaurant, lounge, entertainment, pool, exercise center, in-room refrigerators, microwaves and coffee makers, children free with parents, VCRs, wheelchair access, NS rooms, TV, A/C, children free with parents, no pets, local transportation, meeting facilities, senior rates, CC. SGL/DBL$75-$105.

Ramada Inn East (25 Hotel Circle Northeast, 87123; 271-1000, Fax 291-9028, 800-2-RAMADA) 204 rooms and suites, restaurant, lounge, entertainment, pool, wheelchair access, NS rooms, airport transportation, pets OK, A/C, TV, children under 18 free with parents, room service, laundry facilities, meeting facilities, senior rates, CC. SGL/DBL$60-$84, STS$125.

Ramada Hotel Classic (6815 Menaul Northeast, 87110; 881-0000, Fax 881-3736, 800-2-RAMADA) 296 rooms and suites, restaurant, lounge, entertainment, indoor pool, whirlpools, spa, exercise center, wheelchair access, NS rooms, pets OK, A/C, airline ticket office, TV, children under 18 free with parents, room service, laundry facilities, meeting facilities, senior rates, CC. SGL/DBL$90-$120, STS$125.

Residence Inn (3300 Prospect Ave., Northeast, 87107; 881-2661, Fax 884-5551, 800-331-3131) 112 rooms and 2-bedroom suites, free breakfast, in-room refrigerators, coffee makers and microwaves, laundry facilities, TV, A/C, VCRs, pets OK, complimentary newspaper, fireplaces, children free with parents, NS rooms, wheelchair access, meeting facilities, CC. SGL/DBL$110-$135.

Rio Grande Inn (1015 Rio Grande Northwest, 87104; 843-9500, 800-959-4726) 170 rooms, restaurant, heated pool, free local calls, children free with parents, pets OK, A/C, TV, NS rooms, wheelchair access, senior rates, CC. SGL/DBL$25-$65.

Rodeway Inn Midtown (2108 Menaul Blvd. Northeast, 87107; 884-2480, 800-424-4777) 99 rooms, restaurant, free breakfast, pool, wheelchair access, NS rooms, children free with parents, A/C, TV, senior rates, CC. SGL/DBL$30-$75.

Sandcastle (327 Arizona Southeast, 87108; 256-9462) free breakfast, A/C, TV, NS, no pets, private baths, children over 12 welcome, CC. SGL/DBL$75-$85.

Sheraton Old Town (800 Rio Grande Blvd. Northwest, 87104; 843-6300, Fax 842-9863, 800-325-3535) 190 rooms and suites, restaurant, lounge, entertainment, pool, exercise center, NS rooms, A/C, TV, children free with parents, wheelchair access, airport courtesy car, boutiques, barber and beauty shop, no pets, in-room refrigerators, meeting facilities, senior rates, CC. SGL/DBL$90-$200.

Super 8 Downtown Motel (2500 University Blvd. Northeast, 87107; 888-4884, 800-800-8000) 198 rooms and suites, pets OK, children under 12 free with parents, free local calls, laundry facilities, A/C, TV, in-room refrigerators and microwaves, fax, NS rooms, senior rates, wheelchair access, meeting facilities, CC. SGL/DBL$35-$50.

Super 8 Motel West (6030 Iliff Northwest, 87121; 836-5560, Fax 836-5560 ext 350, 800-800-8000) 98 rooms and suites, pets OK, children under 12 free with parents, free local calls, A/C, TV, in-room refrigerators and micro-waves, fax, NS rooms, airport transportation, senior rates, wheelchair access, meeting facilities, CC. SGL/DBL$35-$48.

Travelers Inn (411 McKnight Ave., Northwest 87102; 242-5228) 99 rooms, heated pool, whirlpools, airport transportation, in-room refrigerators, children free with parents, no pets, A/C, TV, NS rooms, wheelchair access, CC. SGL/DBL$41-$47.

TraveLodge Tramway (13139 Central Ave. Northeast, 87123; 292-4878, Fax 299-1822, 800-578-7878) 40 rooms, restaurant, wheelchair access, com-plimentary newspaper, laundry service, TV, A/C, free local calls, fax, NS rooms, in-room refrigerators and microwaves, airport transportation, chil-dren under 18 free with parents, pets OK, meeting facilities, CC. SGL/DBL$35-$68.

TraveLodge Midtown (1635 Candelaria Northeast, 87102; 800-578-7878) 87 rooms, restaurant, lounge, free breakfast, indoor heated pool, exercise center, wheelchair access, complimentary newspaper, laundry service, TV, A/C, free local calls, fax, NS rooms, in-room refrigerators and micro-waves, children under 18 free with parents, no pets, meeting facilities for 20, CC. SGL/DBL$39-$82.

W.J. Marsh Home (301 Edith Southeast, 87102; 247-1001) free breakfast, A/C, wheelchair access, TV, CC. SGL/DBL$36-$46.

Alto
Area Code 505

High Country Lodge (Alto 88312; 336-4321) 32 2-bedroom apartments, indoor pool, sauna, whirlpools, game room, fireplaces, kitchenettes, TV, NS rooms, wheelchair access, pets OK, senior rates, CC. SGL/DBL$65-$80.

Shadow Mountain Lodge (107 Main St., 88312; 257-4886, 800-441-4331) 19 efficiencies, A/C, TV, NS rooms, wheelchair access, in-room coffee mak-ers, children free with parents, no pets, meeting facilities, senior rates, CC. SGL/DBL$85-$93.

Sierra Mesa Lodge (Alto 88312; 336-4514) 5 rooms, free breakfast, fire-places, NS, TV, NS rooms, wheelchair access, antique furnishings, chil-dren free with parents, CC. SGL/DBL$80-$90.

Arroyo Seco
Area Code 505

Villacito Condominiums (Arroyo Seco 87514; 776-8778) 4 2-bedroom condominiums, A/C, TV, NS rooms, wheelchair access, CC. SGL/DBL$100-$260.

Artesia

Area Code 505

Best Western Pecos Inn (2209 West Main St., 88210; 748-3324, Fax 748-2868, 800-528-1234) 81 rooms, restaurant, lounge, indoor heated pool, exercise center, whirlpools, sauna, children free with parents, A/C, NS rooms, TV, laundry facilities, wheelchair access, no pets, in-room refrigerators, local transportation, senior rates, meeting facilities, CC. SGL/DBL$50-$110.

Aztec

Area Code 505

Enchantment Lodge (1800 West Aztec Blvd., 87410; 334-6143, 800-847-2194) 20 rooms, heated pool, laundry facilities, gift shop, no pets, A/C, TV, NS rooms, wheelchair access, CC. SGL/DBL$28-$40.

Belen

Area Code 505

Budget Host Rio Communities Resort Motel (502 Rio Communities Blvd., 87002; 864-4451, 800-283-4678) 21 rooms, restaurant, pool, pets OK, laundry facilities, NS rooms, wheelchair access, A/C, TV, senior rates, children free with parents, CC. SGL/DBL$28-$33.

Super 8 Motel (428 South Main St., 87002; 864-8188, Fax 864-1243, 800-800-8000) 43 rooms and suites, restaurant, no pets, children under 12 free with parents, free local calls, A/C, TV, in-room refrigerators and microwaves, fax, NS rooms, senior rates, wheelchair access, meeting facilities, CC. SGL/DBL$38-$49.

Bernalillo

Area Code 505

Super 8 Motel (265 Hwy. 44 East, 87004; 867-0766, 800-800-8000) 38 rooms and suites, restaurant, pets OK, children under 12 free with parents, free local calls, A/C, TV, in-room refrigerators and microwaves, fax, NS rooms, senior rates, wheelchair access, meeting facilities, CC. SGL/DBL$35-$48.

Bloomfield

Area Code 505

Super 8 Motel (501 West Broadway, 87413; 632-8826. 800-800-8000) 42 rooms and suites, restaurant, pets OK, children under 12 free with parents, free local calls, A/C, TV, in-room refrigerators and microwaves, fax, NS

rooms, senior rates, wheelchair access, meeting facilities, CC.
SGL/DBL$33-$46.

Carlsbad

Area Code 505

Best Western Motel (1829 South Canal St., 88220; 887-2851, Fax 887-800-
528-1234) 203 rooms, restaurant, lounge, entertainment, free breakfast,
lounge, pool, exercise center, children free with parents, A/C, NS rooms,
TV, laundry facilities, room service, in-room refrigerators, wheelchair
access, pets OK, senior rates, meeting facilities, CC. SGL/DBL$45-$65.

Continental Inn (3820 National Parks Hwy. 88220; 887-0341) 58 rooms,
restaurant, heated pool, no pets, local transportation, in-room refrigerators, A/C, TV, NS rooms, wheelchair access, CC. SGL/DBL$33-$43.

Holiday Inn (601 South Canal, 88220; 885-8500, Fax 887-5999, 800-HOLI-
DAY) 112 rooms and suites, restaurant, lounge, pool, exercise center, spa,
airport transportation, children under 19 free with parents, wheelchair
access, A/C, TV, NS rooms, fax, room service, pets OK, laundry service,
meeting facilities for 350, senior rates, CC. SGL/DBL$65-$75.

Lorlodge Motel (2019 South Canal St., 88220; 887-1171, Fax 887-6577) 30
rooms, heated pool, children free with parents, pets OK, in-room refrigerators and microwaves, A/C, TV, VCRs, NS rooms, wheelchair access,
CC. SGL/DBL$25-$43.

Motel 6 (3824 National Parks Hwy., 88220; 885-0011, 505-891-6161) 80
rooms, pool, free local calls, children under 17 free with parents, NS
rooms, wheelchair access, pets OK, A/C, TV, CC. SGL/DBL$38-$44.

Park Inn International (3706 National Parks Hwy., 88220; 887-2861, Fax
887-2861, 800-437-PARK) 124 rooms and suites, restaurant, lounge, entertainment, outdoor pool, spa, airport transportation, A/C, in-room refrigerators, microwaves and coffee makers, TV, wheelchair access, NS rooms,
children free with parents, pets OK, meeting facilities for 300, senior rates,
CC. SGL/DBL$40-$66.

Parkview Motel (401 East Green St., 88220; 885-3117) 26 rooms, pool, pets
OK, A/C, TV, NS rooms, wheelchair access, in-room coffee makers, senior
rates, CC. SGL/DBL$30-$38.

Rodeway Inn (3804 National Parks Hwy., 88220; 887-5535, 800-424-4777)
107 rooms, restaurant, lounge, indoor heated pool, whirlpools, sauna,
in-room refrigerators and microwaves, wheelchair access, NS rooms, children free with parents, A/C, TV, senior rates, CC. SGL/DBL$45-$62.

Stagecoach Inn (1819 South Canal St., 88220; 887-1148) 55 rooms, restaurant, pool, whirlpools, in-room refrigerators, pets OK, A/C, TV, NS rooms, wheelchair access, CC. SGL/DBL$26-$55.

TraveLodge South (3817 National Parks Hwy., 88220; 887-8888, Fax 885-0126, 800-578-7878) 60 rooms, restaurant, lounge, free breakfast, heated pool, jacuzzi, wheelchair access, complimentary newspaper, laundry service, TV, A/C, free local calls, fax, NS rooms, in-room refrigerators and microwaves, airport transportation, children under 18 free with parents, pets OK, meeting facilities, senior rates, CC. SGL/DBL$37-$53.

Carrizozo
Area Code 505

The Old Adobe Inn (911 12th St., 88301; 648-2149) free breakfast, A/C, TV, 1904 home, NS, no pets, no children, antique furnishings, CC. SGL/DBL$75.

Cedar Crest
Area Code 505

Elaine's Bed and Breakfast (Cedar Crest 87008; 281-2467) free breakfast, A/C, TV, no pets, NS, private baths. SGL/DBL$65-$90.

Chama
Area Code 505

The Candy Dancer (299 Maple St., 87520; 756-2191) 3 rooms, free breakfast, children free with parents, no pets, TV, CC. SGL/DBL$55-$85.

Elk Horn Lodge (Route 1, 87520; 756-2105, 800-532-8874) 22 rooms and cottages, restaurant, local transportation, A/C, TV, NS rooms, wheelchair access, pets OK, CC. SGL/DBL$38-$55.

Cimarron
Area Code 505

The Kit Carson Inn (Hwy. 64, 87714; 376-2288) 39 rooms, restaurant, lounge, pool, pets OK, A/C, TV, VCRs, NS rooms, wheelchair access, CC. SGL/DBL$35-$50.

St. James Hotel (Route 1, 87714; 376-2664, Fax 376-2378, 800-748-2694) 25 rooms and suites, restaurant, pool, gift shop, A/C, TV, NS rooms, wheelchair access, pets OK, antique furnishings, gift shop, game room, CC. SGL/DBL$35-$80.

Clayton
Area Code 505

Holiday Motel (Hwy. 87 North, 88415; 374-2558) 30 rooms, pets OK, A/C, TV, NS rooms, wheelchair access, senior rates, CC. SGL/DBL$27-$39.

Sunset Motel (701 South 1st St., 88415; 374-2589) 35 rooms and 2-bedroom suites, children free with parents, A/C, TV, NS rooms, wheelchair access, pets OK, in-room computer hookups, CC. SGL/DBL$25-$44.

Cloudcroft
Area Code 505

The Lodge Inn (Hwy. 82, 88317; 682-2566, 800-395-6343) 59 rooms and suites, restaurant, lounge, entertainment heated pool, hot tubs, sauna, gift shop, TV, children free with parents, NS rooms, wheelchair access, no pets, 1890s inn, meeting facilities, CC. SGL/DBL$60-$165.

Summitt Inn (100 Chipmonk, 88317; 682-2814) 10 efficiencies and cabins, A/C, TV, NS rooms, wheelchair access, kitchenettes, pets OK, CC. SGL/DBL$40-$95.

Clovis
Area Code 505

Best Western La Vista Inn (1516 Mabry Dr., 88101; 762-3808, Fax 762-1422, 800-528-1234) 47 rooms, heated pool, game room, children free with parents, A/C, NS rooms, TV, laundry facilities, wheelchair access, pets OK, airport transportation, in-room refrigerators, senior rates, meeting facilities, CC. SGL/DBL$30-$45.

Clovis Inn (2912 Mabry Dr., 88101; 762-5600) 97 rooms and suites, heated pool, whirlpools, laundry facilities, pets OK, in-room refrigerators and microwaves, children free with parents, A/C, TV, NS rooms, wheelchair access, CC. SGL/DBL$30-$38, STS$45-$50.

Comfort Inn (1616 Mabry Dr., 88101; 762-4591, 800-221-2222) 50 rooms, restaurant, free breakfast, pool, wheelchair access, NS rooms, no pets, children under 18 free with parents, A/C, TV, meeting facilities, senior rates, CC. SGL/DBL$52-$58.

Days Inn (1720 Mabry Dr., 88101; 762-2971, Fax 762-2735, 800-325-2525) 95 rooms and suites, free breakfast, outdoor heated pool, children free with parents, room service, laundry service, A/C, TV, free local calls, pets OK, game room, fax, wheelchair access, NS rooms, senior rates, CC. SGL/DBL$26-$50.

Holiday Inn (2700 Mabry Dr., 88101; 762-4491, Fax 769-0564, 800-HOLI-DAY) 119 rooms, restaurant, lounge, indoor and outdoor pool, exercise center, whirlpools, children under 19 free with parents, wheelchair access, A/C, TV, NS rooms, fax, room service, no pets, laundry service, meeting facilities, senior rates, CC. SGL/DBL$45-$50.

Motel 6 (2620 Mabry Dr., 88101; 762-2995, 505-891-6161) 82 rooms, pool, free local calls, children under 17 free with parents, NS rooms, wheelchair access, pets OK, A/C, TV, CC. SGL/DBL$40-$48.

Coolidge
Area Code 505

Navajo Lodge (Coolidge 87312; 862-7553) free breakfast, A/C, TV, CC. SGL/DBL$40-$60.

Deming
Area Code 505

Best Western Chilton Inn (1709 Spruce St., 88031; 546-8813, 800-528-1234) 57 rooms and suites, restaurant, pool, exercise center, children free with parents, A/C, NS rooms, TV, laundry facilities, wheelchair access, pets OK, beauty shop, senior rates, meeting facilities, CC. SGL/DBL$40-$55.

Deming Motel (500 West Pine St., 88030; 546-2737) 28 rooms, pool, TV, pets OK, CC. SGL/DBL$24-$30.

Grand Motor Inn (1721 East Spruce St., 88031; 546-2632, Fax 546-4446) 62 rooms and suites, restaurant, lounge, heated pool, pets OK, A/C, TV, NS rooms, children free with parents, wheelchair access, meeting facilities, CC. SGL/DBL$42-$65.

Holiday Inn (Deming 88030; 546-2661, Fax 546-6308, 800-HOLIDAY) 80 rooms, restaurant, lounge, entertainment, heated pool, exercise center, children under 19 free with parents, wheelchair access, A/C, TV, NS rooms, fax, room service, no pets, laundry service, meeting facilities for 100, senior rates, CC. SGL/DBL$44-$50.

Motel 6 (Deming 88031; 546-2623, 505-891-6161) 102 rooms, pool, free local calls, children under 17 free with parents, NS rooms, wheelchair access, pets OK, A/C, TV, CC. SGL/DBL$36-$66.

Super 8 Motel (1217 West Pines, 88030; 546-0481, 800-800-8000) 43 rooms and suites, restaurant, no pets, children under 12 free with parents, free local calls, A/C, TV, in-room refrigerators and microwaves, fax, NS rooms, senior rates, wheelchair access, meeting facilities, CC. SGL/DBL$35-$48.

Wagon Wheel Motel (1109 West Pine St., 88030; 546-2681) 18 rooms, heated pool, in-room refrigerators, pets OK, laundry facilities, A/C, TV, NS rooms, wheelchair access, CC. SGL/DBL$22-$30.

Dulce
Area Code 505

Best Western Inn (Hwy. 64, 87528; 759-3663, Fax 759-3170, 800-528-1234) 42 rooms, restaurant, lounge, pool, exercise center, children free with parents, A/C, NS rooms, TV, laundry facilities, wheelchair access, pets OK, gift shop, airport transportation, in-room refrigerators, senior rates, meeting facilities, CC. SGL/DBL$50-$75.

Eagle Nest
Area Code 505

Horseshoe Cabins (Hwy. 64, 87718; 800-752-7933) 45 cabins, children free with parents, CC. SGL/DBL$25-$190.

El Prado
Area Code 505

Salsa del Salto Inn (El Prado 87529; 776-2422) 6 rooms, free breakfast, heated pool, whirlpools, tennis courts, no pets, NS, TV, fireplaces, antique furnishings, wheelchair access, CC. SGL/DBL$95-$160.

Espanola
Area Code 505

Casa del Rio (Espanola 87532; 753-6049) 2 rooms, free breakfast, NS, no pets, CC. SGL/DBL$85-$100.

Comfort Inn (2975 South Riverside Dr., 87532; 753-2419, 800-221-2222) 41 rooms, restaurant, free breakfast, indoor pool, sauna, wheelchair access, NS rooms, no pets, children under 18 free with parents, A/C, TV, meeting facilities, senior rates, CC. SGL/DBL$42-$73.

Park Inn (920 North Riverside Dr., 87532; 753-7291, Fax 753-1218, 800-766-7943) 51 rooms and suites, free breakfast, lounge, heated pool, A/C, pets OK, TV, NS rooms, in-room refrigerators, children free with parents, wheelchair access, meeting facilities, senior rates, CC. SGL/DBL$55-$80.

Western Holiday (Hwy. 68, 87532; 753-2491) 23 rooms, restaurant, A/C, TV, NS rooms, wheelchair access, in-room coffee makers, no pets, CC. SGL/DBL$35-$52.

Super 8 Motel (298 South Riverside, 87532; 753-5374, Fax 753-5339, 800-800-8000) 50 rooms and suites, pets OK, children under 12 free with parents, free local calls, A/C, TV, in-room refrigerators and microwaves, fax, NS rooms, senior rates, wheelchair access, meeting facilities, CC. SGL/DBL$39-$58.

Farmington
Area Code 505

Basin Lodge (701 Airport Dr., 87401; 325-5061) 21 rooms, A/C, TV, children free with parents, pets OK, NS rooms, wheelchair access, CC. SGL/DBL$30-$37.

Best Western Inn (700 Scott Ave., 87401; 327-5221, 800-528-1234) 194 rooms, restaurant, lounge, indoor pool, exercise center, children free with parents, A/C, NS rooms, TV, airport courtesy car, game room, room service, laundry facilities, wheelchair access, pets OK, senior rates, meeting facilities, CC. SGL/DBL$50-$70.

Comfort Inn (555 Scott Ave., 87401; 325-2626, 800-221-2222) 60 rooms, restaurants, free breakfast, pool, wheelchair access, NS rooms, pets OK, children under 18 free with parents, A/C, in-room refrigerators, TV, meeting facilities, senior rates, CC. SGL/DBL$53-$73.

Days Inn (2530 Bloomfield Hwy., 87401; 327-4433, 800-325-2525) 52 rooms and suites, restaurant, lounge, outdoor pool, children free with parents, room service, laundry service, A/C, TV, free local calls, pets OK, fax, wheelchair access, NS rooms, airport transportation, meeting facilities, senior rates, CC. SGL/DBL$35-$55.

Farmington Lodge (1510 West Main St., 87401; 325-0233, 800-833-4792) 31 rooms, pool, in-room refrigerators and coffee makers, A/C, TV, NS rooms, wheelchair access, no pets, CC. SGL/DBL$28-$35.

Holiday Inn (600 East Broadway, 87401; 327-9811, Fax 325-2288, 800-HOLIDAY) 140 rooms and suites, restaurant, lounge, pool, exercise center, whirlpools, airport transportation, children under 19 free with parents, wheelchair access, A/C, TV, NS rooms, fax, room service, pets OK, laundry service, meeting facilities for 300, senior rates, CC. SGL/DBL$56-$65.

La Quinta Inn (675 Scott Ave., 87401; 327-4706, 800-531-5900) 106 rooms, restaurant, free breakfast, lounge, pool, complimentary newspaper, free local calls, fax, laundry service, NS rooms, wheelchair access, remote control TV, A/C, in-room refrigerators, pets OK, meeting facilities, CC. SGL/DBL$65-$75.

Motel 6 (510 Scott Ave., 87401; 327-0242, 505-891-6161) 98 rooms, pool, free local calls, children under 17 free with parents, NS rooms, wheelchair access, pets OK, A/C, TV, CC. SGL/DBL$38-$44.

Motel 6 (1600 Bloomfield Hwy., 87401; 326-4501, 505-891-6161) 134 rooms, pool, free local calls, children under 17 free with parents, NS rooms, wheelchair access, pets OK, A/C, TV, CC. SGL/DBL$36-$48.

Silver Rose Inn (3151 West Main St., 87401; 325-8219) free breakfast, A/C, TV, NS, no pets, no children, private baths, CC. SGL/DBL$65-$80.

Super 8 Motel (1601 Bloomfield Hwy., 87401; 325-1813, Fax 325-1813 ext 199, 800-800-8000) 60 rooms and suites, pets OK, children under 12 free with parents, game room, free local calls, A/C, TV, in-room refrigerators and microwaves, fax, NS rooms, senior rates, wheelchair access, meeting facilities, CC. SGL/DBL$28-$44.

Gallup
Area Code 505

Ambassador Motel (1601 West Hwy. 66, 87301; 722-3843) 45 rooms and 2-bedroom suites, heated pool, A/C, TV, NS rooms, wheelchair access, pets OK, CC. SGL/DBL$25-$31.

Best Western Inn (3009 Hwy. 66 West, 87301; 722-2221, Fax 722-7442, 800-528-1234) 126 rooms and suites, restaurant, lounge, indoor pool, exercise center, whirlpools, sauna, lighted tennis courts, game room, gift shop, airport transportation, children free with parents, A/C, NS rooms, TV, laundry facilities, wheelchair access, in-room refrigerators, pets OK, senior rates, meeting facilities, CC. SGL/DBL$55-$135.

Best Western Royal Holiday (1903 West Hwy. 66, 87301; 722-4900, 800-528-1234) 50 rooms, restaurant, pool, exercise center, sauna, whirlpools, children free with parents, A/C, NS rooms, TV, laundry facilities, wheelchair access, pets OK, meeting facilities, senior rates, CC. SGL/DBL$40-$85.

Budget Inn (2806 West Hwy. 66, 87301; 722-6631, 800-527-0700) pool, NS rooms, children free with parents, pets OK, A/C, TV, meeting facilities, CC. SGL/DBL$32-$44.

Colonial Motel (1007 West Coal Ave., 87301; 863-6821) 26 rooms, A/C, TV, NS rooms, wheelchair access, airport transportation, pets OK, CC. SGL/DBL$18-$30.

Comfort Inn (3208 West Hwy. 66, 87301; 722-0982, 800-221-2222) 51 rooms, restaurant, free breakfast, indoor heated pool, whirlpools, wheelchair access, NS rooms, no pets, children under 18 free with parents, A/C, TV, meeting facilities, senior rates, CC. SGL/DBL$43-$68.

Days Inn (3201 West Hwy. 66, 87301; 863-6889, 800-325-2525) 74 rooms and suites, free breakfast, indoor pool, children free with parents, room service, laundry service, A/C, TV, free local calls, pets OK, fax, wheelchair access, NS rooms, senior rates, CC. SGL/DBL$30-$45, STS$60-$80.

Days Inn (1603 West Hwy. 66, 87301; 863-3891, 800-325-2525) 78 rooms and suites, free breakfast, outdoor pool, children free with parents, room service, laundry service, A/C, TV, free local calls, pets OK, fax, wheelchair access, NS rooms, senior rates, CC. SGL/DBL$30-$45.

Econo Lodge (3101 West Hwy. 66, 87301; 722-3800, 800-4-CHOICE) 51 rooms, children under 12 free with parents, no pets, NS rooms, in-room coffee makers, wheelchair access, A/C, TV, senior rates, CC. SGL/DBL$35-$65.

El Capitan Motel (1300 East Hwy. 66, 87301; 863-6828, 800-543-6351) 42 rooms and 2-bedroom suites, A/C, TV, NS rooms, wheelchair access, pets OK, in-room computer hookups, senior rates, CC. SGL/DBL$22-$36.

El Rancho Hotel (1000 East Hwy. 66, 87301; 863-9311, 800-543-6351) 80 rooms and efficiencies, restaurant, lounge, pool, gift shop, A/C, TV, NS rooms, wheelchair access, pets OK, local transportation, laundry facilities, CC. SGL/DBL$56-$80.

HoJo Inn (I-40 and Hwy. 66, 87305; 863-6801, Fax 722-5106, 800-I-GO-HOJO) 42 rooms, restaurant, lounge, pool, children free with parents, wheelchair access, NS rooms, TV, A/C, gift shop, no pets, laundry facilities, senior rates, meeting facilities, CC. SGL/DBL$20-$35.

Holiday Inn (2915 West Hwy. 66, 87301; 722-2201, Fax 722-9616, 800-HOLIDAY) 212 rooms, restaurant, lounge, entertainment, indoor pool, exercise center, children under 19 free with parents, wheelchair access, A/C, TV, NS rooms, fax, room service, game room, airport courtesy car, pets OK, gift shop, laundry service, meeting facilities, senior rates, CC. SGL/DBL$65-$75.

Motel 6 (3306 West Hwy. 66, 87301; 863-4491, 505-891-6161) 80 rooms and suites, pool, free local calls, children under 17 free with parents, NS rooms, wheelchair access, pets OK, A/C, TV, CC. SGL/DBL$36-$48.

Roadrunner Motel (3012 East Hwy. 66, 87301; 863-3804) 31 rooms, restaurant, heated pool, pets OK, A/C, TV, NS rooms, wheelchair access, children free with parents, CC. SGL/DBL$24-$34.

Rodeway Inn (2003 West Hwy. 66, 87301; 863-9386, Fax 863-6532, 800-424-4777) 92 rooms, restaurant, heated pool, whirlpools, sauna, wheelchair access, NS rooms, children free with parents, A/C, TV, no pets, meeting facilities, senior rates, CC. SGL/DBL$33-$40.

Super 8 Motel (1715 Hwy. 66, 87301; 722-5300, Fax 722-6200, 800-800-8000) 75 rooms and suites, indoor pool, sauna, whirlpools, no pets, children under 12 free with parents, free local calls, A/C, TV, in-room refrigerators and microwaves, fax, NS rooms, senior rates, wheelchair access, meeting facilities, CC. SGL/DBL$44-$56.

Travelers Inn (3304 West Hwy. 66, 87301; 722-7765, 800-633-8300) 108 rooms and suites, heated pool, A/C, TV, NS rooms, wheelchair access, in-room refrigerators, children free with parents, pets OK, senior rates, CC. SGL/DBL$30-$65.

TraveLodge (1709 West 66th Ave., 87301; 863-9301, Fax 722-5933, 800-578-7878) 50 rooms and suites, restaurant, lounge, pool, sauna, wheelchair access, complimentary newspaper, laundry service, TV, A/C, free local calls, fax, NS rooms, in-room refrigerators and microwaves, children under 18 free with parents, pets OK, meeting facilities, CC. SGL/DBL$34-$50.

Glenwood
Area Code 505

Los Olmos Guest Ranch (Glenwood 88039; 539-2311) 13 rooms, restaurant, pool, whirlpools, pets OK, NS rooms, CC. SGL/DBL$45-$80.

Grants
Area Code 505

Best Western Inn (1501 East Santa Fe Ave., 87020; 287-7901, 800-528-1234) 126 rooms, restaurant, free breakfast, lounge, entertainment, pool, exercise center, children free with parents, A/C, NS rooms, TV, laundry facilities, wheelchair access, pets OK, meeting facilities, senior rates, CC. SGL/DBL$56-$76.

Days Inn (1504 East Santa Fe Ave., 87020; 287-8883, Fax 287-7772, 800-325-2525) 62 rooms and suites, outdoor pool, children free with parents, room service, laundry service, A/C, TV, free local calls, pets OK, fax, wheelchair access, NS rooms, senior rates, CC. SGL/DBL$39-$79.

Econo Lodge (1509 East Santa Fe Ave., 87020; 287-4426, 800-4-CHOICE) 155 rooms, restaurant, lounge, entertainment, pool, children under 12 free with parents, no pets, free local calls, fax, NS rooms, wheelchair access, A/C, TV, senior rates, CC. SGL/DBL$28-$50.

Leisure Lodge (1204 East Santa Fe Ave., 87020; 287-2991) 32 rooms, heated pool, A/C, TV, NS rooms, wheelchair access, in-room refrigerators, children free with parents, pets OK, senior rates, CC. SGL/DBL$27-$43.

Motel 6 (1505 East Santa Fe Ave., 87020; 285-4607, 505-891-6161) 103 rooms, pool, free local calls, children under 17 free with parents, NS rooms, wheelchair access, pets OK, A/C, TV, CC. SGL/DBL$38-$44.

Sands Motel (112 McArthur St., 87020; 287-2996) 24 rooms, pets OK, children free with parents, in-room refrigerators, A/C, TV, NS rooms, wheelchair access, CC. SGL/DBL$27-$45.

Super 8 Motel (1604 East Santa Fe Ave., 87020; 287-8811, 800-800-8000) 46 rooms and suites, restaurant, indoor pool, whirlpools, no pets, children under 12 free with parents, free local calls, A/C, TV, in-room refrigerators and microwaves, fax, NS rooms, senior rates, wheelchair access, meeting facilities, CC. SGL/DBL$35-$50.

Hobbs
Area Code 505

Best Western Leawood Inn (1301 East Broadway, 88240; 313-4900, 800-528-1234) 68 rooms, restaurant, free breakfast, lounge, pool, exercise center, children free with parents, A/C, NS rooms, TV, laundry facilities, airport transportation, in-room refrigerators, wheelchair access, pets OK, senior rates, meeting facilities, CC. SGL/DBL$37-$45.

Hobbs Motor Inn (501 North Marland Blvd., 88240; 397-3251, 800-635-6639) 75 rooms and suites, restaurant, lounge, entertainment, heated pool, pets OK, A/C, TV, in-room refrigerators, children free with parents, NS rooms, wheelchair access, meeting facilities, CC. SGL/DBL$35-$85.

Inn Keepers of New Mexico (309 North Marland Blvd., 88240; 397-7171) 63 rooms, pool, A/C, TV, NS rooms, wheelchair access, in-room refrigerators, pets OK, CC. SGL/DBL$35-$45.

Super 8 Motel (722 North Marland, 88240; 397-7511, 800-800-8000) 61 rooms and suites, pets OK, children under 12 free with parents, free local calls, A/C, TV, in-room refrigerators and microwaves, fax, NS rooms, senior rates, wheelchair access, meeting facilities, CC. SGL/DBL$25-$37.

Zia Motel (619 North Marland, 88240; 397-3591) 38 rooms, heated pool, A/C, TV, pets OK, NS rooms, wheelchair access, senior rates, CC. SGL/DBL$33-$40.

Las Cruces
Area Code 505

Best Western Mesilla Valley Inn (901 Avenida de Mesilla, 88005; 524-8603, Fax 526-8437, 800-528-1234) 167 rooms, restaurant, lounge, entertainment, heated pool, exercise center, whirlpools, children free with parents, A/C, NS rooms, TV, laundry facilities, wheelchair access, pets OK, senior rates, meeting facilities for 350, CC. SGL/DBL$50-$60.

Best Western Mission Inn (1765 South Main St., 88005; 524-8591, 800-528-1234) 70 rooms, restaurant, free breakfast, lounge, heated pool, exercise center, children free with parents, A/C, NS rooms, TV, laundry facilities, wheelchair access, pets OK, meeting facilities for 75, senior rates, CC. SGL/DBL$48-$60.

Bruce Motel (800 South Main St., 88005; 526-1644) 21 rooms, kitchenettes, A/C, TV, CC. SGL/DBL$18-$30.

Budget Inn (2255 West Picacho Ave., 88005; 523-0365, 800-527-0700) 57 rooms, pool, NS rooms, children free with parents, pets OK, A/C, TV, meeting facilities, CC. SGL/DBL$15-$28.

Century 21 Motel (2454 North Main St., 88005; 524-9626) 48 rooms and efficiencies, A/C, TV, NS rooms, wheelchair access, CC. SGL/DBL$26-$65.

Coachlight Inn (301 South Motel Blvd., 88005; 526-3301) 98 rooms, pool, A/C, TV, NS rooms, wheelchair access, CC. SGL/DBL$98.

Comfort Inn (Lapasada Lane, 88005; 800-221-2222) 41 rooms, free breakfast, pool, whirlpools, wheelchair access, NS rooms, no pets, children under 18 free with parents, A/C, TV, meeting facilities, senior rates, CC. SGL/DBL$43-$76.

Days End Lodge (755 North Valley Dr., 88005; 524-7753, Fax 523-2127) 32 rooms, heated pool, A/C, TV, NS rooms, wheelchair access, senior rates, CC. SGL/DBL$37-$41.

Days Inn (2600 South Valley Dr., 88001; 526-4441, Fax 526-3713, 800-325-2525) 132 rooms and suites, restaurant, lounge, indoor pool, game room, children free with parents, room service, laundry service, A/C, TV, free local calls, airport transportation, in-room refrigerators, no pets, fax, wheelchair access, NS rooms, meeting facilities for 230, senior rates, CC. SGL/DBL$40-$60.

Desert Lodge (1900 West Picacho Ave., 88001; 524-1925) 10 rooms, pool, A/C, TV, children free with parents, NS rooms, wheelchair access, pets OK, CC. SGL/DBL$18-$27.

Desert Oasis Inn (1765 West Picacho Ave., 88001; 524-6858) 18 rooms, pool, kitchenettes, A/C, TV, NS rooms, wheelchair access, CC. SGL/DBL$20-$25.

Dunes Motel (2200 South Valley Dr., 88005; 524-4960) 12 rooms, A/C, TV, NS rooms, wheelchair access, CC. SGL/DBL$20-$60.

Economy Inn (2160 West Picacho, 88005; 524-8627, 800-826-0778) 90 rooms and suites, restaurant, heated pool, free local calls, wheelchair access, A/C, children free with parents, TV, NS rooms, no pets, meeting facilities for 200, senior rates, CC. SGL/DBL$20-$45.

Hampton Inn (755 Avenida de Mesilla, 88005; 526-8311, 800-HAMPTON) 118 rooms, restaurant, free breakfast, pool, exercise center, children under 18 free with parents, NS rooms, wheelchair access, in-room computer hookups, fax, TV, A/C, free local calls, pets OK, meeting facilities for 12, CC. SGL/DBL$45-$55.

Hilton Hotel (705 South Telshor Blvd., 88001; 522-4300, Fax 521-4707, 800-HILTONS) 203 rooms and suites, restaurant, lounge, entertainment, pool, exercise center, children free with parents, NS rooms, wheelchair access, no pets, room service, laundry facilities, A/C, TV, gift shop, in-room refrigerators and coffee makers, no pets, meeting facilities, senior rates, CC. SGL/DBL$60-$275.

Holiday Inn de Las Cruces (201 University Ave., 88001; 526-4411, Fax 524-0530, 800-HOLIDAY) 110 rooms and suites, restaurant, lounge, entertainment, indoor pool, exercise center, children under 19 free with parents, wheelchair access, A/C, TV, NS rooms, game room, gift shop, fax, airport courtesy car, room service, no pets, laundry service, meeting facilities for 1,000, senior rates, CC. SGL/DBL$55-$80, STS$250.

Imperial Sky Motel (1865 West Picacho Ave., 88005; 524-3591) 29 rooms and efficiencies, A/C, TV, NS rooms, wheelchair access, CC. SGL/DBL$15-$28.

La Quinta Inn (790 Ave. de Mesilla, 88005; 524-0331, 800-531-5900) 100 rooms, pool, complimentary newspaper, free local calls, fax, laundry service, NS rooms, wheelchair access, remote control TV, A/C, meeting facilities for 25, CC. SGL/DBL$46-$65.

Lundeen Inn (618 South Alameda Blvd., 88005; 526-3327) 8 rooms, free breakfast, A/C, TV, private baths, in-room refrigerators and microwaves, pets OK, CC. SGL/DBL$50-$90.

Meson de Mesilla (1803 Avenida de Mesilla, 88046; 525-9212, 800-732-6025) 12 rooms and suites, restaurant, free breakfast, pool, antique furnishings, pets OK, A/C, TV, NS rooms, airport courtesy car, wheelchair access, modified American plan available, CC. SGL/DBL$45-$90.

Motel 6 (235 La Posada Lane, 88001; 525-1010, 505-891-6161) 118 rooms, pool, free local calls, children under 17 free with parents, NS rooms, wheelchair access, pets OK, A/C, TV, CC. SGL/DBL$30-$42.

Paradise Motel (2040 West Picacho Ave., 88005; 526-5583) 32 rooms and efficiencies, pool, A/C, TV, NS rooms, wheelchair access, CC. SGL/DBL$18-$27.

Plaza Suites (301 East University Ave., 88001; 525-5500) 83 rooms and efficiencies, heated pool, A/C, TV, NS rooms, wheelchair access, CC. SGL/DBL$45-$50.

Royal Host Motel (2146 West Picacho Ave., 88005; 524-8536) 26 rooms, pool, A/C, children free with parents, pets OK, TV, NS rooms, wheelchair access, senior rates, CC. SGL/DBL$24-$42.

Sands Motel (1655 South Main St., 88001; 524-7791) 13 rooms, heated pool, A/C, TV, NS rooms, wheelchair access, CC. SGL/DBL$22-$35.

Super 8 Motel South (245 La Posada Lane, 88001; 523-8695, Fax 527-2914, 800-800-8000) 61 rooms and suites, pets OK, children under 12 free with parents, free local calls, A/C, TV, in-room refrigerators and microwaves, fax, NS rooms, senior rates, wheelchair access, meeting facilities, CC. SGL/DBL$37-$57.

Super 8 Motel East (4411 North Main St., 88001; 382-1490, Fax 382-1849, 800-800-8000) 59 rooms and suites, restaurant, outdoor pool, no pets, children under 12 free with parents, free local calls, A/C, TV, in-room refrigerators and microwaves, fax, NS rooms, senior rates, wheelchair access, meeting facilities, CC. SGL/DBL$37-$50.

Town House Motel (2205 West Picacho Ave., 88005; 524-7733) 21 rooms and efficiencies, pool, A/C, TV, NS rooms, wheelchair access, CC. SGL/DBL$15-$28.

Villa Motel (1785 South Main St., 88001; 526-5573) 19 rooms, heated pool, kitchenettes, A/C, TV, NS rooms, wheelchair access, CC. SGL/DBL$22-$30.

Western Inn (2155 West Picacho Ave., 88005; 523-5399) 48 rooms, restaurant, heated pool, A/C, TV, NS rooms, wheelchair access, CC. SGL/DBL$18-$48.

Las Vegas
Area Code 505

Comfort Inn (2500 North Grand Ave., 87701; 425-1100, 800-221-2222) 101 rooms, restaurant, free breakfast, indoor pool, whirlpools, wheelchair access, NS rooms, no pets, children under 18 free with parents, A/C, TV, meeting facilities, senior rates, CC. SGL/DBL$40-$63.

El Camino Motel (1152 North Grand Ave., 87701; 425-5994) 23 rooms, lounge, children free with parents, pets OK, A/C, TV, NS rooms, wheelchair access, senior rates, CC. SGL/DBL$30-$45.

The Inn on the Santa Fe Trail (1133 North Grand Ave., 87701; 425-6791) 38 rooms, pets OK, in-room refrigerators and microwaves, rooms, children free with parents, senior rates, CC. SGL/DBL$40-$65.

Plaza Hotel (230 Old Town Plaza, 87701; 425-3591, 800-328-1882) 38 rooms and suites, restaurant, lounge, 1880s inn, A/C, TV, NS rooms, wheelchair access, pets OK, local transportation, meeting facilities, senior rates, CC. SGL/DBL$55-$90.

Scottish Inns (1216 North Grand Ave., 87701; 425-9357, 800-251-1962) 45 rooms, restaurant, A/C, TV, wheelchair access, NS rooms, children under age 3 free with parents, free local calls, local transportation, senior rates, CC. SGL/DBL$25-$65.

Super 8 Motel (2029 North Hwy. 85, 87701; 425-5288, 800-800-8000) 36 rooms and suites, restaurant, no pets, children under 12 free with parents, free local calls, A/C, TV, in-room refrigerators and microwaves, fax, NS rooms, senior rates, wheelchair access, meeting facilities, CC. SGL/DBL$35-$48.

Town House Motel (1215 Grand Ave., 87701; 425-6717) 42 rooms, A/C, TV, NS rooms, wheelchair access, CC. SGL/DBL$35-$40.

Lincoln
Area Code 505

Case de Patron (Hwy. 380 East, 88338; 653-4676) 5 rooms and 1- and 2-bedroom cottages, free breakfast, TV, in-room refrigerators and coffee makers, NS, no pets, private baths, no pets, CC. SGL/DBL$65-$95.

Lordsburg
Area Code 505

Best Western Inn (944 East Motel Dr., 88045; 542-3591, 800-528-1234) 88 rooms, restaurant, lounge, pool, exercise center, children free with parents, A/C, NS rooms, TV, laundry facilities, wheelchair access, pets OK, meeting facilities, VCRs, senior rates, CC. SGL/DBL$40-$54.

Best Western Inn (1303 South Main St., 88045; 542-8807, 800-528-1234) 40 rooms, restaurant, heated pool, exercise center, children free with parents, A/C, NS rooms, TV, laundry facilities, wheelchair access, pets OK, meeting facilities, senior rates, CC. SGL/DBL$42-$48.

Super 8 Motel (110 East Maple St., 88045; 542-8882, 800-800-8000) 41 rooms and suites, no pets, children under 12 free with parents, free local calls, A/C, TV, in-room refrigerators and microwaves, fax, NS rooms, senior rates, wheelchair access, meeting facilities, CC. SGL/DBL$35-$46.

Los Alamos
Area Code 505

Hilltop House (400 Trinity Dr., 87544; 662-2441, Fax 662-5913, 800-462-0936) 100 rooms and suites, restaurant, free breakfast, indoor heated pool, A/C, TV, NS rooms, in-room coffee makers, kitchenettes, VCRs, pets OK, airport transportation, pets OK, beauty shop, children free with parents, room service, wheelchair access, CC. SGL/DBL$65-$85.

Los Alamos Inn (2201 Trinity Dr., 87544; 662-7211, 800-279-9279) 115 rooms, restaurant, lounge, pool, sauna, A/C, no pets, TV, NS rooms, wheelchair access, airport transportation, children free with parents, in-room refrigerators and coffee makers, senior rates, meeting facilities, CC. SGL/DBL$65-$80.

The Orange Street Inn (3496 Orange St., 87544; 662-2651) 7 rooms, free breakfast, children free with parents, NS, antique furnishings, TV, airport transportation, CC. SGL/DBL$50-$75.

Los Lunas
Area Code 505

Comfort Inn (1711 Main St. Southwest, 87031; 865-5100, 800-221-2222) 44 rooms, pool, whirlpools, wheelchair access, NS rooms, no pets, children under 18 free with parents, A/C, TV, meeting facilities, senior rates, CC. SGL/DBL$43-$68.

Los Ojos
Area Code 505

Casa de Martinez (Los Ojos 87551; 588-7858) 6 rooms, free breakfast, 1860s home, NS, shared baths, no pets, senior rates, CC. SGL/DBL$45-$85.

Mescalero
Area Code 505

The Inn of the Mountain Gods (Mescalero 88340; 257-5141, Fax 257-6173, 800-545-9011) 250 rooms and suites, restaurant, lounge, entertainment, heated pool, exercise center, sauna, whirlpools, A/C, TV, NS rooms, wheelchair access, airport transportation, in-room refrigerators and coffee makers, gift shop, laundry facilities, children free with parents, no pets, senior rates, meeting facilities, CC. SGL/DBL$95-125.

Mesilla
Area Code 505

Happy Trails Bed and Breakfast (1857 Paisaho Rd., 88005; 527-8471) 3 rooms, free breakfast, A/C, NS, laundry facilities, pets OK, shared baths, senior rates, CC. SGL/DBL$75-$100.

Moriarty
Area Code 505

Days Inn (Route 66 West, 87035; 832-4451, Fax 832-6464, 800-325-2525) 41 rooms and suites, free breakfast, children free with parents, room service, laundry service, A/C, TV, free local calls, pets OK, fax, wheelchair access, NS rooms, senior rates, CC. SGL/DBL$32-$54.

Howard Johnson Lodge (1316 Central Ave., 87305; 832-4457, Fax 832-4965, 800-I-GO-HOJO) 29 rooms, free breakfast, children free with parents, wheelchair access, NS rooms, TV, A/C, no pets, laundry facilities, senior rates, meeting facilities, CC. SGL/DBL$30-$42.

Sunset Motel (Moriarty 87035; 832-4234) 18 rooms, A/C, TV, NS rooms, pets OK, CC. SGL/DBL$30-$35.

Super 8 Motel (Central Ave., 87035; 832-6730, 800-800-8000) 42 rooms and suites, pets OK, children under 12 free with parents, free local calls, A/C, TV, in-room refrigerators and microwaves, fax, NS rooms, senior rates, wheelchair access, meeting facilities, CC. SGL/DBL$35-$47.

Ojo Caliente
Area Code 505

Ojo Caliente Mineral Springs (Ojo Caliente 87549; 583-2233) 27 rooms, spa, CC. SGL/DBL$45-$60.

Placitas
Area Code 505

Kensington House (Placitas 87043; 867-5586) free breakfast, A/C, TV, NS, private baths, CC. SGL/DBL$70-$110.

Portales
Area Code 505

Dunes Motel (Hwy. 70 West, 88130; 356-6668, Fax 356-6668 ext 13) 41 rooms and suites, restaurant, heated pool, pets OK, in-room refrigerators and coffee makers, A/C, TV, NS rooms, wheelchair access, airport transportation, senior rates, CC. SGL/DBL$65-$105.

Portales Inn (218 West 3rd St., 88130; 359-1208) 39 rooms, restaurant, A/C, TV, NS rooms, in-room refrigerators, pets OK, wheelchair access, meeting facilities, senior rates, CC. SGL/DBL$30-$40.

Super 8 Motel (1805 West 2nd St., 88130; 356-8518, Fax 359-0431, 800-800-8000) 45 rooms and suites, whirlpools, no pets, children under 12 free with parents, free local calls, A/C, TV, in-room refrigerators and microwaves, fax, NS rooms, senior rates, wheelchair access, meeting facilities, CC. SGL/DBL$38-$52.

Questa
Area Code 505

Fagerquists Cottonwood Park - The Last Resort (Questa, 87556; 586-0285) 22 rooms, restaurant, TV, CC. SGL/DBL$40-$80.

Sangre de Cristo Motel (Hwys. 522 and 38, 87556, 800-459-0300) 18 rooms, A/C, TV, NS rooms, wheelchair access, CC. SGL/DBL$40.

Ranchos de Taos
Area Code 505

Rose Garden Inn (Ranchos de Taos, 87557; 758-4121) 2 rooms, A/C, TV, NS rooms, wheelchair access, no pets, children free with parents, CC. SGL/DBL$37-$47.

Taos Motel (Ranchos de Taos, 87557; 758-2524, 800-323-6009) 28 rooms, A/C, TV, NS rooms, wheelchair access, children free with parents, senior rates, CC. SGL/DBL$29-$48.

Raton
Area Code 505

Best Western Sands Manor Inn (300 Clayton Rd., 87740; 445-2737, 800-528-1234) 50 rooms, restaurant, heated pool, exercise center, children free with parents, A/C, NS rooms, local transportation, TV, laundry facilities, wheelchair access, no pets, senior rates, meeting facilities, CC. SGL/DBL$70-$75.

El Kapp Motel (200 Clayton Rd., 87740; 445-2791, 800-748-2482) 26 rooms, A/C, TV, NS rooms, no pets, children free with parents, wheelchair access, CC. SGL/DBL$28.

Harmony Manor Motel (351 Clayton Rd., 87740; 445-2763, 800-922-0347) 18 rooms, A/C, TV, children free with parents, pets OK, NS rooms, wheelchair access, CC. SGL/DBL$36-$60.

Holiday Classic Motel (473 Clayton Rd., 87740; 445-5555, 800-255-8879) 87 rooms, restaurant, lounge, indoor heated pool, game room, airport transportation, pets OK, A/C, TV, NS rooms, VCRs, laundry facilities, wheelchair access, children free with parents, senior rates, CC. SGL/DBL$60-$70.

Master Hosts Melody Lane Inn (136 Canyon Dr., 87740; 445-3655, Fax 445-3655 ext 100, 800-251-1962) 26 rooms, lounge, pool, saunas, in-room refrigerators, NS rooms, A/C, TV, children under 18 free with parents, pets OK, senior rates, meeting facilities, CC. SGL/DBL$35-$55.

Motel 6 (1600 Cedar St., 87740; 445-2777, 505-891-6161) 103 rooms, pool, free local calls, children under 17 free with parents, NS rooms, wheelchair access, pets OK, A/C, TV, CC. SGL/DBL$38-$49.

The Red Violet Inn (344 North 2nd St., 87740; 445-9778, 800-624-9778) 4 rooms, restaurant, free breakfast, antique furnishings, NS, 1902 inn, TV, A/C, senior rates, CC. SGL/DBL$45-$65.

Red River
Area Code 505

Alpine Lodge (Main St., 87558; 754-2952, 800-252-2333) 45 rooms and efficiencies, restaurant, lounge, entertainment, A/C, TV, NS rooms, wheelchair access, kitchenettes, no pets, CC. SGL/DBL$30-$135.

Arrowhead Ski Lodge (Pioneer Rd., 87558; 754-2255) 19 rooms and efficiencies, A/C, TV, NS rooms, wheelchair access, no pets, senior rates, CC. SGL/DBL$40-$80.

Bitter Creek Guest Ranch (Bitter Creek Rd., 87558; 754-2587, 800-562-9462) 10 1- to 4-bedroom cabins, TV, no pets OK, CC. 1BR/2BR$65, 3BR/4BR$85.

Lifts West Condominiums (Main St., 87558; 754-2778, 800-221-1859) 75 condominiums, restaurant, pool, whirlpools, laundry facilities, no pets, boutiques, A/C, VCRs, TV, NS rooms, wheelchair access, fireplaces, meeting facilities, senior rates, CC. SGL/DBL$60-$350.

The Lodge at Red River (West Main St., 87558; 754-6280) 24 rooms, restaurant, lounge, no pets, modified American plan available, TV, NS rooms, wheelchair access, meeting facilities, senior rates, CC. SGL/DBL$65-$80.

Ponderosa Lodge (Main St., 87558; 754-2988, 800-336-7787) 17 rooms and apartments, restaurant, whirlpools, sauna, no pets, children free with parents, TV, NS rooms, wheelchair access, kitchenettes, CC. SGL/DBL$60-$220.

Red River Inn (300 West Main St., 87558; 754-2930, 800-365-2930) 16 rooms, A/C, TV, NS rooms, wheelchair access, CC. SGL/DBL$36-$46.

River Ranch (West Main St., 87558; 754-2227) 21 cabins and apartments, A/C, TV, NS rooms, wheelchair access, no pets, children free with parents, CC. SGL/DBL$55-$90.

Riverside Motel and Cabins (Main St., 87558; 754-2252, Fax 754-2495, 800-432-9999) 38 rooms and cabins, restaurant, whirlpools, kitchenettes, no pets, fireplaces, TV, NS rooms, wheelchair access, meeting facilities, CC. SGL/DBL$50-$105.

Tall Pine Resort (Red River 87558; 754-2241) 19 1- and 2-bedroom cabins, TV, NS rooms, wheelchair access, pets OK, laundry facilities, CC. SGL/DBL$60-$95.

Terrace Towers Lodge (West Main St., 87558; 754-2962, 800-69-LODGE) 30 1- to 3-bedroom efficiencies, pets OK, laundry facilities, A/C, TV, NS rooms, children free with parents, kitchenettes, pets OK, VCRs, wheelchair access, CC. SGL/DBL$35-$65.

Valley Lodge (Red River 87558; 754-2262, 800-951-2262) 8 rooms, A/C, TV, NS rooms, wheelchair access, pets OK, children free with parents, CC. SGL/DBL$40.

Rio Rancho

Area Code 505

Best Western Inn (1465 Rio Rancho Dr., 87124; 892-1700, 800-528-1234) 106 rooms and suites, restaurant, lounge, pool, exercise center, children free with parents, A/C, NS rooms, TV, laundry facilities, wheelchair access, in-room coffee makers, local transportation, pets OK, senior rates, meeting facilities, CC. SGL/DBL$40-$65.

Road Forks

Area Code 505

Desert West Motel (Road Forks 88045; 542-8810) 59 rooms and efficiencies, pool, children free with parents, in-room refrigerators, A/C, TV, pets OK, meeting facilities, senior rates, CC. SGL/DBL$40-$45.

Roswell

Area Code 505

Best Western Inn (2000 North Main St., 88201; 622-6430, 800-528-1234) 124 rooms, restaurant, lounge, indoor heated pool, exercise center, sauna, whirlpools, lighted tennis courts, airport transportation, children free with parents, A/C, NS rooms, TV, laundry facilities, in-room refrigerators, wheelchair access, pets OK, meeting facilities, senior rates, CC. SGL/DBL$52-$68.

Days Inn (1310 North Main St, 88201; 623-4021, Fax 623-0079, 800-325-2525) 62 rooms and suites, restaurant, lounge, free breakfast, outdoor pool, children free with parents, room service, laundry service, A/C, TV, free local calls, pets OK, fax, wheelchair access, NS rooms, senior rates, CC. SGL/DBL$34-$46.

Frontier Motel (3010 North Main St., 88201; 623-9440, 800-678-1401) 58 rooms and efficiencies, restaurant, free breakfast, heated pool, A/C, TV, NS rooms, wheelchair access, in-room refrigerators, pets OK, CC. SGL/DBL$30-$45.

Roswell Inn (1815 North Main St., 88201; 623-4920, 800-323-0913) 121 rooms, restaurant, lounge, heated pool, airport transportation, no pets, A/C, airport courtesy car, room service, TV, NS rooms, wheelchair access, meeting facilities, senior rates, CC. SGL/DBL$55-$155.

Royal Motel (2001 North Main St., 88201; 622-0110) 67 rooms, pool, no pets, children free with parents, A/C, TV, NS rooms, wheelchair access, senior rates, CC. SGL/DBL$29-$40.

Ruidoso

Area Code 505

Best Western Swiss Chalet Inn (Ruidoso 88345; 258-3333, 800-528-1234) 82 rooms and suites, restaurant, free breakfast, lounge, indoor pool, exercise center, whirlpools, airport courtesy car, children free with parents, A/C, NS rooms, TV, laundry facilities, wheelchair access, pets OK, meeting facilities, senior rates, meeting facilities, CC. SGL/DBL$60-$190.

Dan Dee Cabins (Ruidoso 88345; 257-2165) 12 rooms and 1- to 3-bedroom cabins, kitchenettes, fireplaces, pets OK, TV, CC. SGL/DBL$56-$75.

Enchantment Inn (307 Hwy. 70 West, 88345; 80 rooms and suites, restaurant, free breakfast, lounge, indoor and outdoor pool, whirlpools, A/C, TV, NS rooms, in-room refrigerators and microwaves, wheelchair access, room service, no pets, meeting facilities, senior rates, CC. SGL/DBL$45-$125.

The Inn at Pine Springs (Ruidos 88346; 378-8100) 100 rooms, whirlpools, pets OK, A/C, TV, children free with parents, CC. SGL/DBL$40-$78.

Ruidoso Lodge Cabins (300 Main St., 88345; 257-2510) 8 cabins, kitchenettes, pets OK, TV, fireplaces, CC. SGL/DBL$50-$95.

Story Book Cabins (Ruidos 88345; 257-2115) 10 rooms and 1- to 3-bedroom cabins, kitchenettes, no pets, TV, CC. SGL/DBL$65-$75.

Super 8 Motel (100 Cliff Dr., 88345; 378-8180, 800-800-8000) 63 rooms and suites, restaurant, whirlpools, sauna, no pets, children under 12 free with parents, free local calls, A/C, TV, in-room refrigerators and microwaves, fax, NS rooms, senior rates, wheelchair access, meeting facilities, CC. SGL/DBL$33-$47.

Village Lodge (Ruidoso 88345; 258-5442, 800-722-8779) 28 efficiencies, heated pool, laundry facilities, A/C, TV, NS rooms, wheelchair access, children free with parents, in-room refrigerators, microwaves and coffee makers, pets OK, laundry facilities, senior rates, CC. SGL/DBL$60-$100.

Villa Inn (Ruidoso 88345; 378-4471) 60 rooms, heated pool, no pets, children free with parents, A/C, TV, NS rooms, wheelchair access, CC. SGL/DBL$30-$55.

West Winds Lodge and Condominiums (208 Eagle Dr., 88345; 257-4031, 800-421-0691) 30 rooms and condominiums, pool, local transportation, kitchenettes, TV, NS rooms, wheelchair access, CC. SGL/DBL$45-$170.

Santa Fe
Area Code 505

Rental and Reservation Services:

Santa Fe Accommodations (320 Artist Rd., 87501; 800-745-9910) rental condominiums and casitas.

□□□

Alexander's Inn (529 East Palace Ave., 87501; 986-1431) 7 rooms, free breakfast, A/C, TV, NS, no pets, 1903 inn, private baths, in-room coffee makers, CC. SGL/DBL$65-$140.

Best Western High Mesa Inn (3347 Cerrilos Rd., 87501; 473-2800, 800-528-1234) 211 rooms, restaurant, lounge, entertainment, indoor pool, exercise center, whirlpools, children free with parents, A/C, NS rooms, TV, laundry facilities, wheelchair access, pets OK, in-room refrigerators, no senior rates, meeting facilities, CC. SGL/DBL$85-$110.

Best Western Inn (211 Old Santa Fe Trail, 87504; 988-5531, Fax 984-7988, 800-528-1234) 136 rooms, restaurant, free breakfast, lounge, pool, exercise center, children free with parents, A/C, NS rooms, room service, TV, laundry facilities, wheelchair access, no pets, barber and beauty shop, senior rates, meeting facilities, CC. SGL/DBL$180-$200.

Bishop's Lodge (Santa Fe 87504; 983-6377) 74 rooms and 2-bedroom suites, restaurant, lounge, heated pool, exercise center, whirlpools, A/C, TV, modified American plan available, in-room refrigerators, local transportation, no pets, NS rooms, wheelchair access, CC. SGL/DBL$125-$355.

Cactus Lodge Motel (2864 Cerrillos Rd., 87501; 471-7699) 25 rooms and 2-bedroom efficiencies, A/C, TV, NS rooms, wheelchair access, no pets, CC. SGL/DBL$32-$75.

Canyon Road Casitas Inn (652 Canyon Rd., 87501; 988-5888, 800-279-0755) 2 efficiencies, free breakfast, fireplaces, NS, no pets, wheelchair access, private baths, CC. SGL/DBL$100-$170.

Comfort Inn (4300 Cerrillos Rd., 87504; 800-221-2222) 60 rooms, restaurant, free breakfast, indoor pool, whirlpools, wheelchair access, NS rooms, no pets, children under 18 free with parents, A/C, TV, meeting facilities, senior rates, CC. SGL/DBL$43-$92.

Days Inn (Cerrillos Rd., 87502; 438-3822, Fax 438-3795, 800-325-2525) 96 rooms and suites, free breakfast, indoor pool, children free with parents, room service, laundry service, A/C, TV, free local calls, pets OK, fax, wheelchair access, NS rooms, senior rates, CC. SGL/DBL$45-$63.

Dos Casas Viejas Inn (610 Aqua Friar St., 87501; 983-1636) 3 rooms and suites, free breakfast, heated pool, TV, wheelchair access, NS, in-room coffee makers, CC. SGL/DBL$125-$185.

El Dorado Motel (309 West San Francisco, 87501; 988-4455, 800-955-4455) 218 rooms and suites, restaurant, lounge, entertainment, heated pool, whirlpools, sauna, in-room coffee makers, A/C, children free with parents, TV, NS rooms, wheelchair access, meeting facilities, senior rates, CC. SGL/DBL$135-$225.

El Paradero Inn (220 West Manhattan, 87501; 988-1177) 14 rooms and suites, kitchenettes, children free with parents, A/C, TV, NS rooms, wheelchair access, pets OK, fireplaces, antique furnishings, CC. SGL/DBL$50-$130.

El Rey Inn (1862 Cerrillos Rd., 87502; 982-1931, Fax 989-9249) 55 rooms and suites, free breakfast, pool, whirlpools, laundry facilities, A/C, TV, NS rooms, in-room refrigerators, fireplaces, wheelchair access, no pets, children free with parents, CC. SGL/DBL$55-$145.

Fort Marcy Condominiums (320 Artist Rd., 87501; 982-6636) 80 rooms and 1- to 3-bedroom condominiums, indoor heated pool, whirlpools, kitchenettes, in-room refrigerators and microwaves, A/C, TV, wheelchair access, CC. SGL/DBL$83-$160.

Four Kachinas Inn (512 Webber St., 87501; 982-2550) 4 rooms, free breakfast, TV, NS, no pets, CC. SGL/DBL$80-$110.

Garrett's Desert Inn (311 Old Santa Fe Trail, 87501; 982-1851) 82 rooms, heated pool, A/C, TV, NS rooms, wheelchair access, no pets, CC. SGL/DBL$80-$100.

Grant Corner Inn (122 Grant Ave., 87501; 983-6678) 13 rooms, free breakfast, A/C, TV, NS, wheelchair access, children free with parents, antique furnishings, private baths, room service, no pets, CC. SGL/DBL$65-$140.

Hilton Hotel (100 Sandoval St., 87501; 800-HILTONS) 155 rooms and suites, restaurant, lounge, entertainment, heated pool, exercise center, whirlpools, children free with parents, NS rooms, wheelchair access, pets OK, in-room refrigerators and coffee makers, pets OK, in-room computer hookups, room service, laundry facilities, A/C, TV, meeting facilities, senior rates, CC. SGL/DBL$125-$250.

Holiday Inn (4048 Cerrillos Rd., 87505; 473-4646, Fax 473-4646 ext 510, 800-HOLIDAY) 130 rooms and suites, restaurant, lounge, indoor and outdoor pool, exercise center, jacuzzi, sauna, whirlpools, gift shop, fireplaces, children under 19 free with parents, wheelchair access, A/C, airport transportation, TV, NS rooms, fax, room service, pets OK, laundry service, meeting facilities for 200, senior rates, CC. SGL/DBL$85-$275.

Howard Johnson Lodge (4044 Cerrillos Rd., 87501; 438-8950, Fax 471-9129, 800-I-GO-HOJO) 47 rooms and suites, jacuzzis, children free with parents, wheelchair access, NS rooms, TV, A/C, no pets, laundry facilities, senior rates, meeting facilities, CC. SGL/DBL$56-$88.

The Inn of the Anasazi (113 Washington Ave., 87501; 988-3030, Fax 988-3277, 800-688-8100) 59 rooms and suites, restaurant, A/C, TV, children free with parents, NS rooms, wheelchair access, in-room coffee makers, pets OK, CC. SGL/DBL$230-$260, STS$390-$400.

The Inn of the Animal Tracks (7070 Paseo de Peralta, 87501; 988-1546) 47 rooms and suites, free breakfast, TV, NS, wheelchair access, CC. SGL/DBL$90-$115.

The Inn on the Alameda (303 East Alameda, 87501; 984-2121, Fax 986-8325, 800-289-2122) 47 rooms and suites, free breakfast, lounge, whirlpools, A/C, TV, NS rooms, wheelchair access, fireplaces, pets OK, CC. SGL/DBL$145-$325.

The Inn on the Paseo (630 Paseo de Peralto, 87501; 984-8200, 800-457-9045) 19 rooms and suites, free breakfast, A/C, TV, NS, no pets, wheelchair access, CC. SGL/DBL$100-$180.

The Inn of the Governors (234 Don Gaspar Ave., 87501; 982-4333, Fax 989-9149, 800-234-4534) 100 rooms, restaurant, lounge, entertainment, heated pool, A/C, TV, NS rooms, wheelchair access, no pets, rooms service, meeting facilities, senior rates, CC. SGL/DBL$90-$250.

Jean's Place (2407 Camino Capitan, 87505; 471-4053) 1 room, free breakfast, A/C, TV, NS, private bath, no pets, CC. SGL/DBL$40-$45.

La Fonda Hotel (100 East San Francisco St., 87501; 982-5511, Fax 988-2952, 800-523-5002) 160 rooms and suites, restaurant, lounge, entertainment, pool, whirlpools, fireplaces, A/C, TV, NS rooms, wheelchair access, no pets, beauty shop, antique furnishings, meeting facilities, senior rates, CC. SGL/DBL$150-$450.

La Posada de Santa Fe (330 East Palace Ave., 87501; 986-0000, Fax 982-6850, 800-727-5276) 119 rooms and suites, restaurant, lounge, pool, fireplaces, A/C, TV, NS rooms, wheelchair access, no pets, beauty shop, meeting facilities, senior rates, CC. SGL/DBL$115-$400.

La Quinta Inn (4298 Cerrillos Rd., 87505; 471-1142, Fax 438-7219, 800-531-5900) 130 rooms and suites, restaurant, free breakfast, lounge, pool, complimentary newspaper, free local calls, fax, laundry service, NS rooms, wheelchair access, remote control TV, A/C, pets OK, in-room refrigerators, meeting facilities, CC. SGL/DBL$75-$84.

Motel 6 (3007 Cerrillos Rd., 87501; 473-1380, 505-891-6161) 104 rooms, pool, free local calls, children under 17 free with parents, NS rooms, wheelchair access, pets OK, A/C, TV, CC. SGL/DBL$36-$44.

Motel 6 (3695 Cerrillos Rd., 87501; 471-4140, 505-891-6161) 121 rooms, pool, free local calls, children under 17 free with parents, NS rooms, wheelchair access, pets OK, A/C, TV, CC. SGL/DBL$38-$44.

Park Inn International (2900 Cerrillos Rd, 87501; 473-4281, 800-437-PARK) 83 rooms and suites, pool, A/C, TV, wheelchair access, NS rooms, meeting facilities for 50, senior rates, CC. SGL/DBL$58-$80.

Picacho Plaza (750 North St. Francis Dr., 87501; 982-5591, 800-441-5591) 129 rooms and suites, restaurant, lounge, entertainment, heated pool, whirlpools, A/C, TV, NS rooms, in-room refrigerators and coffee makers, local transportation, wheelchair access, meeting facilities, senior rates, CC. SGL/DBL$78-$390.

Plaza Real Hotel (125 Washington Ave., 87501; 988-4900, 800-279-REAL) 56 rooms and suites, restaurant, free breakfast, lounge, exercise center, whirlpools, tennis courts, children free with parents, no pets, A/C, TV, NS rooms, in-room refrigerators, wheelchair access, in-room refrigerators, room service, meeting facilities, senior rates, CC. SGL/DBL$135-$600.

Preston House (106 Faithway St., 87501; 982-3465) 15 rooms and suites, free breakfast, A/C, TV, NS, 1880s inn, antique furnishings, fireplaces, pets OK, wheelchair access, CC. SGL/DBL$58-$130.

Pueblo Bonito (138 West Manhattan, 87501; 984-8001) 18 rooms and suites, free breakfast, kitchenettes, fireplaces, TV, NS rooms, wheelchair access, antique furnishings, CC. SGL/DBL$85-$130.

Quality Inn (3011 Cerrillos Rd., 87501; 471-1211, 800-221-2222) 99 rooms and suites, restaurant, lounge, pool, exercise center, children free with parents, A/C, TV, room service, laundry service, NS rooms, pets OK, in-room refrigerators, airport transportation, meeting facilities, senior rates, CC. SGL/DBL$55-$96.

Ramada Inn (2907 Cerrillos Rd., 87501; 471-3000, Fax 471-6034, 800-2-RAMADA) 107 rooms and suites, restaurant, lounge, outdoor pool, wheelchair access, NS rooms, pets OK, A/C, TV, children under 18 free with parents, room service, laundry facilities, meeting facilities, senior rates, CC. SGL/DBL$68-$93.

Residence Inn by Marriott (1698 Galisteo St., 87501; 988-6300, 800-331-3131) 120 suites, free breakfast, in-room refrigerators, coffee makers and microwaves, laundry facilities, TV, A/C, VCRs, pets OK, complimentary newspaper, fireplaces, children free with parents, NS rooms, wheelchair access, meeting facilities, CC. SGL/DBL$155.

St. Francis Hotel (210 Don Gaspar Ave., 87501; 983-5700, Fax 989-7690, 800-666-5700) 83 rooms and suites, restaurant, lounge, A/C, TV, NS rooms, wheelchair access, in-room refrigerators, children free with parents, kitchenettes, no pets, antique furnishings, CC. SGL/DBL$80-$170, STS$200-$300.

Santa Fe Hotel (1501 Paseo de Peralta, 87501; 982-1200, 800-825-9876) 131 rooms and suites, restaurant, lounge, entertainment, pool, laundry facilities, gift shop, no pets, A/C, TV, NS rooms, wheelchair access, meeting facilities, senior rates, CC. SGL/DBL$115-$225.

Stage Coach Motel (3360 Cerrillos Rd., 87501; 471-0707) 14 rooms, A/C, TV, NS rooms, no pets, in-room refrigerators and microwaves, wheelchair access, CC. SGL/DBL$47-$60.

Sunset House (436 Sunset St., 87501; 983-3523) free breakfast, A/C, TV, no pets, NS, fireplaces, private baths, CC. SGL/DBL$66-$80.

Super 8 Motel (3358 Cerrillos Rd., 87501; 471-8811, Fax 471-3239, 800-800-8000) 96 rooms and suites, no pets, children under 12 free with parents, free local calls, A/C, TV, in-room refrigerators and microwaves, fax, NS rooms, senior rates, wheelchair access, meeting facilities, CC. SGL/DBL$33-$47.

Territorial Inn (215 Washington Ave., 87501; 989-7737, Fax 986-1411) 11 rooms, free breakfast, TV, NS rooms, wheelchair access, 1890s inn, antique furnishings, children free with parents, no pets, CC. SGL/DBL$80-$150.

TraveLodge Santa Fe Plaza (646 Cerrillos Rd., 87501; 982-3551, Fax 983-8624, 800-578-7878) 49 rooms, restaurant, pool, wheelchair access, complimentary newspaper, laundry service, TV, A/C, free local calls, fax, NS rooms, in-room refrigerators and microwaves, children under 18 free with parents, no pets, meeting facilities, CC. SGL/DBL$78-$98.

TraveLodge South (3450 Cerrillos Road, 87501; 800-578-7878) 78 rooms and suites, restaurant, lounge, free breakfast, pool, sauna, room service, wheelchair access, complimentary newspaper, laundry service, TV, A/C, free local calls, fax, NS rooms, in-room refrigerators and microwaves, children under 18 free with parents, no pets, meeting facilities, CC. SGL/DBL$40-$140.

Water Street Inn (427 West Water St., 87501; 984-1193) 7 rooms, free breakfast, NS, A/C, TV, fireplaces, wheelchair access, CC. SGL/DBL$110-$135.

Santa Rosa
Area Code 505

Best Western Adobe Inn (Will Rogers Dr., 88435; 472-3446, 800-528-1234) 58 rooms, heated pool, exercise center, children free with parents, A/C, NS rooms, TV, laundry facilities, wheelchair access, gift shop, airport transportation, no pets, senior rates, meeting facilities, CC. SGL/DBL$38-$58.

Budget Host American Inn (924 Will Rogers Dr., 88435; 472-3481, 800-283-4678) 30 rooms, restaurant, lounge, laundry facilities, NS rooms, wheelchair access, A/C, TV, no pets, senior rates, children free with parents, CC. SGL/DBL$23-$34.

Days Inn (Santa Rosa 88435; 472-5985, 800-325-2525) 60 rooms and suites, children free with parents, room service, laundry service, A/C, TV, free local calls, pets OK, fax, wheelchair access, NS rooms, senior rates, CC. SGL/DBL$35-$65.

Holiday Inn (3300 Will Rogers Dr., 88435; 472-5411, Fax 472-3537, 800-HOLIDAY) 50 rooms, restaurant, lounge, pool, exercise center, children under 19 free with parents, wheelchair access, A/C, TV, NS rooms, fax, room service, pets OK, laundry service, meeting facilities, senior rates, CC. SGL/DBL$22-$40.

Motel 6 (3400 Will Rogers Dr., 88435; 472-3045, 505-891-6161) 90 rooms, pool, free local calls, children under 17 free with parents, NS rooms, wheelchair access, pets OK, A/C, TV, CC. SGL/DBL$36-$48.

Super 8 Motel (1201 Will Rogers Dr., 88435; 472-5388, 800-800-8000) 88 rooms and suites, restaurant, no pets, children under 12 free with parents, free local calls, A/C, TV, in-room refrigerators and microwaves, fax, NS rooms, senior rates, wheelchair access, meeting facilities, CC. SGL/DBL$33-$45.

Silver City

Area Code 505

Bear Mountain Guest Ranch (Silver City 88061; 538-2538) 3 rooms, free breakfast, A/C, TV, American plan available, private baths, senior rates, CC. SGL/DBL$58-$110.

Carter House (101 North Cooper St., 88061; 388-5485) 5 rooms, free breakfast, NS, laundry facilities, no pets, shared baths, 1906 home, CC. SGL/DBL$50-$65.

Copper Manor (710 Silver Heights Blvd., 88061; 538-5392) 68 rooms, restaurant, indoor pool, A/C, TV, NS rooms, wheelchair access, no pets, senior rates, CC. SGL/DBL$35-$50.

Drifter Motel (711 Silver Heights Blvd., 88061; 538-2916) 69 rooms, restaurant, lounge, entertainment, heated pool, A/C, TV, NS rooms, wheelchair access, CC. SGL/DBL$36-$45.

Holiday Motor Hotel (Silver City 88061; 538-3711, 800-828-8291) 79 rooms, restaurant, pool, pets OK, A/C, TV, NS rooms, wheelchair access, children free with parents, no pets, laundry facilities, meeting facilities, senior rates, CC. SGL/DBL$40-$48.

Super 8 Motel (1040 East Hwy. 180, 88061; 388-1983, 800-800-8000) 69 rooms and suites, pets OK, children under 12 free with parents, free local calls, A/C, TV, in-room refrigerators and microwaves, fax, NS rooms, senior rates, wheelchair access, meeting facilities, CC. SGL/DBL$36-$58.

Socorro

Area Code 505

Best Western Golden Manor Inn (507 North California St., 87801; 835-0230, 800-528-1234) 40 rooms, restaurant, heated pool, exercise center, children free with parents, A/C, NS rooms, TV, laundry facilities, wheelchair access, pets OK, senior rates, meeting facilities, CC. SGL/DBL$42-$50.

Motel 6 (807 Hwy. 85, 87801; 835-4300, 505-891-6161) 123 rooms, pool, free local calls, children under 17 free with parents, NS rooms, wheelchair access, pets OK, A/C, TV, CC. SGL/DBL$36-$46.

San Miguel Motel (916 California St. Northeast, 87801; 835-0211, 800-548-7938) 40 rooms, restaurant, heated pool, A/C, TV, NS rooms, wheelchair access, in-room refrigerators, laundry facilities, pets OK, CC. SGL/DBL$25-$35.

Super 8 Motel (1121 Frontage Rd. Northwest 87801; 835-4626, Fax 835-3988, 800-800-8000) 88 rooms and suites, outdoor heated pool, whirlpools, laundry facilities, no pets, children under 12 free with parents, free local calls, A/C, TV, in-room refrigerators and microwaves, fax, NS rooms, senior rates, wheelchair access, meeting facilities, CC. SGL/DBL$40-$55.

Taos
Area Code 505

Rental and Reservation Services:

Affordable Meetings and Accommodations (715 Pueblo Sur, 87571; 751-1292, 800-290-5384)

Del Norte Reservations (Taos 87571; 758-2031, 800-258-8436)

Taos Accommodations Limited (Taos 87571; 758-8899, 800-548-2146)

Taos Bed and Breakfast Association (Taos 87571; 758-4747, 800-876-7857)

Taos Central Reservations (Taos 87571; 758-9767, 800-821-2437) rental hotels, resort, condominiums and cabins.

Taos Enchanted Circle Reservations (Taos 87571; 758-2600, 800-8914)

Taos Mountain Reservations (Taos 87571; 751-1350, 800-291-1350)

Taos Vacation Home Rentals (206 Lund St., 87571; 800-858-3820) rental homes.

Traditional Taos Bed and Breakfast Association (Taos 87571; 758-8245, 800-525-8267)

ᢁᢁᢁ

Abominable Snow Mansion (Taos 87571; 776-8298, Fax 776-2107) 95 beds, free breakfast, TV, kitchen, CC. SGL$15-$22, DBL$30-$44.

Alpine Village (Taos 87571; 776-8540, Fax 776-8542, 800-322-8267) 7 1- and 2-bedroom condominiums, A/C, TV, NS rooms, wheelchair access, CC. SGL/DBL$78-$260.

American Artists Gallery House (132 Frontier Rd., 87571; 758-4446) 5 rooms, free breakfast, A/C, TV, no pets, private baths, NS, fireplaces, hot tub, CC. SGL/DBL$60-$90.

Best Western Kachina Lodge (Taos 87571; 758-2275, Fax 758-9207, 800-528-1234) 118 rooms, restaurant, entertainment, pool, exercise center, children free with parents, A/C, NS rooms, TV, laundry facilities, wheelchair access, pets OK, meeting facilities, senior rates, CC. SGL/DBL$65-$105.

Brooks Street Inn (119 Brooks St., 87571; 758-1486) 6 rooms, free breakfast, local transportation, no pets, NS, children free with parents, airport transportation, in-room refrigerators and microwaves, A/C, TV, NS rooms, wheelchair access, fireplace, CC. SGL/DBL$70-$100.

Casa de las Chimeneas (405 Cordoba Lane, 87571; 758-4777) 4 rooms and suites, free breakfast, no pets, fireplaces, TV, NS rooms, wheelchair access, hot tub, private baths, antique furnishings, in-room coffee makers, CC. SGL/DBL$110-$145.

Casa Europa (157 Upper Ranchitos Rd., 87571; 758-9798) 6 rooms, free breakfast, whirlpools, sauna, TV, NS rooms, wheelchair access, airport courtesy car, no pets, antique furnishings, CC. SGL/DBL$65-$110.

Casa Feliz (137 Bent St., 87571; 758-9790) free breakfast, A/C, TV, private baths, NS, CC. SGL/DBL$95-$125.

Casa Otero (215 Ranchitos Rd., 87571; 758-5434, Fax 758-0799, 800-776-1961) 4 apartments, A/C, TV, NS rooms, wheelchair access, CC. SGL/DBL$65-$85.

Dancing Dog Guesthouse (815 North Witt Rd., 87571; 758-0078, 800-353-0078) 1 room, A/C, TV, no pets, children free with parents, NS rooms, wheelchair access, CC. SGL/DBL$45-$60.

Days Inn (1333 Paseo Del Pueblo, 87571; 758-2230, Fax 461-2259, 800-325-2525) 37 rooms and suites, free breakfast, children free with parents, room service, laundry service, A/C, TV, free local calls, pets OK, fax, wheelchair access, NS rooms, senior rates, CC. SGL/DBL$45-$67.

El Monte Lodge (317 Kit Carson Rd., 87571; 758-3171, 800-828-TAOS) 13 rooms, A/C, TV, NS rooms, in-room refrigerators, airport transportation, fireplaces, kitchenettes, laundry facilities, wheelchair access, pets OK, CC. SGL/DBL$60-$100.

El Pueblo Lodge (412 Paseo del Pueblo Norte, 87571; 758-8700, Fax 758-6321, 800-433-9612) 43 rooms and apartments, restaurant, free breakfast, heated pool, whirlpools, kitchenettes, A/C, TV, NS rooms, wheelchair access, in-room refrigerators, pets OK, senior rates, CC. SGL/DBL$50-$60, STS$100-$200.

El Rincon Inn (114 East Kit Carson, 87571; 758-4874) 12 rooms, free breakfast, A/C, TV, NS rooms, wheelchair access, pets OK, antique furnishings, in-room coffee makers, fireplaces, CC. SGL/DBL$45-$125.

Guest Quarters and Gallery at Touchstone (110 Mabel Dodge Lane, 87571; 758-0192) 4 rooms, A/C, TV, NS rooms, wheelchair access, CC. SGL/DBL$65-$90.

Hacienda del Sol (109 Mabel Dodge Lane, 87571; 758-0287) free breakfast, A/C, TV, 1800s home, NS, no pets, private baths, fireplace, hot tub, CC. SGL/DBL$45-$130.

Hacienda Inn (1321 Paseo del Pueblo, 87571; 758-8610, 800-858-8543) 51 rooms, free breakfast, indoor heated pool, sauna, A/C, TV, NS rooms, wheelchair access, children free with parents, CC. SGL/DBL$95-$185.

Holiday Inn (1005 Paseo del Pueblo, 87571; 758-4444, Fax 758-0055, 800-759-2736, 800-HOLIDAY) 126 rooms and suites, restaurant, lounge, entertainment, pool, exercise center, children under 19 free with parents, wheelchair access, A/C, TV, NS rooms, fireplaces, fax, room service, no pets, laundry service, meeting facilities for 150, senior rates, CC. SGL/DBL$59-$125.

Indian Hills Inn (Taos 87571; 758-4293, 800-444-2346) 48 rooms, free breakfast, pool, A/C, TV, NS rooms, wheelchair access, CC. SGL/DBL$37-$60.

Koshari Inn (910 East Kit Carson Rd., 87571; 758-7199) 12 rooms, heated pool, TV, NS rooms, wheelchair access, pets OK, CC. SGL/DBL$50-$82.

La Posada de Taos (309 Juanita Lane, 87571; 758-8164) 6 rooms, free breakfast, no pets, whirlpools, TV, CC. SGL/DBL$65-$150.

Moonlight Inn (Taos 87571; 776-8474) 2 rooms, free breakfast, TV, NS rooms, wheelchair access, no pets, children free with parents, senior rates, CC. SGL/DBL$35-$65.

Park Inn International (1321 South Santa Fe Rd., 87581; 758-8610, 800-437-PARK) 51 rooms and suites, lounge, indoor heated pool, spa, A/C, TV, wheelchair access, NS rooms, airport transportation, meeting facilities for 450, senior rates, CC. SGL/DBL$50-$73.

Quail Ridge Inn (Taos 87571; 776-2211, 800-624-4448) 110 condominiums, restaurant, lounge, heated pool, lighted tennis courts, exercise center, whirlpools, sauna, fireplaces, no pets, children free with parents, kitchenettes, laundry facilities, TV, no pets, NS rooms, wheelchair access, meeting facilities, senior rates, CC. SGL/DBL$80-$300.

Quality Inn (1043 Camino Del Pueblo, 87571; 758-2200, Fax 758-9009, 800-221-2222) 99 rooms and suites, restaurant, lounge, pool, exercise center, whirlpools, children free with parents, A/C, TV, room service, pets OK, in-room refrigerators, laundry service, NS rooms, meeting facilities, senior rates, CC. SGL/DBL$53-$93, STS$135.

Rancho Ramada de Taos (615 Paseo del Pueblo, 87571; 758-2900) 124 rooms and suites, restaurant, lounge, indoor pool, whirlpools, fireplaces, no pets, A/C, TV, NS rooms, room service, wheelchair access, children free with parents, meeting facilities, senior rates, CC. SGL/DBL$60-$175.

Ruby Slipper Inn (416 La Lomita, 87571; 758-0613) 7 rooms, whirlpools, free breakfast, TV, NS rooms, no pets, wheelchair access, CC. SGL/DBL$70-$95.

Sagebrush Inn (Taos 87571; 758-2254, 800-428-3626) 80 rooms and suites, restaurant, free breakfast, lounge, entertainment, pool, whirlpools, tennis courts, antique furnishings, fireplaces, A/C, TV, NS rooms, pets OK, in-room refrigerators, wheelchair access, meeting facilities, senior rates, CC. SGL/DBL$50-$150.

Sonterra Condominiums (Taos 87571; 758-7989) 9 condominiums, kitchenettes, A/C, TV, NS rooms, wheelchair access, CC. SGL/DBL$53-$200.

Stewart House Gallery and Inn (Taos 87571; 776-2913) free breakfast, A/C, TV, NS, no pets, private baths, CC. SGL/DBL$60-$90.

Sun God Lodge (Taos 87571; 758-3162, Fax 758-1716, 800-821-2437) 56 rooms and suites, A/C, TV, NS rooms, wheelchair access, free local calls, fireplaces, in-room refrigerators and microwaves, children free with parents, pets OK, CC. SGL/DBL$38-$99.

Super 8 Motel (Hwy. 68, 87571; 758-1088, 800-800-8000) 50 rooms and suites, whirlpools, no pets, children under 12 free with parents, free local calls, A/C, TV, in-room refrigerators and microwaves, fax, NS rooms, senior rates, wheelchair access, meeting facilities, CC. SGL/DBL$42-$65.

Taos Country Inn (Taos 87571; 866-6548) free breakfast, A/C, TV, fireplaces, antique furnishings, no pets, NS, no children, private baths, CC. SGL/DBL$95-$150.

Taos Inn (125 Paseo del Pueblo, 87571; 758-2233, Fax 758-5776, 800-826-7466) 39 rooms, restaurant, lounge, entertainment, heated pool, whirlpools, A/C, TV, NS rooms, fireplaces, antique furnishings, no pets, wheelchair access, CC. SGL/DBL$80-$155.

Taos Ski Valley

Area Code 505

Rental and Reservation Services:

Taos Valley Resort Association (Taos Ski Valley 87525; 776-2233, Fax 776-8842, 800-776-1111) rental homes and condominiums.

❑❑❑

Amizette Inn (Taos Ski Valley, 87525; 776-2451, 800-446-8267) 12 rooms, restaurant, free breakfast, sauna, TV, CC. SGL/DBL$50-$120.

Austing Haus (Taos Ski Valley 87525; 776-2649, Fax 776-8751, 800-748-2932) 34 rooms, restaurant, free breakfast, pool, children free with parents, TV, NS rooms, wheelchair access, pets OK, game room, laundry facilities, CC. SGL/DBL$90-$110.

Chalet Montesano (Taos Ski Valley 87525; 776-8226) 4 rooms and suites, spa, children over 14 welcome, A/C, TV, NS rooms, wheelchair access, CC. SGL/DBL$66-$237.

Columbine Inn (Taos Ski Valley 87525; 776-1437) 20 rooms, free breakfast, sauna, pets OK, TV, CC. SGL/DBL$50-$145.

The Inn at Snakedance (Taos Ski Valley 87525; 776-2277, Fax 776-1410, 800-322-9815) 60 rooms and suites, restaurant, lounge, free breakfast, pool, exercise center, A/C, TV, NS rooms, wheelchair access, CC. SGL/DBL$70-$195.

Innsbruck Lodge and Condominiums (Taos Ski Valley 87527; 776-2313, Fax 776-8510, 800-243-5253) 24 rooms and suites, kitchenettes, A/C, TV, NS rooms, wheelchair access, CC. SGL/DBL$130.

Kandahar Condominiums (Taos Ski Valley 87527; 776-2226, Fax 776-2481, 800-756-2226) 27 1- and 2-bedroom condominiums, A/C, TV, NS rooms, wheelchair access, CC. SGL/DBL$250.

Powderhorn Condominiums (Taos Ski Valley 87527; 776-2341, 800-776-2346) 9 condominiums, hot tubs, fireplaces, A/C, TV, NS rooms, wheelchair access, CC. SGL/DBL$60-$155.

Rio Hondo Condominiums (Taos Ski Valley 87527; 776-2646, Fax 776-2825) 18 2- to 4-bedroom condominiums, outdoor pool, sauna, VCRs, fireplaces, no pets, TV, NS rooms, wheelchair access, CC. SGL/DBL$80-$280.

Sierra del Sol Condominiums (Taos Ski Valley 87525; 776-2981, 800-523-3954) 32 condominiums, sauna, jacuzzis, fireplaces, A/C, TV, NS rooms, wheelchair access, CC. SGL/DBL$65-$147.

Taos East Condominiums (Taos Ski Valley, 87525; 776-2271, Fax 776-8240, 800-238-SNOW) 11 condominiums, whirlpools, A/C, TV, NS rooms, wheelchair access, pets OK, CC. SGL/DBL$45-$195.

Taos Mountain Lodge (Taos Ski Valley, 87525; 776-2229, 800-530-8098) 10 rooms and suites, A/C, TV, NS rooms, wheelchair access, CC. SGL/DBL$50-$175.

Twining Condominiums (Taos Ski Valley 87525; 776-8873, 800-828-2472) 19 2-bedroom condominiums, A/C, TV, NS rooms, wheelchair access, CC. SGL/DBL$55-$135.

Thoreau
Area Code 505

Zuni Mountain Lodge (Thoreau 87323; 862-7769) free breakfast, A/C, TV, CC. SGL/DBL$35-$70.

Truchas
Area Code 505

Rancho Arriba (Truchas 87578; 689-2374) free breakfast, A/C, TV, NS, no pets, shared baths, CC. SGL/DBL$45-$50.

Truth or Consequences
Area Code 505

Ace Lodge (1014 North Date St., 87901; 894-2515) 38 rooms, restaurant, heated pool, A/C, TV, NS rooms, wheelchair access, airport transportation, senior rates, CC. SGL/DBL$50-$60.

Best Western Hot Springs Inn (2270 North Date St., 87901; 894-6665, 800-528-1234) 40 rooms, restaurant, heated pool, exercise center, children free with parents, A/C, NS rooms, TV, laundry facilities, wheelchair access, no pets, senior rates, meeting facilities, CC. SGL/DBL$42-$50.

Elephant Butte Resort Inn (Truth or Consequences 87901; 744-5431) 48 rooms, restaurant, lounge, A/C, TV, NS rooms, children free with parents, pets OK, wheelchair access, senior rates, CC. SGL/DBL$50-$60.

Super 8 Motel (2701 North Date St., 87901; 894-7888, Fax 894-7883, 800-800-8000) 40 rooms and suites, restaurant, no pets, children under 12 free with parents, free local calls, A/C, TV, in-room refrigerators and microwaves, fax, NS rooms, senior rates, wheelchair access, meeting facilities, CC. SGL/DBL$37-$50.

Tucumcari
Area Code 505

Best Western Inn (200 East Estrella, 88401; 461-4884, Fax 461-2463, 800-528-1234) 107 rooms, restaurant, lounge, pool, exercise center, children free with parents, A/C, NS rooms, TV, laundry facilities, wheelchair access, pets OK, game room, senior rates, meeting facilities, CC. SGL/DBL$50-$60.

Days Inn (2623 South 1st St., 88401; 461-3158, 800-325-2525) 40 rooms and suites, restaurant, free breakfast, children free with parents, room service, laundry service, A/C, TV, free local calls, pets OK, fax, wheelchair access, NS rooms, senior rates, CC. SGL/DBL$29-$42.

Econo Lodge (3400 East Tucumcari Blvd., 88401; 461-4194, 800-4-CHOICE) 41 rooms, restaurant, pool, children under 12 free with parents, pets OK, free local calls, NS rooms, wheelchair access, A/C, TV, meeting facilities, senior rates, CC. SGL/DBL$22-$45.

Friendship Inn (315 East Tucumcari Blvd., 88401; 461-0330, 800-424-4777) 31 rooms, restaurant, pool, exercise center, A/C, TV, no pets, NS rooms, children free with parents, wheelchair access, senior rates, CC. SGL/DBL$22-$36.

Holiday Inn (East Tucumcari Blvd., 88401; 461-3780, Fax 461-3931, 800-HOLIDAY) 100 rooms, restaurant, lounge, entertainment, outdoor heated pool, exercise center, children under 19 free with parents, wheelchair access, A/C, TV, NS rooms, fax, room service, airport transportation, pets OK, laundry service, meeting facilities, senior rates, CC. SGL/DBL$55-$73.

Howard Johnson Lodge (3604 Tucumcari Blvd., 88401; 461-2747, Fax 461-2259, 800-I-GO-HOJO) 32 rooms, free breakfast, children free with parents, wheelchair access, NS rooms, TV, A/C, no pets, laundry facilities, senior rates, meeting facilities, CC. SGL/DBL$32-$44.

Motel 6 (2900 East Tucumcari Blvd., 88401; 461-4791, 505-891-6161) 122 rooms, pool, free local calls, children under 17 free with parents, NS rooms, wheelchair access, pets OK, A/C, TV, CC. SGL/DBL$38-$45.

Rodeway Inn East (1023 East Tucumcari Blvd., 88401; 461-0360, 800-424-4777) pool, wheelchair access, NS rooms, children free with parents, A/C, TV, senior rates, CC. SGL/DBL$28-$50.

Rodeway Inn West (1302 West Tucumcari Blvd., 88401; 461-3140, 800-424-4777) 60 rooms, restaurant, pool, wheelchair access, NS rooms, children free with parents, A/C, TV, senior rates, CC. SGL/DBL$26-$39.

Safari Motel (722 East Tucumcari Blvd., 88401; 461-3642) 23 rooms, heated pool, A/C, TV, NS rooms, wheelchair access, laundry facilities, children free with parents, pets OK, senior rates, CC. SGL/DBL$24-$36.

Super 8 Motel (4001 East Tucumcari Blvd., 88401; 461-4444, Fax 461-4320, 800-800-8000) 63 rooms and suites, restaurant, indoor heated pool, laundry facilities, no pets, children under 12 free with parents, free local calls,

A/C, TV, in-room refrigerators and microwaves, fax, NS rooms, senior rates, wheelchair access, meeting facilities, CC. SGL/DBL$33-$48.

TraveLodge (1214 East Tucumcari Blvd., 88401; 461-1401, Fax 461-4329, 800-578-7878) 38 rooms, restaurant, lounge, pool, wheelchair access, complimentary newspaper, laundry service, TV, A/C, free local calls, fax, NS rooms, in-room refrigerators and microwaves, children under 18 free with parents, no pets, meeting facilities, CC. SGL/DBL$25-$48.

Valdito
Area Code 505

Mountain Village (Route 22, 87579; 587-2259, 800-445-0724) TV, A/C, TV, CC. SGL/DBL$40-$60.

Sipapu Lodge (Hwy. 518, 87589; 587-2240) 30 rooms and suites, A/C, no pets, children free with parents, TV, NS rooms, wheelchair access, CC. SGL/DBL$40-$84.

Walton Mountain Inn (Valdito 87579; 587-2297) 10 rooms, A/C, TV, NS rooms, wheelchair access, meeting facilities, senior rates, CC. SGL/DBL$35-$48.

Vaughn
Area Code 505

Bel-Air Motel (Vaughn 88353; 584-2241) 21 rooms, no pets, A/C, TV, NS rooms, wheelchair access, CC. SGL/DBL$25-$36.

Whites City
Area Code 505

Best Western Inn (12 Carlsbad Caverns Hwy., 88268; 785-2291, 800-528-1234) 63 rooms, heated pool, exercise center, whirlpools, tennis courts, children free with parents, A/C, NS rooms, TV, laundry facilities, wheelchair access, pets OK, no pets, meeting facilities, senior rates, CC. SGL/DBL$50-$80.

Oklahoma

Ada
Area Code 405

Best Western Raintree Motor Inn (1100 North Mississippi, 74820; 332-6262, 800-528-1234) 40 rooms, restaurant, lounge, indoor pool, exercise center, children free with parents, A/C, NS rooms, TV, laundry facilities, wheelchair access, no pets, airport transportation, fax, senior rates, meeting facilities, CC. SGL/DBL$45-$55.

Afton

Area Code 918

Shangri-La Resort and Conference Center (Afton 74331; 257-9300, Fax 257-5619) 452 rooms and suites restaurant, lounge, entertainment, pool, exercise center, sauna, whirlpools, tennis courts, A/C, TV, NS rooms, wheelchair access, airport transportation, in-room refrigerators and coffee makers, laundry facilities, children free with parents, no pets, senior rates, meeting facilities, CC. SGL/DBL$60-$125.

Altus

Area Code 405

Holiday Inn (2804 North Main St., 73521; 482-9300, 800-HOLIDAY) 102 rooms, restaurant, lounge, indoor and outdoor pool, exercise center, whirlpools, sauna, airport transportation, children under 19 free with parents, wheelchair access, A/C, TV, NS rooms, fax, room service, pets OK, laundry service, meeting facilities, senior rates, CC. SGL/DBL$42-$56.

Ramada Inn (2515 East Broadway, 73521; 477-3000, Fax 477-0078, 800-2-RAMADA) 122 rooms and suites, restaurant, lounge, heated pool, jacuzzi, wheelchair access, NS rooms, free breakfast, pets OK, A/C, TV, children under 18 free with parents, room service, laundry facilities, meeting facilities for 400, senior rates, CC. SGL/DBL$40-$60, STS$80.

Alva

Area Code 405

Holiday Motel (701 East Oklahoma Blvd., 73717; 327-3333) 20 rooms, pool, in-room refrigerators, no pets, A/C, TV, NS rooms, wheelchair access, CC. SGL/DBL$30-$40.

Ranger Inn (420 East Oklahoma Blvd., 73717; 327-19813) 41 rooms, restaurant, children free with parents, pets OK, A/C, TV, NS rooms, wheelchair access, CC. SGL/DBL$26-$32.

Western Motel (608 East Oklahoma Blvd., 73717; 327-1362) 21 rooms, pool, in-room refrigerators, no pets, A/C, TV, NS rooms, wheelchair access, CC. SGL/DBL$27-$35.

Wharton's Vista Motel (1330 West Oklahoma Blvd., 73717; 327-3232) 20 rooms and 1- and 2-bedroom efficiencies, A/C, TV, NS rooms, wheelchair access, pets OK, CC. SGL/DBL$20-$26.

Ardmore
Area Code 405

Best Western Inn (2519 West Hwy. 142, 73401; 223-1234, 800-528-1234) 80 rooms, restaurant, pool, exercise center, children free with parents, A/C, NS rooms, TV, laundry facilities, wheelchair access, local transportation, pets OK, senior rates, meeting facilities, CC. SGL/DBL$36-$55.

Days Inn (2432 Veterans Blvd., 73401; 223-7976, 800-325-2525) 65 rooms and suites, free breakfast, children free with parents, room service, laundry service, A/C, TV, free local calls, pets OK, fax, wheelchair access, NS rooms, senior rates, CC. SGL/DBL$36-$44.

Dorchester Inn (2614 West Broadway, 73401; 226-1761) 50 rooms and suites, A/C, TV, NS rooms, wheelchair access, no pets, senior rates, CC. SGL/DBL$45-$50, STS$50-$82.

Holiday Inn (2705 Holiday Dr., 73401; 223-7130, Fax 223-7130 ext 390, 800-HOLIDAY) 169 rooms and suites, restaurant, lounge, entertainment, heated pool, exercise center, children under 19 free with parents, wheelchair access, A/C, TV, NS rooms, fax, room service, pets OK, laundry service, meeting facilities for 75, senior rates, CC. SGL/DBL$45-$75.

Lake Murray Resort (Ardmore 73402; 223-6600, Fax 223-6154, 800-654-8240) 135 rooms and cottages, pool, restaurant, lounge, A/C, TV, NS rooms, wheelchair access, room service, pets OK, game room, kitchenettes, children free with parents, in-room refrigerators, fireplaces, CC. SGL/DBL$50-$150.

Motel 6 (120 Holiday Dr., 73401; 226-7666, 891-6161) 126 rooms, pool, free local calls, children under 17 free with parents, NS rooms, wheelchair access, pets OK, A/C, TV, CC. SGL/DBL$39-$44.

Ramada Inn (2700 West Broadway, 73401; 226-1250, 800-2-RAMADA) 108 rooms and suites, restaurant, lounge, pool, exercise center, sauna, wheelchair access, NS rooms, pets OK, A/C, TV, children under 18 free with parents, room service, laundry facilities, meeting facilities, senior rates, CC. SGL/DBL$45-$55, STS$85.

Red Carpet Inn (2120 Veterans Blvd., 73401; 223-2201, 800-251-1962) 68 rooms, children free with parents, TV, A/C, NS rooms, free local calls, in-room refrigerators, pets OK, meeting facilities, senior rates, CC. SGL/DBL$20-$38.

Atoka
Area Code 405

Best Western Inn (2101 South Mississippi, 74525; 889-7381, 889-6695, 800-528-1234) 54 rooms, restaurant, pool, exercise center, children free with parents, A/C, NS rooms, TV, laundry facilities, wheelchair access, pets OK, senior rates, meeting facilities, CC. SGL/DBL$38-$53.

Thunderbird Lodge (402 North Mississippi Ave., 74525; 889-3315) 24 rooms, pool, A/C, TV, NS rooms, wheelchair access, children free with parents, no pets, CC. SGL/DBL$25-$35.

Bartlesville
Area Code 405

Best Western Inn (222 Southeast Washington Blvd., 74006; 335-7755, Fax 335-7763, 800-336-2415, 800-528-1234) 110 rooms, restaurant, free breakfast, lounge, pool, exercise center, children free with parents, A/C, complimentary newspaper, NS rooms, TV, laundry facilities, wheelchair access, pets OK, senior rates, meeting facilities, CC. SGL/DBL$43-$66.

Holiday Inn (1410 Southeast Washington Blvd., 74006; 333-8320, Fax 333-8979, 800-HOLIDAY) 106 rooms and suites, restaurant, lounge, indoor pool, whirlpools, exercise center, children under 19 free with parents, wheelchair access, A/C, TV, NS rooms, fax, room service, airport transportation, kitchenettes, pets OK, laundry service, meeting facilities for 200, senior rates, CC. SGL/DBL$45-$63.

Phillips Hotel (821 Johnstone, 74003; 336-5600, Fax 336-0350, 800-331-0706) 165 rooms and suites, restaurant, lounge, entertainment, exercise equipment, A/C, gift shop, TV, NS rooms, wheelchair access, senior rates, CC. SGL/DBL$75-$185.

Travelers Motel (3105 East Frank Phillips Blvd., 74006; 333-1900) 24 rooms, free breakfast, no pets, A/C, TV, NS rooms, wheelchair access, CC. SGL/DBL$26-$32.

Blackwell
Area Code 405

Days Inn (4302 West Doolin, 74631; 363-2911, 800-325-2525) 50 rooms and suites, restaurant, children free with parents, room service, laundry service, A/C, TV, free local calls, pets OK, fax, wheelchair access, NS rooms, senior rates, CC. SGL/DBL$29-$44.

Super 8 Motel (1014 West Doolin, 74631; 363-5945, 800-800-8000) 43 rooms and suites, pets OK, children under 12 free with parents, free local calls,

A/C, TV, in-room refrigerators and microwaves, fax, NS rooms, senior rates, wheelchair access, meeting facilities, CC. SGL/DBL$35-$46.

Boise City
Area Code 405

Townsman Motel (Hwy. 287, 73933; 544-2506) 40 rooms, restaurant, pets OK, A/C, TV, NS rooms, wheelchair access, in-room refrigerators, CC. SGL/DBL$35-$36.

Broken Arrow
Area Code 918

Econo Lodge (1401 North Elm Pl., 74011; 258-6617, Fax 251-5660, 800-4-CHOICE) 40 rooms, restaurant, free breakfast, children under 12 free with parents, no pets, NS rooms, wheelchair access, A/C, TV, free local calls, fax, senior rates, CC. SGL/DBL$35-$48.

Broken Bow
Area Code 405

Charles Wesley Motor Lodge (302 North Park Dr., 74728; 584-3303) 50 rooms, restaurant, pool, A/C, TV, NS rooms, wheelchair access, pets OK, meeting facilities, senior rates, CC. SGL/DBL$30-$40.

Chandler
Area Code 405

Econo Lodge (600 North Price, 78434; 258-2131, Fax 258-3090, 800-441-6502, 800-4-CHOICE) 40 rooms, restaurant, pool, children under 12 free with parents, no pets, NS rooms, wheelchair access, A/C, TV, free local calls, room service, meeting facilities, senior rates, CC. SGL/DBL$34-$44.

Checotah
Area Code 918

Best Western La Donna Inn (Checotah 74426; 473-2376, 800-528-1234) 48 rooms, free breakfast, pool, exercise center, children free with parents, A/C, NS rooms, TV, laundry facilities, wheelchair access, pets OK, senior rates, meeting facilities, CC. SGL/DBL$38-$60.

Fountainhead Resort (Checotah 74426; 689-9173, Fax 689-9493, 800-345-6343) 205 rooms, suites and cabins, restaurant, lounge, entertainment, pool, lighted tennis courts, exercise center, sauna, gift shop, A/C, TV, NS rooms, gift shop, laundry facilities, in-room refrigerators, no pets, wheelchair access, senior rates, CC. SGL/DBL$75-$95, STS$200-$250.

Fountainhead Resort Hotel (Checotah 74426; 689-9493) 202 rooms and efficiencies, restaurant, lounge, entertainment, heated pool, sauna, whirlpools, pets OK, A/C, TV, NS rooms, wheelchair access, senior rates, CC. SGL/DBL$55-$85.

Chickasha

Area Code 405

Best Western Inn (2101 South 4th St., 73202; 224-4890, Fax 224-3411, 800-528-1234) 154 rooms, restaurant, free local calls, local transportation, children free with parents, A/C, NS rooms, TV, laundry facilities, wheelchair access, pets OK, senior rates, meeting facilities, CC. SGL/DBL$65-$75.

Claremore

Area Code 405

Best Western Will Rogers Inn (940 South Lynn Riggs Blvd., 74017; 341-4410, Fax 341-6045, 800-528-1234) 52 rooms, restaurant, lounge, entertainment, pool, exercise center, children free with parents, A/C, NS rooms, TV, laundry facilities, wheelchair access, pets OK, senior rates, meeting facilities, CC. SGL/DBL$45-$55.

Claremore Motel (812 East Will Rogers Blvd., 74017; 341-3254) 16 rooms and 2-bedroom efficiencies, A/C, TV, NS rooms, wheelchair access, pets OK, CC. SGL/DBL$32-$38.

Clinton

Area Code 405

Best Western Trade Winds Courtyard Inn (2128 Gary Blvd., 73601; 323-2601, Fax 323-4655, 800-528-1234) 66 rooms, restaurant, free breakfast, lounge, pool, hot tubs, in-room refrigerators, children free with parents, A/C, NS rooms, TV, laundry facilities, wheelchair access, pets OK, senior rates, meeting facilities, CC. SGL/DBL$30-$65.

Budget Host Inn (1413 Neptune Dr., 73601; 323-9333, 800-283-4678) 123 rooms and efficiencies, restaurant, laundry facilities, NS rooms, wheelchair access, A/C, TV, children free with parents, pets OK, senior rates, CC. SGL/DBL$18-$30.

Comfort Inn (2247 Gary Freeway, 73601; 323-6840, Fax 323-4067, 800-221-2222) 80 rooms, restaurant, free breakfast, pool, wheelchair access, NS rooms, no pets, children under 18 free with parents, A/C, TV, meeting facilities, senior rates, CC. SGL/DBL$36-$47.

Holiday Inn (1200 South 10th St., 73601; 323-5550, Fax 323-7648, 800-HOLIDAY) 70 rooms, restaurant, lounge, outdoor pool, exercise center, children under 19 free with parents, wheelchair access, A/C, TV, NS rooms, fax, room service, no pets, laundry service, meeting facilities, senior rates, CC. SGL/DBL$35-$50.

Park Inn International (2140 Gary Blvd., 73601; 323-2010, Fax 323-7552, 800-437-PARK) 100 rooms, restaurant, lounge, lighted tennis courts, airport courtesy car, A/C, TV, wheelchair access, NS rooms, meeting facilities for 140, senior rates, CC. SGL/DBL$28-$40.

Super 8 Motel (1120 South 10th St., 73601; 323-4979, 800-800-8000) 26 rooms and suites, restaurant, no pets, children under 12 free with parents, free local calls, A/C, TV, in-room refrigerators and microwaves, fax, NS rooms, senior rates, wheelchair access, meeting facilities, CC. SGL/DBL$32-$50.

Travel Inn (1116 South 10th St., 73601; 323-1888) 20 rooms, restaurant, A/C, TV, NS rooms, wheelchair access, CC. SGL/DBL$20-$25.

Duncan
Area Code 405

The Duncan Inn (3402 North Hwy. 81, 73533; 252-5210) 92 rooms, pool, A/C, TV, NS rooms, pets OK, laundry facilities, wheelchair access, meeting facilities, senior rates, CC. SGL/DBL$25-$36.

Heritage Inn (1515 Hwy. 81, 73533; 252-5612, Fax 252-5620) 37 rooms, restaurant, children free with parents, no pets, A/C, TV, NS rooms, wheelchair access, CC. SGL/DBL$25-$30.

Holiday Inn (1015 North Hwy. 81, 73533; 252-1500, 800-HOLIDAY) 138 rooms, restaurant, lounge, indoor pool, exercise center, children under 19 free with parents, wheelchair access, A/C, TV, NS rooms, fax, room service, no pets, laundry service, meeting facilities for 50, senior rates, CC. SGL/DBL$45-$55.

TraveLodge (2535 North Hwy. 81, 73533; 252-0810, Fax 255-6591, 800-578-7878) 69 rooms and suites, restaurant, lounge, pool, wheelchair access, complimentary newspaper, laundry service, TV, A/C, free local calls, fax, NS rooms, in-room refrigerators and microwaves, children under 18 free with parents, no pets, meeting facilities for 60, CC. SGL/DBL$40-$54.

Durant
Area Code 405

Best Western Inn (2401 West Main St., 74701; 924-7676, Fax 924-3060, 800-528-1234) 60 rooms, restaurant, pool, exercise center, children free with parents, A/C, NS rooms, TV, laundry facilities, wheelchair access, no pets, senior rates, meeting facilities, CC. SGL/DBL$25-$35.

Holiday Inn (2121 West Main St., 74701; 924-5432, Fax 924-9721, 800-HOLIDAY) 81 rooms, restaurant, lounge, pool, exercise center, children under 19 free with parents, wheelchair access, A/C, TV, NS rooms, fax, room service, no pets, laundry service, meeting facilities for 60, senior rates, CC. SGL/DBL$58-$75.

Elk City
Area Code 405

Best Western Inn (2015 West 3rd St., 73648; 225-2331, 800-528-1234) 83 rooms, restaurant, pool, exercise center, children free with parents, A/C, NS rooms, TV, laundry facilities, wheelchair access, pets OK, airport transportation, meeting facilities, senior rates, CC. SGL/DBL$30-$45.

Days Inn (1100 Hwy. 34, 73644; 225-9210, 800-325-2525) 140 rooms and suites, free breakfast, outdoor pool, children free with parents, room service, laundry service, A/C, TV, free local calls, pets OK, fax, wheelchair access, NS rooms, senior rates, CC. SGL/DBL$26-$42, STS$75.

Econo Lodge (108 Meadow Ridge, 73644; 225-5120, Fax 225-0908, 800-4-CHOICE) 45 rooms, children under 12 free with parents, pets OK, NS rooms, wheelchair access, A/C, TV, senior rates, CC. SGL/DBL$28-$38.

Flamingo Inn (2000 West 3rd St., 73644; 225-1811, 800-466-1811) 151 rooms and suites, restaurant, lounge, entertainment, pool, whirlpools, sauna, A/C, TV, airport transportation, pets OK, NS rooms, wheelchair access, pets OK, meeting facilities, senior rates, CC. SGL/DBL$25-$45.

Holiday Inn (Elk City 73648; 225-6637, Fax 225-6637 ext 168, 800-HOLIDAY) 151 rooms and suites, restaurant, lounge, entertainment, indoor heated pool, exercise center, whirlpools, in-room refrigerators, children under 19 free with parents, wheelchair access, A/C, TV, NS rooms, fax, room service, pets OK, laundry service, meeting facilities for 350, senior rates, CC. SGL/DBL$45-$65.

Motel 6 (2500 East Hwy. 66, 73644; 225-6661, 891-6161) 120 rooms, pool, free local calls, children under 17 free with parents, NS rooms, wheelchair access, pets OK, A/C, TV, CC. SGL/DBL$39-$46.

Quality Inn (102 B.J. Hughes Access Rd., 73648; 225-8140, 800-221-2222) 55 rooms and suites, restaurant, free breakfast, indoor pool, exercise center, whirlpools, children free with parents, A/C, TV, room service, laundry service, NS rooms, meeting facilities, senior rates, CC. SGL/DBL$30-$45.

Red Carpet Inn (2604 East Hwy. 66, 73644; 225-2241, Fax 243-0455, 800-251-1962) 65 rooms, restaurant, lounge, pool, children free with parents, TV, A/C, NS rooms, pets OK, meeting facilities, senior rates, CC. SGL/DBL$25-$35.

TraveLodge (301 Sleep Hollow Ct., 73644; 243-0150, 800-578-7878) 44 rooms, restaurant, lounge, free breakfast, pool, wheelchair access, complimentary newspaper, laundry service, TV, A/C, free local calls, fax, NS rooms, in-room refrigerators and microwaves, children under 18 free with parents, no pets, meeting facilities, senior rates, CC. SGL/DBL$26-$35.

El Reno
Area Code 405

Best Western Inn (El Reno 73036; 262-6490, 800-528-1234) 60 rooms, heated pool, children free with parents, A/C, NS rooms, TV, laundry facilities, wheelchair access, pets OK, meeting facilities, senior rates, CC. SGL/DBL$35-$55.

Days Inn (2700 South Country Club Rd., 73036; 262-8720, 800-325-2525) 53 rooms and suites, children free with parents, room service, laundry service, A/C, TV, free local calls, pets OK, fax, wheelchair access, NS rooms, senior rates, CC. SGL/DBL$29-$37.

Merit Inn (2820 Hwy. 81, 73036; 262-8240, Fax 262-6560, 800-262-8240) 50 rooms, restaurant, pool, children free with parents, laundry facilities, A/C, TV, NS rooms, wheelchair access, senior rates, CC. SGL/DBL$27-$40.

Enid
Area Code 405

Best Western Inn (2828 South Van Burn, 73703; 242-7100, Fax 242-6202, 800-528-1234) 100 rooms, restaurant, lounge, indoor pool, exercise center, children free with parents, A/C, NS rooms, TV, laundry facilities, wheelchair access, no pets, local transportation, senior rates, meeting facilities, CC. SGL/DBL$40-$54.

Econo Lodge (2523 Mercer Dr., 73701; 237-3090, 800-4-CHOICE) 69 rooms, children under 12 free with parents, no pets, NS rooms, wheelchair access, A/C, TV, senior rates, CC. SGL/DBL$29-$45.

Holiday Inn (2901 South Van Buren, 73703; 237-6000, 800-HOLIDAY) 100 rooms, restaurant, lounge, pool, exercise center, children under 19 free with parents, wheelchair access, A/C, TV, NS rooms, fax, room service, no pets, laundry service, meeting facilities for 250, senior rates, CC. SGL/DBL$35-$58.

Ramada Inn (3005 West Garriott Rd., 73703; 234-0440, Fax 233-1402, 800-2-RAMADA) 124 rooms and suites, restaurant, lounge, indoor heated pool, whirlpool tubs, sauna, wheelchair access, NS rooms, pets OK, A/C, TV, children under 18 free with parents, room service, laundry facilities, airport transportation, meeting facilities, senior rates, CC. SGL/DBL$55-$65.

Erick

Area Code 405

Econo Lodge (Route 1, 73645; 526-3315, Fax 526-8165, 800-4-CHOICE) 32 rooms, children under 12 free with parents, no pets, NS rooms, wheelchair access, A/C, TV, senior rates, CC. SGL/DBL$28-$38.

Frederick

Area Code 405

Scottish Inns (1015 South Main St., 73542; 335-2129, 800-251-1962) pool, A/C, TV, wheelchair access, NS rooms, children free with parents, in-room refrigerators, free local calls, senior rates, CC. SGL/DBL$26-$33.

Grove

Area Code 918

Grand Motel (2100 South Main St., 74344; 786-6124) 20 rooms, restaurant, A/C, TV, NS rooms, wheelchair access, no pets, CC. SGL/DBL$24-$38.

Guthrie

Area Code 405

Best Western Territorial Inn (2323 Territorial Trail, 73044; 282-8831, 800-528-1234) 84 rooms, restaurant, free breakfast, lounge, pool, exercise center, children free with parents, A/C, NS rooms, TV, laundry facilities, wheelchair access, pets OK, senior rates, meeting facilities, CC. SGL/DBL$44-$62.

Harrison House (124 West Harrison, 73044; 282-1000, Fax 282-0287) 34 rooms, restaurant, free breakfast, antique furnishings, 1890s inn, A/C, TV, CC. SGL/DBL$50-$85.

Town House Motel (221 East Oklahoma Ave., 73044; 282-2000) 22 rooms, restaurant, in-room coffee makers, A/C, TV, NS rooms, wheelchair access, children free with parents, pets OK, senior rates, CC. SGL/DBL$27-$38.

Guymon

Area Code 405

Ambassador Inn (Guymon 73942; 338-5555) 70 rooms, restaurant, lounge, entertainment, pool, A/C, TV, NS rooms, wheelchair access, no pets, meeting facilities, CC. SGL/DBL$35-$55.

Best Western Townsman Motel (Guymon 73942; 338-6556, Fax 338-1374, 800-528-1234) 65 rooms, restaurant, free breakfast, lounge, indoor pool, exercise center, spa, children free with parents, A/C, NS rooms, TV, laundry facilities, wheelchair access, pets OK, senior rates, meeting facilities, CC. SGL/DBL$38-$46.

Lodge USA (923 Hwy. 54, 73942; 338-5431) 40 rooms, restaurant, A/C, TV, NS rooms, wheelchair access, airport transportation, CC. SGL/DBL$27-$35.

Henryetta

Area Code 918

HoJo Inn (Hwy. 75 and Trudgeon Rd., 74437; 652-4448, 800-I-GO-HOJO) 38 rooms, free breakfast, outdoor pool, children free with parents, wheelchair access, NS rooms, free local calls, TV, A/C, no pets, laundry facilities, senior rates, meeting facilities, CC. SGL/DBL$35-$50.

Holiday Inn (Henryetta 74437; 652-2581, Fax 652-2581, 800-HOLIDAY) 84 rooms and suites, restaurant, lounge, indoor heated pool, exercise center, whirlpools, sauna, children under 19 free with parents, wheelchair access, A/C, TV, NS rooms, fax, room service, pets OK, laundry service, meeting facilities, senior rates, CC. SGL/DBL$65-$75.

Le Baron Motel (East Main St., 74437; 652-2531) 24 rooms, whirlpools, A/C, TV, NS rooms, wheelchair access, pets OK, CC. SGL/DBL$28-$35.

Super 8 Motel (I-40 and Dewey Bartlett Rd., 74437; 652-2533, 800-800-8000) 50 rooms and suites, restaurant, pets OK, children under 12 free with parents, free local calls, A/C, TV, in-room refrigerators and microwaves, fax, NS rooms, senior rates, wheelchair access, meeting facilities, CC. SGL/DBL$30-$46.

Hooker

Area Code 405

Sunset Motel (710 Hwy. 54, 73945; 652-3250) 15 rooms, A/C, TV, NS rooms, wheelchair access, senior rates, CC. SGL/DBL$22-$30.

Hugo

Area Code 405

The Village Inn (610 West Jackson St., 74743; 326-3333) 50 rooms, restaurant, pool, A/C, TV, NS rooms, wheelchair access, meeting facilities, CC. SGL/DBL$25-$28.

Idabel

Area Code 405

Holiday Inn (Hwy. 70 West, 74745; 286-6501, Fax 286-7482, 800-HOLIDAY) 99 rooms and suites, restaurant, lounge, pool, exercise center, children under 19 free with parents, wheelchair access, A/C, TV, NS rooms, fax, room service, no pets, laundry service, meeting facilities, senior rates, CC. SGL/DBL$45-$55.

Kingston
Area Code 405

Lake Texoma Resort (Kingston 73439; 564-2311, 800-654-8240) 187 rooms and cottages, restaurant, pool, whirlpools, exercise center, sauna, in-room refrigerators, no pets, fireplaces, children free with parents, modified American plan, A/C, TV, NS rooms, wheelchair access, CC. SGL/DBL$54-$95.

Lawton
Area Code 405

Best Western Sandpiper Inn (2202 North Hwy. 277, 73507; 353-0310, Fax 357-7388, 800-749-0310, 800-528-1234) 120 rooms, restaurant, lounge, pool, exercise center, children free with parents, free local calls, airport transportation, A/C, NS rooms, TV, laundry facilities, wheelchair access, pets OK, senior rates, meeting facilities, CC. SGL/DBL$40-$55.

Days Inn Fort Sill (1201 Northwest Cache Rd., 73507; 248-7099, Fax 248-0298, 800-325-2525) 71 rooms and suites, free breakfast, outdoor pool, children free with parents, room service, laundry service, A/C, TV, free local calls, pets OK, fax, wheelchair access, NS rooms, senior rates, CC. SGL/DBL$22-$45, STS$45-$65.

Executive Inn (3110 Northwest Cache Rd., 73507; 353-3104, Fax 353-0992) 96 rooms, restaurant, pool, sauna, A/C, TV, NS rooms, wheelchair access, pets OK, airport courtesy car, in-room refrigerators, senior rates, CC. SGL/DBL$40-$55.

Holiday Inn (3134 Cache Rd., 73505; 353-1682, Fax 353-2872, 800-HOLI-DAY) 170 rooms, restaurant, lounge, entertainment, pool, exercise center, children under 19 free with parents, airport transportation, wheelchair access, A/C, TV, NS rooms, fax, room service, no pets, laundry service, meeting facilities, senior rates, CC. SGL/DBL$38-$50.

Hospitality Inn (202 East Lee Blvd., 73501; 355-9765) 106 rooms, free breakfast, pool, A/C, laundry facilities, pets OK, in-room coffee makers, TV, NS rooms, wheelchair access, children free with parents, senior rates, CC. SGL/DBL$33-$40.

Howard Johnson Hotel (1125 East Gore Blvd., 73501; 353-0200, Fax 353-6801, 800-I-GO-HOJO) 142 rooms, restaurant, lounge, indoor pool, tennis courts, children free with parents, wheelchair access, NS rooms, TV, A/C, pets OK, laundry facilities, senior rates, meeting facilities for 450, CC. SGL/DBL$40-$70.

Park Inn International (3110 Cache Rd., 73505; 353-3104, Fax 357-0544, 800-437-PARK) 97 rooms, restaurant, pets OK, indoor and outdoor pool, sauna, whirlpools, airport transportation, A/C, TV, wheelchair access, NS rooms, meeting facilities for 50, senior rates, CC. SGL/DBL$40-$48.

Ramada Inn (601 North 2nd, 73507; 355-7155, Fax 353-6162, 800-2-RAMADA) 101 rooms and suites, restaurant, lounge, pool, wheelchair access, NS rooms, pets OK, A/C, TV, children under 18 free with parents, in-room coffee makers, airport transportation, room service, laundry facilities, meeting facilities, senior rates, CC. SGL/DBL$39-$80.

McAlester
Area Code 918

Comfort Inn (1215 George Nigh Expressway, 74502; 426-0115, 800-221-2222) 58 rooms, restaurant, pool, wheelchair access, NS rooms, no pets, children under 18 free with parents, A/C, TV, meeting facilities, senior rates, CC. SGL/DBL$38-$46.

Days Inn (1217 South George Nigh Expwy., 74501; 426-5050, Fax 426-5055, 800-325-2525) 100 rooms and suites, restaurant, lounge, indoor pool, jacuzzi, children free with parents, room service, laundry service, A/C, TV, free local calls, pets OK, fax, wheelchair access, NS rooms, meeting facilities, senior rates, CC. SGL/DBL$39-$69.

Holiday Inn (1500 George Nigh Expressway, 74501; 423-7766, Fax 426-0068, 800-HOLIDAY) 160 rooms and suites, restaurant, lounge, indoor pool, exercise center, children under 19 free with parents, wheelchair access, A/C, TV, NS rooms, fax, airport transportation, in-room refrigerators and microwaves, room service, no pets, laundry service, meeting facilities, senior rates, CC. SGL/DBL$45-$55, STS$90-$180.

Valley Inn (2400 South Main St., 74501; 426-5400, Fax 426-5400) 32 rooms, restaurant, lounge, pool, laundry facilities, no pets, in-room refrigerators, A/C, TV, NS rooms, wheelchair access, CC. SGL/DBL$30-$40.

Miami
Area Code 918

Best Western Inn (2225 East Steve Owens Blvd., 74354; 542-6681, Fax 542-3777, 800-528-1234) 80 rooms and 2-room suites, restaurant, pool, exercise center, children free with parents, A/C, NS rooms, airport transportation, TV, laundry facilities, wheelchair access, pets OK, senior rates, meeting facilities, CC. SGL/DBL$40-$59.

Super 8 Motel (2120 East Steve Owens Blvd., 74354; 542-3382, 800-800-8000) 32 rooms and suites, no pets, children under 12 free with parents, free local calls, A/C, TV, in-room refrigerators and microwaves, fax, NS rooms, senior rates, wheelchair access, meeting facilities, CC. SGL/DBL$33-$46.

Midwest City

Area Code 405

Motel 6 (5801 Tinker Diagonal, 73110; 737-8851, 891-6161) 100 rooms, pool, free local calls, children under 17 free with parents, NS rooms, wheelchair access, pets OK, A/C, TV, CC. SGL/DBL$38-$44.

Motel 6 (6166 Tinker Diagonal, 73110; 737-6676, 891-6161) 93 rooms, pool, free local calls, children under 17 free with parents, NS rooms, wheelchair access, pets OK, A/C, TV, CC. SGL/DBL$36-$48.

Moore

Area Code 405

Best Western Inn (2600 North Broadway, 73160; 794-6611, 800-528-1234) 80 rooms, restaurant, free breakfast, lounge, pool, exercise center, children free with parents, A/C, NS rooms, TV, laundry facilities, wheelchair access, pets OK, senior rates, meeting facilities, CC. SGL/DBL$33-$43.

Motel 6 (1417 North Moore Ave., 73160; 799-6616, 891-6161) 122 rooms, pool, free local calls, children under 17 free with parents, NS rooms, wheelchair access, pets OK, A/C, TV, CC. SGL/DBL$39-$44.

Super 8 Motel (1520 North Moore Ave., 73160; 794-4030, 800-800-8000) 40 rooms and suites, whirlpools, no pets, children under 12 free with parents, free local calls, A/C, TV, in-room refrigerators and microwaves, fax, NS rooms, senior rates, wheelchair access, meeting facilities, CC. SGL/DBL$35-$49.

Muskogee

Area Code 918

Best Western Trade Winds Inn (534 South 32nd St., 74401; 683-2951, 800-528-1234) 109 rooms, restaurant, free breakfast, lounge, entertainment, pool, exercise center, children free with parents, A/C, NS rooms, TV, laundry facilities, wheelchair access, complimentary newspaper, free local calls, pets OK, senior rates, meeting facilities, CC. SGL/DBL$45-$78.

Days Inn (900 South 32nd St., 74401; 683-3911, Fax 683-5744, 800-325-2525) 43 rooms and suites, free breakfast, outdoor pool, children free with parents, room service, laundry service, A/C, TV, free local calls, pets OK, fax, wheelchair access, NS rooms, senior rates, CC. SGL/DBL$39-$48.

Econo Lodge (2018 West Shawnee Ave., 74401; 683-0101, 800-4-CHOICE) 45 rooms, restaurant, free breakfast, pool, children under 12 free with parents, no pets, NS rooms, wheelchair access, A/C, TV, senior rates, CC. SGL/DBL$35-$60.

Motel 6 (903 South 32nd St., 74401; 683-8369, 891-6161) 81 rooms, pool, free local calls, children under 17 free with parents, NS rooms, wheelchair access, pets OK, A/C, TV, CC. SGL/DBL$38-$46.

Quality Inn (2300 East Shawnee Ave., 74403; 683-6551, 800-221-2222) 122 rooms and suites, restaurant, lounge, pool, exercise center, children free with parents, A/C, TV, room service, laundry service, NS rooms, meeting facilities, senior rates, CC. SGL/DBL$38-$55.

Ramada Inn (800 South 32nd St., 74401; 682-4341, Fax 682-7400, 800-2-RAMADA) 142 rooms and suites, restaurant, lounge, indoor pool, exercise center, sauna, whirlpools, game room, wheelchair access, NS rooms, pets OK, A/C, TV, children under 18 free with parents, room service, laundry facilities, airport transportation, meeting facilities for 500, senior rates, CC. SGL/DBL$48-$130.

Super 8 Motel (2430 South 32nd St., 74401; 683-8888, 800-800-8000) 56 rooms and suites, restaurant, laundry facilities, pets OK, children under 12 free with parents, free local calls, A/C, TV, in-room refrigerators and microwaves, fax, NS rooms, senior rates, wheelchair access, meeting facilities, CC. SGL/DBL$30-$45.

Norman
Area Code 405

Days Inn (609 North Interstate Dr., 73069; 360-4380, Fax 321-5767, 800-325-2525) 72 rooms and suites, free breakfast, children free with parents, room service, laundry service, A/C, TV, free local calls, pets OK, fax, wheelchair access, NS rooms, senior rates, CC. SGL/DBL$30-$50, STS$50-$79.

Holiday Inn (2600 West Main St., 73069; 329-1624, 800-HOLIDAY) 144 rooms, restaurant, lounge, entertainment, indoor heated pool, exercise center, whirlpools, children under 19 free with parents, wheelchair access, A/C, TV, NS rooms, fax, room service, pets OK, laundry service, meeting facilities, senior rates, CC. SGL/DBL$45-$55.

Ramada Inn (1200 24th Ave. Southwest, 73072; 321-0110, Fax 360-5629, 800-2-RAMADA) 151 rooms and suites, restaurant, lounge, entertainment, pool, wheelchair access, game room, car rental desk, free local calls, NS rooms, pets OK, A/C, TV, children under 18 free with parents, room service, laundry facilities, meeting facilities, senior rates, CC. SGL/DBL$50-$100.

Residence Inn (2681 Jefferson, 73069; 366-0900, Fax 360-6552, 800-331-3131) 125 rooms and suites, free breakfast, in-room refrigerators, coffee makers and microwaves, laundry facilities, TV, A/C, VCRs, pets OK, complimentary newspaper, fireplaces, children stay free with parents, NS rooms, wheelchair access, meeting facilities for 50, CC. SGL/DBL$80-$110.

Sheraton Inn Norman (1000 North Interstate Dr., 73069; 364-2882, Fax 321-5264, 800-325-3535) 151 rooms and suites, restaurant, lounge, entertainment, indoor heated pool, jacuzzi, exercise center, spa, gift shop, airport courtesy car, A/C, TV, laundry facilities, wheelchair access, NS rooms, room service, 5,300 square feet of meeting and exhibition space, 9 meeting rooms, meeting facilities for 500, CC. SGL/DBL$75-$100.

Stratford House Inn (225 North Interstate Dr., 73069; 329-7194) 40 rooms, free breakfast, whirlpools, A/C, TV, NS rooms, wheelchair access, senior rates, CC. SGL/DBL$25-$40.

Thunderbird Lodge (1430 24th Ave. Southwest, 73072; 329-6990, Fax 360-4072) 98 rooms, heated pool, kitchenettes, A/C, TV, NS rooms, wheelchair access, in-room refrigerators, no pets, CC. SGL/DBL$30-$33.

Oklahoma City
Area Code 405

Airport Hilton West (401 South Meridian, 73108; 947-7681, Fax 947-7681 ext 7360, 800-HILTONS) 507 rooms and suites, restaurant, lounge, 3 indoor and outdoor pools, exercise center, sauna, whirlpools, jogging track, lighted tennis courts, wheelchair access, NS rooms, business services, meeting facilities for 1,000, A/C, TV, CC. 5 miles from the airport and the downtown area, 2 miles from the State Fairgrounds. SGL/DBL$99-$109.

Best Valu Inn (4800 South I-35, 73129; 670-3815) 158 rooms, free breakfast, pool, pets OK, laundry service, NS rooms, A/C, TV, CC. SGL/DBL$45-$55.

Best Western Saddleback Inn (4300 Southwest Third St., 73108; 947-7000, Fax 948-7636, 800-228-3903, 800-5281234, 800-522-6626 in Oklahoma) 220 rooms and suites, restaurant, lounge, heated pool, free local calls, pets OK, local transportation, children under 18 free with parents, wheelchair access, NS rooms, fax, meeting facilities for 300, A/C, TV, CC. 5 miles from the downtown area. SGL/DBL$44-$60.

Best Western Trade Winds Central Inn (1800 East Reno, 73117; 235-4531, Fax 235-1861, 800-528-1234) 198 rooms and suites, restaurant, lounge, pool, children under 12 free with parents, free local calls, local transportation, NS rooms, A/C, TV, meeting facilities, senior rates, CC. In the downtown area. SGL$43-$60.

Clarion Hotel (4445 North Lincoln Blvd., 73105; 528-2741, 800-221-2222) 50 rooms, restaurant, free breakfast, pool, no pets, NS rooms, children under 18 free with parents, senior rates, meeting facilities, A/C, TV, CC. SGL/DBL$41-$62.

Comfort Inn East (5653 Tinker Diagonal, 73110; 733-1339, 800-221-2222) 150 rooms, restaurant, free breakfast, lounge, pool, wheelchair access, NS rooms, no pets, children under 18 free with parents, A/C, TV, meeting facilities, senior rates, CC. SGL/DBL$46-$63.

Comfort Inn (4017 Northwest 39th Expressway, 73112; 947-0038, Fax 946-7450, 800-221-2222) 114 rooms, restaurant, free breakfast, pool, exercise facilities, wheelchair access, children free with parents, NS rooms, A/C, TV, CC. 7 miles from the Cowboy Hall of Fame, 3 miles from the State Fairgrounds, 5 miles from the downtown area. SGL/DBL$43-$73.

Comfort Inn Airport South (2200 South Meridian, 73108; 681-9000, 800-2285150) 100 rooms, restaurant, pool, wheelchair access, no pets, NS rooms, A/C, TV children free with parents, meeting facilities, CC. SGL$46-$52, DBL$52-$58.

Comfort Inn (4240 West I-40, 73108; 943-4400, 800-221-2222) 51 rooms, free breakfast, pool, wheelchair access, NS rooms, no pets, children under 18 free with parents, A/C, TV, meeting facilities, senior rates, CC. SGL/DBL$43-$56.

Courtyard by Marriott (4301 Highline Rd., 73108; 946-6500, Fax 946-7638, 800-321-2211) 149 rooms, restaurant, lounge, pool, jacuzzi, children free with parents, in-room refrigerators, wheelchair access, NS rooms, A/C, TV, airport courtesy car, meeting facilities, CC. SGL/DBL$65-$115.

Days Inn Meridian Airport (4712 West I-40, 73128; 947-8721, Fax 9425020, 800-325-2525) 152 rooms and suites, free breakfast, lounge, laundry service, children under 12 free with parents, cable TV, free local calls, airport transportation, pets OK, wheelchair access, fax, NS rooms, meeting facilities for 650, A/C, CC. 4 miles from the airport. SGL/DBL$32-$40.

Days Inn Northwest (2801 Northwest 39th St., 73112; 946-0741, Fax 942-0180, 800-325-2525) 192 rooms and suites, restaurant, lounge, in-room refrigerators, wheelchair access, NS rooms, fax, pets OK, in-room refrigerators and coffee makers, free local calls, 7 meeting rooms, A/C, TV, CC. 12 miles from the airport, 6 minutes from the Cowboy Hall of Fame and the State Fairgrounds. SGL/DBL$39-$55, STS$69-$75.

Days Inn (2616 South I-35, 73129; 677-0521, 800-325-2525) 88 rooms, restaurant, free breakfast, lounge, pool, children under 12 free with parents, cable TV, free local calls, pets OK, laundry service, wheelchair access, NS rooms, airport transportation, meeting facilities for 650, A/C, TV, CC. 8 miles from the State Fairgrounds, 5 miles from the State Capital, 10 miles from the airport. SGL/DBL$35-$55.

Econo Lodge (1307 Southeast 44th St., 73129; 672-4533, 800-4-CHOICE) 70 rooms, restaurant, pool, children under 12 free with parents, no pets, NS rooms, wheelchair access, A/C, TV, senior rates, CC. SGL/DBL$27-$45.

Econo Lodge Airport (820 South MacArthur Blvd., 73128; 947-8651, 800-4-CHOICE) 70 rooms, pool, children under 12 free with parents, no pets, NS rooms, wheelchair access, A/C, TV, senior rates, CC. SGL/DBL$29-$46.

Econo Lodge (8200 West I-40, 73128; 787-7051, 800-4-CHOICE) 60 rooms and efficiencies, pool, children under 12 free with parents, no pets, NS rooms, wheelchair access, A/C, TV, senior rates, free local calls, CC. SGL/DBL$21-$39.

Embassy Suites (1815 South Meridian Ave., 73108; 942-8511, Fax 682-9835, 800-465-4329) 236 2-room suites, restaurant, lounge, free breakfast, pool, sauna, jacuzzi, exercise center, NS rooms, gift shop, room service, laundry service, wheelchair access, airport courtesy car, meeting facilities, A/C, TV, CC. 2 miles from the airport, 12 miles from the Cowboy Hall of Fame, 20 miles from the University of Oklahoma. SGL/DBL$61-$65.

Fifth Season Inn (6200 North Robinson, 73118; 843-5558, Fax 843-5558 ext 2641, 800-682-0049, 800-522-9458 in Oklahoma) 202 rooms and suites, restaurant, lounge, pool, whirlpools, exercise center, gift shop, laundry service, local transportation, complimentary newspaper, pets OK, wheelchair access, NS rooms, A/C, TV meeting facilities, CC. SGL/DBL$95.

Hampton Inn Airport (1905 South Meridian Ave., 73108; 682-2080, Fax 682-3662, 800-HAMPTON) 129 rooms, free breakfast, pool, airport transportation, children under 18 free with parents, NS rooms, wheelchair access, A/C, TV, computer hookups, fax, free local calls, airport transportation, meeting facilities, CC. SGL/DBL$60-$73.

Hilton Inn Northwest (2945 Northwest Expressway, 73112; 848-4811, Fax 843-4829, 800-HILTONS) 213 rooms and suites, restaurant, lounge, entertainment, outdoor pool, exercise center, wheelchair access, NS rooms, airport courtesy car, business services, meeting facilities for 300, A/C, TV, CC. In the northwest business district, 12 miles from the airport, 8 miles from the downtown area. SGL$99, DBL$109, STS$175-$250.

Holiday Inn (12001 Northeast Expressway, 73111; 478-0400, Fax 478-2774, 800-HOLIDAY) 210 rooms and suites, restaurant, lounge, indoor pool, whirlpools, children under 12 free with parents, wheelchair access, NS rooms, fax, room service, laundry service, meeting facilities for 200, A/C, TV, CC. Near Frontier City, 3 miles from the Cowboy Hall of Fame and the State Capital. SGL/DBL$75-$89.

Holiday Inn Northwest (3535 Northwest 39th St., 73112; 947-2351, Fax 948-7752, 800-HOLIDAY) 243 rooms and suites, restaurant, lounge, children under 12 free with parents, wheelchair access, NS rooms, fax, room service, airport transportation, gift shop, meeting facilities for 400, A/C, TV, CC. 8 miles from the airport, 2 miles from the State Fairgrounds. SGL/DBL$75-$95.

Holiday Inn West Airport (801 South Meridian Ave., 73108; 942-8511, Fax 946-7126, 800-HOLIDAY) 486 rooms, restaurant, lounge, 2 indoor pools, children under 12 free with parents, wheelchair access, NS rooms, fax, room service, gift shop, meeting facilities for 1,500, A/C, TV, CC. 5 miles from the Convention Center, 15 miles from Remington Park Racetrack. SGL/DBL$65-$75.

Holiday Inn East (5701 Tinker Diagonal Rd., 73110; 737-4481, Fax 732-5706, 800-HOLIDAY) 156 rooms and suites, restaurant, lounge, exercise center, children under 12 free with parents, wheelchair access, NS rooms, fax, room service, meeting facilities for 150, A/C, TV, CC. 13 miles from the airport, 5 minutes from the Sports Stadium, 10 minutes from the State Capital and Fairgrounds. SGL/DBL$68-$84.

Howard Johnson (5301 North Lincoln Blvd., 73112; 528-7563, 800-I-GO-HOJO) 132 rooms, restaurant, free breakfast, lounge, pool, children free with parents, wheelchair access, NS rooms, TV, A/C, no pets, laundry facilities, senior rates, meeting facilities for 200, CC. SGL/DBL$39-$80.

Howard Johnson Lodge (400 South Meridian, 73108; 943-9841, Fax 943-9841 ext 152, 800-I-GO-HOJO) 96 rooms, restaurant, free breakfast, pool, children under 12 free with parents, NS rooms, laundry service, fax, car rental desk, airport transportation, A/C, TV, CC. 5 miles from airport and the downtown area. SGL/DBL$34-$70.

La Quinta Inn South (8315 South I-35, 73149; 631-8661, Fax 631-1892, 800-531-5900) 122 rooms, restaurant, lounge, heated pool, complimentary newspaper, free local calls, fax, laundry service, NS rooms, wheelchair access, meeting facilities, A/C, TV, CC. 6 miles from the airport, within 5 miles of the Convention Center, Crossroads Mall and downtown area, 12 miles from the Cowboy Hall of Fame. SGL/DBL$43-$50.

Lexington Hotel Suites (1200 South Meridian, 73108; 943-7800, 943-8346) 144 suites, free breakfast, heated outdoor pool, laundry service, airport courtesy car, wheelchair access, NS rooms, meeting facilities, CC. SGL$40-$70, DBL$45-$75.

Marriott Hotel (3233 Northwest Expressway, 73112; 842-6633, Fax 842-3152, 800-229-9290) 354 rooms and suites, Concierge Level, restaurant, lounge, entertainment, indoor and outdoor pools, exercise center, sauna, whirlpools, airport courtesy car, NS rooms, wheelchair access, gift shop, airline ticket desk, meeting facilities, A/C, TV, CC, 15 minutes from downtown area and airport. SGL/DBL$109.

Meridian Plaza (2101 South Meridian Ave., 73108; 685-4000, Fax 685-0574, 800-622-7666) 249 rooms, restaurant, lounge, entertainment, pool, sauna, jacuzzi, exercise center, gift shop, wheelchair access, NS rooms, A/C, TV, in-room refrigerators, airport courtesy car, meeting facilities, CC. SGL/DBL$45, STS$66.

Motel 6 (820 South Meridian Ave., 73108; 946-6662, 891-6161) 129 rooms, pool, free local calls, children under 17 free with parents, NS rooms, wheelchair access, pets OK, A/C, TV, CC. SGL/DBL$38-$44.

Motel 6 (4200 West I-40, 73108; 947-6550, 891-6161) 114 rooms, pool, free local calls, children under 17 free with parents, NS rooms, wheelchair access, pets OK, A/C, TV, CC. SGL/DBL$39-$46.

Plaza Inn (3200 South Prospect, 73129; 672-2341, Fax 670-3497) 205 rooms and suites, restaurant, pool, room service, laundry service, NS rooms, A/C, TV, wheelchair access, meeting facilities, CC. SGL/DBL$30-$40, STS$50-$75.

Marriott Residence Inn Central Plaza (112 South Martin Luther King Blvd., 73117; 235-2761, 800-221-2222) 192 rooms, restaurant, lounge, pool, wheelchair access, NS rooms, meeting facilities, A/C, TV, CC. 12 miles from the airport, 5 miles from the Remington Park Race Track and State Fairgrounds. SGL/DBL$54-$64.

Quality Inn West (720 South MacArthur Blvd., 73128; 943-2393, 800-221-2222) 65 rooms and suites, restaurant, free breakfast, pool, exercise center, children free with parents, A/C, TV, room service, laundry service, NS rooms, meeting facilities, senior rates, CC. SGL/DBL$39-$60.

Ramada Inn Airport South (6800 South I-35, 73149; 631-3321, Fax 6313489, 800-2-RAMADA) 120 rooms, restaurant, lounge, entertainment, pool, children under 18 free with parents, wheelchair access, NS rooms, airport courtesy car, A/C, TV, CC. Near the downtown area and Fairgrounds. SGL/DBL$48-$53.

Ramada Inn Airport West (800 South Meridian, 73108; 942-0040, Fax 942-0638, 800-2-RAMADA) 170 rooms, restaurant, lounge, outdoor pool, children under 18 free with parents, wheelchair access, NS rooms, airport transportation, free local calls, meeting facilities, A/C, TV, CC. 5 miles from downtown area, 3 miles from the Fairgrounds, 5 miles from airport. SGL/DBL$45-$55.

Ramada Inn (3709 Northwest 39th, 73112; 942-7730, Fax 948-6238, 800-2-RAMADA) 90 rooms, free breakfast, airport transportation, complimentary newspaper, laundry service, NS rooms, wheelchair access, beauty shop, meeting facilities for 100, A/C, TV, CC. 2 miles from the Cowboy Hall of Fame. SGL/DBL$43-$58.

Red Carpet Inn (11901 Northeast Expressway, 73111; 478-0243, 800-251-1962) 32 rooms, restaurant, lounge, pool, whirlpools, kitchenettes, children under 12 stay free with parents, NS rooms, wheelchair access, no pets, meeting facilities, A/C, gift shop, free local calls, TV, CC. 3 miles from the Cowboy Hall of Fame, State Capital and Fairgrounds, 25 miles from the airport. SGL/DBL$48-$68.

Rodeway Inn (4601 Southwest Third, 73108; 947-2400, Fax 947-2931, 800-292-7929, 800-228-1200) 184 rooms and suites, restaurant, free breakfast, wheelchair access, NS rooms, A/C, TV, laundry service, airport transportation, pets OK, senior rates, CC. SGL/DBL$34-$50.

Sheraton Century Center Hotel (Broadway at Main, 73102; 235-2780, Fax 272-0396, 800-325-3535) 400 rooms and suites, 3 restaurants, lounge, entertainment, pool, wheelchair access, NS rooms, airport courtesy car, 15 meeting rooms, 17,000 square feet of meeting and exhibition space, meeting facilities for 1,000, A/C, TV, CC. Near the entertainment district and Convention Center, 12 miles from the airport. SGL/DBL$68-$138.

Super 8 Central (3030 South I-35, 73129; 677-1000, Fax 672-0016, 800-800-8000) 99 rooms, jacuzzis, no pets, children under 18 free with parents, NS rooms, wheelchair access, computer hookups, fax, free local calls, meeting facilities, A/C, TV, CC. 6 miles from Remington Park, 3 miles from The Medical Complex. SGL/DBL$33-$43.

Super 8 Motel (1117 Northeast 13th St., 73117; 232-0404, 800-800-8000) 25 rooms, free breakfast, children under 18 free with parents, NS rooms, no pets, in-room refrigerators, wheelchair access, computer hookups, fax, free local calls, meeting facilities, A/C, TV, CC. Near the State Capital and Oklahoma Health Center. SGL/DBL$35-$49.

Super 8 Motel (311 South Meridian, 73108; 947-7801, 800-800-8000) 160 rooms and suites, restaurant, laundry facilities, no pets, children under 12 free with parents, free local calls, A/C, TV, in-room refrigerators and microwaves, fax, NS rooms, senior rates, wheelchair access, meeting facilities, CC. SGL/DBL$30-$46.

Travelers Inn (I-40 and Meridian 73108; 942-8294, 800-633-8300) 139 rooms and suites, pool, free local calls, NS rooms, wheelchair access, meeting facilities, A/C, TV, CC. Near the airport. SGL/DBL$45-$55.

The Waterford Hotel (6300 Waterford Blvd., 73118; 848-4782, Fax 843-9161, 800-992-2009) 197 rooms and suites, restaurant, lounge, entertainment, pool, exercise center, tennis, gift shop, airport transportation, A/C, TV, children free with parents, in-room refrigerators, wheelchair access, NS rooms, meeting facilities, CC. SGL$102, STS$122.

Okmulgee
Area Code 918

Best Western Inn (3499 North Wood Dr., 74447; 756-9200, 800-528-1234) 49 rooms, restaurant, lounge, pool, exercise center, children free with parents, A/C, NS rooms, TV, laundry facilities, wheelchair access, pets OK, senior rates, meeting facilities for 100, CC. SGL/DBL$38-$68.

Pauls Valley
Area Code 405

Amish Inn Motel (Pauls Valley 73075; 238-7545) 30 rooms, restaurant, A/C, TV, NS rooms, no pets, wheelchair access, CC. SGL/DBL$20-$40.

Best Western Four Sands Inn (Pauls Valley 73075; 238-6416, 800-528-1234) 50 rooms, free breakfast, pool, exercise center, children free with parents, A/C, NS rooms, TV, laundry facilities, wheelchair access, pets OK, senior rates, meeting facilities, CC. SGL/DBL$36-$45.

Days Inn (Pauls Valley 73075; 238-7548, 800-325-2525) 54 rooms and suites, children free with parents, room service, laundry service, A/C, TV, free local calls, pets OK, fax, wheelchair access, NS rooms, senior rates, CC. SGL/DBL$32-$47.

Garden Inn Motel (Pauls Valley 73075; 238-7313) 55 rooms, restaurant, indoor heated pool, pets OK, A/C, TV, NS rooms, wheelchair access, CC. SGL/DBL$20-$30.

Perry
Area Code 405

Best Western Cherokee Strip Inn (Perry 73077; 336-2218, Fax 336-9753, 800-528-1234) 90 rooms, restaurant, lounge, indoor pool, children free with parents, A/C, NS rooms, complimentary newspaper, TV, laundry facilities, wheelchair access, pets OK, senior rates, meeting facilities, CC. SGL/DBL$40-$46.

Dan-D Motel (515 Fir St., 73077; 336-4463) 26 rooms and efficiencies, restaurant, pool, A/C, TV, NS rooms, wheelchair access, no pets, in-room refrigerators, CC. SGL/DBL$18-$25.

Days Inn (Perry 73077; 336-2277, 800-325-2525) 43 rooms and suites, free breakfast, children free with parents, room service, laundry service, A/C, TV, free local calls, pets OK, fax, wheelchair access, NS rooms, senior rates, CC. SGL/DBL$27-$40.

First Interstate Inn (Perry 73077; 336-2277, 800-462-4667) 45 rooms, A/C, TV, NS rooms, wheelchair access, pets OK, laundry facilities, senior rates, CC. SGL/DBL$27-$35.

Ponca City
Area Code 405

Best Western Thunderbird Motel (407 South 14th St., 74601; 765-6671, Fax 765-6673, 800-528-1234) 40 rooms, restaurant, free breakfast, lounge, pool, exercise center, children free with parents, A/C, NS rooms, TV, laundry facilities, wheelchair access, pets OK, senior rates, meeting facilities, CC. SGL/DBL$29-$47.

Days Inn (1415 East Bradley, 74606; 767-1406, Fax 762-9589, 800-325-2525) 60 rooms and suites, free breakfast, outdoor pool, children free with parents, room service, laundry service, A/C, TV, free local calls, pets OK, fax, wheelchair access, NS rooms, senior rates, CC. SGL/DBL$34-$40, STS$46-$50.

Econo Lodge (212 South 14th St., 74601; 762-3401, Fax 762-4550, 800-4-CHOICE) 88 rooms, pool, children under 12 free with parents, no pets, NS rooms, wheelchair access, A/C, TV, senior rates, CC. SGL/DBL$30-$38.

Holiday Inn (2215 North 14th St., 74606; 800-HOLIDAY) 139 rooms and suites, restaurant, lounge, pool, exercise center, children under 19 free with parents, wheelchair access, A/C, TV, NS rooms, fax, room service, no pets, laundry service, meeting facilities, senior rates, CC. SGL/DBL$40-$60.

Marland Estate Conference Center Hotel (901 Mountain Rd., 74604; 767-0422, Fax 767-0344) 35 rooms and suites, pool, in-room refrigerators, no pets, A/C, TV, NS rooms, wheelchair access, CC. SGL/DBL$40-$46.

Surrey Motel (116 South 14th St., 74601; 765-5563) 21 rooms, restaurant, A/C, TV, NS rooms, wheelchair access, no pets, CC. SGL/DBL$25-$30.

Pryor
Area Code 918

Days Inn (Hwy. 69 South, 74362; 825-7600, 800-325-2525) 55 rooms and suites, restaurant, outdoor pool, children free with parents, room service, laundry service, A/C, TV, free local calls, pets OK, fax, wheelchair access, NS rooms, senior rates, CC. SGL/DBL$30-$75.

Holiday Motel (701 South Mill St., 74362; 825-1204) 25 rooms, pool, A/C, TV, NS rooms, wheelchair access, pets OK, in-room refrigerators, children free with parents, senior rates, CC. SGL/DBL$25-$35.

Pryor House Inn (123 South Mill St., 74632; 35 rooms and suites, restaurant, free breakfast, pool, A/C, TV, NS rooms, wheelchair access, pets OK, children free with parents, CC. SGL/DBL$33-$45.

Purcell
Area Code 405

Econo Lodge (2500 Hwy. 74 South, 73080; 527-5603, 800-4-CHOICE) 32 rooms, outdoor pool, children under 12 free with parents, no pets, NS rooms, free local calls, wheelchair access, A/C, TV, senior rates, CC. SGL/DBL$30-$40.

Quartz Mountain State Park
Area Code 405

Quartz Mountain Lodge (Route 1, 73655; 563-2424, Fax 563-9125) 59 rooms, suites and cottages, restaurant, indoor and outdoor pool, lighted tennis courts, no pets, A/C, TV, NS rooms, wheelchair access, modified American plan available, senior rates, CC. SGL/DBL$50-$88.

Ramona
Area Code 918

Jarrett Farm Country Inn (Ramona 74061; 371-9868) free breakfast, NS, no pets, private baths, modified American plan available, A/C, TV, CC. SGL/DBL$100-$150.

Roman Nose State Park
Area Code 405

Roman Nose Resort (Watonga 73772; 623-7281, 800-654-8240) 57 rooms and cottages, restaurant, pool, lighted tennis courts, A/C, TV, NS rooms, wheelchair access, children free with parents, senior rates, CC. SGL/DBL$50-$65.

Sallisaw
Area Code 918

Best Western Blue Ribbon Motor Inn (706 South Kerr Blvd., 74955; 776-6294, Fax 775-5151, 800-528-1234) 51 rooms, restaurant, free breakfast, lounge, indoor and outdoor pool, exercise center, children free with parents, A/C, NS rooms, TV, laundry facilities, wheelchair access, pets OK, senior rates, meeting facilities, CC. SGL/DBL$33-$48.

Days Inn (Sallisaw 74955; 775-4406, 800-325-2525) 33 rooms and suites, restaurant, whirlpools, children free with parents, room service, laundry service, A/C, TV, free local calls, pets OK, fax, wheelchair access, NS rooms, senior rates, CC. SGL/DBL$32-$40, STS$40-$46.

Golden Spur Inn (Sallisaw 74955; 775-4443) 27 rooms, pool, hot tubs, A/C, TV, NS rooms, wheelchair access, pets OK, senior rates, CC. SGL/DBL$25-$35.

Holiday Inn (1300 East Cherokee, 74955; 775-7791, Fax 775-7795, 800-HOLIDAY) 50 rooms, restaurant, lounge, pool, exercise center, children under 19 free with parents, wheelchair access, A/C, TV, NS rooms, fax, room service, pets OK, laundry service, meeting facilities for 150, senior rates, CC. SGL/DBL$35-$43.

McKnight Motel (1611 West Ruth St., 74955; 775-9126, 800-842-9442) 39 rooms and 2-bedroom suites, restaurant, pool, whirlpools, A/C, TV, NS rooms, wheelchair access, in-room coffee makers, no pets, laundry facilities, senior rates, CC. SGL/DBL$40-$50.

Super 8 Motel (924 South Kerr Blvd., 74955; 775-8900, 800-800-8000) 98 rooms and suites, restaurant, outdoor pool, pets OK, children under 12 free with parents, free local calls, A/C, TV, in-room refrigerators and microwaves, fax, NS rooms, senior rates, wheelchair access, meeting facilities, CC. SGL/DBL$33-$43.

Sapulpa
Area Code 918

Super 8 Motel (1505 New Sapulpa Rd., 74066; 227-3300, 800-800-8000) 60 rooms and suites, outdoor pool, no pets, children under 12 free with parents, free local calls, A/C, TV, in-room refrigerators and microwaves, fax, NS rooms, senior rates, wheelchair access, meeting facilities, CC. SGL/DBL$32-$45.

Savanna
Are Code 918

Budget Host Colonial Inn (Savanna 74565; 548-3506, 800-283-4678) 30 rooms and 1- and 2-bedroom efficiencies, laundry facilities, NS rooms, wheelchair access, A/C, TV, senior rates, children free with parents, pets OK, CC. SGL/DBL$22-$28.

Seminole
Area Code 405

Oxford Inn (2323 State St., 74868; 382-6800) 69 rooms, restaurant, lounge, pool, laundry facilities, no pets, A/C, TV, NS rooms, wheelchair access, CC. SGL/DBL$40-$45.

Rexdale Inn (2151 Hwy. 9, 74868; 382-7002) 20 rooms, A/C, TV, NS rooms, wheelchair access, no pets, senior rates, CC. SGL/DBL$25-$30.

Shawnee
Area Code 405

Best Western Cinderella Motor Inn (623 Kickapoo Spur, 74801; 273-7010, 800-528-1234) 92 rooms, restaurant, lounge, indoor pool, exercise center, children free with parents, A/C, NS rooms, TV, laundry facilities, wheelchair access, pets OK, senior rates, meeting facilities, CC. SGL/DBL$45-$60.

Budget Host Inn (Hwy. 177, 74801; 275-8430, 800-283-4678) 30 rooms, laundry facilities, NS rooms, wheelchair access, no pets, A/C, TV, senior rates, children free with parents, senior rates, CC. SGL/DBL$25-$44.

Comfort Inn (4981 North Harrison, 74801; 275-5310, 800-221-2222) 60 rooms, restaurant, pool, wheelchair access, NS rooms, no pets, children under 18 free with parents, A/C, TV, meeting facilities, senior rates, CC. SGL/DBL$35-$45.

Econo Lodge (5107 North Harrison St., 74801; 275-6720, 800-4-CHOICE) 53 rooms, restaurant, children under 12 free with parents, no pets, NS rooms, wheelchair access, A/C, TV, senior rates, CC. SGL/DBL$35-$60.

Fleetwood Motel (1301 North Harrison St., 74801; 273-7561) 17 rooms, A/C, TV, NS rooms, CC. SGL/DBL$25-$30.

Super 8 Motel (4900 North Harrison, 74801; 275-0089, 800-800-8000) 36 rooms and suites, restaurant, pets OK, children under 12 free with parents, free local calls, A/C, TV, in-room refrigerators and microwaves, fax, NS rooms, senior rates, wheelchair access, meeting facilities, CC. SGL/DBL$35-$53.

Stillwater
Area Code 405

Best Western Inn (600 McElroy, 74075; 377-7010, Fax 743-1686, 800-528-1234) 122 rooms, restaurant, indoor heated pool, exercise center, whirlpools, sauna, children free with parents, A/C, NS rooms, in-room refrigerators, airport transportation, TV, laundry facilities, wheelchair access, pets OK, senior rates, meeting facilities, CC. SGL/DBL$45-$110.

Executive Inn (5010 West 6th St., 74074; 743-2570) 79 rooms, restaurant, pool, pets OK, A/C, TV, NS rooms, wheelchair access, CC. SGL/DBL$38-$45.

Holiday Inn (2515 West 6th Ave., 74074; 372-0800, Fax 377-8212, 800-HOLIDAY) 141 rooms and suites, restaurant, lounge, pool, exercise center, children under 19 free with parents, wheelchair access, A/C, airport transportation, game room, TV, NS rooms, fax, room service, no pets, laundry service, meeting facilities, senior rates, CC. SGL/DBL$45-$120.

Motel 6 (5122 West 6th Ave., 74074; 624-0433, 891-6161) 121 rooms, pool, free local calls, children under 17 free with parents, NS rooms, wheelchair access, pets OK, A/C, TV, CC. SGL/DBL$36-$40.

Stroud
Area Code 918

Best Western Inn (1200 North 8th Ave., 74079; 968-9515, 800-528-1234) 44 rooms, restaurant, pool, exercise center, children free with parents, A/C, NS rooms, TV, laundry facilities, wheelchair access, pets OK, meeting facilities, senior rates, CC. SGL/DBL$35-$44.

Sulphur
Area Code 405

Chickasaw Motor Inn (Sulphur 73086; 622-2156) 71 rooms, restaurant, pool, no pets, A/C, TV, NS rooms, wheelchair access, meeting facilities, senior rates, CC. SGL/DBL$30-$40.

Super 8 Motel (2110 West Broadway, 73086; 622-6500, 800-800-8000) 40 rooms and suites, restaurant, laundry facilities, pets OK, children under 12 free with parents, free local calls, A/C, TV, in-room refrigerators and microwaves, fax, NS rooms, senior rates, wheelchair access, meeting facilities, CC. SGL/DBL$32-$42.

Tahlequah
Area Code 918

Tahlequah Motor Lodge (2501 South Muskogee, 74464; 456-2350, Fax 456-4580) 53 rooms, restaurant, pool, A/C, TV, NS rooms, no pets, wheelchair access, meeting facilities, senior rates, CC. SGL/DBL$32-$52.

Tonkawa
Area Code 405

Western Inn (Tonkawa 74653; 628-2577) 17 rooms, restaurant, A/C, TV, NS rooms, pets OK, wheelchair access, CC. SGL/DBL$28-$35.

Tulsa

Area Code 918

Downtown Tulsa

Adam's Mark Hotel (100 East Second St., 74103; 582-9000, Fax 560-2232, 800-444-ADAM) 450 rooms and suites, restaurant, lounge, indoor and outdoor pools, exercise center, hot tub, 24-hour room service, gift shop, laundry service, airport courtesy car, 15 meeting rooms, 9,216 square feet of meeting and exhibition space, meeting facilities for 1,300, A/C, TV, CC. Near the Convention Center, 8 miles from the airport. SGL/DBL$105-$125.

DoubleTree Hotel Downtown (616 West Seventh St., 74127; 587-8000, Fax 587-1642, 800-828-7447) 418 rooms and suites, 2 restaurants, lounge, spa, whirlpools, sauna, exercise center, airport courtesy car, business service, room service, 13 meeting rooms, meeting facilities for 1,300, A/C, TV, CC. Near the Tulsa Convention Center, 12 miles from the airport. SGL/DBL$125-$145.

Doubletree Hotel Downtown (6110 South Yale Ave., 74136; 495-1000, Fax 495-1944, 800-528-0444) 371 rooms and suites, Executive Floor, 2 restaurants, lounge, indoor pool, sauna, whirlpools, jogging trail, room service, children under 12 free with parents, NS rooms, airport courtesy car, 26 meeting rooms, meeting facilities for 950, A/C, TV, CC. 20 minutes from the airport. SGL/DBL$134-$144.

Howard Johnson Hotel (17 West 7th St., 74119; 585-5898, 800-I-GO-HOJO) 200 rooms, restaurant, lounge, pool, children free with parents, wheelchair access, NS rooms, TV, A/C, no pets, room service, laundry facilities, senior rates, meeting facilities, CC. SGL/DBL$32-$80.

Ramada Inn Riverview (7900 South Lewis Ave., 74136; 492-5000, 800-228-2828, 800-272-6232) 300 rooms, Executive Floor, pool, tennis courts, exercise center, sauna, airport courtesy car, meeting facilities, A/C, TV, CC. SGL/DBL$73-$135.

Sheraton Kensington Hotel (1902 East 71st St., 74136; 493-7000, Fax 481-7147, 800-325-3535) 383 rooms, restaurant, 2 lounges, indoor pool, jacuzzi, exercise center, jogging track, 6 lighted tennis courts, wheelchair access, NS rooms, airport courtesy car, 12 meeting rooms, 34,000 square feet of meeting and exhibition space, meeting facilities for 1,500, A/C, TV, CC. Near the Kensington Galleria Shopping area, 5 miles from the Convention Center, 15 miles from the airport. SGL/DBL$68-$95.

Airport Area

Best Western Roadside Inn (7475 East Admiral Place, 74115; 836-8101, 800-528-1234) 100 rooms, pool, exercise center, sauna, airport courtesy car, meeting facilities, A/C, TV, CC. SGL/DBL$54-$68.

Days Inn (1016 North Garnett Rd., 74116; 438-5050, Fax 438-8314, 800-325-2525) 98 rooms, restaurant, children under 12 free with parents, cable TV, free local calls, pets OK, wheelchair access/rooms, NS rooms, A/C, meeting facilities, CC. 4 miles from the airport. SGL/DBL$26-$38.

Days Inn (8201 East Skelly Dr., 74129; 665-6800, Fax 665-6800 ext 108) 192 rooms and suites, free breakfast, pool, saunas, in-room refrigerators, wheelchair access, NS rooms, children free with parents, A/C, TV, airport transportation, kitchenettes, meeting facilities, CC. SGL/DBL$38-$55.

Holiday Inn Airport (8181 East Skelly Dr., 74129; 663-4541, Fax 665-7109, 800-HOLIDAY) 211 rooms, restaurant, lounge, entertainment, pool, whirlpools, exercise center, children under 12 free with parents, wheelchair access, NS rooms, fax, room service, gift shop, airport transportation, meeting facilities for 250, A/C, TV, CC. 7 miles from the downtown area. SGL/DBL$65-$75.

Holiday Inn Airport (1010 North Garnett, 74116; 437-7660, Fax 438-7538, 800-HOLIDAY) 158 rooms and suites, restaurant, lounge, indoor pool, children under 12 free with parents, wheelchair access, NS rooms, fax, room service, airport transportation, meeting facilities for 400, A/C, TV, CC. 9 miles from the downtown area, 2 miles from the Raceway. SGL/DBL$64-$85.

La Quinta Inn Airport (35 North Sheridan Rd., 74115; 836-3931, Fax 836-5428, 800-531-5900) 101 rooms, restaurant, lounge, heated pool, complimentary newspaper, free local calls, fax, laundry service, NS rooms, wheelchair access, A/C, TV, meeting facilities, CC. 4 miles from the Civic Center, Fairgrounds and downtown area, 3 miles from the airport. SGL/DBL$48-$68.

Quality Inn Airport (222 North Garnett Rd., 74116; 438-0780, 800-221-2222) 118 rooms and suites, restaurant, lounge, entertainment, pool, exercise center, children free with parents, A/C, TV, room service, laundry service, NS rooms, meeting facilities, senior rates, CC. SGL/DBL$40-$49.

Sheraton Inn Airport (2201 North 77th East Ave., 74115; 835-9911, Fax 8382452, 800-325-3535) 170 rooms and suites, 2 restaurants, lounge, outdoor pool, sauna, exercise center, NS rooms, wheelchair access, complimentary airport transportation, 9 meeting rooms, 7,200 square feet of meeting and exhibition space, meeting facilities for 800, A/C, TV, CC. Near the Tulsa Fairgrounds, 8 miles from the downtown area, .5 miles from the airport. SGL/DBL$75$95, STS$105.

Super 8 Motel (6616 East Archer St., 74115; 836-1981, Fax 836-1981 ext 7, 800-800-8000) 55 rooms and suites, outdoor pool, no pets, wheelchair access, NS rooms, fax, free local calls, A/C, TV, CC. 5 miles from the downtown area. SGL/DBL$32-$45.

Other Locations

Best Western Trade Winds East Inn (3337 East Skelly Dr., 74135; 743-7931, Fax 749-6312, 800-528-1234) 158 rooms, restaurant, lounge, entertainment, pool, cable TV, airport courtesy car, fax, children under 12 free with parents, NS rooms, A/C, CC. SGL/DBL$55-$73.

Camelot Hotel (4956 South Peoria Ave., 74105; 747-8811) 330 rooms, Executive Floor, pool, exercise center, sauna, airport courtesy car, meeting facilities, A/C, TV, CC. SGL/DBL$85-$125.

Comfort Inn (4717 South Yale Ave., 74135; 622-6776, Fax 622-1809, 800-235-8937, 800-221-2222) 109 rooms, restaurant, free breakfast, pool, wheelchair access, NS rooms, no pets, children under 18 free with parents, A/C, TV, meeting facilities, senior rates, CC. SGL/DBL$39-$45.

Days Inn (5525 West Skelly Dr., 74107; 446-1561, 800-325-2525) 96 rooms and suites, restaurant, lounge, outdoor pool, children free with parents, room service, laundry service, A/C, TV, free local calls, pets OK, fax, wheelchair access, NS rooms, senior rates, CC. SGL/DBL$32-$50.

Econo Lodge (11620 East Skelley Dr., 74128; 437-9200, 800-4-CHOICE) 80 rooms, restaurant, lounge, free breakfast, indoor and outdoor pool, whirlpools, children under 12 free with parents, no pets, NS rooms, wheelchair access, A/C, TV, meeting facilities, senior rates, CC. SGL/DBL$29-$50.

Embassy Suites (3332 South 79th East Ave., 74145; 622-4000, 800-362-2779) 248 suites, pool, exercise center, sauna, airport courtesy car, meeting facilities, A/C, TV, CC. SGL/DBL$69-$135.

Hampton Inn (3209 South 79th Ave., 74145; 663-1000, Fax 663-0587, 800-HAMPTON) 148 rooms, restaurant, free breakfast, pool, exercise center, children under 18 free with parents, NS rooms, wheelchair access, in-room computer hookups, fax, TV, A/C, free local calls, pets OK, meeting facilities, CC. SGL/DBL$55-$65.

Hawthorne Suites (3509 South 79th East Ave., 74145; 663-3900, Fax 663-3900, 800-527-1133) 131 suites, free breakfast, pool, exercise center, sauna, airport courtesy car, pets OK, wheelchair access, complimentary newspaper, airport transportation, meeting facilities, A/C, TV, CC. 10 miles from the downtown area, 5 miles from the airport and University of Tulsa. SGL/DBL$85-$95.

Holiday Inn (3131 East 51st St., 74105; 743-9811, Fax 743-6599, 800-HOLI-DAY) 117 rooms, restaurant, lounge, heated indoor pool, sauna, exercise center, children under 12 free with parents, wheelchair access, NS rooms, fax, room service, free local calls, airport transportation, no pets, meeting facilities for 125, A/C, TV, CC. 4 miles from the Fairgrounds, 3.5 miles from Expo Square, 4.5 miles from Fairmeadows. SGL/DBL$68-$78.

La Quinta Inn South (12525 East 52nd St. South, 74146; 254-1626, Fax 252-3408, 800-531-5900) 129 rooms, restaurant, lounge, heated pool, complimentary newspaper, free local calls, fax, laundry service, NS rooms, wheelchair access, meeting facilities, A/C, TV, CC. 3 miles from the Eastland Mall and Outlet Mall, 11 miles from the downtown area and Civic Center, 10 miles from the airport. SGL/DBL$40-$60.

La Quinta Inn (10829 East 41st St., 74146; 665-0220, Fax 664-4810, 800-531-5900) 115 rooms, free breakfast, pool, whirlpools, airport courtesy car, pets OK, wheelchair access, NS rooms, children free with parents, meeting facilities, A/C, TV, CC. SGL/DBL$43-$58.

Lexington Hotel Suites (8525 East 41st St., 74145; 627-0030, Fax 627-0587) 162 suites, free breakfast, pool, airport courtesy car, laundry service, wheelchair access, NS rooms, children free with parents, meeting facilities, A/C, TV, CC. SGL/DBL$40-$70.

Marriott Hotel (10918 East 41st St., 74146; 627-5000, 800-228-9290) 336 rooms and suites, restaurant, lounge, pool, exercise center, sauna, whirlpools, game room, gift shop, airport courtesy car, A/C, TV, NS rooms, wheelchair access, senior rates, meeting facilities, A/C, TV, CC. SGL/DBL$55-$75.

Motel 6 East (1011 South Garnett Rd., 74128; 234-6200, 891-6161) 153 rooms, pool, free local calls, children under 17 free with parents, NS rooms, wheelchair access, pets OK, A/C, TV, CC. SGL/DBL$35-$48.

Motel 6 West (5828 West Skelly Dr., 74107; 4450-223, 891-6161) 155 rooms, pool, free local calls, children under 17 free with parents, NS rooms, wheelchair access, pets OK, A/C, TV, CC. SGL/DBL$38-$45.

Ramada Inn (5000 East Skelly Dr., 74135; 622-6000, Fax 664-9353, 800-2-RAMADA) 320 rooms and suites, restaurant, lounge, entertainment, outdoor heated pool, wheelchair access, NS rooms, pets OK, A/C, TV, children under 18 free with parents, gift shop, beauty shop, airport courtesy car, room service, laundry facilities, meeting facilities, senior rates, CC. SGL/DBL$50-$106.

Quality Inn (6030 East Skelly Dr., 74135; 665-2630, 800-221-2222) 131 rooms, restaurant, free breakfast, pool, exercise center, children free with parents, A/C, TV, room service, laundry service, NS rooms, meeting facilities, senior rates, CC. SGL/DBL$41-$58.

Residence Inn (8181 East 41st St. South, 74145; 6647241, 800-331-3131) 136 rooms and suites, free breakfast, in-room refrigerators, coffee makers and microwaves, laundry facilities, TV, A/C, VCRs, pets OK, complimentary newspaper, fireplaces, children free with parents, NS rooms, wheelchair access, meeting facilities, CC. SGL/DBL$85-$119.

Shangri La Resort (Route 3, 74331; 257-4204, 800-331-4060) 500 rooms and cottages, restaurant, lounge, tennis courts, golf course, pool, exercise center, sauna, airport courtesy car, meeting facilities. SGL$75, DBL$85-$135.

Skyline East (6333 East Skeely Dr., 74135; 927-1000) 270 rooms, pool, exercise center, sauna, airport courtesy car, meeting facilities. SGL/DBL$45.

Super 8 Motel (11521 East Skelly Dr., 74128; 438-7700, 800-800-8000) 112 rooms and suites, restaurant, outdoor pool, laundry facilities, no pets, children under 12 free with parents, free local calls, A/C, TV, in-room refrigerators and microwaves, fax, NS rooms, senior rates, wheelchair access, meeting facilities, CC. SGL/DBL$29-$37.

Super 8 Motel (1347 East Skelly Dr., 74150; 743-4431, Fax 743-2661, 800-800-8000) 60 rooms, restaurant, outdoor pool, no pets, wheelchair access/rooms, NS rooms, fax, free local calls, A/C, TV, CC. 1 mile from the downtown area. SGL/DBL$33-$50.

Travelers Inn (I-44 and 193rd East Ave., 74145; 266-7000, 800-633-8300) 117 rooms, pool, free local calls, NS rooms, wheelchair access, meeting facilities, A/C, TV, CC. 4 miles from the downtown area, 10 miles from Phoenix Sky Harbor International Airport and State Capital Building. SGL/DBL$25-$35.

Travelers Inn (I-44 and 49th West Ave., 74107; 446-6000, 800-633-8300) 125 rooms and suites, pool, free local calls, NS rooms, wheelchair access, meeting facilities, A/C, TV, CC. 6 miles from the downtown area, 10 minutes from the Fairgrounds. SGL$22, DBL$28.

Vinita
Area Code 918

Park Hills Motel (Vinita 74301; 256-5511) 21 rooms and 1- and 2-bedroom efficiencies, A/C, TV, NS rooms, wheelchair access, pets OK, CC. SGL/DBL$20-$28.

Wagoner
Area Code 918

Indian Lodge Motel (Wagoner 74467; 485-3184) 25 rooms and efficiencies, pool, A/C, TV, NS rooms, wheelchair access. SGL/DBL$45-$70.

Super 8 Motel (805 South Dewey St., 74467; 485-4818, 800-800-8000) 40 rooms and suites, restaurant, pets OK, children under 12 free with parents, free local calls, A/C, TV, in-room refrigerators and microwaves, fax, NS rooms, senior rates, wheelchair access, meeting facilities, CC. SGL/DBL$30-$45.

Western Hills Ranch (Wagoner 74467; 772-2545, 800-654-8240) 142 rooms and 1- and 2-bedroom cottages, restaurant, lounge, entertainment, pool, lighted tennis courts, A/C, TV, NS rooms, wheelchair access, children free with parents, gift shop, room service, no pets, meeting facilities, senior rates, CC. SGL/DBL$65-$175.

Watonga
Area Code 405

Roman Nose Resort (Watonga 73772; 623-7281, Fax 623-2538) 57 rooms, suites and cottages, restaurant, pool, tennis courts, A/C, TV, NS rooms, wheelchair access, pets OK, senior rates, CC. SGL/DBL$50-$65.

Weatherford
Area Code 405

Best Western Mark Motor Hotel (525 East Main St., 73096; 772-3325, 800-528-1234) 59 rooms, restaurant, pool, exercise center, children free with parents, A/C, NS rooms, TV, laundry facilities, wheelchair access, airport transportation, pets OK, meeting facilities, senior rates, CC. SGL/DBL$32-$45.

Days Inn (1019 East Main St., 73096; 772-5592, 800-325-2525) 70 rooms and suites, free breakfast, outdoor pool, children free with parents, room service, laundry service, A/C, TV, free local calls, pets OK, fax, wheelchair access, NS rooms, senior rates, CC. SGL/DBL$35-$50.

Econo Lodge (I-40 and Hwy. 54, 73096; 772-7711, 800-4-CHOICE) 44 rooms, restaurant, pool, children under 12 free with parents, no pets, NS rooms, wheelchair access, A/C, TV, senior rates, CC. SGL/DBL$27-$41.

Travel Inn (3401 East Main St., 73096; 772-6238) 25 rooms, A/C, TV, NS rooms, wheelchair access, CC. SGL/DBL$22-$25.

Webbers Falls
Area Code 918

Super 8 Motel (I-40 and Hwy. 100, 74470; 464-2272, 800-800-8000) 40 rooms and suites, restaurant, pets OK, children under 12 free with parents, free local calls, A/C, TV, in-room refrigerators and microwaves, fax, NS rooms, senior rates, wheelchair access, meeting facilities, CC. SGL/DBL$30-$45.

Woodward
Area Code 405

Hospitality Inn (4120 Williams Ave., 73801; 254-2964) 60 rooms and efficiencies, free breakfast, pool, A/C, TV, NS rooms, wheelchair access, pets OK, meeting facilities, CC. SGL/DBL$25-$36.

Northwest Inn (Woodward 73801; 256-7600, Fax 254-2274, 800-727-7606) 123 rooms, restaurant, lounge, entertainment, pool, exercise center, game room, in-room refrigerators, A/C, TV, NS rooms, wheelchair access, pets OK, CC. SGL/DBL$40-$50.

Yukon
Area Code 405

Comfort Inn West (321 North Mustang Rd., 73099; 324-1000, 800-221-2222) 108 rooms, restaurant, free breakfast, pool, wheelchair access, NS rooms, no pets, children under 18 free with parents, A/C, TV, meeting facilities, senior rates, CC. SGL/DBL$41-$59.

Texas

Abilene
Area Code 915

Best Western Inn (3950 Ridgemont Dr., 79606; 695-1262, 800-528-1234) 61 rooms, restaurant, pool, exercise center, children free with parents, A/C, NS rooms, TV, laundry facilities, in-room refrigerators and coffee makers, wheelchair access, pets OK, meeting facilities, senior rates, CC. SGL/DBL$45-$50.

Best Western Inn (3210 Pine St., 79601; 677-2683, 800-528-1234) 105 rooms, restaurant, pool, exercise center, children free with parents, A/C, NS rooms, TV, laundry facilities, VCRs, wheelchair access, pets OK, meeting facilities, senior rates, CC. SGL/DBL$36-$50.

Econo Lodge (1633 West Stamford 79601; 673-5424, 800-4-CHOICE) 34 rooms, pool, children under 12 free with parents, no pets, NS rooms, wheelchair access, A/C, TV, senior rates, CC. SGL/DBL$26-$40.

Embassy Suites (4250 Ridgemont Dr., 79606; 698-1234, Fax 698-2771, 800-EMBASSY) 176 2-room suites, restaurant, lounge, free breakfast, lounge, entertainment, heated pool, whirlpool, exercise center, sauna, room service, laundry service, wheelchair access, complimentary newspaper, free local calls, pets OK, NS rooms, gift shop, local transportation, meeting facilities, senior rates, CC. SGL/DBL$85-$95.

Executive Inn (1702 East I-20, 79601; 672-6433, Fax 676-0105) 98 rooms, pool, VCRs, A/C, TV, NS rooms, wheelchair access, children free with parents, no pets, senior rates, CC. SGL/DBL$38-$50.

Holiday Inn (1625 Hwy. 351, 79601; 673-5271, Fax 673-8240, 800-HOLI-DAY) 160 rooms, exercise center, children under 19 free with parents, wheelchair access, A/C, TV, NS rooms, fax, room service, airport transportation, pets OK, laundry service, meeting facilities, senior rates, CC. SGL/DBL$45-$56.

Kiva Motel (5403 South 1st St., 79605; 695-2150) 201 rooms and suites, restaurant, lounge, indoor and outdoor pools, whirlpools tubs, sauna, A/C, pets OK, room service, in-room refrigerators, TV, NS rooms, wheelchair access, meeting facilities, senior rates, CC. SGL/DBL$50-$125.

Ramada Inn (3450 South Clack, 79606; 695-7700, Fax 698-0546, 800-2-RAMADA) 148 rooms and suites, restaurant, lounge, entertainment, pool, wheelchair access, NS rooms, pets OK, A/C, TV, children under 18 free with parents, room service, laundry facilities, 3 meeting rooms, meeting facilities for 250, senior rates, CC. SGL/DBL$50-$69.

Red Carpet Inn (2202 I-20, 79603; 677-2463, 800-251-1962) 46 rooms, restaurant, lounge, pool, whirlpools, children free with parents, TV, A/C, NS rooms, gift shop, free local calls, laundry facilities, pets OK, meeting facilities, senior rates, CC. SGL/DBL$33-$45.

Royal Inn (5695 South 1st St., 79605; 692-3022, 800-588-4386) 150 rooms and suites, restaurant, lounge, entertainment, pool, A/C, TV, NS rooms, wheelchair access, pets OK, room service, meeting facilities, senior rates, CC. SGL/DBL$30-$45.

Super 8 Motel (I-20 and Hwy. 351, 79601; 673-5251, 800-800-8000) 96 rooms and suites, no pets, children under 12 free with parents, free local calls, A/C, TV, in-room refrigerators and microwaves, fax, NS rooms, senior rates, wheelchair access, meeting facilities, CC. SGL/DBL$36-$47.

Addison

Area Code 214

Courtyard by Marriott (4165 Proton Dr., 75244; 490-7390, 800-331-3131) 145 rooms and suites, free breakfast, in-room refrigerators, coffee makers and microwaves, laundry facilities, TV, A/C, VCRs, laundry facilities, pets OK, complimentary newspaper, fireplaces, children free with parents, NS rooms, wheelchair access, meeting facilities, CC. SGL/DBL$48-$90.

Hampton Inn (4555 Beltway, 75244; 991-2800, Fax 991-7691, 800-HAMP-TON) 160 rooms, restaurant, free breakfast, pool, exercise center, children under 18 free with parents, NS rooms, wheelchair access, in-room computer hookups, fax, TV, A/C, free local calls, pets OK, meeting facilities, CC. SGL/DBL$55-$63.

Harvey Hotel (14315 Midway Rd., 75244; 980-8877, Fax 788-2758) 420 rooms and suites, restaurant, lounge, pool, exercise center, whirlpools, children free with parents, A/C, TV, NS rooms, wheelchair access, in-room refrigerators and coffee makers, local transportation, pets OK, laundry facilities, meeting facilities, senior rates, CC. SGL/DBL$55-$120.

Holiday Inn North Dallas (4099 Valley View Rd., 75244; 395-9000, Fax 788-1174, 800-HOLIDAY) 298 rooms and suites, restaurant, lounge, whirlpool, exercise center, children free with parents, wheelchair access, NS rooms, A/C, TV, fax, room service, airport transportation, gift shop, meeting facilities for 1,000, CC. SGL/DBL$65-$85.

Homewood Suites (4451 Belt Line Rd., 75244; 788-1342, 800-CALL-HOME) 120 1 and 2-bedroom suites, free breakfast, pool, whirlpools, exercise center, in-room refrigerators, coffee makers and microwaves, fireplace, fax, pets OK, TV, pets OK, A/C, complimentary newspaper, VCRs, NS rooms, wheelchair access, senior rates, meeting facilities, CC. SGL/DBL$70-$100.

Marriott Hotel (14901 Dallas Pkwy., 75240; 661-2800, Fax 934-1731, 800-331-3131) 547 rooms and suites, free breakfast, in-room refrigerators, coffee makers and microwaves, laundry facilities, TV, A/C, VCRs, pets OK, complimentary newspaper, fireplaces, children free with parents, NS rooms, wheelchair access, meeting facilities, CC. SGL/DBL$80-$135.

Ramada Limited (4151 Beltway, 75244; 233-2525, Fax 404-8066, 800-2-RAMADA) 78 rooms and suites, restaurant, lounge, pool, wheelchair access, NS rooms, pets OK, A/C, TV, children under 18 free with parents, airport transportation, room service, laundry facilities, meeting facilities, senior rates, CC. SGL/DBL$40-$60.

Alice

Area Code 512

Days Inn (555 North Johnson, 78332; 664-6616, Fax 664-8016, 800-325-2525) 97 rooms and suites, restaurant, free breakfast, children free with parents, room service, laundry service, A/C, TV, free local calls, pets OK, fax, wheelchair access, NS rooms, senior rates, CC. SGL/DBL$35-$41.

Kings Inn (815 Hwy. 281 South, 78332; 664-4351) 103 rooms, restaurant, lounge, pool, in-room refrigerators and microwaves, children free with parents, pets OK, A/C, TV, NS rooms, wheelchair access, meeting facilities, CC. SGL/DBL$30-$35.

Alpine
Area Code 915

Sunday House Inn (Alpine 79830; 837-3363) 80 rooms, restaurant, pool, A/C, TV, NS rooms, wheelchair access, pets OK, airport courtesy car, meeting facilities, CC. SGL/DBL$35-$44.

Alvin
Area Code 713

Homeplace Inn (1588 South Hwy. 35 Bypass, 77511; 331-0335, Fax 585-3352) 40 rooms, pool, laundry facilities, A/C, TV, NS rooms, wheelchair access, pets OK, children free with parents, laundry facilities, in-room refrigerators, VCRs, CC. SGL/DBL$36-$45.

Amarillo
Area Code 806

AmeriSuites (6800 I-40 West, 79106; 358-7943, 800-833-1516) 126 suites, free breakfast, pool, exercise center, A/C, TV, wheelchair access, children free with parents, kitchenettes, complimentary newspaper, NS rooms, laundry facilities, in-room refrigerators and microwaves, meeting facilities, CC. SGL/DBL$68-$80.

Best Western Inn (1610 Coulter Dr., 79106; 358-7861, 800-528-1234) 103 rooms, restaurant, indoor heated pool, exercise center, whirlpools, children free with parents, A/C, NS rooms, TV, laundry facilities, wheelchair access, no pets, in-room refrigerators, microwaves and coffee makers, meeting facilities, senior rates, CC. SGL/DBL$50-$65.

Big Texan Motel (7701 I-40, 79120; 372-5000) 55 rooms, restaurant, heated pool, whirlpools, sauna, children free with parents, laundry facilities, pets OK, A/C, TV, NS rooms, wheelchair access, CC. SGL/DBL$40-$50.

Comfort Inn Airport (1515 I-40 East, 79102; 376-9993, 800-221-2222) 112 rooms, free breakfast, pool, wheelchair access, NS rooms, no pets, children under 18 free with parents, A/C, TV, meeting facilities, senior rates, CC. SGL/DBL$45-$91.

Days Inn (Ross-Osage St., 79102; 379-6255, Fax 379-8204, 800-325-2525) 119 rooms and suites, free breakfast, outdoor pool, children free with parents, room service, laundry service, A/C, TV, free local calls, pets OK, fax, wheelchair access, NS rooms, meeting facilities for 85, senior rates, CC. SGL/DBL$42-$65.

Econo Lodge (2801 I-40 West, 79109; 355-9171, 800-4-CHOICE) 118 rooms, restaurant, lounge, entertainment, pool, children under 12 free with parents, no pets, NS rooms, wheelchair access, A/C, TV, senior rates, CC. SGL/DBL$31-$46.

Fifth Season Inn (6801 I-40 West, 79106; 358-7881) 237 rooms and suites, restaurant, lounge, entertainment, indoor heated pool, whirlpools, sauna, A/C, TV, NS rooms, wheelchair access, in-room refrigerators, no pets, children free with parents, airport transportation, CC. SGL/DBL$50-$150.

Friendship Inn (6005 Amarillo Blvd. West, 79106; 355-3321, 800-424-4777) 27 rooms, pool, exercise center, A/C, TV, no pets, NS rooms, children free with parents, wheelchair access, senior rates, CC. SGL/DBL$26-$38.

Hampton Inn (1700 I-40 East, 79103; 372-1425, Fax 379-8807, 800-HAMPTON) 116 rooms, restaurant, free breakfast, pool, exercise center, children under 18 free with parents, NS rooms, wheelchair access, in-room computer hookups, fax, TV, A/C, free local calls, pets OK, meeting facilities, CC. SGL/DBL$40-$56.

Harvey Hotel (3100 I-40 West, 79102; 358-6161) 265 rooms, restaurant, free breakfast, lounge, entertainment, pool, whirlpools, exercise center, A/C, TV, in-room refrigerators, pets OK, airport transportation, NS rooms, wheelchair access, meeting facilities, senior rates, CC. SGL/DBL$70-$75.

Holiday Inn (1191 Ross Osage St., 79102; 372-8741, Fax 372-214, 800-HOLIDAY) 247 rooms and suites, restaurant, lounge, indoor pool, exercise center, whirlpools, sauna, jacuzzis, airport transportation, game room, children under 19 free with parents, wheelchair access, A/C, TV, NS rooms, fax, room service, no pets, laundry service, meeting facilities, senior rates, CC. SGL/DBL$65-$85.

Super 8 Motel (I-40 and Lakeside Dr., 79101; 335-2836, 800-800-8000) 80 rooms and suites, restaurant, no pets, children under 12 free with parents, free local calls, A/C, TV, in-room refrigerators and microwaves, fax, NS rooms, senior rates, wheelchair access, meeting facilities, CC. SGL/DBL$35-$46.

TraveLodge East (3205 I-40 East, 79104; 372-8171, Fax 372-2815, 800-578-7878) 96 rooms, restaurant, lounge, pool, wheelchair access, complimentary newspaper, laundry service, TV, A/C, free local calls, fax, NS rooms, in-room refrigerators and microwaves, children under 18 free with parents, no pets, meeting facilities for 200, CC. SGL/DBL$40-$55.

TraveLodge West (2035 Paramount Blvd., 79109; 353-3541, Fax 353-0201, 800-578-7878) 100 rooms, restaurant, lounge, pool, exercise center, wheelchair access, complimentary newspaper, laundry service, TV, A/C, free local calls, fax, NS rooms, in-room refrigerators and microwaves, children under 18 free with parents, no pets, meeting facilities for 35, CC. SGL/DBL$20-$48.

Anthony
Area Code 915

Super 8 Motel (100 Park North Dr., 79821; 886-2888, 800-800-8000) 49 rooms and suites, no pets, children under 12 stay free with parents, free local calls, A/C, TV, in-room refrigerators and microwaves, fax, NS rooms, pets OK, senior rates, wheelchair access, meeting facilities, CC. SGL/DBL$38-$46.

Aransas Pass
Area Code 512

Days Inn (410 Goodnight Ave., 78336; 758-7375, Fax 758-8105, 800-325-2525) 32 rooms and suites, free breakfast, children free with parents, room service, laundry service, A/C, TV, free local calls, pets OK, game room, fax, wheelchair access, NS rooms, senior rates, CC. SGL/DBL$50-$150.

Homeport Inn (1515 Wheeler Ave., 78336; 758-3213) 63 rooms, pool, whirlpools, A/C, TV, NS rooms, wheelchair access, children free with parents, pets OK, senior rates, CC. SGL/DBL$31-$37.

Arlington
Area Code 817

Best Western Great Southwest (3501 East Division St., 76011; 640-7722, 640-9043, 800-528-1234) 122 rooms, restaurant, pool, jacuzzi, pets OK, NS rooms, A/C, TV, wheelchair access, laundry service, airport courtesy car, meeting facilities, CC. SGL$38-$48, DBL$48-$60.

Charlie Club Fitness Center and Hotel (117 South Watson, 76011; 633-4000) 192 rooms and suites, 15 meeting rooms, 4,200 square feet of meeting and exhibition space, meeting facilities for 200, CC. SGL$55, DBL$63.

Comfort Inn (1601 East Division, 76011; 261-2300, 800-221-2222) 156 rooms and apartments, restaurant, lounge, pool, exercise center, wheelchair access, NS rooms, A/C, TV, meeting facilities, CC. SGL/DBL$44-$55.

Courtyard by Marriott (1500 West Stadium Dr., 76011; 277-2774, 800-321-2211) 145 rooms, restaurant, indoor and outdoor pool, exercise center, jacuzzi, in-room refrigerators and coffee makers, A/C, TV, no pets, 2 meeting rooms, 600 square feet of meeting and exhibition space, meeting facilities for 100, senior rates, CC. SGL/DBL$72-$82.

Courtyard by Marriott (2201 Airport Freeway, 76021; 267-3737, Fax 545-2319, 800-321-2211) 145 rooms, restaurant, lounge, heated pool, jacuzzi, laundry service, children free with parents, wheelchair access, NS rooms, A/C, TV, in-room refrigerators, meeting facilities, CC. SGL/DBL$88-$135.

Days Inn (1195 North Watson Rd., 76011; 649-0147, 800-325-2525) 124 rooms, pool, meeting facilities, A/C, TV, NS rooms, wheelchair access, children free with parents, CC. SGL/DBL$35-$55.

Fairfield Inn (2500 East Lamar, 76006; 640-1808) 109 rooms, A/C, TV, NS rooms, wheelchair access, no pets, children free with parents, CC. SGL/DBL$55-$68.

Flagship Inn (601 Ave. H East, 76011; 640-1666, 800-346-1666) 295 rooms and cottages, pool, airport courtesy car, A/C, TV, NS rooms, wheelchair access, children free with parents, CC. SGL$52, DBL$57.

Hampton Inn Arlington South (I-20 and Matlock Rd., 76018; 467-3535, Fax 467-5570, 800-HAMPTON) 142 rooms, free breakfast, pool, children free with parents, NS rooms, A/C, TV, wheelchair access, computer hookups, fax, free local calls, meeting facilities. SGL/DBL$65-$78.

Holiday Inn Great Southwest (Hwy. 360 and Brown Blvd., 76011; 640-7712, 800-465-4329) 237 rooms, restaurant, lounge, indoor and outdoor pools, tennis courts, exercise center, golf, airport transportation, wheelchair access, NS rooms, A/C, TV, 6 meeting rooms, 4,000 square feet of meeting and exhibition space, meeting facilities for 200, senior rates, CC. SGL$74, DBL$79.

Howard Johnson at Six Flags (903 North Collins St., 76011; 261-3621, 800-446-4656) 185 rooms, restaurant, lounge, entertainment, pool, exercise center, laundry service, NS rooms, A/C, TV, 4 meeting rooms, 2,700 square feet of meeting and exhibition space, meeting facilities for 200, CC. SGL$60, DBL$70.

Inn Townelodge (1181 North Watson Rd., 76006; 649-0993) 114 rooms, pool, in-room refrigerators and coffee makers, children free with parents, no pets, A/C, TV, NS rooms, wheelchair access, laundry facilities, senior rates, CC. SGL/DBL$50-$60.

Park Inn International (703 Benge Dr., 76013; 860-2323, 800-437-PARK) 60 rooms, restaurant, lounge, pool, A/C, TV, VCRs, complimentary newspaper, wheelchair access, NS rooms, pets OK, meeting facilities, senior rates, CC. SGL/DBL$35-$48.

Quality Inn Airport (1607 North Watson Rd., 76006; 640-4444, 800-221-2222) 178 rooms and suites, free breakfast, pool, sauna, whirlpool, exercise center, in-room refrigerators and microwaves, wheelchair access, NS-rooms, A/C, TV, local transportation, meeting facilities, CC. SGL/DBL$45-$65.

Radisson Suites (700 Ave. H East, 76011; 640-0400, 800-228-9822) 202 suites, pool, sauna, jacuzzi, A/C, TV, NS rooms, no pets, in-room refrigerators and coffee makers, wheelchair access, children free with parents, 5 meeting rooms, 3,000 square feet of meeting and exhibition space, meeting facilities for 220, CC. SGL/DBL$80-$119.

Ramada Inn (700 East Lamar Blvd., 76001; 265-7711, 800-272-6232) 175 rooms and suites, restaurant, lounge, pool, A/C, TV, NS rooms, wheelchair access, no pets, children free with parents, pets OK, 3,100 square feet of meeting and exhibition space, meeting facilities for 250, senior rates, CC. SGL/DBL$40-$77.

Sheraton Centre Park (1500 Stadium Dr. East, 76011; 261-8200, 800-325-3535) 320 rooms, pool, jacuzzi, exercise center, sauna, A/C, TV, room service, no pets, room service, gift shop, airline ticket desk, NS rooms, wheelchair access, 12 meeting rooms, 3,200 square feet of meeting and exhibition space, meeting facilities for 700, CC. SGL/DBL$82.

Athens
Area Code 903

Best Western Inn and Suites (Athens 75751; 675-9214, Fax 675-5963, 800-528-1234) 80 rooms, restaurant, lounge, entertainment, pool, exercise center, children free with parents, A/C, NS rooms, TV, laundry facilities, wheelchair access, pets OK, meeting facilities, senior rates, CC. SGL/DBL$35-$48.

Spanish Trace Inn (716 East Tyler St., 75751; 675-5173, 800-488-5173) 80 rooms and suites, restaurant, lounge, A/C, TV, NS rooms, pets OK, children free with parents, room service, wheelchair access, meeting facilities, senior rates, CC. SGL/DBL$40-$50.

Atlanta
Area Code 903

Best Western Inn (801 Loop 59N, 75551; 796-7121, 800-528-1234) 65 rooms, pool, exercise center, children free with parents, A/C, NS rooms, TV, laundry facilities, wheelchair access, pets OK, in-room coffee makers, meeting facilities, senior rates, CC. SGL/DBL$31-$42.

Butler's Inn (1100 West Main St., 75551; 796-8235) 58 rooms, pool, pets OK, in-room refrigerators, A/C, children free with parents, pets OK, TV, NS rooms, wheelchair access, CC. SGL/DBL$30-$38.

Austin
Area Code 512

Downtown Austin

Austin Creek (111 East First St., 78701; 478-9611) 287 rooms, pool, sauna, exercise center, airport courtesy car, meeting facilities, CC. SGL/DBL$65.

Driskill Hotel (604 Brazos St., 78701; 474-5911) 185 rooms, pool, sauna, exercise center, airport courtesy car, meeting facilities, CC. SGL/DBL$65.

Embassy Suites Downtown (300 South Congress Ave., 78704; 469-9000, Fax 480-9164, 800-362-2779) 127 2-room suites, restaurant, lounge, free breakfast, pool, sauna, whirlpools, exercise center, NS rooms, A/C, TV, gift shop, room service, laundry service, wheelchair access, airport courtesy car, meeting facilities. Near the Convention Center, 2 miles from the State Capital, 7 miles from the airport, CC. SGL/DBL$75-$125.

Four Seasons Hotel (98 San Jacinto Blvd., 78701; 478-4500, 800-332-3442) 308 rooms and suites, restaurant, lounge, pool, sauna, exercise center, airport courtesy car, meeting facilities, CC. SGL/DBL$165-$205.

Guest Quarters Suites (303 West 15th St., 78701; 478-7000, 800-429-2900) 191 1-bedroom suites, restaurant, pool, exercise center, sauna, whirlpools, TV, A/C, in-room refrigerators, local transportation, laundry service, fax, NS rooms, wheelchair access, meeting facilities, CC. SGL/DBL$139-$159.

Marriott Hotel at the Capitol (701 East 11th St., 78701; 478-1111, Fax 478-3700, 800-228-9290) 365 rooms and suites, restaurant, lounge, entertainment, indoor and outdoor pool, exercise center, whirlpools, sauna, game room, airport transportation, wheelchair access, TV, A/C, NS rooms, laundry service, gift shop, children free with parents, meeting facilities, senior rates, CC. SGL/DBL$85-$165.

Omni Hotel (700 San Jacinto, 78701; 476-3700, Fax 320-5882, 800-THE-OMNI) 324 rooms and suites, restaurant, lounge, entertainment, outdoor pool, sauna, exercise center, hot tub, laundry service, wheelchair access, NS rooms, A/C, TV, 21,900 square feet of meeting and exhibition space, senior rates, CC. SGL/DBL$70-$95, STS$100-$165.

Passport Inn University (3105 North I-35, 78722; 478-1631, 800-251-1962) pool, A/C, TV, NS rooms, wheelchair access, free local calls, children stay free with parents, pets OK, senior rates, CC. SGL/DBL$40-$72.

Quality Inn South (2200 South Interregional, 78704; 444-0561, 800-221-2222) 125 rooms, pool, whirlpools, sauna, exercise center, wheelchair access, NS rooms, meeting facilities. 7 miles from the airport, 2 miles from the Municipal Auditorium, CC. SGL/DBL$51-$66.

Ramada Inn South (1212 West Ben White Blvd., 78704; 447-0150, Fax 441-2051, 800-2-RAMADA) 107 rooms and suites, restaurant, lounge, pool, jacuzzi, children under 18 free with parents, wheelchair access, NS rooms, A/C, TV, airport transportation, meeting facilities for 200. 2 miles from the University of Texas, 4 miles from the State Capital, 8 miles from the airport, CC. SGL$60, DBL$60-$68, STS$115, X$8.

Airport Area

Best Western Chariot Inn (7300 I-35 North, 78752; 452-9371, 800-528-1234) 161 rooms, restaurant, lounge, children free with parents, NS rooms, A/C, TV, meeting facilities. 3 miles from the State Capital, CC. SGL$35-$47, DBL$39-$51, X$4.

Doubletree Hotel (6505 I-35 North, 78752; 454-3737, Fax 454-6915, 800-828-7447) 350 rooms and suites, Concierge Floor, restaurant, lounge, outdoor pool, whirlpools, sauna, room service, A/C, TV, room service, 14 meeting rooms, meeting facilities for 1,000. 10 minutes from the airport, CC. SGL/DBL$125-$138.

Econo Lodge North (820 East Anderson Lane, 78752; 835-4311, 800-4-CHOICE) 148 rooms, restaurant, free breakfast, pool, children under 12 free with parents, no pets, NS rooms, wheelchair access, A/C, TV, senior rates, CC. SGL/DBL$31-$53.

Embassy Suites Airport North (5901 I-35 North, 78723; 454-8004, Fax 454-9047, 800-EMBASSY) 165 2-room suites, restaurant, lounge, free breakfast, pool, sauna, whirlpools, exercise center, NS rooms, A/C, TV, gift shop, room service, laundry service, wheelchair access, airport courtesy car, meeting facilities. 4 miles from the airport, 5 miles from the State Capital, CC. SGL/DBL$69-$135.

Friendship Inn (6201 Hwy. 290 East, 78723; 458-4759, 800-424-4777) 48 rooms, restaurant, free breakfast, pool, exercise center, A/C, TV, no pets, NS rooms, children free with parents, wheelchair access, in-room refrigerators and microwaves, senior rates, CC. SGL/DBL$34-$54.

Hampton Inn North (7619 I35 North, 78752; 452-3300, Fax 452-3124, 800-HAMPTON) 122 rooms, free breakfast, pool, exercise center, children under 18 free with parents, NS rooms, A/C, TV, wheelchair access, computer hookups, fax, free local calls, meeting facilities. 1 mile from Highland Mall, 5 miles from the State Capital, 4 miles from the University of Texas, 4 miles from the airport, CC. SGL/DBL$55-$75.

Hawthorn Suites Central (935 La Posada Dr., 78752; 459-3335, Fax 467-9736, 800-527-1133) 71 suites, free breakfast, pool, exercise center, whirlpools, airport transportation, wheelchair access, NS rooms, A/C, TV, complimentary newspaper, laundry service, pets OK, meeting facilities for 50. 5 miles from the airport, CC. SGL/DBL$85-$95.

Hilton Hotel Airport (6000 Middle Fiskville Rd., 78752; 451-5757, Fax 467-7644, 800-HILTONS) 332 rooms and suites, restaurant, lounge, pool, airport courtesy car, NS rooms, A/C, TV, wheelchair access, concierge, meeting facilities for 900. 3 minutes from the airport, 5 miles from the downtown area and the University of Texas, CC. SGL/DBL$99-$129.

Holiday Inn Airport (6911 North Interregional Hwy., 78752; 459-4251, Fax 459-9274, 800-HOLIDAY) 293 rooms, restaurant, lounge, children under 12 free with parents, wheelchair access, NS rooms, A/C, TV, fax, room service, local transportation, meeting facilities for 100. Near Highland Mall, 5 miles from the downtown area and State Capital, CC. SGL/DBL$78-$109.

Hyatt Regency (208 Barton Springs, 78704; 477-1234, Fax 480-2069, 800-233-1234) 448 rooms and suites, restaurant, Regency Club Floor, lounge, entertainment, outdoor heated pool, whirlpools, jogging track, NS rooms, A/C, TV, complimentary newspaper, wheelchair access, 18 meeting rooms, 20,000 square feet of meeting and exhibition space. Near the Municipal Auditorium, 10 minutes from the airport, 6 minutes from the theater district, CC. SGL/DBL$134-$154.

La Quinta Inn (300 East 11th St., 78701; 476-7151, Fax 476-8503, 800-531-5900) 147 rooms, restaurant, free breakfast, lounge, pool, complimentary newspaper, free local calls, fax, laundry service, NS rooms, airport transportation, wheelchair access, TV, A/C, meeting facilities, CC. SGL/DBL$50-$66.

La Quinta Inn (7100 I-35 North, 78752; 452-9401, Fax 452-0856, 800-531-5900) 115 rooms, restaurant, free breakfast, lounge, pool, complimentary newspaper, free local calls, fax, laundry service, NS rooms, wheelchair access, TV, A/C, meeting facilities, CC. SGL/DBL$54-$68.

Sheraton Austin Hotel (500 I-35 North, 78701; 480-8181, Fax 482-0660, 800-325-3535) 246 rooms and suites, restaurant, lounge, entertainment, outdoor pool, hot tubs, exercise center, wheelchair access, NS rooms, A/C, TV, airport courtesy car, 4 meeting rooms, 4,000 square feet of meeting and exhibition space, meeting facilities for 150. Near the State Capital, the Convention Center and the entertainment district, 3 miles from the airport, CC. SGL/DBL$65-$95.

Other Locations

Barton Creek Club (8212 Barton Club Dr., 78735; 328-2500) 150 rooms, pool, sauna, exercise center, airport courtesy car, beauty shop, meeting facilities, CC. SGL/DBL$95-$115.

Best Western South (3909 I-35 South, 78741; 444-0532, Fax 445-4141, 800-528-1234) 180 rooms, restaurant, lounge, whirlpools, children free with parents, NS rooms, A/C, TV, wheelchair access, meeting facilities, CC. SGL$39-$49, DBL$42-$52, X$3.

Best Western Seville Plaza Inn (4323 I-35 South, 78744; 447-5511, Fax 4438055, 800-528-1234) 92 rooms and suites, restaurant, lounge, pool, children free with parents, NS rooms, A/C, TV, meeting facilities, CC. SGL$38-$50, DBL$45-$80, X$5.

Comfort Inn (7928 Gessner Dr., 78753; 339-7311, 800-221-2222) 125 rooms, restaurant, free breakfast, indoor pool, whirlpools, sauna, wheelchair access, NS rooms, A/C, TV, meeting facilities, CC. SGL/DBL$40-$67.

Holiday Inn Town Lake (20 North Interregional Hwy., 78741; 448-2444, Fax 448-4999, 800-HOLIDAY) 210 rooms, restaurant, lounge, entertainment, outdoor pool, spa, children under 12 free with parents, wheelchair access, NS rooms, A/C, TV, fax, room service, in-room refrigerators, pets OK, meeting facilities for 400, CC. SGL/DBL$68-$88.

Howard Johnson Plaza Hotel (7800 I35 North, 78753; 836-8520, Fax 837-0897, 800-800-I-GO-HOJO) 188 rooms, restaurant, free breakfast, lounge, pool, exercise center, spa, children under 12 free with parents, wheelchair access, NS rooms, A/C, TV, airport transportation, in-room refrigerators, meeting facilities for 350, CC. SGL/DBL$49-$86.

La Quinta Inn (1603 East Oltorf Blvd., 78741; 447-6661, Fax 447-1744, 800-531-5900) 104 rooms, restaurant, lounge, heated pool, complimentary newspaper, free local calls, fax, laundry service, NS rooms, A/C, TV, wheelchair access, meeting facilities, CC. SGL/DBL$43-$63.

La Quinta Inn (4200 I-35 South, 78745; 443-17747151, Fax 447-1555, 800-5315900) 130 rooms, restaurant, lounge, heated pool, complimentary newspaper, free local calls, fax, laundry service, NS rooms, A/C, TV, wheelchair access, meeting facilities, CC. SGL/DBL$40-$60.

La Quinta Inn Highland Mall (5812 I-35 North, 78751; 459-4381, Fax 452-3917, 800-531-5900) 122 rooms, restaurant, lounge, heated pool, complimentary newspaper, free local calls, fax, laundry service, NS rooms, A/C, TV, wheelchair access, meeting facilities, CC. SGL/DBL$43-$58.

Hawthorn Suites Northwest (8888 Tailwood Dr., 78759; 343-0008, Fax 343-6532, 800-527-1133) 103 suites, free breakfast, pool, whirlpools, laundry service, wheelchair access, NS rooms, A/C, TV, pets OK, airport transportation, meeting facilities for 50, CC. SGL/DBL$85-$95.

Ramada Inn Airport (5660 I-35 North, 78751; 458-2340, Fax 458-8525, 800-2RAMADA) 195 rooms, restaurant, free breakfast, lounge, pool, children under 18 free with parents, wheelchair access, NS rooms, A/C, TV, airport transportation, CC. SGL$77-$87, DBL$87-$97, STS$125, X$10.

Stouffer Hotel (9721 Arboretum Blvd., 78759; 343-2626, 800-468-3571) 478 rooms and suites, pool, sauna, exercise center, A/C, TV, airport courtesy car, meeting facilities, CC. SGL/DBL$100-$175.

TraveLodge (8300 I-35 North, 78753; 835-5050, Fax 835-0347, 800-578-7878) 141 rooms and 1- and 2-bedroom suites, restaurant, lounge, free breakfast, pool, wheelchair access, complimentary newspaper, laundry service, TV, A/C, free local calls, fax, NS rooms, in-room refrigerators and microwaves, children under 18 free with parents, no pets, meeting facilities, CC. SGL/DBL$39-$85.

Woodfin Suites Hotel and Business Center (7685 Northcross Dr., 78757; 452-9391, 800-237-8811) 198 1- and 2-bedroom suites, free breakfast, outdoor heated pool, jacuzzi, limousine service, laundry service, meeting facilities. 1BR$129, 2BR$169.

Wyndham Austin At Southpark (4140 Governor's Row, 78744; 448-2222, Fax 448-4744, 800-822-4200) 315 rooms and suites, restaurant, indoor and outdoor pool, sauna, whirlpools, exercise center, 13,000 square feet of meeting and exhibition space, meeting facilities for 185, CC. SGL/DBL$85-$109, STS$115.

Bandera

Area Code 210

Dixie Dude Ranch (Bandera 78003; 796-7771, 800-375-9255) 18 rooms and cottages, restaurant, pool, A/C, TV, laundry facilities, no pets, children free with parents, American plan available, NS rooms, wheelchair access, CC. SGL/DBL$80-$160.

The Flying L Ranch (Bandera 78003; 796-3001, Fax 796-8455, 800-292-5134) 38 1- and 2-bedroom cottages, restaurant, lounge, entertainment, pool, whirlpools, lighted tennis courts, A/C, TV, NS rooms, children free with parents, wheelchair access, no pets, gift shop, laundry facilities, senior rates, CC. SGL/DBL$95-$125.

Mayan Ranch (Bandera 78003; 796-3312) 67 1- to 4-bedroom cottages, restaurant, lounge, pool, exercise center, tennis courts, fireplaces, no pets, game room, children free with parents, A/C, TV, NS rooms, American plan available, wheelchair access, airport transportation, CC. SGL/DBL$90-$180.

Bay City

Area Code 409

Econo Lodge (3712 7th St., 77414; 245-5115, 800-4-CHOICE) 60 rooms, restaurant, free breakfast, pool, whirlpools, free local calls, children under 12 free with parents, no pets, NS rooms, wheelchair access, A/C, TV, senior rates, CC. SGL/DBL$32-$45.

Baytown

Area Code 713

Holiday Inn (300 South Hwy. 146, 77520; 427-7481, Fax 427-7877, 800-HOLIDAY) 173 rooms and suites, restaurant, lounge, pool, exercise center, children under 19 free with parents, wheelchair access, A/C, TV, NS rooms, in-room refrigerators, fax, room service, no pets, laundry service, meeting facilities for 250, senior rates, CC. SGL/DBL$55-$105.

La Quinta Inn (4911 East I-10, 77521; 421-5566, Fax 421-4009, 800-531-5900) 130 rooms, restaurant, free breakfast, lounge, pool, complimentary newspaper, free local calls, fax, laundry service, NS rooms, wheelchair access, TV, A/C, meeting facilities, CC. SGL/DBL$55-$80.

Sleep Inn (5222 I-10 East, 77521; 800-221-2222) 72 rooms, free breakfast, indoor heated pool, whirlpools, wheelchair access, NS rooms, no pets, children under 18 free with parents, senior rates, A/C, TV, meeting facilities, CC. SGL/DBL$40-$58.

Beaumont

Area Code 409

Best Western Jefferson Inn (I-10 South, 77707; 842-0037, Fax 842-0057, 800-528-1234) 120 rooms, restaurant, free breakfast, lounge, pool, exercise center, children free with parents, A/C, NS rooms, TV, laundry facilities, wheelchair access, kitchenettes, pets OK, in-room refrigerators, meeting facilities, senior rates, meeting facilities, CC. SGL/DBL$45-$55.

Best Western Inn (2155 North 11th St., 77703; 898-8150, Fax 898-0078, 800-528-1234) 152 rooms, pool, exercise center, children free with parents, A/C, NS rooms, TV, laundry facilities, wheelchair access, pets OK, meeting facilities, senior rates, CC. SGL/DBL$30-$45.

Days Inn (852B Harrison Ave., 77702; 838-0581, 800-325-2525) 150 rooms and suites, outdoor pool, children free with parents, room service, laundry service, A/C, TV, free local calls, pets OK, fax, wheelchair access, NS rooms, senior rates, CC. SGL/DBL$29-$42.

Hilton Hotel (2355 I-10 South, 77705; 842-3600, Fax 842-1355, 800-HIL-TONS) 285 rooms and suites, restaurant, lounge, entertainment, pool, jacuzzis, exercise center, children free with parents, NS rooms, wheelchair access, no pets, room service, laundry facilities, A/C, airport transportation, TV, meeting facilities, CC. SGL/DBL$60-$250.

Holiday Inn (2095 North 11th St., 77703; 892-2222, Fax 892-2231, 800-HOLIDAY) 190 rooms, restaurant, lounge, pool, exercise center, children under 19 free with parents, wheelchair access, A/C, TV, NS rooms, fax, room service, pets OK, laundry service, meeting facilities, senior rates, CC. SGL/DBL$55-$68.

Holiday Inn (3950 I-10 South, 77705; 842-5995, Fax 842-0315, 800-HOLIDAY) 253 rooms and suites, restaurant, lounge, indoor pool, exercise center, children under 19 free with parents, wheelchair access, A/C, TV, game room, gift shop, airport transportation, NS rooms, fax, room service, pets OK, laundry service, meeting facilities, senior rates, CC. SGL/DBL$70-$105.

La Quinta Inn (220 I-10 North, 77702; 838-9991, Fax 832-1266, 800-531-5900) 122 rooms, restaurant, free breakfast, lounge, pool, complimentary newspaper, free local calls, fax, laundry service, NS rooms, pets OK, wheelchair access, TV, A/C, meeting facilities, CC. SGL/DBL$45-$63.

Quality Inn (1295 North 11th St., 77702; 892-7722, 800-221-2222) 125 rooms and suites, restaurant, pool, exercise center, children free with parents, A/C, TV, room service, laundry service, NS rooms, in-room refrigerators and microwaves, pets OK, meeting facilities, senior rates, CC. SGL/DBL$43-$50.

Bedford
Area Code 817

Courtyard by Marriott (2201 West Airport Freeway, 76021; 545-2202, Fax 545-2319, 800-331-3131) 145 rooms and suites, free breakfast, heated pool, whirlpools, in-room refrigerators, coffee makers and microwaves, laundry facilities, TV, A/C, VCRs, pets OK, complimentary newspaper, fireplaces, children free with parents, NS rooms, wheelchair access, meeting facilities, CC. SGL/DBL$70-$90.

Hampton Inn (1450 Hwy. 121, 76022; 267-5200, 800-426-7866) 118 rooms, free breakfast, pool, pets OK, children free with parents, NS rooms, A/C, TV, wheelchair access, computer hookups, fax, free local calls, meeting facilities, CC. SGL/DBL$87-$105.

Holiday Inn (3005 Airport Freeway, 76021; 267-3181, 800-465-4329) 158 rooms and suites, restaurant, lounge, pool, sauna, whirlpools, A/C, TV, NS rooms, wheelchair access, children free with parents, in-room refrigerators, pets OK, airport courtesy car, meeting facilities, CC. SGL/DBL$68-$88.

La Quinta Inn (1450 West Airport Freeway, 76022; 267-5200, Fax 283-1682, 800-531-5900) 118 rooms, restaurant, free breakfast, lounge, pool, complimentary newspaper, free local calls, fax, laundry service, NS rooms, wheelchair access, TV, A/C, meeting facilities, CC. SGL/DBL$55-$68.

Beeville
Area Code 512

Best Western Inn (400 Hwy. 181 South, 78102; 358-4000, 800-528-1234) 60 rooms, pool, exercise center, children free with parents, A/C, NS rooms, TV, laundry facilities, wheelchair access, pets OK, meeting facilities, senior rates, CC. SGL/DBL$40-$46.

Bellmead
Area Code 817

Motel 6 (1509 Hogan Lane, 76705; 799-4957, 505-891-6161) pool, free local calls, children under 17 free with parents, NS rooms, wheelchair access, pets OK, A/C, TV, CC. SGL/DBL$33-$36.

Red Carpet Inn (1320 Behrens Circle, 76705; 799-5786, 800-251-1962) pool, children free with parents, TV, A/C, NS rooms, free local calls, pets OK, meeting facilities, senior rates, CC. SGL/DBL$25-$33.

Belton
Area Code 817

Best Western Inn (Belton 76513; 939-5711, Fax 939-5711, 800-528-1234) 49 rooms, pool, exercise center, children free with parents, A/C, NS rooms, TV, laundry facilities, wheelchair access, no pets, in-room refrigerators and microwaves, meeting facilities, senior rates, CC. SGL/DBL$35-$55.

Ramada Limited (1102 East 2nd, 76513; 939-3745, 800-2-RAMADA) 65 rooms and suites, restaurant, lounge, pool, wheelchair access, NS rooms, pets OK, A/C, TV, children under 18 free with parents, room service, laundry facilities, meeting facilities, senior rates, CC. SGL/DBL$33-$78.

Rodeway Inn (1520 South I-35, 76513; 939-0754, 800-424-4777) 50 rooms, pool, wheelchair access, NS rooms, children free with parents, A/C, TV, senior rates, CC. SGL/DBL$33-$45.

Big Bend National Park
Area Code 915

Chisos Mountain Lodge (Big Bend National Park 79834; 477-2291, Fax 477-2352) 72 rooms, restaurant, pets OK, children free with parents, A/C, CC. SGL/DBL$53-$70.

Big Sandy
Area Code 903

Annie's Bed and Breakfast (Big Sandy 75755; 636-4355) 13 rooms, free breakfast, A/C, TV, NS, in-room refrigerators, no pets, senior rates, CC. SGL/DBL$45-$115.

Big Spring
Area Code 915

Best Western Mid-Continent Inn (Big Spring 79720; 267-1601, 800-528-1234) 153 rooms, restaurant, lounge, heated pool, exercise center, children free with parents, A/C, NS rooms, TV, laundry facilities, wheelchair access, pets OK, senior rates, meeting facilities, CC. SGL/DBL$40-$60.

Days Inn (300 Tulane Ave., 79720; 263-7621, Fax 263-2790, 800-325-2525) 101 rooms and suites, restaurant, lounge, outdoor pool, children free with parents, room service, laundry service, A/C, TV, free local calls, pets OK, fax, wheelchair access, NS rooms, meeting facilities, senior rates, CC. SGL/DBL$42-$54.

Ponderosa Motor Inn (2701 South Gregg St., 79720; 267-5237) 27 rooms, restaurant, A/C, TV, NS rooms, wheelchair access, CC. SGL/DBL$25-$33.

Boerne
Area Code 210

Best Western Inn (35150 I-10, 78006; 249-9791, 800-528-1234) 81 rooms, pool, exercise center, children free with parents, A/C, NS rooms, TV, laundry facilities, wheelchair access, pets OK, laundry facilities, meeting facilities, senior rates, CC. SGL/DBL$42-$60.

Key to the Hills Motel (1228 South Main St., 78006; 249-3562) 40 rooms, A/C, TV, children free with parents, pets OK, NS rooms, wheelchair access, senior rates, CC. SGL/DBL$46-$63.

Bonham
Area Code 903

Days Inn (1515 Old Ector Rd., 75418; 583-3121, 800-325-2525) 53 rooms and suites, restaurant, free breakfast, outdoor pool, children free with parents, room service, laundry service, A/C, TV, free local calls, pets OK, in-room refrigerators, fax, wheelchair access, NS rooms, senior rates, CC. SGL/DBL$32-$38.

Borger
Area Code 806

The Inn Place of Borger (100 Bulldog Blvd., 79007; 273-9556) 92 rooms, heated pool, pets OK, in-room coffee makers, kitchenettes, A/C, TV, NS rooms, wheelchair access, CC. SGL/DBL$40-$46.

Bowie
Area Code 817

Days Inn (Hwys. 287 and 58, 76230; 872-5426, 800-325-2525) 60 rooms and suites, outdoor pool, children free with parents, room service, laundry service, A/C, TV, free local calls, pets OK, fax, wheelchair access, NS rooms, senior rates, meeting facilities, CC. SGL/DBL$28-$49.

Park Lodge (708 Park Ave., 76230; 872-1111) 40 rooms, pool, children free with parents, A/C, TV, NS rooms, pets OK, in-room refrigerators, wheelchair access, CC. SGL/DBL$28-$44.

Brady
Area Code 915

Plateau Motel (Brady 76825; 597-2185) 85 rooms, pool, A/C, pets OK, children free with parents, TV, NS rooms, wheelchair access, CC. SGL/DBL$28-$40.

Sunset Inn (2108 South Bridge, 76825; 597-0789) 44 rooms, pool, children free with parents, in-room refrigerators, pets OK, A/C, TV, NS rooms, wheelchair access, senior rates, CC. SGL/DBL$40-$44.

Brownsville
Area Code 512

Best Western Inn and Suites (845 North Expressway, 78520; 546-5501, 800-528-1234) 121 rooms, restaurant, pool, children free with parents, parents, A/C, NS rooms, TV, laundry facilities, wheelchair access, pets OK, meeting facilities, senior rates, CC. SGL/DBL$42-$78.

Days Inn (715 North Frontage Rd., 78520; 541-2201, Fax 541-6011, 800-325-2525) 117 rooms and suites, restaurant, outdoor pool, children free with parents, room service, laundry service, A/C, TV, free local calls, pets OK, fax, wheelchair access, NS rooms, meeting facilities, senior rates, CC. SGL/DBL$38-$70.

Flamingo Motel (1741 Central Blvd., 78520; 546-2478) pool, kitchenettes, A/C, TV, NS rooms, wheelchair access, CC. SGL/DBL$35-$45.

Fort Brown Hotel and Resort (Brownsville 78520; 546-2201, Fax 546-0756, 800-582-333) 278 rooms and suites, restaurant, lounge, entertainment, heated pool, exercise center, sauna, whirlpools, lighted tennis courts, A/C, TV, NS rooms, wheelchair access, in-room refrigerators and coffee makers, laundry facilities, gift shop, children free with parents, no pets, senior rates, meeting facilities, CC. SGL/DBL$69-$75, STS$85-$200.

La Quinta Inn (55 Sam Perl Blvd., 78520; 546-0381, Fax 541-5313, 800-531-5900) 143 rooms, restaurant, free breakfast, lounge, pool, complimentary newspaper, free local calls, fax, laundry service, NS rooms, wheelchair access, TV, A/C, meeting facilities, CC. SGL/DBL$45-$60.

Motel 6 (22655 North Expressway, 78520; 546-4699, 505-891-6161) pool, free local calls, children under 17 free with parents, NS rooms, wheelchair access, pets OK, A/C, TV, CC. SGL/DBL$38-$45.

Ranch Viejo Resort (Brownsville 78520; 350-4000, Fax 350-9681) 100 rooms and 1- to 3-bedroom villas, restaurant, lounge, entertainment, pool, whirlpools, lighted tennis courts, A/C, TV, NS rooms, wheelchair access, local transportation, children free with parents, no pets, meeting facilities, CC. SGL/DBL$88-$106.

Sheraton Inn Plaza Royale (3777 North Expressway, 78520; 350-9191, Fax 350-4153, 800-325-3535) 142 rooms and suites, restaurant, lounge, entertainment, indoor and outdoor pool, exercise center, NS rooms, A/C, TV, children stay free with parents, wheelchair access, in-room refrigerators and coffee makers, pets OK, 2,500 square feet of meeting and exhibition space, 3 meeting rooms, meeting facilities for 200, senior rates, CC. SGL/DBL$80-$105.

Brownwood

Area Code 915

Days Inn (1205 C.C. Woodson Rd., 76801; 643-5611, 800-325-2525) 30 rooms and suites, free breakfast, outdoor pool, children free with parents, room service, laundry service, A/C, TV, free local calls, pets OK, fax, wheelchair access, NS rooms, senior rates, CC. SGL/DBL$30-$50.

Holiday Inn (515 East Commerce, 76801; 646-2551, Fax 646-0912, 800-HOLIDAY) 141 rooms, restaurant, free breakfast, lounge, pool, exercise center, children under 19 free with parents, wheelchair access, A/C, TV, NS rooms, fax, in-room coffee makers, room service, no pets, laundry service, meeting facilities, senior rates, CC. SGL/DBL$45-$50.

Post Oak Inn (606 Early Blvd., 76801; 643-5621) 42 rooms, free breakfast, pool, A/C, TV, NS rooms, wheelchair access, senior rates, CC. SGL/DBL$27-$35.

Buffalo

Area Code 903

Best Western Inn (Buffalo 75831; 322-5831, 800-528-1234) 45 rooms, heated pool, exercise center, whirlpools, kitchenettes, children free with parents, A/C, NS rooms, TV, laundry facilities, in-room refrigerators, wheelchair access, pets OK, meeting facilities, senior rates, CC. SGL/DBL$37-$44.

Burleson

Area Code 903

Days Inn (Hwy. 19, 75103; 567-6588, 800-325-2525) 43 rooms and suites, outdoor pool, children free with parents, room service, laundry service, A/C, TV, free local calls, pets OK, fax, wheelchair access, NS rooms, senior rates, CC. SGL/DBL$33-$44.

Burnet
Area Code 512

HoJo Inn (908 Buchanan Dr., 78611; 756-4747, Fax 756-7839, 800-I-GO-HOJO) 46 rooms, restaurant, lounge, outdoor pool, children free with parents, wheelchair access, NS rooms, TV, A/C, no pets, laundry facilities, local transportation, senior rates, meeting facilities, senior rates, CC. SGL/DBL$45-$60.

Canton
Area Code 903

Best Western Inn (Canton 75103; 567-6591, 800-528-1234) 60 rooms, pool, exercise center, children free with parents, A/C, NS rooms, TV, laundry facilities, wheelchair access, pets OK, meeting facilities, senior rates, CC. SGL/DBL$40-$75.

Canyon
Area Code 806

Buffalo Inn (300 23rd St., 79015; 655-2124) 21 rooms, no pets, children free with parents, A/C, TV, NS rooms, wheelchair access, CC. SGL/DBL$25-$44.

Carrollton
Area Code 214

Red Roof Inn (1720 South Broadway, 75006; 245-1700, Fax 245-4402, 800-843-7663) 134 rooms, NS rooms, A/C, TV, fax, wheelchair access, complimentary newspaper, free local calls, in-room computer hookups, CC. SGL/DBL$24-$45.

Carthage
Area Code 903

Carthage Motel (321 South Shelby, 75633; 693-3814) 13 rooms, A/C, TV, NS rooms, wheelchair access, pets OK, senior rates, CC. SGL/DBL$29-$36.

Castroville
Area Code 210

Best Western Inn (1650 Hwy. 90 West, 78009; 538-2262, Fax 538-9732, 800-528-1234) 40 rooms, pool, exercise center, children free with parents, A/C, NS rooms, TV, laundry facilities, wheelchair access, pets OK, meeting facilities, senior rates, CC. SGL/DBL$45-$60.

Landmark Inn (402 Florence St., 78009; 538-2133) 8 rooms, no pets, TV, CC. SGL/DBL$35-$40.

Center
Area Code 409

Best Western Inn (1005 Hurst St., 75935; 598-3384, 800-528-1234) 72 rooms, pool, exercise center, children free with parents, A/C, NS rooms, TV, laundry facilities, wheelchair access, pets OK, in-room refrigerators and microwaves, meeting facilities, senior rates, CC. SGL/DBL$35-$45.

Channelview
Area Code 713

Econo Lodge (17011 I-10 East, 77530; 457-2966, 800-4-CHOICE) 100 rooms, restaurant, pool, children under 12 free with parents, no pets, NS rooms, wheelchair access, A/C, TV, senior rates, CC. SGL/DBL$30-$90.

Holiday Inn East Belt (15157 I-10 East, 77530; 452-7304, Fax 452-7304 ext 395, 800-HOLIDAY) 182 rooms, restaurant, lounge, pool, exercise center, children under 19 free with parents, wheelchair access, A/C, TV, in-room refrigerators and microwaves, NS rooms, fax, room service, no pets, laundry service, meeting facilities for 250, senior rates, CC. SGL/DBL$58-$66.

Ramada Limited (16939 I-10 East, 77530; 457-1640, 800-2-RAMADA) 60 rooms and suites, restaurant, free breakfast, wheelchair access, NS rooms, pets OK, A/C, TV, children under 18 free with parents, room service, laundry facilities, meeting facilities, senior rates, CC. SGL/DBL$32-$73.

Childress
Area Code 817

Best Western Classic Inn (1805 Ave. F Northwest, 79201; 937-6353, 800-528-1234) 116 rooms, restaurant, lounge, pool, exercise center, children free with parents, A/C, NS rooms, TV, laundry facilities, wheelchair access, pets OK, senior rates, meeting facilities, senior rates, CC. SGL/DBL$45-$50.

Econo Lodge (1612 Northwest Hwy. 287, 79201; 937-3695, 800-4-CHOICE) 28 rooms, restaurant, pool, children under 12 stay free with parents, no pets, NS rooms, wheelchair access, A/C, TV, senior rates, CC. SGL/DBL$33-$52.

Cisco

Area Code 817

Oak Motel (300 I-20 East, 76437; 442-2100) 30 rooms, A/C, TV, NS rooms, wheelchair access, children stay free with parents, pets OK, CC. SGL/DBL$20-$30.

Clarendon

Area Code 806

Western Skies Motel (Clarendon 79226; 874-3501) 23 rooms, heated pool, no pets, A/C, TV, NS rooms, wheelchair access, CC. SGL/DBL$30-$38.

Claude

Area Code 806

L A Motel (200 East 1st St., 79019; 226-4981) 15 rooms, A/C, TV, NS rooms, pets OK, wheelchair access, senior rates, CC. SGL/DBL$22-$35.

Cleburne

Area Code 817

Days Inn (101 North Ridgeway Dr., 76031; 645-8836, Fax 645-4813, 800-325-2525) 45 rooms and suites, free breakfast, outdoor pool, children free with parents, room service, laundry service, A/C, TV, free local calls, pets OK, fax, wheelchair access, NS rooms, senior rates, CC. SGL/DBL$32-$45.

Sagamar Inn (2107 North Main St., 76031; 556-0848) 28 rooms, pool, whirlpools, in-room refrigerators, A/C, TV, pets OK, meeting facilities, CC. SGL/DBL$35-$40.

Clute

Area Code 409

Days Inn (805 West Hwy. 332, 77531; 265-3301, 800-325-2525) 100 rooms and suites, free breakfast, outdoor pool, children free with parents, room service, laundry service, A/C, TV, free local calls, pets OK, fax, wheelchair access, NS rooms, meeting facilities, senior rates, CC. SGL/DBL$35-$45.

La Quinta Inn (1126 Hwy. 332 West, 77531; 265-7461, Fax 265-3804, 800-531-5900) 136 rooms, restaurant, free breakfast, lounge, pool, complimentary newspaper, free local calls, fax, laundry service, NS rooms, wheelchair access, TV, A/C, meeting facilities, CC. SGL/DBL$55-$60.

Coldspring
Area Code 409

San Jacinto Inn (Coldspring 77331; 653-3008) 13 rooms, children free with parents, A/C, TV, pets OK, NS rooms, wheelchair access, CC. SGL/DBL$35-$40.

College Station
Area Code 409

Comfort Inn (104 Texas Ave. South, 77840; 846-7333, Fax 846-5479, 800-221-2222) 114 rooms, free breakfast, pool, whirlpools, wheelchair access, NS rooms, laundry facilities, pets OK, children under 18 free with parents, A/C, TV, airport transportation, in-room refrigerators, meeting facilities, senior rates, CC. SGL/DBL$45-$75.

Hampton Inn (320 Texas Ave. South, 77840; 846-0184, Fax 846-0184 ext. 104, 800-HAMPTON) 134 rooms, restaurant, free breakfast, pool, exercise center, children under 18 free with parents, NS rooms, wheelchair access, in-room computer hookups, fax, TV, A/C, airport transportation, free local calls, no pets, meeting facilities, CC. SGL/DBL$50-$75.

Hilton Hotel and Conference Center (801 University Drive East, 77840, 800-HILTONS) 303 rooms and suites, restaurant, lounge, entertainment, pool, exercise center, jacuzzi, children free with parents, NS rooms, wheelchair access, no pets, room service, laundry facilities, A/C, airport transportation, TV, meeting facilities, CC. SGL/DBL$50-$250.

Holiday Inn (1502 Texas Ave. South, 77840; 693-1736, 800-HOLIDAY) 126 rooms, restaurant, lounge, pool, exercise center, children under 19 free with parents, wheelchair access, A/C, TV, NS rooms, airport transportation, fax, room service, no pets, laundry service, meeting facilities for 200, senior rates, CC. SGL/DBL$50-$66.

La Quinta Inn (607 Texas Ave., 77840; 696-7777, Fax 696-0531, 800-531-5900) 176 rooms, restaurant, free breakfast, lounge, pool, complimentary newspaper, free local calls, fax, laundry service, NS rooms, wheelchair access, TV, pets OK, A/C, airport transportation, meeting facilities, CC. SGL/DBL$50-$56.

Manor House Motel (2504 Texas Ave. South, 77840; 764-9540, Fax 693-2430) 117 rooms, restaurant, free breakfast, pool, pets OK, airport transportation, A/C, TV, NS rooms, wheelchair access, airport courtesy car, senior rates, CC. SGL/DBL$40-$65.

Super 8 Motel (Cooner and Texas Ave., 77840; 800-800-8000) 90 rooms and suites, no pets, children under 12 free with parents, free local calls,

A/C, TV, in-room refrigerators and microwaves, fax, NS rooms, senior rates, wheelchair access, meeting facilities, CC. SGL/DBL$40-$56.

Colorado City
Area Code 915

Days Inn (Colorado City 79512; 728-2638, Fax 728-2132, 800-325-2525) 52 rooms and suites, outdoor pool, children free with parents, room service, laundry service, A/C, TV, free local calls, pets OK, fax, wheelchair access, NS rooms, senior rates, CC. SGL/DBL$34-$41, STS$50-$55.

Villa Inn (2310 Hickory St., 79512; 728-5217) 40 rooms, pool, no pets, A/C, TV, NS rooms, wheelchair access, CC. SGL/DBL$27-$38.

Columbus
Area Code 409

Columbus Inn (2208 Hwy. 71, 78934; 732-5723) 50 rooms, heated pool, whirlpools, NS rooms, children free with parents, pets OK, airport transportation, A/C, TV, NS rooms, wheelchair access, CC. SGL/DBL$40-$45.

Homeplace Inn (2436 Hwy. 71 South, 78934; 732-6293) 40 rooms, A/C, TV, NS rooms, wheelchair access, children free with parents, laundry facilities, pets OK, CC. SGL/DBL$45-$52.

Conroe
Area Code 409

Holiday Inn (160 I-45 South, 77301; 756-8941, Fax 756-8984, 800-HOLI-DAY) 138 rooms, restaurant, lounge, pool, exercise center, children under 19 free with parents, wheelchair access, A/C, TV, NS rooms, fax, room service, no pets, laundry service, meeting facilities for 250, senior rates, CC. SGL/DBL$60-$73.

Ramada Inn (1520 South Frazier, 77301; 756-8939, 800-2-RAMADA) 81 rooms and suites, restaurant, free breakfast, lounge, pool, wheelchair access, NS rooms, pets OK, A/C, TV, children under 18 free with parents, room service, laundry facilities, meeting facilities, senior rates, CC. SGL/DBL$39-$60.

Conway
Area Code 806

S&S Motor Inn (Conway 79068; 537-5111) 10 rooms, restaurant, A/C, TV, NS rooms, pets OK, wheelchair access, CC. SGL/DBL$35-$45.

Copperas Cove
Area Code 817

HoJo Inn (302 West Hwy. 190, 76522; 547-2345, Fax 547-5124, 800-I-GO-HOJO) 50 rooms, free breakfast, outdoor pool, children free with parents, wheelchair access, NS rooms, TV, A/C, no pets, laundry facilities, senior rates, meeting facilities, CC. SGL/DBL$35-$52.

Corpus Christi
Area Code 512

Bayfront Inn (601 North Shoreline Blvd., 78401; 883-7271) 120 rooms, restaurant, pool, A/C, TV, NS rooms, wheelchair access, pets OK, senior rates, meeting facilities, CC. SGL/DBL$60-$68.

Best Western Sandy Shores Beach Hotel (3200 Surfside, 78401; 883-7456, Fax 883-1437, 800-528-1234) 251 rooms and suites, restaurant, lounge, heated pool, exercise center, whirlpools, sauna, children free with parents, A/C, NS rooms, TV, laundry facilities, wheelchair access, no pets, room service, meeting facilities, senior rates, CC. SGL/DBL$50-$180.

Best Western Inn (11217 I-37, 78410; 241-6675, Fax 241-6733, 800-528-1234) 40 rooms, pool, sauna, whirlpools, pets OK, in-room computer hookups, children free with parents, A/C, NS rooms, TV, laundry facilities, wheelchair access, pets OK, in-room refrigerators and microwaves, VCRs, meeting facilities, senior rates, CC. SGL/DBL$50-$65.

Best Western Inn (2838 South Padre Island Dr., 78415; 854-0005, 800-528-1234) 140 rooms, pool, exercise center, whirlpools, no pets, children free with parents, A/C, NS rooms, TV, laundry facilities, wheelchair access, pets OK, meeting facilities, senior rates, CC. SGL/DBL$45-$73.

Christy Estate Suites (3942 Holly Rd., 78415; 854-1091, Fax 854-4766, 800-6-SUITE6) 98 rooms and 2-bedroom suites, pool, whirlpools, kitchenettes, no pets, A/C, TV, NS rooms, wheelchair access, senior rates, CC. SGL/DBL$70-$110.

Comfort Inn Airport (6301 I-37, 78409; 289-6925, 800-221-2222) 138 rooms, free breakfast, outdoor pool, hot tub, wheelchair access, NS rooms, no pets, children under 18 free with parents, free local calls, game room, laundry facilities, A/C, TV, airport transportation, meeting facilities, senior rates, CC. SGL/DBL$36-$55.

Days Inn (4302 Surfside Blvd., 78402; 882-3297, Fax 882-6865, 800-325-2525) 56 rooms and suites, free breakfast, children free with parents, room service, laundry service, A/C, TV, free local calls, no pets, fax, wheelchair access, in-room refrigerators and microwaves, NS rooms, senior rates, CC. SGL/DBL$35-$75, STS$75-$100.

Days Inn Airport (901 Navigation Blvd., 78408; 888-8599, Fax 888-5746, 800-325-2525) 121 rooms and suites, restaurant, outdoor pool, children free with parents, room service, laundry service, A/C, TV, free local calls, pets OK, fax, wheelchair access, NS rooms, meeting facilities, senior rates, CC. SGL/DBL$30-$85.

Drury Inn (2021 North Padre Island Dr., 78408; 289-8200, 800-325-8300) 150 2-room suites, free breakfast, pool, TV, children under 18 free with parents, NS rooms, A/C, in-room refrigerators and microwaves, pets OK, wheelchair access, fax, in-room computer hookups, free local calls, meeting facilities, senior rates, CC. SGL/DBL$50-$60.

Embassy Suites (4337 Padre Island Dr., 78411; 853-7899, 800-EMBASSY) 150 2-room suites, free breakfast, lounge, heated pool, whirlpool, exercise center, sauna, room service, laundry service, wheelchair access, complimentary newspaper, free local calls, pets OK, game room, NS rooms, gift shop, local transportation, meeting facilities, senior rates, CC. SGL/DBL$95-$105.

Gulf Beach Luxury Motor Inn (3500 Surfside Blvd., 78402; 882-3500) 39 rooms, children free with parents, laundry facilities, pets OK, A/C, TV, NS rooms, wheelchair access, CC. SGL/DBL$50-$70.

Gulfstream Motel (14810 Windward Dr., 78418; 949-8061, 800-542-7368) 96 efficiencies, heated pool, children free with parents, no pets, game room, laundry facilities, A/C, TV, NS rooms, wheelchair access, CC. SGL/DBL$110-$145.

Harbor Inn (411 North Shoreline Blvd., 78401; 884-4815) 98 rooms, pool, A/C, pets OK, VCRs, TV, NS rooms, wheelchair access, meeting facilities, CC. SGL/DBL$28-$65.

Holiday Inn (5549 Leopard St., 78408; 289-5100, 800-HOLIDAY) 247 rooms and suites, restaurant, lounge, indoor pool, exercise center, whirlpools, tennis, gift shop, airport transportation, children under 19 free with parents, wheelchair access, in-room computer hookups, A/C, TV, NS rooms, fax, room service, no pets, laundry service, in-room refrigerators and coffee makers, meeting facilities, senior rates, CC. SGL/DBL$70-$125.

Holiday Inn Emerald Beach (1102 South Shoreline, 78401; 883-5731, 800-HOLIDAY) 368 rooms, restaurant, lounge, entertainment, indoor heated pool, exercise center, whirlpools, children under 19 free with parents, wheelchair access, A/C, airport transportation, gift shop, water view, TV, NS rooms, in-room refrigerators and coffee makers, fax, room service, pets OK, laundry service, meeting facilities, senior rates, CC. SGL/DBL$85-$100.

Holiday Inn Padre Island Beachfront (15202 Windward Dr., 78418; 949-8041, Fax 949-9139, 800-HOLIDAY) 148 rooms, restaurant, lounge, entertainment, pool, exercise center, children under 19 free with parents, wheelchair access, gift shop, water view, A/C, TV, NS rooms, fax, room service, no pets, laundry service, meeting facilities for 250, senior rates, CC. SGL/DBL$55-$68.

The Island House (15340 Leeward Dr., 78418; 949-8166, 800-333-8806) 61 apartments, heated pool, laundry facilities, A/C, TV, NS rooms, wheelchair access, children free with parents, no pets, meeting facilities, senior rates, CC. SGL/DBL$65-$150.

La Quinta Inn North (5155 I-37 North, 78408; 888-5721, Fax 888-5401, 800-531-5900) 123 rooms, restaurant, free breakfast, lounge, pool, complimentary newspaper, free local calls, fax, laundry service, NS rooms, wheelchair access, TV, A/C, airport transportation, meeting facilities, CC. SGL/DBL$45-$75.

La Quinta Inn South (6225 South Padre Island Dr., 78412; 991-5730, Fax 993-4011, 800-531-5900) 129 rooms, restaurant, free breakfast, lounge, pool, complimentary newspaper, free local calls, fax, laundry service, NS rooms, wheelchair access, TV, A/C, meeting facilities, CC. SGL/DBL$45-$85.

Marriott Bayfront Hotel (900 North Shoreline Blvd., 78401; 887-1600, Fax 887-6715, 800-228-9290) 474 rooms and suites, restaurant, lounge, entertainment, indoor and outdoor pool, exercise center, whirlpools, sauna, airport transportation, airline ticket desk, car rental desk, wheelchair access, TV, A/C, NS rooms, laundry service, gift shop, children free with parents, meeting facilities, senior rates, CC. SGL/DBL$400-$500.

Quality Hotel (601 North Water St., 78401; 882-8100, Fax 888-6540, 800-221-2222) 200 rooms and suites, restaurant, lounge, entertainment, pool, exercise center, children free with parents, A/C, TV, room service, laundry service, NS rooms, gift shop, airport courtesy car, game room, meeting facilities, senior rates, CC. SGL/DBL$50-$175.

Radisson Marina Hotel (300 North Shoreline Dr., 78401; 883-5111, Fax 883-7702, 800-333-3333) 174 rooms and suites, restaurant, lounge, entertainment, pool, exercise center, sauna, gift shop, airport courtesy car, in-room refrigerators, microwaves and coffee makers, children free with parents, VCRs, wheelchair access, NS rooms, TV, A/C, pets OK, CC. SGL/DBL$80-$180.

Ramada Inn Greyhound Racetrack (5501 I-37, 78408, 800-2-RAMADA) 153 rooms and suites, restaurant, lounge, pool, hot tub, sauna, game room, wheelchair access, NS rooms, pets OK, A/C, airport courtesy car, TV, children under 18 free with parents, room service, laundry facilities, meeting facilities, senior rates, CC. SGL/DBL$45-$55, STS$180-$225.

Sea Shell Inn (202 Kleberg Pl., 78402; 888-5391) 25 rooms and 2-bedroom suites, heated pool, kitchenettes, no pets, children free with parents, in-room refrigerators and microwaves, A/C, TV, NS rooms, wheelchair access, CC. SGL/DBL$32-$74.

Sheraton Bayfront Hotel (707 North Shoreline Blvd., 78401; 882-1700, Fax 884-1074, 800-325-3535) 346 rooms and suites, restaurant, lounge, entertainment, indoor and outdoor heated pool, exercise center, whirlpools, sauna, lighted tennis courts, gift shop, airport courtesy car, NS rooms, A/C, TV, children free with parents, wheelchair access, 10,000 square feet of meeting and exhibition space, 11 meeting rooms, meeting facilities for 400, CC. SGL/DBL$75-$275.

Surfside Condominiums (15005 Windward Dr., 78418; 949-8128) 34 condominiums, laundry facilities, children free with parents, A/C, TV, NS rooms, wheelchair access, pets OK, kitchenettes, CC. SGL/DBL$75-$100.

TraveLodge (910 Corn Products Rd., 78409; 289-5666, Fax 289-0932, 800-578-7878) 100 rooms, restaurant, lounge, entertainment, free breakfast, pool, exercise center, wheelchair access, complimentary newspaper, laundry service, TV, A/C, free local calls, fax, airport transportation, gift shop, NS rooms, in-room refrigerators and microwaves, children under 18 free with parents, no pets, meeting facilities, CC. SGL/DBL$44-$54.

Villa del Sol (3938 Surfside Blvd., 78402; 883-9748, 800-242-3291) 283 1-bedroom condominiums, heated pool, whirlpools, laundry facilities, children free with parents, no pets, kitchenettes, A/C, TV, NS rooms, wheelchair access, CC. SGL/DBL$65-$120.

Corsicana
Area Code 903

Days Inn (287 South Corsicana, 75110; 872-0659, Fax 874-1245, 800-325-2525) 60 rooms and suites, restaurant, lounge, outdoor pool, children free with parents, room service, laundry service, A/C, TV, free local calls, pets OK, fax, wheelchair access, NS rooms, meeting facilities, senior rates, CC. SGL/DBL$35-$70, STS$70-$125.

Econo Lodge (2021 Regal Dr., 75110; 874-4751, 800-4-CHOICE) 96 rooms, restaurant, lounge, pool, whirlpools, free local calls, children under 12 free with parents, no pets, NS rooms, wheelchair access, A/C, TV, senior rates, CC. SGL/DBL$30-$35.

Crockett
Area Code 409

Embers Motor Inn (1401 Loop 304 East, 75835; 544-5681) 60 rooms, pool, A/C, TV, NS rooms, wheelchair access, pets OK, children free with parents, senior rates, CC. SGL/DBL$25-$38.

Dalhart
Area Code 806

Best Western Inn (Hwy. 87, 79022; 249-5637, Fax 249-5803, 800-528-1234) 55 rooms, restaurant, lounge, heated pool, children free with parents, A/C, NS rooms, TV, laundry facilities, wheelchair access, pets OK, senior rates, meeting facilities, senior rates, CC. SGL/DBL$35-$50.

Best Western Inn (623 Denver Ave., 79022; 249-4538, 800-528-1234) 48 rooms, heated pool, exercise center, children free with parents, A/C, NS rooms, TV, laundry facilities, wheelchair access, pets OK, meeting facilities, senior rates, CC. SGL/DBL$35-$45.

Comfort Inn (Dalhart 79022; 249-8585, 800-221-2222) 36 rooms, restaurant, heated pool, wheelchair access, NS rooms, pets OK, children under 18 free with parents, A/C, TV, local transportation, in-room refrigerators and coffee makers, meeting facilities, senior rates, CC. SGL/DBL$32-$50.

Econo Lodge (123 Liberal St., 79022; 249-6464, 800-4-CHOICE) 46 rooms, children under 12 free with parents, no pets, NS rooms, wheelchair access, free local calls, airport transportation, A/C, TV, senior rates, CC. SGL/DBL$29-$36.

Friendship Inn (400 Liberal St., 79022; 249-4557, 800-424-4777) 24 rooms, A/C, TV, no pets, NS rooms, children free with parents, wheelchair access, senior rates, CC. SGL/DBL$25-$35.

Sands Motel (301 Liberal St., 79022; 249-4568) 36 rooms, pool, A/C, TV, NS rooms, wheelchair access, pets OK, CC. SGL/DBL$20-$35.

Super 8 Motel (East Hwy. 54, 79022; 249-8526, 800-800-8000) 45 rooms and suites, whirlpools, sauna, pets OK, children under 12 free with parents, free local calls, A/C, TV, in-room refrigerators and microwaves, fax, NS rooms, senior rates, wheelchair access, meeting facilities, CC. SGL/DBL$32-$42.

Dallas
Area Code 214

Downtown Dallas

Holiday Inn Downtown (1015 Elm St., 75202; 748-9951, 800-HOLIDAY) 311 rooms and suites, restaurant, lounge, exercise center, children free with parents, wheelchair access, NS rooms, A/C, TV, fax, room service, meeting facilities for 750, CC. Near the Convention Center and Reunion Arena, 7 miles from Love Field Airport, 17 miles from the Dallas-Fort Worth International Airport. SGL/DBL$65-$75.

Ramada Hotel Downtown Convention Center (1011 South Akard, 75215; 421-1083, Fax 428-6827, 800-2-RAMADA) 238 rooms and suites, restaurant, lounge, indoor pool, children free with parents, wheelchair access, NS rooms, A/C, TV, pets OK, local transportation, CC. In the business district near the Convention Center and the Cotton Bowl. SGL$45-$125, DBL$55-$135, STS$450+, X$10.

Airport Area

Clarion Hotel (1241 West Mockingbird Lane, 75247; 630-7000, Fax 638-6943, 800-221-2222) 350 rooms, restaurant, lounge, pool, exercise center, wheelchair access, NS rooms, A/C, TV, no pets, airport transportation, 13,000 square feet of meeting and exhibition space, CC. 2 miles from Love Field Airport and the Market Center, 5 miles from the business district and Convention Center. SGL/DBL$58-$68.

Holiday Inn Love Field (7050 Stemmons Freeway, 75247; 630-8500, 800-HOLIDAY) 356 rooms and suites, Concierge Floor, restaurant, lounge, entertainment, indoor pool, whirlpool, exercise center, children free with parents, wheelchair access, NS rooms, A/C, TV, fax, room service, airport transportation, meeting facilities for 1,000, CC. 5 miles from the downtown area, 3 miles from Love Field Airport, 13 miles from the Dallas-Fort Worth International Airport, 2.5 miles from Texas Stadium. SGL/DBL$58-$98.

Hyatt Regency Airport (International Pkwy., 75261; 453-1234, Fax 456-8668, 800-233-1234) 1,400 rooms and suites, Regency Club Floor, 4 restaurants, 3 lounges, outdoor heated pool, golf, 7 tennis courts, exercise center, airport courtesy car, NS rooms, A/C, TV, complimentary newspaper, wheelchair access, 80 meeting rooms, 130,000 square feet of meeting and exhibition space, senior rates, CC. At the Dallas-Fort Worth International Airport, 20 minutes from the downtown area. SGL$134-$159, DBL$159-$184.

Ramada Hotel Love Field (3232 West Mockingbird Lane, 75235; 357-5601, Fax 357-0104; 800-2-RAMADA) 104 rooms and suites, restaurant, lounge, entertainment, pool, children free with parents, wheelchair access, NS rooms, A/C, TV, airport transportation, pets OK, 19,000 square feet of meeting and exhibition space, CC. At Love Field Airport, 4 miles from Texas Stadium and the Market Center. SGL/DBL$64-$91.

Northeast Dallas

Bristol Suites (7800 Alpha Rd., 75240; 233-7600, Fax 701-8618, 800-922-9222) 295 rooms and suites, restaurant, free breakfast, indoor and outdoor pool, exercise center, jacuzzi, room service, pets OK, wheelchair access, NS rooms, A/C, TV, children free with parents, local transportation, 11,500 square feet of meeting and exhibition space, CC. SGL$99, DBL$114.

Colony Park Hotel (6060 North Central Expressway, 75206; 750-6060, Fax 750-6060 ext 7105) 288 rooms, pool, exercise center, jacuzzi, beauty shop, children free with parents, pets OK, wheelchair access, NS rooms, A/C, TV, local transportation, in-room refrigerators, airport courtesy car, meeting facilities, CC. SGL/DBL$85-$105.

Days Inn (8051 LBJ Freeway, 75251; 680-3000, Fax 680-3200, 800-325-2525) 200 rooms and suites, restaurant, free breakfast, lounge, entertainment, pool, children free with parents, local transportation, free local calls, fax, no pets, wheelchair access, local transportation, NS rooms, A/C, TV, meeting facilities, senior rates, CC. In the business and entertainment district, 20 miles from the Dallas-Fort Worth International Airport. SGL/DBL$39-$70.

Doubletree Hotel At Campbell Centre (8250 North Central Expressway, 75206; 691-8700, Fax 369-0432, 800-528-0444) 302 rooms and suites, restaurant, lounge, whirlpools, exercise center, tennis, putting green, room service, 11 meeting rooms, A/C, TV, meeting facilities for 800, CC. 21 miles from the Dallas-Fort Worth International Airport, 8 miles from Love Field Airport. SGL/DBL$48-$65.

Doubletree Hotel At Lincoln Centre (5410 LBJ Freeway, 75240; 934-8400, Fax 701-5244, 800-528-0444) 525 rooms and suites, Gold Leaf Floors, 4 restaurants, 2 lounges, pool, whirlpool, exercise center, room service, A/C, TV, 23 meeting rooms, meeting facilities for 1,800, CC. Near the North Dallas Lincoln Centre, 20 minutes from the Dallas-Fort Worth International Airport. SGL$134, DBL$144.

Embassy Suites Park Central (13131 North Central Expressway, 75243; 234-3300, Fax 437-4247, 800-EMBASSY) 233 2-room suites, restaurant, lounge, free breakfast, pool, exercise center, jacuzzi, sauna, NS rooms, A/C, TV, laundry service, wheelchair access, airport courtesy car, meeting facilities, CC. 15 miles from the Love Field Airport and downtown area, 18 miles from the Dallas-Fort Worth International Airport. SGL/DBL$119-$130.

Fairmont Hotel (1717 North Akard St., 75201; 720-2020, Fax 720-2020, 800-527-4727) 550 rooms and 1-bedroom suites, restaurant, lounge, entertainment, pool, beauty shop, boutiques, wheelchair access, NS rooms, A/C, TV, meeting facilities, CC. SGL$69-$99, STS$109.

Grand Kempinski Hotel (15201 Dallas North Pkwy., 75248; 386-6000, Fax 991-6937, 800-426-3135) 529 rooms, indoor and outdoor pool, sauna, lighted tennis courts, exercise center, beauty shop, A/C, TV, airport courtesy car, meeting facilities for 3,600, CC. 25 minutes from the Dallas-Fort Worth International Airport and the downtown area. SGL/DBL$115, STS$250-$450.

Harvey Park Central (7815 LBJ Freeway, 75240; 960-7000, 800-922-9222) 313 rooms, pool, exercise center, jacuzzi, 10,000 square feet of meeting and exhibition space, CC. SGL$65-$74, DBL$75-$84.

Hilton Parkway (4801 LBJ Freeway, 75240; 661-3600, Fax 661-1060, 800-HILTONS) 310 rooms and suites, restaurant, lounge, indoor and heated outdoor pool, exercise center, jacuzzi, sauna, local transportation, wheelchair access, NS rooms, A/C, TV, in-room computer hookups, business services, 23 meeting rooms, meeting facilities for 500, CC. 10 miles from the downtown area, 17 miles from the Dallas-Fort Worth International Airport. SGL/DBL$100-$135.

Hilton Central (5600 North Central Expressway, 75206; 827-4100, 800-445-8667) 400 rooms and suites, restaurant, lounge, pool, exercise center, jacuzzi, beauty shop, airport courtesy car, A/C, TV, meeting facilities, CC. SGL/DBL$99-$139.

Holiday Inn Park Central (8102 LBJ and Colt Rd., 75251; 239-7211, 800-HOLIDAY) 201 rooms and suites, restaurant, lounge, children free with parents, wheelchair access, NS rooms, A/C, TV, fax, room service, meeting facilities, CC. 18 miles from the Dallas-Fort Worth International Airport, 10 miles from Love Field Airport, 11 miles from the downtown area. SGL/DBL$58-$68.

Holiday Inn Northeast (LBJ Freeway and I-35, 75243; 341-5400, Fax 553-9349, 800-HOLIDAY) 164 rooms and suites, restaurant, lounge, entertainment, exercise center, jogging track, children free with parents, wheelchair access, NS rooms, A/C, TV, fax, room service, pets OK, meeting facilities for 350, CC. SGL$75, DBL$85-$105.

Holiday Inn North Park Plaza (10650 North Central Expressway, 75231; 373-6000, Fax 373-1037, 800-HOLIDAY) 279 rooms and suites, restaurant, lounge, indoor pool, exercise center, children free with parents, wheelchair access, NS rooms, A/C, TV, fax, room service, airport transportation, pets OK, meeting facilities for 400, CC. 8 miles from the downtown area, 18 miles from the Dallas-Fort Worth International Airport. SGL/DBL$75-$90.

La Quinta Inn Central (4440 North Central Expressway, 75206; 821-4220, Fax 821-7685, 800-531-5900) 101 rooms, restaurant, lounge, heated pool, complimentary newspaper, free local calls, fax, laundry service, NS-rooms, A/C, TV, wheelchair access, meeting facilities, CC. 4 miles from the Fair Park, downtown area and Cotton Bowl, 21 miles from the West End Marketplace, 30 miles from the Dallas-Fort Worth International Airport. SGL/DBL$50-$65.

La Quinta Inn Northpark (10001 North Central Expressway, 75231; 361-8200, Fax 691-0482, 800-531-5900) 129 rooms, restaurant, lounge, heated pool, complimentary newspaper, free local calls, fax, laundry service, NS rooms, A/C, TV, wheelchair access, meeting facilities, CC. 5 miles from the Northpark Mall, Biblical Art Center and Southern Methodist University, 15 miles from Texas Stadium, 8 miles from the downtown area, 7 miles from Love Field Airport, 32 miles from Dallas-Fort Worth International Airport. SGL/DBL$40-$60.

Mansion On Turtle Creek (2821 Turtle Creek Blvd., 75219; 559-2100, Fax 528-4187, 800-323-7500) 205 rooms and suites, restaurant, lounge, entertainment, heated pool, exercise center, concierge, 24-hour room service, wheelchair access, NS rooms, A/C, TV, meeting facilities for 200, CC. 5 minutes from the business district. SGL$230-$320, DBL$270-$360, STS$485-$1,250.

Marriott Park Central (7750 LBJ Freeway, 75251; 233-4421, Fax 233-3679, 800-228-9290) 445 rooms and suites, restaurant, lounge, outdoor pool, exercise center, jacuzzi, whirlpool, jogging track, NS rooms, A/C, TV, wheelchair access, airline ticket desk, gift shop, car rental desk, airport courtesy car, meeting facilities, CC. 25 minutes from the Dallas-Fort Worth International airport and Love Field Airport. SGL/DBL$90-$115.

Marriott Residence Inn (US 75 at Meadow Rd., 75231; 750-8220, 800-331-3131) 134 suites, free breakfast, exercise center, kitchens, in-room refrigerators, laundry service, wheelchair access, NS rooms, A/C, TV, pets OK, VCRs, meeting facilities for 30, CC. 16 miles from the Dallas-Fort Worth International Airport, 8 miles from downtown. SGL$85, DBL$95.

Omni Melrose Hotel (3015 Oaklawn Ave., 75219; 521-5151, Fax 521-2470, 800-843-6664) 184 rooms and suites, restaurant, lounge, entertainment, exercise center, laundry service, meeting facilities, A/C, TV, local transportation, limousine service, 2,400 square feet of meeting and exhibition space, CC. 5 miles from the Dallas Market Center and business district, 3 miles from Love Field Airport, 18 miles from the Dallas-Fort Worth International Airport. SGL/DBL$89.

Park Cities Inn (6101 Hillcrest Ave., 75205; 521-0330, Fax 522-5400) 53 rooms, free breakfast, children free with parents, in-room refrigerators, A/C, TV, meeting facilities, CC. SGL/DBL$50-$80.

Preston Suites Hotel (6104 LBJ Freeway, 75240; 458-2626, Fax 395-8331, 800-524-7038) 92 1-, 2-, and 3-bedroom suites, free breakfast, outdoor pool, exercise center, jacuzzi, children free with parents, in-room refrigerators and microwaves, complimentary newspaper, laundry service, A/C, TV, free local calls, pets OK, airport transportation, fax, 900 square feet of meeting and exhibition space, meeting facilities for 75, CC. Located 15 minutes from the downtown area, 20 minutes from the airport. 1BR$83, 2BR$103, 3BR$123.

Red Roof Inn (1550 Empire Central Dr., 75235; 638-5151, Fax 638-3920, 800-843-7663) 111 rooms, NS rooms, A/C, TV, fax, wheelchair access, complimentary newspaper, free local calls, in-room computer hookups, CC. 10 miles from the Dallas-Fort Worth International Airport, 6 miles from the downtown area, 3 miles from the Market Center. SGL$33-$37, DBL$39.

Residence Inn North Central (13636 Goldmark Dr., 75240; 669-0478, 800-331-3131) 70 rooms, pool, exercise center, jacuzzi, wheelchair access, in-room refrigerators, NS rooms, A/C, TV, laundry service, pets OK, meeting facilities, CC. SGL/DBL$75-$88.

Rodeway Inn (3140 West Mockingbird Lane, 75235; 357-1701, 800-228-2000) 42 rooms, restaurant, pool, A/C, TV, airport courtesy car, CC. SGL/DBL$41-$55.

Sheraton Park Central Hotel (12720 Merit Dr., 75251, 385-3000, Fax 991-4557, 800-325-3535) 545 rooms and suites, 3 restaurants, 3 lounges, entertainment, outdoor pool, jacuzzi, 2 tennis courts, wheelchair access, NS rooms, A/C, TV, business services, 21 meeting rooms, 25,000 square feet of meeting and exhibition space, meeting facilities for 2,200, CC. 20 miles from the Dallas-Fort Worth International Airport. SGL/DBL$75-$105.

Sheraton Mockingbird Hotel West (1893 West Mockingbird Lane, 75235; 634-8850, Fax 634-8805 ext 7189, 800-325-2525) 301 rooms and suites, 2 restaurants, lounge, outdoor pool, whirlpool, sauna, exercise center, jogging track, wheelchair access, NS rooms, A/C, TV, complimentary airport transportation, 14 meeting rooms, 16,000 square feet of meeting and exhibition space, meeting facilities for 750, CC. Near the West End, Dallas Market Center and Texas Stadium, 12 miles from the Dallas-Fort Worth International Airport. SGL/DBL$69-$85.

TraveLodge Market Center (4500 Harry Hines Blvd., 75219; 522-6650, Fax 526-0049, 800-255-3050) 22 rooms and suites, restaurant, lounge, pool, exercise center, airport courtesy car, NS rooms, A/C, TV, room service, meeting facilities for 60, CC. Near the World Trade Center and Dallas Market Center, 1.5 miles from the downtown area, 4 miles from the Cowboy Stadium. SGL/DBL$41-$58.

Westin Hotel Galleria (13340 Dallas Pkwy., 75240; 934-9494, Fax 851-2869, 800-228-3000) 430 rooms, Executive Club Level, restaurant, lounge, outdoor heated pool, jogging track, sauna, exercise center, 24-hour room service, wheelchair access/room, NS rooms, A/C, TV, car rental desk, airline ticket desk, concierge, pets OK, 21 meeting rooms, meeting facilities for 1,690, CC. Near the Galleria Shopping Complex, 12 minutes from the downtown area, 10 minutes from Love Field Airport, 20 minutes from the Dallas-Fort Worth International Airport. SGL$170-$210, DBL$195-$240, STS$350-$1250, X$25.

Southeast Dallas

Aristocrat Hotel (1933 Main St., 75201; 741-7700, Fax 939-3639, 800-231-4235) 172 rooms and suites, restaurant, lounge, free breakfast, exercise center, children free with parents, room service, in-room refrigerators, complimentary newspaper, airport transportation, business services, 3,000 square feet of meeting and exhibition space, meeting facilities for

120, CC. In the historic district, 8 miles from Love Field, 25 miles from Dallas-Fort Worth International Airport. SGL/DBL$89-$130, STS$130.

Best Western Market Center (2023 Market Center Blvd., 75207; 741-9000, Fax 741-6100, 800-528-1234) 95 rooms, restaurant, lounge, free breakfast, pool, complimentary newspaper, NS rooms, A/C, TV, local transportation, children free with parents, no pets, laundry service, CC. 2 miles from the downtown area. SGL$58-$63, DBL$63-$78, X$10.

Courtyard by Marriott (2382 Stemmons Trail, 75207; 352-7676, Fax 352-4914, 800-321-2211) 145 rooms, restaurant, lounge, pool, exercise center, jacuzzi, children free with parents, wheelchair access, NS rooms, A/C, TV, laundry service, meeting facilities, CC. SGL/DBL$95-$115.

Crescent Court Hotel (400 Crescent Court, 75201; 871-3200, Fax 871-3272, 800-654-6541, 800-323-7500) 218 rooms and 1 and 2-bedroom suites, restaurant, outdoor heated pool, sauna, exercise center, wheelchair access, NS rooms, A/C, TV, boutiques, meeting facilities for 400, CC. Near the West End Marketplace and the Dallas Museum of Art. SGL$220-$310, DBL$250-$340, 1BR$400-$800, 2BR$1,000-$1,200.

Embassy Suites Market Center (2727 Stemmons Freeway, 75207; 630-5332, Fax 630-3446, 800-362-2779) 248 2-room suites, restaurant, lounge, free breakfast, pool, exercise center, jacuzzi, sauna, NS rooms, A/C, TV, gift shop, room service, laundry service, wheelchair access, airport courtesy car, meeting facilities, CC. 5 miles from the Love Field Airport and downtown area, 15 miles from the Dallas-Fort Worth International Airport, 6 miles from the Texas Stadium. SGL/DBL$69-$135.

Hampton Inn (12670 East Northwest Hwy., 75228; 613-5000, Fax 613-4535, 800-HAMPTON) 125 rooms, free breakfast, pool, children free with parents, NS rooms, A/C, TV, wheelchair access, computer hookups, fax, free local calls, meeting facilities, CC. 12 miles from the downtown area, 8 miles from the Fairgrounds, 12 miles from Love Field Airport, 25 miles from the Dallas-Fort Worth International Airport. SGL/DBL$45-$60.

Holiday Inn Market Center (1955 Market Center Blvd., 75207; 747-9551, Fax 747-9551 ext 7369, 800-HOLIDAY) 246 rooms, restaurant, lounge, children free with parents, wheelchair access, NS rooms, A/C, TV, fax, room service, no pets, meeting facilities for 250, CC. Near the World Trade Center, 3 miles from the Convention Center, 12 miles from the Dallas-Fort Worth International Airport, 4 miles from Love Field. SGL/DBL$85.

Hyatt Regency At Reunion (300 Reunion Blvd., 75207; 651-1234, Fax 742-8126, 800-233-1234) 943 rooms and suites, Regency Club, restaurant, lounge, exercise center, 24-hour room service, NS rooms, A/C, TV, complimentary newspaper, wheelchair access, CC. Near the Convention Center and the West End Historic District, 20 minutes from the Dallas-Fort Worth International Airport. SGL/DBL$134-$159.

La Quinta Inn East (8303 East R.L. Thornton Freeway, 75228; 324-3731, Fax 324-1652, 800-531-5900) 102 rooms, restaurant, lounge, heated pool, complimentary newspaper, free local calls, fax, laundry service, NS rooms, A/C, TV, wheelchair access, meeting facilities, CC. 23 miles from the Dallas-Fort Worth International Airport, 15 miles from Love Field , within 5 miles of the Cotton Bowl and downtown area. SGL$43, DBL$53-$63.

Loew's Anatole Hotel (2201 Stemmons Freeway, 75207; 748-1200, Fax 761-7520, 800-223-0888) 1,620 rooms and suites, restaurants, lounges, entertainment, indoor and outdoor pool, exercise center, jogging track, beauty shop, wheelchair access, NS rooms, A/C, TV, in-room refrigerators, boutiques, local transportation, meeting facilities, CC. SGL/DBL$115-$155, DBL$135-$175.

Park Plaza (1914 Commerce St., 75201; 747-7000, Fax 742-1337) 710 rooms and suites, restaurant, lounge, entertainment, free breakfast, indoor pool, exercise center, sauna, whirlpool, in-room refrigerators, wheelchair access, NS rooms, A/C, TV, meeting facilities, CC. SGL/DBL$110-$145.

Plaza of the Americas (650 North Pearl St., 75201; 979-9000, Fax 953-1931, 800-225-5843) 442 rooms and suites, restaurant, lounge, entertainment, exercise center, tennis courts, local transportation, boutiques, children free with parents, wheelchair access, NS rooms, A/C, TV, room service, beauty shop, meeting facilities, CC. SGL/DBL$150-$195, STS$199-$325.

Quality Hotel Market Center (2015 Market Center Blvd., 75207; 741-7481, Fax 747-6191, 800-221-2222) 280 rooms, restaurant, lounge, pool, exercise center, wheelchair access, NS rooms, A/C, TV, no pets, meeting facilities, CC. Near the Market Center, 5 miles from the Cotton Bowl and Love Field Airport, 3 miles from the Convention Center. SGL/DBL$35-$65.

Red Roof Inn (8108 East R.L. Thornton Freeway, 75228; 388-8741, Fax 3888741 ext 444, 800-843-7663) 119 rooms, NS rooms, A/C, TV, fax, wheelchair access, complimentary newspaper, free local calls, in-room computer hookups, CC. 5 miles from the downtown area and Convention Center, 28 miles from the Dallas-Fort Worth International Airport. SGL/DBL$35-$43.

Rodeway Inn (2027 Market Center Blvd., 75207; 748-2243, 800-424-4777) 82 rooms, restaurant, free breakfast, pool, wheelchair access, NS rooms, children free with parents, A/C, TV, senior rates, CC. SGL/DBL$50-$75.

Sheraton Suites Market Center (2101 Stemmons Freeway, 75207; 747-3000, Fax 742-5713, 800-325-3535) 253 rooms and suites, restaurant, lounge, indoor and outdoor pool, whirlpool, exercise center, wheelchair access, NS rooms, A/C, TV, 5 meeting rooms, 2,856 square feet of meeting and exhibition space, meeting facilities for 200, CC. Near the Market Center, World Trade Center, 3 miles from the Convention Center, 18 miles from the Dallas-Fort Worth International Airport. SGL/DBL$125-$250.

The Sheraton Adolphus Hotel (1321 Commerce St., 75202; 742-8200, Fax 747-3532, 800-221-9083, 800-325-3535) 431 rooms and 1- and 2-bedroom suites, 3 restaurants, 2 lounges, entertainment, 24-hour room service, exercise center, gift shop, business services, 15 meeting rooms, 22,000 square feet of meeting and exhibition space, meeting facilities for 2,400. Near the Convention Center, the Dallas Arts and Museum District and the Historic West End, 17 miles from the Dallas-Fort Worth International Airport. SGL$175-$235, DBL$200-$260, 1BR$475, 2BR$575.

Southland Center (400 North Olive, 75201; 922-8000, Fax 969-7650) 506 rooms and suites, restaurant, lounge, exercise center, boutiques, wheelchair access, pets OK, NS rooms, A/C, TV, meeting facilities, CC. SGL/DBL$85-$190, STS$200-$425.

StoneLeigh (2927 Maple Ave., 75201; 871-7111, Fax 871-7111 ext 1213, 800336-4242) 158 rooms and suites, restaurant, lounge, pool, lighted tennis courts, airport transportation, wheelchair access, NS rooms, A/C, TV, in-room refrigerators, CC. SGL/DBL$125-$160, STS$220.

Stouffer Hotel (2222 Stemmons Freeway, 75207; 631-2222, Fax 905-3814) 540 rooms and suites, restaurant, lounge, entertainment, heated pool, wheelchair access, gift shop, NS rooms, A/C, TV, gift shop, local transportation, pets OK, in-room refrigerators, CC. SGL/DBL$140-$175, STS$185.

Southwest Dallas

Classic Motor Inn (9229 Carpenter Freeway, 75247; 631-6663, Fax 631-6616, 800-253-7377) 135 rooms and suites, restaurant, free breakfast, pool, exercise center, sauna, wheelchair access, NS rooms, A/C, TV, in-room refrigerators, CC. SGL/DBL$35-$50.

Northwest Dallas

Best Western Windsor Suites Hotel (2363 Stemmons Trail, 75220; 350-2300, Fax 350-5144, 800-528-1234) 95 2-room suites, restaurant, free breakfast, pool, spa, jacuzzi, NS rooms, A/C, TV, complimentary newspaper, in-room refrigerators and microwaves, children free with parents, fax, CC. 3 miles from the Dallas-Fort Worth International Airport. SGL$55-$80, DBL$65-$90, X$10.

Days Inn (1575 Regal Row, 75247; 638-6100, 800-325-2525) 200 rooms, free breakfast, lounge, pool, children free with parents, pets OK, fax, free local calls, wheelchair access, NS rooms, A/C, airport transportation, TV, meeting facilities for 300, senior rates, CC. 8 miles from the downtown area, 12 miles from the Dallas-Fort Worth International Airport. SGL/DBL$40-$85.

Embassy Suites Love Field (3880 West Northwest Hwy., 75220; 357-4500, Fax 357-0683, 800-362-2779) 248 2-room suites, restaurant, lounge, free breakfast, pool, exercise center, jacuzzi, sauna, gift shop, NS rooms, A/C,

TV, wheelchair access, laundry service, room service, airport courtesy car, CC. 13 miles from the Dallas-Fort Worth International Airport, 6 miles from the World Trade Center. SGL/DBL$75-$125.

Embassy Park Suites (13131 North Central Expressway, 75243; 234-3300, Fax 437-4247, 800-EMBASSY) 280 rooms, restaurant, free breakfast, lounge, entertainment, pool, exercise center, jacuzzi, wheelchair access, NS rooms, A/C, TV, in-room refrigerators, meeting facilities, CC. SGL/DBL$65-$88.

La Quinta Inn (1625 Regal Row, 75247; 630-5701, Fax 634-2315, 800-531-5900) 132 rooms, restaurant, lounge, heated pool, complimentary newspaper, free local calls, fax, laundry service, NS rooms, A/C, TV, wheelchair access, airport transportation, meeting facilities, CC. 3 miles from the Convention Center, Cotton Bowl and downtown area, 11 miles from the Dallas-Fort Worth International Airport, 3 miles from Love Field. SGL/DBL$45-$60.

Le Baron (1055 Regal Row, 75247; 634-8550, Fax 634-9512) 333 rooms and suites, restaurant, lounge, entertainment, pool, exercise center, lighted tennis courts, wheelchair access, in-room refrigerators, NS rooms, A/C, TV, pets OK, meeting facilities, CC. SGL/DBL$75-$95, STS$160.

Marriott Residence Inn (6950 North Stemmons Freeway, 75247; 631-2472, Fax 634-9645, 800-331-3131) 253 suites, restaurant, lounge, indoor and outdoor pool, exercise center, whirlpool, in-room refrigerators, laundry service, in-room computer hookups, wheelchair access, NS rooms, A/C, TV, pets OK, VCRs, gift shop, meeting facilities for 35, CC. 6 miles from the downtown area, 2.5 miles from the World Trade Center and Info Mart, 3 miles from Texas Stadium and 10 miles from the Dallas-Fort Worth International Airport. SGL/DBL$98-$138.

Rodeway (13900 North Central Expressway, 75243; 231-5181, 800-228-2000) 177 rooms, pool, exercise center, jacuzzi, meeting facilities, CC. SGL$35, DBL$37.

Radisson Stemmons (2230 West Northwest Hwy., 75220; 351-4477, Fax 351-4499, 800-228-9822) 195 rooms, restaurant, lounge, pool, exercise center, jacuzzi, gift shop, local transportation, wheelchair access, NS rooms, A/C, TV, pets OK, in-room refrigerators, airport courtesy car, meeting facilities, CC. SGL/DBL$95-$115.

Red Roof Inn (10335 Gardner Rd., 75220; 506-8100, Fax 556-0072, 800-843-7663) 112 rooms, NS rooms, A/C, TV, fax, wheelchair access, complimentary newspaper, free local calls, in-room computer hookups, pets OK, senior rates, CC. 8 miles from the Dallas-Fort Worth International Airport, 8 miles from the downtown area, 6 miles from the World Trade Center. SGL$35-$37, DBL$38-$40.

Summitt Hotel (2645 LBJ Freeway, 75234; 243-3363, Fax 484-7082, 800-228-3555) 376 rooms and suites, restaurants, lounge, entertainment, indoor and outdoor pool, exercise center, jacuzzi, meeting facilities, CC. SGL$105, DBL$115.

Other Locations

Drury Inn (2421 Walnut Hill, 75229; 484-3330, Fax 484-3330 ext 240, 800-325-8300) 130 rooms and suites, restaurant, free breakfast, pool, wheelchair access, NS rooms, A/C, TV, pets OK, CC. SGL/DBL$55-$70.

Hampton Inn Walnut Hill (11069 Composite Dr., 75229; 484-6557, Fax 484-6557, 800-HAMPTON) 116 rooms, free breakfast, pool, pets OK, children free with parents, NS rooms, A/C, TV, wheelchair access, computer hookups, fax, free local calls, meeting facilities. 2 miles from Texas Stadium, 3 miles from the Galleria, 12 miles from Love Field Airport, 20 miles from the Dallas-Fort Worth International Airport. SGL/DBL$55-$70.

Motel 6 Southeast (9626 C.F. Hawn Expressway, 75217; 286-7952) 125 rooms, A/C, TV, CC. SGL/DBL$36-$42.

Scottish Inns (4150 North Central Expressway, 75204; 827-4310) 80 rooms, restaurant, pool, children free with parents, no pets, CC. 3 miles from the Cotton Bowl, Fairgrounds and the downtown area, 20 miles from the Dallas-Fort Worth International Airport. SGL/DBL$50-$65.

Sheraton LBJ Northeast (11350 LBJ Freeway, 75238; 341-5400, 800-325-3535) 246 rooms, restaurant, lounge, pool, exercise center, jacuzzi, room service, children free with parents, NS rooms, A/C, TV, meeting facilities, CC. SGL/DBL$68-$88.

Decatur

Area Code 817

Comfort Inn (1709 Hwy. 287, 76234; 627-6919, 800-221-2222) 43 rooms, free breakfast, pool, whirlpools, sauna, exercise center, wheelchair access, NS rooms, no pets, children under 18 free with parents, A/C, TV, meeting facilities, senior rates, CC. SGL/DBL$40-$55.

Del Rio

Area Code 210

Best Western Inn (810 Ave. F., 78840; 775-7511, Fax 774-2194, 800-528-1234) 62 rooms, pool, exercise center, children free with parents, A/C, NS rooms, TV, laundry facilities, wheelchair access, pets OK, meeting facilities, pets OK, senior rates, CC. SGL/DBL$45-$61.

Best Western Inn (2000 Ave. F, 78840; 775-6323, 800-528-1234) 58 rooms, restaurant, pool, exercise center, children free with parents, A/C, in-room computer hookups, NS rooms, TV, laundry facilities, in-room refrigerators, microwaves and coffee makers, wheelchair access, pets OK, meeting facilities, senior rates, CC. SGL/DBL$45-$75.

Ramada Inn (2101 Ave. F, 78840; 775-1511, Fax 775-1551 ext 113, 800-2-RAMADA) 127 rooms and suites, restaurant, free breakfast, lounge, entertainment, heated pool, jacuzzi, exercise center, wheelchair access, NS rooms, pets OK, A/C, in-room refrigerators and coffee makers, TV, children under 18 free with parents, room service, laundry facilities, 3 meeting rooms, meeting facilities for 200, senior rates, CC. SGL/DBL$55-$66, STS$113.

Remington Inn (3808 Hwy. 90 West, 78840; 775-0585) 96 rooms and 2-bedroom suites, heated pool, A/C, pets OK, children free with parents, TV, NS rooms, wheelchair access, CC. SGL/DBL$25-$45.

Twin City Inn (2005 Ave. F., 78840; 775-7591) 100 rooms, pool, A/C, TV, NS rooms, wheelchair access, children free with parents, in-room refrigerators, pets OK, CC. SGL/DBL$40-$45.

Denison
Area Code 903

Holiday Inn (Denison 75020; 465-6800, 800-HOLIDAY) 100 rooms, restaurant, lounge, pool, exercise center, children under 19 free with parents, wheelchair access, A/C, TV, in-room coffee makers, NS rooms, fax, room service, no pets, laundry service, meeting facilities for 300, senior rates, CC. SGL/DBL$48-$60.

Denton
Area Code 817

Exel Inn (4211 I-35 East North, 76201; 383-1471) 114 rooms, pool, laundry facilities, whirlpool tubs, laundry facilities, pets OK, VCRs, A/C, TV, NS rooms, wheelchair access, in-room refrigerators, senior rates, CC. SGL/DBL$27-$40.

Holiday Inn (1500 Dallas Dr., 76205; 387-3511, 800-HOLIDAY) 144 rooms and suites, restaurant, lounge, pool, exercise center, children under 19 free with parents, wheelchair access, A/C, TV, free local calls, airport transportation, in-room refrigerators, microwaves and coffee makers, NS rooms, fax, room service, no pets, laundry service, meeting facilities, senior rates, CC. SGL/DBL$50-$65.

La Quinta Inn (700 Fort Worth Dr., 76201; 387-5840, Fax 387-2493, 800-531-5900) 100 rooms, restaurant, free breakfast, lounge, pool, complimentary newspaper, free local calls, pets OK, in-room refrigerators, fax, laundry service, NS rooms, wheelchair access, TV, A/C, meeting facilities, CC. SGL/DBL$41-$46.

Quality Inn (820 South I-35, 76205; 387-0591, 800-221-2222) 61 rooms and suites, restaurant, free breakfast, pool, exercise center, whirlpools, children free with parents, A/C, TV, room service, laundry service, NS rooms, meeting facilities, senior rates, CC. SGL/DBL$40-$200.

Radisson Hotel and Conference Center (2211 I-35 North, 76205; 565-8499, 800-333-3333) 150 rooms and suites, restaurant, lounge, entertainment, pool, exercise center, in-room refrigerators, microwaves and coffee makers, VCRs, wheelchair access, pets OK, TV, A/C, children free with parents, pets OK, CC. SGL/DBL$65-$75.

Desoto
Area Code 214

Holiday Inn (151 North Beckley, 75115; 224-9100, Fax 228-8283, 800-HOLIDAY) rooms and suites, restaurant, lounge, pool, exercise center, children under 19 free with parents, wheelchair access, A/C, TV, NS rooms, fax, room service, no pets, laundry service, meeting facilities, senior rates, CC. SGL/DBL$58-$64.

Dublin
Area Code 817

Central Motor Inn (723 North Patrick, 76446; 445-2138) 21 rooms, pool, in-room refrigerators, A/C, TV, NS rooms, wheelchair access, children free with parents, no pets, CC. SGL/DBL$25-$35.

Dumas
Area Code 806

Best Western Inn (1712 South Dumas Ave., 79029; 935-6441, 800-528-1234) 103 rooms, indoor heated pool, exercise center, whirlpools, in-room refrigerators and microwaves, children free with parents, A/C, NS rooms, TV, laundry facilities, wheelchair access, in-room computer hookups, VCRs, pets OK, meeting facilities, senior rates, CC. SGL/DBL$45-$75.

Econo Lodge (1719 South Dumas Ave., 79029; 935-9098, 800-4-CHOICE) 41 rooms, restaurant, free breakfast, pool, whirlpools, children under 12 free with parents, no pets, NS rooms, wheelchair access, A/C, TV, senior rates, CC. SGL/DBL$28-$48.

Super 8 Motel (119 West 17th, 79029; 935-6222, 800-800-8000) 30 rooms and suites, restaurant, pets OK, children under 12 free with parents, free local calls, A/C, TV, in-room refrigerators and microwaves, fax, in-room computer hookups, pets OK, NS rooms, senior rates, wheelchair access, meeting facilities, CC. SGL/DBL$34-$46.

Duncanville
Area Code 214

Hampton Inn (4154 Preferred Pl., 75116; 298-4747, 800-HAMPTON) 120 rooms, restaurant, free breakfast, pool, exercise center, children under 18 free with parents, NS rooms, wheelchair access, in-room computer hookups, fax, TV, A/C, free local calls, pets OK, meeting facilities, CC. SGL/DBL$47-$60.

Holiday Inn Southwest (711 East Camp Wisdom Rd., 75116; 298-8911, Fax 298-8983, 800-HOLIDAY) 122 rooms and suites, restaurant, lounge, exercise center, children stay free with parents, wheelchair access, NS rooms, A/C, TV, fax, room service, pets OK, meeting facilities, CC. SGL/DBL$65-$96.

Eagle Pass
Area Code 512

Eagle Pass Inn (2150 North Hwy. 277, 78852; 773-9531) 56 rooms, restaurant, lounge, pool, A/C, TV, NS rooms, wheelchair access, children free with parents, pets OK, local transportation, CC. SGL/DBL$28-$45.

La Quinta Inn (2525 Main St., 78852; 773-7000, Fax 773-8852, 800-531-5900) 130 rooms, restaurant, free breakfast, lounge, pool, complimentary newspaper, free local calls, fax, laundry service, NS rooms, wheelchair access, TV, A/C, local transportation, pets OK, meeting facilities, CC. SGL/DBL$47-$55.

Eastland
Area Code 817

Budget Host Motor Inn (I-20 and Hwy. 570, 76448; 629-2655, Fax 629-1914, 800-283-4678) 66 rooms, restaurant, lounge, pool, pets OK, laundry facilities, NS rooms, wheelchair access, A/C, TV, senior rates, children free with parents, CC. SGL/DBL$32-$48.

Econo Lodge (2001 I-20 West, 76448; 629-3324, 800-4-CHOICE) 46 rooms, restaurant, lounge, free breakfast, pool, children under 12 free with parents, no pets, NS rooms, wheelchair access, A/C, TV, senior rates, CC. SGL/DBL$32-$40.

Sleephouse Motel (3900 I-20 East, 76448; 629-3336) 30 rooms, pets OK, in-room refrigerators and microwaves, children free with parents, A/C, TV, NS rooms, wheelchair access, CC. SGL/DBL$24-$35.

Edinburg
Area Code 210

Rodeway Inn University (1400 West University Dr., 78539; 381-5400, 800-424-4777) 95 rooms, restaurant, pool, wheelchair access, NS rooms, children free with parents, A/C, TV, senior rates, CC. SGL/DBL$36-$65.

El Campo
Area Code 409

El Campo Inn (210 West Hwy. 59, 77437; 543-1110) 60 rooms, pool, whirlpool tub, pets OK, in-room refrigerators, children free with parents, laundry facilities, A/C, TV, NS rooms, wheelchair access, CC. SGL/DBL$35-$48.

El Paso
Area Code 915

Best Western Airport Inn (7144 Gateway East, 79915; 779-7700, Fax 772-1920, 800-528-1234) 175 rooms, restaurant, free breakfast, lounge, pool, exercise center, children free with parents, A/C, NS rooms, TV, laundry facilities, wheelchair access, pets OK, meeting facilities, senior rates, CC. SGL/DBL$41-$75.

Beverly Crest Motor Inn (8709 Dyer St., 79904; 755-7631) 49 rooms, pool, kitchenettes, A/C, TV, pets OK, NS rooms, wheelchair access, CC. SGL/DBL$28-$40.

Budgetel Inn (7620 North Mesa St., 79912; 585-2999, 800-428-3438) 107 rooms and suites, free breakfast, children under 18 free with parents, A/C, wheelchair access, in-room refrigerators and microwaves, NS rooms, free local calls, in-room computer hookups, pets OK, fax, VCRs, TV, meeting facilities, CC. SGL/DBL$38-$50.

Camino Real Paso del Norte (101 South El Paso St., 79901; 534-3000, 800-722) 375 rooms and suites, restaurant, lounge, entertainment, heated pool, exercise center, sauna, whirlpools, A/C, TV, children free with parents, no pets, in-room refrigerators and microwaves, NS rooms, wheelchair access, senior rates, CC. SGL/DBL$115-$135.

Cliff Inn (1600 Cliff Dr., 79902; 533-6700, Fax 544-2127, 800-333-2543) 80 rooms, A/C, TV, no pets, children free with parents, NS rooms, wheelchair access, CC. SGL/DBL$52-$62.

Comfort Inn (900 Yarborough Dr., 79915; 594-9111, 800-221-2222) 185 rooms and suites, free breakfast, pool, whirlpools, wheelchair access, NS rooms, no pets, children under 18 free with parents, in-room refrigerators, local transportation, kitchenettes, A/C, TV, meeting facilities, senior rates, CC. SGL/DBL$42-$46.

Coral Motel (6420 Montana Ave., 79925; 772-3263) 32 rooms and 2-bedroom efficiencies, no pets, A/C, TV, NS rooms, wheelchair access, CC. SGL/DBL$32-$44.

Days Inn Airport (6308 Montana Ave., 79925; 778-6661, Fax 778-7926, 800-325-2525) 69 rooms and suites, outdoor pool, children free with parents, room service, laundry service, A/C, TV, free local calls, pets OK, fax, wheelchair access, NS rooms, senior rates, CC. SGL/DBL$39-$48.

Days Inn (9125 West Gateway Dr., 79925; 593-8400, Fax 599-1268, 800-325-2525) 115 rooms and suites, free breakfast, outdoor pool, children free with parents, room service, laundry service, A/C, TV, free local calls, pets OK, airport transportation, fax, wheelchair access, NS rooms, senior rates, CC. SGL/DBL$42-$64.

Econo Lodge (6363 Montana Ave., 79925; 778-3311, 800-4-CHOICE) 59 rooms, pool, children under 12 free with parents, no pets, airport transportation, NS rooms, wheelchair access, A/C, TV, senior rates, CC. SGL/DBL$30-$50.

El Parador Hotel (6400 Montana, 79925; 772-4231, 800-772-4231) 100 rooms, restaurant, whirlpools, A/C, TV, NS rooms, wheelchair access, airport transportation, no pets, children free with parents, meeting facilities, CC. SGL/DBL$35-$45.

Embassy Suites (6100 Gateway East, 79905; 770-6222, Fax 779-8846, 800-EMBASSY) 185 2-room suites, restaurant, lounge, free breakfast, lounge, heated pool, whirlpool, exercise center, sauna, room service, laundry service, wheelchair access, complimentary newspaper, free local calls, in-room refrigerators and coffee makers, airport transportation, pets OK, NS rooms, gift shop, local transportation, business services, meeting facilities, CC. SGL/DBL$90-$104.

Hilton El Paso Airport Hotel (2027 Airway Blvd., 79925; 778-4241, Fax 772-6871, 800-HILTONS) 275 rooms and suites, restaurant, lounge, entertainment, pool, exercise center, sauna, jacuzzi, children free with parents, NS rooms, wheelchair access, no pets, gift shop, in-room refrigerators, room service, laundry facilities, A/C, TV, airport transportation, business services, meeting facilities, CC. SGL/DBL$85-$95.

Holiday Inn (900 Sunland Park Dr., 79922; 833-2900, 800-HOLIDAY) 175 rooms, restaurant, lounge, pool, exercise center, children under 19 free with parents, wheelchair access, A/C, TV, NS rooms, fax, room service, airport transportation, VCRs, no pets, laundry service, meeting facilities for 120, senior rates, CC. SGL/DBL$65-$78.

wheelchair access, A/C, TV, NS rooms, fax, room service, no pets, laundry service, meeting facilities, senior rates, CC. SGL/DBL$65-$125.

Howard Johnson Lodge (8887 Gateway West, 79925; 591-9471, Fax 591-5602, 800-I-GO-HOJO) 140 rooms, restaurant, lounge, pool, children free with parents, wheelchair access, NS rooms, TV, A/C, room service, no pets, laundry facilities, airport transportation, senior rates, meeting facilities for 135, CC. SGL/DBL$45-$60.

La Quinta Inn (6140 Gateway Blvd. East, 79905; 778-9321, Fax 779-1505, 800-531-5900) 121 rooms, restaurant, free breakfast, lounge, pool, complimentary newspaper, free local calls, fax, laundry service, NS rooms, wheelchair access, TV, airport transportation, A/C, meeting facilities, CC. SGL/DBL$50-$55.

La Quinta Inn (11033 Gateway Blvd. West, 79935; 591-2244, Fax 592-9300, 800-531-5900) 138 rooms, restaurant, free breakfast, lounge, pool, complimentary newspaper, free local calls, fax, laundry service, NS rooms, wheelchair access, TV, A/C, meeting facilities, CC. SGL/DBL$45-$50.

La Quinta Inn (7550 Remcon Circle, 79912; 833-2522, Fax 581-9303, 800-531-5900) 130 rooms, restaurant, free breakfast, lounge, pool, complimentary newspaper, free local calls, fax, in-room refrigerators, pets OK, laundry service, NS rooms, wheelchair access, TV, A/C, meeting facilities, CC. SGL/DBL$50-$55.

Marriott Hotel (1600 Airway Boulevard, 79925; 779-3300, Fax 772-0915, 800-228-9290) 296 rooms and suites, restaurant, lounge, entertainment, indoor and outdoor pool, exercise center, whirlpools, sauna, airport courtesy car, airline ticket desk, car rental desk, wheelchair access, TV, A/C, in-room refrigerators and coffee makers, NS rooms, laundry service, gift shop, children free with parents, meeting facilities, senior rates, CC. SGL/DBL$65-$110.

Motel 6 Mid-City (4800 Gateway East, 79905; 533-7521, 505-891-6161) pool, free local calls, children under 17 free with parents, NS rooms, wheelchair access, pets OK, A/C, TV, CC. SGL/DBL$42-$48.

Motel 6 (1330 Lomaland, 79935; 592-6386, 505-891-6161) pool, free local calls, children under 17 free with parents, NS rooms, wheelchair access, pets OK, A/C, TV, CC. SGL/DBL$36-$44.

Park Inn International (6099 Montana, 79925; 778-3341, Fax 772-3249, 800-437-PARK) 120 rooms, suites, restaurant, airport transportation, A/C, TV, wheelchair access, NS rooms, meeting facilities for 150, CC. SGL/DBL$35-$48.

Quality Inn (6201 Gateway West, 79925; 778-6611, 800-221-2222) 307 rooms and suites, restaurant, lounge, entertainment, pool, exercise center, children free with parents, A/C, airport transportation, in-room refrigerators and microwaves, VCRs, TV, room service, laundry service, NS rooms, meeting facilities, senior rates, CC. SGL/DBL$45-$93.

Radisson Suite Inn (1770 Airway Blvd., 79925; 772-3333, Fax 779-3323, 800-333-3333) 149 rooms and suites, restaurant, lounge, entertainment, pool, exercise center, in-room refrigerators, microwaves and coffee makers, children free with parents, VCRs, wheelchair access, airport transportation, no pets, NS rooms, TV, A/C, senior rates, CC. SGL/DBL$80-$95.

Residence Inn (6791 Montana Ave., 79925; 772-8000, 800-331-3131) 200 rooms and suites, free breakfast, in-room refrigerators, coffee makers and microwaves, laundry facilities, TV, A/C, VCRs, no pets, complimentary newspaper, fireplaces, children free with parents, NS rooms, wheelchair access, airport transportation, meeting facilities for 130, CC. SGL/DBL$90-$125.

Sunset Heights Bed and Breakfast (717 West Yandell, 79902; 544-1743, 800-767-8513) 5 rooms, free breakfast, no pets, children free with parents, A/C, TV, CC. SGL/DBL$80-$145.

Travelers Inn (10635 Gateway West, 79935; 595-1913, Fax 591-8307, 800-633-8300) 127 rooms, heated pool, whirlpools, A/C, TV, in-room refrigerators, no pets, children free with parents, NS rooms, wheelchair access, CC. SGL/DBL$34-$44.

Westar Suites (8250 Gateway East, 79935; 591-9600, Fax 591-3262, 800-255-1755) 126 suites, heated pool, whirlpools, airport transportation, no pets, children stay free with parents, in-room refrigerators and microwaves, VCRs, A/C, TV, NS rooms, wheelchair access, senior rates, CC. SGL/DBL$65-$74.

Ennis

Area Code 214

Quality Inn (107 Wagon Wheel Dr., 75119; 875-9641, 800-221-2222) 68 rooms and suites, restaurant, lounge, pool, exercise center, children free with parents, A/C, TV, VCRs, no pets, room service, laundry service, NS rooms, meeting facilities, senior rates, CC. SGL/DBL$40-$60.

Euless

Area Code 817

La Quinta Inn (1001 West Airport Freeway, 76040; 540-0233, Fax 283-8712, 800-531-5900) 130 rooms, restaurant, free breakfast, lounge, pool, complimentary newspaper, free local calls, fax, laundry service, NS rooms, wheelchair access, TV, pets OK, airport transportation, A/C, meeting facilities, CC. SGL/DBL$50-$56.

Ramada Inn (2201 West Airport Freeway, 76040; 800-2-RAMADA) 150 rooms and suites, restaurant, lounge, pool, wheelchair access, NS rooms, pets OK, A/C, TV, children under 18 free with parents, kitchenettes, airport transportation, room service, laundry facilities, 2,000 square feet of meeting and exhibition space, meeting facilities, senior rates, CC. SGL/DBL$45-$75, STS$60-$80.

Farmers Branch
Area Code 214

Best Western Oak Tree Inn (13333 Stemmons Freeway, 75234; 241-8521, Fax 243-4103, 800-528-1234) 186 rooms and suites, restaurant, lounge, free breakfast, pool, sauna, room service, children free with parents, free local calls, airport courtesy car, pets OK, laundry service, fax, meeting facilities, CC. SGL$44-$59, DBL$49-$64, STS$88-$104, X$5.

Doubletree Hotel (1590 LBJ Freeway, 75234; 869-4300, Fax 869-3295, 800-828-7447) 339 rooms and suites, restaurant, lounge, heated pool, whirlpools, sauna, NS rooms, children under 18 free with parents, senior rates, CC, A/C, TV, in-room refrigerators, pets OK, business services, fax, in-room computer hookups, meeting facilities, CC. SGL/DBL$68-$100.

Econo Lodge (2275 Valley View Lane, 75234; 243-5500, Fax 243-8738, 800-4-CHOICE) 105 rooms, restaurant, pool, children under 12 free with parents, no pets, NS rooms, laundry facilities, wheelchair access, A/C, TV, senior rates, CC. SGL/DBL$38-$46.

La Quinta Inn (13235 Stemmons Freeway, 75234; 620-7333, 800-531-5900) 122 rooms, pool, complimentary newspaper, free local calls, fax, laundry service, NS rooms, wheelchair access, TV, A/C, pets OK, children free with parents, meeting facilities, CC. SGL/DBL$45-$49.

Fort Davis
Area Code 915

Indian Lodge (Hwy. 118 North, 79734; 426-3254) 39 rooms, restaurant, heated pool, no pets, children free with parents, A/C, TV, NS rooms, wheelchair access, CC. SGL/DBL$40-$55.

Limpia Hotel (Fort Davis 79734; 426-3237) 22 rooms, restaurant, lounge, entertainment, in-room refrigerators, no pets, A/C, TV, NS rooms, wheelchair access, CC. SGL/DBL$49-$68.

Prude Guest Ranch (Fort Davis 79734; 426-3202) 41 rooms, indoor heated pool, exercise center, lighted tennis courts, A/C, TV, NS rooms, wheelchair access, pets OK, CC. SGL/DBL$45-$75.

Fort Hancock
Area Code 915

Fort Hancock Motel (Fort Hancock 79839; 769-3981) 27 rooms, A/C, TV, NS rooms, wheelchair access, pets OK, laundry facilities, CC. SGL/DBL$35-$44.

Fort Stockton
Area Code 915

Comfort Inn (2601 I-10 West, 79735; 336-9781, 800-221-2222) 97 rooms, restaurant, free breakfast, pool, wheelchair access, NS rooms, no pets, in-room refrigerators, children under 18 free with parents, A/C, TV, meeting facilities, senior rates, CC. SGL/DBL$47-$58.

Econo Lodge (800 East Dickinson Blvd., 79735; 336-9711, 800-4-CHOICE) 70 rooms, restaurant, lounge, pool, children under 12 free with parents, no pets, NS rooms, wheelchair access, A/C, TV, senior rates, pets OK, CC. SGL/DBL$38-$48.

Texan Inn (3200 West Dickinson Blvd., 79735; 336-8531, Fax 336-6789) 100 rooms, restaurant, pool, pets OK, A/C, TV, NS rooms, wheelchair access, CC. SGL/DBL$65.

Fort Worth
Area Code 817

Downtown/Central

Best Western Plaza (2000 Beach St., 76103; 534-4801, Fax 534-4801, 800-528-1234) 164 rooms and suites, restaurant, lounge, whirlpool, children free with parents, NS rooms, A/C, TV, meeting facilities, CC. SGL$45-$89, DBL$52-$99, X$10.

CareALot Inn (1111 West Lancaster, 76102; 338-0215, 800-952-3011) 60 rooms, restaurant, lounge, entertainment, free local calls, children free with parents, 1,800 square feet of meeting and exhibition space, meeting facilities for 100, CC. SGL/DBL$45-$65.

Comfort Inn (2050 Beach St., 76103; 535-2591, 800-221-2222) 99 rooms, restaurant, free breakfast, lounge, pool, exercise center, wheelchair access, NS rooms, no pets, children under 18 free with parents, A/C, TV, meeting facilities, senior rates, CC. SGL/DBL$50-$68.

Downtown Motor Inn (600 North Henderson St., 76102; 332-6187, 800-952-3011, 800-221-4049) 60 rooms, restaurant, lounge, entertainment, wheelchair access, children free with parents, 1,875 square feet of meeting and exhibition space, meeting facilities for 100, CC. SGL/DBL$40-$65.

Park Central Hotel (1010 Houston St., 76102; 336-2011) 120 rooms, restaurant, lounge, pool, children free with parents, A/C, TV, 500 square feet of meeting and exhibition space, meeting facilities for 70, CC. SGL/DBL$30-$85.

Radisson Plaza (815 Main St., 76102; 870-1234, Fax 335-3408, 800-333-3333, 800-233-1234) 516 rooms, 3 restaurants, lounge, entertainment, pool, exercise center, children free with parents, concierge, room service, 18 meeting rooms, 14,000 square feet of meeting and exhibition space, meeting facilities for 1,300, CC. SGL/DBL$99-$143.

Ramada Inn Downtown (1701 Commerce St., 76102; 335-7000, 800-2-RAMADA) 254 rooms and suites, restaurant, lounge, entertainment, indoor pool, airport transportation, NS rooms, A/C, TV, children free with parents, free local calls, wheelchair access, 8,750 square feet of meeting and exhibition space, meeting facilities for 1,000, CC. In the business district near the Convention Center, 15 minutes from the Will Rogers Auditorium. SGL$62-$76, DBL$72-$86, STS$200, X$10.

Remington Hotel and Conference Center (600 Commerce St., 76102; 332-6900, Fax 332-6048, 800-677-4373) 300 rooms and suites, restaurant, lounge, entertainment, free local calls, children free with parents, 12 meeting rooms, 4,900 square feet of meeting and exhibition space, meeting facilities for 500, CC. SGL/DBL$61-$103.

Worthington Hotel (200 Main St., 76102; 870-1000, Fax 332-5679, 800-433-5677) 509 rooms and suites, 3 restaurants, 3 lounges, entertainment, pool, jacuzzi, sauna, exercise center, wheelchair access, NS rooms, A/C, TV, children free with parents, free local calls, tennis courts, 12,600 square feet of meeting and exhibition space, meeting facilities for 1,200, CC. SGL/DBL$89-$144.

North Fort Worth

Comfort Inn (4850 North Freeway 76106; 834-8001, 800-221-2222) 64 rooms, restaurant, free breakfast, pool, wheelchair access, NS rooms, no pets, children under 18 free with parents, A/C, TV, meeting facilities, senior rates, CC. SGL/DBL$40-$68.

Days Inn South (4213 South Freeway, 76115; 923-1987, 800-325-2525) 55 rooms, restaurant, free breakfast, children free with parents, NS rooms, A/C, TV, wheelchair access, fax, no pets, CC. 15 miles from the downtown area, 20 minutes from the airport. SGL$32-$38, DBL$36-$46, X$8.

HoJo Inn (4201 South Freeway, 76115; 923-8281, 800-I-GO-HOJO) 98 rooms, restaurant, lounge, pool, children free with parents, wheelchair access, NS rooms, TV, A/C, no pets, room service, airport transportation, laundry facilities, senior rates, meeting facilities, CC. SGL/DBL$37-$40.

Holiday Inn North (2540 Meacham Blvd., 76106; 625-9911, Fax 625-5132, 800-HOLIDAY) 247 rooms and suites, restaurant, lounge, indoor pool, exercise center, children free with parents, wheelchair access, NS rooms, A/C, TV, fax, room service, 8,000 square feet of meeting and exhibition space, meeting facilities for 1,000, CC. 18 miles from the airport, 5 miles from the downtown area, 9 miles from the Convention Center. SGL/DBL$60-$160.

Miss Molley's Bed and Breakfast (109 West Exchange Ave., 76106; 626-1522) 8 rooms, free breakfast, CC. SGL/DBL$45-$65.

Motel 6 North (3271 Interstate 35 West, 76106; 625-4359) 106 rooms, A/C, TV, CC. SGL/DBL$33-$38.

Sandpiper Inn (4000 North Main St., 76106; 625-5531, Fax 625-5531 ext 415) 83 rooms, lounge, pool, children free with parents, 1,700 square feet of meeting and exhibition space, meeting facilities for 100, CC. SGL/DBL$40-$60.

Stockyards Inn (109 East Exchange St., 76106; 625-6427, Fax 624-2571, 800-423-8471) 52 rooms, restaurant, lounge, entertainment, pool, exercise center, whirlpool, beauty shop, children free with parents, wheelchair access, NS rooms, A/C, TV, 1,500 square feet of meeting and exhibition space, meeting facilities for 75. SGL/DBL$65-$95.

West Forth Worth

Best Western West Branch Inn (7301 West Freeway, 76116; 244-7444, Fax 244-7902, 800-528-1234) 120 rooms and suites, restaurant, lounge, entertainment, pool, children free with parents, free local calls, in-room refrigerators, fax, NS rooms, A/C, TV, meeting facilities for 125, CC. 5 miles from the downtown area. SGL$38-$60, DBL$43-$65, X$5.

Clayton House Inn (1551 South University Dr., 76107; 336-9823, Fax 877-0735, 800-486-2162) 99 rooms, pool, children free with parents, free local calls, 2,500 square feet of meeting and exhibition space, CC. Near the Will Rogers Auditorium. SGL/DBL$29-$39.

Country Hotel Suites (8401 I-30 West, 76117; 560-0060, Fax 244-3047, 800-456-4000) 99 rooms and suites, pool, free local calls, children free with parents, 300 square feet of meeting and exhibition space, meeting facilities for 20, CC. SGL/DBL$44-$75.

Courtyard by Marriott (3150 Riverfront Dr., 76107; 335-1300, Fax 336-6926, 800-321-2211) 130 rooms, restaurant, lounge, pool, wheelchair access, children free with parents, A/C, TV, 2 meeting rooms, 800 square feet of meeting and exhibition space, meeting facilities for 100, CC. SGL/DBL$79-$109.

Deluxe Inn (3800 Hwy. 377, 76116; 560-2831) 64 rooms, children free with parents, free local calls, A/C, TV, CC. SGL/DBL$64.

Green Oaks Inn (6901 West Freeway, 76116; 738-7311, Fax 377-1308, 800-433-2174, 800-772-2341 in Texas) 282 rooms, restaurant, lounge, entertainment, 2 pools, sauna, jacuzzi, exercise center, lighted tennis courts, wheelchair access, free local calls, children free with parents, 6,000 square feet of meeting and exhibition space, 16 meeting rooms, meeting facilities for 1,000, CC. SGL/DBL$59-$98.

Hampton Inn (2700 Cherry Lane, 76116; 560-4180, Fax 560-8032, 800-HAMPTON) 125 rooms, free breakfast, pool, pets OK, children free with parents, NS rooms, A/C, TV, wheelchair access, computer hookups, fax, free local calls, meeting facilities, CC. 28 miles from the airport, 12 miles from Astroworld, 5 miles from the downtown area. SGL$48-$51, DBL$54-$57.

Lexington Hotel Suites (8409 West Airport Freeway, 76116; 560-0060, Fax 244-3047, 800-53-SUITES) 144 rooms and efficiencies, free breakfast, pool, wheelchair access, NS rooms, A/C, TV, pets OK, children free with parents, laundry services, CC. SGL/DBL$50-$75.

Marriott Residence Inn (1701 South University Dr., 76107; 870-1011, Fax 877-5500, 800-331-3131) 120 suites, pool, kitchens, in-room refrigerators, laundry service, wheelchair access, children free with parents, NS rooms, A/C, TV, pets OK, VCRs, 400 square feet of meeting and exhibition space, CC. 3 miles from the downtown area, 27 miles from the airport. SGL/DBL$105-$155.

Motel 6 West (8701 Interstate 20 West, 76116; 244-9740) 118 rooms, A/C, TV, CC. SGL/DBL$38-$42.

Ramada Inn Fort Worth Midtown (1401 South University Dr., 76107; 336-9311, Fax 877-3023, 800-2-RAMADA) 181 rooms and suites, restaurant, lounge, pool, NS rooms, A/C, TV, children free with parents, 4 meeting rooms, 1,550 square feet of meeting and exhibition space, meeting facilities for 150, CC. In the historic area, 1 mile from the Will Rogers Auditorium, 2 miles from the downtown area and Convention Center. SGL$50-$60, DBL$55-$65, STS$100, X$10.

Fredericksburg
Area Code 210

Budget Host Deluxe Inn (901 East Main St., 78624; 997-3344, Fax 997-4381, 800-283-4678) 25 rooms and suites, restaurant, laundry facilities, NS rooms, wheelchair access, A/C, TV, senior rates, in-room microwaves, pets OK, airport transportation, free local calls, children free with parents, CC. SGL/DBL$28-$55.

Comfort Inn (908 South Adams St., 78624; 997-9811, 800-221-2222) 46 rooms and suites, restaurant, free breakfast, pool, wheelchair access, NS rooms, no pets, children under 18 free with parents, A/C, TV, meeting facilities, senior rates, CC. SGL/DBL$50-$63.

Econo Lodge (810 South Adams St., 78624; 997-3437, 800-4-CHOICE) 36 rooms, pool, whirlpools, children under 12 free with parents, no pets, NS rooms, free local calls, wheelchair access, A/C, TV, senior rates, CC. SGL/DBL$46-$65.

Gainesville
Area Code 817

Best Western Inn (2103 I-35 North, 76240; 665-7737, 800-528-1234) 35 rooms, pool, exercise center, children free with parents, A/C, NS rooms, TV, laundry facilities, wheelchair access, pets OK, in-room coffee makers, no pets, meeting facilities, senior rates, CC. SGL/DBL$32-$41.

Comfort Inn (1936 I-35 North, 76240; 665-5599, 800-221-2222) 61 rooms, free breakfast, pool, wheelchair access, NS rooms, no pets, children under 18 free with parents, A/C, TV, meeting facilities, senior rates, CC. SGL/DBL$36-$42.

Holiday Inn (600 Fair Park Blvd., 76240; 665-8800, Fax 665-8709, 800-HOLIDAY) 118 rooms, restaurant, lounge, pool, exercise center, children under 19 free with parents, wheelchair access, A/C, TV, NS rooms, fax, room service, game room, pets OK, laundry service, meeting facilities for 185, senior rates, CC. SGL/DBL$45-$50.

Galveston
Area Code 409

Casa del Mar Lexington Hotels Suites and Inns (6102 Sewall Blvd., 77552; 740-2431, Fax 744-8896, 800-927-8483) 175 1-bedroom suites, free breakfast, heated pool, A/C, TV, fax, laundry facilities, children free with parents, kitchenettes, no pets, NS rooms, wheelchair access, CC. SGL/DBL$55-$135.

Commodore on the Beach (3618 Seawall Blvd., 77552; 763-2375) 90 rooms, pool, in-room refrigerators, pets OK, airport transportation, A/C, TV, NS rooms, wheelchair access, CC. SGL/DBL$40-$95.

Days Inn (6107 Broadway, 77551; 740-2491, Fax 740-1958, 800-325-2525) 88 rooms and suites, outdoor pool, children free with parents, room service, laundry service, A/C, TV, free local calls, in-room refrigerators, pets OK, fax, wheelchair access, NS rooms, senior rates, CC. SGL/DBL$25-$80.

Econo Lodge (2825 61st St., 77551; 744-7133, 800-4-CHOICE) 96 rooms, pool, children under 12 free with parents, no pets, NS rooms, wheelchair access, A/C, TV, free local calls, senior rates, CC. SGL/DBL$25-$90.

Gaido's Seaside Inn (3828 Seawall Blvd., 77550; 762-9625, Fax 762-4825) 108 rooms and suites, restaurant, lounge, pool, kitchenettes, A/C, TV, NS rooms, wheelchair access, meeting facilities, CC. SGL/DBL$40-$80.

Galvez Hotel (2024 Seawall Blvd., 77550; 765-7721) 228 rooms and suites, restaurant, lounge, indoor and outdoor pool, sauna, whirlpools, A/C, TV, NS rooms, wheelchair access, children free with parents, no pets, in-room refrigerators, senior rates, CC. SGL/DBL$100-$130.

Harbor View Inn (928 Ferry Rd., 77550; 762-3311) 49 rooms and efficiencies, A/C, TV, NS rooms, wheelchair access, no pets, kitchenettes, meeting facilities, CC. SGL/DBL$45-$85.

Holiday Inn On The Beach (5002 Seawall Blvd., 77551; 740-3581, Fax 744-6677, 800-HOLIDAY) 180 rooms and suites, restaurant, lounge, entertainment, pool, exercise center, whirlpools, sauna, children under 19 free with parents, wheelchair access, A/C, in-room refrigerators, TV, NS rooms, fax, room service, no pets, laundry service, meeting facilities, senior rates, CC. SGL/DBL$55-$115.

The Inn at San Luis (5400 Seawall Blvd., 77550; 744-5000, Fax 740-2209) 153 rooms and suites, restaurant, lounge, heated pool, whirlpools, children free with parents, A/C, TV, NS rooms, wheelchair access, CC. SGL/DBL$60-$120.

La Quinta Inn (1402 Seawall Blvd., 77550; 763-1224, 800-531-5900) 117 rooms, pool, complimentary newspaper, free local calls, fax, laundry service, NS rooms, wheelchair access, TV, A/C, pets OK, in-room refrigerators, meeting facilities, CC. SGL/DBL$51-$70.

Ramada Inn Resort (600 Strand, 77550; 765-5544, Fax 765-8601, 800-2-RAMADA) 241 rooms and suites, restaurant, lounge, pool, wheelchair access, NS rooms, pets OK, A/C, TV, children under 18 free with parents, room service, laundry facilities, meeting facilities, senior rates, CC. SGL/DBL$45-$125.

San Luis Hotel (5222 Seawall Blvd., 77551; 744-1500) 244 rooms, restaurant, lounge, heated pool, whirlpools, sauna, lighted tennis courts, in-room refrigerators, no pets, A/C, TV, NS rooms, wheelchair access, meeting facilities, CC. SGL/DBL$86-$168.

Tremont House (2300 Ships Mechanic Row, 77550; 763-0300, Fax 763-1539) 117 rooms, restaurant, lounge, A/C, TV, in-room refrigerators, VCRs, no pets, antique furnishings, NS rooms, wheelchair access, CC. SGL/DBL$130-$175.

Victorian Condominium Hotel (6300 Seawall Blvd., 77551; 740-3555) 235 rooms and 1- and 2-bedroom condominiums, heated pool, whirlpools, lighted tennis courts, kitchenettes, no pets, A/C, TV, NS rooms, wheelchair access, senior rates, CC. SGL/DBL$50-$195.

Victorian Inn (511 17th St., 77550; 762-3235) 3 rooms, free breakfast, A/C, TV, 1899 home, children over 12 welcome, no pets, private baths, fireplaces, senior rates, CC. SGL/DBL$105-$150.

Garland
Area Code 214

Catnap Creek Bed and Breakfast (417 Glen Canyon Dr., 75041; 530-0819) 3 rooms, free breakfast, hot tub, private baths, no children, no pets, NS, A/C, TV, CC. SGL/DBL$45-$65.

Comfort Inn (3536 West Kingsley Rd., 75041; 340-3501, 800-221-2222) 103 rooms, free breakfast, indoor heated pool, exercise center, whirlpools, sauna, kitchenettes, wheelchair access, NS rooms, no pets, children under 18 free with parents, A/C, TV, meeting facilities, senior rates, CC. SGL/DBL$48-$58.

Days Inn (6222 Beltline Rd., 75043; 226-7621, Fax 226-3617, 800-325-2525) 120 rooms, free breakfast, pool, jacuzzi, pets OK, children free with parents, free local calls, wheelchair access, NS rooms, A/C, TV, senior rates, meeting facilities, CC. 12 miles from the downtown area. SGL/DBL$32-$70.

La Quinta Inn (12721 I-35, 75041; 271-7581, Fax 271-1388, 800-531-5900) 122 rooms, restaurant, pool, free local calls, NS rooms, A/C, TV, wheelchair access, fax, complimentary magazines, laundry service, meeting facilities, CC. 25 miles from the Dallas-Fort Worth International Airport. SGL/DBL$40-$65.

Gatesville
Area Code 817

Regency Motor Inn (2307 Main St., 76528; 865-8405) 30 rooms, pool, whirlpools, no pets, A/C, TV, NS rooms, wheelchair access, CC. SGL/DBL$33-$43.

Georgetown
Area Code 512

Comfort Inn (1005 Leander Rd., 78628; 863-7504, 800-221-2222) 50 rooms, free breakfast, pool, wheelchair access, NS rooms, no pets, children under 18 free with parents, A/C, TV, meeting facilities, senior rates, CC. SGL/DBL$45-$82.

Historic Page House (1000 Leander Rd., 78628; 863-8979) 6 rooms, free breakfast, A/C, TV, NS, no pets, antique furnishings, local transportation, CC. SGL/DBL$70-$85.

Ramada Inn (333 North I-35, 78628; 869-2541, Fax 863-7073, 800-2-RAMADA) 97 rooms and suites, restaurant, lounge, pool, wheelchair access, NS rooms, airport transportation, pets OK, A/C, TV, children under 18 free with parents, room service, laundry facilities, 7 meeting rooms, meeting facilities for 250, senior rates, CC. SGL/DBL$60-$90.

Giddings
Area Code 409

Best Western Inn (3556 East Austin, 78942; 542-5791, 800-528-1234) 60 rooms, pool, exercise center, whirlpools, children free with parents, A/C, NS rooms, TV, laundry facilities, wheelchair access, pets OK, in-room coffee makers, pets OK, meeting facilities, senior rates, CC. SGL/DBL$35-$48.

Econo Lodge (Hwy. 290 East, 78942; 542-9666, 800-4-CHOICE) 62 rooms, pool, children under 12 free with parents, no pets, NS rooms, wheelchair access, A/C, TV, senior rates, CC. SGL/DBL$30-$42.

Giddings Sands Motel (1600 East Austin, 78942; 542-3111) 51 rooms, pool, whirlpools, in-room refrigerators, A/C, TV, NS rooms, wheelchair access, airport transportation, children free with parents, senior rates, CC. SGL/DBL$31-$46.

Granbury
Area Code 817

Best Western Inn (1204 East Hwy. 377, 76048; 573-8874, 800-528-1234) 42 rooms, pool, exercise center, children free with parents, A/C, NS rooms, TV, laundry facilities, wheelchair access, pets OK, in-room refrigerators, meeting facilities, senior rates, CC. SGL/DBL$40-$65.

Comfort Inn (1201 Hwy. 377 Bypass, 76048; 573-2611, 800-221-2222) 48 rooms, free breakfast, pool, wheelchair access, NS rooms, no pets, children under 18 free with parents, A/C, TV, meeting facilities, senior rates, CC. SGL/DBL$48-$58.

Days Inn (1339 North Plaza Dr., 76048; 573-2691, Fax 573-7662, 800-325-2525) 67 rooms and suites, restaurant, free breakfast, lounge, outdoor pool, children free with parents, room service, laundry service, A/C, TV, free local calls, pets OK, fax, wheelchair access, NS rooms, meeting facilities, senior rates, CC. SGL/DBL$59-$69.

Grand Prairie
Area Code 214

Hampton Inn (2050 North Hwy. 360, 75050; 988-8989, Fax 988-8989 ext 300, 800-HAMPTON) 140 rooms, restaurant, free breakfast, pool, exercise center, children under 18 free with parents, NS rooms, wheelchair access, in-room computer hookups, fax, TV, A/C, free local calls, airport transportation, pets OK, meeting facilities, CC. SGL/DBL$58-$74.

La Quinta Inn (1410 Northwest 19th St., Grand Prairie 75050; 641-3021, Fax 660-3041, 800-531-5900) 122 rooms, restaurant, lounge, heated pool, complimentary newspaper, free local calls, fax, laundry service, NS-rooms, A/C, TV, wheelchair access, meeting facilities. 5 miles from the Great Southwest Industrial District, 10 miles from the University of Dallas, 11 miles from the Dallas-Fort Worth International Airport, 17 miles from Love Field. SGL$45, DBL$48-$60.

Grapevine
Area Code 817

Dallas-Fort Worth Hilton Executive Conference Center (1800 Hwy. 26 East, 76051; 481-8444, Fax 481-3160, 800-HILTONS) 400 rooms and suites, 3 restaurants, 2 lounges, entertainment, indoor and outdoor pools, tennis courts, exercise center, wheelchair access, NS rooms, A/C, TV, 40,000 square feet of meeting and exhibition space, CC. SGL/DBL$119-$149.

Hilton Hotel and Conference Center (1800 Hwy. E, 76051; 481-8444, Fax 481-3160, 800-HILTONS) 395 rooms and suites, restaurant, lounge, entertainment, pool, exercise center, lighted tennis courts, whirlpools, sauna, airport transportation, children free with parents, NS rooms, wheelchair access, no pets, room service, in-room refrigerators and microwaves, laundry facilities, A/C, TV, business services, meeting facilities, CC. SGL/DBL$70-$150.

Hyatt Regency (Grapevine 75051; 453-1234, 800-233-1234) 1,367 rooms and suites, restaurant, lounge, entertainment, pool, whirlpools, exercise center, in-room refrigerators and coffee makers, children free with parents, no pets, airport transportation, room service, TV, A/C, NS rooms, wheelchair access, CC. SGL/DBL$80-$170.

Greenville
Area Code 903

Days Inn (5118 I-30, 75401; 455-8462, 800-325-2525) 57 rooms and suites, free breakfast, outdoor pool, children free with parents, room service, laundry service, A/C, TV, free local calls, pets OK, fax, wheelchair access,

NS rooms, in-room refrigerators, meeting facilities, senior rates, CC. SGL/DBL$28-$45.

Holiday Inn (1215 I-30, 75401; 454-7000, 800-HOLIDAY) 137 rooms, restaurant, lounge, pool, exercise center, whirlpools, in-room refrigerators and coffee makers, free local calls, children under 19 free with parents, wheelchair access, A/C, TV, NS rooms, fax, room service, no pets, laundry service, meeting facilities, senior rates, CC. SGL/DBL$45-$50.

Royal Inn (Greenville 75401; 455-9600) 60 rooms and 2-bedroom suites, pool, A/C, TV, NS rooms, wheelchair access, pets OK, children free with parents, CC. SGL/DBL$27-$40.

Harlingen
Area Code 512

Best Western Inn (6779 West Expressway 83, 78550; 425-7070, 800-528-1234) 102 rooms, restaurant, free breakfast, lounge, pool, exercise center, children free with parents, A/C, NS rooms, TV, laundry facilities, wheelchair access, airport transportation, limousine service, pets OK, meeting facilities, senior rates, CC. SGL/DBL$50-$60.

Fishermans Lodging (Harlingen 78551; 748-3581) 6 1-, 2- and 3-bedroom apartments, A/C, no pets, TV, airport transportation, kitchenettes, CC. SGL/DBL$65-$125.

Holiday Inn (1901 West Tyler, 78550; 324-1810, Fax 425-7227, 800-HOLIDAY) 148 rooms and suites. restaurant, lounge, entertainment, outdoor pool, exercise center, children under 19 free with parents, wheelchair access, A/C, kitchenettes, airport transportation, TV, NS rooms, fax, room service, no pets, laundry service, meeting facilities for 300, senior rates, CC. SGL/DBL$55-$76.

Holiday Vista Motel (1738 North Sunshine Strip, 78550; 423-6000) 49 rooms and efficiencies, pool, A/C, TV, NS rooms, wheelchair access, laundry facilities, no pets, CC. SGL/DBL$38-$44.

Hudson House Motel (500 Ed Cary Dr., 78550; 428-8911) 37 rooms, pool, A/C, TV, NS rooms, wheelchair access, airport transportation, kitchenettes, no pets, laundry facilities, CC. SGL/DBL$60.

La Quinta Inn (1002 South Expressway 83, 78550; 428-6888, 800-531-5900) 130 rooms, restaurant, pool, airport transportation, free local calls, fax, laundry service, no pets, NS rooms, wheelchair access, TV, children free with parents, A/C, meeting facilities, CC. SGL/DBL$50-$56.

Ramada Limited (4401 South Express 83, 78551; 800-2-RAMADA) 45 rooms and suites, restaurant, lounge, pool, whirlpools, in-room refrigerators and microwaves, wheelchair access, NS rooms, pets OK, A/C, TV, children under 18 free with parents, room service, laundry facilities, meeting facilities, senior rates, CC. SGL/DBL$55-$78.

Rodeway Inn (1821 West Tyler, 78550; 425-1040, 800-424-4777) 110 rooms, restaurant, lounge, pool, wheelchair access, NS rooms, children free with parents, A/C, no pets, TV, in-room coffee makers, airport transportation, senior rates, laundry facilities, CC. SGL/DBL$38-$48.

Ross Haus (Harlingen 78550; 425-1717) 4 rooms and suites, A/C, TV, NS rooms, children free with parents, no pets, kitchenettes, CC. SGL/DBL$28-$33.

Super 8 Motel (1201 South Expressway 83, 78552; 800-800-8000) 59 rooms and suites, restaurant, outdoor heated pool, pets OK, children under 12 free with parents, free local calls, A/C, TV, in-room refrigerators and microwaves, fax, NS rooms, senior rates, wheelchair access, meeting facilities, CC. SGL/DBL$40-$55.

Save Inn (1800 West Harrison, 78550; 425-1212) 120 rooms and efficiencies, A/C, no pets, TV, kitchenettes, CC. SGL/DBL$28-$36.

Sun Valley Motor Hotel (1900 South Sunshine Strip, 78550; 423-7222) 100 rooms and efficiencies, restaurant, lounge, entertainment, pool, in-room coffee makers, local transportation, beauty shop, free local calls, children free with parents, no pets, A/C, TV, NS rooms, wheelchair access, CC. SGL/DBL$48-$65.

Henderson
Area Code 903

Days Inn (1500 Hwy. 259 South, 75652; 657-9561, 800-325-2525) 81 rooms and suites, restaurant, free breakfast, outdoor pool, children free with parents, room service, laundry service, A/C, TV, free local calls, pets OK, fax, wheelchair access, NS rooms, meeting facilities, senior rates, CC. SGL/DBL$36-$42.

Hillsboro
Area Code 817

Ramada Inn (Hwy. 22, 76645; 582-3493, Fax 582-2755, 800-2-RAMADA) 98 rooms and suites, restaurant, lounge, pool, wheelchair access, NS rooms, pets OK, A/C, TV, children under 18 free with parents, airport transportation, room service, laundry facilities, meeting facilities, senior rates, CC. SGL/DBL$40-$56.

Hondo
Area Code 210

Whitetail Lodge (Hondo 78861; 426-3031) 53 rooms, pool, pets OK, children free with parents, A/C, TV, NS rooms, wheelchair access, CC. SGL/DBL$42-$58.

Houston
Area Code 713

Rental and Reservation Services:

Downtown Houston Bed and Breakfast (1200 Southmore Ave., 77004; 523-1114, Fax 523-0790)

Downtown Houston

Allen Park Inn (2121 Allen Pkwy., 77019; 521-9321, Fax 521-9321, 800-231-6310) 269 rooms and suites, restaurant, lounge, outdoor pool, exercise center, jacuzzi, sauna, children free with parents, in-room refrigerators, laundry service, NS rooms, A/C, TV, barber and beauty shop, 24-hour room service, wheelchair, no pets, fax business service, 7,000 square feet of meeting and exhibition space, meeting facilities for 350, CC. 1.6 miles from the Convention Center, 11 miles from Hobby Airport, 23 miles from the Houston Intercontinental Airport. SGL$78, DBL$86, STS$125-$250.

Days Inn Downtown (801 Calhoun, 77022; 659-2222, Fax 659-8348, 800-325-2525) 309 rooms, free breakfast, outdoor pool, spa, exercise center, local transportation, fax, children free with parents, free local calls, wheelchair access, NS rooms, A/C, TV, meeting facilities, CC. 24 miles from the Houston Intercontinental Airport, 1 mile from the Convention Center. SGL$45-$80, DBL$60-$90, X$10.

Doubletree Hotel At Allen Center (400 Dallas St., 77056; 759-0202, Fax 759-1166, 800-528-0444) 341 rooms and suites, 2 restaurants, lounge, children free with parents, airport courtesy car, wheelchair access, NS rooms, A/C, TV, business services, 14 meeting rooms, meeting facilities for 600, CC. 35 minutes from the Houston Intercontinental Airport, 25 minutes from Hobby Airport. SGL/DBL$95-$105.

Howard Johnson Lodge (4225 North Freeway, 77022; 695-6011, Fax 695-7567, 800-I-GO-HOJO) 200 rooms and suites, restaurant, lounge, entertainment, pool, jacuzzis, children free with parents, wheelchair access, NS rooms, TV, room service, A/C, no pets, laundry facilities, senior rates, meeting facilities, CC. SGL/DBL$39-$58.

Hyatt Regency (1200 Louisiana St., 77002; 654-1234, Fax 951-0934, 800-233-1234) 959 rooms and suites, Regency Club and Gold Passport Floors, restaurant, lounge, entertainment, outdoor pool, exercise center, NS-rooms, A/C, TV, complimentary newspaper, wheelchair access, business services, local transportation, CC. Near the Convention Center and the theater district. SGL/DBL$85-$135.

Lancaster Hotel (701 Texas Ave., 77002; 228-9500, Fax 223-0336, 800-231-0336) 93 rooms and suites, restaurant, lounge, exercise center, wheelchair access, airport courtesy car, A/C, TV, meeting facilities, CC. In the financial and theater district. SGL/DBL$145, STS$250.

The Lovett Inn (501 Lovett Blvd., 77066; 522-5224, Fax 528-6708, 800-779-5224) 6 rooms, free breakfast, pool, private bath, fax, meeting facilities, CC. SGL/DBL$50.

Robin's Nest (4104 Greeley, 77006; 528-5821, Fax 522-0708, 800-622-8343) 12 rooms, free breakfast, private bath, CC. SGL$60-$70.

Airport Area

Best Western Intercontinental Airport (6900 Will Clayton Pkwy., 77061; 446-3041, Fax 446-1468, 800-528-1234) 219 rooms and suites, restaurant, lounge, pool, airport courtesy car, gift shop, fax, children free with parents, laundry service, NS rooms, A/C, TV, no pets, CC. 1 mile from the Houston Intercontinental Airport. SGL/DBL$43.

Clarion Inn (500 North Sam Houston Pkwy., 77060; 931-0101, 800-221-2222) 378 rooms, restaurant, lounge, free breakfast, pool, whirlpools, no pets, NS rooms, children under 18 free with parents, senior rates, meeting facilities, A/C, TV, CC. SGL/DBL$45-$105.

Days Inn (8611 Airport Blvd., 77061; 947-0000, Fax 944-0357, 800-325-2525) 198 rooms, restaurant, jacuzzi, pool, children free with parents, free local calls, fax, no pets, airport transportation, exercise center, wheelchair access, NS rooms, A/C, TV, meeting facilities, CC. At the airport, 10 miles from the downtown area, 12 miles from the Astrodome. SGL/DBL$55-$70.

Days Inn (2200 South Wayside, 77023; 928-2800, Fax 928-3473, 800-325-2525) 100 rooms, free breakfast, pool, children free with parents, fax, pets OK, free local calls, wheelchair access, NS rooms, A/C, TV, CC. 5 miles from the Houston Intercontinental Airport and the downtown area. SGL/DBL$34-$47.

Days Inn Airport (17607 Eastex Freeway, 77061; 446-4611, Fax 446-4765, 800-325-2525) 152 rooms, restaurant, lounge, pool, wheelchair access, pets OK, NS rooms, A/C, TV, fax, children free with parents, meeting facilities for 70, CC. SGL/DBL$39-$54.

Doubletree Hotel At Intercontinental Airport (15747 JFK Blvd., 77032; 442-8000, Fax 590-8461, 800-528-0444) 325 rooms and suites, restaurant, lounge, outdoor pool, room service, airport courtesy car, children free with parents, NS rooms, A/C, TV, 19 meeting rooms, meeting facilities for 800, CC. 6 minutes from the Houston Intercontinental Airport. SGL/DBL$113, STS$175.

Hobby Airport Hilton (8181 Airport Blvd., 77061; 645-3000, Fax 645-3000 ext 902, 800-HILTONS) 310 rooms and 2bedroom suites, restaurant, lounge, outdoor pool, exercise center, jogging track, wheelchair access, NS rooms, A/C, TV, airport courtesy car, business services, meeting facilities for 1,200, CC. At the Hobby Airport, 9 miles from the downtown area and Convention Center. SGL/DBL$98, 2BR$168.

Holiday Inn Airport Express (702 Sam Houston Pkwy., 77060; 999-9942, Fax 999-9942, 800-HOLIDAY) 200 rooms, restaurant, lounge, outdoor pool, children free with parents, wheelchair access, NS rooms, A/C, TV, fax, room service, airport transportation, no pets, meeting facilities for 100. 3 miles from the Houston Intercontinental Airport, 16 miles from the downtown area, 20 miles from the Astrodome, CC. SGL/DBL$89.

Holiday Inn Airport (15222 JFK Boulevard, 77032; 449-2311, Fax 449-6833, 800-HOLIDAY) 400 rooms, restaurant, lounge, pool, exercise center, lighted tennis courts, children under 19 free with parents, wheelchair access, A/C, TV, car rental desk, NS rooms, fax, room service, airport transportation, pets OK, laundry service, meeting facilities, senior rates, CC. SGL/DBL$65-$90.

Holiday Inn Hobby Airport (9100 Gulf Freeway, 77061; 943-7979, 800-465-4329) 289 rooms and suites, restaurant, lounge, entertainment, indoor heated pool, exercise center, spa, local transportation, children under 19 free with parents, wheelchair access, A/C, TV, NS rooms, fax, room service, no pets, laundry service, meeting facilities, senior rates, CC. SGL/DBL$65-$125.

Howard Johnson Lodge (7777 Airport Blvd., 77061; 644-1261, Fax 644-9559, 800-800-I-GO-HOJO) 148 rooms, restaurant, lounge, entertainment, pool, exercise center, children free with parents, NS rooms, A/C, laundry facilities, TV, fax, airport courtesy car, car rental desk, room service, CC. At the Hobby Airport, 9 miles from the downtown area, 10 miles from NASA, 12 miles from the Astrodome. SGL/DBL$42-$65.

La Quinta Inn Intercontinental Airport (6 North Belt East, 77060; 447-6888, Fax 847-3921, 800-531-5900) 122 rooms, restaurant, lounge, heated pool, complimentary newspaper, free local calls, fax, laundry service, NS rooms, A/C, TV, wheelchair access, meeting facilities, CC. 5 miles from the Northpoint Business Center, 20 miles from the downtown area. SGL/DBL$58-$67.

Marriott Houston Airport (18700 Kennedy Blvd., 77032; 443-2310, Fax 443-5295, 800-228-9290) 566 rooms and suites, restaurant, lounge, outdoor pool, sauna, whirlpools, exercise center, room service, gift shop, laundry service, A/C, TV, NS rooms, wheelchair access, airport courtesy car, beauty shop, meeting facilities, senior rates, CC. SGL/DBL$115-$235.

Park Inn International (14819 Eastex Freeway, 77096; 441-4000, 800-437-PARK) 51 rooms, restaurant, pool, complimentary newspaper, NS rooms, CC. 4 miles from the Houston Intercontinental Airport and Deerbrook Mall, 12 miles from the Astrodome. SGL/DBL$39.

Quality Inn Airport (6115 Will Clayton Pkwy., 77025; 446-9131, Fax 446-2251, 800-231-6134, 800-221-2222) 172 rooms, restaurant, lounge, entertainment, pool, exercise center, room service, car rental desk, pets OK, wheelchair access, NS rooms, A/C, TV, meeting facilities, CC. 2 miles from the Houston Intercontinental Airport. SGL$56-$78.

Quality Inn Hobby Airport (1505 College Ave., 77087; 946-5900, 800-221-2222) 124 rooms, restaurant, pool, wheelchair access, NS rooms, A/C, TV, no pets, CC. 3 miles from the downtown area, 1 mile from the Houston Intercontinental Airport. SGL$58, DBL$65.

Sheraton Crown Hotel and Conference Center (15700 John F. Kennedy Blvd., 77032; 442-5100, Fax 987-9130, 800-325-3535) 419 rooms and suites, 3 restaurants, lounge, indoor and outdoor pools, whirlpools, spa, exercise center, wheelchair access, NS rooms, A/C, TV, airport courtesy car, 32,000 square feet of meeting and exhibition space, meeting facilities for 800, CC. 20 miles from the museum and theater district, 1.5 miles from the Houston Intercontinental Airport. SGL/DBL$70-$100.

West Houston

Adam's Mark Hotel (2900 Briarpark Dr., 77042; 978-7400, Fax 735-2726, 800-444-2326) 604 rooms, 2 restaurants, 3 lounges, entertainment, indoor and outdoor pools, sauna, exercise center, children stay free with parents, NS rooms, A/C, TV, in-room refrigerators, airport transportation, gift shop, wheelchair access, 21 meeting rooms, 31,000 square feet of meeting and exhibition space, CC. SGL$115, DBL$130, STS$190-$275.

Comfort Inn Greenspoint (12500 North Freeway, 77060; 876-3888, 800-221-2222) 175 rooms, free breakfast, pool, sauna, wheelchair access, NS rooms, A/C, TV, no pets, airport courtesy car, CC. 10 miles from the downtown area, 15 miles from the Convention Center, 9 miles from the Houston Intercontinental Airport. SGL/DBL$42-$71.

Days Inn (9799 Katy Freeway, 77024; 468-7801, 800-325-2525) 192 rooms, free breakfast, lounge, pool, children free with parents, fax, free local calls, pets OK, wheelchair access, NS rooms, A/C, TV, meeting facilities for 200, CC. 9 miles from the downtown area and Convention Center, 2 miles from the Town and Country Mall. SGL/DBL$45-$50, STS$55-$65.

Doubletree Hotel At Post Oak (2001 Post Oak Blvd., 77056; 961-9300, Fax 961-1557, 800-528-0444) 450 rooms, 2 restaurants, 2 lounges, outdoor pool, sauna, children free with parents, NS rooms, A/C, TV, wheelchair access, 21 meeting rooms, meeting facilities for 900, CC. 15 minutes from the downtown area, 30 minutes from the Houston Intercontinental Airport. SGL/DBL$105-$125.

Galleria Inn (4723 West Alabama, 77027; 621-2797, 800-448-8355) 50 suites, pool, in-room refrigerators and microwaves, A/C, TV, NS rooms, CC. Near the Galleria Shopping Center. STS$75.

Guest Quarters Suite Hotel (5353 Westheimer Rd., 77056; 961-9000, 800-424-2900) 335 1- and 2-bedroom suites, pool, exercise center, whirlpools, gift shop, NS rooms, A/C, TV, airport transportation, children free with parents, wheelchair access, meeting facilities for 200, CC. Near the Galleria Shopping Center. 1BR$124, 2BR$234.

Holiday Inn Crowne Plaza (2222 West Loop St., 77027; 961-7272, Fax 962-3327, 800-327-6213) 477 rooms and suites, restaurant, lounge, entertainment, indoor pool, exercise center, children under 19 free with parents, wheelchair access, A/C, TV, NS rooms, fax, airport transportation, car rental desk, room service, no pets, laundry service, meeting facilities, senior rates, CC. SGL/DBL$65-$86.

Holiday Inn (I-10 and Hwy. 6, 77079; 558-5580, Fax 496-4150, 800-HOLI-DAY) 344 rooms and suites, restaurant, lounge, indoor pool, exercise center, children under 19 free with parents, wheelchair access, A/C, TV, NS rooms, fax, room service, gift shop, pets OK, laundry service, meeting facilities, senior rates, CC. SGL/DBL$55-$76.

Houstonian Hotel and Conference Center (1111 North Post Oak Lane, 77024; 680-2626, Fax 680-2993, 800-231-2759, 800-392-0784 in Texas) 295 rooms and suites, 4 restaurants, 2 lounges, outdoor heated pools, sauna, exercise center, lighted tennis courts, children free with parents, in-room refrigerators, laundry service, complimentary newspaper, barber, limousine service, airport transportation, wheelchair access, audiovisual equipment, business service, fax, 35,000 square feet of meeting and exhibition space, CC. 2 miles from the Galleria, 45 minutes from Houston Intercontinental Airport, 30 minutes from Hobby Airport. SGL$139, STS$199-$800.

La Quinta Inn (8017 Katy Freeway, 77024; 688-8941, Fax 683-8410, 800-531-5900) 100 rooms, restaurant, lounge, heated pool, complimentary newspaper, free local calls, fax, laundry service, NS rooms, A/C, TV, wheelchair access, meeting facilities, CC. 5 miles from the Galleria Shopping Center, Memorial Center and University of Houston, 28 miles from the Houston Intercontinental Airport, 15 miles from Hobby Airport. SGL$53-$58.

Marriott Hotel (5150 Westheimer Rd., 77056; 961-1500, Fax 961-5045, 800-327-0200) 498 rooms and suites, restaurant, lounge, entertainment, indoor and outdoor pool, sauna, exercise center, whirlpools, NS rooms, A/C, TV, wheelchair access, gift shop, business services, meeting facilities, CC. Near the Galleria Shopping Center, 20 minutes from the downtown area and Astrodome. SGL$129$139, DBL$139-$149.

Marriott Westside (13210 Katy Freeway, 77079; 558-1234, Fax 558-0268, 800-233-1234) 400 rooms and suites, restaurant, lounge, entertainment, pool, exercise center, wheelchair access, A/C, TV, NS rooms, meeting facilities, CC. SGL/DBL$115-$140.

Ramada Inn (7787 Katy Freeway, 77024; 681-5000, Fax 682-8400, 800-2-RAMADA) 287 rooms and suites, restaurant, lounge, entertainment, pool, airport transportation, pets OK, NS rooms, A/C, TV, wheelchair access, 11 meeting rooms, meeting facilities for 400, CC. Near the Astrodome and Astroworld. SGL$49-$89, DBL$49-$99, STS$69, X$10.

Ritz Carlton (1919 Briar Oaks Lane, 77027; 840-7600, Fax 840-7600 ext 6175, 800-241-3333) 232 rooms and suites, Ritz Carlton Club, restaurant, lounge, entertainment, heated pool, exercise center, jogging track, A/C, TV, NS rooms, wheelchair access, 24-hour room service, 12 meeting rooms. CC. 15 minutes from the downtown business district. SGL/DBL$170, STS$270.

Sheraton Grande Hotel (2525 West Loop South, 77027; 961-3000, Fax 961-1490, 800-325-3535) 321 rooms and suites, restaurant, lounge, 24-hour room service, pool, spa, exercise center, gift shop, car rental desk, wheelchair access, NS rooms, A/C, TV, 9 meeting rooms, 10,000 square feet of meeting and exhibition space, meeting facilities for 500, CC. Near Memorial Park, the Astrodome and Galleria Shopping Center, 32 miles from the Houston Intercontinental Airport. SGL/DBL$139-$159.

Marriott Hotel (255 North Sam Houston Pkwy., 77060; 875-4000, Fax 875-6208, 800-289-2929) 391 rooms and suites, Concierge Level, restaurant, lounge, indoor and outdoor pool, sauna, whirlpools, exercise center, room service, airport courtesy car, NS rooms, A/C, TV, wheelchair access, gift shop, airline ticket desk, laundry service, meeting facilities, CC. 10 minutes from the Houston Intercontinental Airport, 25 minutes from the downtown area. SGL$65, DBL$75.

Sofitel Hotel (425 North Beltway 8, 77060; 445-9000, Fax 445-0629, 800-231-4612) 338 rooms, 2 restaurants, outdoor pool, sauna, exercise center, beauty shop, airport courtesy car, meeting facilities for 1,000, CC. 7 miles from the Houston Intercontinental Airport, 15 miles from the downtown area. SGL/DBL$145-$155.

Stouffer Presidente Hotel (6 Greenway Plaza East, 77046; 629-1200, Fax 629-4702, 800-468-3571) 400 rooms and suites, pool, sauna, exercise center, 24-hour room service, wheelchair access, complimentary newspaper, meeting facilities, CC. SGL$114-$159, DBL$124-$169.

TraveLodge Greenway Plaza (2828 Southwest Freeway, 77098; 526-4571, Fax 526-8709, 800-255-3050) 210 rooms, Executive Floor, restaurant, lounge, pool, exercise center, local transportation, room service, fax, A/C, TV, meeting facilities for 200, senior rates, CC. Near Summit Plaza, 10 minutes from the Astrodome and AstroWorld. SGL/DBL$45-$110.

Westin Hotel Galleria (5060 West Alabama Ave., 77056; 960-8100, Fax 960-6553, 800-228-3000) 485 rooms and suites, restaurant, lounge, pool, whirlpools, sauna, exercise center, jogging track, concierge, gift shop, pets OK, 24-hour room service, wheelchair access/room, NS rooms, A/C, TV, 30,000 square feet of meeting and exhibition space, meeting facilities for 2,500. Near the Galleria Shopping Center, 15 minutes from the downtown area and Convention Center, 25 miles from the Houston Intercontinental Airport. SGL$155, DBL$180, STS$300-$1,000, X$15.

Westin Hotel Oaks (5011 Westheimer, 77056; 960-8100, Fax 960-6554, 800-228-3000) 406 rooms and suites, restaurant, lounge, entertainment, pool, whirlpools, sauna, exercise center, tennis, jogging track, car rental desk, pets OK, gift shop, concierge, airport courtesy car, 24-hour room service, wheelchair access/room, NS rooms, A/C, TV, meeting facilities for 1,200, CC. 25 miles from the Houston Intercontinental Airport. SGL$165-$180, DBL$180-$195, STS$400-$1,300, X$15.

White House Motor Hotel (9300 South Main St., 77025; 666-2261, Fax 668-7697) 220 rooms, free breakfast, pool, wheelchair access. SGL/DBL$45-$65.

Wyndham Greenspoint (12400 Greenspoint Dr., 77060; 875-2222, Fax 875-1652, 800-822-4200) 472 rooms and suites, restaurant, lounge, pool, jogging track, whirlpools, exercise center, airport courtesy car, wheelchair access, 38,000 square feet of meeting and exhibition space, CC. Near the Greenspoint Mall. SGL/DBL$80-$125.

Wyndham Warwick (5701 Main St., 77005; 526-1991, Fax 639-4545, 800-822-4200, 800-323-7500, 800-822-4200) 307 rooms and suites, restaurant, lounge, pool, sauna, exercise center, 10 meeting rooms, 15,000 square feet of meeting and exhibition space, CC. In the museum district, 3 miles from the downtown area, near the Convention Center. SGL/DBL$77-$105.

Northwest Houston

Durham House Bed and Breakfast (921 Heights Blvd., 77008; 868-4654) 8 rooms, free breakfast, private baths, NS, no pets, antique furnishings, CC. SGL/DBL$65-$85.

Rodeway Inn Memorial Park (5820 Katy Freeway, 77007; 869-9211, Fax 869-9211, 800-228-2000) 100 rooms, restaurant, pool, children free with parents, free local calls, A/C, TV, CC. SGL$40, DBL$42.

Southwest Houston

Alamo Plaza Hotel (4343 Old Spanish Trail, 77021; 747-6900) 57 rooms, restaurant, A/C, TV, CC. Near the Astrodome. SGL/DBL$20.

Days Inn (8500 Kirby Dr., 77054; 796-8383, 800-325-2525) 130 rooms, children free with parents, free local calls, wheelchair access, airport transportation, NS rooms, A/C, TV, fax, no pets, meeting facilities, CC. Near the Astrodome, 5 miles from the Galleria Shopping Center, 10 miles from the Houston Intercontinental Airport. SGL/DBL$49-$78.

Embassy Suites (9090 Southwest Freeway, 77074; 995-3415, Fax 779-0703, 800-362-2779) 243 2-room suites, restaurant, lounge, free breakfast, pool, sauna, exercise center, NS rooms, A/C, TV, gift shop, wheelchair access, meeting facilities, CC. 25 miles from the Hobby Airport, 30 miles from the Houston Intercontinental Airport, 15 miles from the downtown area. SGL/DBL$65.

Harvey Suites Medical Center (6800 South Main St., 77030; 528-7744, Fax 528-6983, 800-922-9222) 200 rooms and suites, restaurant, lounge, pool, exercise center, gift shop, wheelchair access, NS rooms, A/C, TV, local transportation, laundry service, meeting facilities, CC. SGL/DBL$60-$80.

Hilton Southwest (6780 South West Freeway, 77074; 977-7911, Fax 974-5805, 800-HILTONS) 300 rooms and suites, restaurant, lounge, outdoor pool, exercise center, NS rooms, A/C, TV, wheelchair access, gift shop, car rental desk, airline ticket desk, business services, 10,000 square feet of meeting and exhibition space, meeting facilities for 500, CC. 4 miles from the Galleria Shopping Center, 3 miles from the Summit Sports Arena, 30 miles from the Houston Intercontinental Airport, 22 miles from the Hobby Airport. SGL$95-$105, DBL$105-$135, STS$150-$250.

Holiday Inn Astrodome (8111 Kirby Dr., 77054; 790-1900, 800-HOLIDAY) 235 rooms, restaurant, lounge, pool, exercise center, whirlpools, children under 19 free with parents, wheelchair access, A/C, TV, NS rooms, fax, room service, no pets, laundry service, 3,200 square feet of meeting and exhibition space, senior rates, CC. SGL/DBL$58-$98.

Holiday Inn Medical Center (6701 South Main St., 77030; 797-1110, Fax 797-1034, 800-HOLIDAY) 296 rooms, restaurant, lounge, pool, exercise center, children under 19 free with parents, wheelchair access, A/C, TV, NS rooms, local transportation, gift shop, fax, room service, no pets, laundry service, meeting facilities for 500, senior rates, CC. SGL/DBL$$73-$86.

Holiday Inn West Loop (3131 West Loop St., 77027; 621-1900, Fax 439-0989, 800-HOLIDAY) 318 rooms and suites, restaurant, free breakfast, lounge, pool, exercise center, children under 19 free with parents, wheelchair access, A/C, local transportation, gift shop, TV, NS rooms, fax, room service, no pets, laundry service, meeting facilities for 300, senior rates, CC. SGL/DBL$65-$75.

Houston Plaza Hilton (6633 Travis St., 77030; 524-6633, Fax 529-6806, 800-HILTONS) 185 suites, restaurant, lounge, entertainment, outdoor pool, exercise center, jogging track, in-room refrigerators, NS rooms, A/C, TV, wheelchair access, business services, meeting facilities for 600. 1.5 miles from the Astrodome, 3.5 miles from the downtown area, 11 miles from the Hobby Airport, 25 miles from the Houston Intercontinental Airport. STS$130.

La Quinta Inn Astrodome (9911 Buffalo Speedway, 77054; 668-8082, Fax 668-0821, 800-531-5900) 115 rooms, restaurant, lounge, free breakfast, heated pool, complimentary newspaper, free local calls, fax, laundry service, NS rooms, wheelchair access, meeting facilities. 5 miles from the Astrodome, Museum of Fine Art and Rice University, 13 miles from the downtown area, 38 miles from the Houston Intercontinental Airport. SGL/DBL$53-$67.

Marriott West Loop (1750 West Loop South, 77027; 960-0111, Fax 960-0111 ext 1601, 800-228-9290) 304 rooms and suites, restaurant, lounge, entertainment, indoor pool, sauna, whirlpools, jogging track, exercise center, wheelchair access, NS rooms, A/C, TV, complimentary newspaper, gift shop, local transportation. 15 minutes from the downtown area and Convention Center. SGL/DBL$105-$135.

Marriott Medical Center (6580 Fannin St., 77030; 796-0080, Fax 796-0080 ext 6694, 800-242-2121) 389 rooms and suites, restaurant, lounge, indoor pool, sauna, whirlpools, jogging track, exercise center, NS rooms, wheelchair access, A/C, TV, local transportation, beauty shop, gift shop, laundry service, wheelchair access. 3 miles from the Astrodome and the downtown area, 25 miles from the Houston Intercontinental Airport. SGL$105, DBL$115.

Marriott Astrodome (2100 South Braeswood Blvd., 77030; 797-9000, Fax 799-8362, 800-228-9290) 339 rooms and suites, restaurant, lounge, entertainment, outdoor pool, sauna, exercise center, NS rooms, A/C, TV, wheelchair access, gift shop, meeting facilities. Near the Astrodome and

Texas Medical Center, 3 miles from the downtown area, 27 miles from the Houston Intercontinental Airport. SGL$95-$105, DBL$115-$235.

Marriott Residence Inn Astrodome (7710 South Main St., 77030; 660-7993, Fax 660-8019, 800-331-3131) 165 suites, in-room refrigerators, laundry room, wheelchair access, NS rooms, A/C, TV, pets OK, in-room VCRs, meeting facilities for 40, CC. 5 miles from the downtown area, 12 miles from the Houston Intercontinental Airport. SGL/DBL$78.

Park Inn International (6700 South Main St., 77030; 522-2811, Fax 522-2607, 800-437-PARK) 194 rooms, restaurant, outdoor pool, complimentary newspaper, laundry service, airport transportation, NS rooms, meeting facilities for 200, CC. Near the Texas Medical Center, 3 miles from Astroworld, Waterworld and the Astrodome. SGL$39, DBL$44.

Radisson Suite Hotel (1400 Old Spanish Trail, 77054; 796-1000, Fax 796-8055, 800-333-3333) 1- and 2-room suites, restaurant, lounge, free breakfast, pool, wheelchair access, CC. SGL/DBL$89-$99.

Sheraton Astrodome Hotel (8686 Kirby Dr., 77054; 748-3221, Fax 790-9676, 800-325-3535) 756 rooms and suites, 2 restaurants, 2 lounges, entertainment, exercise center, gift shop, barber shop, tour and sports ticket office, wheelchair access, NS rooms, A/C, TV, business services, 33 meeting rooms, 50,000 square feet of meeting and exhibition space, CC. Near the Astrodome and Astroworld. SGL$95, DBL$105, STS$125-$250.

Other Locations

Best Western Greenspoint Plaza Inn (11211 North Freeway, 77037; 447-6311, Fax 447-3719, 800-528-1234) 144 rooms and suites, restaurant, lounge, pool, airport courtesy car, fax, children free with parents, NS rooms, A/C, TV, meeting facilities, CC. 10 miles from the downtown area. SGL/DBL$45-$58.

Brookhollow Hilton Inn (2504 North Loop West, 77092; 688-7711, Fax 688-3561, 800-HILTONS) 230 rooms and suites, restaurant, lounge, heated outdoor pool, exercise center, NS rooms, A/C, TV, wheelchair access, complimentary newspaper, local transportation, business services, meeting facilities for 200, CC. 18 miles from the Houston Intercontinental Airport and Hobby Airport, 7 miles from the downtown area and Convention Center. SGL/DBL$105-$135.

Charlie Fitness and Hotel (9009 Boone Rd., 77099; 530-0000) 86 rooms, pool, sauna, exercise center, A/C, TV, meeting facilities, CC. SGL/DBL$85-$115.

Comfort Inn (9041 Westheimer Rd., 77063; 783-1400, 800-221-2222) 69 rooms and suites, free breakfast, lounge, entertainment, pool, sauna, wheelchair access, NS rooms, A/C, TV, no pets, laundry service, meeting facilities, CC. 35 miles from the Houston Intercontinental Airport, 12 miles from the Astrodome, 25 miles from Hobby Airport, 9 miles from the downtown area. SGL/DBL$48-$63.

Days Inn (9015 I-40 North Freeway, 77037; 820-1500, 800-325-2525) 100 rooms and suites, restaurant, free breakfast, lounge, pool, children free with parents, fax, free local calls, wheelchair access, NS rooms, CC. 9 miles from the Houston Intercontinental Airport and the downtown area, 18 miles from Astroworld. SGL/DBL$38-$49.

Days Inn Central (100 West Cavalcade, 77009; 869-7121, Fax 868-5167, 800-325-2525) 140 rooms, restaurant, free breakfast, pool, children free with parents, local transportation, free local calls, wheelchair access, NS rooms, senior rates, CC. 15 miles from the Houston Intercontinental Airport, 3 miles from the downtown area, Convention Center and Park Mall. SGL/DBL$40-$54.

Days Inn (10155 East Freeway, 77029; 675-2711, 800-325-2525) 156 rooms, restaurant, lounge, pool, free breakfast, children free with parents, free local calls, fax, pets OK, wheelchair access, NS rooms, A/C, TV, meeting facilities for 100, senior rates, CC. 18 miles from the Houston Intercontinental Airport, 10 miles from the Hobby Airport, 8 miles from the downtown area. SGL/DBL$49-$58.

Days Inn (6060 Hooton Rd., 77081; 777-9955, Fax 777-3443, 800-325-2525) 74 rooms, free breakfast, pool, children free with parents, free local calls, fax, wheelchair access, no pets, NS rooms, CC. 8 miles from the downtown area and the Astrodome, 3 miles from the Galleria Shopping Center. SGL/DBL$38-$54.

Econo Lodge (7905 South Main St., 77025; 667-8200, 800-4-CHOICE) 78 rooms, pool, children under 12 free with parents, no pets, NS rooms, wheelchair access, A/C, TV, senior rates, CC. SGL/DBL$35-$55.

Four Seasons On The Park (4 Riverview, 77056; 871-8181, 800-332-3442) 383 rooms, restaurant, lounge, pool, sauna, A/C, TV, exercise center, meeting facilities, CC. SGL/DBL$55-$125.

Four Seasons Hotel (1300 Lamar, 77010; 650-1300, Fax 650-8169, 800-332-3442) 399 rooms and suites, restaurant, lounge, entertainment, heated pool, exercise center, whirlpools, sauna, local transportation, boutiques, wheelchair access, NS rooms, A/C, TV, meeting facilities, CC. SGL/DBL$95-$265.

Grand Hotel (2425 West Loop South, 77027; 961-3000, 800-231-2579) 300 rooms, pool, exercise center, A/C, TV, meeting facilities, CC. SGL/DBL$100.

Hampton Inn (828 Mercury Dr., 77013; 673-4200, Fax 673-4200 ext 101, 800-HAMPTON) 89 rooms, free breakfast, pool, children free with parents, NS rooms, A/C, TV, wheelchair access, computer hookups, fax, free local calls, meeting facilities, CC. 5 miles from the downtown area, 13 miles from the Astrodome, 20 miles from the Houston Intercontinental Airport. SGL/DBL$55-$68.

Hilton Inn West (12401 Katy Freeway, 77079; 496-9090, Fax 496-5623, 800-HILTONS) 165 rooms and suites, restaurant, lounge, outdoor pool, exercise center, NS rooms, A/C, TV, wheelchair access, business services, meeting facilities for 150, CC. 40 miles from the Houston Intercontinental Airport, 20 minutes from the downtown area. SGL/DBL$95-$105, 1BR$155-$215, 2BR$225.

HoJo Inn (4602 Katy Freeway, 77007; 861-9000, 800-865-9122) 30 rooms, free breakfast, children free with parents, wheelchair access, NS rooms, fax, free local calls, meeting facilities, CC. 4 miles from the Convention Center, 22 miles from Houston Intercontinental Airport, 2 miles from the downtown area. SGL/DBL$40-$52.

Holiday Inn (2712 Southwest Freeway, 77098; 523-8448, Fax 523-8448 ext 1918, 800-HOLIDAY) 364 rooms, restaurant, lounge, entertainment, pool, exercise center, children under 19 free with parents, wheelchair access, A/C, TV, NS rooms, fax, gift shop, local transportation, room service, no pets, laundry service, meeting facilities, senior rates, CC. SGL/DBL$66-$80.

Holiday Inn (16510 I-45 North, 77090; 821-2570, Fax 821-1304, 800-HOLIDAY) 250 rooms, restaurant, lounge, free breakfast, entertainment, children free with parents, wheelchair access, NS rooms, A/C, TV, fax, room service, airport transportation, no pets, meeting facilities, CC. 8 miles from the Houston Intercontinental Airport, 15 miles from the downtown area, 4 miles from Old Town Spring. SGL/DBL$64-$74.

Holiday Inn Northwest (14996 Northwest Freeway, 77040; 939-9955, Fax 939-9955 ext 7138, 800-HOLIDAY) 196 rooms, restaurant, lounge, children free with parents, wheelchair access, NS rooms, A/C, TV, fax, room service, no pets, meeting facilities for 200, CC. 22 miles from the airport, 16 miles from the downtown area, 19 miles from the Astrodome. SGL$65-$75.

Holiday Inn (11160 Southwest Freeway, 77031; 530-1400, Fax 530-2919, 800-HOLIDAY) 240 rooms and suites, restaurant, lounge, entertainment, indoor pool, exercise center, whirlpools, in-room coffee makers, children under 19 free with parents, wheelchair access, A/C, TV, NS rooms, fax, room service, no pets, laundry service, meeting facilities for 400, senior rates, CC. SGL/DBL$58-$125.

Holiday Inn (1300 NASA Blvd., 333-2500, Fax 335-1587, 800-682-3193, 800-HOLIDAY) 225 rooms and suites, restaurant, lounge, pool, exercise center, children under 19 free with parents, wheelchair access, A/C, TV,

NS rooms, fax, room service, no pets, laundry service, meeting facilities for 300, senior rates, CC. SGL/DBL$60-$100.

Howard Johnson Lodge (6855 Southwest Freeway, 77074; 771-0641, Fax 771-5310, 800-800-I-GO-HOJO) 110 rooms, restaurant, lounge, entertainment, pool, children free with parents, NS rooms, A/C, TV, meeting facilities, senior rates, CC. 10 miles from the Astrodome and Astroworld. SGL/DBL$39-$60.

Inn On The Park (4 Riverway, 77056; 871-8181, Fax 871-8116) 381 rooms and suites, restaurant, lounge, entertainment, 3 pools, exercise center, sauna, whirlpools, 24-hour room service, local transportation, wheelchair access, pets OK, NS rooms, A/C, TV, meeting facilities, CC. SGL/DBL$65-$85.

La Colombe D'Or (3410 Montrose Blvd., 77006; 524-7990, Fax 524-8923) 6 suites, restaurant, lounge, free breakfast, A/C, TV, whirlpools, CC. STS$165-$650.

La Quinta Inn Sharpstown (8201 Southwest Freeway, 77074; 772-3626, Fax 995-1270, 800-531-5900) 130 rooms, restaurant, lounge, heated pool, exercise center, complimentary newspaper, free local calls, fax, laundry service, NS rooms, wheelchair access, meeting facilities, CC. 5 miles from the Galleria Shopping Center and Summit Arena, 10 miles from the downtown area, 13 miles from the Astrodome, 40 miles from the Houston Intercontinental Airport, 20 miles from the Hobby Airport. SGL/DBL$53-$67.

La Quinta Inn Southwest (10552 Southwest Freeway, 77074; 270-9559, Fax 270-0219, 800-531-5900) 115 rooms, restaurant, lounge, free breakfast, heated pool, jacuzzi, complimentary newspaper, free local calls, fax, laundry service, NS rooms, A/C, TV, wheelchair access, meeting facilities, CC. 5 miles from the Sharpstown Mall and Arena Theater, 13 miles from the downtown area and Convention Center, 23 miles from Hobby Airport, 45 miles from the Houston Intercontinental Airport. SGL/DBL$55-$65.

La Quinta Inn Wilcrest (11113 Katy Freeway, 77079; 932-0808, Fax 973-2352, 800-531-5900) 177 rooms, restaurant, lounge, heated pool, complimentary newspaper, free local calls, fax, laundry service, NS rooms, A/C, TV, wheelchair access, meeting facilities, CC. 35 miles from the Houston Intercontinental Airport, 25 miles from the Hobby Airport, within 5 miles of the Memorial Center and Town and Country Plaza, 16 miles from the downtown area, CC. SGL/DBL$53-$55.

La Quinta Inn (13290 FM 1960 West, 77065; 469-4018, Fax 955-6350, 800-531-5900) 130 rooms, restaurant, lounge, heated pool, complimentary newspaper, free local calls, fax, laundry service, NS rooms, A/C, TV, wheelchair access, meeting facilities, CC. 5 miles from Easton Commons Center and Cypress Plaza and Houston Indoor Sports Center, 25 miles from the Houston Intercontinental Airport, 35 miles from Hobby Airport. SGL/DBL$58-$62.

La Quinta Inn Loop (17111 North Freeway, 77090; 444-7500, Fax 893-6271, 800-531-5900) 138 rooms, restaurant, lounge, heated pool, complimentary newspaper, free local calls, fax, laundry service, NS rooms, A/C, TV, wheelchair access, meeting facilities, CC. 11 miles from the Houston Intercontinental Airport, 22 miles from the downtown area. SGL/DBL$55-$65.

La Quinta Inn Hobby Airport (9902 Gulf Freeway, 77034; 941-0900, Fax 946-1987, 800-531-5900) 129 rooms, restaurant, lounge, heated pool, complimentary newspaper, free local calls, fax, laundry service, NS rooms, A/C, TV, wheelchair access, meeting facilities, CC. 4 miles from the Port of Houston and Convention Center, 9 miles from the downtown area, 11 miles from the Astrodome, 1 mile from the Hobby Airport, 25 miles from the Houston Intercontinental Airport. SGL/DBL$53-$67.

La Quinta Inn Greenway Plaza (4015 Southwest Freeway, 77027; 623-4750, Fax 963-0599, 800-531-5900) 128 rooms, restaurant, lounge, heated pool, complimentary newspaper, free local calls, fax, laundry service, NS rooms, A/C, TV, wheelchair access, meeting facilities, CC. 4 miles from the Convention Center, downtown area and the Astrodome, 35 miles from the Houston Intercontinental Airport. SGL/DBL$53-$67.

La Quinta Inn Brookhollow (11002 North West Freeway, 77092; 688-2581, Fax 686-2146, 800-531-5900) 122 rooms, restaurant, lounge, free breakfast, heated pool, complimentary newspaper, free local calls, fax, laundry service, NS rooms, wheelchair access, meeting facilities, CC. 25 miles from the Houston Intercontinental Airport and Hobby Airport, within 10 miles of the Convention Center, Galleria Shopping Center and downtown area, 15 miles from the Astrodome. SGL/DBL$53-$67.

La Quinta Inn East (11999 East Freeway, 77029; 453-5425, Fax 451-8374, 800-531-5900) 122 rooms, restaurant, lounge, heated pool, complimentary newspaper, free local calls, fax, laundry service, NS rooms, A/C, TV, wheelchair access, meeting facilities, CC. 17 miles from Hobby Airport, 24 miles from the Houston Intercontinental Airport, within 10 miles of AstroWorld, the Convention Center and the downtown area. SGL/DBL$55-$65.

Lexington Hotel Suites (16140 I-45 North, 77090; 821-1000, Fax 821-1420) 248 suites, restaurant, free breakfast, pool, children free with parents, wheelchair access, NS rooms, A/C, TV, local transportation, airport courtesy car, meeting facilities, CC. STS$40-$80.

Marriott Residence Inn (6910 Southwest Freeway, 77074; 785-3415, Fax 785-1130, 800-331-3131) 151 suites, outdoor heated pool, local transportation, exercise center, in-room refrigerators and microwaves, laundry service, wheelchair access, NS rooms, A/C, TV, pets OK, VCRs, meeting facilities for 40, CC. SGL/DBL$89.

Medallion Hotel (3000 North Loop West, 77092; 688-0100, Fax 688-9224, 800-688-3000) 382 rooms, Concierge Floor, restaurant, 2 lounges, heated outdoor pool, exercise center, A/C, TV, wheelchair access, meeting facilities, CC. SGL/DBL$90.

Motel 6 (9638 Plainfield Rd., 77036; 778-0008) 345 rooms, pool, A/C, TV, CC. SGL/DBL$38-$42.

Ramada Inn Northwest (1280 Northwest Freeway, 77040; 462-9977, Fax 462-9977 ext 345, 800-2-RAMADA) 296 rooms and suites, restaurant, lounge, entertainment, pool, jacuzzi, exercise center, sauna, airport courtesy car, 18 meeting rooms. 12 miles from the Astrodome, 7 miles from the Galleria Shopping Center, CC. SGL$75-$85, DBL$85-$95, STS$90, X$10.

Residence Inn (525 Bay Area Blvd., 77058; 486-2424, Fax 488-8179, 800-331-3131) 110 rooms and 2-bedroom suites, free breakfast, pool, exercise center, whirlpools, local transportation, in-room refrigerators, children free with parents, wheelchair access, NS rooms, A/C, TV, meeting facilities, CC. SGL/DBL$79, 2BR$109.

Rodeway Inn Southwest (3135 Southwest Freeway, 77098; 526-1071, 800-228-2000) 84 rooms, pool, children free with parents, A/C, TV, free local calls, CC. SGL$41-$45.

Sarah's Bed and Breakfast (941 Heights Blvd., 77008; 868-1130, 800-593-1130) 10 rooms and suites, free breakfast, free local calls, NS, private baths. 20 minutes from the Hobby Airport. SGL/DBL$50-$75, STS$120.

Sheraton Town and Country (10655 Katy Freeway, 77024; 467-6411, 800-325-3535) 228 rooms and suites, restaurant, lounge, pool, sauna, exercise center, NS rooms, A/C, TV, wheelchair access, children free with parents, meeting facilities, CC. SGL$95, DBL$105.

Stouffer Hotel (Greenway Plaza East, 77046; 629-1200, Fax 629-4702, 800-HOTELS-1) 389 rooms, restaurant, lounge, outdoor pool, exercise center, room service, fax, A/C, TV, wheelchair access, NS rooms, children free with parents, 10,000 square feet of meeting and exhibition space, 15 meeting rooms, CC. SGL/DBL$85.

Super 8 Motel (4020 Southwest Freeway, 77027; 623-4720, Fax 963-8526, 800-800-8000) 180 rooms and suites, restaurant, lounge, outdoor pool, whirlpools, exercise center, sauna, pets OK, children under 12 free with parents, free local calls, A/C, TV, in-room refrigerators and microwaves, fax, NS rooms, senior rates, wheelchair access, meeting facilities, CC. SGL/DBL$40-$55.

Super 8 Airport (JFK Blvd., 77032; 442-1830, Fax 787-8032, 800-800-8000) 128 rooms, restaurant, outdoor pool, spa, sauna, exercise center, free breakfast, children free with parents, pets OK, NS rooms, A/C, TV, wheelchair access, computer hookups, fax, free local calls, meeting facilities, CC. 18 miles from Astroworld and Waterworld, 2 miles from the Houston Intercontinental Airport and the Greenspoint Mall. SGL/DBL$44-$63.

TraveLodge (4726 FM 1960 West, 77069; 587-9171, Fax 587-0258, 800-255-3050) 70 rooms, restaurant, lounge, pool, fax, no pets, NS rooms, A/C, TV, wheelchair access, CC. SGL/DBL$38-$42.

TraveLodge West (4204 Hwy. 6 North, 77084; 859-2233, 800-255-3050) 68 rooms and suites, restaurant, lounge, pool, sauna, whirlpools, laundry service, meeting facilities, game room, A/C, TV, meeting facilities, senior rates, CC. 3 miles from the Willowbrook Mall, 3 miles from the Texas Renaissance Festival. SGL/DBL$38-$55.

Westchase Hilton & Towers (9999 Westheimer Rd., 77041; 974-1000, Fax 974-1000 ext 257, 800-HILTONS) 305 rooms and suites, restaurant, lounge, entertainment, outdoor pool, exercise center, spa, complimentary newspaper, airport transportation, wheelchair access, NS rooms, business services, meeting facilities for 625, CC. 4 miles from the Galleria Shopping Center, 35 miles from the Hobby Airport and Houston Intercontinental Airport. SGL/DBL$135.

Hunt
Area Code 512

Joy Spring Ranch (Hunt 78024; 238-4531) 4 rooms, free breakfast, A/C, TV, NS, no pets, no children, private baths, CC. SGL/DBL$65-$75.

Huntsville
Area Code 409

Baker Motel (845 South Sam Houston Ave., 77340; 295-3761) 23 rooms, rooms, A/C, TV, NS rooms, wheelchair access, CC. SGL/DBL$33-$40.

Blue Bonnet Bed and Breakfast (White Rd., 77341; 295-2072) 3 rooms, free breakfast, A/C, TV, CC. SGL/DBL$30-$60.

Center Motel (1602 Sam Houston Ave., 77340; 295-5401) 29 rooms, A/C, TV, NS rooms, wheelchair access, CC. SGL/DBL$30-$38.

Econo Lodge (1501 North I-45, 77340; 295-6401, 800-4-CHOICE) 57 rooms, pool, children under 12 free with parents, no pets, NS rooms, wheelchair access, A/C, TV, senior rates, CC. SGL/DBL$29-$48.

Huntsville Inn (1300 I-45, 77342; 295-5725, 800-822-7281) 49 rooms, A/C, TV, NS rooms, no pets, children free with parents, wheelchair access, children free with parents, CC. SGL/DBL$35.

Longhorn House Bed and Breakfast (Huntsville 77342; 295-1844) 3 rooms, free breakfast, A/C, TV, CC. SGL/DBL$30-$36.

Motel 6 (1607 I-45, 77342; 291-6927, 505-891-6161) 122 rooms, pool, free local calls, children under 17 free with parents, NS rooms, wheelchair access, pets OK, A/C, TV, CC. SGL/DBL$36-$42.

Park Inn International (1401 I-45 North, 77340; 295-6454, Fax 295-9245, 800-437-PARK) 122 rooms, restaurant, lounge, A/C, TV, wheelchair access, NS rooms, in-room coffee makers, meeting facilities for 450, senior rates, CC. SGL/DBL$45-$65.

Sam Houston Inn (3296 I-45 South, 77342; 295-9151, 800-395-9151) 74 rooms, lounge, A/C, pets OK, children free with parents, TV, NS rooms, wheelchair access, meeting facilities, CC. SGL/DBL$48.

Sunset Inn (3211 I-45, 77342; 295-7595) 43 rooms, A/C, TV, NS rooms, wheelchair access, CC. SGL/DBL$26-$30.

University Hotel (Huntsville 77340; 291-2151) 98 rooms, A/C, TV, NS rooms, no pets, children free with parents, wheelchair access, CC. SGL/DBL$40-$50.

Waterwood National Resort and Country Club (Hwy. 190, 77340; 891-5211, 800-441-5211) 81 rooms, restaurant, lounge, pool, A/C, TV, NS rooms, wheelchair access, meeting facilities, CC. SGL/DBL$65-$90.

The Whistler Bed and Breakfast (Ave. M, 77342; 295-2834) 4 rooms, free breakfast, A/C, no pets, TV, CC. SGL/DBL$35-$70.

Irving
Area Code 214

Best Western DFW Airport (2611 West Airport Freeway, 75062; 570-7500, Fax 594-1693, 800-528-1234) 124 rooms and suites, restaurant, lounge, in-room refrigerators and microwaves, local transportation, children free with parents, computer hookups in rooms, laundry service, fax, airport courtesy car, CC. SGL$44-$89, DBL$49-$99.

Best Western Preference (4325 West John Carpenter Freeway, 75063; 621-8277, 800-528-2779) 144 rooms, pool, sauna, exercise center, airport courtesy car, meeting facilities, CC. SGL$36-$46, DBL$45-55, X$5.

Comfort Inn Airport (8205 Esters Blvd., 75063; 929-0066, 800-221-2222) 152 rooms, free breakfast, pool, wheelchair access, NS rooms, no pets, children under 18 free with parents, A/C, TV, meeting facilities, senior rates, CC. SGL/DBL$43-$93.

Crown Sterling Suites (4650 West Airport Freeway, 75062; 790-0093, Fax 790-4768) 308 suites, restaurant, lounge, free breakfast, indoor heated pool, sauna, children free with parents, gift shop, wheelchair access, NS rooms, airport courtesy car, meeting facilities, CC. SGL/DBL$130-$150.

Courtyard by Marriott Las Colinas (1151 West Walnut Hill, 75038; 550-8100, 800-321-2211) 147 rooms and suites, restaurant, lounge, pool, exercise center, whirlpools, children free with parents, laundry service, A/C, NS rooms, TV, meeting facilities, senior rates, CC. SGL/DBL$84-$106.

Days Inn Texas Stadium (2200 East Airport Freeway, 75062; 438-6666, 800-325-2525) 178 rooms, outdoor pool, children free with parents, room service, laundry service, A/C, TV, free local calls, airport transportation, pets OK, fax, wheelchair access, NS rooms, senior rates, CC. SGL/DBL$34-$65.

Days Inn Airport (Irving 75063; 621-8277, Fax 929-4932, 800-325-2525) 134 rooms and suites, restaurant, free breakfast, outdoor pool, children free with parents, room service, laundry service, A/C, TV, free local calls, pets OK, fax, wheelchair access, NS rooms, meeting facilities, senior rates, CC. SGL/DBL$35-$55.

Drury Inn Airport (4210 Airport Freeway, 75062; 986-1200) 128 rooms, restaurant, free breakfast, pool, wheelchair access, pets OK, NS rooms, A/C, TV, airport transportation, children free with parents, meeting facilities, CC. SGL/DBL$45-$60.

Four Seasons Las Colinas (4150 North MacArthur Blvd., 75062; 570-0700, Fax 717-2550, 800-332-3442) 315 rooms and 1-bedroom suites, restaurant, lounge, pool, tennis courts, sauna, exercise center, wheelchair access, NS rooms, A/C, TV, 24-hour room service, airport courtesy car, meeting facilities, CC. SGL$195-$220, STS$350.

Harvey Dallas-Fort Worth Airport (4545 West John Carpenter Freeway, 75063; 929-4500, Fax 929-0774, 800-922-9222) 512 rooms and suites, pool, sauna, exercise center, airport courtesy car, wheelchair access, laundry service, NS rooms, A/C, TV, gift shop, children free with parents, meeting facilities, CC. SGL/DBL$99-$115.

Hawthorn Suites (7900 Brookriver Dr., 75247; 688-1010, Fax 688-1010, 800-527-1133) 97 suites, free breakfast, pool, complimentary newspaper, pets OK, wheelchair access, NS rooms, A/C, TV, laundry service, 2 meeting rooms, meeting facilities for 40, CC. SGL/DBL$85-$95, STS$95.

Holiday Inn Fort Worth Airport South (4440 West Airport Freeway, 75062; 399-1010, Fax 790-8545, 800-HOLIDAY) 241 rooms, restaurant, lounge, whirlpool, exercise facilities, children free with parents, wheelchair access, NS rooms, A/C, TV, fax, room service, no pets, airport courtesy car, meeting facilities for 800, CC. SGL/DBL$65-$75.

Holiday Inn Airport North (Hwy. 144, 75063; 929-8181, Fax 929-8181 ext 7363, 800-HOLIDAY) 275 rooms and suites, restaurant, lounge, entertainment, children free with parents, wheelchair access, NS rooms, A/C, TV, fax, room service, gift shop, airport transportation, meeting facilities for 1,000, CC. SGL/DBL$65-$105.

Homewood Suites (4300 Wingren, 75039; 556-0665, Fax 401-3765, 800-CALL-HOME) 1- and 2-bedroom suites, free breakfast, pool, whirlpools, exercise center, in-room refrigerators, coffee makers and microwaves, fireplace, fax, pets OK, TV, A/C, complimentary newspaper, local transportation, NS rooms, wheelchair access, senior rates, business services, meeting facilities, CC. 1BR$91, 2BR$131.

Howard Johnson (120 West Airport Freeway, 75062; 579-8911, Fax 721-1846, 800-I-GO-HOJO) 120 rooms, restaurant, free breakfast, lounge, pool, children free with parents, wheelchair access, NS rooms, TV, A/C, airport transportation, no pets, laundry facilities, senior rates, meeting facilities for 1,000, CC. SGL/DBL$34-$46.

La Quinta Inn (4105 West Airport Freeway, 75062; 252-6546, Fax 570-4225, 800-531-5900) 166 rooms, restaurant, free breakfast, lounge, pool, complimentary newspaper, free local calls, fax, laundry service, NS rooms, wheelchair access, TV, A/C, meeting facilities, CC. SGL/DBL$65-$75.

Lexington Hotel Suites (4100 West John Carpenter Freeway, 75063; 929-4224, Fax 929-4224) 138 rooms and 1- and 2-bedroom suites, free breakfast, pool, whirlpool, laundry service, airport courtesy car, wheelchair access, children free with parents, NS rooms, A/C, TV, meeting facilities, CC. SGL/DBL$70-$100.

Marriott Residence Inn (950 Walnut Hill Lane, 75038; 580-7773, Fax 550-8824; 800-331-3131) 165 suites, kitchens, in-room refrigerators and microwaves, exercise center, laundry service, wheelchair access, NS-rooms, A/C, TV, pets OK, VCRs, meeting facilities for 40, CC. SGL/DBL$85-$119.

Marriott Airport Hotel (8440 Freeport Pkwy., 75063; 929-8800, Fax 929-6501, 800-228-9290) 492 rooms and suites, restaurant, lounge, entertainment, indoor and outdoor pools, exercise center, whirlpools, sauna, airport courtesy car, car rental desk, wheelchair access, TV, A/C, NS rooms, laundry service, gift shop, children free with parents, meeting facilities, senior rates, CC. SGL/DBL$65-$97, STS$100.

Omni Hotel (221 East Las Colinas Blvd., 75039; 556-0800, Fax 556-0729, 800-843-6664) 420 rooms and suites, Concierge Level, restaurant, lounge, outdoor pool, sauna, exercise center, whirlpool, jogging track, NS rooms,

A/C, TV, wheelchair access, gift shop, airline ticket desk, airport courtesy car, audiovisual equipment, meeting facilities, CC. SGL$135, DBL$145.

Ramada Inn (4110 West Airport Freeway, 75062; 399-2005, Fax 986-7620, 800-2-RAMADA) 138 rooms and suites, restaurant, lounge, pool, wheelchair access, NS rooms, pets OK, A/C, TV, children under 18 free with parents, room service, laundry facilities, airport transportation, in-room refrigerators, meeting facilities, senior rates, CC. SGL/DBL$65-$93.

Sheraton Grand Hotel (Hwy. 114 and Esters Blvd., 75063; 929-8400, 800-325-3535) 300 rooms and suites, restaurant, lounge, entertainment, indoor and outdoor heated pool, exercise center, sauna, hot tub, NS rooms, A/C, TV, children free with parents, airport courtesy car, wheelchair access, 12,200 square feet of meeting and exhibition space, meeting facilities for 600, senior rates, CC. SGL/DBL$100+.

Wyndham Garden (110 West Carpenter Freeway, 75039; 650-1600, 800-822-4200) 166 rooms and suites, restaurant, lounge, outdoor pool, whirlpool, NS rooms, A/C, TV, wheelchair access, meeting facilities, CC. SGL/DBL$106-$116, STS$116-$126.

Jacksboro
Area Code 817

Jacksboro Inn (Jacksboro 76458; 567-3751) 48 rooms, pool, in-room refrigerators, children free with parents, A/C, TV, NS rooms, wheelchair access, CC. SGL/DBL$30-$40.

Jacksonville
Area Code 903

Best Western Inn (1407 East Rusk St., 75766; 586-9841, 800-528-1234) 94 rooms, restaurant, pool, exercise center, children free with parents, A/C, NS rooms, TV, laundry facilities, wheelchair access, pets OK, in-room refrigerators, microwaves and coffee makers, meeting facilities, senior rates, CC. SGL/DBL$45-$55.

Jasper
Area Code 409

Ramada Inn (239 East Gibson, 75961; 384-9021, 800-2-RAMADA) 100 rooms and suites, restaurant, lounge, entertainment, pool, wheelchair access, NS rooms, pets OK, A/C, TV, children under 18 free with parents, room service, laundry facilities, meeting facilities, senior rates, CC. SGL/DBL$55-$85.

Jefferson
Area Code 903

Best Western Inn (400 South Walcott, 76557; 665-3983, 800-528-1234) 65 rooms, pool, exercise center, children free with parents, A/C, NS rooms, TV, laundry facilities, wheelchair access, pets OK, in-room refrigerators and microwaves, meeting facilities, senior rates, CC. SGL/DBL$45-$65.

Johnson City
Area Code 210

Save Inn Motel (107 Hwy. 281, 78636; 868-4044) 53 rooms, restaurant, pool, A/C, TV, children free with parents, pets OK, NS rooms, wheelchair access, meeting facilities, CC. SGL/DBL$36-$45.

Junction
Area Code 915

Carousel Inn (1908 Main St., 76849; 446-3301) 30 rooms, A/C, TV, NS rooms, wheelchair access, pets OK, in-room refrigerators, CC. SGL/DBL$25-$38.

Days Inn (111 South Martinez St., 76849; 446-3730, 800-325-2525) 48 rooms and suites, free breakfast, outdoor pool, children free with parents, room service, laundry service, A/C, TV, free local calls, pets OK, fax, wheelchair access, NS rooms, meeting facilities, senior rates, CC. SGL/DBL$43-$65.

Hills Motel (1520 Main St., 76849; 446-2567) 27 rooms, restaurant, pool, in-room refrigerators, pets OK, children free with parents, A/C, TV, NS rooms, wheelchair access, senior rates, CC. SGL/DBL$28-$38.

La Vista Motel (2040 North Main St., 76849; 446-2191) 8 rooms, pets OK, in-room refrigerators, children free with parents, A/C, TV, CC. SGL/DBL$26-$36.

Katy
Area Code 713

Best Western Inn (Katy 77449; 392-9800, 800-528-1234) 104 rooms, pool, exercise center, children free with parents, A/C, NS rooms, TV, laundry facilities, wheelchair access, children free with parents, local transportation, in-room coffee makers, pets OK, meeting facilities, senior rates, CC. SGL/DBL$44-$55.

Kerrville

Area Code 210

Best Western Inn (2124 Sidney Baker St., 78028; 896-1313, 800-528-1234) 97 rooms, pool, exercise center, children free with parents, A/C, NS rooms, TV, laundry facilities, wheelchair access, pets OK, meeting facilities, senior rates, CC. SGL/DBL$59-$100.

Econo Lodge (2145 Sidney Baker St., 78028; 896-1711, 800-4-CHOICE) 102 rooms, restaurant, lounge, entertainment, pool, children under 12 free with parents, no pets, free local calls, NS rooms, wheelchair access, A/C, TV, senior rates, CC. SGL/DBL$36-$55.

Hill Country Inn (2127 Sidney Baker St., 78028; 896-1511) 98 rooms, restaurant, pool, children free with parents, pets OK, VCRs, A/C, TV, NS rooms, wheelchair access, CC. SGL/DBL$36-$46.

Holiday Inn (2033 Sidney Baker St., 78028; 257-4440, Fax 896-8189, 800-HOLIDAY) 200 rooms, restaurant, lounge, entertainment, outdoor heated pool, exercise center, whirlpools, lighted tennis courts, jacuzzi, children under 19 free with parents, wheelchair access, A/C, TV, NS rooms, fax, room service, airport transportation, pets OK, laundry service, meeting facilities for 1,000, senior rates, CC. SGL/DBL$65-$100.

The Inn of the Hills River Resort (1001 Junction Hwy., 78028; 895-5000) 217 rooms and suites, restaurant, lounge, entertainment, pool, exercise center, sauna, whirlpools, lighted tennis courts, A/C, TV, NS rooms, wheelchair access, airport transportation, in-room refrigerators and coffee makers, laundry facilities, children free with parents, pets OK, senior rates, meeting facilities, CC. SGL/DBL$50-$225.

Sands Motel (1804 Sidney Baker St., 78028; 896-8200, Fax 257-2407) 45 rooms, restaurant, pool, A/C, TV, NS rooms, wheelchair access, children free with parents, pets OK, CC. SGL/DBL$25-$54.

Kilgore

Area Code 903

Ramada Inn (3501 Hwy. 259 North, 75662; 983-3456, Fax 984-3193, 800-2-RAMADA) 80 rooms and suites, restaurant, lounge, outdoor pool, wheelchair access, NS rooms, pets OK, A/C, TV, children under 18 free with parents, room service, laundry facilities, meeting facilities for 50, senior rates, CC. SGL/DBL$45-$68.

Killeen

Area Code 817

Best Western Inn (2709 East Business Hwy. 109, 76541; 526-6651, 800-528-1234) 66 rooms and efficiencies, pool, exercise center, children free with parents, A/C, NS rooms, TV, laundry facilities, wheelchair access, in-room refrigerators, pets OK, meeting facilities, senior rates, CC. SGL/DBL$35-$50.

Cowhouse Motor Inn (605 North Gray, 76541; 634-3151) 77 rooms, restaurant, lounge, pool, A/C, TV, NS rooms, wheelchair access, CC. SGL/DBL$30-$40.

Days Inn (810 Central Texas Expwy., 76541; 634-6644, Fax 634-2751, 800-325-2525) 40 rooms and suites, free breakfast, outdoor pool, children stay free with parents, room service, laundry service, A/C, TV, free local calls, pets OK, fax, wheelchair access, NS rooms, senior rates, CC. SGL/DBL$40-$50.

Econo Lodge (606 East Central Texas Expwy., 76542; 634-6868, 800-4-CHOICE) 40 rooms, free breakfast, pool, children under 12 free with parents, no pets, NS rooms, wheelchair access, A/C, TV, senior rates, CC. SGL/DBL$37-$60.

Economy Motel (817 East Business Hwy. 190, 76542; 634-3128) 40 rooms and efficiencies, A/C, TV, NS rooms, wheelchair access, senior rates, CC. SGL/DBL$28-$33.

Friendship Inn (601 West Hwy. 190, 76541; 526-2232, 800-424-4777) 20 rooms, free breakfast, facilities, A/C, TV, no pets, free local calls, laundry facilities, NS rooms, children free with parents, wheelchair access, senior rates, CC. SGL/DBL$50-$73.

Hallmark Motor Inn (4500 East Central Texas Expressway, 76542; 634-1313, 800-345-9679) 100 rooms and 1- and 2-bedroom suites, restaurant, lounge, pool, A/C, TV, NS rooms, wheelchair access, airport transportation, children free with parents, no pets, in-room refrigerators and microwaves, free local calls, meeting facilities, senior rates, CC. SGL/DBL$36-$48.

Holiday Inn Express (1602 East Central Texas Expressway, 76541; 554-2727, 800-HOLIDAY) 75 rooms, restaurant, free breakfast, lounge, pool, exercise center, children under 19 free with parents, wheelchair access, A/C, TV, NS rooms, fax, room service, no pets, laundry service, meeting facilities, senior rates, CC. SGL/DBL$58-$76.

Holiday Terrace Motel (1708 East Hwy. 90, 76541; 690-4141) 40 rooms and suites, restaurant, pool, jacuzzi, A/C, TV, NS rooms, wheelchair access, CC. SGL/DBL$30-$46.

Ironside Motor Inn (4040 South Fort Hood St., 76541; 526-4632) 55 rooms and suites, free breakfast, pool, jacuzzi, A/C, TV, NS rooms, wheelchair access, CC. SGL/DBL$65, STS$75-$110.

Killeen Motel (511 East Business Hwy. 190, 76541; 634-2654) 32 rooms, pool, A/C, TV, NS rooms, wheelchair access, free local calls, CC. SGL/DBL$40.

La Quinta Inn (1112 Fort Hood St., 76541; 526-8331, Fax 526-0394, 800-531-5900) 105 rooms, restaurant, free breakfast, lounge, pool, complimentary newspaper, free local calls, fax, airport transportation, in-room refrigerators and microwaves, no pets, laundry service, NS rooms, wheelchair access, TV, A/C, meeting facilities, senior rates, CC. SGL/DBL$45-$50.

Liberty Motel (529 East Business Hwy. 190, 76541; 634-2199) 40 rooms and 3- and 4-bedroom suites, A/C, TV, NS rooms, wheelchair access, CC. SGL/DBL$28-$38.

Motel 7 (729 East Business Hwy. 190, 76541; 554-6035) 35 rooms, A/C, TV, NS rooms, wheelchair access, CC. SGL/DBL$36.

Park Inn International (803 Trimmier Rd., 76541; 526-4343, 800-437-PARK) 132 rooms and suites, restaurant, lounge, pool, exercise center, local transportation, fax, in-room refrigerators, A/C, TV, wheelchair access, NS rooms, CC. SGL/DBL$60-$70.

Ramada Inn (1100 South Fort Hood Rd., 76541; 634-3101, Fax 634-8844, 800-2-RAMADA) 164 rooms and suites, restaurant, lounge, entertainment, outdoor pool, wheelchair access, NS rooms, pets OK, A/C, TV, children under 18 free with parents, room service, laundry facilities, 3,500 square feet of meeting and exhibition space, meeting facilities for 200, senior rates, CC. SGL/DBL$40-$56.

Sheraton Inn Plaza Killeen (1721 Central Texas Expressway, 76541; 634-1555, 800-325-3535) 148 rooms and suites, restaurant, lounge, entertainment, outdoor heated pool, exercise center, jacuzzi, NS rooms, A/C, TV, children free with parents, airport transportation, in-room refrigerators, no pets, wheelchair access, 7,200 square feet of meeting and exhibition space, 6 meeting rooms, meeting facilities for 500, senior rates, CC. SGL/DBL$55-$70.

Kingsville
Area Code 512

Best Western Inn (2402 East King Ave., 78363; 595-5656, 800-528-1234) 50 rooms, pool, exercise center, children free with parents, A/C, NS rooms, TV, laundry facilities, wheelchair access, pets OK, meeting facilities, senior rates, CC. SGL/DBL$45-$55.

Econo Lodge (2502 East Kennedy, 78363; 592-5251, 800-4-CHOICE) 117 rooms, restaurant, lounge, entertainment, outdoor pool, whirlpools, sauna, children under 12 free with parents, no pets, NS rooms, wheelchair access, A/C, TV, senior rates, CC. SGL/DBL$36-$75.

Get N'Go Travel Center Motor Inn (3430 Hwy. 77, 78363; 595-5753) 26 rooms, restaurant, pool, children free with parents, pets OK, laundry facilities, A/C, TV, NS rooms, wheelchair access, CC. SGL/DBL$40-$48.

HoJo Inn (105 South 77 Bypass, 78363; 592-6471, Fax 592-6476, 800-I-GO-HOJO) 86 rooms, restaurant, lounge, pool, children free with parents, wheelchair access, NS rooms, TV, A/C, pets OK, laundry facilities, senior rates, meeting facilities, CC. SGL/DBL$39-$49.

Lago Vista
Area Code 512

The Inn on Lake Travis (1900 American Dr., 78645; 267-1102) 54 rooms, restaurant, lounge, pool, lighted tennis courts, no pets, in-room refrigerators, children free with parents, A/C, TV, NS rooms, wheelchair access, CC. SGL/DBL$55-$75.

LaPorte
Area Code 713

La Quinta Inn (1105 Hwy. 146 South, 77571; 470-0760, Fax 471-2116, 800-531-5900) 114 rooms, restaurant, free breakfast, lounge, pool, complimentary newspaper, free local calls, fax, laundry service, NS rooms, wheelchair access, TV, pets OK, A/C, meeting facilities, CC. SGL/DBL$58-$65.

Lake Jackson
Area Code 409

Best Western Inn (915 Hwy. 332 West, 77566; 297-3031, Fax 297-9875, 800-528-1234) 100 rooms, pool, exercise center, children free with parents, A/C, NS rooms, TV, laundry facilities, wheelchair access, pets OK, in-room refrigerators and coffee makers, meeting facilities, senior rates, CC. SGL/DBL$45-$50.

Ramada Inn (925 Hwy. 332, 77566; 297-1161, Fax 297-1249, 800-2-RAMADA) 147 rooms and suites, restaurant, lounge, entertainment, pool, wheelchair access, NS rooms, pets OK, A/C, TV, children under 18 free with parents, room service, laundry facilities, 3,500 square feet of meeting and exhibition space, senior rates, CC. SGL/DBL$70-$95, STS$130.

Lamesa
Area Code 806

Shiloh Inn (1707 Lubbock Hwy., 79331; 872-6721) 50 rooms, A/C, TV, NS rooms, wheelchair access, senior rates, CC. SGL/DBL$35-$45.

Laredo
Area Code 512

Civic Center Inn (2620 Santa Ursula Ave., 78040; 722-6321) 75 rooms and 2-bedroom suites, restaurant, pool, airport transportation, children free with parents, no pets, A/C, TV, NS rooms, wheelchair access, senior rates, CC. SGL/DBL$45-$53.

Family Gardens Inn (5830 San Bernardo, 78041; 723-5300, Fax 723-5300, 800-292-4053) 193 rooms, suites and cottages, restaurant, lounge, heated pool, whirlpools, gift shop, laundry facilities, local transportation, in-room refrigerators, microwaves and coffee makers, pets OK, A/C, TV, NS rooms, wheelchair access, CC. SGL/DBL$50-$75.

Fiesta Inn (Laredo 78040; 723-3603, Fax 724-7697) 150 rooms, pool, laundry facilities, airport transportation, in-room refrigerators and microwaves, children free with parents, no pets, A/C, TV, NS rooms, wheelchair access, CC. SGL/DBL$50-$65.

Holiday Inn (800 Garden St., 78040; 727-5800, Fax 727-0278, 800-HOLIDAY) 200 rooms and suites, restaurant, lounge, entertainment, pool, exercise center, children under 19 free with parents, wheelchair access, A/C, TV, NS rooms, fax, airport transportation, gift shop, room service, no pets, laundry service, meeting facilities, senior rates, CC. SGL/DBL$65-$90.

La Posada (Laredo 78042; 722-1701, 800-531-7156) 224 rooms and suites, restaurant, lounge, entertainment, heated pool, A/C, TV, NS rooms, wheelchair access, in-room refrigerators, room service, boutiques, airport courtesy car, CC. SGL/DBL$70-$150.

La Quinta Inn (3600 Santa Ursula Ave., 78041; 722-0511, Fax 723-6642, 800-531-5900) 152 rooms, restaurant, free breakfast, lounge, pool, complimentary newspaper, free local calls, children free with parents, fax, laundry service, NS rooms, wheelchair access, TV, A/C, meeting facilities, CC. SGL/DBL$55-$70, STS$75-$85.

Siesta Motel (4109 San Bernardo Ave., 78041; 723-3661) 59 rooms, restaurant, lounge, no pets, A/C, TV, NS rooms, wheelchair access, CC. SGL/DBL$32-$48.

League City
Area Code 713

South Shore Harbour Resort and Conference Center (2500 South Shore Blvd., 77573; 334-1000) 250 rooms and suites, restaurant, lounge, entertainment, indoor and outdoor pool, whirlpools, sauna, lighted tennis courts, airport transportation, VCRs, TV, A/C, wheelchair access, NS rooms, in-room refrigerators, no pets, senior rates, meeting facilities, CC. SGL/DBL$100-$150.

Lewisville
Area Code 214

Days Inn (1401 South Stemmons, 75067; 436-0080, 800-325-2525) 100 rooms and suites, free breakfast, hot tubs, children free with parents, room service, laundry service, A/C, TV, free local calls, pets OK, fax, wheelchair access, NS rooms, senior rates, CC. SGL/DBL$38-$48, STS$70-$90.

Hampton Inn (200 North Stemmons Freeway, 75067; 434-1000, Fax 221-1323, 800-HAMPTON) 130 rooms, free breakfast, pool, pets OK, children free with parents, NS rooms, A/C, TV, wheelchair access, computer hookups, fax, free local calls, pets OK, meeting facilities, CC. SGL/DBL$53-$58.

La Quinta Inn (1657 South Stemmons Freeway, 75067; 221-7525, Fax 221-8795, 800-531-5900) 130 rooms, pool, complimentary newspaper, free local calls, fax, laundry service, NS rooms, wheelchair access, TV, pets OK, A/C, meeting facilities, CC. SGL/DBL$40-$45.

Ramada Inn (1102 Texas St., 75067; 221-2121, 800-2-RAMADA) 86 rooms and suites, restaurant, lounge, pool, wheelchair access, NS rooms, pets OK, A/C, TV, children under 18 free with parents, room service, laundry facilities, meeting facilities, senior rates, CC. SGL/DBL$38-$53.

Liberty
Area Code 409

HoJo Inn (1512 Hwy. 90, 77575; 336-5752, Fax 336-9868, 800-I-GO-HOJO) 90 rooms, pool, children free with parents, wheelchair access, NS rooms, TV, A/C, no pets, laundry facilities, senior rates, meeting facilities, CC. SGL/DBL$30-$33.

Live Oak

Area Code 210

La Quinta Inn (Live Oak 78223; 657-5500, 800-531-5900) 80 rooms, restaurant, pool, complimentary newspaper, free local calls, fax, laundry service, NS rooms, wheelchair access, TV, A/C, pets OK, VCRs, meeting facilities, CC. SGL/DBL$35-$40.

Livingston

Area Code 409

Econo Lodge (117 Hwy. 59 Loop, 77351; 327-2451, 800-4-CHOICE) 56 rooms, pool, children under 12 free with parents, no pets, NS rooms, wheelchair access, A/C, TV, senior rates, CC. SGL/DBL$28-$45.

Park Inn International (2500 Hwy. 59 South, 77351; 327-2525, Fax 327-2525 ext 300, 800-437-PARK) 80 rooms and suites, restaurant, lounge, A/C, TV, wheelchair access, NS rooms, meeting facilities for 80, senior rates, CC. SGL/DBL$40-$50.

Ramada Inn (1200 North Washington, 77351; 327-3366, Fax 327-3048, 800-2-RAMADA) 96 rooms and suites, restaurant, lounge, entertainment, outdoor pool, wheelchair access, NS rooms, pets OK, A/C, TV, children under 18 free with parents, room service, laundry facilities, meeting facilities, senior rates, CC. SGL/DBL$50-$66.

Lockhart

Area Code 512

Lockhart Inn (1207 Hwy. 183 South, 78644; 398-5201) 36 rooms, A/C, TV, NS rooms, pets OK, children free with parents, wheelchair access, CC. SGL/DBL$25-$45.

Longview

Area Code 903

Comfort Inn (203 North Spur 63, 75601; 757-7858, Fax 757-7031, 800-221-2222) 63 rooms, restaurant, lounge, entertainment, free breakfast, pool, wheelchair access, NS rooms, no pets, children under 18 free with parents, A/C, TV, meeting facilities, senior rates, CC. SGL/DBL$45-$53.

Days Inn (3103 Estes Pkwy., 75602; 758-1113, Fax 236-7726, 800-325-2525) 36 rooms and 2-room suites, free breakfast, children free with parents, room service, laundry service, A/C, TV, free local calls, pets OK, fax, wheelchair access, NS rooms, meeting facilities, senior rates, CC. SGL/DBL$45-$55.

Econo Lodge (3120 Estes Pkwy., 75602; 753-4884, 800-4-CHOICE) 79 rooms, restaurant, free breakfast, pool, children under 12 free with parents, no pets, NS rooms, wheelchair access, A/C, TV, meeting facilities, senior rates, CC. SGL/DBL$30-$37.

Guest Inn (419 Spur 64 North, 75601; 757-0500) 143 rooms, restaurant, pool, children free with parents, in-room refrigerators and microwaves, pets OK, A/C, TV, NS rooms, wheelchair access, CC. SGL/DBL$37-$50.

Holiday Inn (I-20 and Estes Pkwy., 75602; 758-0700, Fax 758-8705, 800-HOLIDAY) 189 rooms and suites, restaurant, lounge, indoor pool, exercise center, whirlpools, sauna, airport transportation, children under 19 free with parents, wheelchair access, A/C, TV, NS rooms, fax, room service, no pets, laundry service, meeting facilities for 500, senior rates, CC. SGL/DBL$55-$130.

La Quinta Inn (502 South Access Rd., 75602; 757-3663, Fax 753-3780, 800-531-5900) 106 rooms, restaurant, free breakfast, lounge, pool, complimentary newspaper, free local calls, fax, laundry service, NS rooms, wheelchair access, TV, airport transportation, A/C, meeting facilities, CC. SGL/DBL$45-$56.

Longview Inn (605 Access Rd., 75602; 753-0350) 100 rooms, pool, whirlpools, laundry facilities, pets OK, VCRs, A/C, TV, NS rooms, wheelchair access, airport transportation, CC. SGL/DBL$40-$55.

Motel 6 (110 West Access Rd., 75603; 758-5256, 505-891-6161) 78 rooms, pool, free local calls, children under 17 free with parents, NS rooms, wheelchair access, pets OK, A/C, TV, CC. SGL/DBL$35-$48.

Ramada Inn (3304 South Eastman Rd., 75602; 758-0711, Fax 758-2036, 800-2-RAMADA) 63 rooms and suites, restaurant, free breakfast, outdoor pool, exercise center, sauna, wheelchair access, NS rooms, pets OK, A/C, TV, children under 18 free with parents, room service, laundry facilities, meeting facilities, senior rates, CC. SGL/DBL$38-$58.

Lubbock
Area Code 806

Barcelona Court (5215 Loop 289 South, 79424; 794-5353, Fax 798-3630, 800-222-1122) 161 rooms, free breakfast, outdoor heated pool, children free with parents, laundry facilities, gift shop, airport courtesy car, A/C, TV, NS rooms, wheelchair access, CC. SGL/DBL$72-$82.

Days Inn (2401 4th St., 79415; 747-7111, Fax 747-9749, 800-325-2525) 90 rooms and suites, free breakfast, outdoor pool, children free with parents, room service, laundry service, A/C, TV, free local calls, pets OK, fax, wheelchair access, NS rooms, senior rates, CC. SGL/DBL$35-$50.

Econo Lodge (714 Ave. Q, 79401; 765-8847, 800-4-CHOICE) 50 rooms, children under 12 free with parents, no pets, NS rooms, wheelchair access, A/C, TV, senior rates, CC. SGL/DBL$26-$40.

Holiday Inn Civic Center (801 Ave. Q, 79401; 763-1200, Fax 763-2656, 800-HOLIDAY) 293 rooms and suites, restaurant, lounge, entertainment, indoor pool, exercise center, whirlpool, sauna, children under 19 free with parents, wheelchair access, A/C, TV, NS rooms, fax, room service, in-room refrigerators, pets OK, laundry service, meeting facilities, senior rates, CC. SGL/DBL$65-$75.

Holiday Inn South (6624 I-27, 79404; 745-2208, Fax 745-1265, 800-HOLI-DAY) 166 rooms and suites, restaurant, lounge, indoor pool, exercise center, children under 19 free with parents, wheelchair access, A/C, TV, NS rooms, fax, room service, airport transportation, pets OK, laundry service, meeting facilities for 450, senior rates, CC. SGL/DBL$60-$77.

Howard Johnson Lodge (4801 Ave. Q, 79412; 747-1671, Fax 747-4265, 800-I-GO-HOJO) 55 rooms, restaurant, free breakfast, lounge, entertainment, children free with parents, wheelchair access, NS rooms, TV, A/C, no pets, laundry facilities, senior rates, meeting facilities, CC. SGL/DBL$50-$66.

Lubbock Inn (3901 19th St., 79408; 792-5181, 800-545-8226) 147 rooms and suites, free breakfast, heated pool, in-room refrigerators, airport courtesy car, A/C, no pets, children free with parents, TV, NS rooms, wheelchair access, room service, CC. SGL/DBL$48-$68.

Lubbock Plaza Motel (3201 Loop 289 South, 79432; 797-3241, Fax 793-1203) 203 rooms and suites, restaurant, lounge, indoor heated pool, whirlpools, exercise center, sauna, airport courtesy car, in-room refrigerators, microwaves and coffee makers, laundry facilities, pets OK, A/C, TV, NS rooms, wheelchair access, meeting facilities, CC. SGL/DBL$70-$82, STS$100-$225.

Motel 6 (909 66th St., 79412; 745-5541, 505-891-6161) 178 rooms, pool, free local calls, children under 17 free with parents, NS rooms, wheelchair access, pets OK, A/C, TV, CC. SGL/DBL$39-$45.

Paragon Hotel (4115 Brownfield Hwy., 79407; 792-0065, Fax 792-0178) 130 rooms and efficiencies, pool, A/C, TV, NS rooms, children free with parents, pets OK, airport transportation, wheelchair access, senior rates, meeting facilities, CC. SGL/DBL$50-$56.

Residence Inn by Marriott (2551 Loop 289 South, 79423; 745-1963, Fax 748-1183, 800-331-3131) 80 rooms and suites, free breakfast, heated pool, whirlpools, in-room refrigerators, coffee makers and microwaves, laundry facilities, TV, A/C, VCRs, pets OK, complimentary newspaper, fireplaces, children free with parents, NS rooms, wheelchair access, meeting facilities, CC. SGL/DBL$95-$125.

Sheraton Inn at the Civic Center (505 Ave. Q, 79401; 747-0171, Fax 747-9243, 800-325-3535) 145 rooms and suites, restaurant, lounge, entertainment, indoor heated pool, exercise center, in-room refrigerators, NS rooms, A/C, TV, airport courtesy car, children free with parents, wheelchair access, 7,000 square feet of meeting and exhibition space, 6 meeting rooms, meeting facilities for 300, CC. SGL/DBL$65-$80, STS$150-$200.

Super 8 Motel (501 Ave. Q, 79401; 762-8726, 800-800-8000) 34 rooms and suites, restaurant, lounge, no pets, children under 12 free with parents, free local calls, A/C, TV, in-room refrigerators and microwaves, fax, NS rooms, senior rates, wheelchair access, meeting facilities, CC. SGL/DBL$35-$60.

Lufkin
Area Code 409

Best Western Inn (4200 North Medford Dr., 75901; 632-7300, 800-528-1234) 83 rooms, pool, exercise center, whirlpools, children free with parents, A/C, NS rooms, TV, laundry facilities, wheelchair access, pets OK, meeting facilities, senior rates, CC. SGL/DBL$37-$44.

Days Inn (2130 South 1st, 75901; 639-3301, Fax 634-4266, 800-325-2525) 124 rooms and suites, restaurant, lounge, jacuzzis, children free with parents, room service, laundry service, complimentary newspaper, A/C, TV, free local calls, pets OK, fax, wheelchair access, NS rooms, meeting facilities for 350, senior rates, CC. SGL/DBL$38-$75.

Holiday Inn (4306 South First St., 75901; 639-3333, Fax 639-3382, 800-HOLIDAY) 102 rooms, restaurant, lounge, pool, exercise center, whirlpools, children under 19 free with parents, wheelchair access, A/C, TV, NS rooms, fax, room service, no pets, in-room refrigerators, laundry service, airport transportation, meeting facilities for 150, senior rates, CC. SGL/DBL$55-$75.

La Quinta Inn (110 South 10th St., 75901; 634-9475, 800-531-5900) 118 rooms, restaurant, free breakfast, lounge, pool, complimentary newspaper, free local calls, fax, pets OK, laundry service, NS rooms, wheelchair access, TV, A/C, meeting facilities, CC. SGL/DBL$45-$65.

La Quinta Inn (2119 South 1st St., 75901; 634-3351, Fax 634-9475, 800-531-5900) 106 rooms, restaurant, free breakfast, lounge, pool, complimentary newspaper, free local calls, fax, laundry service, NS rooms, wheelchair access, TV, A/C, meeting facilities, CC. SGL/DBL$43-$68.

Motel 6 (1110 South Timberland Dr., 75901; 637-7850, 505-891-6161) 133 rooms, pool, free local calls, children under 17 free with parents, NS rooms, wheelchair access, pets OK, A/C, TV, CC. SGL/DBL$40-$48.

Ramada Inn (2011 South 1st St., 75901; 639-1122, Fax 639-1188, 800-2-RAMADA) 196 rooms and suites, restaurant, lounge, entertainment, pool, wheelchair access, NS rooms, pets OK, A/C, TV, children under 18 free with parents, room service, laundry facilities, meeting facilities for 350, senior rates, CC. SGL/DBL$35-$58, STS$65.

Marble Falls
Area Code 210

Comfort Inn (1206 Hwy. 281 North, 78654; 693-7531, 800-221-2222) 48 rooms, restaurant, pool, whirlpools, wheelchair access, NS rooms, no pets, children under 18 free with parents, A/C, TV, meeting facilities, senior rates, CC. SGL/DBL$45-$75.

Hill Country Motel (1101 Hwy. 281 North, 78654; 693-3637) 67 rooms, pool, whirlpools, pets OK, children free with parents, A/C, TV, NS rooms, wheelchair access, CC. SGL/DBL$30-$39.

La Casita (1908 Redwood Dr., 78654; 598-6448) cottage, free breakfast, A/C, TV, no pets, private bath, NS, CC. SGL/DBL$55-$60.

Quality Inn (1206 Hwy. 281 North, 78654; 590-4646, 800-221-2222) 164 rooms and suites, restaurant, pool, exercise center, sauna, children free with parents, A/C, TV, room service, laundry service, NS rooms, meeting facilities, senior rates, CC. SGL/DBL$50-$130.

Marshall
Area Code 903

Best Western Inn (5555 East End Blvd., 75670; 935-1941, Fax 938-0071, 800-528-1234) 100 rooms, restaurant, lounge, pool, exercise center, children free with parents, A/C, NS rooms, TV, room service, laundry facilities, wheelchair access, pets OK, meeting facilities, senior rates, CC. SGL/DBL$42-$60.

Comfort Inn (I-20 and Hwy. 59, 75670; 935-1135, 800-221-2222) 60 rooms, restaurant, free breakfast, pool, spa, wheelchair access, NS rooms, no pets, children under 18 free with parents, A/C, TV, room service, meeting facilities, senior rates, CC. SGL/DBL$40-$62.

Economy Inn (6002 East End Blvd. South, 75670; 935-1184, 800-826-0778) 40 rooms, free local calls, wheelchair access, pets OK, A/C, children free with parents, TV, NS rooms, in-room refrigerators and microwaves, senior rates, CC. SGL/DBL$30-$36.

Holiday Inn (100 I-20 West, 75670; 935-7923, Fax 938-2675, 800-HOLI-DAY) 94 rooms, restaurant, free breakfast, lounge, pool, exercise center, whirlpools, children under 19 free with parents, wheelchair access, A/C, TV, NS rooms, fax, room service, complimentary newspaper, pets OK; laundry service, meeting facilities for 100, senior rates, CC. SGL/DBL$49-$125.

Motel 6 (300 I-20 East, 75670; 935-4394, 505-891-6161) 121 rooms, pool, free local calls, children under 17 free with parents, NS rooms, wheelchair access, pets OK, A/C, TV, CC. SGL/DBL$36-$44.

Ramada Inn (5301 East End Blvd. South, 75670; 938-9261, Fax 938-9261 ext 368, 800-2-RAMADA) 102 rooms and suites, restaurant, lounge, pool, wheelchair access, NS rooms, pets OK, A/C, TV, children under 18 free with parents, room service, laundry facilities, meeting facilities, senior rates, CC. SGL/DBL$46-$100.

McAllen
Area Code 210

Best Western Inn and Suites (300 East Expressway 83, 78503; 630-3333, 800-528-1234) 92 rooms and suites, pool, exercise center, children free with parents, A/C, NS rooms, TV, laundry facilities, wheelchair access, pets OK, airport transportation, in-room refrigerators, microwaves and coffee makers, meeting facilities, senior rates, CC. SGL/DBL$51-$61.

Doubletree Club Hotel (101 North Main St., 78502; 631-1101, Fax 631-7934, 800-828-7447) 158 rooms and suites, restaurant, free breakfast, lounge, pool, NS rooms, children under 18 free with parents, airport courtesy car, in-room refrigerators, A/C, TV, business services, fax, in-room computer hookups, meeting facilities, senior rates, CC. SGL/DBL$65-$160.

Drury Inn (612 West Expressway 83, 78501; 687-5100, 800-325-8300) 89 rooms and 1- and 2-room suites, free breakfast, pool, TV, children under 18 free with parents, NS rooms, A/C, wheelchair access, fax, in-room computer hookups, free local calls, airport transportation, pets OK, in-room refrigerators and microwaves, meeting facilities, senior rates, CC. SGL/DBL$50-$75.

Embassy Suites (1800 South 2nd St., 78503; 686-3000, Fax 631-8362, 800-EM-BASSY) 168 2-room suites, restaurant, lounge, entertainment, free breakfast, lounge, heated pool, whirlpool, exercise center, sauna, room service, laundry service, wheelchair access, complimentary newspaper, free local calls, gift shop, in-room refrigerators, NS rooms, gift shop, local transportation, business services, meeting facilities, CC. SGL/DBL$90-$110.

Fairway Resort (2105 South 10th St., 78503; 682-2445) 154 rooms, restaurant, lounge, entertainment, heated pool, airport transportation, VCRs, pets OK, children free with parents, laundry facilities, A/C, TV, NS rooms, wheelchair access, CC. SGL/DBL$56-$105.

Hampton Inn (300 West Expressway 83, 78501; 682-4900, 800-HAMP-TON) 91 rooms, restaurant, free breakfast, pool, exercise center, children under 18 free with parents, NS rooms, wheelchair access, in-room computer hookups, fax, TV, A/C, free local calls, pets OK, meeting facilities, CC. SGL/DBL$60-$72.

Hilton Airport Hotel (2721 South 10th St., 78503; 687-1161, Fax 687-8651, 800-HILTONS) 149 rooms and suites, restaurant, lounge, entertainment, heated pool, exercise center, tennis court, jacuzzi, gift shop, children free with parents, NS rooms, wheelchair access, no pets, room service, laundry facilities, airport transportation, A/C, TV, business services, meeting facilities, CC. SGL/DBL$60-$80.

Holiday Inn Civic Center (200 West Hwy. 83, 78501; 686-2471, Fax 686-2038, 800-HOLIDAY) 173 rooms, restaurant, lounge, entertainment, indoor pool, exercise center, children under 19 free with parents, wheelchair access, A/C, TV, NS rooms, fax, room service, game room, pets OK, local transportation, gift shop, laundry service, meeting facilities for 700, senior rates, CC. SGL/DBL$58-$85.

Holiday Inn Airport (2000 South 10th St., 78501; 686-1741, Fax 682-7187, 800-HOLIDAY) 150 rooms, restaurant, lounge, entertainment, pool, exercise center, children under 19 free with parents, wheelchair access, A/C, TV, NS rooms, in-room coffee makers, local transportation, fax, room service, no pets, laundry service, meeting facilities, senior rates, CC. SGL/DBL$56-$72.

La Quinta Inn (1100 South 10th St., 78501; 687-1101, Fax 687-9265, 800-531-5900) 120 rooms, restaurant, free breakfast, lounge, pool, complimentary newspaper, free local calls, fax, laundry service, airport courtesy car, NS rooms, wheelchair access, TV, A/C, meeting facilities, CC. SGL/DBL$55-$68.

Motel 6 (700 Hwy. 83 Expressway, 78501, 687-3700, 505-891-6161) pool, free local calls, children under 17 free with parents, NS rooms, wheelchair access, pets OK, A/C, TV, CC. SGL/DBL$38-$48.

Quality Inn (1401 South 10th St., 78501; 682-8301, 800-221-2222) 111 rooms and suites, restaurant, free breakfast, lounge, entertainment, pool, exercise center, children free with parents, no pets, A/C, free local calls, TV, room service, laundry service, NS rooms, meeting facilities, senior rates, CC. SGL/DBL$46-$70.

Rodeway Inn (1421 South 10th St., 78501; 686-1586, 800-424-4777) 75 rooms, restaurant, free breakfast, pool, wheelchair access, NS rooms, children free with parents, A/C, TV, senior rates, CC. SGL/DBL$36-$50.

Thrifty Inn (620 Expressway 83 West, 78501; 631-6700) 93 rooms, children free with parents, airport transportation, pets OK, A/C, TV, NS rooms, wheelchair access, CC. SGL/DBL$40-$55.

McKinney
Area Code 214

Comfort Inn (2104 North Central Expressway, 75070; 548-8888, 800-221-2222) 82 rooms, free breakfast, pool, wheelchair access, NS rooms, no pets, children under 18 free with parents, A/C, TV, meeting facilities, senior rates, CC. SGL/DBL$35-$62.

Holiday Inn (1300 North Central Expressway, 75069; 542-9471, 800-HOLIDAY) 100 rooms, restaurant, lounge, pool, exercise center, children under 19 free with parents, wheelchair access, A/C, TV, in-room coffee makers, NS rooms, fax, room service, no pets, laundry service, meeting facilities, senior rates, CC. SGL/DBL$55-$74.

Woods Motel (1431 North Tennessee St., 75069; 542-4469) 38 rooms, restaurant, lounge, pool, pets OK, A/C, TV, children free with parents, NS rooms, wheelchair access, CC. SGL/DBL$30-$41.

Memphis
Area Code 806

Best Western Inn (Hwy. 287 North, 79245; 259-3583, 800-528-1234) 37 rooms, restaurant, lounge, pool, children free with parents, A/C, NS rooms, TV, laundry facilities, wheelchair access, pets OK, meeting facilities, senior rates, CC. SGL/DBL$42-$46.

Mesquite
Area Code 214

Days Inn (3601 Hwy. 80, 75150; 279-6561, 800-325-2525) 119 rooms and suites, restaurant, lounge, entertainment, outdoor pool, children free with parents, room service, laundry service, A/C, TV, free local calls, pets OK, fax, wheelchair access, NS rooms, meeting facilities, senior rates, CC. SGL/DBL$30-$40.

Midland
Area Code 915

Airport Hotel (100 South Airport Plaza Dr., 79711; 561-8000, Fax 561-5243) 98 rooms, restaurant, lounge, pool, in-room refrigerators and coffee makers, pets OK, children free with parents, airport transportation, A/C, TV, NS rooms, wheelchair access, CC. SGL/DBL$45-$50.

Days Inn (4714 Hwy. 80, 79703; 699-7727, Fax 699-7813, 800-325-2525) 70 rooms and suites, free breakfast, outdoor pool, children free with parents, room service, laundry service, A/C, TV, free local calls, pets OK, fax, airport transportation, wheelchair access, NS rooms, senior rates, CC. SGL/DBL$27-$32.

Hampton Inn (3904 West Wall, 79703; 694-7774, Fax 694-0134, 800-HAMPTON) 110 rooms, restaurant, free breakfast, outdoor heated pool, exercise center, children under 18 free with parents, NS rooms, no pets, wheelchair access, in-room computer hookups, fax, TV, A/C, free local calls, airport transportation, pets OK, meeting facilities, CC. SGL/DBL$48-$68.

Hilton Hotel and Towers (117 West Wall, 79703; 683-6131, Fax 683-0958, 800-HILTONS) 258 rooms and suites, restaurant, lounge, entertainment, heated pool, spa, exercise center, children free with parents, NS rooms, wheelchair access, no pets, room service, laundry facilities, A/C, free local calls, airport transportation, gift shop, TV, business services, meeting facilities, CC. SGL/DBL$80-$100, STS$180-$255.

Holiday Inn (4300 I-20 West, 79703; 697-3181, Fax 694-7754, 800-HOLIDAY) 280 rooms, restaurant, lounge, indoor pool, exercise center, children whirlpools, under 19 free with parents, wheelchair access, A/C, TV, airport courtesy car, NS rooms, fax, room service, no pets, laundry service, meeting facilities for 1,500, senior rates, CC. SGL/DBL$55-$75.

La Quinta Inn (4130 West Wall St., 79703; 697-9900, Fax 689-0617, 800-531-5900) 146 rooms, restaurant, free breakfast, lounge, pool, complimentary newspaper, free local calls, fax, laundry service, airport transportation, NS rooms, wheelchair access, no pets, TV, A/C, meeting facilities, CC. SGL/DBL$45-$60.

Lexington Hotel Suites (1002 South Midkiff, 79701; 697-3155, Fax 699-2017) 211 efficiencies, free breakfast, heated pool, whirlpools, A/C, TV, NS rooms, wheelchair access, senior rates, CC. SGL/DBL$45-$65.

Motel 6 (1000 South Midkiff, 79701; 697-3197, 505-891-6161) 87 rooms, pool, free local calls, children under 17 free with parents, NS rooms, wheelchair access, pets OK, A/C, TV, CC. SGL/DBL$39-$44.

Plaza Inn (4108 North Big Spring, 79705; 686-8733, Fax 685-2017, 800-365-3222) 115 rooms, free breakfast, pool, sauna, airport courtesy car, A/C, TV, NS rooms, in-room refrigerators, pets OK, children free with parents, wheelchair access, meeting facilities, CC. SGL/DBL$55-$66.

Ramada Hotel (3100 West Wall St., 79701; 699-4144, Fax 699-4405, 800-2-RAMADA) 200 rooms and suites, restaurant, free breakfast, lounge, pool, wheelchair access, NS rooms, pets OK, A/C, TV, children under 18 free with parents, room service, laundry facilities, meeting facilities, senior rates, CC. SGL/DBL$40-$55.

Midlothian
Area Code 214

Best Western Inn (220 North Hwy. 67, 76065; 775-1891, 800-528-1234) 45 rooms, pool, exercise center, children free with parents, A/C, NS rooms, TV, laundry facilities, wheelchair access, pets OK, in-room refrigerators, meeting facilities, senior rates, CC. SGL/DBL$37-$50.

Mineola
Area Code 214

Sellers' Corner (411 East Kilpatrick, 75773; 569-6560) 4 rooms, free breakfast, A/C, TV, 1910 home, antique furnishings, private baths, NS, no pets, senior rates, CC. SGL/DBL$75-$90.

Mineral Wells
Area Code 817

Days Inn (3701 East Hubbard, 76067; 325-6961, Fax 325-9155, 800-325-2525) 78 rooms and suites, restaurant, outdoor pool, children free with parents, room service, laundry service, A/C, TV, free local calls, pets OK, airport transportation, fax, wheelchair access, NS rooms, meeting facilities for 200, senior rates, CC. SGL/DBL$40-$49.

HoJo Inn (2809 Hwy. 180 West, 76067; 328-1111, 800-I-GO-HOJO) 30 rooms, free breakfast, outdoor pool, children free with parents, wheelchair access, NS rooms, TV, A/C, no pets, laundry facilities, free local calls, senior rates, meeting facilities, CC. SGL/DBL$34-$42.

Twelve Oaks Inn (4103 Hwy. 180 East, 76067; 325-6956) 31 rooms, pool, pets OK, in-room refrigerators, airport transportation, A/C, TV, NS rooms, wheelchair access, CC. SGL/DBL$28-$38.

Monahans
Area Code 915

Best Western Inn (702 West I-20, 79756; 943-4345, 800-528-1234) 90 rooms, restaurant, pool, exercise center, pets OK, children free with parents, A/C, NS rooms, TV, laundry facilities, wheelchair access, meeting facilities, senior rates, CC. SGL/DBL$35-$55.

Howard Johnson Lodge (806 West Hwy. 20, 79756; 943-7585, Fax 943-9327, 800-I-GO-HOJO) 47 rooms, restaurant, lounge, outdoor pool, children free with parents, wheelchair access, NS rooms, TV, A/C, no pets, laundry facilities, senior rates, meeting facilities, CC. SGL/DBL$35-$65.

Mount Pleasant

Area Code 903

Best Western Inn (Mount Pleasant 75455; 572-4303, 800-528-1234) 80 rooms, restaurant, lounge, pool, exercise center, children free with parents, A/C, NS rooms, TV, laundry facilities, wheelchair access, in-room refrigerators, pets OK, meeting facilities, senior rates, CC. SGL/DBL$36-$40.

Comfort Inn (I-30 and Hwy. 271, 75455; 800-221-2222) 60 rooms, free breakfast, pool, wheelchair access, NS rooms, no pets, children under 18 free with parents, A/C, TV, meeting facilities, senior rates, CC. SGL/DBL$39-$49.

Holiday Inn (2501 Ferguson Rd., 75455; 572-6611, Fax 572-6640, 800-HOLIDAY) 109 rooms and suites, restaurant, lounge, pool, exercise center, whirlpools, children under 19 free with parents, wheelchair access, A/C, TV, in-room refrigerators and coffee makers, airport transportation, NS rooms, fax, room service, no pets, laundry service, meeting facilities, senior rates, CC. SGL/DBL$45-$60.

Lakewood Motel (204 Lakewood Dr., 75455; 582-9808) 71 rooms, pool, A/C, TV, NS rooms, children free with parents, pets OK, wheelchair access, CC. SGL/DBL$27-$35.

Muleshoe

Area Code 806

Heritage House Inn (2301 West American Blvd., 79347; 272-7575) 51 rooms, outdoor heated pool, laundry facilities, pets OK, children free with parents, in-room refrigerators, A/C, TV, NS rooms, wheelchair access, CC. SGL/DBL$35-$44.

Nacogdoches

Area Code 409

Econo Lodge (2020 Northwest Loop 224, 75961; 569-0880, 800-4-CHOICE) 68 rooms, restaurant, lounge, pool, children under 12 free with parents, no pets, NS rooms, wheelchair access, A/C, TV, senior rates, CC. SGL/DBL$38-$54.

Fredonia Hotel (200 North Fredonia St., 75961; 564-1234, Fax 564-1234 ext 200) 113 rooms and suites, restaurant, lounge, pool, pets OK, gift shop, A/C, TV, in-room coffee makers, NS rooms, wheelchair access, meeting facilities, senior rates, CC. SGL/DBL$50-$165.

Holiday Inn (3400 South St., 75961; 569-8100, Fax 569-0332, 800-HOLIDAY) 126 rooms and suites, restaurant, lounge, indoor and outdoor pool, exercise center, jacuzzis, whirlpools, children under 19 free with parents, wheelchair access, A/C, TV, NS rooms, fax, room service, pets OK, laundry service, meeting facilities for 250, senior rates, CC. SGL/DBL$50-$70.

La Quinta Inn (3215 South St., 75961; 560-5453, Fax 560-4372, 800-531-5900) 106 rooms, restaurant, free breakfast, lounge, pool, complimentary newspaper, free local calls, fax, laundry service, pets OK, NS rooms, wheelchair access, TV, A/C, meeting facilities, CC. SGL/DBL$45-$60.

Nassau Bay
Area Code 713

Days Inn (2020 NASA Rd., 77058; 332-3551, Fax 332-6192, 800-325-2525) 103 rooms and suites, free breakfast, outdoor pool, children free with parents, room service, laundry service, A/C, TV, free local calls, pets OK, fax, wheelchair access, in-room computer hookups, NS rooms, meeting facilities, senior rates, CC. SGL/DBL$55-$60.

Nassau Bay Hilton Hotel (3000 NASA Rd., 77058; 333-9300, Fax 333-3750, 800-HILTONS) 244 rooms and suites, restaurant, lounge, entertainment, pool, exercise center, children free with parents, NS rooms, wheelchair access, no pets, room service, laundry facilities, in-room refrigerators, A/C, TV, business services, meeting facilities, CC. SGL/DBL$100-$120.

Navasoto
Area Code 409

Best Western Inn (818 Hwy. 6 Loop South, 77868; 825-7775, 800-528-1234) 60 rooms, pool, exercise center, children free with parents, A/C, NS rooms, TV, laundry facilities, wheelchair access, VCRs, in-room refrigerators and coffee makers, pets OK, meeting facilities, senior rates, CC. SGL/DBL$35-$45.

Nederland
Area Code 409

Best Western Inn (200 Memorial Hwy. 69, 77627; 727-1631, 800-528-1234) 115 rooms, restaurant, lounge, pool, children free with parents, NS rooms, TV, laundry facilities, wheelchair access, pets OK, meeting facilities, senior rates, CC. SGL/DBL$38-$52.

New Braunfels
Area Code 210

Faust Hotel (240 South Seguin, 78130; 625-7791) 62 rooms, A/C, TV, NS rooms, no pets, 1920s inn, antique furnishings, CC. SGL/DBL$70-$80.

Hill Country Motor Inn (210 Hwy. 81 East, 78130; 625-7373) 61 rooms and 2-bedroom efficiencies, pool, kitchenettes, no pets, A/C, TV, NS rooms, wheelchair access, CC. SGL/DBL$40-$65.

Holiday Inn (1051 I-35, 78130; 625-8017, Fax 625-3130, 800-HOLIDAY) 140 rooms and suites, restaurant, lounge, pool, exercise center, children under 19 free with parents, wheelchair access, A/C, TV, NS rooms, fax, room service, no pets, laundry service, meeting facilities, senior rates, CC. SGL/DBL$65-$75.

Newcombe's Tennis Ranch (New Braunfels 78131; 625-9105) 56 rooms and cottages, restaurant, lounge, entertainment, heated pool, whirlpools, lighted tennis courts, airport transportation, fireplaces, A/C, TV, NS rooms, wheelchair access, CC. SGL/DBL$60-$145.

Prince Solms Inn (295 East San Antonio, 78130; 625-9169) 11 rooms and suites, restaurant, free breakfast, A/C, TV, NS rooms, wheelchair access, no children allowed, antique furnishings, senior rates, CC. SGL/DBL$60-$110.

Rodeway Inn (1209 I-35 South, 78130; 629-6991, 800-424-4777) 130 rooms, pool, wheelchair access, NS rooms, children free with parents, pets OK, laundry facilities, in-room refrigerators and microwaves, A/C, TV, senior rates, CC. SGL/DBL$44-$70.

North Richland Hills

Area Code 817

La Quinta Inn West (7888 I-30 West, 76180; 246-5511, Fax 246-8870, 800-531-5900) 106 rooms, restaurant, lounge, free breakfast, heated pool, free newspaper, free local calls, fax, laundry service, NS rooms, A/C, TV, wheelchair access, meeting facilities, CC. SGL/DBL$58-$105.

La Quinta Inn Northeast (7920 Bedford Euless Rd., 76180; 485-2750, Fax 656-8977, 800-531-5900) 100 rooms, restaurant, lounge, free breakfast, heated pool, free newspaper, free local calls, fax, laundry service, airport transportation, NS rooms, A/C, TV, wheelchair access, meeting facilities, CC. SGL/DBL$65-$95.

Lexington Inn (8709 Airport Freeway, 76180; 656-8881) 115 rooms, pool, whirlpools, children free with parents, airport transportation, pets OK, VCRs, A/C, TV, NS rooms, wheelchair access, CC. SGL/DBL$40-$48.

Odem

Area Code 512

Days Inn (Hwy. 77, 78370; 368-2166, Fax 368-2678, 800-325-2525) 24 rooms and suites, free breakfast, outdoor pool, whirlpools, children free with parents, room service, laundry service, A/C, TV, free local calls, pets OK, fax, wheelchair access, NS rooms, meeting facilities, senior rates, CC. SGL/DBL$30-$65.

Odessa

Area Code 915

Best Western Inn (110 West I-20, 79761; 337-3006, 800-528-1234) 118 rooms and suites, restaurant, lounge, indoor heated pool, exercise center, whirlpools, sauna, children free with parents, A/C, NS rooms, TV, laundry facilities, wheelchair access, pets OK, airport transportation, meeting facilities, senior rates, CC. SGL/DBL$35-$85.

Classic Suites (3031 East I-20, 79761; 333-9678) 113 suites, free breakfast, heated pool, pets OK, laundry facilities, in-room refrigerators, A/C, TV, NS rooms, wheelchair access, children free with parents, senior rates, CC. SGL/DBL$27-$35.

Days Inn (3075 East Business Loop 20, 79761; 335-8000, Fax 335-9562, 800-325-2525) 96 rooms and suites, free breakfast, outdoor pool, children free with parents, room service, laundry service, A/C, TV, free local calls, pets OK, fax, wheelchair access, NS rooms, meeting facilities, senior rates, CC. SGL/DBL$42-$50, STS$60-$65.

Econo Lodge (1518 South Grant, 79761; 333-1486, 800-4-CHOICE) 40 rooms, free breakfast, pool, children under 12 free with parents, no pets, NS rooms, wheelchair access, A/C, TV, senior rates, CC. SGL/DBL$32-$38.

Executive Inn (2505 East 2nd St., 79761; 333-1528, Fax 333-1528) 44 rooms, A/C, TV, NS rooms, wheelchair access, in-room refrigerators and microwaves, pets OK, senior rates, CC. SGL/DBL$25-$35.

Hilton Hotel (5200 East University, 79762; 368-5885, Fax 362-8959, 800-HILTONS) 194 rooms and suites, restaurant, lounge, entertainment, outdoor heated pool, jacuzzi, exercise center, whirlpools, children free with parents, NS rooms, wheelchair access, no pets, room service, laundry facilities, airport transportation, fax, A/C, TV, business services, meeting facilities, CC. SGL/DBL$60-$350.

Holiday Inn (3001 East Hwy. 80, 79760; 333-3931, Fax 333-9961, 800-HOLIDAY) 293 rooms, restaurant, lounge, indoor pool, exercise center, whirlpools, sauna, children under 19 free with parents, wheelchair access, A/C, TV, NS rooms, fax, room service, airport transportation, no pets, laundry service, meeting facilities for 300, senior rates, CC. SGL/DBL$56-$68.

Holiday Inn Centre (6201 East I-20, 79760; 362-2311, Fax 362-9810, 800-HOLIDAY) 273 rooms and suites, restaurant, lounge, pool, exercise center, whirlpools, airport transportation, children under 19 free with parents, wheelchair access, A/C, TV, NS rooms, fax, room service, no pets, laundry service, meeting facilities for 2,500, senior rates, CC. SGL/DBL$55-$160.

La Quinta Inn (5001 East Hwy. 80, 79761; 333-2820, Fax 4208, 800-531-5900) 122 rooms, restaurant, free breakfast, lounge, pool, complimentary newspaper, free local calls, fax, laundry service, NS rooms, wheelchair access, TV, airport transportation, A/C, meeting facilities, CC. SGL/DBL$45-$65.

Motel 6 North (2925 East Hwy. 80, 79761; 126 505-891-6161) pool, free local calls, children under 17 free with parents, NS rooms, wheelchair access, pets OK, A/C, TV, CC. SGL/DBL$39-$45.

Motel 6 South (200 East I-20 Service Rd., 79766; 333-4025, 505-891-6161) pool, free local calls, children under 17 free with parents, NS rooms, wheelchair access, pets OK, A/C, TV, CC. SGL/DBL$38-$46.

Villa West Inn (300 West I-20, 79760; 335-5055) 40 rooms, pets OK, A/C, TV, NS rooms, senior rates, CC. SGL/DBL$20-$30.

Orange

Area Code 409

Best Western Inn (2630 I-10, 77630; 883-6616, 800-528-1234) 60 rooms, pool, children free with parents, A/C, NS rooms, TV, laundry facilities, wheelchair access, pets OK, in-room refrigerators, meeting facilities, senior rates, CC. SGL/DBL$40-$48.

Motel 6 (4407 27th St., 77630; 883-4891, 505-891-6161) 126 rooms, pool, free local calls, children under 17 free with parents, NS rooms, wheelchair access, pets OK, A/C, TV, CC. SGL/DBL$38-$44.

Ramada Inn (2610 I-10, 77630; 883-0231, Fax 883-8839, 800-2-RAMADA) 125 rooms and suites, restaurant, lounge, entertainment, pool, wheelchair access, NS rooms, pets OK, A/C, TV, children under 18 free with parents, room service, laundry facilities, 10 meeting rooms, meeting facilities for 450, senior rates, CC. SGL/DBL$50-$130.

Red Carpet Inn (2900 I-10, 77630; 883-9981, 800-251-1962) 150 rooms, restaurant, lounge, pool, children free with parents, TV, A/C, NS rooms, pets OK, free local calls, complimentary newspaper, meeting facilities, room service, senior rates, CC. SGL/DBL$38-$45.

Ozona

Area Code 915

Best Western Circle Bar Inn (Ozona 76943; 392-2611, 800-528-1234) 52 rooms, restaurant, free breakfast, lounge, pool, exercise center, children free with parents, in-room refrigerators, boutiques, A/C, NS rooms, TV, laundry facilities, wheelchair access, pets OK, meeting facilities, senior rates, CC. SGL/DBL$40-$55.

Comfort Inn (1307 Ave. A, 76943; 392-3791, 800-221-2222) 50 rooms, free breakfast, pool, wheelchair access, NS rooms, no pets, children under 18 free with parents, A/C, TV, meeting facilities, senior rates, CC. SGL/DBL$44-$70.

Days Inn (820 Loop 466, 76943; 392-2631, Fax 392-2633, 800-325-2525) 23 rooms and suites, children free with parents, room service, laundry service, A/C, TV, free local calls, pets OK, fax, in-room computer hookups, wheelchair access, NS rooms, meeting facilities, senior rates, CC. SGL/DBL$28-$53.

Flying W Lodge (Ozona 76943; 392-2656) 40 rooms, pool, A/C, TV, NS rooms, wheelchair access, children free with parents, pets OK, senior rates, CC. SGL/DBL$25-$35.

Palestine
Area Code 903

Best Western Inn (1601 West Palestine Ave., 75801; 723-4655, Fax 723-2519, 800-528-1234) 66 rooms, restaurant, pool, exercise center, children free with parents, A/C, NS rooms, TV, laundry facilities, wheelchair access, pets OK, meeting facilities, senior rates, CC. SGL/DBL$35-$44.

Days Inn (1100 East Palestine Ave., 75801; 729-3151, 800-325-2525) 65 rooms and suites, outdoor pool, children free with parents, room service, laundry service, A/C, TV, free local calls, pets OK, fax, wheelchair access, NS rooms, meeting facilities for 275, senior rates, CC. SGL/DBL$35-$48, STS$59-$79.

Ramada Inn (1101 East Palestine Ave., 75801; 723-7300, Fax 723-3704, 800-2-RAMADA) 99 rooms and suites, restaurant, lounge, pool, wheelchair access, NS rooms, pets OK, A/C, TV, children under 18 free with parents, room service, laundry facilities, meeting facilities, senior rates, CC. SGL/DBL$40-$80.

Pampa
Area Code 806

Coronado Inn (1101 North Hobart St., 79065; 669-2506, 800-388-5650) 120 rooms and suites, restaurant, lounge, entertainment, pool, A/C, TV, NS rooms, game room, wheelchair access, CC. SGL/DBL$35-$90.

Paris
Area Code 903

Best Western Inn (3755 Northeast Loop, 75460; 785-5566, Fax 785-5566, 800-528-1234) 80 rooms, pool, exercise center, children free with parents,

A/C, NS rooms, TV, laundry facilities, wheelchair access, pets OK, meeting facilities, senior rates, CC. SGL/DBL$34-$40.

Comfort Inn (3505 Northeast Loop 286, 75460; 784-7481, 800-221-2222) 65 rooms, free breakfast, pool, wheelchair access, NS rooms, no pets, children under 18 free with parents, A/C, TV, meeting facilities, senior rates, CC. SGL/DBL$37-$53.

Holiday Inn (3560 Northeast Loop 286, 75460; 785-5545, Fax 785-9510, 800-HOLIDAY) 124 rooms, restaurant, lounge, outside pool, exercise center, children under 19 free with parents, wheelchair access, A/C, TV, NS rooms, fax, room service, pets OK, laundry service, airport transportation, meeting facilities, senior rates, CC. SGL/DBL$50-$70.

Pasadena
Area Code 713

Grumpy's Motor Inn (4222 Spencer Hwy., 77504; 944-6652) 44 rooms and 2-bedroom efficiencies, A/C, TV, children free with parents, pets OK, NS rooms, wheelchair access, CC. SGL/DBL$29-$38.

Rodeway Inn (114 South Richey St., 77506; 477-6871, 800-424-4777) 140 rooms, restaurant, free breakfast, lounge, pool, wheelchair access, NS rooms, children free with parents, A/C, TV, meeting facilities, senior rates, CC. SGL/DBL$33-$61.

Pearsall
Area Code 210

Porter House Inn (Pearsall 78061; 334-9466) 42 rooms, restaurant, lounge, pool, A/C, TV, NS rooms, wheelchair access, pets OK, CC. SGL/DBL$35-$40.

Sunset Motel (613 North Oak St., 78061; 334-3693) 21 rooms, pets OK, in-room refrigerators, microwaves and coffee makers, A/C, TV, NS rooms, wheelchair access, senior rates, CC. SGL/DBL$30-$36.

Pecos
Area Code 915

Best Western Sunday House Inn (900 West Palmer, 79772; 447-2215, Fax 447-4463, 800-528-1234) 104 rooms, restaurant, pool, exercise center, children free with parents, A/C, NS rooms, TV, laundry facilities, room service, wheelchair access, pets OK, meeting facilities, senior rates, CC. SGL/DBL$35-$56.

Holiday Inn (4002 Cedar Ave., 79722; 445-5404, Fax 445-2484, 800-HOLIDAY) 96 rooms, restaurant, lounge, outdoor pool, exercise center, children under 19 free with parents, wheelchair access, A/C, TV, NS rooms, fax, room service, no pets, laundry service, meeting facilities for 80, senior rates, CC. SGL/DBL$40-$50.

Motel 6 (3002 South Cedar St., 79772; 445-9034, 505-891-6161) 130 rooms, pool, free local calls, children under 17 free with parents, NS rooms, wheelchair access, pets OK, A/C, TV, CC. SGL/DBL$40-$48.

Pharr
Area Code 201

Pen-Ann Motel (1007 West Hwy. 83, 78577; 787-3267) 38 rooms, children free with parents, A/C, TV, NS rooms, wheelchair access, airport transportation, no pets, CC. SGL/DBL$28-$42.

Plainview
Area Code 806

Best Western Inn (600 North I-27, 79072; 293-9454, Fax 293-9454 ext 200, 800-528-1234) 83 rooms, restaurant, free breakfast, lounge, pool, exercise center, children free with parents, A/C, NS rooms, TV, laundry facilities, wheelchair access, pets OK, meeting facilities, senior rates, CC. SGL/DBL$45-$90.

Holiday Inn (Plainview 79073; 293-4181, 800-HOLIDAY) 98 rooms, restaurant, lounge, complimentary newspaper, airport transportation, children under 19 free with parents, wheelchair access, A/C, TV, NS rooms, in-room refrigerators, microwaves and coffee makers, fax, room service, no pets, laundry service, meeting facilities, senior rates, CC. SGL/DBL$45-$51.

Plano
Area Code 214

Comfort Inn (621 Central Pkwy. East, 75074; 424-5568, 800-221-2222) 102 rooms, free breakfast, pool, wheelchair access, NS rooms, no pets, children under 18 free with parents, A/C, TV, meeting facilities, senior rates, CC. SGL/DBL$45-$60.

Courtyard by Marriott (4901 West Plano Pkwy., 75075; 867-8000, 800-321-2121) 140 rooms, pool, sauna, exercise center, A/C, TV, laundry facilities, A/C, TV, NS rooms, wheelchair access, meeting facilities, senior rates, CC. SGL/DBL$72-$82.

Harvey Hotel (1600 North Central Pkwy., 75074; 578-8558, 800-922-9222) 279 rooms and suites, restaurant, lounge, entertainment, pool, sauna, exercise center, whirlpools, NS rooms, pets OK, A/C, TV, wheelchair access, in-room refrigerators, microwaves and coffee makers, children free with parents, laundry facilities, meeting facilities, CC. SGL/DBL$68-$73, STS$120.

Holiday Inn (700 Central Pkwy. East, 75074; 881-1881, 800-HOLIDAY) 157 rooms, restaurant, lounge, pool, exercise center, children under 19 free with parents, wheelchair access, A/C, TV, NS rooms, fax, in-room coffee makers, room service, pets OK, laundry service, meeting facilities, senior rates, CC. SGL/DBL$80-$93.

La Quinta (1820 North Central Expressway 75074; 423-1300, Fax 423-6593, 800-922-9222) 114 rooms, restaurant, free breakfast, pool, free local calls, NS rooms, pets OK, A/C, TV, laundry service, wheelchair access, meeting facilities, CC. SGL/DBL$49-$68.

Sleep Inn (4921 West Plano Pkwy. 75075; 800-221-2222) 100 rooms, free breakfast, wheelchair access, NS rooms, no pets, children under 18 free with parents, senior rates, A/C, TV, meeting facilities, CC. SGL/DBL$45-$55.

Port Aransas

Area Code 512

Channel View Motel (631 Channel View Dr., 78373; 749-6648, 800-234-8110) 23 1- to 3-bedroom efficiencies, pool, A/C, TV, NS rooms, wheelchair access, laundry facilities, no pets, in-room refrigerators, children free with parents, CC. SGL/DBL$120-$244.

Coral Cay Condominiums (1423 11th St., 78373; 749-5111, 800-221-4981) 55 rooms and 2-bedroom condominiums, heated pool, tennis courts, kitchenettes, no pets OK, A/C, TV, wheelchair access, CC. SGL/DBL$75-$160.

Courtyard by Marriott (622 Access Rd., 78373; 749-5243, 800-331-3131) 58 rooms and suites, complimentary breakfast, pool in-room refrigerators, microwaves and coffee makers, A/C, VCRs, no pets, complimentary newspaper, children free with parents, kitchenettes, A/C, TV, NS rooms, wheelchair access, meeting facilities, senior rates, CC. SGL/DBL$40-$75.

Dunces Condominiums (1000 Lantana Lane, 78373; 749-5155, Fax 749-5930, 800-288-DUNE) 48 1- to 3-bedroom condominiums, heated pool, exercise center, whirlpools, tennis courts, kitchenettes, A/C, TV, NS rooms, wheelchair access, CC. SGL/DBL$90-$125.

El Cortes Villas (Hwy. 361, 78373; 749-6206) 27 rooms and 2-bedroom villas, pool, laundry facilities, A/C, TV, NS rooms, wheelchair access, no pets, CC. SGL/DBL$45-$110.

Executive Keys (820 Access Rd. 1A, 78373; 749-6272) 51 rooms and 2- and 3-bedroom apartments, pool, A/C, TV, NS rooms, wheelchair access, CC. SGL/DBL$38-$175.

Gulf Shore Condominiums (Hwy. 361, 78373; 749-6257) 33 rooms, pool, tennis courts, kitchenettes, A/C, TV, laundry facilities, no pets, CC. SGL/DBL$$70-$130.

Port Arthur

Area Code 409

Holiday Inn (2929 75th St., 777642; 724-5000, Fax 724-7644, 800-HOLI-DAY) 163 rooms and suites, restaurant, lounge, entertainment, pool, exercise center, children under 19 free with parents, wheelchair access, A/C, TV, airport transportation, NS rooms, fax, room service, no pets, laundry service, meeting facilities, senior rates, CC. SGL/DBL$61-$125.

Ramada Inn (3801 Hwy. 73, 77642; 962-9858, Fax 962-3685, 800-2-RAMADA) 125 rooms and suites, restaurant, lounge, entertainment, pool, wheelchair access, NS rooms, pets OK, airport transportation, A/C, TV, children under 18 free with parents, room service, laundry facilities, meeting facilities, senior rates, CC. SGL/DBL$55-$120.

Port Isabel

Area Code 210

Padre Vista Motel (Port Isabel 78578; 943-7866) 58 rooms, restaurant, lounge, pool, whirlpools, pets OK, children free with parents, A/C, TV, NS rooms, wheelchair access, CC. SGL/DBL$30-$120.

Southwind Inn (600 Davis St., 78578; 943-3392) 17 rooms and efficiencies, pets OK, airport transportation, A/C, TV, NS rooms, wheelchair access, laundry facilities, CC. SGL/DBL$30-$50.

Yacht Club Hotel (700 Yturria St., 78578; 943-1301) 24 rooms, restaurant, lounge, heated pool, children free with parents, pets OK, A/C, TV, NS rooms, wheelchair access, CC. SGL/DBL$35-$100.

Port Lavaca

Area Code 512

Days Inn (2100 North Hwy. 35 Bypass, 77979; 552-4511, 800-325-2525) 99 rooms and suites, restaurant, lounge, outdoor pool, children free with parents, room service, laundry service, A/C, TV, free local calls, pets OK, fax, wheelchair access, NS rooms, meeting facilities for 200, senior rates, CC. SGL/DBL$46-$85.

Shell Fish Inn (2621 Hwy. 35 North Bypass, 77979; 552-3393) 50 rooms, pool, in-room refrigerators, children free with parents, no pets, A/C, TV, NS rooms, wheelchair access, CC. SGL/DBL$30-$37.

Portland

Area Code 512

Comfort Inn (1703 North Hwy. 181, 78374; 643-2222, 800-221-2222) 40 rooms, free breakfast, pool, whirlpools, sauna, wheelchair access, NS rooms, pets OK, children under 18 free with parents, A/C, TV, meeting facilities, senior rates, CC. SGL/DBL$47-$58.

Quanah
Area Code 817

Quanah Park Inn (1405 West 11th St., 79252; 663-6366, Fax 663-2593) 38 rooms, children free with parents, laundry facilities, A/C, TV, NS rooms, wheelchair access, CC. SGL/DBL$30-$44.

Rancho Viejo
Area Code 210

Rancho Viejo Resort and Country Club (1 Ranch Viejo Dr., 78520; 350-4000, Fax 350-5696, 800-531-7400) 88 rooms and 2- and 3-bedroom villas, restaurant, lounge, pool, exercise center, tennis courts, boutiques, A/C, no pets, children free with parents, TV, NS rooms, wheelchair access, meeting facilities for 900, CC. SGL/DBL$100-$115, 2BR$216, 3BR$314.

Ranger
Area Code 817

Days Inn (Ranger 76470; 647-1176, Fax 647-1832, 800-325-2525) 30 rooms and suites, free breakfast, outdoor pool, children free with parents, room service, laundry service, A/C, TV, free local calls, pets OK, fax, wheelchair access, NS rooms, meeting facilities, senior rates, CC. SGL/DBL$30-$45.

Raymondville
Area Code 210

Tall Palms Motel (Raymondville 78580; 689-2850) 25 rooms and cottages, children free with parents, no pets, children free with parents, TV, CC. SGL/DBL$28-$32.

Red Oak
Area Code 214

Days Inn (200 South Commercial, 75154; 617-3501, Fax 617-8521, 800-325-2525) 60 rooms and suites, outdoor pool, children free with parents, room service, laundry service, A/C, TV, free local calls, pets OK, fax, wheelchair access, NS rooms, senior rates, CC. SGL/DBL$25-$45.

Richardson
Area Code 214

Clarion Suites Hotel (1981 North Central Expressway 75080; 644-4000, 800-221-2222) 296 rooms and suites, restaurant, lounge, free breakfast, indoor and outdoor pool, exercise center, whirlpools, no pets, NS rooms, children under 18 free with parents, senior rates, meeting facilities, A/C, TV, CC. SGL/DBL$60-$123.

Courtyard by Marriott (1000 South Sherman, 75081; 235-5000, 800-331-3131) 149 rooms and suites, complimentary breakfast, pool, in-room refrigerators, microwaves and coffee makers, A/C, VCRs, no pets, complimentary newspaper, children free with parents, kitchenettes, A/C, TV, NS rooms, wheelchair access, meeting facilities, senior rates, CC. SGL/DBL$50-$80.

Hawthorn Suites (250 Municipal Dr., 75080; 669-1000, Fax 235-2452, 800-527-2360) 72 suites, free breakfast, pool, airport transportation, wheelchair access, NS rooms, A/C, TV, pets OK, laundry service, 3 meeting rooms, meeting facilities for 50. 25 miles from the Dallas-Fort Worth International Airport, 5 miles from the University of Texas. SGL/DBL$67-$71.

Hampton Inn (1577 Gateway Blvd., 75080; 234-5400, Fax 234-8942, 800-HAMPTON) 130 rooms, free breakfast, pool, children free with parents, NS rooms, A/C, TV, wheelchair access, computer hookups, fax, free local calls, meeting facilities, CC. SGL/DBL$50-$60.

Holiday Inn Richardson (1655 North Central Expressway, 75080; 238-1900, Fax 661-1096, 800-HOLIDAY) 221 rooms, restaurant, lounge, indoor pool, exercise center, children free with parents, wheelchair access, NS rooms, A/C, TV, fax, room service, laundry service, meeting facilities for 300, CC. SGL/DBL$75-$83.

Ramada Renaissance (701 East Campbell Rd., 75081; 231-9600, 800-272-6232) 342 rooms and suites, restaurant, lounge, pool, sauna, exercise center, A/C, TV, NS rooms, wheelchair access, in-room refrigerators, children free with parents, no pets, airport courtesy car, meeting facilities, CC. SGL$125-$135, DBL$135-$145.

Sleep Inn (2650 North Central Expressway, 75080; 470-9440, 800-221-2222) 64 rooms, free breakfast, exercise center, whirlpools, wheelchair access, NS rooms, no pets, children under 18 free with parents, senior rates, A/C, TV, meeting facilities, CC. SGL/DBL$38-$68.

Richmond
Area Code 713

Budget Inn (26035 Southwest Freeway, 77469; 342-5387, Fax 342-5387, 800-527-0700) 50 rooms and efficiencies, pool, NS rooms, children free with parents, no pets, A/C, TV, meeting facilities, senior rates, CC. SGL/DBL$29-$39.

Rio Grande City

Area Code 210

Fort Ringold Motor Inn (4350 Hwy. 83 East, 78582; 487-5666) 64 rooms, restaurant, lounge, entertainment, pool, A/C, TV, NS rooms, wheelchair access, children free with parents, no pets, CC. SGL/DBL$50-$60.

Robstown

Area Code 512

Econo Lodge (2225 Hwy. 77 North, 78380; 387-9444, 800-4-CHOICE) 32 rooms, pool, children under 12 free with parents, no pets, NS rooms, free local calls, wheelchair access, A/C, TV, senior rates, CC. SGL/DBL$37-$55.

Royal Motor Inn (Hwy. 77 South, 78380; 367-9416) 24 rooms, pool, whirlpools, pets OK, A/C, TV, NS rooms, wheelchair access, in-room refrigerators, CC. SGL/DBL$28-$36.

Rockport

Area Code 512

Days Inn (1212 Laurel, 78382; 729-6379, Fax 729-5162, 800-325-2525) 29 rooms and suites, free breakfast, outdoor pool, children free with parents, room service, laundry service, A/C, TV, free local calls, pets OK, fax, wheelchair access, NS rooms, meeting facilities, senior rates, CC. SGL/DBL$46-$68.

Laguna Reef (1021 Water St., 78382; 729-1742, 800-248-1057) 69 rooms and 2-bedroom apartments, pool, laundry facilities, kitchenettes, pets OK, children free with parents, A/C, TV, wheelchair access, CC. SGL/DBL$40-$160.

Village Inn (503 North Austin St., 78382; 729-6370) 25 rooms and 2-bedroom efficiencies, restaurant, children free with parents, pets OK, A/C, TV, NS rooms, wheelchair access, CC. SGL/DBL$32-$48.

Rockwall

Area Code 214

The Inn of Rockwall (1130 I-30, 75087; 722-9922) 58 rooms, swimming pool, whirlpools, no pets, A/C, TV, NS rooms, wheelchair access, CC. SGL/DBL$35-$44.

Rosenberg
Area Code 713

Best Western Inn (28382 Southwest Freeway, 77471; 342-6000, Fax 342-6000, 800-528-1234) 104 rooms, pool, exercise center, whirlpools, children free with parents, A/C, NS rooms, TV, laundry facilities, wheelchair access, pets OK, meeting facilities, senior rates, CC. SGL/DBL$35-$50.

Round Rock
Area Code 512

La Quinta Inn (2004 North I-35, 78681; 255-6666, Fax 388-3635, 800-531-5900) 115 rooms, restaurant, free breakfast, lounge, pool, complimentary newspaper, free local calls, fax, in-room refrigerators, laundry service, NS rooms, wheelchair access, TV, A/C, meeting facilities for 100, CC. SGL/DBL$50-$56.

Salado
Area Code 817

HoJo Inn (Salado 76571; 947-5000, 800-I-GO-HOJO) 42 rooms, free breakfast, pool, children free with parents, wheelchair access, NS rooms, TV, A/C, no pets, laundry facilities, senior rates, meeting facilities, CC. SGL/DBL$30-$42.

The Rose Mansion (1 Roseway, 76571; 947-5999) 5 rooms, free breakfast, A/C, TV, fireplaces, NS, no pets, private baths, 1870s home, CC. SGL/DBL$70-$98.

Stagecoach Inn (Salado 76571; 947-5111, 800-732-8994) 82 rooms and suites, restaurant, lounge, pool, whirlpools, lighted tennis courts, children free with parents, no pets, in-room refrigerators and microwaves, A/C, TV, NS rooms, wheelchair access, CC. SGL/DBL$40-$57.

San Angelo
Area Code 915

Best Western Inn (415 West Beauregard, 76903; 653-2995, Fax 653-2995, 800-528-1234) 75 rooms, restaurant, pool, exercise center, children free with parents, A/C, NS rooms, TV, laundry facilities, wheelchair access, room service, pets OK, meeting facilities, senior rates, CC. SGL/DBL$38-$45.

Days Inn (4613 South Jackson, 76903; 658-6594, 800-325-2525) 113 rooms and suites, restaurant, lounge, outdoor pool, children free with parents, room service, laundry service, A/C, TV, free local calls, pets OK, fax, wheelchair access, NS rooms, airport transportation, meeting facilities, senior rates, CC. SGL/DBL$30-$50, STS$60-$70.

El Patio Motel (1901 West Beauregard St., 76901; 655-5711, 800-677-7735) 100 rooms and efficiencies, restaurant, pool, pets OK, A/C, TV, NS rooms, wheelchair access, senior rates, meeting facilities, CC. SGL/DBL$20-$35.

Holiday Inn Convention Center (441 Rio Concho Dr., 76903; 658-2828, Fax 658-8741, 800-HOLIDAY) 149 rooms and suites, restaurant, lounge, entertainment, indoor pool, exercise center, children under 19 free with parents, wheelchair access, A/C, TV, NS rooms, fax, room service, airport transportation, no pets, laundry service, meeting facilities for 400, senior rates, CC. SGL/DBL$60-$160.

Howard Johnson (333 Rio Concho, 76903; 658-5755, 800-I-GO-HOJO) 128 rooms, restaurant, free breakfast, lounge, indoor pool, sauna, hot tub, children free with parents, wheelchair access, NS rooms, TV, A/C, no pets, laundry facilities, senior rates, meeting facilities, CC. SGL/DBL$48-$69.

Inn of the Conchos (2021 North Bryant, 76903; 658-2811, Fax 653-7560) 125 rooms and suites, restaurant, entertainment, pool, room service, in-room refrigerators, pets OK, A/C, TV, NS rooms, wheelchair access, senior rates, meeting facilities, CC. SGL/DBL$36-$56.

La Quinta Inn (2307 Loop 306, 76903; 949-0515, Fax 944-1187, 800-531-5900) 170 rooms, restaurant, free breakfast, lounge, pool, complimentary newspaper, free local calls, fax, laundry service, NS rooms, wheelchair access, TV, A/C, airport transportation, meeting facilities, CC. SGL/DBL$50-$65.

Motel 6 (311 North Bryant, 76903; 658-8061, 505-891-6161) 106 rooms, pool, free local calls, children under 17 free with parents, NS rooms, wheelchair access, pets OK, A/C, TV, CC. SGL/DBL$38-$46.

Ole Coach (4205 South Bryant, 76903; 653-6966, 800-227-6456) 82 rooms, lounge, entertainment, pool, tennis courts, pets OK, children free with parents, A/C, TV, NS rooms, wheelchair access, senior rates, CC. SGL/DBL$30-$40.

Ramada Inn (2502 Loop 306, 76904; 944-2578, Fax 944-4373, 800-2-RAMADA) 101 rooms and suites, restaurant, lounge, entertainment, pool, wheelchair access, NS rooms, pets OK, airport transportation, A/C, TV, children under 18 free with parents, room service, laundry facilities, meeting facilities, senior rates, CC. SGL/DBL$58-$88.

San Antonio

Area Code 210

Downtown San Antonio

Alamo Plaza Hotel (705 East Houston St., 78205; 225-8486, 800-824-6674) 177 rooms, pool, jacuzzi, sauna, A/C, TV, meeting facilities. SGL/DBL$90-$145.

Bed and Breakfast Belle of Monte Vista (505 Belknap Place, 78212; 732-4006) 5 rooms, free breakfast, airport courtesy car, A/C, TV, CC. SGL$40, DBL$50.

Bonner Garden (145 East Agarita, 78212; 733-4222, Fax 733-6129) 5 rooms, bed and breakfast, A/C, TV, CC. SGL/DBL$75-$110.

Brookhaven Manor (128 West Mistletoe, 78212; 733-3939, 800-851-3666) 4 rooms, bed and breakfast, A/C, TV, CC. SGL$70, DBL$80.

Courtyard by Marriott Downtown (600 Santa Rosa South, 78204; 229-9449, Fax 229-1853, 800-321-2211) 149 rooms and suites, restaurant, pool, wheelchair access, A/C, TV, CC. SGL/DBL$80-$90.

Crockett Hotel (320 Bonham St., 78205; 225-6500, Fax 225-6500, 800-292-1050) 202 rooms, pool, jacuzzi, sauna, wheelchair access, A/C, TV, room service, meeting facilities, CC. SGL$85-$120, DBL$94-$140.

Days Inn Riverwalk (902 East Houston St., 78205; 227-6233, Fax 228-0901, 800-325-2525) 81 rooms and suites, free breakfast, free local calls, fax, wheelchair access, NS rooms, A/C, TV, no pets, children free with parents, free local calls, senior rates, CC. Near the Riverwalk and Convention Center, 2 miles from the San Antonio Zoo. SGL/DBL$49-$99, STS$110-$125.

Elmira Motor Inn (1126 East Houston St., 78212; 222-9463) 132 rooms, pool, wheelchair access, A/C, TV, CC. SGL/DBL$25-$27.

Fairmont Hotel (401 South Alamo St., 78205; 224-8800, Fax 224-2767, 800-642-3363) 36 rooms and suites, restaurant, pool, 24-hour room service, wheelchair access, airport courtesy car, meeting facilities, A/C, TV, CC. SGL/DBL$145-$155.

Hilton Palacio del Rio (200 South Alamo St., 78205; 222-1400, Fax 270-0761, 800-445-8667) 482 rooms and suites, 3 restaurants, lounge, pool, jacuzzi, hot tub, room service, wheelchair access, A/C, TV, gift shop, meeting facilities, A/C, TV, CC. SGL/DBL$145-$205.

Holiday Inn Downtown (319 West Durango, 78204; 225-3211, Fax 222-1125, 800-HOLIDAY) 317 rooms, restaurant, lounge, pool, whirlpools, children free with parents, wheelchair access, NS rooms, A/C, TV, fax, room service, pets OK, meeting facilities for 300, CC. Near the Alamo, Riverwalk and Convention Center. SGL$61-$71, DBL$69-$79.

Holiday Inn Riverwalk North (110 Lexington, 78205; 223-9461, Fax 223-9267, 800-HOLIDAY) 323 rooms, restaurant, lounge, entertainment, pool, exercise center, children free with parents, wheelchair access, NS rooms, A/C, TV, fax, room service, meeting facilities for 1,000, CC. Near the Convention Center and business district. SGL/DBL$80-$90.

Holiday Inn Riverwalk (217 North Saint Mary's St., 78205; 224-2500, Fax 223-1302, 800-HOLIDAY) 313 rooms and suites, restaurant, lounge, entertainment, pool, exercise center, children free with parents, wheelchair access, NS rooms, A/C, TV, fax, room service, meeting facilities for 750, CC. 5 miles from the airport, near the Alamo and Convention Center. SGL$95-$108, DBL$105-$118.

Hyatt Regency On The Riverwalk (123 Losoya, 78205; 222-1234, Fax 227-4925; 800-223-1234) 632 rooms and suites, 2 restaurants, lounge, pool, jacuzzi, NS rooms, A/C, TV, complimentary newspaper, 24-hour room service, wheelchair access, meeting facilities for 1500, CC. Near the Alamo and Convention Center, 12 minutes from the airport. SGL/DBL$155-$175.

La Mansion Del Rio (112 College St., 78205; 225-2581, Fax 226-0389, 800-323-7500) 350 rooms and suites, 2 restaurants, lounge, pool, 24-hour room service, concierge, wheelchair access, meeting facilities for 130, A/C, TV, CC. On the San Antonio River near the Convention Center. SGL$135-$225, DBL$155-$245, STS$370-$1,500.

La Quinta Inn Convention Center (1001 East Commerce St., 78205; 222-9189, Fax 228-9816, 800-531-5900) 140 rooms, restaurant, lounge, heated pool, complimentary newspaper, free local calls, fax, laundry service, NS rooms, A/C, TV, wheelchair access, meeting facilities, CC. 8 miles from the airport, within 5 miles of Fort Sam Houston and the Convention Center. SGL/DBL$70-$80.

La Quinta Inn Market Square (900 Dolorosa, 78207; 271-0001, Fax 228-0663, 800-531-5900) 124 rooms, restaurant, lounge, heated pool, complimentary newspaper, free local calls, fax, laundry service, NS rooms, A/C, TV, wheelchair access, meeting facilities, CC. 4 miles from the Alamo and Convention Center, 15 miles from Sea World, 9 miles from the airport. SGL/DBL$64-$75.

Marriott Rivercenter (101 Bowie St., 78205; 223-1000, Fax 223-6239, 800-228-9290) 1,082 rooms and suites, Concierge Level, restaurant, lounge, entertainment, indoor and outdoor pool, exercise center, sauna, whirlpools, wheelchair access, gift shop, airline ticket desk, meeting facilities for

250, A/C, TV, CC. On the Riverwalk near the Alamo, 15 minutes from Sea World. SGL/DBL$155-$165.

Marriott River Walk (711 East Riverwalk, 78205; 224-4555, Fax 224-2754, 800-228-9290) 504 rooms and suites, restaurant, lounge, entertainment, indoor and outdoor pool, exercise center, whirlpools, sauna, NS rooms, A/C, TV, wheelchair access, gift shop, 24-hour room service, airline ticket desk, meeting facilities for 150, CC. Near the Riverwalk and the Alamo, 20 minutes from Sea World. SGL$145-$165, DBL$165-$186.

Menger Hotel (204 Alamo Plaza, 78205; 223-4361, Fax 228-0022, 800-241-3848) 357 rooms and suites, restaurant, pool, wheelchair access, 24-hour room service, beauty shop, meeting facilities for 150, A/C, TV, CC. SGL$74-$94, DBL$94-$118.

Motel 6 (211 North Pecos, 78207; 225-1111) 118 rooms, wheelchair access, pool, A/C, TV, CC. SGL/DBL$32-$38.

Plaza San Antonio (555 South Alamo, 78205; 229-1000, Fax 223-6650, 800-421-1172) 250 rooms and suites, restaurant, pool, jacuzzi, sauna, exercise center, tennis courts, wheelchair access, 24-hour room service, meeting facilities for 120, A/C, TV, CC. SGL$130-$170, DBL$150-$190.

Rodeway Inn Downtown (900 North Main Ave., 78212; 223-2951, Fax 223-9064, 800-228-2000) 128 rooms, restaurant, free breakfast, outdoor pool, exercise center, wheelchair access, airport courtesy car, free local calls, meeting facilities for 80, A/C, TV, CC. SGL/DBL$55-$126.

St. Anthony InterContinental Hotel (300 East Travis St., 78205; 227-4392, Fax 227-0915, 800-327-0200) 350 rooms and suites, restaurant, pool, exercise center, wheelchair access, meeting facilities for 120, A/C, TV, CC. SGL/DBL$106-$126.

Sheraton Gunter Hotel (205 East Houston St., 78205; 227-3241, Fax 227-3241 ext 7761, 800-325-3535) 325 rooms and suites, 2 restaurants, 2 lounges, entertainment, 24-hour room service, heated outdoor pool, jacuzzi, exercise center, gift shop, barber shop, wheelchair access, NS rooms, A/C, TV, 14 meeting rooms, 17,200 square feet of meeting and exhibition space, meeting facilities for 1,110, CC. Near the Riverwalk, Institute of Texan Culture and La Villita, 8 miles from the airport. SGL$89-$116, DBL$99-$139.

Travelers Hotel (220 Broadway, 78205; 226-4381) 106 rooms and suites, pool, wheelchair access, A/C, TV, CC. SGL/DBL$20-$25.

TraveLodge Hotel On The River (100 Villita St., 78205; 226-2271, Fax 226-9453, 800-255-3050) 133 rooms and suites, restaurant, lounge, entertainment, pool, gift shop, car rental desk, airport transportation, no pets, room service, complimentary newspaper, gift shop, meeting facilities for

350, A/C, TV, CC. Near the Alamo, Market Square and the Convention Center. SGL/DBL$75-$210.

TraveLodge Alamo (405 Broadway, 78205; 222-9400, Fax 229-9744, 800-255-3050) 81 rooms and suites, restaurant, lounge, free breakfast, pool, wheelchair access, airport transportation, fax, no pets, A/C, TV, car rental desk, laundry facilities, local transportation, senior rates, CC. SGL/DBL$50-$90.

Airport Area

AmeriSuites Hotel Airport (11221 San Pedro, 78216; 342-4800, Fax 342-1110, 800-255-1755) 118 rooms and suites, pool, wheelchair access, complimentary newspaper, NS rooms, children free with parents, A/C, TV, CC. SGL/DBL$62-$72.

Best Western Town House Motel (942 Northeast Loop 410, 78209; 826-6311, Fax 826-6311, 800-528-1234) 60 rooms, restaurant, lounge, free breakfast, pool, airport courtesy car, free local calls, fax, NS rooms, A/C, TV, CC. 1 mile from the airport. SGL$35-$46, DBL$39-$56.

Courtyard by Marriott Airport (8615 Broadway, 78217; 828-7200, Fax 828-9003, 800-321-2211) 145 rooms and suites, restaurant, pool, airport courtesy car, meeting facilities, A/C, TV, CC. SGL/DBL$72-$82.

Days Inn (2635 Northeast Loop 410, 78217; 653-9110, 800-325-2525) 202 rooms and suites, free breakfast, outdoor pool, children free with parents, room service, laundry service, A/C, TV, free local calls, pets OK, fax, wheelchair access, NS rooms, airport transportation, meeting facilities, senior rates, CC. SGL/DBL$35-$90, STS$80-$160.

Drury Inn Airport (143 Northeast Loop I-410, 78216; 366-4300, Fax 366-4300, 800-325-8300) 125 rooms and suites, pool, A/C, TV, wheelchair access, A/C, TV, airport transportation, meeting facilities, senior rates, CC. SGL/DBL$56-$64.

Embassy Suites Airport (10110 U.S. Hwy. 281 North, 78216; 525-9999, Fax 525-0626, 800-362-2779) 261 2-room suites, restaurant, lounge, free breakfast, pool, jacuzzi, sauna, exercise center, NS rooms, A/C, TV, gift shop, room service, laundry service, airport courtesy car, car rental desk, wheelchair access, business services, meeting facilities, CC. 1 mile from the San Antonio International airport, 7 miles from the downtown area and Riverwalk. SGL/DBL$129-$139.

Executive Guesthouse (12828 U.S. Hwy. 281 North, 78219; 494-7600, Fax 545-4314, 800-362-8700) 126 rooms, pool, sauna, airport courtesy car, wheelchair access, A/C, TV, meeting facilities, CC. SGL/DBL$120-$130.

Hampton Inn Airport (8818 Jones Maltsberger Rd., 78216; 366-1800, Fax 366-1800, 800-HAMPTON) 121 rooms, free breakfast, pool, airport transportation, children free with parents, NS rooms, A/C, TV, room service, wheelchair access, computer hookups, fax, free local calls, meeting facilities, CC. .5 miles from the airport, 7 miles from the Alamo and Riverwalk, 8 miles from the Coliseum. SGL$63-$77.

Holiday Inn Airport (77 Northeast Loop 410, 78216; 349-9900, Fax 349-4660, 800-HOLIDAY) 400 rooms and suites, restaurant, lounge, entertainment, outdoor pool, hot tub, exercise center, children free with parents, wheelchair access, NS rooms, A/C, TV, fax, room service, local transportation, airport transportation, meeting facilities for 500, CC. .7 miles from the airport, 6 miles from the downtown area, 9 miles from Sea World. SGL/DBL$85-$135, DBL$95-$145.

Howard Johnson Airport North (9603 I-35 North, 78233; 655-2120, 800-654-2000) 90 rooms, restaurant, lounge, pool, children free with parents, wheelchair access, NS rooms, TV, A/C, pets OK, laundry facilities, senior rates, meeting facilities, CC. SGL/DBL$30-$70.

La Quinta Inn Airport East (333 Northeast Loop 410, 78216; 828-0781, Fax 826-3445, 800-531-5900) 198 rooms, restaurant, lounge, heated pool, complimentary newspaper, free local calls, fax, laundry service, airport transportation, NS rooms, A/C, TV, wheelchair access, meeting facilities, CC. 4 miles from Trinity University and Fort Sam Houston, 8 miles from the River Walk and downtown area, .5 miles from the airport. SGL/DBL$56-$66.

La Quinta Inn Airport West (219 North Loop 410, 78216; 342-4291, Fax 366-0748, 800-531-5900) 100 rooms, restaurant, lounge, heated pool, complimentary newspaper, free local calls, airport transportation, fax, laundry service, NS rooms, A/C, TV, wheelchair access, meeting facilities, CC. 5 miles from Fort Sam Houston and the downtown area, .5 miles from the airport. SGL/DBL$56-$66.

Quality Inn (10811 I-35 North, 78233; 800-221-2222) 164 rooms and suites, restaurant, lounge, pool, exercise center, whirlpools, children free with parents, A/C, TV, room service, laundry service, NS rooms, meeting facilities, senior rates, CC. SGL/DBL$50-$130.

Radisson Airport Hotel (611 Northwest Loop 410, 78216; 340-6060, Fax 340-7174, 800-333-3333) 387 rooms and suites, restaurant, pool, room service, wheelchair access, A/C, TV, meeting facilities, CC. SGL/DBL$75-$85.

Ramada Inn Airport (1111 Northeast Loop I-410, 78209; 828-9031, 800-288-9031, 800-272-6232) 244 rooms and suites, restaurant, pool, airport courtesy car, A/C, TV, wheelchair access, meeting facilities, CC. SGL/DBL$65-$85.

Sheraton Fiesta San Antonio Hotel (37 Northeast Loop 410, 78216; 366-2424, Fax 341-0410, 800-325-3535) 291 rooms and suites, 2 restaurants, 2 lounges, entertainment, 24-hour room service, gift shop, wheelchair access, NS rooms, A/C, TV, airport courtesy car, business services, 7 meeting rooms, 8,892 square feet of meeting and exhibition space, meeting facilities for 880, CC. 8 miles from the Alamo, 1 mile from the airport. SGL/DBL$110-$125.

Other Locations

Aloha Motel and Apartments (1435 Austin Hwy., 78209; 828-0933, 800-752-6354) 100 rooms and suites, pool, wheelchair access, A/C, TV, CC. SGL/DBL$18-$35.

Bed and Breakfast Beauregard House (215 Beauregard, 78204; 222-1198) 5 rooms, free breakfast, A/C, TV, CC. SGL$60, DBL$70.

Best Western Continental Inn (9735 I-35 North, 78233; 655-3510, Fax 655-0778, 800-528-1234) 161 rooms and suites, restaurant, pool, heated spa, in-room refrigerators and microwaves, no pets, valet laundry, NS rooms, A/C, TV, CC. 8 miles from the downtown area. SGL$42-$58, DBL$50-$66, X$3.

Best Western Ingram Park Inn (6855 North West Loop 410, 78238; 520-8080, Fax 522-0892, 800-528-1234) 60 rooms and suites, restaurant, lounge, pool, jacuzzi, fax, wheelchair access, NS rooms, A/C, TV, meeting facilities. 10 miles from the downtown area. SGL$35-$56, DBL$39-$62.

Comfort Inn (4403 I-10 East, 78219; 333-9430, Fax 359-7201, 800-221-2222) 120 rooms and suites, restaurant, free breakfast, pool, whirlpools, wheelchair access, in-room refrigerators, free local calls, NS rooms, A/C, TV, wheelchair access, meeting facilities, CC. 2 miles from the Coliseum, 10 miles from the Riverwalk and downtown area. SGL/DBL$40-$70.

Days Inn East (4039 East Houston St., 78220; 337-6753, 800-325-2525) 122 rooms, restaurant, free breakfast, wheelchair access, pets OK, fax, NS rooms, A/C, TV, children free with parents, senior rates, CC. 20 minutes from Fiesta Texas, 4 miles from the River Center Mall. SGL$30-$90.

Days Inn Northeast (I-35 and Coliseum Rd., 78219; 225-4521, 800-325-2525) 122 rooms, free breakfast, pool, children stay free with parents, pets OK, NS rooms, A/C, TV, wheelchair access, fax service, CC. 4 miles from the River Center Mall and Riverwalk, 20 minutes from Fiesta Texas. SGL/DBL$44-$98.

Deluxe Inn (3370 I-35 North, 78219; 271-3100, Fax 224-2525) 50 rooms, wheelchair access, A/C, TV, CC. SGL/DBL$40-$58.

Econo Lodge (218 South W.W. White Rd., 78219; 333-3346, 800-4-CHOICE) 40 rooms, free breakfast, pool, exercise center, free local calls, children under 12 free with parents, no pets, NS rooms, fax, wheelchair access, A/C, TV, senior rates, CC. SGL/DBL$28-$95.

Hampton Inn Northwest (4803 Manitou Dr., 78228; 684-9966, Fax 684-6211, 800-HAMPTON) 123 rooms, free breakfast, pool, pets OK, children free with parents, NS rooms, A/C, TV, wheelchair access, computer hook-ups, fax, free local calls, meeting facilities, CC. 6 miles from the airport, 8 miles from Fiesta Texas, the Alamo and Riverwalk. SGL/DBL$48-$65.

Hawthorn Suites Hotel (4041 Bluemel Rd., 78240; 561-9660, Fax 561-9663, 800-527-1133) 127 suites, free breakfast, pool, whirlpools, airport transportation, wheelchair access, complimentary newspaper, NS rooms, A/C, TV, pets OK, 2 meeting rooms, meeting facilities for 20, CC. 7 miles from the San Antonio International Airport, 11 miles from the Alamo and Riverwalk. SGL/DBL$99-$119.

Holiday Inn Coliseum (3855 Pan Am Hwy., 78219; 226-4361, 800-HOLIDAY) 202 rooms, restaurant, lounge, children free with parents, wheelchair access, NS rooms, A/C, TV, fax, room service, meeting facilities for 150, CC. 10 miles from the airport, 1 mile from the Coliseum, 5 miles from the downtown area and Alamo. SGL$99, DBL$119.

Holiday Inn Northwest (3233 Northwest Loop 410, 78213; 377-3900, Fax 377-0120, 800-HOLIDAY) 290 rooms, Executive Level, restaurant, lounge, indoor pool, exercise center, children free with parents, wheelchair access, NS rooms, A/C, TV, fax, room service, airport transportation, pets OK, local transportation, meeting facilities for 450, CC. 4 miles from the airport, 6 miles from the downtown area. SGL/DBL$60-$78.

Holiday Inn (6023 Northwest Expressway, 78201; 736-1900, Fax 734-2253, 800-HOLIDAY) 211 rooms and suites, restaurant, lounge, free breakfast, exercise center, children free with parents, wheelchair access, NS rooms, A/C, TV, fax, room service, laundry service, meeting facilities for 200, CC. 4 miles from the airport, 5 miles from the Alamo and Riverwalk. SGL/DBL$73-$79.

Knights Inn (6370 I-35 North, 78218; 646-6336, 800-843-5644) 134 rooms, kitchenettes, NS rooms, A/C, TV, wheelchair access, in-room refrigerators and microwaves, CC. 8 miles from the downtown area, 5 miles from the San Antonio Zoo, 6 miles from the airport. SGL$37-$42.

La Quinta Inn Windsor Park (6410 I-35 North, 78218; 653-6619, Fax 590-3359, 800-531-5900) 130 rooms, restaurant, pool, meeting facilities, free local calls, NS rooms, A/C, TV, wheelchair access, cable TV, fax, complimentary magazines, valet laundry, free parking. 8 miles from the airport. SGL/DBL$58-$68.

La Quinta Inn South (7202 South Pan Am Expressway, 78224; 922-2111, Fax 923-7979, 800-531-5900) 122 rooms, restaurant, lounge, heated pool, complimentary newspaper, free local calls, fax, laundry service, NS rooms, A/C, TV, wheelchair access, meeting facilities, CC. 3 miles from the Alamo, Convention Center and downtown area, 14 miles from the San Antonio International Airport. SGL/DBL$51-$61.

La Quinta Inn Toepperwein (12822 I-35 North, 78233; 657-5500, Fax 590-3640, 800-531-5900) 134 rooms, restaurant, lounge, heated pool, complimentary newspaper, free local calls, fax, laundry service, NS rooms, A/C, TV, wheelchair access, meeting facilities, CC. 4 miles from the Rolling Oaks Mall and Olympia Park, 14 miles from the downtown area, 9 miles from airport. SGL/DBL$58-$68.

La Quinta Inn Vance Jackson (5922 Northwest Expressway, 78201; 734-7931, Fax 733-6039, 800-531-5900) 111 rooms, restaurant, lounge, heated pool, complimentary newspaper, free local calls, fax, laundry service, NS rooms, A/C, TV, wheelchair access, meeting facilities, CC. 5 miles from the Alamo, Convention Center and downtown area, 7 miles from the airport. SGL/DBL$52-$66.

La Quinta Inn Ingram Park (7134 Northwest Loop 410, 78238; 680-8883, Fax 681-3877, 800-531-5900) 195 rooms, restaurant, lounge, heated pool, complimentary newspaper, free local calls, fax, laundry service, NS-rooms, A/C, TV, wheelchair access, meeting facilities, CC. 5 miles from the Northside Athletic Complex, 10 miles from the downtown area, 11 miles from the airport. SGL/DBL$56-$66.

Motel 6 (4621 Rittiman Rd., 78218; 653-4419) 110 rooms, pool, A/C, TV, wheelchair access, CC. SGL/DBL$30-$33.

Motel 6 (9500 Wurzbach, 78240; 593-0013) 123 rooms, pool, A/C, TV, CC. SGL/DBL$31-$37.

Motel 6 East (138 North W.W. White Rd., 78219; 333-1850) 183 rooms, wheelchair access, A/C, TV, CC. SGL/DBL$33-$37.

Quality Inn Northeast (3817 North Pan Am Expressway, 78219; 224-3030, 800-221-2222) 124 rooms and suites, free breakfast, pool, sauna, wheelchair access, NS rooms, A/C, TV, no pets, senior rates, CC. SGL/DBL$30-$100.

Relay Station Motel (5530 I-70, 78219; 662-6691) 144 rooms, restaurant, pool, wheelchair access, A/C, TV, CC. SGL/DBL$27-$37.

Richman Inn (3617 North Pan American Expressway, 78219; 225-3261, Fax 225-6658, 800-233-9881) 93 rooms, restaurant, pool, A/C, TV, CC. SGL$28-$31, DBL$38-$41.

Rodeway Inn Wonderland (6804 Northwest Expressway, 78201; 734-7111, 800-228-2000) 100 rooms and suites, pool, A/C, TV, CC. SGL/DBL$36-$53.

Rodeway Inn Laredo (15001 I-35 South, 78204; 271-3334, 800-228-2000) 90 rooms, free breakfast, airport courtesy car, meeting facilities, A/C, TV, CC. SGL/DBL$42-$138.

Rodeway Inn Northeast (1259 Austin Hwy., 78209; 824-7321, 800-228-2000) 39 rooms, pool, airport courtesy car, A/C, TV, CC. SGL$74, DBL$80.

San Antonio International Hostel Bullis House Inn (621 Pierce St., 78208; 223-9426) 50 rooms, CC. SGL/DBL$30-$55.

Scotsman Inn (5710 Industry Park Dr., 78218; 662-7400, Fax 662-7400 ext 199, 800-688-7268) 112 rooms, pool, CC. SGL/DBL$28-$36.

7 Oaks Hotel and Conference Center (1400 Austin Hwy., 78209; 824-5371, Fax 829-1477, 800-346-5866) 190 rooms and suites, 2 restaurants, pool, CC. SGL/DBL$55-$65.

Skyline Motel (1401 Austin Hwy., 78209; 824-2305) 68 rooms, pool, A/C, TV, CC. SGL/DBL$28-$43.

Super 8 Motel (11027 I-35 North, 78233; 637-1033, 800-800-8000) 62 rooms and suites, restaurant, outdoor pool, free breakfast, children free with parents, NS rooms, A/C, TV, wheelchair access, no pets, computer hook-ups, fax, free local calls, meeting facilities, CC. 1 mile from Sea Word and the Windsor Park Shopping Center, 12 miles from Fiesta Texas and the Alamo. SGL$33, DBL$37.

Medical Center Area

AmeriSuites Hotel Medical Center (10950 Laureate, 78249; 691-1103, Fax 691-2180, 800-255-1755) 126 suites, pool, A/C, TV, wheelchair access, complimentary newspaper, children free with parents, CC. SGL/DBL$44-$60.

Comfort Inn Northwest (Northwest 410 Loop, 78229; 800-221-2222) 50 rooms, free breakfast, pool, wheelchair access, NS rooms, no pets, children under 18 free with parents, A/C, TV, meeting facilities, senior rates, CC. SGL/DBL$48-$98.

Courtyard by Marriott Medical Center (8585 Marriott Dr., 78229; 696-7100, Fax 696-8905, 800-321-2211) 146 rooms and suites, restaurant, pool, jacuzzi, sauna, pool, wheelchair access, A/C, TV, meeting facilities, CC. SGL/DBL$66-$76.

Embassy Suites (7750 Briaridge St., 78230; 340-5421, Fax 340-1843, 800-362-2779) 217 2-room suites, restaurant, lounge, free breakfast, pool, exercise center, jacuzzi, sauna, airport courtesy car, NS rooms, A/C, TV, meeting facilities, CC. 4.5 miles from the airport, 6 miles from Fiesta Texas, 8 miles from the downtown area and Riverwalk. SGL/DBL$104-$114.

Guesthouse Inn (7500 Louis Pasteur, 78229; 616-0030, Fax 616-0048) 49 rooms and suites, wheelchair access, pool, A/C, TV, CC. SGL/DBL$45-$52.

Hampton Inn (San Antonio 78230; 561-9058, Fax 690-5566, 800-HAMP-TON) 122 rooms, free breakfast, pool, children free with parents, NS rooms, A/C, TV, wheelchair access, computer hookups, fax, free local calls, meeting facilities for 45, CC. 13 miles from Sea World, 10 miles from Market Square, 12 miles from the Alamo and Riverwalk, 6 miles from the airport. SGL/DBL$55-$63.

La Quinta Inn Wurzbach (9542 I-10 West, 78230; 593-0338, Fax 593-0838, 800-531-5900) 106 rooms, restaurant, lounge, heated pool, complimentary newspaper, free local calls, fax, laundry service, NS rooms, A/C, TV, wheelchair access, CC. SGL/DBL$55-$65.

Lexington Hotel Suites (4935 Northwest Loop I410, 78229; 680-3351, Fax 680-5182, 800-53-SUITE) 210 suites, pool, A/C, TV, wheelchair access, CC. SGL/DBL$53-$62.

Oak Hills Motor Inn (7401 Wurzbach, 78229; 614-9900, Fax 696-9900, 800-468-3507) 223 rooms and suites, restaurant, pool, wheelchair access, room service, A/C, TV, CC. SGL/DBL$54-$60.

Wyndham Hotel (9821 Colonnade Blvd., 78230; 691-8888, Fax 691-1128, 800-822-4200) 325 rooms and suites, restaurant, lounge, indoor and outdoor pools, sauna, whirlpools, wheelchair access, exercise center, cable TV, 23,000 square feet of meeting and exhibition space, meeting facilities for 300, CC. In the Colonnade Office Complex, 2 miles from Fiesta Texas, 10 minutes from the airport and the downtown area. SGL/DBL$130-$149.

Suburban Area

Best Western Lackland Lodge (6815 Hwy. 90 West, 78227; 675-9690, Fax 675-9690, 800-528-1234) 185 rooms and suites, restaurant, pool, kitchenettes, fax, children free with parents, no pets, wheelchair access, NS rooms, CC. SGL$40-$65, DBL$70, X$4.

Coachman Inn (3180 Goliad Rd., 78223; 337-7171, 800-FOR-INNS) 120 rooms and suites, pool, wheelchair access, A/C, TV, CC. SGL/DBL$39-$49.

Econo Lodge (6735 Hwy. 90 West, 78227; 674-5711, 800-4-CHOICE) 46 rooms, restaurant, free breakfast, pool, children under 12 free with parents, no pets, NS rooms, free local calls, wheelchair access, A/C, TV, senior rates, CC. SGL/DBL$31-$48.

La Quinta Inn Lackland (6511 Military Dr. West, 78227; 674-3200, Fax 673-6015, 800-531-5900) 140 rooms, restaurant, lounge, heated pool, complimentary newspaper, free local calls, fax, laundry service, local transportation, NS rooms, A/C, TV, wheelchair access, meeting facilities, CC. 19

miles from the airport, within 5 miles of the Westlakes Mall and South Park Mall, 8 miles from Sea World, 15 miles from the downtown area. SGL/DBL$49-$59.

Motel 6 Sea World (2185 Southwest Loop 410, 78227; 673-9020) 122 rooms, pool, wheelchair access, A/C, TV, CC. SGL/DBL$29-$35.

Rodeway Inn O'Conner Road (11591 I-35 North, 78223; 654-9111, Fax 646-0038, 800-228-2000) 92 rooms and suites, restaurant, free breakfast, pool, spa, A/C, TV, wheelchair access, airport courtesy car, meeting facilities, CC. SGL/DBL$55-$126.

Travelers Inn (6861 Hwy. 90 West, 78227; 675-4120, Fax 670-1890, 800-633-8300) 125 rooms and suites, pool, free local calls, NS rooms, A/C, TV, wheelchair access, meeting facilities, CC. SGL/DBL$30-$36.

San Benito
Area Code 210

Budget Host Motel (2055 West Hwy. 77, 78586; 399-6148, 800-283-4678) 22 rooms, pool, whirlpools, sauna, airport transportation, no pets, kitchenettes, laundry facilities, NS rooms, wheelchair access, A/C, TV, in-room refrigerators, senior rates, children stay free with parents, CC. SGL/DBL$33-$50.

San Juan
Area Code 210

San Juan Hotel (125 West Hwy. 83, 78589; 781-5339) 22 rooms, restaurant, pool, in-room refrigerators, children free with parents, pets OK, A/C, TV, NS rooms, wheelchair access, meeting facilities, CC. SGL/DBL$30-$88.

San Marcos
Area Code 512

Aquarena Springs Inn (San Marcos 78667; 396-8901) 24 rooms and efficiencies, restaurant, free breakfast, pool, no pets, in-room refrigerators, children free with parents, laundry service, A/C, TV, NS rooms, wheelchair access, CC. SGL/DBL$65-$80.

Crystal River Inn (326 West Hopkins, 78666; 396-3739) 9 rooms, free breakfast, A/C, TV, NS rooms, wheelchair access, airport transportation, no pets, no children, CC. SGL/DBL$45-$100.

Days Inn (1001 I-35 North, 78666; 353-5050, 800-325-2525) 62 rooms and suites, outdoor pool, children free with parents, room service, laundry service, A/C, TV, free local calls, pets OK, fax, wheelchair access, NS rooms, meeting facilities, senior rates, CC. SGL/DBL$35-$55.

Econo Lodge (811 South Guadalupe St., 78666; 353-5300, 800-4-CHOICE) 57 rooms and efficiencies, pool, children under 12 free with parents, no pets, NS rooms, kitchenettes, free local calls, wheelchair access, A/C, TV, senior rates, CC. SGL/DBL$33-$70.

Executive House Hotel (1433 I-35 North, 78666; 353-7770) 91 rooms and suites, pool, in-room refrigerators and coffee makers, pets OK, children free with parents, A/C, TV, NS rooms, wheelchair access, meeting facilities, senior rates, CC. SGL/DBL$30-$65.

Holiday Inn (1635 Aquarena Springs Dr., 78666; 353-8011, Fax 396-8062, 800-HOLIDAY) 100 rooms, restaurant, lounge, outdoor pool, exercise center, children under 19 free with parents, wheelchair access, A/C, TV, NS rooms, fax, room service, no pets, laundry service, meeting facilities, senior rates, CC. SGL/DBL$45-$65.

Homeplace Inn (1429 I-35 North, 78666; 396-0400) 40 rooms, pool, A/C, TV, NS rooms, meeting facilities, senior rates, CC. SGL/DBL$40-$62.

Motel 6 (1321 I-35 North, 78666; 396-8705, 505-891-6161) 126 rooms, pool, free local calls, children under 17 free with parents, NS rooms, wheelchair access, pets OK, A/C, TV, CC. SGL/DBL$39-$44.

Rodeway Inn (801 I-35 North, 78666; 353-1303, 800-424-4777) 44 rooms, free breakfast, pool, wheelchair access, NS rooms, children free with parents, A/C, TV, senior rates, CC. SGL/DBL$35-$120.

Sanderson
Area Code 915

Desert Air Motel (Sanderson 79848; 345-2572) 16 rooms, A/C, TV, NS rooms, wheelchair access, pets OK, CC. SGL/DBL$22-$34.

Seagoville
Area Code 214

Red Carpet Inn (1920 Hwy. 175, 75159; 287-2600, 800-251-1962) children free with parents, TV, A/C, NS rooms, free local calls, pets OK, meeting facilities, senior rates, CC. SGL/DBL$25-$38.

Segovia
Area Code 915

Best Western Inn (Segovia 76849; 446-3331, 800-528-1234) 33 rooms, pool, exercise center, whirlpools, tennis courts, children free with parents, A/C, NS rooms, TV, laundry facilities, wheelchair access, pets OK, meeting facilities, senior rates, CC. SGL/DBL$46-$50.

Seguin

Area Code 210

Best Western Inn (1603 I-10, 78155; 379-9631, 800-528-1234) 83 rooms, pool, exercise center, children free with parents, A/C, NS rooms, TV, laundry facilities, wheelchair access, pets OK, in-room refrigerators, airport transportation, meeting facilities, senior rates, CC. SGL/DBL$35-$60.

Econo Lodge (3013 North Hwy. 123 Bypass, 78155; 372-3990, 800-4-CHOICE) 60 rooms, restaurant, lounge, pool, whirlpools, children under 12 free with parents, no pets, NS rooms, wheelchair access, A/C, free local calls, TV, senior rates, CC. SGL/DBL$33-$60.

Holiday Inn (2950 North Hwy. 123 Bypass, 78155; 372-0860, Fax 372-3020, 800-HOLIDAY) 139 rooms and suites, restaurant, lounge, whirlpools, exercise center, children under 19 free with parents, wheelchair access, A/C, TV, NS rooms, fax, room service, in-room refrigerators, microwaves and coffee makers, no pets, laundry service, meeting facilities for 150, senior rates, CC. SGL/DBL$55-$90.

Seminole

Area Code 915

Raymond Motor Inn (301 West Ave. A, 79360; 758-3653) 37 rooms and efficiencies, no pets, in-room refrigerators, children free with parents, A/C, TV, CC. SGL/DBL$30-$45.

Seminole Inn (2000 Hobbs Hwy., 79360; 758-9881) 40 rooms, pool, A/C, TV, NS rooms, wheelchair access, in-room refrigerators and microwaves, children free with parents, pets OK, CC. SGL/DBL$35-$40.

Shamrock

Area Code 806

Best Western Inn (301 I-40 East, 79079; 256-2106, 800-528-1234) 157 rooms, restaurant, lounge, indoor heated pool, exercise center, children free with parents, A/C, NS rooms, TV, VCRs, laundry facilities, wheelchair access, in-room refrigerators, pets OK, meeting facilities, senior rates, CC. SGL/DBL$40-$50.

Econo Lodge (1006 East 12th St., 79079; 256-2111, 800-4-CHOICE) 78 rooms and 2-room suites, free breakfast, pool, children under 12 free with parents, no pets, NS rooms, wheelchair access, A/C, TV, senior rates, CC. SGL/DBL$30-$46.

Western Motel (104 East 12th St., 79079; 256-3244) 24 rooms, restaurant, A/C, TV, NS rooms, children free with parents, wheelchair access, pets OK, senior rates, CC. SGL/DBL$23-$33.

Sherman
Area Code 903

Ramada Inn (2105 Texoma Pkwy., 75090; 892-2161, 800-2-RAMADA) 144 rooms and suites, restaurant, lounge, entertainment, outdoor pool, hot tub, free local calls, wheelchair access, NS rooms, pets OK, A/C, TV, children under 18 free with parents, room service, laundry facilities, meeting facilities, senior rates, CC. SGL/DBL$45-$66.

Sheraton Inn Sherman (3605 Hwy. 75 South, 75090; 868-0555, Fax 892-9396, 800-325-3535) 142 rooms and suites, restaurant, lounge, entertainment, outdoor pool, exercise center, hot tub, whirlpools, in-room refrigerators, laundry facilities, NS rooms, A/C, TV, pets OK, children free with parents, wheelchair access, 4,000 square feet of meeting and exhibition space, 8 meeting rooms, meeting facilities for 300, senior rates, CC. SGL/DBL$60-$225.

Super 8 Motel (111 East Hwy. 1417, 75090; 868-9325, 800-800-8000) 47 rooms and suites, pets OK, children under 12 free with parents, free local calls, A/C, TV, in-room refrigerators and microwaves, fax, NS rooms, senior rates, wheelchair access, meeting facilities, CC. SGL/DBL$30-$50.

Snyder
Area Code 915

Great Western Motel (800 East Coliseum Dr., 79550; 573-1166) 56 rooms and suites, restaurant, lounge, pool, A/C, TV, NS rooms, wheelchair access, pets OK, senior rates, CC. SGL/DBL$27-$36.

Purple Sage Motel (Snyder 79550; 573-5491, Fax 573-9027) 45 rooms and suites, free breakfast, indoor heated pool, whirlpools, gift shop, A/C, TV, NS rooms, wheelchair access, microwaves and coffee makers, pets OK, in-room refrigerators, children free with parents, senior rates, CC. SGL/DBL$28-$60.

Willow Park Inn (Snyder 79550; 573-1961) 43 rooms, restaurant, indoor heated pool, whirlpools, pets OK, children free with parents, A/C, TV, NS rooms, wheelchair access, CC. SGL/DBL$48-$58.

Sonora
Area Code 915

Devil's River Motel (Sonora 76950; 387-3516) 99 rooms, restaurant, pool, A/C, TV, NS rooms, wheelchair access, laundry facilities, pets OK, children free with parents, meeting facilities, senior rates, CC. SGL/DBL$30-$50.

Holiday Host Motel (Hwy. 290 East, 76950; 387-2532) 20 rooms, A/C, TV, NS rooms, wheelchair access, CC. SGL/DBL$26-$33.

Twin Oaks Motel (907 Crockett Ave., 76950; 387-2551) 53 rooms, children free with parents, A/C, TV, NS rooms, wheelchair access, pets OK, CC. SGL/DBL$25-$40.

South Padre Island
Area Code 210

Best Western Inn (Padre Blvd., 78597; 761-4913, Fax 761-2719, 800-528-1234) 58 rooms, restaurant, free breakfast, lounge, pool, exercise center, whirlpools, children free with parents, A/C, NS rooms, TV, laundry facilities, wheelchair access, pets OK, meeting facilities, senior rates, CC. SGL/DBL$85-$95.

Days Inn (3913 Padre Blvd., 78597; 761-7831, Fax 761-2033, 800-325-2525) 57 rooms and suites, free breakfast, outdoor pool, hot tubs, kitchenettes, children free with parents, room service, laundry service, A/C, TV, free local calls, pets OK, fax, wheelchair access, NS rooms, meeting facilities, senior rates, CC. SGL/DBL$47-$120.

Holiday Inn (100 Padre Blvd., 78597; 761-5401, 800-HOLIDAY) 227 rooms, restaurant, lounge, pool, whirlpools, hot tubs, children under 19 free with parents, wheelchair access, A/C, TV, NS rooms, fax, room service, no pets, laundry service, 4,000 square feet of meeting and exhibition space, senior rates, CC. SGL/DBL$85-$150.

Radisson Resort (500 Padre Blvd., 78597; 761-6511, Fax 761-1602, 800-333-3333) 182 rooms and suites, restaurant, lounge, entertainment, heated pool, exercise center, whirlpools, lighted tennis courts, in-room refrigerators, microwaves and coffee makers, children free with parents, VCRs, wheelchair access, NS rooms, gift shop, TV, A/C, children free with parents, pets OK, meeting facilities, senior rates, CC. SGL/DBL$90-$240, STS$250-$335.

Sheraton Spa Beach Resort (310 Padre Blvd., 78597; 761-6551, Fax 761-6570, 800-325-3535) 250 rooms and suites, restaurant, lounge, entertainment, indoor and outdoor heated pool, exercise center, whirlpools, tennis courts, NS rooms, A/C, TV, laundry facilities, no pets, airport transportation, children free with parents, gift shop, boutiques, wheelchair access, 6 meeting rooms, meeting facilities for 400, CC. SGL/DBL$90-$250.

Tiki Apartment Hotel (6608 Padre Blvd., 78597; 761-2694, Fax 761-4748) 131 rooms and 2- and 3-bedroom suites, restaurant, lounge, pool, sauna, whirlpools, kitchenettes, children free with parents, pets OK, A/C, TV, NS rooms, wheelchair access, CC. SGL/DBL$65-$119.

Spring
Area Code 713

Days Inn (19606 Cypresswood Court, 77388; 350-6400, Fax 353-6927, 800-325-2525) 108 rooms and suites, restaurant, outdoor pool, children free with parents, room service, laundry service, A/C, TV, free local calls, pets OK, fax, wheelchair access, NS rooms, meeting facilities, senior rates, CC. SGL/DBL$34-$49, STS$49-$60.

TraveLodge (20543 I-45 North, 77388; 353-3547, 800-578-7878) 89 rooms, pool, wheelchair access, complimentary newspaper, laundry service, TV, A/C, free local calls, fax, NS rooms, in-room refrigerators and microwaves, children under 18 free with parents, no pets, VCRs, in-room computer hookups, laundry facilities, meeting facilities, senior rates, CC. SGL/DBL$45-$55.

Stafford
Area Code 713

La Quinta Inn (12727 Southwest Freeway, 77477; 240-2300, Fax 240-6677, 800-531-5900) 129 rooms, pool, complimentary newspaper, free local calls, fax, laundry service, NS rooms, wheelchair access, TV, A/C, in-room refrigerators, pets OK, children free with parents, in-room computer hookups, meeting facilities, CC. SGL/DBL$56-$66.

Stephenville
Area Code 817

Best Western Inn (1625 South Loop 377, 76401; 968-2114, Fax 968-2114 ext 103, 800-528-1234) 50 rooms, restaurant, free breakfast, lounge, pool, exercise center, children free with parents, A/C, NS rooms, TV, laundry facilities, wheelchair access, pets OK, meeting facilities, senior rates, CC. SGL/DBL$40-$70.

Budget Host Texan Motor Inn (Hwy. 377 South, 76401; 968-5003, Fax 968-5060, 800-283-4678) 30 rooms, restaurant, laundry facilities, NS rooms, wheelchair access, A/C, TV, senior rates, pets OK, children free with parents, senior rates, CC. SGL/DBL$31-$40.

Holiday Inn (2865 West Washington, 76401; 968-5256, Fax 968-4255, 800-HOLIDAY) 100 rooms, restaurant, lounge, pool, exercise center, children under 19 free with parents, wheelchair access, A/C, TV, NS rooms, fax, room service, no pets, laundry service, meeting facilities for 250, senior rates, CC. SGL/DBL$40-$150.

Raintree Inn (701 South Loop, 76401; 969-3392, 800-241-3378) 65 rooms, restaurant, pool, children free with parents, pets OK, A/C, TV, NS rooms, wheelchair access, meeting facilities, senior rates, CC. SGL/DBL$33-$45.

Study Butte
Area Code 915

Big Bend Motor Inn (Study Butte 79852; 371-2218) 82 rooms and efficiencies, pool, A/C, TV, NS rooms, in-room refrigerators and microwaves, kitchenettes, no pets, children free with parents, A/C, TV, wheelchair access, CC. SGL/DBL$30-$44.

Longhorn Ranch Motel (Study Butte 79852; 371-2541)24 rooms, restaurant, laundry facilities, no pets, children free with parents, A/C, TV, NS rooms, wheelchair access, CC. SGL/DBL$29-$36.

Sulphur Springs
Area Code 903

Best Western Inn (Sulphur Springs 75483; 885-7515, Fax 885-7515, 800-528-1234) 88 rooms, heated pool, exercise center, children free with parents, A/C, NS rooms, TV, laundry facilities, wheelchair access, pets OK, in-room refrigerators and microwaves, meeting facilities, senior rates, CC. SGL/DBL$38-$44.

Holiday Inn (1495 East Industrial, 75482; 885-0562, Fax 885-3982, 800-HOLIDAY) 100 rooms and suites, restaurant, lounge, pool, exercise center, children under 19 free with parents, wheelchair access, A/C, TV, in-room refrigerators, NS rooms, fax, room service, pets OK, laundry service, meeting facilities for 150, senior rates, CC. SGL/DBL$47-$55.

Sweetwater
Area Code 915

Best Western Sunday House Inn (701 Southwest Georgia St., 79556; 235-4853, Fax 235-8935, 800-528-1234) 131 rooms, restaurant, free breakfast, lounge, pool, exercise center, children free with parents, A/C, NS rooms, TV, laundry facilities, wheelchair access, pets OK, meeting facilities, senior rates, CC. SGL/DBL$36-$46.

Holiday Inn (500 Georgia St., 79556; 236-6887, Fax 236-6887 ext 204, 800-HOLIDAY) 107 rooms, restaurant, lounge, pool, exercise center, children under 19 free with parents, wheelchair access, A/C, TV, NS rooms, fax, room service, pets OK, laundry service, airport transportation, meeting facilities for 150, senior rates, CC. SGL/DBL$45-$58.

Temple
Area Code 817

Days Inn (Temple 76501; 774-9223, 800-325-2525) 60 rooms and suites, outdoor pool, children free with parents, room service, laundry service,

A/C, TV, free local calls, pets OK, fax, wheelchair access, NS rooms, meeting facilities, senior rates, CC. SGL/DBL$29-$55, STS$60-$95.

Econo Lodge (1001 North General Bruce Dr., 76504; 771-1688, 800-4-CHOICE) 60 rooms, free breakfast, pool, children under 12 free with parents, no pets, free local calls, NS rooms, wheelchair access, A/C, TV, senior rates, CC. SGL/DBL$30-$36.

HoJo Inn (1912 South 32nd St., 76504; 778-5521, 800-I-GO-HOJO) 50 rooms, free breakfast, pool, children free with parents, wheelchair access, NS rooms, TV, A/C, no pets, free local calls, laundry facilities, senior rates, meeting facilities, CC. SGL/DBL$45-$65.

Holiday Inn (802 North General Bruce Dr., 76504; 778-4411, Fax 778-8086, 800-HOLIDAY) 132 rooms and suites, restaurant, lounge, pool, exercise center, children under 19 free with parents, wheelchair access, A/C, TV, NS rooms, fax, room service, pets OK, laundry service, meeting facilities for 200, senior rates, CC. SGL/DBL$45-$60.

The Inn at Scott and White (2625 South 31st St., 76504; 778-5511, Fax 773-3161, 800-749-0318) 129 rooms and suites, restaurant, pool, A/C, TV, NS rooms, barber and beauty shop, gift shop, airport courtesy car, no pets, room service, in-room refrigerators, wheelchair access, CC. SGL/DBL$50-$125.

La Quinta Inn (1604 Barton Ave., 76501; 771-2980, Fax 778-7565, 800-531-5900) 106 rooms, restaurant, free breakfast, lounge, pool, complimentary newspaper, free local calls, fax, laundry service, pets OK, NS rooms, wheelchair access, TV, A/C, meeting facilities, senior rates, CC. SGL/DBL$46-$55.

Ramada Inn (400 Southwest Avenue, 76504; 773-1515, 800-2-RAMADA) 108 rooms and suites, restaurant, lounge, pool, wheelchair access, NS rooms, pets OK, A/C, TV, children under 18 free with parents, room service, airport transportation, laundry facilities, 6 meeting rooms, meeting facilities for 200, senior rates, CC. SGL/DBL$50-$63.

Terrell
Area Code 214

Best Western Inn (Terrell 75160; 563-2676, 800-528-1234) 60 rooms, pool, exercise center, children free with parents, A/C, NS rooms, TV, laundry facilities, wheelchair access, pets OK, meeting facilities, senior rates, CC. SGL/DBL$32-$50.

Comfort Inn (1705 Hwy. 34 South, 75160; 563-1511, 800-221-2222) 49 rooms, free breakfast, pool, exercise facilities, wheelchair access, NS rooms, no pets, children under 18 free with parents, A/C, TV, meeting facilities, senior rates, CC. SGL/DBL$40-$75.

Texarkana
Area Code 903

Best Western Inn (4200 State Line Ave., 75502; 774-3851, Fax 772-8440, 800-528-1234) 116 rooms, restaurant, pool, exercise center, children free with parents, A/C, NS rooms, TV, laundry facilities, wheelchair access, pets OK, in-room refrigerators, meeting facilities, senior rates, CC. SGL/DBL$40-$45.

Budgetel Inn (5102 North State Line Ave., 75502; 773-1000, Fax 773-5000, 800-428-3438) 106 rooms and suites, free breakfast, children under 18 free with parents, A/C, wheelchair access, NS rooms, free local calls, in-room computer hookups, fax, in-room refrigerators and microwaves, pets OK, VCRs, TV, meeting facilities, CC. SGL/DBL$35-$44.

Comfort Inn (5105 Stateline Ave., 75501; 792-6688, 800-221-2222) 79 rooms and suites, free breakfast, pool, whirlpools, wheelchair access, NS rooms, no pets, children under 18 free with parents, A/C, TV, meeting facilities, senior rates, CC. SGL/DBL$42-$75.

Days Inn (4415 State Line Ave., 75503; 794-2502, 800-325-2525) 52 rooms and suites, restaurant, free breakfast, children free with parents, room service, laundry service, A/C, TV, free local calls, pets OK, fax, wheelchair access, NS rooms, airport transportation, meeting facilities, senior rates, CC. SGL/DBL$33-$70.

Econo Lodge (4505 North Stateline Ave., 75501; 793-5546, 800-4-CHOICE) 54 rooms, free breakfast, children under 12 free with parents, no pets, NS rooms, wheelchair access, A/C, TV, senior rates, CC. SGL/DBL$35-$38.

Holiday Inn (5401 North State Line Ave., 75503; 792-3366, Fax 792-5649, 800-HOLIDAY) 112 rooms, restaurant, lounge, outdoor pool, hot tub, exercise center, children under 19 free with parents, in-room refrigerators, wheelchair access, A/C, TV, NS rooms, fax, room service, airport transportation, pets OK, laundry service, meeting facilities, senior rates, CC. SGL/DBL$45-$95.

Holiday Inn (5100 North State Line Ave., 75503; 774-3521, Fax 772-3068, 800-HOLIDAY) 210 rooms, restaurant, lounge, indoor heated pool, exercise center, sauna, whirlpools, children under 19 free with parents, wheelchair access, in-room refrigerators and coffee makers, airport transportation, A/C, TV, NS rooms, fax, room service, pets OK, laundry service, meeting facilities, senior rates, CC. SGL/DBL$65-$84.

La Quinta Inn (5201 State Line Ave., 75503; 794-1900, Fax 792-5506, 800-531-5900) 130 rooms, restaurant, free breakfast, lounge, pool, complimentary newspaper, free local calls, fax, laundry service, NS rooms, wheelchair access, TV, A/C, airport transportation, meeting facilities, CC. SGL/DBL$41-$55.

Motel 6 West (1924 Hampton Rd., 75501; 793-1413, 505-891-6161) 100 rooms, pool, free local calls, children under 17 free with parents, NS rooms, wheelchair access, pets OK, A/C, TV, CC. SGL/DBL$38-$44.

Motel 6 East (900 Realtor Ave., 75502; 772-0678, 505-891-6161) 121 rooms, pool, free local calls, children under 17 free with parents, NS rooms, wheelchair access, pets OK, A/C, TV, CC. SGL/DBL$40-$44.

Ramada Inn (I-30 and Summerhill Rd., 75501; 794-3131, Fax 793-0606, 800-2-RAMADA) 126 rooms and suites, restaurant, lounge, entertainment, pool, wheelchair access, NS rooms, pets OK, A/C, beauty shop, airport transportation, TV, children under 18 free with parents, room service, laundry facilities, meeting facilities, senior rates, CC. SGL/DBL$40-$46, STS$85.

Sheraton Inn Texarkana (5301 North Stateline Ave., 75503; 792-3222, Fax 792-3222 ext 263, 800-325-3535) 150 rooms and suites, restaurant, lounge, entertainment, indoor heated pool, exercise center, hot tubs, airport courtesy car, NS rooms, A/C, TV, children free with parents, in-room refrigerators, pets OK, wheelchair access, 5,000 square feet of meeting and exhibition space, 8 meeting rooms, meeting facilities for 500, CC. SGL/DBL$50-$68.

Shoney's Inn (5210 State Line Ave., 75504; 772-0070, 800-222-2222) 72 rooms, pool, whirlpools, A/C, TV, NS rooms, children free with parents, complimentary newspaper, NS rooms, wheelchair access, fax, in-room refrigerators, pets OK, senior rates, CC. SGL/DBL$38-$65.

Texas City
Area Code 409

La Quinta Inn (1121 Hwy. 146 North, 77590; 948-3101, Fax 945-4412, 800-531-5900) 121 rooms, restaurant, free breakfast, lounge, pool, complimentary newspaper, free local calls, fax, laundry service, NS rooms, wheelchair access, TV, in-room refrigerators, VCRs, pets OK, A/C, meeting facilities, CC. SGL/DBL$55-$70.

Three Rivers
Area Code 512

Choke Canyon Bass Inn (Three Rivers 78071; 786-3521) 30 rooms, pool, A/C, TV, NS rooms, wheelchair access, pets OK, in-room refrigerators, CC. SGL/DBL$33-$40.

Staghorn Inn (Three Rivers 78071; 786-3541) 32 rooms, A/C, TV, NS rooms, wheelchair access, no pets, CC. SGL/DBL$29-$39.

Tomball

Area Code 713

Best Western Inn (30130 Hwy. 249, 77375; 351-9700, 800-528-1234) 50 rooms, pool, exercise center, children free with parents, A/C, NS rooms, TV, laundry facilities, wheelchair access, pets OK, in-room refrigerators, microwaves and coffee makers, meeting facilities, senior rates, CC. SGL/DBL$42-$54.

Tyler

Area Code 903

Days Inn (12732 Hwy. 155 North, 75708; 877-9227, 800-325-2525) 50 rooms and suites, free breakfast, children free with parents, room service, laundry service, A/C, TV, free local calls, pets OK, fax, wheelchair access, NS rooms, meeting facilities, senior rates, CC. SGL/DBL$35-$45.

Econo Lodge (3209 West Gentry Pkwy., 75702; 593-0103, 800-4-CHOICE) 51 rooms, restaurant, pool, children under 12 free with parents, no pets, NS rooms, VCRs, wheelchair access, A/C, TV, senior rates, CC. SGL/DBL$30-$50.

Holiday Inn (3310 Troup Hwy., 75701; 593-3600, Fax 593-3600 ext 350, 800-HOLIDAY) 160 rooms, restaurant, lounge, pool, exercise center, children under 19 free with parents, wheelchair access, A/C, TV, NS rooms, fax, room service, no pets, laundry service, meeting facilities for 300, senior rates, CC. SGL/DBL$55-$130.

La Quinta Inn (1601 West Southwest Loop 323, 75701; 561-2223, Fax 581-5708, 800-531-5900) 130 rooms, restaurant, free breakfast, lounge, pool, free newspaper, free local calls, fax, laundry service, NS rooms, wheelchair access, TV, A/C, meeting facilities, CC. SGL/DBL$51-$65.

Motel 6 (3236 Brady Gentry Pkwy., 75702; 595-6691, 505-891-6161) 80 rooms, pool, free local calls, children under 17 free with parents, NS rooms, wheelchair access, pets OK, A/C, TV, CC. SGL/DBL$40-$44.

Park Inn International (2701 West Northwest Loop 323, 75702; 593-7391, Fax 593-2265, 800-437-PARK) 125 rooms and suites, restaurant, lounge, A/C, TV, wheelchair access, airport transportation, complimentary newspaper, NS rooms, meeting facilities for 175, senior rates, CC. SGL/DBL$40-$73.

Quality Hotel and Conference Center (2843 Northwest Loop 323, 75702; 597-1301, 800-221-2222) 136 rooms and suites, restaurant, pool, exercise center, children free with parents, A/C, pets OK, airport transportation, TV, room service, laundry service, NS rooms, meeting facilities, senior rates, CC. SGL/DBL$47-$57.

Ramada Inn (2701 Hwy. 69, 75702; 593-7391, Fax 593-2265, 800-2-RAMADA) 125 rooms and suites, restaurant, lounge, entertainment, pool, wheelchair access, NS rooms, pets OK, free local calls, airport transportation, A/C, TV, children under 18 free with parents, room service, laundry facilities, meeting facilities, senior rates, CC. SGL/DBL$55-$73.

Residence Inn (3303 Troup Hwy., 75701; 595-5188, Fax 595-5719, 800-331-3131) 128 rooms and suites, free breakfast, in-room refrigerators, coffee makers and microwaves, laundry facilities, TV, A/C, VCRs, pets OK, complimentary newspaper, fireplaces, airport transportation, children free with parents, NS rooms, wheelchair access, meeting facilities, senior rates, CC. SGL/DBL$85-$105.

Sheraton Tyler Hotel (5701 South Broadway, 75703; 561-5800, Fax 561-9916, 800-325-3535) 186 rooms and suites, restaurant, lounge, entertainment, outdoor pool, exercise center, jacuzzi, airport courtesy car, pets OK, laundry facilities, in-room refrigerators, NS rooms, A/C, TV, children free with parents, wheelchair access, 9,000 square feet of meeting and exhibition space, meeting facilities for 900, senior rates, CC. SGL/DBL$75-$250.

Stratford House Inn (2600 West Northwest Loop 323, 75702; 597-2756) 40 rooms, restaurant, free breakfast, whirlpools, A/C, TV, NS rooms, wheelchair access, pets OK, senior rates, CC. SGL/DBL$35-$40.

TraveLodge (2616 North Loop 323, 75702; 593-8361, Fax 593-8756, 800-578-7878) 115 rooms, pool, wheelchair access, complimentary newspaper, laundry service, TV, A/C, free local calls, in-room refrigerators and microwaves, pets OK, fax, NS rooms, in-room refrigerators and microwaves, children under 18 free with parents, no pets, meeting facilities, senior rates, CC. SGL/DBL$38-$68.

Universal City
Area Code 210

Comfort Inn Northeast (200 Palisades, 78148; 659-5851, 800-221-2222) 120 rooms, free breakfast, pool, wheelchair access, NS rooms, no pets, children under 18 free with parents, A/C, TV, meeting facilities, senior rates, CC. SGL/DBL$40-$135.

Uvalde
Area Code 210

Best Western Inn (701 East Main St., 78801; 278-5671, 800-528-1234) 87 rooms, pool, exercise center, children free with parents, A/C, NS rooms, TV, laundry facilities, wheelchair access, pets OK, kitchenettes, meeting facilities, senior rates, CC. SGL/DBL$30-$40.

Holiday Inn (920 East Main St., 78801; 278-4511, 800-HOLIDAY) 151 rooms and suites, restaurant, lounge, pool, exercise center, children under

19 free with parents, wheelchair access, A/C, TV, NS rooms, fax, room service, no pets, laundry service, meeting facilities for 200, senior rates, CC. SGL/DBL$42-$85.

Van Horn
Area Code 915

Best Western Inn (Van Horn 79855; 283-2410, 800-528-1234) 60 rooms, restaurant, free breakfast, lounge, pool, exercise center, children free with parents, A/C, NS rooms, TV, laundry facilities, wheelchair access, pets OK, meeting facilities, senior rates, CC. SGL/DBL$35-$60.

Best Western Inn (Van Horn 79855; 283-2030, 800-528-1234) 33 rooms and 2-bedroom suites, children free with parents, A/C, NS rooms, TV, laundry facilities, wheelchair access, pets OK, meeting facilities, senior rates, CC. SGL/DBL$28-$48.

Comfort Inn (1601 West Broadway St., 79855; 283-2211, 800-221-2222) 40 rooms, free breakfast, pool, wheelchair access, NS rooms, no pets, children under 18 free with parents, A/C, TV, meeting facilities, senior rates, CC. SGL/DBL$38-$55.

Days Inn (600 East Broadway, 79855; 283-2401, Fax 283-2382, 800-325-2525) 59 rooms and suites, restaurant, free breakfast, children free with parents, room service, laundry service, A/C, TV, free local calls, pets OK, fax, wheelchair access, NS rooms, meeting facilities, senior rates, CC. SGL/DBL$33-$55.

Economy Inn (Hwy. 80 West, 79885; 283-2754, 800-826-0778) 16 rooms, free local calls, wheelchair access, A/C, children free with parents, TV, NS rooms, no pets, senior rates, CC. SGL/DBL$22-$32.

Friendship Inn (I-10 and Hwy. 80, 79855; 283-2992, 800-424-4777) 40 rooms, pool, exercise center, A/C, TV, pets OK, NS rooms, children free with parents, wheelchair access, senior rates, CC. SGL/DBL$30-$46.

Howard Johnson Lodge (200 Golf Course Dr., 79855; 283-2780, 800-543-8831, 800-I-GO-HOJO) 83 rooms, restaurant, lounge, pool, children free with parents, wheelchair access, NS rooms, TV, A/C, room service, airport transportation, no pets, laundry facilities, senior rates, meeting facilities, CC. SGL/DBL$33-$40.

Plaza Inn (Van Horn 79855; 283-2780, 800-543-8831) 98 rooms, restaurant, lounge, entertainment, pool, A/C, TV, NS rooms, wheelchair access, pets OK, laundry facilities, meeting facilities, senior rates, CC. SGL/DBL$35-$44.

Super 8 Motel (1807 East Service Rd., 79855; 283-2282, 800-800-8000) 41 rooms and suites, no pets, children under 12 free with parents, free local calls, A/C, TV, in-room refrigerators and microwaves, fax, laundry facilities, pets OK, NS rooms, senior rates, wheelchair access, meeting facilities, CC. SGL/DBL$36-$44.

Vega
Area Code 806

Best Western Inn (1800 Vegas Blvd., 79092; 267-2131, 800-528-1234) 41 rooms, restaurant, outdoor heated pool, exercise center, children free with parents, A/C, NS rooms, TV, laundry facilities, wheelchair access, pets OK, meeting facilities, senior rates, CC. SGL/DBL$38-$50.

Vernon
Area Code 817

Best Western Inn (1615 Expressway, 76384; 552-5417, 800-528-1234) 47 rooms, restaurant, pool, exercise center, children free with parents, A/C, NS rooms, TV, laundry facilities, wheelchair access, pets OK, airport transportation, meeting facilities, senior rates, CC. SGL/DBL$36-$46.

Green Tree Inn (3029 Morton, 76384; 552-5421) 30 rooms, free breakfast, pool, children free with parents, pets OK, A/C, TV, NS rooms, wheelchair access, senior rates, CC. SGL/DBL$30-$38.

Sunday House Inn (3110 Frontage Rd., 76384; 552-9982) 62 rooms, restaurant, pool, pets OK, A/C, TV, NS rooms, wheelchair access, CC. SGL/DBL$32-$40.

Western Motel (715 Wilbarger St., 76384; 552-2531) 28 rooms, pool, A/C, TV, NS rooms, wheelchair access, in-room coffee makers, pets OK, children free with parents, senior rates, CC. SGL/DBL$20-$30.

Victoria
Area Code 512

Best Western Inn (2605 Houston Hwy., 77901; 578-9911, 800-528-1234) 104 rooms, pool, exercise center, children free with parents, A/C, NS rooms, TV, laundry facilities, wheelchair access, no pets, meeting facilities, senior rates, CC. SGL/DBL$35-$54.

Hampton Inn (3112 Houston Hwy., 77901; 578-2030, Fax 573-1238, 800-HAMPTON) 1-3 rooms, restaurant, free breakfast, pool, exercise center, children under 18 free with parents, NS rooms, wheelchair access, in-room computer hookups, airport transportation, fax, TV, A/C, free local calls, pets OK, meeting facilities, CC. SGL/DBL$44-$65.

Holiday Inn (2705 East Houston, 77901; 575-0251, Fax 575-8362, 800-HOLIDAY) 226 rooms and suites, restaurant, lounge, indoor and outdoor heated pool, exercise center, sauna, whirlpools, VCRs, game room, children under 19 free with parents, wheelchair access, A/C, TV, NS rooms, fax, airport transportation, room service, no pets, laundry service, meeting facilities for 500, senior rates, CC. SGL/DBL$45-$56.

La Quinta Inn (7603 North Navarro St., 77904; 572-3585, Fax 576-4617, 800-531-5900) 130 rooms, restaurant, free breakfast, lounge, pool, complimentary newspaper, free local calls, fax, in-room refrigerators, pets OK, laundry service, NS rooms, wheelchair access, TV, A/C, meeting facilities, CC. SGL/DBL$45-$65.

Motel 6 (3716 Houston Hwy., 77901; 573-1273, 505-891-6161) 80 rooms, pool, free local calls, children under 17 free with parents, NS rooms, wheelchair access, pets OK, A/C, TV, CC. SGL/DBL$38-$48.

Ramada Inn (3901 East Houston Hwy., 77901; 578-2723, 800-2-RAMADA) 126 rooms and suites, restaurant, lounge, pool, wheelchair access, NS rooms, pets OK, A/C, TV, children under 18 free with parents, airport transportation, room service, laundry facilities, meeting facilities, senior rates, CC. SGL/DBL$44-$56, STS$68.

Waco
Area Code 817

Best Western Inn (Waco 76703; 753-0316, Fax 753-3811, 800-528-1234) 84 rooms, restaurant, pool, exercise center, children free with parents, A/C, NS rooms, TV, laundry facilities, wheelchair access, no pets, in-room refrigerators, meeting facilities, senior rates, CC. SGL/DBL$50-$55.

Best Western Inn (Waco 76712; 776-3194, 800-528-1234) 55 rooms, pool, exercise center, children free with parents, A/C, NS rooms, TV, laundry facilities, in-room refrigerators, microwaves and coffee makers, wheelchair access, pets OK, meeting facilities, senior rates, CC. SGL/DBL$42-$50.

Days Inn (1504 West I-35, 76705; 799-8585, Fax 799-3031, 800-325-2525) 60 rooms and suites, free breakfast, outdoor pool, children free with parents, room service, laundry service, A/C, TV, free local calls, pets OK, fax, wheelchair access, NS rooms, meeting facilities, senior rates, CC. SGL/DBL$40-$55.

Hilton Hotel (113 South University Parks Dr., 76701; 754-8484, Fax 752-2214, 800-HILTONS) 199 rooms and suites, restaurant, lounge, entertainment, pool, exercise center, tennis courts, children free with parents, NS rooms, airport transportation, in-room refrigerators, wheelchair access, no pets, room service, laundry facilities, A/C, TV, business services, meeting facilities, CC. SGL/DBL$65-$75.

Holiday Inn (1001 Lake Brazos Dr., 76704; 753-0261, Fax 753-0227, 800-HOLIDAY) 172 rooms, restaurant, lounge, pool, exercise center, children under 19 free with parents, wheelchair access, A/C, TV, NS rooms, fax, room service, no pets, in-room coffee makers, laundry service, meeting facilities, senior rates, CC. SGL/DBL$60-$65.

Howard Johnson Lodge (101 North I-35, 76704; 752-8222, Fax 752-3723, 800-I-GO-HOJO) 160 rooms, free breakfast, pool, children free with parents, wheelchair access, NS rooms, TV, A/C, no pets, airport transportation, laundry facilities, senior rates, meeting facilities for 250, CC. SGL/DBL$39-$50.

La Quinta University Inn (1110 South 9th St., 76706; 752-9741, Fax 757-1600, 800-531-5900) 102 rooms, restaurant, free breakfast, lounge, pool, complimentary newspaper, free local calls, fax, laundry service, NS rooms, wheelchair access, TV, in-room refrigerators and microwaves, pets OK, A/C, meeting facilities, CC. SGL/DBL$50-$57.

Lexington Hotels Suites and Inns (115 Jack Kultgen, 76706; 754-1266, Fax 755-8612, 800-927-8483) 113 suites, free breakfast, pool, A/C, TV, fax, laundry facilities, no pets, children free with parents, airport transportation, in-room refrigerators, microwaves and coffee makers, NS rooms, wheelchair access, senior rates, CC. SGL/DBL$89-$129.

Motel 6 (3120 Jack Kultgen Freeway, 76706; 662-4611, 505-891-6161) 110 rooms, pool, free local calls, children under 17 free with parents, NS rooms, wheelchair access, pets OK, A/C, TV, CC. SGL/DBL$39-$46.

Quality Inn (801 South 4th St., 76706; 757-2000, Fax 757-1110, 800-ASK-WACO, 800-221-2222) 150 rooms and suites, restaurant, free breakfast, lounge, pool, exercise center, whirlpools, children free with parents, A/C, TV, room service, in-room refrigerators, microwaves and coffee makers, laundry service, NS rooms, meeting facilities, senior rates, CC. SGL/DBL$55-$69.

Ramada Inn (4201 Franklin Ave., 76710; 772-9440, 800-2-RAMADA) 123 rooms and suites, restaurant, lounge, pool, wheelchair access, NS rooms, pets OK, A/C, TV, children under 18 free with parents, room service, laundry facilities, in-room refrigerators, microwaves and coffee makers, meeting facilities, senior rates, CC. SGL/DBL$48-$54.

Super 8 Motel (I-35 and South 13th St., 76710; 800-800-8000) 78 rooms and suites, no pets, children under 12 free with parents, free local calls, A/C, TV, in-room refrigerators and microwaves, fax, NS rooms, senior rates, wheelchair access, meeting facilities, CC. SGL/DBL$37-$51.

Waxahachie

Area Code 214

Buffalo Creek Inn (795 South I-35 East, 75165; 937-4982) 94 rooms, pool, whirlpools, pets OK, children free with parents, laundry facilities, A/C, TV, NS rooms, wheelchair access, CC. SGL/DBL$34-$40.

Comfort Inn (200 I-35 East, 75165, 800-221-2222) 60 rooms, restaurant, free breakfast, pool, wheelchair access, NS rooms, no pets, children under 18 free with parents, A/C, TV, meeting facilities, senior rates, CC. SGL/DBL$42-$54.

Weatherford
Area Code 817

Best Western Inn (1927 Santa Fe Dr., 76086; 599-8683, 800-528-1234) 42 rooms, pool, exercise center, children free with parents, A/C, NS rooms, TV, laundry facilities, in-room refrigerators, microwaves and coffee makers, wheelchair access, no pets, meeting facilities, senior rates, CC. SGL/DBL$40-$55.

Comfort Inn (809 Palo Pinto St., 76086; 599-8683, 800-221-2222) 42 rooms, free breakfast, pool, wheelchair access, NS rooms, no pets, children under 18 free with parents, A/C, TV, meeting facilities, senior rates, CC. SGL/DBL$38-$57.

Holiday Inn (I-20 and Hwy. 51, 76087; 599-3700, 800-HOLIDAY) 45 rooms and suites, restaurant, lounge, pool, exercise center, jacuzzis, whirlpools, children under 19 free with parents, wheelchair access, A/C, TV, NS rooms, fax, room service, pets OK, laundry service, meeting facilities, senior rates, CC. SGL/DBL$56-$74.

Webster
Area Code 713

Best Western Inn (889 West Bay Area Blvd., 77598; 338-6000, 800-528-1234) 80 rooms, pool, exercise center, children free with parents, A/C, NS rooms, TV, laundry facilities, wheelchair access, in-room refrigerators, microwaves and coffee makers, pets OK, meeting facilities, senior rates, CC. SGL/DBL$45-$65.

Quality Inn (904 East NASA Rd., 77598; 800-221-2222) 112 rooms and suites, restaurant, free breakfast, pool, exercise center, children free with parents, A/C, TV, room service, laundry service, NS rooms, meeting facilities, senior rates, CC. SGL/DBL$49-$60.

Ramada Inn (1301 NASA Rd., 77598, 488-0220, Fax 488-1759, 800-2-RAMADA) 196 rooms and suites, restaurant, free breakfast, lounge, heated pool, wheelchair access, NS rooms, pets OK, A/C, TV, children under 18 free with parents, room service, airport transportation, in-room computer hookups, laundry service, in-room refrigerators, microwaves and coffee makers, laundry facilities, meeting facilities, senior rates, CC. SGL/DBL$78-$88.

Weslaco
Area Code 210

Vali-Ho Motel (2100 Hwy. 83, 78596; 968-2173) 37 rooms and efficiencies, heated pool, A/C, TV, in-room refrigerators, no pets, NS rooms, wheelchair access, CC. SGL/DBL$35-$44.

West Columbia
Area Code 409

Homeplace Inn (714 Columbia Dr., 77486; 345-2399) 40 rooms, pool, pets OK, VCRs, A/C, TV, children free with parents, fireplace, laundry facilities, NS rooms, wheelchair access, senior rates, CC. SGL/DBL$44-$55.

Westlake
Area Code 817

Marriott Solana (5 Village Circle, 76262; 430-3848, Fax 4304870, 800-228-9290) 200 rooms and 2-bedroom suites, restaurant, lounge, outdoor pool, exercise center, jogging track, whirlpool, wheelchair access, NS rooms, A/C, in-room refrigerators, TV, gift shop, CC. SGL/DBL$60-$115.

Wharton
Area Code 409

Homeplace Inn (Wharton 77488; 532-1152) 40 rooms, A/C, TV, NS rooms, laundry facilities, pets OK, children free with parents, wheelchair access, meeting facilities, senior rates, CC. SGL/DBL$40-$50.

Whitesboro
Area Code 903

Swiss Villa Motel (Whitesboro 76273; 564-5662) 34 rooms, pool, A/C, TV, NS rooms, wheelchair access, pets OK, CC. SGL/DBL$25-$33.

Wichita Falls
Area Code 816

Best Western Inn (1601 8th St., 76301; 322-1182, 800-528-1234) 42 rooms, pool, exercise center, children free with parents, A/C, NS rooms, TV, laundry facilities, wheelchair access, pets OK, meeting facilities, senior rates, CC. SGL/DBL$30-$36.

Days Inn Airport (1211 Century Expwy., 76305; 723-5541, 800-325-2525) 100 rooms and suites, restaurant, lounge, outdoor pool, children free with parents, room service, laundry service, A/C, TV, free local calls, pets OK, fax, wheelchair access, NS rooms, meeting facilities, senior rates, CC. SGL/DBL$32-$78.

Econo Lodge (1700 5th St., 76301; 761-1889, 800-4-CHOICE) 115 rooms, free breakfast, pool, children under 12 free with parents, no pets, NS rooms, wheelchair access, A/C, TV, meeting facilities, senior rates, CC. SGL/DBL$30-$43.

Hampton Inn (1317 Kenley, 76305; 766-3300, Fax 723-8226, 800-HAMP-TON) 120 rooms, restaurant, free breakfast, pool, exercise center, children under 18 free with parents, NS rooms, wheelchair access, in-room computer hookups, fax, TV, A/C, free local calls, pets OK, meeting facilities, CC. SGL/DBL$45-$56.

La Quinta Inn (1128 Central Freeway North, 76305; 322-6971, 800-531-5900) 139 rooms, restaurant, free breakfast, lounge, pool, complimentary newspaper, free local calls, fax, laundry service, NS rooms, wheelchair access, TV, A/C, pets OK, meeting facilities, senior rates, CC. SGL/DBL$45-$65.

Motel 6 (1812 Maurine St., 76304; 322-8817, 505-891-6161) 82 rooms, pool, free local calls, children under 17 free with parents, NS rooms, wheelchair access, pets OK, A/C, TV, CC. SGL/DBL$39-$44.

Ramada Inn (401 Broad St., 76301; 766-6000, Fax 766-5942, 800-2-RAMADA) 248 rooms and suites, restaurant, lounge, indoor and outdoor pool, jacuzzi, wheelchair access, NS rooms, pets OK, A/C, TV, children under 18 free with parents, room service, laundry facilities, 10,000 square feet of meeting and exhibition space, senior rates, CC. SGL/DBL$49-$105.

Sheraton Inn Wichita Falls (100 Central Freeway, 76305; 761-6000, Fax 766-1488, 800-325-3535) 166 rooms and suites, restaurant, lounge, entertainment, indoor and outdoor pool, whirlpools, game rooms, in-room refrigerators, NS rooms, A/C, TV, children free with parents, gift shop, wheelchair access, airport courtesy car, 6,000 square feet of meeting and exhibition space, 7 meeting rooms, meeting facilities for 600, senior rates, CC. SGL/DBL$65-$80, STS$85-$160.

Utah

Alta

Area Code 801

Alta Lodge (Alta 84092; 742-3500, 800-748-5025) 57 rooms, restaurant, lounge, whirlpools, sauna, fireplaces, children under 5 free with parents, TV, NS rooms, wheelchair access, modified American plan available, CC. SGL/DBL$100-$225.

Rustler Lodge (Little Cottonwood Canyon Rd., 84092; 742-2200, 800-451-5223) 57 rooms and suites, restaurant, lounge, heated pool, sauna, whirlpools, laundry facilities, A/C, TV, modified American plan available, NS rooms, wheelchair access, meeting facilities, CC. SGL/DBL$100-$225.

Beaver
Area Code 801

Best Western Inn (161 South Main St., 84713; 438-2438, 800-528-1234) 24 rooms, restaurant, heated pool, exercise center, whirlpools, sauna, children free with parents, A/C, NS rooms, TV, laundry facilities, wheelchair access, pets OK, senior rates, meeting facilities, senior rates, CC. SGL/DBL$38-$48.

Best Western Inn (Beaver 84713; 439-2455, 800-528-1234) 53 rooms, restaurant, lounge, entertainment, indoor heated pool, whirlpools, children free with parents, A/C, NS rooms, TV, laundry facilities, wheelchair access, pets OK, meeting facilities, senior rates, CC. SGL/DBL$40-$48.

Comfort Inn Downtown (645 North Main St., 84713; 438-2409, 800-221-2222) 51 rooms and suites, free breakfast, pool, wheelchair access, NS rooms, no pets, children under 18 free with parents, A/C, TV, meeting facilities, senior rates, CC. SGL/DBL$36-$52.

De Lano Motel (480 North Main St., 84713; 438-2418) 10 rooms, pets OK, laundry facilities, A/C, laundry facilities, TV, NS rooms, wheelchair access, pets OK, meeting facilities, senior rates, CC. SGL/DBL$30-$38.

Quality Inn (1540 South Hwy. 450, 84713; 438-5426, 800-221-2222) 52 rooms and suites, restaurant, indoor heated pool, exercise center, hot tub, children free with parents, A/C, TV, room service, laundry service, NS rooms, meeting facilities, senior rates, CC. SGL/DBL$36-$59.

Sleepy Lagoon Motel (Beaver 84713; 438-5681) 21 rooms, heated pool, A/C, TV, NS rooms, wheelchair access, no pets, senior rates, CC. SGL/DBL$40-$50.

Blanding
Area Code 801

Best Western Gateway Motel (88 East Center, 84511; 678-2278, 800-528-1234) 59 rooms, restaurant, heated pool, exercise center, children free with parents, A/C, NS rooms, TV, laundry facilities, wheelchair access, pets OK, meeting facilities, senior rates, CC. SGL/DBL$36-$60.

Comfort Inn (711 South Main St., 84511; 678-3271, Fax 678-3219, 800-221-2222) 52 rooms, free breakfast, indoor heated pool, exercise center, sauna, wheelchair access, NS rooms, no pets, children under 18 free with parents, A/C, TV, meeting facilities, senior rates, CC. SGL/DBL$41-$83.

Bluff
Area Code 801

Recapture Lodge and Pioneer House (Bluff 84512; 672-2281) 28 rooms and efficiencies, restaurant, heated pool, whirlpools, in-room refrigerators, pets OK, TV, NS rooms, wheelchair access, CC. SGL/DBL$26-$46.

Brigham City
Area Code 801

Budget Host Inn (505 North Main St., 84302; 723-8584, 800-283-4678) 17 rooms, no pets, airport transportation, laundry facilities, NS rooms, wheelchair access, A/C, TV, senior rates, children free with parents, CC. SGL/DBL$25-$44.

HoJo Inn (1167 South Main, 84302; 723-8511, 800-I-GO-HOJO) 44 rooms, restaurant, free breakfast, lounge, indoor pool, whirlpools, children free with parents, wheelchair access, NS rooms, TV, A/C, no pets, laundry facilities, senior rates, meeting facilities, CC. SGL/DBL$36-$46.

Brighton
Area Code 801

Brighton Chalets (Brighton 84121; 942-8824, 800-748-4824) 5 chalets, whirlpool baths, kitchenettes, A/C, TV, fireplaces, NS rooms, no pets, wheelchair access, CC. SGL/DBL$50, 1BR$65, 2BR$80.

Brighton Lodge (Brighton 84121; 532-4731, 800-873-5512) 22 rooms, restaurant, lounge, heated pool, whirlpools, no pets, boutiques, game room, in-room refrigerators, children free with parents, A/C, TV, NS rooms, wheelchair access, CC. SGL/DBL$85-$115.

Das Alpen Haus (Star Route, 84121; 649-0565) 4 suites, free breakfast, sauna, jacuzzi, fireplaces, no pets, A/C, TV, CC. SGL/DBL$60-$70.

Bryce
Area Code 801

Best Western Ruby's Inn (Bryce 84764; 834-5341, 800-528-1234) 316 rooms and suites, restaurant, lounge, indoor heated pool, exercise center, children free with parents, A/C, NS rooms, TV, laundry facilities, wheelchair access, pets OK, senior rates, meeting facilities, CC. SGL/DBL$70-$105.

Bryce Canyon Lodge (Bryce 84764; 586-7686) 110 rooms and cabins, restaurant, lounge, laundry facilities, no pets, TV, CC. SGL/DBL$67-$80.

Bryce Canyon Pines (Bryce 84764; 834-5441, Fax 834-5330) 50 rooms, suites and cottages, restaurant, heated pool, fireplaces, A/C, TV, NS rooms, wheelchair access, CC. SGL/DBL$50-$85.

Bullfrog
Area Code 801

Defiance House (Bullfrog 84553; 684-2233) 48 rooms, restaurant, lounge, no pets, laundry facilities, A/C, TV, NS rooms, wheelchair access, CC. SGL/DBL$47-$90.

Cedar City
Area Code 801

Abbey Inn (200 North 940 West, 84720; 586-9966, 800-325-5411) 80 rooms, restaurant, free breakfast, indoor heated pool, spa, whirlpools, in-room refrigerators and microwaves, laundry facilities, A/C, TV, CC. SGL/DBL$35-$70.

Best Western Town and Country Inn (189 North Main St., 84720; 586-9900, Fax 586-1664, 800-528-1234) 157 rooms and suites, restaurant, lounge, indoor and outdoor pool, exercise center, whirlpools, children free with parents, A/C, NS rooms, TV, laundry facilities, airport courtesy car, game room, wheelchair access, pets OK, senior rates, meeting facilities, CC. SGL/DBL$50-$140.

Best Western Inn (80 South Main St., 84720; 586-6518, Fax 586-7257, 800-528-1234) 75 rooms and suites, restaurant, lounge, heated pool, exercise center, whirlpools, children free with parents, A/C, NS rooms, TV, laundry facilities, wheelchair access, no pets, meeting facilities, senior rates, CC. SGL/DBL$35-$75.

Bryce Canyon Lodge (Cedar City 84720; 834-5361) 114 cabins, restaurant, A/C, TV, NS rooms, wheelchair access, laundry facilities, gift shop, CC. SGL/DBL$65-$100.

Budget Inn (323 South Main St., 84720; 586-6557) 30 rooms, restaurant, heated pool, sauna, pets OK, A/C, TV, children free with parents, airport transportation, NS rooms, wheelchair access, CC. SGL/DBL$23-$50.

Comfort Inn (250 North 1100 West, 84720; 586-2081, Fax 586-3193, 800-221-2222) 94 rooms, free breakfast, heated pool, wheelchair access, NS rooms, airport courtesy car, pets OK, children under 18 free with parents, A/C, TV, meeting facilities, senior rates, CC. SGL/DBL$55-$65.

Days Inn (479 South Main St., 84720; 586-9471, Fax 586-2688, 800-325-2525) 30 rooms and suites, free breakfast, children free with parents, room service, laundry service, A/C, TV, free local calls, pets OK, fax, wheelchair access, NS rooms, meeting facilities, senior rates, CC. SGL/DBL$34-$59.

Holiday Inn (1575 West 200 North, 84720; 586-8888, 800-432-8828, 800-HOLIDAY) 100 rooms and suites, restaurant, lounge, pool, exercise center, whirlpools, airport transportation, children under 19 free with parents, wheelchair access, A/C, TV, NS rooms, fax, room service, no pets, laundry service, meeting facilities, senior rates, CC. SGL/DBL$75-$88, STS$95-$163.

Quality Inn (18 South Main St., 84720; 586-2433, 800-221-2222) 50 rooms and suites, restaurant, pool, exercise center, children free with parents, A/C, TV, room service, complimentary newspaper, free local calls, airport transportation, in-room refrigerators and microwaves, laundry service, NS rooms, meeting facilities, senior rates, CC. SGL/DBL$40-$78.

Paxman's Summer House (170 North 400 West, 84720; 586-3755) 4 rooms, free breakfast, no pets, TV, antique furnishings, A/C, NS, CC SGL/DBL$55-$70.

Raycap Motel (2555 North Main St., 84720; 586-7435) 36 rooms, restaurant, heated pool, whirlpools, A/C, TV, NS rooms, wheelchair access, CC. SGL/DBL$32-$45.

Rodeway Inn (281 South Main St., 84720; 586-9916, 800-424-4777) 48 rooms and 2-bedroom suites, restaurant, pool, whirlpools, sauna, game room, wheelchair access, NS rooms, children free with parents, airport transportation, A/C, TV, senior rates, CC. SGL/DBL$40-$72.

Super 7 Motel (190 South Main St., 84720; 586-6566) 27 rooms, A/C, TV, NS rooms, wheelchair access, no pets, CC. SGL/DBL$20-$53.

Super 8 Motel (145 North 1550 West, 84720; 586-8880, Fax 586-8880, 800-800-8000) 55 rooms and suites, restaurant, lounge, whirlpools, pets OK, children under 12 free with parents, free local calls, A/C, TV, in-room refrigerators and microwaves, fax, NS rooms, senior rates, wheelchair access, meeting facilities, CC. SGL/DBL$40-$55.

Thrifty Motel (344 South Main St., 84720; 586-9114) 29 rooms, restaurant, pool, kitchenettes, pets OK, A/C, TV, NS rooms, wheelchair access, CC. SGL/DBL$20-$50.

Woodbury Guest House (237 South 300 West, 84720; 586-6696) 5 rooms, free breakfast, whirlpools, no pets, NS rooms, A/C, TV, CC. SGL/DBL$55-$80.

Zion Inn (222 South Main St., 84720; 586-9487) 24 rooms, kitchenettes, A/C, TV, NS rooms, wheelchair access, CC. SGL/DBL$22-$38.

Delta
Area Code 801

Best Western Inn (527 East Topaz Blvd., 84624; 864-3882, 800-528-1234) 83 rooms, restaurant, heated pool, exercise center, children free with parents, A/C, NS rooms, TV, laundry facilities, wheelchair access, pets OK, meeting facilities, in-room refrigerators, senior rates, CC. SGL/DBL$40-$50.

Budget Motel (75 South 350 East, 84624; 864-4533) 20 rooms and efficiencies, A/C, TV, NS rooms, wheelchair access, in-room refrigerators, CC. SGL/DBL$23-$38.

Killpack Motor Motel (201 West Main St., 84624; 864-2734) 16 rooms and 2-bedroom efficiencies, A/C, TV, NS rooms, wheelchair access, CC. SGL/DBL$25-$32.

Enterprise
Area Code 801

Sleep E Motel (735 East Main St., 84725; 878-2603) 6 rooms, restaurant, free breakfast, A/C, TV, NS rooms, wheelchair access, CC. SGL/DBL$30-$50.

Fillmore
Area Code 801

Best Western Paradise Inn (1025 North Main St., 84631; 743-6895, 800-528-1234) 80 rooms, restaurant, free breakfast, lounge, heated pool, exercise center, whirlpools, children free with parents, A/C, NS rooms, TV, laundry, wheelchair access, pets OK, senior rates, meeting facilities, CC. SGL/DBL$40-$50.

Fillmore Motel (61 North Main St., 84631; 743-5454) 20 rooms and 2-bedroom efficiencies, pets OK, A/C, TV, NS rooms, wheelchair access, CC. SGL/DBL$22-$38.

Spinning Wheel Motel (65 South Main St., 84631; 743-6260) 16 rooms and 1- and 2-bedroom efficiencies, A/C, TV, pets OK, wheelchair access, CC. SGL/DBL$25-$30.

Garden City
Area Code 801

Bear Lake Motor Lodge (50 South Bear Lake Blvd, 84028; 946-3271) 10 rooms, restaurant, A/C, TV, pets OK, kitchenettes, NS rooms, meeting facilities for 50, CC. SGL/DBL$32-$62.

Blue Water Beach Motel (2126 South Hwy. 250 East, 84028; 946-3333) 15 rooms and suites, kitchenettes, A/C, TV, NS rooms, wheelchair access, pets OK, kitchenettes, laundry facilities, CC. SGL/DBL$49-$80.

Greek Goddess Motel (205 North Bear Lake Blvd., 84028; 946-3233) 8 rooms, restaurant, A/C, TV, NS rooms, wheelchair access, meeting facilities for 30, CC. SGL/DBL$28-$40.

Ideal Beach Resort (2176 South Bear Lake Blvd., 84028; 946-3364) 55 rooms, restaurant, sauna, jacuzzi, kitchenettes, laundry facilities, A/C, TV, NS rooms, wheelchair access, meeting facilities for 35, CC. SGL/DBL$55.

The Inn at Harbor Village (785 North Bear Lake Blvd., 84028; 800-364-6840) 50 rooms, restaurant, jacuzzi, laundry facilities, A/C, TV, NS rooms, wheelchair access, meeting facilities for 550, CC. SGL/DBL$85-$125.

The Inn of the Three Bears (135 South Bear Lake Blvd., 84028; 946-8590) 3 rooms, free breakfast, A/C, TV, laundry facilities, CC. SGL/DBL$48-$60.

Sweetwater Condominiums (757 Bear Lake Blvd., 84028; 800-272-UTAH) 13 1- to 3-bedroom condominiums, restaurant, A/C, TV, no pets, children free with parents, NS rooms, wheelchair access, pets OK, CC. SGL/DBL$500W-$750W.

Green River
Area Code 801

Bankurz Hatt Bed and Breakfast (214 Farrer St., 84525; 564-3382) rooms, free breakfast, 1890s home, A/C, TV, CC. SGL/DBL$75-$120.

Best Western River Terrace Inn (880 East Main St., 84525; 564-3401, 800-528-1234) 51 rooms, restaurant, heated pool, exercise center, children free with parents, A/C, NS rooms, TV, laundry facilities, wheelchair access, pets OK, local transportation, senior rates, meeting facilities, CC. SGL/DBL$50-$100.

Bookcliff Lodge (395 East Main St., 84525; 564-3406) 97 rooms, restaurant, heated pool, pets OK, A/C, TV, NS rooms, wheelchair access, CC. SGL/DBL$30-$70.

Budget Host Bookcliff Lodge (395 East Main St., 84525; 564-3650, 800-283-4678) 97 rooms, restaurant, laundry facilities, NS rooms, wheelchair access, A/C, TV, senior rates, children free with parents, CC. SGL/DBL$30-$45.

Cottage Motel (60 East Main St., 84525; 564-3441) 31 rooms, A/C, TV, NS rooms, wheelchair access, CC. SGL/DBL$35-$40.

Motel 6 (946 East Main St., 84525; 564-3436, 505-891-6161) 103 rooms, pool, free local calls, children under 17 free with parents, NS rooms, wheelchair access, pets OK, A/C, TV, CC. SGL/DBL$36-$44.

National 9 Inn (357 West Main St., 84525; 564-8237, 800-524-9999) 35 rooms, free breakfast, pool, NS rooms, wheelchair access, A/C, TV, children free with parents, pets OK, senior rates, CC. SGL/DBL$25-$45.

Oasis Motel (118 West Main St., 84525; 564-3471) 20 rooms, A/C, TV, NS rooms, wheelchair access, CC. SGL/DBL$18-$28.

Robber's Roost Motel (125 West Main St., 84525; 564-2452) 20 rooms, pool, A/C, TV, NS rooms, wheelchair access, CC. SGL/DBL$30-$60.

Rodeway Inn (525 East I-70 Business Loop, 84525; 564-3421, 800-424-4777) 42 rooms, restaurant, pool, wheelchair access, NS rooms, children free with parents, A/C, game room, TV, senior rates, CC. SGL/DBL$48-$70.

Ruby Ranch House (Green River 84525; 564-3538) 3 rooms. SGL/DBL$45-$80.

Sleepy Hollow Motel (94 East Main St., 84525; 564-8189) 17 rooms, A/C, TV, NS rooms, wheelchair access, CC. SGL/DBL$32-$50.

Hatch
Area Code 801

New Bryce Motel (Hatch 84735; 735-4265) 20 rooms, restaurant, A/C, TV, NS rooms, wheelchair access, CC. SGL/DBL$37-$49.

Riverside Motel (Hatch 84735; 735-4223) 8 rooms, A/C, TV, NS rooms, wheelchair access, laundry facilities, CC. SGL/DBL$35-$45.

Heber City
Area Code 801

Danish Viking Lodge (989 South Main St., 84032; 654-2202, Fax 654-2770, 800-544-4066) 34 rooms and efficiencies, outdoor heated pool, sauna, whirlpools, A/C, TV, NS rooms, in-room refrigerators, laundry facilities, children free with parents, wheelchair access, senior rates, CC. SGL/DBL$32-$75.

The Homestead Resort (700 North Homestead Dr., 84049; 654-1102, Fax 654-5087, 800-327-7220) 117 rooms and suites, restaurant, lounge, indoor and outdoor pool, whirlpools, sauna, lighted tennis court, A/C, TV, NS rooms, wheelchair access, gift shop, no pets, meeting facilities, senior rates, CC. SGL/DBL$150-$225.

Hy Lander Motel (425 South Main St., 84032; 654-2150) 22 rooms and 2-bedroom efficiencies, restaurant, heated pool, A/C, TV, NS rooms, wheelchair access, CC. SGL/DBL$25-$42.

National 9 High Country Inn (1000 South Main St., 84032; 654-0201, 800-345-9198, 800-524-9999) 38 rooms, restaurant, free breakfast, heated pool, whirlpools, laundry facilities, in-room refrigerators, no pets, NS rooms, wheelchair access, A/C, TV, children free with parents, senior rates, CC. SGL/DBL$38-$48.

Swiss Alps Inn (167 South Main St., 84032; 654-0722) 14 rooms and 2-bedroom efficiencies, restaurant, heated pool, whirlpools, sauna, A/C, TV, NS rooms, wheelchair access, CC. SGL/DBL$30-$48.

Huntsville
Area Code 801

Jackson Fork Inn (7345 East 900 South, 84317; 745-0051, 800-255-0672) 8 rooms, restaurant, pets OK, A/C, TV, NS rooms, wheelchair access, CC. SGL/DBL$40-$110.

Hurricane
Area Code 801

Best Western Lamplighter Inn (280 West State St., 84737; 635-4647, Fax 635-0840, 800-528-1234) 63 rooms, restaurant, pool, jacuzzis, children free with parents, A/C, NS rooms, TV, laundry facilities, wheelchair access, pets OK, meeting facilities, senior rates, CC. SGL/DBL$35-$50.

Park Villa Motel (650 West State St., 84737; 635-4010, Fax 635-9483, 800-682-6336) 24 rooms and 2-bedroom efficiencies, heated pool, spa, whirlpools, pets OK, kitchenettes, laundry facilities, A/C, TV, NS rooms, wheelchair access, CC. SGL/DBL$36-$46.

Kanab
Area Code 801

Best Western Red Hills Inn (125 West Center St., 84741; 644-2675, 800-528-1234) 72 rooms, restaurant, heated pool, exercise center, children free with parents, A/C, NS rooms, TV, laundry facilities, wheelchair access, pets OK, in-room refrigerators, senior rates, meeting facilities, CC. SGL/DBL$65-$70.

Budget Host K Motel (330 South 100 East, 84741; 644-2611, Fax 644-2788, 800-283-4678) 17 rooms, restaurant, laundry facilities, NS rooms, wheelchair access, A/C, TV, airport transportation, senior rates, children free with parents, CC. SGL/DBL$27-$49.

Four Seasons Motor Inn (22 North 300 West, 84741; 644-2635) 41 rooms, restaurant, pool, gift shop, pets OK, A/C, TV, NS rooms, wheelchair access, CC. SGL/DBL$56-$65.

Parry Lodge (89 East Center st., 84741; 644-2601, 800-748-4104) 89 rooms, restaurant, heated pool, A/C, kitchenettes, TV, NS rooms, wheelchair access, pets OK, laundry facilities, senior rates, CC. SGL/DBL$55-$65.

Quail Park Lodge (125 North 300 West, 84741; 644-2639) 12 rooms, restaurant, heated pool, pets OK, A/C, TV, NS rooms, wheelchair access, CC. SGL/DBL$28-$45.

Shilo Inn (296 West 100 North, 84741; 644-2562, 800-222-2244) 119 rooms and suites, restaurant, lounge, heated pool, whirlpools, laundry facilities, spa, complimentary newspaper, gift shop, airport courtesy car, in-room refrigerators, A/C, TV, NS rooms, wheelchair access, VCRs, children under 12 free with parents, meeting facilities for 150, senior rates, CC. SGL/DBL$50-$70.

Super 8 Motel (70 South 200 West, 84741; 644-5500, Fax 644-5576, 800-800-8000) 36 rooms and suites, restaurant, pets OK, children under 12 free with parents, free local calls, A/C, TV, in-room refrigerators and microwaves, fax, NS rooms, senior rates, wheelchair access, meeting facilities, CC. SGL/DBL$31-$50.

Layton
Area Code 801

La Quinta Inn (1965 North 1200 West, 84041; 776-6700, Fax 776-2677, 800-531-5900) 100 rooms, restaurant, free breakfast, lounge, indoor heated pool, sauna, jacuzzi, complimentary newspaper, free local calls, fax, laundry service, NS rooms, wheelchair access, TV, A/C, meeting facilities, CC. SGL/DBL$48-$56.

Loa
Area Code 801

Road Creek Inn (90 South Main St., 84747; 836-2485, 800-388-7688) 12 rooms, restaurant, free breakfast, whirlpools, sauna, A/C, no pets, TV, NS rooms, wheelchair access, CC. SGL/DBL$44-$76.

Logan

Area Code 801

Alta Motel (51 East Hwy. 500 North, 84321; 752-6300) 19 rooms and suites, indoor and outdoor pool, exercise center, kitchenettes, laundry facilities, A/C, TV, NS rooms, wheelchair access, meeting facilities for 50, CC. SGL/DBL$25-$30.

Best Western Inn (153 South Main St., 84321; 752-5220, Fax 462-4154, 800-462-4154, 800-528-1234) 77 rooms, restaurant, free breakfast, lounge, pool, exercise center, children free with parents, A/C, NS rooms, TV, laundry facilities, wheelchair access, pets OK, senior rates, meeting facilities, CC. SGL/DBL$36-$60.

Best Western Inn (250 South Main St., 84321; 752-5700, Fax 752-9719, 800-528-1234) 89 rooms, indoor pool, whirlpools, sauna, children free with parents, A/C, NS rooms, TV, laundry facilities, wheelchair access, pets OK, meeting facilities, senior rates, CC. SGL/DBL$35-$44.

Center Street Bed and Breakfast (169 East Center St., 84321; 752-3443) 12 rooms and suites, free breakfast, whirlpools, indoor heated pool, A/C, TV, antique furnishings, NS, no pets, meeting facilities for 15, CC. SGL/DBL$40-$50, STS$65-$150.

Comfort Inn (447 North Main St., 84321; 752-9141, 800-221-2222) 83 rooms, restaurant, free breakfast, indoor heated, pool, whirlpools, exercise center, wheelchair access, NS rooms, no pets, children under 18 free with parents, A/C, TV, meeting facilities for 100, senior rates, CC. SGL/DBL$50.

Days Inn Downtown (364 South Main St., 84321; 753-5623, 800-325-2525) 48 rooms and suites, free breakfast, outdoor pool, children free with parents, kitchenettes, room service, laundry service, A/C, TV, free local calls, pets OK, fax, wheelchair access, NS rooms, meeting facilities, senior rates, CC. SGL/DBL$32-$55.

Logan House Inn (168 North Hwy. 100 East, 84321; 752-7727) 5 rooms, free breakfast, A/C, TV, NS rooms, wheelchair access, CC. SGL/DBL$80-$150.

Super 8 Motel (865 Hwy. 89, 84321; 753-8883, 800-800-8000) 61 rooms and suites, pets OK, children under 12 free with parents, free local calls, A/C, TV, in-room refrigerators and microwaves, fax, NS rooms, senior rates, wheelchair access, meeting facilities, CC. SGL/DBL$31-$50.

University Inn (Utah State University, 84321; 750-1153, 800-231-5634) 74 rooms and suites, restaurant, A/C, TV, NS rooms, wheelchair access, meeting facilities for 100, CC. SGL/DBL$38-$52.

Zanavoo Lodge (250 North Main St., 84321; 752-0085) 11 rooms, restaurant, A/C, TV, NS rooms, wheelchair access, meeting facilities for 200, CC. SGL/DBL$25-$50.

Manila
Area Code 801

Niki's Inn (Manila 84086; 784-3117) 10 rooms, restaurant, A/C, TV, NS rooms, CC. SGL/DBL$30-$48.

Manti
Area Code 801

Country Village (145 North Main St., 84642; 835-9300) 23 rooms and 2-bedroom suites, restaurant, whirlpools, A/C, TV, NS rooms, wheelchair access, CC. SGL/DBL$33-$38.

Manti House Inn (401 North Main St., 84642; 835-0161) 6 rooms and 2-bedroom suites, restaurant, A/C, no pets, antique furnishings, TV, NS rooms, wheelchair access, CC. SGL/DBL$45-$100.

Old Brigham House (123 East Union St., 84642; 835-8381) 4 rooms, free breakfast, whirlpools, NS rooms, TV, no pets, CC. SGL/DBL$35-$60.

Mexican Hat
Area Code 801

San Juan Inn (Mexican Hat 84531; 683-2220, Fax 683-2210) 33 rooms and apartments, restaurant, lounge, pets OK, A/C, TV, NS rooms, wheelchair access, senior rates, CC. SGL/DBL$38-$55.

Midvale
Area Code 801

Best Western Executive Inn (280 West 7200 South St., 84047; 566-4141, Fax 566-5142, 800-528-1234) 112 rooms and suites, restaurant, heated pool, whirlpools, children free with parents, A/C, NS rooms, TV, laundry facilities, wheelchair access, pets OK, meeting facilities, senior rates, CC. SGL/DBL$50-$150.

Discovery Motor Inn (380 West 7200 South, 84047; 561-2256, 800-444-6969) 89 rooms and suites, restaurant, pool, whirlpools, A/C, TV, NS rooms, wheelchair access, CC. SGL/DBL$47-$56.

La Quinta Inn (530 Catalpa Rd., 84047; 566-3291, Fax 562-5934, 800-531-5900) 122 rooms, restaurant, free breakfast, lounge, pool, complimentary newspaper, free local calls, fax, laundry service, NS rooms, wheelchair access, TV, A/C, meeting facilities, CC. SGL/DBL$48-$63.

Motel 6 (496 North Catalpa St., 84047; 561-0058, 505-891-6161) 128 rooms, pool, free local calls, children under 17 free with parents, NS rooms, wheelchair access, pets OK, A/C, TV, CC. SGL/DBL$35-$38.

Moab

Area Code 801

Rental and Reservation Services:

Arches Reservation Central (76 South Main St., 84321; 259-4737, 800-775-4RES)

Moab/Canyonlands Central Reservations (92 East Center, 84321; 259-5125, 800-748-4386)

□□□

Apache Motel (166 South 400 East, 84532; 259-5727, Fax 259-8989, 800-228-6882) 34 rooms and 1- and 2-bedroom efficiencies, pool, kitchenettes, A/C, TV, NS rooms, wheelchair access, no pets, CC. SGL/DBL$26-$63.

Best Western Green Well Inn (105 South Main St., 84532; 259-6151, 800-528-1234) 72 rooms, restaurant, heated pool, exercise center, children free with parents, A/C, NS rooms, TV, laundry facilities, wheelchair access, pets OK, senior rates, meeting facilities, CC. SGL/DBL$40-$90.

Best Western Canyonlands Inn (16 South Main St., 84532; 259-2300, Fax 259-2301, 800-528-1234) 77 rooms, restaurant, free breakfast, lounge, pool, exercise center, children free with parents, A/C, NS rooms, TV, laundry facilities, wheelchair access, pets OK, meeting facilities, senior rates, CC. SGL/DBL$83-$140.

Bowen Motel (169 North Main St., 84532; 259-7132, 800-874-5439) 40 rooms, heated pool, A/C, TV, NS rooms, wheelchair access, CC. SGL/DBL$50-$60.

Canyon Creek Bed and Breakfast (590 North 500 West, 84532; 259-5262, 800-435-0284) 5 rooms, free breakfast, heated pool, hot tub, A/C, no pets, laundry facilities, TV, CC. SGL/DBL$45-$110.

Castle Valley Inn (Castle Valley, 84532; 259-6012) 8 rooms, free breakfast, restaurant, A/C, TV, VCRs, no pets, NS rooms, CC. SGL/DBL$65-$105.

Circle A Ranch (128 West 200 North, 84532; 259-7632) 6 rooms and apartments, free breakfast, A/C, TV, no pets, children free with parents, CC. SGL/DBL$60-$100.

Comfort Suites (800 South Main St., 84532; 259-5252, Fax 259-7110, 800-221-2222) 75 suites, free breakfast, indoor heated pool, exercise center, whirlpools, wheelchair access, NS rooms, no pets, children under 18 free with parents, in-room refrigerators and microwaves, A/C, TV, meeting facilities, senior rates, CC. SGL/DBL$50-$105.

Cottage Inn Motel (488 North Main St., 84532; 259-5738, Fax 259-5738) 4 rooms and efficiencies, TV, NS, no pets, CC. SGL/DBL$24-$65.

Dark Canyon Recreation (1265 East Knutson Corner, 84532; 259-8389) 4 cabins, CC. SGL/DBL$20-$50.

Days Inn (426 North Main St., 84532; 259-4468, Fax 259-4018, 800-325-2525) 33 rooms and suites, free breakfast, outdoor pool, children free with parents, room service, laundry service, A/C, TV, free local calls, pets OK, fax, wheelchair access, NS rooms, meeting facilities, senior rates, CC. SGL/DBL$48-$59, STS$60-$75.

Desert Chalet (1275 San Juan Dr., 84532; 259-5793) 5 rooms, free breakfast, hot tubs, NS, no pets, A/C, TV, CC. SGL/DBL$35-$75.

Inca Inn Motel (570 North Main St., 84532; 259-7261) 23 rooms and 2-bedroom efficiencies, restaurant, A/C, TV, NS rooms, wheelchair access, CC. SGL/DBL$23-$56.

JR's Inn (1075 South Hwy. 191, 84532; 259-8000, Fax 259-6980) 10 rooms and efficiencies, restaurant, A/C, TV, NS rooms, wheelchair access, in-room refrigerators and microwaves, NS, no pets, CC. SGL/DBL$40-$80.

Kane Creek Bed and Breakfast (490 Kane Creek, 84532; 259-7345) 1 rooms, free breakfast, A/C, private bath, NS, no pets, TV, CC. SGL/DBL$55-$65.

Kokopelli Lodge (72 South 100 East, 84532; 259-7615) 8 rooms, free breakfast, pets are OK, A/C, TV, NS rooms, wheelchair access, CC. SGL/DBL$30-$65.

La Sal Mountain Huts (452 North Main St., 84532; 259-8946, 800-453-8946) 2 cabins, CC. SGL/DBL$28-$56.

Landmark Motel (168 North Main St., 84532; 259-6147, Fax 259-5556, 800-441-6147) 35 rooms and suites, restaurant, heated pool, whirlpools, A/C, TV, laundry facilities, NS rooms, wheelchair access, no pets, meeting facilities, CC. SGL/DBL$65-$88.

Lazy Lizard International Hostel (1213 South Hwy. 191, 84532; 259-6057) 10 rooms, hot tubs, A/C, TV, NS rooms, wheelchair access, CC. SGL/DBL$7-$10.

Matterhorn Guest House (3601 East Matterhorn Heights, 84532; 259-8000) 4 condominiums, free breakfast, A/C, TV, NS rooms, wheelchair access, no pets, CC. SGL/DBL$40-$80.

Mayor's House Bed and Breakfast (505 Rose Tree Lane., 84532; 259-6015) 5 rooms, free breakfast, pool, kitchenettes, NS, no children, game room, A/C, TV, CC. SGL/DBL$40-$125.

Mill Creek Inn (497 Millcreek Dr., 84532; 259-7014) 2 apartments, free breakfast, A/C, TV, NS rooms, wheelchair access, CC. SGL/DBL$40-$50.

Moab Guest House (300 West 400 North, 84532; 259-4458) 4-bedroom rental home, pool, A/C, TV, wheelchair access, CC. SGL/DBL$150-$200.

Moab Valley Inn (711 South Main St., 84532; 259-4419, Fax 259-4332, 800-831-6622) 127 rooms and suites, restaurant, lounge, outdoor heated pool, spa, A/C, TV, NS rooms, wheelchair access, meeting facilities for 650, CC. SGL/DBL$47-$125.

Nichols Lane Accommodations (543 Nichols Lane, 84532; 259-5047) 4 1- and 2-bedroom condominiums, laundry facilities, A/C, TV, NS rooms, wheelchair access, CC. SGL/DBL$40-$60.

Off Center Hotel (96 East Center, 84532; 259-4244, Fax 259-4244, 800-237-HOTL) 10 rooms, no pets, A/C, TV, NS rooms, wheelchair access, CC. SGL/DBL$25-$50.

Pack Creek Ranch (Moab 84532; 259-5505) 9 1-, 2- and 3-bedroom cottages, heated pool, sauna, whirlpools, pets OK, American plan available, A/C, TV, NS rooms, wheelchair access, meeting facilities, CC. SGL/DBL$100-$125.

Pioneer Spring Bed and Breakfast (1275 South Boulder, 84532; 259-4663) 3 rooms, free breakfast, swimming pool, hot tub, no pets, A/C, TV, CC. SGL/DBL$30-$70.

Prospector Lodge (186 North 100 West, 84532; 259-5145) 35 rooms, A/C, TV, NS rooms, wheelchair access, CC. SGL/DBL$30-$55.

Purple Sage Bed and Breakfast (1150 Duchesne, 84532; 259-3310) 3 rooms, free breakfast, A/C, TV, NS, private baths, CC. SGL/DBL$50-$60.

Ramada Inn (182 South Main St., 84532; 259-7141, Fax 259-8989, 800-2-RAMADA) 84 rooms and suites, restaurant, lounge, heated pool, hot tub, jacuzzi, wheelchair access, NS rooms, pets OK, A/C, TV, children under 18 free with parents, room service, laundry facilities, meeting facilities, senior rates, CC. SGL/DBL$45-$85.

Red Rock Lodge Motel (51 North 100 West, 84532; 259-5431) 23 rooms, pool, whirlpools, pets OK, A/C, TV, NS rooms, wheelchair access, in-room refrigerators and coffee makers, CC. SGL/DBL$34-$58.

Red Stone Inn (535 South Main St., 84532; 259-3500, Fax 259-2717, 800-772-1972) 50 rooms, pool, hot tub, kitchenettes, no pets, laundry facilities, A/C, TV, NS rooms, wheelchair access, CC. SGL/DBL$30-$60.

Red Valley Homes (201 East 100 North, 84532; 259-5408) 2- and 3-bedroom rental homes, local transportation, A/C, TV, wheelchair access, CC. SGL/DBL$60-$1,000.

River Lodge (512 North Main St., 84532; 259-6122) 22 rooms, A/C, TV, NS rooms, wheelchair access, no pets, CC. SGL/DBL$40-$61.

Ron-Tez Guest Condominiums (450 East 2nd St., 84532; 259-7599) 8 condominiums, A/C, TV, wheelchair access, CC. SGL/DBL$50-$60.

Rosetree Inn (41 West 100 North, 84532; 259-4305, Fax 259-5192, 800-421-5614) 4 1- and 2-bedroom condominiums, whirlpools, hot tubs, A/C, laundry facilities, NS rooms, TV, wheelchair access, no pets, CC. SGL/DBL$49-$129.

Rustic Inn Motel (120 East 100 South, 84532; 259-6177, Fax 259-2642, 800-281-8184) 35 rooms, free breakfast, TV, NS rooms, wheelchair access, CC. SGL/DBL$20-$75.

Sandi's Bed and Breakfast (450 Walker, 84532; 259-6359) 4 rooms, free breakfast, A/C, TV, no pets, CC. SGL/DBL$40-$80.

Shiloh Country Inn (2390 Old City Park Rd., 84532; 259-8684) 6 rooms, shared baths, A/C, TV, NS rooms, wheelchair access, no pets, fireplaces, CC. SGL/DBL$40-$175.

Silver Sage Inn (840 South Main St., 84532; 259-4420) 12 rooms, A/C, TV, NS rooms, wheelchair access, CC. SGL/DBL$25-$44.

Slick Rock House (1121 Jackson St., 84532; 259-4275) 4-bedroom rental house, A/C, TV, wheelchair access, CC. SGL/DBL$125-$165.

Slickrock Inn (286 South 400 East, 84532; 259-2266) 5-room rental home, NS, A/C, TV, wheelchair access, CC. SGL/DBL$185-$225.

Sundance (208 East 200 South, 84532; 259-8429) 2-bedroom condominiums, A/C, TV, NS rooms, wheelchair access, CC. SGL/DBL$40-$50.

Sunflower Hill Bed and Breakfast (185 North 300 East, 84532; 259-2974) 7 rooms, free breakfast, hot tub, whirlpools, NS rooms, no pets, fireplaces, A/C, TV, antique furnishings, CC. SGL/DBL$54-$86.

Sunset Motel (41 West 100 North, 84532; 259-5191, 800-421-5614) 37 rooms, heated pool, pets OK, A/C, TV, NS rooms, wheelchair access, CC. SGL/DBL$35-$110.

Super 8 Motel (889 North Main St., 84532; 259-8868, Fax 259-8968, 800-800-8000) 146 rooms and suites, restaurant, outdoor pool, whirlpools, no pets, children under 12 free with parents, free local calls, A/C, TV, in-room refrigerators and microwaves, fax, NS rooms, senior rates, wheelchair access, meeting facilities, CC. SGL/DBL$36-$70.

TraveLodge (550 South Main St., 84532; 259-6171, 800-578-7878) 57 rooms, restaurant, lounge, pool, wheelchair access, complimentary newspaper, laundry service, TV, A/C, free local calls, fax, NS rooms, in-room refrigerators and microwaves, children under 18 free with parents, no pets, meeting facilities for 25, CC. SGL/DBL$32-$82.

Virginian Motel (70 East 200 South, 84532; 259-5951) 38 rooms and efficiencies, A/C, TV, NS rooms, wheelchair access, CC. SGL/DBL$30-$50.

Westwood Guest House (81 East 100 South, 84532; 259-7283, 800-526-5690) 7 1- and 2-bedroom apartments, hot tub, free breakfast, A/C, TV, NS rooms, wheelchair access, CC. SGL/DBL$35-$59.

Monroe
Area Code 901

Petersons Bed and Breakfast (95 North 300 West, 84754; 527-4830) 3 rooms, free breakfast, no pets, in-room refrigerators, A/C, TV, senior rates, CC. SGL/DBL$39-$60.

Monticello
Area Code 801

Best Western Wayside Inn (195 East Central, 84535; 587-2261, 800-528-1234) 35 rooms, restaurant, pool, exercise center, children free with parents, A/C, NS rooms, TV, laundry facilities, wheelchair access, pets OK, meeting facilities, senior rates, CC. SGL/DBL$35-$80.

Canyonland Motor Inn (197 North Main St., 84535; 587-2266) 32 rooms, indoor heated pool, whirlpool, sauna, A/C, TV, laundry facilities, pets OK, NS rooms, wheelchair access, senior rates, CC. SGL/DBL$20-$50.

Days Inn (Monticello 84535; 587-2458, 800-325-2525) 43 rooms and suites, free breakfast, indoor heated pool, whirlpools, children free with parents, room service, laundry service, A/C, TV, free local calls, pets OK, fax, wheelchair access, NS rooms, meeting facilities, senior rates, CC. SGL/DBL$35-$65.

Grist Mill Inn Bed and Breakfast (64 South 300 East, 84535; 800-645-3762) 9 rooms, free breakfast, A/C, TV, no pets, children free with parents, CC. SGL/DBL$56.

Triangle H Motel (Monticello 84535; 587-2274, 800-657-6622) 26 rooms and 2-bedroom suites, restaurant, A/C, TV, no pets, NS rooms, wheelchair access, in-room refrigerators, senior rates, CC. SGL/DBL$22-$60.

National 9 Navajo Trail Inn (248 West Main St., 84535; 587-2252, 800-524-9999) 21 rooms and efficiencies, restaurant, NS rooms, wheelchair access, A/C, TV, children free with parents, senior rates, CC. SGL/DBL$25-$52.

Nephi
Area Code 801

Best Western Paradise Inn (1025 South Main St., 84648; 623-0624, 800-528-1234) 40 rooms, pool, exercise center, children free with parents, A/C, NS rooms, TV, laundry facilities, wheelchair access, pets OK, senior rates, meeting facilities, CC. SGL/DBL$40-$50.

Budget Host Roberta's Cove (2250 South Main St., 84648; 623-2629, 800-283-4678) 43 rooms, restaurant, whirlpools, laundry facilities, NS rooms, wheelchair access, A/C, airport transportation, no pets, TV, senior rates, children free with parents, CC. SGL/DBL$26-$41.

Safari Motel (413 South Main St., 84648; 623-1071) 28 rooms, heated pool, in-room refrigerators, A/C, TV, NS rooms, wheelchair access, CC. SGL/DBL$22-$40.

Super 8 Motel (1901 South Main St., 84648; 623-0888, Fax 623-5025, 800-800-8000) 41 rooms and suites, restaurant, no pets, children under 12 free with parents, free local calls, A/C, TV, in-room refrigerators and micro-waves, fax, NS rooms, senior rates, wheelchair access, meeting facilities, CC. SGL/DBL$32-$45.

Whitmore Mansion (110 South Main St., 84648; 623-2047) 6 rooms and 2-bedroom suites, free breakfast, antique furnishings, A/C, private baths, TV, NS rooms, wheelchair access, 1890s inn, no pets, CC. SGL/DBL$45-$75.

Ogden
Area Code 801

Best Western High Country Inn (1335 West 1200 South, 84401; 394-9474, 800-528-1234) 110 rooms, restaurant, free breakfast, lounge, pool, exercise center, hot tubs, children free with parents, A/C, NS rooms, TV, in-room microwaves, laundry facilities, wheelchair access, pets OK, meeting facilities, senior rates, CC. SGL/DBL$44-$105.

Best Western Ogden Park Hotel (247 24th St., 84401; 627-1190; Fax 621-0321, 800-528-1234) 290 rooms and suites, restaurant, free breakfast, indoor pool, exercise center, whirlpools, children free with parents, A/C, NS rooms, TV, laundry facilities, gift shop, beauty shop, local transportation, game room, in-room refrigerators, wheelchair access, pets OK, senior rates, meeting facilities, CC. SGL/DBL$65-$95, STS$95-$125.

Flying J Inn (1206 West 2100 South, 84401; 393-8644, 800-343-8644) 100 rooms, restaurant, lounge, entertainment, heated pool, exercise center, A/C, TV, VCRs, in-room microwaves, pets OK, NS rooms, wheelchair access, CC. SGL/DBL$40-$46.

Holiday Inn (3306 Washington Blvd., 84401; 399-5671, Fax 621-0321, 800-999-6841, 800-HOLIDAY) 109 rooms, restaurant, lounge, indoor pool, exercise center, whirlpools, children under 19 free with parents, wheelchair access, A/C, TV, NS rooms, fax, in-room microwaves, room service, no pets, laundry service, meeting facilities, senior rates, CC. SGL/DBL$58-$68.

Motel 6 Downtown (1455 Washington Blvd., 84404; 627-4560, 505-891-6161) 72 rooms, pool, free local calls, children under 17 free with parents, NS rooms, wheelchair access, pets OK, A/C, TV, CC. SGL/DBL$36-$40.

Motel 6 (1500 West Riverdale Rd., 84405; 627-2880, 505-891-6161) 110 rooms, restaurant, lounge, entertainment, heated pool, tennis courts, whirlpools, free local calls, children under 17 free with parents, NS rooms, wheelchair access, pets OK, A/C, TV, CC. SGL/DBL$40-$50.

Radisson Suite Hotel (2510 Washington Blvd., 84401; 627-1900, Fax 394-5342, 800-333-3333) 144 rooms and suites, restaurant, lounge, entertainment, exercise center, in-room refrigerators, microwaves and coffee makers, in-room refrigerators, gift shop, laundry facilities, children free with parents, VCRs, wheelchair access, NS rooms, TV, A/C, children free with parents, pets OK, CC. SGL/DBL$55-$195.

Sleep Inn (1155 South 1700 West, 84404; 894-5000, 800-221-2222) 68 rooms, free breakfast, pool, whirlpools, wheelchair access, NS rooms, no pets, children under 18 free with parents, senior rates, A/C, TV, meeting facilities, CC. SGL/DBL$40-$50.

Super 8 Motel (1508 West 2100 South, 84401; 731-7100, Fax 731-2627, 800-800-8000) 60 rooms and suites, restaurant, pets OK, children under 12 free with parents, free local calls, A/C, TV, in-room refrigerators and microwaves, fax, NS rooms, senior rates, wheelchair access, meeting facilities, CC. SGL/DBL$33-$40.

TraveLodge (2110 Washington Blvd., 84401; 394-4563, Fax 394-4568, 800-578-7878) 76 rooms, restaurant, lounge, pool, exercise center, wheelchair access, complimentary newspaper, laundry service, TV, A/C, free local calls, fax, game room, NS rooms, in-room refrigerators and microwaves, children under 18 free with parents, no pets, meeting facilities, CC. SGL/DBL$40-$60.

Panguitch
Area Code 801

Best Western New Western Inn (2 East Center St., 84759; 676-8876, 800-528-1234) 55 rooms and suites, pool, exercise center, children free with parents, A/C, NS rooms, TV, laundry facilities, wheelchair access, in-room refrigerators, pets OK, senior rates, meeting facilities, CC. SGL/DBL$40-$100.

Color Country Motel (526 North Main St., 84759; 676-2386, Fax 676-8484) 26 rooms and 2-bedroom efficiencies, restaurant, pool, pets OK, A/C, TV, NS rooms, wheelchair access, CC. SGL/DBL$22-$48.

Horizon Motel (730 North Main St., 84759; 676-2651) 12 rooms and 2-bedroom efficiencies, A/C, TV, NS rooms, wheelchair access, CC. SGL/DBL$30-$70.

Lamp Lighter Inn (581 North Main St., 84759; 676-8392) 12 rooms, restaurant, no pets, A/C, TV, NS, wheelchair access, CC. SGL/DBL$35-$55.

Marianna Inn Motel (600 North Main St., 84759; 676-8844) 24 rooms and 2-bedroom efficiencies, restaurant, whirlpools, pets OK, A/C, TV, NS rooms, wheelchair access, CC. SGL/DBL$25-$55.

Park City
Area Code 801

Best Western Inn (6550 North Landmark Dr., 84060; 649-7300, 800-528-1234) 106 rooms, restaurant, indoor heated pool, exercise center, whirlpools, pets OK, children free with parents, A/C, NS rooms, TV, laundry facilities, wheelchair access, fireplaces, meeting facilities, senior rates, CC. SGL/DBL$50-$110.

Deer Valley Lodging (1375 Deer Valley Dr., 84060; 649-4040, Fax 645-8419, 800-453-3833) 275 1- to 6-bedroom condominiums, heated pool, whirlpools, A/C, TV, NS rooms, wheelchair access, in-room refrigerators, meeting facilities, senior rates, CC. SGL/DBL$$250-$1,600.

Edelweiss Haus (1482 Empire Ave., 84060; 649-9342, 800-438-3855) 45 2-bedroom efficiencies, restaurant, indoor heated pool, whirlpools, sauna, A/C, TV, NS rooms, fireplaces, pets OK, wheelchair access, laundry facilities, CC. SGL/DBL$55-$300.

The Imperial Hotel (221 Main St., 84060; 649-1904, 800-669-UTAH) 11 rooms and suites, restaurant, free breakfast, whirlpools, TV, NS rooms, wheelchair access, senior rates, CC. SGL/DBL$85-$145.

Old Miner's Lodge (615 Woodside Ave., 84060; 645-8068, 800-648-8068) 10 rooms and suites, free breakfast, hot tub, A/C, TV, wheelchair access, 1890s inn, fireplaces, antique furnishings, NS, in-room refrigerators, no pets, CC. SGL/DBL$85-$155.

Olympia Parak Hotel and Conference Center (1895 Sidewinder Dr., 84060; 649-2900, 800-234-9003) 206 rooms and suites, restaurant, lounge, indoor heated pool, sauna, whirlpools, game room, gift shop, A/C, TV, NS rooms, pets OK, wheelchair access, meeting facilities, senior rates, CC. SGL/DBL$60-$250.

Prospect Square Hotel (2200 Sidewinder Dr., 84060; 649-7100, 800-453-3812) 230 rooms and 1- and 2-bedroom apartments, restaurant, lounge, A/C, in-room refrigerators, children free with parents, TV, NS rooms, wheelchair access, senior rates, CC. SGL/DBL$$100-$200.

Resort Center Lodge (1415 Lowell Dr., 84060; 649-0800, Fax 649-1464, 800-824-5331) 123 rooms and suites, restaurant, lounge, indoor and outdoor pool, whirlpools, sauna, in-room refrigerators, A/C, TV, NS rooms, wheelchair access, meeting facilities, CC. SGL/DBL$125-$200, STS$175-$825.

Shadow Ridge Resort Hotel (50 Shadow Ridge Dr., 84060; 649-4300, 800-451-3031) 150 rooms and suites, heated pool, whirlpools, sauna, laundry facilities, fireplaces, in-room refrigerators, A/C, TV, NS rooms, wheelchair access, CC. SGL/DBL$130-$550.

Silver King Hotel (1485 Empire Ave., 84060; 649-5500, Fax 649-6647) 64 rooms and 2-bedroom suites, indoor and outdoor heated pools, whirlpools, sauna, laundry facilities, no pets, A/C, TV, NS rooms, wheelchair access, senior rates, CC. SGL/DBL$90-$460.

Stein Eriksen Lodge (7700 Stein Way, 84060; 649-3700, Fax 648-5825, 800-453-1302) 120 rooms and suites, restaurant, lounge, entertainment, heated pool, whirlpools, exercise center, children free with parents, boutiques, no pets, airport transportation, A/C, TV, NS rooms, wheelchair access, senior rates, CC. SGL/DBL$250-$500.

Washington School Inn (543 Park Ave., 84060; 649-3800, Fax 649-3802, 800-824-1672) 15 rooms and 2- to 4-bedroom suites, free breakfast, heated pool, whirlpools, sauna, A/C, game room, antique furnishings, children free with parents, TV, NS rooms, wheelchair access, meeting facilities, senior rates, CC. SGL/DBL$200-$275.

Yarrow Resort Hotel and Conference Center (1800 Park Ave., 84060; 649-7000, Fax 645-7007, 800-327-2332) 181 rooms and suites, restaurant, lounge, heated pool, whirlpools, A/C, TV, transportation to local attraction, no pets, NS rooms, wheelchair access, meeting facilities, senior rates, CC. SGL/DBL$90-$190.

Parowan

Area Code 801

Best Western Inn (580 North Main St., 84761; 477-3391, Fax 477-8642, 800-528-1234) 28 rooms, restaurant, pool, exercise center, whirlpools, children free with parents, A/C, NS rooms, TV, laundry facilities, wheelchair access, pets OK, meeting facilities, senior rates, CC. SGL/DBL$40-$68.

Jedediah's Inn (625 West 200 South, 84761; 477-3326) 44 rooms, restaurant, lounge, A/C, TV, NS rooms, wheelchair access, CC. SGL/DBL$55-$60.

Pine Valley

Area Code 801

Pine Valley Lodge (960 East Main St., 84722; 574-2544) 10 rooms and cabins, A/C, TV, NS rooms, wheelchair access, laundry facilities, CC. SGL/DBL$35-$50.

Price

Area Code 801

Carriage House Inn (590 East Main St., 84501; 637-5660, Fax 637-5660) 42 rooms, restaurant, indoor and outdoor heated pool, whirlpools, in-room refrigerators and microwaves, A/C, TV, NS rooms, wheelchair access, no pets, CC. SGL/DBL$30-$45.

Crest Motel (625 East Main St., 84501; 637-1532) 85 rooms and 2-bedroom efficiencies, restaurant, A/C, TV, NS rooms, wheelchair access, airport transportation, CC. SGL/DBL$38-$60.

Days Inn (838 Westwood Blvd., 84501; 637-8880, Fax 637-7707, 800-325-2525) 148 rooms and suites, restaurant, lounge, indoor pool, whirlpools, game room, children free with parents, room service, laundry service, A/C, TV, free local calls, pets OK, fax, wheelchair access, NS rooms, meeting facilities, senior rates, CC. SGL/DBL$40-$55, STS$56-$125.

El Rancho Motel (145 North Carbonville Rd., 84501; 637-2424) 33 rooms, heated pool, A/C, TV, NS rooms, wheelchair access, kitchenettes, in-room refrigerators, CC. SGL/DBL$20-$32.

Green Well Motel (655 East Main St., 84501; 637-3520) 97 rooms, restaurant, A/C, TV, NS rooms, wheelchair access, pets OK, CC. SGL/DBL$25-$45.

Mr. Sleep Motel (641 West Price River Dr., 84501; 637-7000) 94 rooms, restaurant, A/C, TV, VCRs, NS rooms, wheelchair access, CC. SGL/DBL$30-$45.

Provo
Area Code 801

Best Western Inn (70 East 300 South, 84604; 373-8973, 800-528-1234) 80 rooms, restaurant, heated pool, exercise center, whirlpools, children free with parents, A/C, NS rooms, TV, laundry facilities, wheelchair access, pets OK, meeting facilities, senior rates, CC. SGL/DBL$56-$158.

Best Western Cottontree Inn (2230 North University Pkwy., 84604; 373-7044, Fax 375-5250, 800-528-1234) 80 rooms and suites, restaurant, heated pool, whirlpools, children free with parents, A/C, NS rooms, beauty shop, TV, laundry facilities, wheelchair access, pets OK, senior rates, meeting facilities, CC. SGL/DBL$60-$150.

Comfort Inn University (1555 Canyon Rd., 84604; 374-6020, Fax 374-0015, 800-221-2222) 100 rooms and suites, free breakfast, indoor heated pool, whirlpools, complimentary newspaper, free local calls, gift shop, wheelchair access, NS rooms, no pets, children under 18 free with parents, A/C, TV, meeting facilities, senior rates, CC. SGL/DBL$50-$125.

Days Inn (200 West, 84604; 375-8600, Fax 374-6654, 800-325-2525) 49 rooms and suites, free breakfast, outdoor pool, children free with parents, room service, laundry service, A/C, TV, free local calls, pets OK, fax, airport transportation, wheelchair access, NS rooms, meeting facilities, senior rates, CC. SGL/DBL$48-$56.

East Bay Inn (1292 South University Ave., 84601; 374-2500, 800-326-0025) 116 rooms and suites, restaurant, heated pool, exercise center, whirlpools, laundry facilities, pets OK, A/C, TV, NS rooms, wheelchair access, CC. SGL/DBL$30-$65.

Fairfield Inn by Marriott (1500 South University Ave., 84601; 377-9500, 800-228-2800) 72 rooms, restaurant, indoor heated pool, jacuzzi, whirlpools, exercise center, children under 18 free with parents, NS rooms, remote control TV, free cable TV, free local calls, laundry service, A/C, wheelchair access, no pets, fax, meeting facilities, senior rates, CC. SGL/DBL$40-$55.

Holiday Inn (1460 South University Ave., 84601; 374-9750, 800-HOLI-DAY) 54 rooms, restaurant, lounge, pool, exercise center, children under 19 free with parents, wheelchair access, A/C, TV, NS rooms, fax, room service, no pets, laundry service, meeting facilities for 300, senior rates, CC. SGL/DBL$45-$60.

Motel 6 (1600 South University Ave., 84601; 375-5064, 505-891-6161) 119 rooms, pool, free local calls, children under 17 free with parents, NS rooms, wheelchair access, pets OK, A/C, TV, CC. SGL/DBL$35-$40.

National 9 Colony Inn Suites (1380 South University Ave., 84601; 374-6800, 800-524-9999) 80 rooms, restaurant, pool, sauna, NS rooms, kitchenettes, wheelchair access, A/C, TV, children free with parents, senior rates, CC. SGL/DBL$26-$43.

Seven Peaks Resort (101 West 100 North, 84601; 377-4700, Fax 377-4708, 800-777-7144) 232 rooms and suites, restaurant, lounge, entertainment, heated pool, whirlpools, sauna, exercise center, local transportation, no pets, A/C, TV, NS rooms, wheelchair access, in-room refrigerators, meeting facilities, senior rates, CC. SGL/DBL$70-$300.

Sundance Resort (Provo 84604; 225-4107, Fax 226-1937) 80 efficiencies and cottages, restaurant, A/C, TV, NS rooms, wheelchair access, CC. SGL/DBL$90-$450.

Super 8 Motel (1288 South University, 84601; 375-8766, Fax 377-7569, 800-800-8000) 60 rooms and suites, no pets, children under 12 free with parents, free local calls, A/C, TV, in-room refrigerators and microwaves, fax, NS rooms, senior rates, wheelchair access, meeting facilities, CC. SGL/DBL$32-$45.

TraveLodge (124 South University Ave., 84601; 373-1974, Fax 373-1974 ext 145, 800-578-7878) 60 rooms and suites, restaurant, lounge, pool, wheelchair access, complimentary newspaper, laundry service, TV, A/C, free local calls, fax, NS rooms, in-room refrigerators and microwaves, children under 18 free with parents, no pets, meeting facilities, CC. SGL/DBL$30-$54.

Uptown Motel (469 West Center St., 84601; 373-8248) 28 rooms, restaurant, heated pool, kitchenettes, pets OK, A/C, TV, NS rooms, wheelchair access, senior rates, CC. SGL/DBL$22-$38.

The Whitney House (415 South University Ave., 84601; 377-3111) 4 rooms, free breakfast, A/C, 1890s inn, NS, TV, CC. SGL/DBL$45-$65.

Richfield
Area Code 801

Best Western Apple Tree Inn (145 South Main St., 84701; 896-5481, 800-528-1234) 62 rooms and suites, free breakfast, heated pool, exercise center, children free with parents, A/C, NS rooms, TV, laundry facilities, wheelchair access, pets OK, senior rates, meeting facilities, CC. SGL/DBL$45-$95.

Budget Host Knights Inn (69 South Main St., 84701; 896-8228, Fax 896-8228 ext 301, 800-283-4678) 50 rooms and suites, restaurant, heated pool, pets OK, airport transportation, laundry facilities, NS rooms, wheelchair access, A/C, TV, senior rates, children free with parents, CC. SGL/DBL$26-$46.

Days Inn (333 North Main St., 84701; 896-6476, 800-325-2525) 51 rooms and suites, restaurant, outdoor pool, exercise center, saunas, children free with parents, room service, laundry service, A/C, TV, free local calls, pets OK, fax, wheelchair access, NS rooms, meeting facilities, senior rates, CC. SGL/DBL$34-$56.

New West Motel (447 South Main St., 84701; 896-4076) 15 rooms, A/C, TV, pets OK, NS rooms, wheelchair access, CC. SGL/DBL$25-$35.

Quality Inn (540 South Main St., 84701; 896-5465, 800-221-2222) 57 rooms and suites, restaurant, free breakfast, pool, exercise center, whirlpools, kitchenettes, children free with parents, A/C, TV, room service, laundry service, NS rooms, meeting facilities, senior rates, CC. SGL/DBL$32-$68.

Romanico Inn (1170 South Main St., 84701; 896-8471) 57 rooms and suites, restaurant, pool, whirlpools, exercise center, A/C, TV, laundry facilities, pets OK, NS rooms, wheelchair access, senior rates, CC. SGL/DBL$25-$45.

Super 8 Motel (1575 North Main St., 84701; 896-9204, Fax 896-9204, 800-800-8000) 42 rooms and suites, no pets, children under 12 free with parents, free local calls, A/C, TV, in-room refrigerators and microwaves, fax, NS rooms, senior rates, wheelchair access, meeting facilities, CC. SGL/DBL$36-$55.

Weston Inn (647 South Main St., 84701; 896-9271) 40 rooms, restaurant, indoor heated pool, whirlpools, room service, local transportation, children free with parents, in-room refrigerators and microwaves, no pets, A/C, TV, NS rooms, wheelchair access, meeting facilities, senior rates, CC. SGL/DBL$38-$50.

Rockville
Area Code 801

Handcart House (244 West Main St., 84763; 772-3867) 3 rooms, free breakfast, antique furnishings, NS, no pets, CC. SGL/DBL$30-$50.

Roosevelt
Area Code 801

Best Western Inn (Roosevelt 84066; 722-4644, 800-528-1234) 40 rooms, restaurant, heated pool, exercise center, children free with parents, A/C, NS rooms, TV, in-room refrigerators, laundry facilities, wheelchair access, pets OK, meeting facilities, senior rates, CC. SGL/DBL$38-$42.

Frontier Motel (75 South 2nd East, 84006; 722-2201) 53 rooms and efficiencies, restaurant, lounge, kitchenettes, A/C, TV, NS rooms, wheelchair access, CC. SGL/DBL$30-$48.

National 9 Western Inn (737 East 200 North, 84066; 722-5115, 800-524-9999) 38 rooms, pool, NS rooms, wheelchair access, A/C, TV, children free with parents, CC. SGL/DBL$28-$36.

Roy
Area Code 801

Circle R Motel (5223 South 1900 West, 84067; 773-7432) pool, laundry facilities, A/C, TV, NS rooms, wheelchair access, CC. SGL/DBL$30-$60.

St. George
Area Code 801

Green Valley Resort Condominiums Rental (1515 West Canyon View Dr., 84770; 628-8060, Fax 673-4084, 800-237-1068) rental 1- to 4-bedroom condominiums.

Ancestor Inn (60 West St. George Blvd., 84770; 673-4666, 800-864-6882) 60 rooms, pool, sauna, in-room refrigerators and microwaves, A/C, TV, NS rooms, wheelchair access, CC. SGL/DBL$39-$50.

Best Western Coral Hills Inn (126 East St. George Blvd., 84770; 673-4844, Fax 673-5352, 800-528-1234) 98 rooms, spa, exercise center, children free with parents, A/C, game room, NS rooms, TV, laundry facilities, wheelchair access, pets OK, senior rates, meeting facilities, senior rates, CC. SGL/DBL$31-$53.

Best Western Travel Inn (316 East St. George Blvd., 84770; 673-3541, 800-528-1234) 30 rooms, restaurant, heated pool, spa, children free with parents, A/C, NS rooms, TV, laundry facilities, wheelchair access, pets OK, meeting facilities, senior rates, CC. SGL/DBL$30-$50.

Bloomington Townhouses (141 Brigham Rd., 84770; 673-6172, Fax 628-6175) 18 1- to 4-bedroom townhouses, restaurant, lounge, pool, tennis courts, kitchenettes, A/C, TV, NS rooms, wheelchair access, CC. SGL/DBL$50-$100.

Bluff's Motel (1140 South Bluff St., 84770; 628-6699) 33 rooms and suites, free breakfast, heated pool, jacuzzi, A/C, TV, NS rooms, in-room microwaves, laundry facilities, wheelchair access, CC. SGL/DBL$30-$50.

Budget Inn (1221 South Main St., 84770; 673-6661) 78 rooms, free breakfast, heated pool, jacuzzi, A/C, TV, NS rooms, wheelchair access, CC. SGL/DBL$30-$50.

Budget 8 Motel (1230 South Bluff St., 84770; 628-5234, 800-275-3494) 53 rooms, heated pool, jacuzzi, A/C, TV, NS rooms, wheelchair access, CC. SGL/DBL$28-$56.

Chalet Motel (664 East George Blvd., 84770; 628-6272) 30 rooms and suites, pool, A/C, TV, no pets, NS rooms, wheelchair access, kitchenettes, CC. SGL/DBL$30-$55.

Claridge Inn (1187 South Bluff St., 84770; 673-7222) 50 rooms, heated pool, whirlpools, A/C, TV, wheelchair access, NS, CC. SGL/DBL$35-$53.

Comfort Inn Suites (1239 South Main St., 84770; 673-7000, 800-221-2222) 123 suites, free breakfast, outdoor heated pool, whirlpools, wheelchair access, NS rooms, no pets, children under 18 free with parents, A/C, TV, meeting facilities, senior rates, CC. SGL/DBL$45-$89.

Coronada Family Inn (559 East St. George Blvd., 84770; 548-6007, 800-628-4436) 60 suites, indoor heated pool, jacuzzi, laundry facilities, A/C, TV, pets OK, NS rooms, wheelchair access, CC. SGL/DBL$35-$55.

Days Inn and Four Seasons Convention Center (747 East St. George Blvd., 84770; 673-611, Fax 673-0994, 800-325-2525) 96 rooms and suites, restaurant, free breakfast, indoor pool, whirlpools, children free with parents, room service, laundry service, A/C, TV, free local calls, pets OK, fax, wheelchair access, NS rooms, airport transportation, meeting facilities, senior rates, CC. SGL/DBL$39-$75, STS$100-$150.

Desert Edge Inn (525 East St. George, 84770; 673-6137) 35 1- and 2-bedroom suites, pool, spa, laundry facilities, A/C, TV, NS rooms, wheelchair access, CC. SGL/DBL$35-$55.

Dixie Palm Motel (185 East St. George Blvd., 84770; 673-3531, Fax 673-5352) 15 rooms, A/C, TV, NS rooms, wheelchair access, CC. SGL/DBL$26-$30.

Green Gate Village Bed and Breakfast (76 West Tabernackle, 84770; 628-6999, 800-350-6999) 16 rooms, free breakfast, pool, tennis courts, whirlpools, 1870s inn, local transportation, fireplaces, antique furnishings, A/C, NS, TV, meeting facilities, CC. SGL/DBL$50-$65.

whirlpools, 1870s inn, local transportation, fireplaces, antique furnishings, A/C, NS, TV, meeting facilities, CC. SGL/DBL$50-$65.

Hilton Inn of St. George (1450 South Hilton Dr., 84770; 628-0463, Fax 628-1501, 800-HILTONS) 164 rooms and suites, restaurant, lounge, entertainment, indoor and outdoor pool, pool, exercise center, whirlpools, tennis courts, game room, children free with parents, NS rooms, wheelchair access, no pets, room service, laundry facilities, A/C, TV, meeting facilities for 500, senior rates, CC. SGL/DBL$50-$125.

Holiday Inn (850 South Bluff St., 84770; 628-4235, Fax 628-8157, 800-457-9800, 800-HOLIDAY) 164 rooms and suites, restaurant, lounge, indoor and outdoor pool, exercise center, children under 19 free with parents, wheelchair access, A/C, TV, NS rooms, fax, room service, no pets, laundry service, airport transportation, meeting facilities for 500, senior rates, CC. SGL/DBL$60-$120.

Motel 6 (205 North 1000 East St., 84770; 628-7979, 505-891-6161) 103 rooms, pool, free local calls, children under 17 free with parents, NS rooms, wheelchair access, pets OK, A/C, TV, CC. SGL/DBL$23-$30.

Oasis Motel (231 West St. George Blvd., 84770; 673-3551) 24 rooms, pool, no pets, kitchenettes, A/C, TV, NS rooms, wheelchair access, CC. SGL/DBL$24-$28.

Ramada Inn (1440 East St. George Blvd., 84770; 628-2828, Fax 628-0505, 800-2-RAMADA) 90 rooms and suites, restaurant, free breakfast, lounge, outdoor heated pool, jacuzzi, game room, wheelchair access, NS rooms, pets OK, A/C, TV, children under 18 free with parents, room service, laundry facilities, meeting facilities for 75, senior rates, CC. SGL/DBL$50-$80.

Ranch Inn (1040 South Main St., 84770; 628-8000) 35 suites, heated pool, jacuzzi, sauna, free local calls, laundry facilities, A/C, TV, NS rooms, wheelchair access, no pets, CC. SGL/DBL$35-$50.

Red Cliff Inn (912 Red Cliff Dr., 84770; 673-3537, Fax 628-0145) 46 rooms, restaurant, heated pool, sauna, whirlpools, pets OK, A/C, TV, NS rooms, wheelchair access, pets OK, CC. SGL/DBL$35-$48.

Red Mesa Motel (247 East St. George Blvd., 84770; 673-3163) 17 rooms and efficiencies, pool, A/C, TV, NS rooms, wheelchair access, CC. SGL/DBL$20-$30.

Regency Inn (770 East St. George Blvd., 84770; 673-6119) 49 rooms and efficiencies, pool, sauna, kitchenettes, A/C, TV, NS rooms, wheelchair access, CC. SGL/DBL$30-$46.

Rococco Inn (511 South Airport Rd., 84770; 628-3671) 27 rooms, restaurant, heated pool, whirlpools, in-room refrigerators, airport transportation, A/C, TV, NS rooms, wheelchair access, no pets, CC. SGL/DBL$28-$40.

Sands Friendship Inn (581 East St. George Blvd., 84770; 673-3501) 20 rooms, pool, A/C, TV, NS rooms, wheelchair access, CC. SGL/DBL$30-$50.

The 7 Wives Inn (217 North 100 West, 84770; 628-3737) 12 rooms, free breakfast, heated pool, no pets, antique furnishings, A/C, TV, NS rooms, wheelchair access, CC. SGL/DBL$50-$68.

Singletree Inn (260 East St. George Blvd., 84770; 673-6161, Fax 673-7453, 800-528-8890) 48 rooms, restaurant, free breakfast, pool, jacuzzi, A/C, TV, NS rooms, wheelchair access, senior rates, CC. SGL/DBL$33-$55.

Sleep Inn (1481 South Sunland Dr., 84770; 673-7900, 800-627-5337, 800-221-2222) 68 rooms, free breakfast, pool, whirlpools, wheelchair access, NS rooms, no pets, children under 18 free with parents, A/C, TV, airport transportation, meeting facilities, CC. SGL/DBL$30-$50.

Southside Inn (750 East St. George Blvd., 84770; 628-9000) 40 rooms, heated pool, jacuzzi, A/C, TV, NS rooms, wheelchair access, children free with parents, free local calls, CC. SGL/DBL$33-$50.

Sun Time Inn (420 St. George Blvd., 84770; 673-6181, 800-237-6253) 46 rooms, restaurant, free breakfast, heated pool, jacuzzi, kitchenettes, A/C, TV, NS rooms, children free with parents, in-room refrigerators, wheelchair access, senior rates, CC. SGL/DBL$33-$50.

Super 8 Motel (915 South Bluff St., 84770; 628-4251, Fax 628-6534, 800-800-8000) 82 rooms and suites, pets OK, children under 12 free with parents, free local calls, A/C, TV, in-room refrigerators and microwaves, fax, NS rooms, senior rates, wheelchair access, meeting facilities, CC. SGL/DBL$40-$47.

Thunderbird Inn (150 North 1000 East, 84770; 673-6123) 200 rooms, restaurant, heated pool, sauna, whirlpools, no pets, A/C, TV, NS rooms, wheelchair access, CC. SGL/DBL$30-$43.

TraveLodge East (175 North 1000 East, 84770; 673-4621, Fax 628-1874, 800-578-7878) 40 rooms and suites, restaurant, lounge, pool, wheelchair access, complimentary newspaper, laundry service, TV, A/C, free local calls, fax, NS rooms, in-room refrigerators and microwaves, children under 18 free with parents, no pets, meeting facilities, CC. SGL/DBL$36-$60.

Western Safari Motel (310 West St. George Blvd., 84770; 673-5283) 16 rooms and efficiencies, A/C, TV, NS rooms, wheelchair access, CC. SGL/DBL$23-$28.

Weston's Lamplighter Inn (460 East St. George Blvd., 84770; 673-4861, Fax 673-4858) 49 rooms, restaurant, pool, sauna, A/C, TV, NS rooms, wheelchair access, meeting facilities, CC. SGL/DBL$30-$50.

Salina
Area Code 801

Best Western Inn (1225 South State St., 84654; 529-7455, 800-528-1234) 40 rooms, restaurant, heated pool, children free with parents, A/C, NS rooms, TV, laundry facilities, wheelchair access, pets OK, meeting facilities, senior rates, CC. SGL/DBL$46-$56.

Budget Host Scenic Hills Motel (75 East 1500 South, 84654; 529-7483, 800-283-4678) 39 rooms, restaurant, laundry facilities, NS rooms, wheelchair access, A/C, TV, senior rates, children free with parents, CC. SGL/DBL$28-$47.

Cedar Creek Inn (60 North State St., 84654; 529-7467) 40 rooms, restaurant, heated pool, whirlpools, pets OK, laundry facilities, A/C, TV, NS rooms, wheelchair access, CC. SGL/DBL$33-$50.

Lone Star Motel (785 West Main St., 84654; 529-3642) 15 rooms, restaurant, A/C, TV, pets OK, NS rooms, wheelchair access, CC. SGL/DBL$32-$56.

Safari Motel (1425 South State St., 84654; 529-7447) 28 rooms, restaurant, heated pool, pets OK, children free with parents, A/C, TV, NS rooms, wheelchair access, senior rates, CC. SGL/DBL$37-$55.

Salt Lake City
Area Code 801

Rental and Reservation Services:

Home Away From Home (5060 South Mile High Dr., 84124; 272-0965) rental homes.

Wasatch Front Ski Accommodations (2020 East 3300 South 23, 84109; 486-4296, 800-762-7606) rental 1- to 7-bedroom homes.

□□□

Airport Inn (2333 West North Temple, 84116; 539-0438) 100 rooms and suites, restaurant, lounge, pool, whirlpools, exercise center, limousine service, A/C, TV, NS rooms, wheelchair access, room service, meeting facilities for 200, CC. SGL/DBL$41-$65.

Alpine Cottage (164 South 900 East, 84102; 533-8184, 800-733-8184) 5 rooms and suites, no pets, free breakfast, A/C, TV, CC. SGL/DBL$55-$109.

Anton Boxrud Bed and Breakfast (57 South 600 East, 84102; 363-8035, 800-524-5511) 6 rooms, free breakfast, A/C, TV, NS, airport transportation, no pets, CC. SGL/DBL$35-$60.

The Avenues (107 F St., 84103; 363-8137) 14 rooms, A/C, TV, NS rooms, wheelchair access, laundry facilities, CC. SGL/DBL$12-$28.

Best Western Olympus Inn (161 West 600 South St., 84101; 571-7373 Fax 524-0354, 800-528-1234) 392 rooms, restaurant, free breakfast, lounge, pool, exercise center, children free with parents, A/C, NS rooms, TV, laundry facilities, airport transportation, wheelchair access, pets OK, meeting facilities for 1,000, senior rates, CC. SGL/DBL$69-$79.

Brigham Street Inn (1135 East South Temple, 84102; 364-4461) 9 rooms and suites, 1890s inn, whirlpools, fireplaces, no pets, A/C, TV, NS rooms, wheelchair access, CC. SGL/DBL$75-$150.

The Carlton Hotel (140 East South Temple, 84102; 355-3418, 800-633-3500) 45 rooms and suites, restaurant, whirlpools, exercise center, limousine service, A/C, TV, room service, laundry facilities, NS rooms, wheelchair access, CC. SGL/DBL$44-$74.

Clarion Hotel and Suites (999 South Main St., 84111; 359-8600) 263 rooms and suites, restaurant, lounge, heated pool, sauna, whirlpools, tennis courts, airport transportation, A/C, TV, NS rooms, no pets, in-room refrigerators and microwaves, wheelchair access, senior rates, CC. SGL/DBL$70-$125.

Colonial Village Motel (1530 South Main St., 84115; 486-8171) 34 rooms and suites, restaurant, A/C, TV, NS rooms, wheelchair access, CC. SGL/DBL$33-$66.

Comfort Inn Airport (200 North Admiral Byrd Rd., 84116; 537-7444, 800-221-2222) 154 rooms and suites, restaurant, lounge, pool, whirlpools, wheelchair access, NS rooms, in-room refrigerators, airport transportation, pets OK, children under 18 free with parents, A/C, TV, meeting facilities, senior rates, CC. SGL/DBL$70-$85.

Courtyard by Marriott (400 South 150 West, 84101; 531-6000, 800-331-3131) 97 rooms and suites, free breakfast, pool, whirlpools, exercise center, in-room refrigerators, coffee makers and microwaves, laundry facilities, TV, A/C, VCRs, pets OK, complimentary newspaper, fireplaces, children free with parents, NS rooms, wheelchair access, meeting facilities for 100, CC. SGL/DBL$65-$75.

Crystal Inn (230 West 500 South, 84101; 328-4466, 800-366-4466) 175 rooms and suites, pool, exercise center, whirlpools, limousine service, A/C, TV, NS rooms, wheelchair access, laundry facilities, meeting facilities for 150, CC. SGL/DBL$55-$105.

Days Inn Airport (1900 West North Temple, 84116; 539-8538, 800-325-2525) 110 rooms and suites, free breakfast, outdoor pool, children free with parents, room service, laundry service, A/C, TV, free local calls, pets OK, fax, wheelchair access, NS rooms, meeting facilities, senior rates, CC. SGL/DBL$37-$52, STS$70-$80.

Days Inn Central (315 West 3300 South, 84115; 486-8780, Fax 486-6611, 800-325-2525) 64 rooms and suites, exercise center, jacuzzis, sauna, in-room refrigerators, children free with parents, room service, laundry service, A/C, TV, free local calls, pets OK, fax, wheelchair access, NS rooms, meeting facilities, senior rates, CC. SGL/DBL$35-$62, STS$69-$99.

Dean's Motor Lodge (1821 South Main St., 84115; 486-7495) 47 rooms and suites, A/C, TV, NS rooms, wheelchair access, CC. SGL/DBL$27-$40.

Deseret Inn (500 West 500 South, 84101; 532-2900) 88 rooms and 2-bedroom suites, restaurant, pool, whirlpools, no pets, A/C, TV, NS rooms, wheelchair access, meeting facilities for 50, CC. SGL/DBL$37-$41.

Doubletree Hotel (215 West South Temple, 84101; 531-7500, Fax 531-7442, 800-828-7447) 374 rooms and suites, restaurant, lounge, entertainment, indoor heated pool, whirlpools, sauna, exercise center, NS rooms, children under 18 free with parents, limousine services, senior rates, CC, A/C, TV, airport transportation, fax, in-room computer hookups, 14 meeting rooms, meeting facilities for 750, CC. SGL/DBL$69-$139.

Econo Lodge (715 West North Temple, 84116; 363-0062, 800-4-CHOICE) 121 rooms, restaurant, pool, children under 12 free with parents, no pets, NS rooms, wheelchair access, A/C, TV, senior rates, CC. SGL/DBL$44-$60.

Embassy Suites (600 South, 84101; 359-7800, Fax 359-3753, 800-EM-BASSY) 241 2-room suites, restaurant, lounge, free breakfast, lounge, heated pool, whirlpool, exercise center, sauna, room service, laundry service, wheelchair access, complimentary newspaper, limousine service, free local calls, NS rooms, gift shop, local transportation, meeting facilities, CC. SGL/DBL$70-$130.

Emerald Inn (476 South State, 84111; 533-9300) 49 rooms, heated pool, no pets, kitchenettes, A/C, TV, NS rooms, wheelchair access, CC. SGL/DBL$34-$45.

Hilton Airport Hotel (5151 Wiley Post Way, 84116; 539-1515, 800-HIL-TONS) 292 rooms and suites, restaurant, lounge, entertainment, pool, exercise center, children free with parents, NS rooms, wheelchair access, no pets, room service, limousine service, laundry facilities, A/C, TV, meeting facilities for 350, CC. SGL/DBL$80-$125.

Holiday Inn Airport (1659 West North Temple, 84116; 533-9000, Fax 364-0614, 800-HOLIDAY) 191 rooms, restaurant, lounge, pool, exercise center, whirlpools, hot tub, children under 19 free with parents, wheelchair access, A/C, TV, NS rooms, fax, room service, airport transportation, no pets, laundry service, meeting facilities for 250, senior rates, CC. SGL/DBL$55-$100.

Howard Johnson Hotel (122 West South Temple, 84101; 521-0130, 800-366-3684, 800-I-GO-HOJO) 226 rooms, restaurant, lounge, outdoor heated pool, exercise center, jacuzzis, gift shop, children free with parents, wheelchair access, NS rooms, TV, A/C, no pets, laundry facilities, senior rates, meeting facilities, CC. SGL/DBL$49-$108.

The Inn at Temple Square (71 West South Temple St., 84101; 531-1000, 800-843-4668) 90 rooms and suites, restaurant, free breakfast, pool, whirlpools, A/C, TV, NS, wheelchair access, 1920s inn, antique furnishings, airport courtesy car, limousine service, no pets, room service, in-room refrigerators, meeting facilities for 100, senior rates, CC. SGL/DBL$85-$220.

Kendell Kitchens Motel (667 North 300 West, 84103; 355-0293) 15 rooms, A/C, TV, NS rooms, wheelchair access, CC. SGL/DBL$20-$50.

The Kimball (150 North Main St., 84103; 363-4000) 1- and 2-bedroom condominiums, A/C, TV, CC. SGL/DBL$60-$120.

Little America Hotel and Towers (500 South Main St., 84101; 363-6781, 800-662-5888) 850 rooms and suites, restaurant, lounge, entertainment, pool, exercise center, sauna, whirlpools, A/C, TV, NS rooms, wheelchair access, limousine service, airport transportation, in-room refrigerators and coffee makers, laundry facilities, children free with parents, no pets, senior rates, meeting facilities for 1,000, CC. SGL/DBL$65-$450.

Marriott Hotel (75 South West Temple, 84101; 531-0800, Fax 532-4127, 800-345-ISKI, 800-228-9290) 510 rooms and suites, restaurant, lounge, entertainment, indoor and outdoor pool, exercise center, whirlpools, tennis courts, sauna, local transportation, car rental desk, wheelchair access, TV, A/C, NS rooms, laundry service, gift shop, children free with parents, meeting facilities, senior rates, CC. SGL/DBL$58-$87.

Motel 6 Downtown (176 West 6th South St., 84101; 531-1252, 505-891-6161) 109 rooms, pool, free local calls, children under 17 free with parents, NS rooms, wheelchair access, pets OK, A/C, TV, CC. SGL/DBL$32-$40.

Motel 6 West (1990 West North Temple St., 84116; 364-1053, 505-891-6161) 104 rooms, pool, free local calls, children under 17 free with parents, NS rooms, wheelchair access, pets OK, A/C, TV, CC. SGL/DBL$36-$46.

National 9 Inn (I-15 and North 9th, 84116; 364-6591, 800-524-9999) 32 rooms, NS rooms, wheelchair access, A/C, TV, children free with parents, senior rates, CC. SGL/DBL$23-$35.

Nendels Inn (2080 West North Temple, 84116; 355-0088, 800-626-2824) 92 rooms and suites, restaurant, pool, laundry facilities, A/C, TV, NS rooms, wheelchair access, meeting facilities for 25, CC. SGL/DBL$47-$53.

Overniter Motor Inn (1500 West North Temple, 84116; 533-8300) 52 rooms, restaurant, pool, A/C, TV, NS rooms, wheelchair access, CC. SGL/DBL$34-$38.

Peery Hotel (110 West 300 South, 84101; 521-4300, 800-331-0073) 77 rooms, restaurant, free breakfast, lounge, exercise center, whirlpools, gift shop, airport courtesy car, children stay free with parents, A/C, TV, NS rooms, no pets, wheelchair access, senior rates, meeting facilities, CC. SGL/DBL$65-$110.

Pinecrest Bed and Breakfast (6211 Emigration Canyon Rd., 84108; 583-6663) 6 rooms, free breakfast, no pets, A/C, TV, CC. SGL/DBL$65-$160.

Quality Inn Midvalley (4465 Century Dr., 84123; 268-2533, 800-221-2222) 131 rooms and suites, restaurant, free breakfast, pool, exercise center, whirlpools, kitchenettes, children free with parents, A/C, TV, room service, laundry service, pets OK, game room, NS rooms, meeting facilities, senior rates, CC. SGL/DBL$50-$79.

Quality Inn Airport (5575 West Amelia Earhart Dr., 84116; 537-7020, Fax 537-7701, 800-522-5575, 800-221-2222) 188 rooms and suites, restaurant, lounge, pool, exercise center, whirlpools, gift shop, airport transportation, car rental desk, children free with parents, A/C, TV, room service, laundry service, NS rooms, meeting facilities, senior rates, CC. SGL/DBL$65-$78.

Quality Inn City Center (154 West 600 South, 84101; 521-2930, 800-221-2222) 247 rooms and suites, restaurant, lounge, pool, exercise center, whirlpools, local transportation, children free with parents, A/C, TV, room service, laundry service, NS rooms, meeting facilities, senior rates, CC. SGL/DBL$59-$60.

Radisson Airport Hotel (2177 West Temple St., 84116; 364-5800, 800-333-3333) 127 rooms and suites, restaurant, free breakfast, heated pool, exercise center, in-room refrigerators, microwaves and coffee makers, children free with parents, VCRs, wheelchair access, NS rooms, airport transportation, TV, A/C, children free with parents, pets OK, meeting facilities, senior rates, CC. SGL/DBL$70-$150.

Ramada Inn (230 West 600 South, 84101; 364-5200, Fax 364-0974, 800-2-RAMADA) 160 rooms and suites, restaurant, lounge, indoor pool, whirlpools, airport transportation, wheelchair access, NS rooms, pets OK, A/C, TV, children under 18 free with parents, room service, laundry facilities, meeting facilities, senior rates, CC. SGL/DBL$55-$78.

Red Lion Inn (255 South West Temple, 84101; 328-2000, Fax 532-1953, 800-547-8010) 500 rooms and suites, restaurant, lounge, entertainment, pool, sauna, spa, exercise center, gift shop, airport courtesy car, A/C, TV, wheelchair access, NS rooms, laundry facilities, 15 meeting rooms, meeting facilities for 1,100, senior rates, CC. SGL/DBL$100-$1,000.

Residence Inn (765 East 400 South St., 84102; 532-5511, Fax 531-0416, 800-331-3131) 128 suites, free breakfast, in-room refrigerators, coffee makers and microwaves, laundry facilities, TV, A/C, VCRs, pets OK, complimentary newspaper, fireplaces, airport courtesy car, children free with parents, NS rooms, wheelchair access, meeting facilities, senior rates, CC. SGL/DBL$130-$178.

Reston Hotel (5335 College Dr., 84123; 264-1054, 800-231-9710) 98 rooms and suites, restaurant, lounge, pool, whirlpools, exercise center, A/C, TV, NS rooms, VCRs, airport transportation, wheelchair access, room service, limousine service, meeting facilities for 40, CC. SGL/DBL$54-$61.

Royal Executive Inn (121 North 300 West, 84103; 521-3450) 56 rooms and suites, restaurant, lounge, heated pool, laundry facilities, A/C, TV, NS rooms, wheelchair access, airport transportation, pets OK, room service, meeting facilities for 35, CC. SGL/DBL$43-$48.

Scenic Motel (1345 South Forthill Dr., 84108; 582-1527) 23 rooms, A/C, TV, NS rooms, wheelchair access, CC. SGL/DBL$29-$44.

Se Rancho Motor Lodge (640 West North Temple, 84116; 532-3300) 56 rooms, restaurant, pool, A/C, TV, NS rooms, wheelchair access, CC. SGL/DBL$21-$35.

Shilo Inn (206 South West Temple, 84101; 521-9500, 800-334-1049) 200 rooms and suites, restaurant, lounge, entertainment, free breakfast, heated pool, sauna, whirlpools, pets OK, airport courtesy car, children under 12 free with parents, gift shop, A/C, TV, NS rooms, wheelchair access, CC. SGL/DBL$47-$77.

Sky Harbor Suites (1876 West North Temple, 85116; 539-8420, 800-677-8483) 1- and 2-bedroom suites, exercise center, A/C, no pets, children free with parents, TV, kitchenettes, CC. 1BR$130W-$450W, 2BR$550W.

Skyline Inn (2475 East 1700 South, 84108; 582-5350) 25 rooms, indoor heated pool, whirlpools, pets OK, A/C, TV, NS rooms, wheelchair access, senior rates, CC. SGL/DBL$40-$50.

Spruce's Bed and Breakfast (6151 South 900 East St., 84121; 268-8762) 4 rooms, free breakfast, NS, kitchenettes, A/C, TV, CC. SGL/DBL$55-$135.

Super 8 Motel (616 South 200 West, 84101; 534-0808, Fax 355-7735, 800-800-8000) 123 rooms and suites, restaurant, no pets, children under 12 free with parents, free local calls, A/C, TV, in-room refrigerators and microwaves, fax, NS rooms, senior rates, wheelchair access, meeting facilities, CC. SGL/DBL$48-$73.

TraveLodge at Temple Square (144 West North Temple St., 84103; 533-8200, Fax 596-0332, 800-578-7878) 55 rooms, restaurant, lounge, pool, wheelchair access, complimentary newspaper, laundry service, TV, A/C, free local calls, fax, NS rooms, in-room refrigerators and microwaves, children under 18 free with parents, no pets, car rental desk, meeting facilities, CC. SGL/DBL$40-$59.

TraveLodge City Center (524 SouthWest Temple St., 84101; 531-7100, Fax 359-3814, 800-578-7878) 60 rooms, restaurant, lounge, pool, jacuzzi, car rental desk, wheelchair access, complimentary newspaper, laundry service, TV, A/C, free local calls, fax, NS rooms, in-room refrigerators and microwaves, children under 18 free with parents, airport transportation, no pets, meeting facilities, CC. SGL/DBL$40-$60.

University Park Hotel (480 Wakara Way, 84108; 581-1000, Fax 583-7641, 800-637-4390) 220 rooms and suites, restaurant, lounge, entertainment, indoor heated pool, whirlpools, exercise center, game room, children free with parents, airport courtesy car, gift shop, A/C, TV, NS rooms, wheelchair access, CC. SGL/DBL$150-$185.

Sandy

Area Code 801

Comfort Inn (8955 South 255 West, 84070; 255-4919, 800-221-2222) 98 rooms, free breakfast, lounge, indoor heated pool, whirlpools, wheelchair access, NS rooms, no pets, children under 18 free with parents, A/C, TV, meeting facilities, senior rates, CC. SGL/DBL$49-$65.

Hampton Inn (10690 South Holiday Park Dr., 84070; 571-0800, 800-HAMPTON) 131 rooms, restaurant, free breakfast, pool, exercise center, children under 18 free with parents, NS rooms, wheelchair access, in-room computer hookups, fax, TV, A/C, local transportation, free local calls, pets OK, meeting facilities, senior rates, CC. SGL/DBL$60-$74.

Mountain Hollow Inn (10209 South Dimple Dell Rd., 84092; 942-3428) 9 rooms and suites, free breakfast, whirlpools, VCRs, no pets, NS, airport transportation, laundry facilities, game room, A/C, TV, CC. SGL/DBL$50-$63.

Snowbird

Area Code 801

Cliff Lodge (Snowbird 84092; 742-2222, 800-453-3000) 532 rooms and suites, restaurant, lounge, entertainment, heated pool, exercise center, whirlpools, sauna, game room, laundry facilities, barber and beauty shop, gift shop, in-room refrigerators, A/C, TV, NS rooms, wheelchair access, CC. SGL/DBL$150-$740.

The Inn (Snowbird 84092; 742-2222, 800-453-3000) 41 rooms and suites, restaurant, heated pool, sauna, A/C, TV, NS rooms, laundry facilities, fireplaces, children free with parents, wheelchair access, CC. SGL/DBL$150-$385.

Iron Blossom Lodge (Snowbird 84092; 742-2222, Fax 742-3445, 800-453-3000) 159 rooms and suites, restaurant, heated pool, whirlpools, sauna, game room, children free with parents, kitchenettes, fireplaces, A/C, TV, NS rooms, wheelchair access, CC. SGL/DBL$150-$495.

The Lodge at Snowbird (Snowbird 84092; 742-2222, 800-453-3000) 160 rooms and suites, restaurant, lounge, heated pool, sauna, whirlpools, children free with parents, fireplaces, TV, NS rooms, wheelchair access, CC. SGL/DBL$150-$350.

South Jordon

Area Code 801

Sleep Inn (10676 South 300 West St., 84065; 572-2020, 800-221-2222) 68 rooms, free breakfast, pool, wheelchair access, NS rooms, no pets, children under 18 free with parents, senior rates, A/C, TV, meeting facilities, CC. SGL/DBL$40-$55.

Springdale

Area Code 801

Best Western Driftwood Lodge (1515 Zion Park Blvd., 84767; 772-3262, Fax 772-3702, 800-528-1234) 48 rooms, restaurant, heated pool, exercise center, children free with parents, A/C, NS rooms, TV, laundry facilities, wheelchair access, pets OK, gift shop, meeting facilities, senior rates, CC. SGL/DBL$53-$65.

The Blue House Bed and Breakfast (Springdale 84767; 772-3912) 4 rooms, free breakfast, A/C, TV, no pets, no children CC. SGL/DBL$30-$50.

Blumberry Inn (897 Zion Park Blvd., 84767; 772-3224) 24 rooms, restaurant, heated pool, TV, NS rooms, pets OK, wheelchair access, CC. SGL/DBL$40-$55.

Canyon Ranch Motel (668 Zion Park Blvd., 84767; 772-3357) 21 rooms and cottages, pool, jacuzzi, kitchenettes, pets OK, A/C, TV, NS rooms, wheelchair access, no pets, CC. SGL/DBL$39-$51.

Cliffrose Lodge and Gardens (281 Zion Park Blvd., 84767; 772-3234, Fax 772-3900, 800-243-UTAH) 36 rooms, pool, A/C, TV, NS rooms, wheelchair access, meeting facilities, laundry facilities, CC. SGL/DBL$50-$100.

The El Rio Lodge (995 Zion Park Blvd., 84767; 772-3205) 11 rooms, A/C, TV, NS rooms, wheelchair access, CC. SGL/DBL$28-$46.

Flannagan's Inn (428 Zion Park Blvd., 84767; 772-3244, 800-756-RSVP) 40 rooms, restaurant, lounge, pool, no pets, A/C, TV, NS rooms, wheelchair access, meeting facilities, CC. SGL/DBL$35-$55.

Harvest House (29 Canyon View Dr., 84767; 772-3880) 4 rooms, restaurant, free breakfast, A/C, TV, private baths, NS, no pets, VCRs, CC. SGL/DBL$50-$80.

Pioneer Lodge (838 Zion Park Blvd., 84767; 772-3233) 41 rooms and 3-bedroom apartment, heated pool, spa, kitchenettes, A/C, TV, NS rooms, wheelchair access, CC. SGL/DBL$36-$48.

Terrace Brook Lodge (990 Zion Park Blvd., 84767; 772-3932, 800-342-6779) 24 rooms, heated pool, A/C, no pets, TV, NS rooms, wheelchair access, CC. SGL/DBL$36-$53.

Under The Eaves Guest House (980 Zion Park Blvd., 84767; 772-3457) 5 rooms, free breakfast, whirlpools, pets OK, A/C, TV, NS, wheelchair access, CC. SGL/DBL$50-$80.

Zion Canyon Campground Cabins (481 Zion Park Blvd., 84767; 772-3237, Fax 772-3844) 11 cabins, restaurant, laundry facilities, TV, CC. SGL/DBL$36-$48.

Zion House Bed and Breakfast (801 Zion Park Blvd., 84767; 772-3281) 4 rooms, free breakfast, NS, A/C, TV, NS, no pets, VCRs, wheelchair access, CC. SGL/DBL$50-$85.

Zion Park Motel (855 Zion Park Blvd., 84767; 772-3902) 21 rooms and 2-bedroom efficiencies, restaurant, heated pool, laundry facilities, A/C, TV, NS rooms, wheelchair access, CC. SGL/DBL$35-$55.

Springville

Area Code 801

Mountain Springs Motel (1560 North 1900 West, 84663; 489-3641) 62 rooms and 2-bedroom apartments, restaurant, heated pool, whirlpools, no pets, A/C, TV, NS rooms, wheelchair access, CC. SGL/DBL$34-$49.

Sterling

Area Code 801

Cedar Crest Inn (819 Palisade Lake Rd., 84665; 835-6352) 9 rooms, restaurant, whirlpools, no pets, fireplaces, A/C, TV, NS rooms, wheelchair access, CC. SGL/DBL$36-$60.

Sunset

Area Code 801

Crystal Cottage Inn (815 North Main St., 84015; 825-9500) 37 rooms, restaurant, whirlpools, exercise center, kitchenettes, no pets, A/C, TV, VCRs, NS rooms, wheelchair access, CC. SGL/DBL$35-$38.

Tooele

Area Code 801

Best Western Inn (365 North Main St., 84074; 882-5010, Fax 882-5746, 800-528-1234) 30 rooms and efficiencies, restaurant, indoor heated pool, whirlpools, exercise center, children free with parents, A/C, NS rooms, TV, laundry facilities, wheelchair access, in-room refrigerators and microwaves, no pets, meeting facilities, senior rates, CC. SGL/DBL$42-$50.

Toquerville

Area Code 801

Your Inn (650 Springs Dr., 84774; 635-9964) 4 rooms, free breakfast, A/C, no children, private baths, TV, NS rooms, wheelchair access, CC. SGL/DBL$45-$55.

Torrey

Area Code 801

Capitol Reef Inn (360 West Main St., 84775; 425-3271) 10 rooms, restaurant, pets OK, A/C, TV, NS rooms, wheelchair access, gift shop, CC. SGL/DBL$35-$45.

Pinewood Resort (Torrey 84775; 800-848-2525) 6 rooms and suites, restaurant, spa, TV, A/C, CC. SGL/DBL$50.

Wonderland Inn (Torrey 84775; 800-458-0216) 50 rooms and suites, restaurant, A/C, TV, NS rooms, wheelchair access, CC. SGL/DBL$44-$54.

Tremonton
Area Code 801

Marble Motel (116 North Tremont St., 84337; 257-3524) 10 rooms and 2-bedroom efficiencies, A/C, no pets, TV, NS rooms, wheelchair access, CC. SGL/DBL$25-$35.

Sandman Motel (585 West Main St., 84337; 257-5675) 38 rooms, A/C, TV, NS rooms, wheelchair access, pets OK, CC. SGL/DBL$30-$39.

Western Inn (2301 West Main St., 84337; 257-3399) 46 rooms, restaurant, A/C, TV, NS rooms, wheelchair access, no pets, CC. SGL/DBL$35-$45.

Tropic
Area Code 801

Bryce Point Bed and Breakfast (Tropic 84776; 679-8629) 5 rooms, free breakfast, A/C, TV, no pets, CC. SGL/DBL$55-$65.

Valley Inn (200 North Main St., 84776; 670-8811) 63 rooms, restaurant, lounge, whirlpools, TV, pets OK, CC. SGL/DBL$45-$65.

Vernal
Area Code 801

Best Western Inn (423 West Main St., 84078; 789-1202, 800-528-1234) 49 rooms, restaurant, heated pool, exercise center, children free with parents, A/C, NS rooms, TV, airport transportation, laundry facilities, wheelchair access, no pets, meeting facilities, senior rates, CC. SGL/DBL$35-$65.

Best Western Inn (251 East Main St., 84078; 789-2660, 800-528-1234) 59 rooms, restaurant, lounge, heated pool, exercise center, whirlpools, VCRs, no pets, airport transportation, children free with parents, A/C, NS rooms, TV, laundry facilities, wheelchair access, meeting facilities, senior rates, CC. SGL/DBL$40-$68.

Days Inn (260 West Main St., 84078; 789-1011, Fax 789-0172, 800-325-2525) 42 rooms and suites, free breakfast, outdoor pool, children free with parents, room service, laundry service, A/C, TV, free local calls, pets OK, airport transportation, fax, wheelchair access, NS rooms, meeting facilities, senior rates, CC. SGL/DBL$29-$58.

Econo Lodge (311 East Main St., 84078; 789-2000, 800-4-CHOICE) 50 rooms, pool, children under 12 free with parents, no pets, NS rooms, wheelchair access, A/C, TV, airport transportation, senior rates, CC. SGL/DBL$34-$52.

Split Mountain Motel (1015 Hwy. 40 East, 84078; 789-9020) 40 rooms, A/C, TV, NS rooms, wheelchair access, no pets, CC. SGL/DBL$25-$46.

Wellington
Area Code 801

National 9 Inn (720 East Main St., 84542; 637-7980, Fax 637-8929, 800-524-9999) 48 rooms, restaurant, indoor heated pool, NS rooms, wheelchair access, A/C, TV, children free with parents, pets OK, in-room refrigerators, senior rates, CC. SGL/DBL$25-$50.

Wellsville
Area Code 801

Sherwood Hills (Hwy. 89, 84339) 245-6424) 60 rooms, restaurant, indoor and outdoor pools, sauna, jacuzzi, kitchenettes, laundry facilities, A/C, TV, NS rooms, wheelchair access, meeting facilities for 200, CC. SGL/DBL$48-$95.

Wendover
Area Code 801

Best Western Inn (Wendover 84083; 665-7811, 800-528-1234) 24 rooms, pool, exercise center, whirlpools, sauna, children free with parents, A/C, NS rooms, TV, laundry facilities, wheelchair access, no pets, meeting facilities, senior rates, CC. SGL/DBL$30-$75.

Motel 6 (561 East Wendover Blvd., 84083; 665-2297, 505-891-6161) 130 rooms, pool, free local calls, children under 17 free with parents, NS rooms, wheelchair access, pets OK, A/C, TV, CC. SGL/DBL$36-$48.

State Line Inn (295 East Wendover Blvd., 84083; 665-2226) 101 rooms, heated pool, whirlpools, A/C, TV, NS rooms, wheelchair access, no pets, CC. SGL/DBL$30-$48.

Western Ridge Motel (895 East Wendover Blvd., 84083; 665-2211) 55 rooms and 2-bedroom suites, heated pool, A/C, TV, NS rooms, wheelchair access, no pets, CC. SGL/DBL$26-$70.

Woods Cross
Area Code 801

Motel 6 (2433 South 800 West, 84087; 298-0289, 505-891-6161) 125 rooms, pool, free local calls, children under 17 free with parents, NS rooms, wheelchair access, pets OK, A/C, TV, CC. SGL/DBL$35-$45.

Additional Reading

from Hunter Publishing

INSIDER'S GUIDE TO WESTERN CANADA
$15.95, ISBN 1-55650-580-9, 205pp

".... The lively, sometimes whimsical text makes reading a pleasure... major sites and attractions are intelligently discussed; there's an emphasis on fine arts and performing arts, and culture...." *Travel Books Worldwide.*

INSIDER'S GUIDE TO EASTERN CANADA
$15.95, ISBN 1-55650-581-7, 256pp

"... text and abundant photographs [are] so outstanding.... This would make a fine addition to most libraries." *Library Journal.*

Filled with history, tour information, local museums and galleries, where to shop, where to eat, these are the most complete guides to Canada in the bookstores. Superb color photos and maps complement the text. Complete accommodation information, from the most luxurious hotels to places for the traveller on a shoestring budget. As with all the books in this series, a free pull-out color map makes planning your days easy.

Among other guides in this series:

FLORIDA $15.95, ISBN 1-55650-452-7, 256pp
HAWAII $15.95, ISBN 1-55650-495-0, 230pp
NEW ENGLAND $17.95, ISBN 1-55650-455-1, 256pp
MEXICO $18.95, ISBN 1-55650-454-3, 320pp
RUSSIA $17.95, ISBN 1-55650-558-2, 224pp
CALIFORNIA $14.95, ISBN 1-55650-163-3, 192pp
INDONESIA $15.95, ISBN 1-55650-453-5, 224pp
TURKEY $17.95, ISBN 1-55650-283-4, 209pp
INDIA $16.95, ISBN 1-55650-164-1, 360pp
NEW ZEALAND $15.95, ISBN 1-55650-624-4, 224pp

ADVENTURE GUIDE TO THE HIGH SOUTHWEST
$14.94, ISBN 1-55650-633-3, 384pp

"... a conscientious and beautifully written guide...."

Hiking, mountaineering, trail riding, cycling, camping, river running, ski touring, wilderness trips – a guide to enjoying the natural attractions of the Four Corners area of Northwest New Mexico, Southwest Colorado, Southern Utah, Northern Arizona, and the Navajo Nation and Hopiland. Includes all practical details on transportation, services, where to eat, where to stay and travel tips on how to cope with the harsh terrain and climate. The most adventurous guide to this region on the market. Maps.

Among other guides in the Adventure Guide series:

COSTA RICA 2nd Ed. $15.95, ISBN 1-55650-598-1, 470pp
PUERTO RICO 2nd Ed. $14.95, ISBN 1-55650-628-7, 304pp
CANADA $15.95, ISBN 1-55650-315-6, 320pp
VIRGIN ISLANDS 3rd Ed. $14.95, ISBN 1-55650-597-3, 280pp
EVERGLADES & THE FLORIDA KEYS $14.95,
  ISBN 1-55650-494-2, 192pp
BAJA CALIFORNIA $11.95, ISBN 1-55650-590-6, 280pp

THE GREAT AMERICAN WILDERNESS: TOURING AMERICA'S NATIONAL PARKS
$11.95, ISBN 1-55650-567-1, 320pp

The 41 most scenic parks throughout the US including Acadia, the Great Smokey Mountains, Yellowstone, Hawaii Volcanoes, the Grand Canyon, Big Bend, the Everglades and many more. This tells you where to stay, where to eat, which roads are most crowded or most beautiful, how much time to allow, what you can safely skip and what you must not miss. Detailed maps of each park show all the surrounding access routes and special sections tell you how to make the most of your time if you only have a couple of hours.

CANADIAN ROCKIES ACCESS GUIDE 3rd Ed.
15.95, ISBN 0-91943-392-8, 369pp

The ultimate guide to outdoor adventure from Banff to Lake Louise to Jasper National Park. This book covers walking and canoeing routes, climbs, cycling and hiking in one of the most spectacular regions on earth. Maps, photos and contact numbers.

WHERE TO STAY IN NEW ENGLAND
$11.95, ISBN 1-55650-602-3, 512pp

"... isn't just your usual B&B or hotel listing, but a selection of almost all hotels, motels, country houses, condos and cottages for rent in the region.... Highly recommended: much more comprehensive in scope than competitors." *Reviewer's Bookwatch.*

Over 5,000 places are listed in this all-inclusive guide. Brief descriptions are supplemented by address, phone number (toll-free when available) and prices. Special sections are dedicated to chain hotels and deals they offer to business travellers, school groups, government workers and senior citizens.

Among other guides in the *Where to Stay* series:

AMERICA'S EASTERN CITIES $11.95, ISBN 1-55650-600-7, 416pp
AMERICA'S WESTERN CITIES $11.95, ISBN 1-55650-420-9, 416pp
MID-ATLANTIC STATES $12.95, ISBN 1-55650-631-7, 446pp
AMERICA'S HEARTLAND $13.93, ISBN 1-55650-632-5, 572pp
THE AMERICAN SOUTHEAST $12.95, ISBN 1-55650-651-1, 512 pp
SOUTHERN CALIFORNIA $12.95, ISBN 1-55650-573-6, 394pp
NORTHERN CALIFORNIA $12.95, ISBN 1-55650-572-8, 280pp

ARIZONA, COLORADO & UTAH: A TOURING GUIDE
$11.95, ISBN 1-55650-656-2, 160pp

A compact guide written for those eager to see the unforgettable attractions of these three states. Driving tours begin in the state capital and cover the museums, parks, zoos and historical buildings in each city. They then lead the reader out into the fascinating land of giant arches, pinnacles, natural bridges, canyons and deserts for which the region is so well known. All the sights are described, along with the best routes to reach them whether on a daytrip or as part of a month-long tour. Accommodations and attractions are listed with opening times and fees. State and city maps make planning easy.

STATE PARKS OF THE SOUTH
$13.95, ISBN 1-55650-655-4, 224pp

This book takes you to 250 state parks in the states of Georgia, Alabama, Tennessee, Kentucky and Florida. From small ones that are largely undiscovered by the public, to others whose names you will recognize – each offers something unique. History, background on the ecosystem, lodges, camping facilities, local attractions, activities, maps and photos put this guide way above any other for practical tips and usability.

HUGO'S SPANISH FOR BUSINESS

If you're heading to Latin America for an important meeting, try our Spanish for Business course. Business courses are available in several languages and consist of four one-hour audio cassettes and a book, with the accent on commercial vocabulary and dialog. Real-life scenarios featuring native speakers teach the use of the language in a wide variety of business situations, from placing ads to handling a job interview to negotiating a loan.

CASSETTE & BOOK $39.95, ISBN 0-8585-208-8
BOOK ALONE (220pp) $9.95, ISBN 0-85285-207-0

HUGO'S LATIN-AMERICAN TRAVEL PACK
$14.95, ISBN 0-85285-219-3, 128pp

A new title in the series that is the perfect learning tool for those taking a vacation in a foreign country. These packs contain a 128-page phrasebook

with mini-dictionary and menu guide, plus a 60-minute cassette with all
the key phrases spoken by natives.

HUGO'S 3 MONTHS LANGUAGE COURSES

"Our personal favorites... Hugo actually teaches you the building blocks
of the language so you have a fighting chance of participating in a real live
conversation." *Conde Nast Traveller.*

Hugo's come in Three Months courses, At The Wheel courses, Business
courses, Conversational courses, Travel Packs, Phrasebooks, Dictionaries
and Verb books and something is available in all of the following languages:

ARABIC
CHINESE
CZECH
DANISH
DUTCH
EL INGLES/ENGLISH FOR SPANISH SPEAKERS
FRENCH
GERMAN
HEBREW
HUNGARIAN
INDONESIAN
ITALIAN
JAPANESE
L'ANGLAIS SIMPLIFIE/ENGLISH FOR FRENCH SPEAKERS
LATIN-AMERICAN SPANISH
NORWEGIAN
POLISH
PORTUGUESE
ROMANIAN
RUSSIAN
SERBO-CROAT
SPANISH
SWEDISH
THAI
TURKISH
YUGOSLAV

All of these titles plus thousands more are available from Hunter Publishing. To receive our free color catalog or to find out more about our books
and maps, contact Hunter Publishing, 300 Raritan Center Parkway,
Edison NJ 08818, or call (908) 225 1900.